Aviation Maintenance Technician Handbook–Airframe

Volume 2

2012

U.S. Department of Transportation
FEDERAL AVIATION ADMINISTRATION
Flight Standards Service

Volume Contents

Volume 1

Preface v

Acknowledgments vii

Table of Contents xiii

Chapter 1
Aircraft Structures 1-1

Chapter 2
Aerodynamics, Aircraft Assembly, and
Rigging 2-1

Chapter 3
Aircraft Fabric Covering 3-1

Chapter 4
Aircraft Metal Structural Repair 4-1

Chapter 5
Aircraft Welding 5-1

Chapter 6
Aircraft Wood 6-1

Chapter 7
Advanced Composite Materials 7-1

Chapter 8
Airoraft Painting and Finishing 8-1

Chapter 9
Aircraft Electrical System 9-1

Glossary G-1

Index I-1

Volume 2

Chapter 10
Aircraft Instrument 10-1

Chapter 11
Communication and Navigation 11-1

Chapter 12
Hydraulic and Pneumatic 12-1

Chapter 13
Aircraft Landing 13-1

Chapter 14
Aircraft Fuel System 14-1

Chapter 15
Ice and Rain Protection 15-1

Chapter 16
Cabin Environmental 16-1

Chapter 17
Fire Protection Systems 17-1

Glossary G-1

Index I-1

Preface

The Aviation Maintenance Technician Handbook–Airframe (FAA-H-8083-31) is one of a series of three handbooks for persons preparing for certification as an airframe or powerplant mechanic. It is intended that this handbook provide the basic information on principles, fundamentals, and technical procedures in the subject matter areas relating to the airframe rating. It is designed to aid students enrolled in a formal course of instruction, as well as the individual who is studying on his or her own. Since the knowledge requirements for the airframe and powerplant ratings closely parallel each other in some subject areas, the chapters which discuss fire protection systems and electrical systems contain some material which is also duplicated in the Aviation Maintenance Technician Handbook–Powerplant (FAA-H-8083-32).

This volume contains information on airframe construction features, assembly and rigging, fabric covering, structural repairs, and aircraft welding. The handbook also contains an explanation of the units that make up the various airframe systems. Because there are so many different types of aircraft in use today, it is reasonable to expect that differences exist in airframe components and systems. To avoid undue repetition, the practice of using representative systems and units is carried out throughout the handbook. Subject matter treatment is from a generalized point of view and should be supplemented by reference to manufacturer's manuals or other textbooks if more detail is desired. This handbook is not intended to replace, substitute for, or supersede official regulations or the manufacturer's instructions. Occasionally the word "must" or similar language is used where the desired action is deemed critical. The use of such language is not intended to add to, interpret, or relieve a duty imposed by Title 14 of the Code of Federal Regulations (14 CFR).

This handbook is available for download, in PDF format, from www.faa.gov.

The subject of Human Factors is contained in the Aviation Maintenance Technician Handbook–General (FAA-H-8083-30).

This handbook is published by the United States Department of Transportation, Federal Aviation Administration, Airman Testing Standards Branch, AFS-630, P.O. Box 25082, Oklahoma City, OK 73125.

Comments regarding this publication should be sent, in email form, to the following address:

AFS630comments@faa.gov

Acknowledgments

The Aviation Maintenance Technician Handbook–Airframe (FAA-H-8083-31) was produced by the Federal Aviation Administration (FAA) with the assistance of Safety Research Corporation of America (SRCA). The FAA wishes to acknowledge the following contributors:

Mr. Chris Brady (www.b737.org.uk) for images used throughout this handbook

Captain Karl Eiríksson for image used in Chapter 1

Cessna Aircraft Company for image used in Chapter 1

Mr. Andy Dawson (www.mossie.org) for images used throughout Chapter 1

Mr. Bill Shemley for image used in Chapter 1

Mr. Bruce R. Swanson for image used in Chapter 1

Mr. Burkhard Domke (www.b-domke.de) for images used throughout Chapter 1 and 2

Mr. Chris Wonnacott (www.fromtheflightdeck.com) for image used in Chapter 1

Mr. Christian Tremblay (www.zodiac640.com) for image used in Chapter 1

Mr. John Bailey (www.knots2u.com) for image used in Chapter 1

Mr. Rich Guerra (www.rguerra.com) for image used in Chapter 1

Mr. Ronald Lane for image used in Chapter 1

Mr. Tom Allensworth (www.avsim.com) for image used in Chapter 1

Navion Pilots Association's Tech Note 001 (www.navionpilots.org) for image used in Chapter 1

U.S. Coast Guard for image used in Chapter 1

Mr. Tony Bingelis and the Experimental Aircraft Association (EAA) for images used throughout Chapter 2

Mr. Benoit Viellefon (www.johnjohn.co.uk/compare-tigermothflights/html/tigermoth_bio_aozh.html) for image used in Chapter 3

Mr. Paul Harding of Safari Seaplanes–Bahamas (www.safariseaplanes.com) for image used in Chapter 3

Polyfiber/Consolidated Aircraft Coatings for images used throughout Chapter 3

Stewart Systems for images used throughout Chapter 3

Superflite for images used throughout Chapter 3

Cherry Aerospace (www.cherryaerospace.com) for images used in Chapters 4 and 7

Raytheon Aircraft (Structural Inspection and Repair Manual) for information used in Chapter 4

Mr. Scott Allen, Kalamazoo Industries, Inc. (www.kalamazooind.com) for image used in Chapter 4

Miller Electric Mfg. Co. (www.millerwelds.com) for images used in Chapter 5

Mr. Aaron Novak, contributing engineer, for charts used in Chapter 5

Mr. Bob Hall (www.pro-fusiononline.com) for image used in Chapter 5

Mr. Kent White of TM Technologies, Inc. for image used in Chapter 5

Safety Supplies Canada (www.safetysuppliescanada.com) for image used in Chapter 5

Smith Equipment (www.smithequipment.com) for images used in Chapter 5

Alcoa (www.alcoa.com) for images used in Chapter 7

Mr. Chuck Scott (www.itwif.com) for images used throughout Chapter 8

Mr. John Lagerlof, Paasche Airbrush Co. (paascheairbrush.com) for image used in Chapter 8

Mr. Philip Love of Turbine Products, LLC (www.turbineproducts.com) for image used in Chapter 8

Consolidated Aircraft Coatings for image used in Chapter 8

Tianjin Yonglida Material Testing Machine Co., Ltd for image used in Chapter 8

Mr. Jim Irwin of Aircraft Spruce & Specialty Co. (www.aircraftspruce.com) for images used in Chapters 9, 10, 11, 13, 14, 15

Mr. Kevan Hashemi for image used in Chapter 9

Mr. Michael Leasure, Aviation Multimedia Library (www2.tech.purdue.edu/at/courses/aeml) for images used in Chapters 9, 13, 14

Cobra Systems Inc. (www.cobrasys.com) for image used in Chapter 10

www.free-online-private-pilot-ground-school.com for image used in Chapters 10, 16

DAC International (www.dacint.com) for image used in Chapter 10

Dawson Aircraft, Inc. (www.aircraftpartsandsalvage.com) for images used throughout Chapter 10

Mr. Kent Clingaman for image used in Chapter 10

TGH Aviation-FAA Instrument Repair Station (www.tghaviation.com) for image used in Chapter 10

The Vintage Aviator, Ltd. (www.thevintageaviator.co.nz) for image used in Chapter 10

ACK Technologies, Inc. (www.ackavionics.com) for image used in Chapter 11

ADS-B Technologies, LLC. (www.ads-b.com) for images used in Chapter 11

Aviation Glossary (www.aviationglossary.com) for image used in Chapter 11

AT&T Archives and History Center for image used in Chapter 11

Electronics International, Inc. (www.buy-ei.com) for image used in Chapter 11

Excelitas Technologies (www.excelitas.com) for image used in Chapter 11

Freestate Electronics, Inc. (www.fse-inc.com) for image used in Chapter 11

AirTrafficAtlanta.com for image used in Chapter 11

Western Historic Radio Museum, Virginia City, Nevada (www.radioblvd.com) for image used in Chapter 11

Avidyne Corporation (www.avidyne.com) for image used in Chapter 11

Kintronic Laboratories (www.kintronic.com) for image used in Chapter 11

Mr. Dan Wolfe (www.flyboysalvage.com) for image used in Chapter 11

Mr. Ken Shuck (www.cessna150.net) for image used in Chapter 11

Mr. Paul Tocknell (www.askacfi.com) for image used in Chapter 11

Mr. Stephen McGreevy (www.auroralchorus.com) for image used in Chapter 11

Mr. Todd Bennett (www.bennettavionics.com) for image used in Chapter 11

National Oceanic and Atmospheric Administration, U.S. Department of Commerce for image used in Chapter 11

RAMI (www.rami.com) for image used in Chapter 11

Rockwell Collins (www.rockwellcollins.com) for image used in Chapter 11

Sarasota Avionics International (www.sarasotaavionics.com) for images used in Chapter 11

Southeast Aerospace, Inc. (www.seaerospace.com) for image used in Chapter 11

Sporty's Pilot Shop (www.sportys.com) for image used in Chapter 11

Watts Antenna Company (www.wattsantenna.com) for image used in Chapter 11

Wings and Wheels (www.wingsandwheels.com) for image used in Chapter 11

Aeropin, Inc. (www.aeropin.com) for image used in Chapter 13

Airplane Mart Publishing (www.AirplaneMart.com) for image used in Chapter 13

Alberth Aviation (www.alberthaviation.com) for image used in Chapter 13

AVweb (www.avweb.com) for image used in Chapter 13

Belle Aire Aviation, Inc. (www.belleaireaviation.com) for image used in Chapter 13

Cold War Air Museum (www.coldwarairmuseum.org) for image used in Chapter 13

Comanche Gear (www.comanchegear.com) for image used in Chapter 13

CSOBeech (www.csobeech.com) for image used in Chapter 13

Desser Tire & Rubber Co., Inc. (www.desser.com) for image used in Chapter 13

DG Flugzeugbau GmbH (www.dg-flugzeugbau.de) for image used in Chapter 13

Expedition Exchange, Inc. (www.expeditionexchange.com) for image used in Chapter 13

Fiddlers Green (www.fiddlersgreen.net) for image used in Chapter 13

Hitchcock Aviation (hitchcockaviation.com) for image used in Chapter 13

KUNZ GmbH aircraft equipment (www.kunz-aircraft.com) for images used in Chapter 13

Little Flyers (www.littleflyers.com) for images used in Chapter 13

Maple Leaf Aviation Ltd. (www.aircraftspeedmods.ca) for image used in Chapter 13

Mr. Budd Davisson (Airbum.com) for image used in Chapter 13

Mr. C. Jeff Dyrek (www.yellowairplane.com) for images used in Chapter 13

Mr. Jason Schappert (www.m0a.com) for image used in Chapter 13

Mr. John Baker (www.hangar9aeroworks.com) for image used in Chapter 13

Mr. Mike Schantz (www.trailer411.com) for image used in Chapter 13

Mr. Robert Hughes (www.escapadebuild.co.uk) for image used in Chapter 13

Mr. Ron Blachut for image used in Chapter 13

Owls Head Transportation Museum (www.owlshead.org) for image used in Chapter 13

PPI Aerospace (www.ppiaerospace.com) for image used in Chapter 13

Protective Packaging Corp. (www.protectivepackaging.net, 1-800-945-2247) for image used in Chapter 13

Ravenware Industries, LLC (www.ravenware.com) for image used in Chapter 13

Renold (www.renold.com) for image used in Chapter 13

Rotor F/X, LLC (www.rotorfx.com) for image used in Chapter 13

SkyGeek (www.skygeek.com) for image used in Chapter 13

Taigh Ramey (www.twinbeech.com) for image used in Chapter 13

Texas Air Salvage (www.texasairsalvage.com) for image used in Chapter 13

The Bogert Group (www.bogert-av.com) for image used in Chapter 13

W. B. Graham, Welded Tube Pros, LLC (www.thefabricator.com) for image used in Chapter 13

Zinko Hydraulic Jack (www.zinkojack.com) for image used in Chapter 13

Aviation Institute of Maintenance (www.aimschool.com) for image used in Chapter 14

Aviation Laboratories (www.avlab.com) for image used in Chapter 14

AVSIM (www.avsim.com) for image used in Chapter 14

Eggenfellner (www.eggenfellneraircraft.com) for image used in Chapter 14

FlightSim.Com, Inc. (www.flightsim.com) for image used in Chapter 14

Fluid Components International, LLC (www.fluidcomponents.com) for image used in Chapter 14

Fuel Quality Services, Inc. (www.fqsinc.com) for image used in Chapter 14

Hammonds Fuel Additives, Inc. (www.biobor.com) for image used in Chapter 14

Jeppesen (www.jeppesen.com) for image used in Chapter 14

MGL Avionics (www.mglavionics.com) for image used in Chapter 14

Mid-Atlantic Air Museum (www.maam.org) for image used in Chapter 14

MISCO Refractometer (www.misco.com) for image used in Chapter 14

Mr. Gary Brossett via the Aircraft Engine Historical Society (www.enginehistory.org) for image used in Chapter 14

Mr. Jeff McCombs (www.heyeng.com) for image used in Chapter 14

NASA for image used in Chapter 14

On-Track Aviation Limited (www.ontrackaviation.com) for image used in Chapter 14

Stewart Systems for image used in Chapter 14

Prist Aerospace Products (www.pristaerospace.com) for image used in Chapter 14

The Sundowners, Inc. (www.sdpleecounty.org) for image used in Chapter 14

Velcon Filters, LLC (www.velcon.com) for image used in Chapter 14

Aerox Aviation Oxygen Systems, Inc. (www.aerox.com) for image used in Chapter 16

Biggles Software (www.biggles-software.com) for image used in Chapter 16

C&D Associates, Inc. (www.aircraftheater.com) for image used in Chapter 16

Cobham (Carleton Technologies Inc.) (www.cobham.com) for image used in Chapter 16

Cool Africa (www.coolafrica.co.za) for image used in Chapter 16

Cumulus Soaring, Inc. (www.cumulus-soaring.com) for image used in Chapter 16

Essex Cryogenics of Missouri, Inc. (www.essexind.com) for image used in Chapter 16

Flightline AC, Inc. (www.flightlineac.com) for image used in Chapter 16

IDQ Holdings (www.idqusa.com) for image used in Chapter 16

Manchester Tank & Equipment (www.mantank.com) for image used in Chapter 16

Mountain High E&S Co. (www.mhoxygen.com) for images used throughout Chapter 16

Mr. Bill Sherwood (www.billzilla.org) for image used in Chapter 16

Mr. Boris Comazzi (www.flightgear.ch) for image used in Chapter 16

Mr. Chris Rudge (www.warbirdsite.com) for image used in Chapter 16

Mr. Richard Pfiffner (www.craggyaero.com) for image used in Chapter 16

Mr. Stephen Sweet (www.stephensweet.com) for image used in Chapter 16

Precise Flight Inc. (www.preciseflight.com) for image used in Chapter 16

SPX Service Solutions (www.spx.com) for image used in Chapter 16

SuperFlash Compressed Gas Equipment (www.oxyfuelsafety.com)

Mr. Tim Mara (www.wingsandwheels.com) for images used in Chapter 16

Mr. Bill Abbott for image used in Chapter 17

Additional appreciation is extended to Dr. Ronald Sterkenburg, Purdue University; Mr. Bryan Rahm, Dr. Thomas K. Eismain, Purdue University; Mr. George McNeill, Mr. Thomas Forenz, Mr. Peng Wang, and the National Oceanic and Atmospheric Administration (NOAA) for their technical support and input.

Table of Contents

Volume Contents iii

Preface v

Acknowledgments vii

Table of Contents xiii

Chapter 10
Aircraft Instrument Systems 10-1
Introduction 10-1
Classifying Instruments 10-3
   Flight Instruments 10-3
   Engine Instruments 10-3
   Navigation Instruments 10-4
Pressure Measuring Instruments 10-5
   Types of Pressure 10-7
   Pressure Instruments 10-8
      Engine Oil Pressure 10-8
      Manifold Pressure 10-9
      Engine Pressure Ratio (EPR) 10-9
      Fuel Pressure 10-10
      Hydraulic Pressure 10-10
      Vacuum Pressure 10-11
      Pressure Switches 10-11
   Pitot-Static Systems 10-12
      Pitot Tubes and Static Vents 10-12
      Air Data Computers (ADC) and Digital Air
      Data Computers (DADC) 10-14
   Pitot-Static Pressure-Sensing Flight Instruments ... 10-16
      Altimeters and Altitude 10-16
      Vertical Speed Indicator 10-22
      Airspeed Indicators 10-24
Remote Sensing and Indication 10-26
   Synchro-Type Remote-Indicating Instruments ... 10-26
      DC Selsyn Systems 10-26
      AC Synchro Systems 10-28
      Remote Indicating Fuel and Oil Pressure
      Gauges 10-28

Mechanical Movement Indicators 10-29
   Tachometers 10-29
      Mechanical Tachometers 10-29
      Electric Tachometers 10-30
   Synchroscope 10-32
   Accelerometers 10-32
   Stall Warning and Angle of Attack (AOA)
   Indicators 10-34
Temperature Measuring Instruments 10-35
   Non-Electric Temperature Indicators 10-36
   Electrical Temperature Measuring Indication ... 10-36
      Electrical Resistance Thermometer 10-36
      Ratiometer Electrical Resistance
      Thermometers 10-38
   Thermocouple Temperature Indicators 10-38
      Turbine Gas Temperature Indicating Systems ... 10-39
   Total Air Temperature Measurement 10-42
Direction Indicating Instruments 10-43
   Magnetic Compass 10-43
   Vertical Magnetic Compass 10-45
   Remote Indicating Compass 10-45
   Remote Indicating Slaved Gyro Compass (Flux
   Gate Compass) 10-45
   Solid State Magnetometers 10-46
Sources of Power for Gyroscopic Instruments 10-46
   Vacuum Systems 10-48
      Venturi Tube Systems 10-48
      Engine-Driven Vacuum Pump 10-48
      Typical Pump-Driven System 10-49
      Twin-Engine Aircraft Vacuum System
      Operation 10-50
   Pressure-Driven Gyroscopic Instrument Systems .. 10-51
   Electrically-Driven Gyroscopic Instrument
   Systems 10-51
Principles of Gyroscopic Instruments 10-52
   Mechanical Gyros 10-52
   Solid State Gyros and Related Systems 10-54
      Ring Laser Gyros (RLG) 10-54

Microelectromechanical Based Attitude and
Directional Systems 10-55
　Other Attitude and Directional Systems 10-55
Common Gyroscopic Instruments 10-56
　Vacuum-Driven Attitude Gyros 10-56
　Electric Attitude Indicators 10-57
　Gyroscopic Direction Indicator or Directional
　Gyro (DG) 10-58
　Turn Coordinators 10-58
　Turn-and-Slip Indicator 10-58
Autopilot Systems 10-60
　Basis for Autopilot Operation 10-60
Autopilot Components 10-61
　Sensing Elements 10-61
　Computer and Amplifier 10-61
　Output Elements 10-61
　Command Elements 10-63
　Feedback or Follow-up Element 10-63
　Autopilot Functions 10-64
　Yaw Dampening 10-65
Automatic Flight Control System (AFCS) 10-65
Flight Director Systems 10-65
Electronic Instruments 10-67
　Electronic Attitude Director Indicator (EADI) 10-67
　Electronic Horizontal Situation
　Indicators (EHSI) 10-68
Electronic Flight Information Systems 10-68
　Electronic Flight Instrument System (EFIS) 10-70
　Electronic Centralized Aircraft Monitor
　(ECAM) 10-71
　Engine Indicating and Crew Alerting
　System (EICAS) 10-72
Flight Management System (FMS) 10-73
Warnings and Cautions 10-74
　Annunciator Systems 10-74
　Aural Warning Systems 10-75
Clocks 10-76
Instrument Housings and Handling 10-77
Instrument Installations and Markings 10-78
　Instrument Panels 10-78
　Instrument Mounting 10-80
　Instrument Power Requirements 10-81
　Instrument Range Markings 10-81
Maintenance of Instruments and Instrument
Systems 10-81
　Altimeter Tests 10-82
　Pitot-Static System Maintenance and Tests 10-83
　Tachometer Maintenance 10-84
　Magnetic Compass Maintenance and
　Compensation 10-84
　Vacuum System Maintenance 10-85

Autopilot System Maintenance 10-85
LCD Display Screens 10-86

Chapter 11
Communication and Navigation 11-1
Introduction 11-1
　Avionics in Aviation Maintenance 11-2
　History of Avionics 11-2
　Fundamentals of Electronics 11-3
　　Analog Versus Digital Electronics 11-3
　　Analog Electronics 11-4
　　Digital Electronics 11-26
Radio Communication 11-30
　Radio Waves 11-31
　　Types of Radio Waves 11-32
　Loading Information onto a Radio Wave 11-32
　　Amplitude Modulation (AM) 11-34
　　Frequency Modulation (FM) 11-35
　　Single Side Band (SSB) 11-36
　Radio Transmitters and Receivers 11-37
　　Transmitters 11-37
　　Receivers 11-37
　　Transceivers 11-38
　Antennas 11-38
　　Length 11-38
　　Polarization, Directivity, and Field Pattern 11-39
　　Types 11-40
　　Transmission Lines 11-41
Radio Navigation 11-41
　VOR Navigation System 11-42
　Automatic Direction Finder (ADF) 11-46
　Radio Magnetic Indicator (RMI) 11-48
　Instrument Landing Systems (ILS) 11-49
　　Localizer 11-49
　　Glideslope 11-49
　　Compass Locators 11-51
　　Marker Beacons 11-52
　Distance Measuring Equipment (DME) 11-52
　Area Navigation (RNAV) 11-54
　Radar Beacon Transponder 11-54
　　Transponder Tests and Inspections 11-58
　　Altitude Encoders 11-58
　Collision Avoidance Systems 11-58
　　Traffic Collision Avoidance Systems (TCAS) ...11-59
　　ADS-B 11-60
　Radio Altimeter 11-62
　Weather Radar 11-64
　Emergency Locator Transmitter (ELT) 11-66

Long Range Aid to Navigation System
(LORAN) 11-69
Global Positioning System (GPS) 11-69
Wide Area Augmentation System (WAAS) 11-71
Inertial Navigation System (INS)/Inertial Reference
System (IRS) 11-71
Installation of Communication and Navigation
Equipment 11-72
Approval of New Avionics Equipment
Installations 11-72
Considerations 11-72
Cooling and Moisture 11-73
Vibration Isolation 11-73
Reducing Radio Interference 11-74
Shielding 11-74
Isolation 11-74
Bonding 11-74
Static Discharge Wicks 11-75
Installation of Aircraft Antenna Systems 11-75
Transmission Lines 11-76
Maintenance Procedure 11-76

Chapter 12
Hydraulic and Pneumatic Power Systems 12-1
Aircraft Hydraulic Systems 12-1
Hydraulic Fluid 12-2
Viscosity 12-2
Chemical Stability 12-2
Flash Point 12-3
Fire Point 12-3
Types of Hydraulic Fluids 12-3
Mineral-Based Fluids 12-3
Polyalphaolefin-Based Fluids 12-3
Phosphate Ester-Based Fluid (Skydrol®) 12-3
Intermixing of Fluids 12-3
Compatibility with Aircraft Materials 12-3
Hydraulic Fluid Contamination 12-4
Contamination Check 12-4
Contamination Control 12-5
Hydraulic System Flushing 12-5
Health and Handling 12-5
Basic Hydraulic Systems 12-6
Open Center Hydraulic Systems 12-6
Closed-Center Hydraulic Systems 12-7
Hydraulic Power Systems 12-7
Evolution of Hydraulic Systems 12-7
Hydraulic Power Pack System 12-7
Hydraulic System Components 12-8
Reservoirs 12-8
Filters 12-12
Micron-Type Filters 12-14

Maintenance of Filters 12-14
Filter Bypass Valve 12-14
Filter Differential Pressure Indicators 12-14
Pumps 12-15
Hand Pumps 12-15
Power-Driven Pumps 12-16
Classification of Pumps 12-16
Constant-Displacement Pumps 12-17
Gear-Type Power Pump 12-17
Gerotor Pump 12-17
Piston Pump 12-18
Vane Pump 12-19
Variable-Displacement Pump 12-20
Valves 12-23
Flow Control Valves 12-23
Pressure Control Valves 12-27
Shuttle Valves 12-29
Accumulators 12-30
Types of Accumulators 12-30
Heat Exchangers 12-32
Actuators 12-32
Linear Actuators 12-32
Rotary Actuators 12-33
Hydraulic Motor 12-34
Ram Air Turbine (RAT) 12-35
Power Transfer Unit (PTU) 12-35
Hydraulic Motor-Driven Generator (HMDG) 12-35
Seals 12-35
V-Ring Packings 12-35
U-Ring 12-35
O-Rings 12-35
Backup Rings 12-37
Gaskets 12-37
Seal Materials 12-37
O-Ring Installation 12-38
Wipers 12-38
Large Aircraft Hydraulic Systems 12-38
Boeing 737 Next Generation Hydraulic System 12-38
Reservoirs 12-38
Pumps 12-38
Filter Units 12-40
Power Transfer Unit (PTU) 12-40
Landing Gear Transfer Unit 12-41
Standby Hydraulic System 12-42
Indications 12-42
Boeing 777 Hydraulic System 12-42
Left and Right System Description 12-43
Center Hydraulic System 12-45

Aircraft Pneumatic Systems..................................12-47
   High-Pressure Systems..................................12-48
      Pneumatic System Components 12-48
      Emergency Backup Systems...............12-51
   Medium-Pressure Systems 12-52
   Low-Pressure Systems 12-52
   Pneumatic Power System Maintenance 12-52

Chapter 13
Aircraft Landing Gear Systems........................13-1
Landing Gear Types...13-1
   Landing Gear Arrangement..............................13-2
      Tail Wheel-Type Landing Gear 13-3
      Tandem Landing Gear 13-3
      Tricycle-Type Landing Gear 13-3
   Fixed and Retractable Landing Gear................13-5
   Shock Absorbing and Non-Shock Absorbing
   Landing Gear 13-5
      Leaf-Type Spring Gear 13-6
      Rigid 13-6
      Bungee Cord 13-7
      Shock Struts 13-7
   Shock Strut Operation 13-11
   Servicing Shock Struts 13-12
   Bleeding Shock Struts 13-13
Landing Gear Alignment, Support, and Retraction ...13-14
   Alignment..13-14
   Support 13-15
   Small Aircraft Retraction Systems 13-16
   Large Aircraft Retraction Systems 13-20
   Emergency Extension Systems 13-22
   Landing Gear Safety Devices...........................13-22
      Safety Switch 13-22
      Ground Locks 13-23
      Landing Gear Position Indicators 13-24
      Nose Wheel Centering 13-24
   Landing Gear System Maintenance 13-25
      Landing Gear Rigging and Adjustment....13-26
      Gear Door Clearances 13-28
      Drag and Side Brace Adjustment 13-28
      Landing Gear Retraction Test 13-29
Nose Wheel Steering Systems 13-30
   Small Aircraft 13-30
   Large Aircraft 13-30
   Shimmy Dampers 13-32
      Steering Damper 13-33
      Piston-Type 13-33
      Vane-Type 13-33
      Non-Hydraulic Shimmy Damper........13-34

Aircraft Wheels...13-34
   Wheel Construction..13-34
      Inboard Wheel Half 13-35
      Outboard Wheel Half.........................13-35
   Wheel Inspection 13-35
      On Aircraft Inspection 13-35
      Proper Installation...............................13-35
      Off Aircraft Wheel Inspection 13-37
Aircraft Brakes...13-42
   Types and Construction of Aircraft Brakes 13-43
      Single Disc Brakes...............................13-43
      Dual-Disc Brakes.................................13-45
      Multiple-Disc Brakes...........................13-46
      Segmented Rotor-Disc Brakes 13-47
      Carbon Brakes 13-50
      Expander Tube Brakes........................13-50
   Brake Actuating Systems 13-52
      Independent Master Cylinders 13-52
      Boosted Brakes 13-55
      Power Brakes 13-56
   Emergency Brake Systems 13-59
      Parking Brake 13-61
      Brake Deboosters...............................13-61
   Anti-Skid 13-61
      System Operation...............................13-61
      Wheel Speed Sensors.........................13-62
      Control Units 13-63
      Anti-Skid Control Valves 13-64
      Touchdown and Lock Wheel Protection 13-66
      Auto Brakes 13-66
      Anti-Skid System Tests 13-66
      Anti-Skid System Maintenance 13-68
   Brake Inspection and Service 13-68
      On Aircraft Servicing 13-68
      Lining Wear 13-68
      Air in the Brake System......................13-69
      Bleeding Master Cylinder Brake Systems..........13-69
      Bleeding Power Brake Systems..........13-71
      Off Aircraft Brake Servicing and Maintenance...13-72
      Replacement of Brake Linings 13-73
   Brake Malfunctions and Damage 13-74
      Overheating 13-74
      Dragging 13-75
      Chattering or Squealing 13-76
Aircraft Tires and Tubes 13-76
   Tire Classification..13-76
      Types...13-76
      Ply Rating 13-77

Tube-Type or Tubeless 13-77
    Bias Ply or Radial 13-78
Tire Construction 13-78
    Bead 13-78
    Carcass Plies 13-79
    Tread 13-79
    Sidewall 13-80
Tire Inspection on the Aircraft 13-80
    Inflation 13-80
    Tread Condition 13-82
    Sidewall Condition 13-86
Tire Removal 13-86
Tire Inspection Off of the Aircraft 13-88
Tire Repair and Retreading 13-88
Tire Storage 13-89
Aircraft Tubes 13-89
    Tube Construction and Selection 13-89
    Tube Storage and Inspection 13-90
    Tire Inspection 13-90
Tire Mounting 13-90
    Tubeless Tires 13-90
    Tube-Type Tires 13-91
Tire Balancing 13-93
Operation and Handling Tips 13-93
    Taxiing 13-94
    Braking and Pivoting 13-94
    Landing Field and Hangar Floor Condition ... 13-94
    Takeoffs and Landings 13-94
    Hydroplaning 13-94

Chapter 14
Aircraft Fuel System 14-1
Basic Fuel System Requirements 14-1
    Fuel System Independence 14-2
    Fuel System Lightning Protection 14-2
    Fuel Flow 14-3
    Flow Between Interconnected Tanks 14-3
    Unusable Fuel Supply 14-3
    Fuel System Hot Weather Operation 14-3
Fuel Tanks 14-3
    Fuel Tank Tests 14-3
    Fuel Tank Installation 14-4
    Fuel Tank Expansion Space 14-4
    Fuel Tank Sump 14-4
    Fuel Tank Filler Connection 14-4
    Fuel Tank Vents and Carburetor Vapor Vents ... 14-4
    Fuel Tank Outlet 14-5
    Pressure Fueling Systems 14-5
    Fuel Pumps 14-5
    Fuel System Lines and Fittings 14-5
    Fuel System Components 14-5

Fuel Valves and Controls 14-5
Fuel Strainer or Filter 14-6
Fuel System Drains 14-6
Fuel Jettisoning System 14-6
Types of Aviation Fuel 14-7
    Reciprocating Engine Fuel—AVGAS 14-7
    Volatility 14-7
    Vapor Lock 14-7
    Carburetor Icing 14-7
    Aromatic Fuels 14-8
    Detonation 14-8
    Surface Ignition and Preignition 14-9
    Octane and Performance Number Rating ... 14-9
    Fuel Identification 14-10
    Purity 14-10
Turbine Engine Fuels 14-11
    Turbine Fuel Volatility 14-12
    Turbine Engine Fuel Types 14-13
    Turbine Engine Fuel Issues 14-13
Aircraft Fuel Systems 14-13
    Small Single-Engine Aircraft Fuel Systems ... 14-13
    Gravity Feed Systems 14-13
    Pump Feed Systems 14-14
    High-Wing Aircraft With Fuel Injection
    System 14-14
    Small Multiengine (Reciprocating) Aircraft
    Fuel Systems 14-15
    Low-Wing Twin 14-15
    High-Wing Twin 14-16
    Large Reciprocating-Engine Aircraft Fuel
    Systems 14-16
    Jet Transport Aircraft Fuel Systems 14-17
    Helicopter Fuel Systems 14-22
Fuel System Components 14-22
    Fuel Tanks 14-22
    Rigid Removable Fuel Tanks 14-23
    Bladder Fuel Tanks 14-25
    Integral Fuel Tanks 14-25
    Fuel Lines and Fittings 14-26
    Fuel Valves 14-26
    Hand-Operated Valves 14-28
    Cone Valves 14-28
    Poppet Valves 14-29
    Manually-Operated Gate Valves 14-29
    Motor-Operated Valves 14-30
    Solenoid-Operated Valves 14-31
    Fuel Pumps 14-31
    Hand-Operated Fuel Pumps 14-31
    Ejector Pumps 14-32

Pulsating Electric Pumps 14-34
    Vane-Type Fuel Pumps 14-35
Fuel Filters 14-36
Fuel Heaters and Ice Prevention 14-39
Fuel System Indicators 14-40
    Fuel Quantity Indicating Systems 14-40
    Fuel Flowmeters 14-44
    Fuel Temperature Gauges 14-46
    Fuel Pressure Gauges 14-47
    Pressure Warning Signal 14-48
    Valve-In-Transit Indicator Lights 14-48
Fuel System Repair 14-49
    Troubleshooting the Fuel System 14-49
    Location of Leaks and Defects 14-49
    Fuel Leak Classification 14-50
    Replacement of Gaskets, Seals, and Packings 14-50
Fuel Tank Repair 14-50
    Welded Tanks 14-51
    Riveted Tanks 14-51
    Soldered Tanks 14-51
    Bladder Tanks 14-51
    Integral Tanks 14-52
    Fire Safety 14-52
Fuel System Servicing 14-54
    Checking for Fuel System Contaminants 14-54
    Water 14-54
    Solid Particle Contaminants 14-55
    Surfactants 14-55
    Microorganisms 14-55
    Foreign Fuel Contamination 14-56
    Detection of Contaminants 14-56
    Fuel Contamination Control 14-58
Fueling and Defueling Procedures 14-59
    Fueling 14-59
    Defueling 14-61
    Fire Hazards When Fueling or Defueling 14-61

Chapter 15
Ice and Rain Protection 15-1
Ice Control Systems 15-1
    Icing Effects 15-2
Ice Detector System 15-3
    Ice Prevention 15-3
Wing and Horizontal and Vertical Stabilizer
Anti-Icing Systems 15-4
    Thermal Pneumatic Anti-icing 15-4
        Wing Anti-Ice (WAI) System 15-4
        Leading Edge Slat Anti-Ice System 15-6
    Thermal Electric Anti-Icing 15-10
    Chemical Anti-Icing 15-10

Wing and Stabilizer Deicing Systems 15-12
    Sources of Operating Air 15-12
        Turbine Engine Bleed Air 15-12
    Pneumatic Deice Boot System for GA Aircraft 15-12
        GA System Operation 15-13
    Deice System for Turboprop Aircraft 15-14
    Deicing System Components 15-14
        Wet-Type Engine-Driven Air Pump 15-14
        Dry-Type Engine-Driven Air Pump 15-16
        Oil Separator 15-17
        Control Valve 15-17
        Deflate Valve 15-18
        Distributor Valve 15-18
        Timer/Control Unit 15-18
        Regulators and Relief Valves 15-18
        Manifold Assembly 15-19
        Inlet Filter 15-19
    Construction and Installation of Deice Boots 15-19
    Inspection, Maintenance, and Troubleshooting
    of Rubber Deicer Boot Systems 15-19
        Operational Checks 15-19
        Adjustments 15-21
        Troubleshooting 15-21
        Inspection 15-21
    Deice Boot Maintenance 15-21
    Electric Deice Boots 15-22
Propeller Deice System 15-23
    Electrothermal Propeller Device System 15-23
    Chemical Propeller Deice 15-23
Ground Deicing of Aircraft 15-23
    Frost Removal 15-25
        Deicing and Anti-icing of Transport Type
        Aircraft 15-25
    Ice and Snow Removal 15-27
Rain Control Systems 15-27
    Windshield Wiper Systems 15-27
    Chemical Rain Repellant 15-27
        Windshield Surface Seal Coating 15-28
    Pneumatic Rain Removal Systems 15-28
Windshield Frost, Fog, and Ice Control Systems 15-28
    Electric 15-28
    Pneumatic 15-30
    Chemical 15-31
Portable Water Tank Ice Prevention 15-32

Chapter 16
Cabin Environmental Control Systems 16-1
Physiology of Flight 16-1
    Composition of the Atmosphere 16-1
    Human Respiration and Circulation 16-2

Oxygen and Hypoxia 16-2
Carbon Monoxide Poisoning 16-3
Aircraft Oxygen Systems 16-3
Forms of Oxygen and Characteristics 16-4
Gaseous Oxygen 16-4
Liquid Oxygen 16-4
Chemical or Solid Oxygen 16-5
Onboard Oxygen Generating Systems
(OBOGS) 16-5
Oxygen Systems and Components 16-6
Gaseous Oxygen Systems 16-6
Chemical Oxygen Systems 16-16
LOX Systems 16-16
Oxygen System Servicing 16-16
Servicing Gaseous Oxygen 16-16
Filling LOX Systems 16-19
Inspection of Masks and Hoses 16-19
Replacing Tubing, Valves, and Fittings 16-20
Prevention of Oxygen Fires or Explosions 16-20
Oxygen System Inspection and Maintenance 16-20
Aircraft Pressurization Systems 16-21
Pressure of the Atmosphere 16-21
Temperature and Altitude 16-22
Pressurization Terms 16-23
Pressurization Issues 16-23
Sources of Pressurized Air 16-24
Reciprocating Engine Aircraft 16-25
Turbine Engine Aircraft 16-26
Control of Cabin Pressure 16-27
Pressurization Modes 16-27
Cabin Pressure Controller 16-28
Cabin Air Pressure Regulator and Outflow
Valve 16-30
Cabin Air Pressure Safety Valve Operation 16-31
Pressurization Gauges 16-32
Pressurization Operation 16-32
Air Distribution 16-34
Cabin Pressurization Troubleshooting 16-34
Air Conditioning Systems 16-34
Air Cycle Air Conditioning 16-35
System Operation 16-36
Pneumatic System Supply 16-36
Component Operation 16-36
Water Separator 16-39
Cabin Temperature Control System 16-39
Vapor Cycle Air Conditioning 16-40
Theory of Refrigeration 16-41
Vapor Cycle Air Conditioning System
Components 16-46

Vapor Cycle Air Conditioning Servicing
Equipment 16-51
System Servicing 16-55
Technician Certification 16-58
Aircraft Heaters 16-58
Bleed Air Systems 16-58
Electric Heating Systems 16-58
Exhaust Shroud Heaters 16-58
Combustion Heaters 16-60
Combustion Air System 16-60
Ventilating Air System 16-60
Fuel System 16-61
Ignition System 16-61
Controls 16-61
Safety Features 16-62
Maintenance and Inspection 16-62

Chapter 17
Fire Protection Systems 17-1
Introduction 17-1
Classes of Fires 17-2
Requirements for Overheat and Fire Protection
Systems 17-2
Fire Detection/Overheat Systems 17-2
Thermal Switch System 17-2
Thermocouple System 17-3
Continuous-Loop Systems 17-4
Fenwal System 17-4
Kidde System 17-4
Pressure Type Sensor Responder Systems 17-6
Pneumatic Continuous-Loop Systems 17-6
Fire Zones 17-8
Smoke, Flame, and Carbon Monoxide Detection
Systems 17-8
Smoke Detectors 17-8
Light Refraction Type 17-8
Ionization Type 17-8
Flame Detectors 17-9
Carbon Monoxide Detectors 17-9
Extinguishing Agents and Portable Fire
Extinguishers 17-10
Halogenated Hydrocarbons 17-10
Inert Cold Gases 17-10
Dry Powders 17-10
Water 17-11
Cockpit and Cabin Interiors 17-11
Extinguisher Types 17-11
Installed Fire Extinguishing Systems 17-11
CO_2 Fire Extinguishing Systems 17-11

xix

Halogenated Hydrocarbons Fire Extinguishing Systems 17-11
Containers 17-12
Discharge Valves 17-13
Pressure Indication 17-13
Two-Way Check Valve 17-13
Discharge Indicators 17-13
    Thermal Discharge Indicator (Red Disk) 17-13
    Yellow Disk Discharge Indicator 17-14
Fire Switch 17-14
Cargo Fire Detection 17-14
    Cargo Compartment Classification 17-15
        Class A 17-15
        Class B 17-15
        Class C 17-15
        Class E 17-15
    Cargo and Baggage Compartment Fire Detection and Extinguisher System 17-15
        Smoke Detector System 17-16
        Cargo Compartment Extinguishing System 17-16
Lavatory Smoke Detectors 17-17
    Lavatory Smoke Detector System 17-17
    Lavatory Fire Extinguisher System 17-18
Fire Detection System Maintenance 17-18
Fire Detection System Troubleshooting 17-19
Fire Extinguisher System Maintenance 17-20
    Container Pressure Check 17-20
    Discharge Cartridges 17-20
    Agent Containers 17-20
Fire Prevention 17-21

Glossary **G-1**

Index **I-1**

Chapter 10
Aircraft Instrument Systems

Introduction

Since the beginning of manned flight, it has been recognized that supplying the pilot with information about the aircraft and its operation could be useful and lead to safer flight. The Wright Brothers had very few instruments on their Wright Flyer, but they did have an engine tachometer, an anemometer (wind meter), and a stop watch. They were obviously concerned about the aircraft's engine and the progress of their flight. From that simple beginning, a wide variety of instruments have been developed to inform flight crews of different parameters. Instrument systems now exist to provide information on the condition of the aircraft, engine, components, the aircraft's attitude in the sky, weather, cabin environment, navigation, and communication. *Figure 10-1* shows various instrument panels from the Wright Flyer to a modern jet airliner.

The ability to capture and convey all of the information a pilot may want, in an accurate, easily understood manner, has been a challenge throughout the history of aviation. As the range of desired information has grown, so too have the size and complexity of modern aircraft, thus expanding even further the need to inform the flight crew without sensory overload or overcluttering the cockpit. As a result, the old flat panel in the front of the cockpit with various individual instruments attached to it has evolved into a sophisticated computer-controlled digital interface with flat-panel display screens and prioritized messaging. A visual comparison between a conventional cockpit and a glass cockpit is shown in *Figure 10-2*.

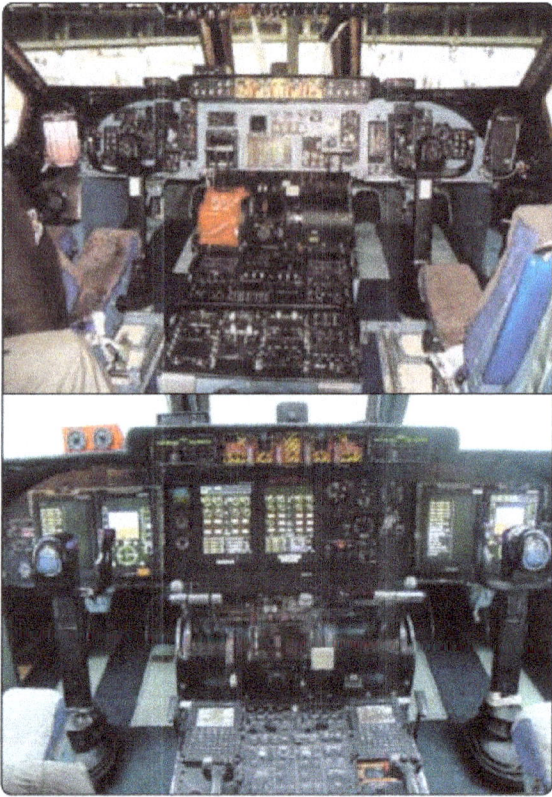

Figure 10-2. *A conventional instrument panel of the C-5A Galaxy (top) and the glass cockpit of the C-5B Galaxy (bottom).*

There are usually two parts to any instrument or instrument system. One part senses the situation and the other part displays it. In analog instruments, both of these functions often take place in a single unit or instrument (case). These are called direct-sensing instruments. Remote-sensing requires the information to be sensed, or captured, and then sent to a separate display unit in the cockpit. Both analog and digital instruments make use of this method. *[Figure 10-3]*

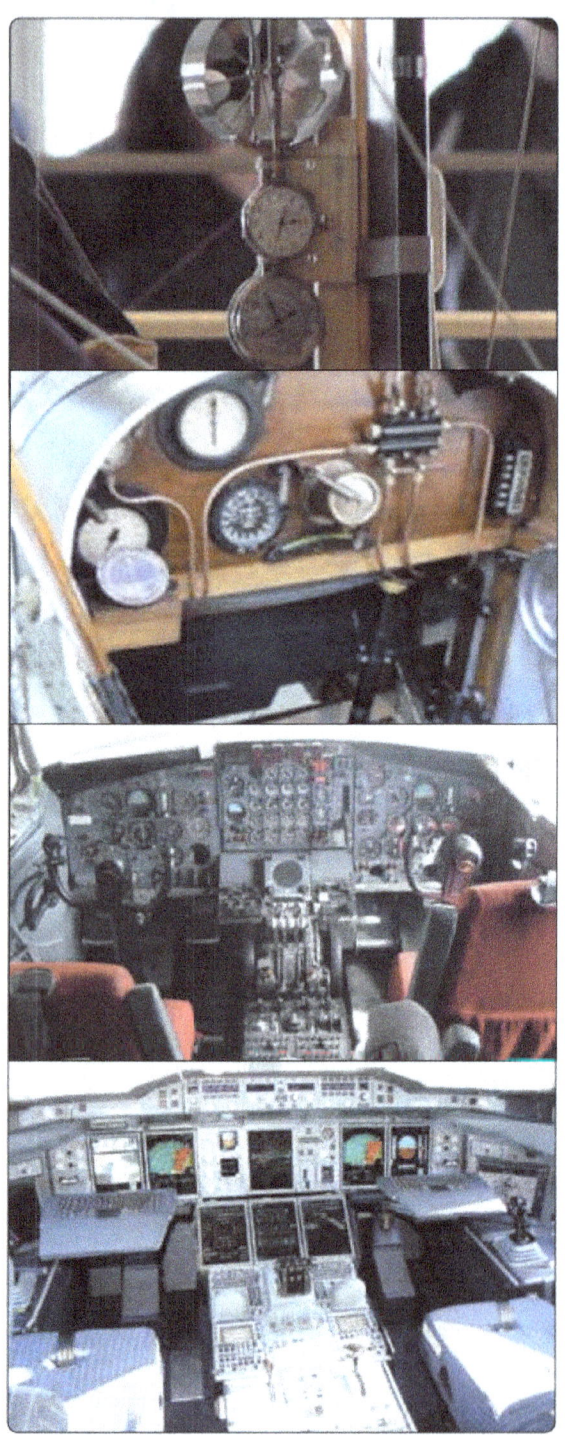

Figure 10-1. *From top to bottom: instruments of the Wright Flyer, instruments on a World War I era aircraft, a late 1950s/early 1960s Boeing 707 airliner cockpit, and an Airbus A380 glass cockpit.*

Figure 10-3. *There are two parts to any instrument system—the sensing mechanism and the display mechanism.*

The relaying of important bits of information can be done in various ways. Electricity is often used by way of wires that carry sensor information into the cockpit. Sometimes pneumatic lines are used. In complex, modern aircraft, this can lead to an enormous amount of tubing and wiring terminating behind the instrument display panel. More efficient information transfer has been accomplished via the use of digital data buses. Essentially, these are wires that share message carrying for many instruments by digitally encoding the signal for each. This reduces the number of wires and weight required to transfer remotely sensed information for the pilot's use. Flat-panel computer display screens that can be controlled to show only the information desired are also lighter in weight than the numerous individual gauges it would take to display the same information simultaneously. An added bonus is the increased reliability inherent in these solid-state systems.

It is the job of the aircraft technician to understand and maintain all aircraft, including these various instrument systems. Accordingly, in this chapter, discussions begin with analog instruments and refer to modern digital instrumentation when appropriate.

Classifying Instruments

There are three basic kinds of instruments classified by the job they perform: flight instruments, engine instruments, and navigation instruments. There are also miscellaneous gauges and indicators that provide information that do not fall into these classifications, especially on large complex aircraft. Flight control position, cabin environmental systems, electrical power, and auxiliary power units (APUs), for example, are all monitored and controlled from the cockpit via the use of instruments systems. All may be regarded as position/condition instruments since they usually report the position of a certain moveable component on the aircraft, or the condition of various aircraft components or systems not included in the first three groups.

Flight Instruments

The instruments used in controlling the aircraft's flight attitude are known as the flight instruments. There are basic flight instruments, such as the altimeter that displays aircraft altitude; the airspeed indicator; and the magnetic direction indicator, a form of compass. Additionally, an artificial horizon, turn coordinator, and vertical speed indicator are flight instruments present in most aircraft. Much variation exists for these instruments, which is explained throughout this chapter. Over the years, flight instruments have come to be situated similarly on the instrument panels in most aircraft. This basic T arrangement for flight instruments is shown in *Figure 10-4*. The top center position directly in front of the pilot and copilot is the basic display position for the artificial horizon even in modern glass cockpits (those with solid-state, flat-panel screen indicating systems).

Figure 10-4. *The basic T arrangement of analog flight instruments. At the bottom of the T is a heading indicator that functions as a compass but is driven by a gyroscope and not subject to the oscillations common to magnetic direction indicators.*

Original analog flight instruments are operated by air pressure and the use of gyroscopes. This avoids the use of electricity, which could put the pilot in a dangerous situation if the aircraft lost electrical power. Development of sensing and display techniques, combined with advanced aircraft electrical systems, has made it possible for reliable primary and secondary instrument systems that are electrically operated. Nonetheless, often a pneumatic altimeter, a gyro artificial horizon, and a magnetic direction indicator are retained somewhere in the instrument panel for redundancy. [Figure 10-5]

Engine Instruments

Engine instruments are those designed to measure operating parameters of the aircraft's engine(s). These are usually quantity, pressure, and temperature indications. They also include measuring engine speed(s). The most common engine instruments are the fuel and oil quantity and pressure gauges, tachometers, and temperature gauges. *Figure 10-6* contains various engine instruments found on reciprocating and turbine-powered aircraft.

Figure 10-5. *This electrically operated flat screen display instrument panel, or glass cockpit, retains an analog airspeed indicator, a gyroscope-driven artificial horizon, and an analog altimeter as a backup should electric power be lost, or a display unit fails.*

Engine instrumentation is often displayed in the center of the cockpit where it is easily visible to the pilot and copilot. *[Figure 10-7]* On light aircraft requiring only one flight crewmember, this may not be the case. Multiengine aircraft often use a single gauge for a particular engine parameter, but it displays information for all engines through the use of multiple pointers on the same dial face.

Navigation Instruments

Navigation instruments are those that contribute information used by the pilot to guide the aircraft along a definite course. This group includes compasses of various kinds, some of which incorporate the use of radio signals to define a specific course while flying the aircraft en route from one airport to another. Other navigational instruments are designed specifically to direct the pilot's approach to landing at an airport. Traditional navigation instruments include a clock and a magnetic compass. Along with the airspeed indicator and wind information, these can be used to calculate navigational progress. Radios and instruments sending locating information via radio waves have replaced these manual efforts in modern aircraft. Global position systems (GPS) use satellites to pinpoint the location of the aircraft via geometric triangulation. This technology is built into some aircraft instrument packages for navigational purposes.

Reciprocating engines	Turbine engines
Oil pressure	Oil pressure
Oil temperature	Exhaust gas temperature (EGT)
Cylinder head temperature (CHT)	Turbine inlet temperature (TIT) or turbine gas temperature (TGT)
Manifold pressure	Engine pressure ratio (EPR)
Fuel quantity	Fuel quantity
Fuel pressure	Fuel pressure
	Fuel flow
Tachometer	Tachometer (percent calibrated)
	N_1 and N_2 compressor speeds
Carburetor temperature	Torquemeter (on turboprop and turboshaft engines)

Figure 10-6. *Common engine instruments. Note: For example purposes only. Some aircraft may not have these instruments or may be equipped with others.*

Figure 10-7. *An engine instrumentation located in the middle of the instrument panel is shared by the pilot and co-pilot.*

Many of these aircraft navigational systems are discussed in chapter 11 of this handbook. *[Figure 10-8]*

To understand how various instruments work and can be repaired and maintained, they can be classified according to the principle upon which they operate. Some use mechanical methods to measure pressure and temperature. Some utilize magnetism and electricity to sense and display a parameter. Others depend on the use of gyroscopes in their primary workings. Still others utilize solid state sensors and computers to process and display important information. In the following sections, the different operating principles for sensing parameters are explained. Then, an overview of many of the engine, flight, and navigation instruments is given.

Pressure Measuring Instruments

A number of instruments inform the pilot of the aircraft's condition and flight situations through the measurement of pressure. Pressure-sensing instruments can be found in the flight group and the engine group. They can be either direct reading or remote sensing. These are some of the most critical instruments on the aircraft and must accurately inform the pilot to maintain safe operations. Pressure measurement involves some sort of mechanism that can sense changes in pressure. A technique for calibration and displaying the information is then added to inform the pilot. The type of pressure needed to be measured often makes one sensing mechanism more suited for use in a particular instance. The three fundamental pressure-sensing mechanisms used in aircraft instrument systems are the Bourdon tube, the diaphragm or bellows, and the solid-state sensing device.

A Bourdon tube is illustrated in *Figure 10-9*. The open end of this coiled tube is fixed in place and the other end is sealed and free to move. When a fluid that needs to be measured is directed into the open end of the tube, the unfixed portion

Figure 10-9. *The Bourdon tube is one of the basic mechanisms for sensing pressure.*

of the coiled tube tends to straighten out. The higher the pressure of the fluid, the more the tube straightens. When the pressure is reduced, the tube recoils. A pointer is attached to this moving end of the tube, usually through a linkage of small shafts and gears. By calibrating this motion of the straightening tube, a face or dial of the instrument can be created. Thus, by observing the pointer movement along the scale of the instrument face positioned behind it, pressure increases and decreases are communicated to the pilot.

The Bourdon tube is the internal mechanism for many pressure gauges used on aircraft. When high pressures need to be measured, the tube is designed to be stiff. Gauges used to indicate lower pressures use a more flexible tube that uncoils and coils more readily. Most Bourdon tubes are made from brass, bronze, or copper. Alloys of these metals can be made to coil and uncoil the tube consistently numerous times.

Bourdon tube gauges are simple and reliable. Some of the instruments that use a Bourdon tube mechanism include the engine oil pressure gauge, hydraulic pressure gauge, oxygen tank pressure gauge, and deice boot pressure gauge. Since the pressure of the vapor produced by a heated liquid

Figure 10-8. *Navigation instruments.*

or gas increases as temperature increases, Bourdon tube mechanisms can also be used to measure temperature. This is done by calibrating the pointer connecting linkage and relabeling the face of the gauge with a temperature scale. Oil temperature gauges often employ Bourdon tube mechanisms. *[Figure 10-10]*

Figure 10-10. *The Bourdon tube mechanism can be used to measure pressure or temperature by recalibrating the pointer's connecting linkage and scaling instrument face to read in degrees Celsius or Fahrenheit.*

Since the sensing and display of pressure or temperature information using a Bourdon tube mechanism usually occurs in a single instrument housing, they are most often direct reading gauges. But the Bourdon tube sensing device can also be used remotely. Regardless, it is necessary to direct the fluid to be measured into the Bourdon tube. For example, a common direct-reading gauge measuring engine oil pressure and indicating it to the pilot in the cockpit is mounted in the instrument panel. A small length of tubing connects a pressurized oil port on the engine, runs though the firewall, and into the back of the gauge. This setup is especially functional on light, single-engine aircraft in which the engine is mounted just forward of the instrument panel in the forward end of the fuselage. However, a remote sensing unit can be more practical on twin-engine aircraft where the engines are a long distance from the cockpit pressure display. Here, the Bourdon tube's motion is converted to an electrical signal and carried to the cockpit display via a wire. This is lighter and more efficient, eliminating the possibility of leaking fluids into the passenger compartment of the aircraft.

The diaphragm and bellows are two other basic sensing mechanisms employed in aircraft instruments for pressure measurement. The diaphragm is a hollow, thin-walled metal disk, usually corrugated. When pressure is introduced through an opening on one side of the disk, the entire disk expands. By placing linkage in contact against the other side of the disk, the movement of the pressurized diaphragm can be transferred to a pointer that registers the movement against the scale on the instrument face. *[Figure 10-11]*

Figure 10-11. *A diaphragm used for measuring pressure. An evacuated sealed diaphragm is called an aneroid.*

Diaphragms can also be sealed. The diaphragm can be evacuated before sealing, retaining absolutely nothing inside. When this is done, the diaphragm is called an aneroid. Aneroids are used in many flight instruments. A diaphragm can also be filled with a gas to standard atmospheric pressure and then sealed. Each of these diaphragms has their uses, which are described in the next section. The common factor in all is that the expansion and contraction of the side wall of the diaphragm is the movement that correlates to increasing and decreasing pressure.

When a number of diaphragm chambers are connected together, the device is called a bellows. This accordion-like assembly of diaphragms can be very useful when measuring the difference in pressure between two gases, called differential pressure. Just as with a single diaphragm, it is the movement of the side walls of the bellows assembly that correlates with changes in pressure and to which a pointer linkage and gearing is attached to inform the pilot. *[Figure 10-12]*

Figure 10-12. *A bellows unit in a differential pressure gauge compares two different pressure values. End movement of the bellows away from the side with the highest pressure input occurs when the pressures in the bellows are not equal. The indicator linkage is calibrated to display the difference.*

Diaphragms, aneroids, and bellows pressure sensing devices are often located inside the single instrument housing that contains the pointer and instrument dial read by the pilot on the instrument panel. Thus, many instruments that make use of these sensitive and reliable mechanisms are direct reading gauges. But, many remote sensing instrument systems also make use of the diaphragm and bellows. In this case, the sensing device containing the pressure sensitive diaphragm or bellows is located remotely on the engine or airframe. It is part of a transducer that converts the pressure into an electrical signal. The transducer, or transmitter, sends the signal to the gauge in the cockpit, or to a computer, for processing and subsequent display of the sensed condition. Examples of instruments that use a diaphragm or bellows in a direct reading or remote sensing gauge are the altimeter, vertical speed indicator, cabin differential pressure gauge (in pressurized aircraft), and manifold pressure gauge.

Solid-state microtechnology pressure sensors are used in modern aircraft to determine the critical pressures needed for safe operation. Many of these have digital output ready for processing by electronic flight instrument computers and other onboard computers. Some sensors send microelectric signals that are converted to digital format for use by computers. As with the analog sensors described above, the key to the function of solid-state sensors is their consistent property changes as pressure changes.

The solid-state sensors used in most aviation applications exhibit varying electrical output or resistance changes when pressure changes occur. Crystalline piezoelectric, piezoresistor, and semiconductor chip sensors are most common. In the typical sensor, tiny wires are embedded in the crystal or pressure-sensitive semiconductor chip. When pressure deflects the crystal(s), a small amount of electricity is created or, in the case of a semiconductor chip and some crystals, the resistance changes. Since the current and resistance changes vary directly with the amount of deflection, outputs can be calibrated and used to display pressure values.

Nearly all of the pressure information needed for engine, airframe, and flight instruments can be captured and/or calculated through the use of solid-state pressure sensors in combination with temperature sensors. But continued use of aneroid devices for comparisons involving absolute pressure is notable. Solid-state pressure-sensing systems are remote sensing systems. The sensors are mounted on the aircraft at convenient and effective locations.

Types of Pressure

Pressure is a comparison between two forces. Absolute pressure exists when a force is compared to a total vacuum, or absolutely no pressure. It is necessary to define absolute pressure, because the air in the atmosphere is always exerting pressure on everything. Even when it seems there is no pressure being applied, like when a balloon is deflated, there is still atmospheric pressure inside and outside of the balloon. To measure that atmospheric pressure, it is necessary to compare it to a total absence of pressure, such as in a vacuum. Many aircraft instruments make use of absolute pressure values, such as the altimeter, the rate-of-climb indicator, and the manifold pressure gauge. As stated, this is usually done with an aneroid.

The most common type of pressure measurement is gauge pressure. This is the difference between the pressure to be measured and the atmospheric pressure. The gauge pressure inside the deflated balloon mentioned above is therefore 0 pounds per square inch (psi). Gauge pressure is easily measured and is obtained by ignoring the fact that the atmosphere is always exerting its pressure on everything. For example, a tire is filled with air to 32 psi at a sea level location and checked with a gauge to read 32 psi, which is the gauge pressure. The approximately 14.7 psi of air pressing on the outside of the tire is ignored. The absolute pressure in the tire is 32 psi plus the 14.7 psi that is needed to balance the 14.7 psi on the outside of the tire. So, the tire's absolute pressure is approximately 46.7 psi. If the same tire is inflated to 32 psi at a location 10,000 feet above sea level, the air pressure on the outside of the tire would only be approximately 10 psi, due to the thinner atmosphere. The pressure inside the tire required to balance this would be 32 psi plus 10 psi, making the absolute pressure of the tire 42 psi. So, the same tire with the same amount of inflation and performance characteristics has different absolute pressure values. Gauge pressure, however, remains the same, indicating the tires are inflated identically. It this case, gauge pressure is more useful in informing us of the condition of the tire.

Gauge pressure measurements are simple and widely useful. They eliminate the need to measure varying atmospheric pressure to indicate or monitor a particular pressure situation. Gauge pressure should be assumed, unless otherwise indicated, or unless the pressure measurement is of a type known to require absolute pressure.

In many instances in aviation, it is desirable to compare the pressures of two different elements to arrive at useful information for operating the aircraft. When two pressures are compared in a gauge, the measurement is known as differential pressure and the gauge is a differential pressure gauge. An aircraft's airspeed indicator is a differential pressure gauge. It compares ambient air pressure with ram air pressure to determine how fast the aircraft is moving through the air. A turbine's engine pressure ratio (EPR) gauge is also a differential pressure gauge. It compares the pressure at the inlet of the engine with that at the outlet to indicate the thrust developed by the engine. Both of these differential pressure gauges and others are discussed further in this chapter and throughout this handbook.

In aviation, there is also a commonly used pressure known as standard pressure. Standard pressure refers to an established or standard value that has been created for atmospheric pressure. This standard pressure value is 29.92 inches of mercury ("Hg), 1,013.2 hectopascal (hPa), or 14.7 psi. It is part of a standard day that has been established that includes a standard temperature of 15 °C at sea level. Specific standard day values have also been established for air density, volume, and viscosity. All of these values are developed averages since the atmosphere is continuously fluctuating. They are used by engineers when designing instrument systems and are sometimes used by technicians and pilots. Often, using a standard value for atmospheric pressure is more desirable than using the actual value. For example, at 18,000 feet and above, all aircraft use 29.92 "Hg as a reference pressure for their instruments to indicate altitude. This results in altitude indications in all cockpits being identical. Therefore, an accurate means is established for maintaining vertical separation of aircraft flying at these high altitudes.

Pressure Instruments
Engine Oil Pressure

The most important instrument used by the pilot to perceive the health of an engine is the engine oil pressure gauge. *[Figure 10-13]* Oil pressure is usually indicated in psi. The normal operating range is typically represented by a green arc on the circular gauge. For exact acceptable operating range, consult the manufacturer's operating and maintenance data. In reciprocating and turbine engines, oil is used to lubricate and cool bearing surfaces where parts are rotating or sliding past each other at high speeds. A loss of pressurized oil to these areas would rapidly cause excessive friction and over temperature conditions, leading to catastrophic engine failure. As mentioned, aircraft using analog instruments often use direct reading Bourdon tube oil pressure gauges. *Figure 10-13* shows the instrument face of a typical oil pressure gauge of this type. Digital instrument systems use an analog or digital remote oil pressure sensing unit that sends output to the computer, driving the display of oil pressure value(s) on the aircraft's cockpit display screens. Oil pressure may be displayed in a circular or linear gauge fashion and may even include a numerical value on screen. Often, oil pressure is grouped with other engine parameter displays on the same page or portion of a page on the display. *Figure 10-14* shows this grouping on a Garmin G1000 digital instrument display system for general aviation aircraft.

Figure 10-13. *An analog oil pressure gauge is driven by a Bourdon tube. Oil pressure is vital to engine health and must be monitored by the pilot.*

Figure 10-14. *Oil pressure indication with other engine-related parameters shown in a column on the left side of this digital cockpit display panel.*

Manifold Pressure

In reciprocating engine aircraft, the manifold pressure gauge indicates the pressure of the air in the engine's induction manifold. This is an indication of power being developed by the engine. The higher the pressure of the fuel air mixture going into the engine, the more power it can produce. For normally aspirated engines, this means that an indication near atmospheric pressure is the maximum. Turbocharged or supercharged engines pressurize the air being mixed with the fuel, so full power indications are above atmospheric pressure.

Most manifold pressure gauges are calibrated in inches of mercury, although digital displays may have the option to display in a different scale. A typical analog gauge makes use of an aneroid described above. When atmospheric pressure acts on the aneroid inside the gauge, the connected pointer indicates the current air pressure. A line running from the intake manifold into the gauge presents intake manifold air pressure to the aneroid, so the gauge indicates the absolute pressure in the intake manifold. An analog manifold pressure gauge, along with its internal workings, is shown in *Figure 10-15*. The digital presentation of manifold pressure is at the top of the engine instruments displayed on the Garmin G1000 multifunctional display in *Figure 10-14*. The aircraft's operating manual contains data on managing manifold pressure in relation to fuel flow and propeller pitch and for achieving various performance profiles during different phases of run-up and flight.

Engine Pressure Ratio (EPR)

Turbine engines have their own pressure indication that relates the power being developed by the engine. It is called the engine pressure ratio (EPR) indicator (EPR gauge). This gauge compares the total exhaust pressure to the pressure of the ram air at the inlet of the engine. With adjustments for temperature, altitude, and other factors, the EPR gauge presents an indication of the thrust being developed by the engine. Since the EPR gauge compares two pressures, it is a differential pressure gauge. It is a remote-sensing instrument that receives its input from an engine pressure ratio transmitter or, in digital instrument systems displays, from a computer. The pressure ratio transmitter contains the bellows arrangement that compares the two pressures and converts the ratio into an electric signal used by the gauge for indication. *[Figure 10-16]*

Figure 10-15. *Engine pressure ratio gauges.*

Figure 10-16. *An analog manifold pressure indicator instrument dial calibrated in inches of mercury (left). The internal workings of an analog manifold pressure gauge are shown on the right. Air from the intake manifold surrounds the aneroid causing it to deflect and indicate pressure on the dial through the use of linkage to the pointer (right).*

Fuel Pressure

Fuel pressure gauges also provide critical information to the pilot. *[Figure 10-17]* Typically, fuel is pumped out of various fuel tanks on the aircraft for use by the engines. A malfunctioning fuel pump, or a tank that has been emptied beyond the point at which there is sufficient fuel entering the pump to maintain desired output pressure, is a condition that requires the pilot's immediate attention. While direct-sensing fuel pressure gauges using Bourdon tubes, diaphragms, and bellows sensing arrangements exist, it is particularly undesirable to run a fuel line into the cockpit, due to the potential for fire should a leak develop. Therefore, the preferred arrangement is to have whichever sensing mechanism that is used be part of a transmitter device that uses electricity to send a signal to the indicator in the cockpit. Sometimes, indications monitoring the fuel flow rate are used instead of fuel pressure gauges. Fuel flow indications are discussed in the fuel system chapter of this handbook.

Hydraulic Pressure

Numerous other pressure monitoring gauges are used on complex aircraft to indicate the condition of various support systems not found on simple light aircraft. Hydraulic systems are commonly used to raise and lower landing gear, operate flight controls, apply brakes, and more. Sufficient pressure in the hydraulic system developed by the hydraulic pump(s) is

Figure 10-17. *A typical analog fuel pressure gauge.*

required for normal operation of hydraulic devices. Hydraulic pressure gauges are often located in the cockpit and at or near the hydraulic system servicing point on the airframe. Remotely located indicators used by maintenance personnel are almost always direct reading Bourdon tube type gauges. Cockpit gauges usually have system pressure transmitted from sensors or computers electrically for indication. *Figure 10-18* shows a hydraulic pressure transmitter in place in a high-pressure aircraft hydraulic system.

Figure 10-18. *A hydraulic pressure transmitter senses and converts pressure into an electrical output for indication by the cockpit gauge or for use by a computer that analyzes and displays the pressure in the cockpit when requested or required.*

Vacuum Pressure

Gyro pressure gauge, vacuum gauge, or suction gauge are all terms for the same gauge used to monitor the vacuum developed in the system that actuates the air driven gyroscopic flight instruments. Air is pulled through the instruments, causing the gyroscopes to spin. The speed at which the gyros spin needs to be within a certain range for correct operation. This speed is directly related to the suction pressure that is developed in the system. The suction gauge is extremely important in aircraft relying solely on vacuum-operated gyroscopic flight instruments.

Vacuum is a differential pressure indication, meaning the pressure to be measured is compared to atmospheric pressure through the use of a sealed diaphragm or capsule. The gauge is calibrated in inches of mercury. It shows how much less pressure exists in the system than in the atmosphere. *Figure 10-19* shows a suction gauge calibrated in inches of mercury.

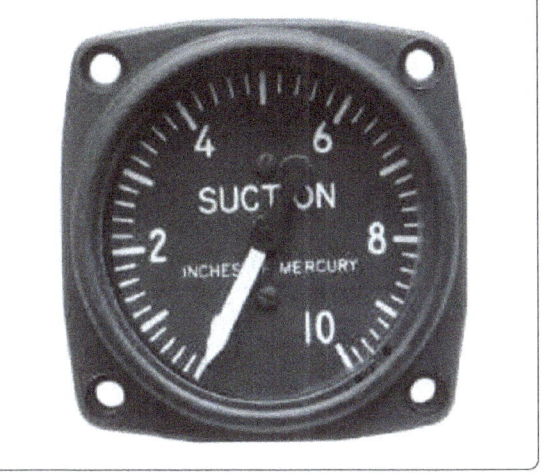

Figure 10-19. *Vacuum suction gauge.*

Pressure Switches

In aviation, it is often sufficient to simply monitor whether the pressure developed by a certain operating system is too high or too low, so that an action can take place should one of these conditions occur. This is often accomplished through the use of a pressure switch. A pressure switch is a simple device usually made to open or close an electric circuit when a certain pressure is reached in a system. It can be manufactured so that the electric circuit is normally open and can then close when a certain pressure is sensed, or the circuit can be closed and then opened when the activation pressure is reached. [*Figure 10-20*]

Pressure switches contain a diaphragm to which the pressure being sensed is applied on one side. The opposite side of the diaphragm is connected to a mechanical switching mechanism for an electric circuit. Small fluctuations or a buildup of pressure against the diaphragm move the diaphragm, but not enough to throw the switch. Only when

Figure 10-20. *A pressure switch can be used in addition to, or instead of, a pressure gauge.*

Figure 10-21. *A normally open pressure switch positioned in an electrical circuit causes the circuit to be open as well. The switch closes, allowing electricity to flow when pressure is applied beyond the switch's preset activation point. Normally, closed pressure switches allow electricity to flow through the switch in a circuit but open when pressure reaches a preset activation point, thus opening the electrical circuit.*

pressure meets or exceeds a preset level designed into the structure of the switch does the diaphragm move far enough for the mechanical device on the opposite side to close the switch contacts and complete the circuit. *[Figure 10-21]* Each switch is rated to close (or open) at a certain pressure, and must only be installed in the proper location.

A low oil pressure indication switch is a common example of how pressure switches are employed. It is installed in an engine so pressurized oil can be applied to the switch's diaphragm. Upon starting the engine, oil pressure increases and the pressure against the diaphragm is sufficient to hold the contacts in the switch open. As such, current does not flow through the circuit and no indication of low oil pressure is given in the cockpit. Should a loss of oil pressure occur, the pressure against the diaphragm becomes insufficient to hold the switched contacts open. When the contacts close, they close the circuit to the low oil pressure indicator, usually a light, to warn the pilot of the situation.

Pressure gauges for various components or systems work similarly to those mentioned above. Some sort of sensing device, appropriate for the pressure being measured or monitored, is matched with an indicating display system. If appropriate, a properly rated pressure switch is installed in the system and wired into an indicating circuit. Further discussion of specific instruments occurs throughout this handbook as the operation of various systems and components are discussed.

Pitot-Static Systems

Some of the most important flight instruments derive their indications from measuring air pressure. Gathering and distributing various air pressures for flight instrumentation is the function of the pitot-static system.

Pitot Tubes and Static Vents

On simple aircraft, this may consist of a pitot static system head or pitot tube with impact and static air pressure ports and leak-free tubing connecting these air pressure pick-up points to the instruments that require the air for their indications. The altimeter, airspeed indicator, and vertical speed indicator are the three most common pitot-static instruments. *Figure 10-22* illustrates a simple pitot-static system connected to these three instruments.

A pitot tube is shown in *Figure 10-23*. It is open and faces into the airstream to receive the full force of the impact air pressure as the aircraft moves forward. This air passes through a baffled plate designed to protect the system from moisture and dirt entering the tube. Below the baffle, a drain hole is provided, allowing moisture to escape. The ram air is directed aft to a chamber in the shark fin of the assembly. An upright tube, or riser, leads this pressurized air out of the pitot assemble to the airspeed indicator.

Figure 10-22. *A simple pitot-static system is connected to the primary flight instruments.*

The aft section of the pitot tube is equipped with small holes on the top and bottom surfaces that are designed to collect air pressure that is at atmospheric pressure in a static, or still, condition. *[Figure 10-23]* The static section also contains a riser tube and the air is run out the pitot assembly through tubes and is connected to the altimeter, the airspeed indicator, and the vertical speed indicator.

Many pitot-static tube heads contain heating elements to prevent icing during flight. The pilot can send electric current to the element with a switch in the cockpit when ice-forming conditions exist. Often, this switch is wired through the ignition switch so that when the aircraft is shut down, a pitot tube heater inadvertently left on does not continue to draw current and drain the battery. Caution should be exercised when near the pitot tube, as these heating elements make the tube too hot to be touched without receiving a burn.

The pitot-static tube is mounted on the outside of the aircraft at a point where the air is least likely to be turbulent. It is pointed in a forward direction parallel to the aircraft's line of flight. The location may vary. Some are on the nose of the fuselage and others may be located on a wing. A few may even be found on the empennage. Various designs exist but the function remains the same, to capture impact air pressure and static air pressure and direct them to the proper instruments. *[Figure 10-24]*

Most aircraft equipped with a pitot-static tube have an alternate source of static air pressure provided for emergency use. The pilot may select the alternate with a switch in the cockpit should it appear the flight instruments are not providing accurate indications. On low-flying unpressurized aircraft, the alternate static source may simply be air from

Figure 10-23. *A typical pitot-static system head, or pitot tube, collects ram air and static pressure for use by the flight instruments.*

Figure 10-24. *Pitot-static system heads, or pitot tubes, can be of various designs and locations on airframes.*

the cabin. *[Figure 10-25]* On pressurized aircraft, cabin air pressure may be significantly different than the outside ambient air pressure. If used as an alternate source for static air, instrument indications would be grossly inaccurate. In this case, multiple static vent pickup points are employed. All are located on the outside of the aircraft and plumbed so the pilot can select which source directs air into the instruments. On electronic flight displays, the choice is made for which source is used by the computer or by the flight crew.

Figure 10-25. *On unpressurized aircraft, an alternate source of static air is cabin air.*

Another type of pitot-static system provides for the location of the pitot and static sources at separate positions on the aircraft. The pitot tube in this arrangement is used only to gather ram air pressure. Separate static vents are used to collect static air pressure information. Usually, these are located flush on the side of the fuselage. *[Figure 10-26]* There may be two or more vents. A primary and alternate source vent is typical, as well as separate dedicated vents for the pilot and first officer's instruments. Also, two primary vents may be located on opposite sides of the fuselage and connected with Y tubing for input to the instruments. This is done to compensate for any variations in static air pressure on the vents due to the aircraft's attitude. Regardless of the number and location of separate static vents, they may be heated as well as the separate ram air pitot tube to prevent icing.

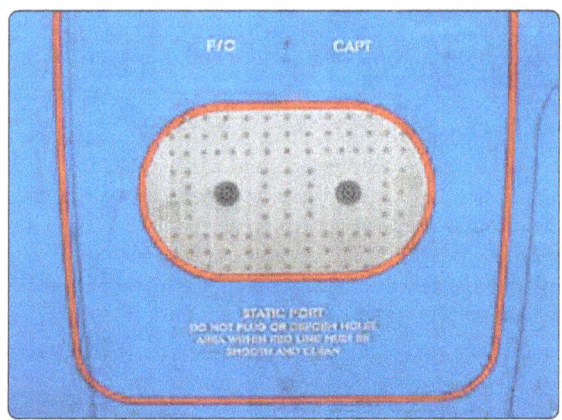

Figure 10-26. *Heated primary and alternate static vents located on the sides of the fuselage.*

The pitot-static systems of complex, multiengine, and pressurized aircraft can be elaborate. Additional instruments, gauges, the autopilot system, and computers may need pitot and static air information. *Figure 10-27* shows a pitot-static system for a pressurized multiengine aircraft with dual analog instrument panels in the cockpit. The additional set of flight instruments for the copilot alters and complicates the pitot-static system plumbing. Additionally, the autopilot system requires static pressure information, as does the cabin pressurization unit. Separate heated sources for static air pressure are taken from both sides of the airframe to feed independent static air pressure manifolds; one each for the pilot's flight instruments and the copilot's flight instruments. This is designed to ensure that there is always one set of flight instruments operable in case of a malfunction.

Air Data Computers (ADC) and Digital Air Data Computers (DADC)

High performance and jet transport category aircraft pitot-static systems may be more complicated. These

Figure 10-27. *Schematic of a typical pitot-static system on a pressurized multiengine aircraft.*

aircraft frequently operate at high altitude where the ambient temperature can exceed 50 °F below zero. The compressibility of air is also altered at high speeds and at high altitudes. Airflow around the fuselage changes, making it difficult to pick up consistent static pressure inputs. The pilot must compensate for all factors of air temperature and density to obtain accurate indications from instruments. While many analog instruments have compensating devices built into them, the use of an air data computer (ADC) is common for these purposes on high-performance aircraft. Moreover, modern aircraft utilize digital air data computers (DADC). The conversion of sensed air pressures into digital values makes them more easily manipulated by the computer to output accurate information that has compensated for the many variables encountered. *[Figure 10-28]*

Figure 10-28. *Teledyne's 90004 TAS/Plus air data computer (ADC) computes air data information from the pitot-static pneumatic system, aircraft temperature probe, and barometric correction device to help create a clear indication of flight conditions.*

Essentially, all pressures and temperatures captured by sensors are fed into the ADC. Analog units utilize transducers to convert these to electrical values and manipulate them in various modules containing circuits designed to make the proper compensations for use by different instruments and systems. A DADC usually receives its data in digital format. Systems that do not have digital sensor outputs will first convert inputs into digital signals via an analog-to-digital converter. Conversion can take place inside the computer or in a separate unit designed for this function. Then, all calculation and compensations are performed digitally by the computer. Outputs from the ADC are electric to drive servo motors or for use as inputs in pressurization systems, flight control units, and other systems. DADC outputs are distributed to these same systems and the cockpit display using a digital data bus.

There are numerous benefits of using ADCs. Simplification of pitot-static plumbing lines creates a lighter, simpler, system with fewer connections, so it is less prone to leaks and easier to maintain. One-time compensation calculations can be done inside the computer, eliminating the need to build compensating devices into numerous individual instruments or units of the systems using the air data. DADCs can run a number of checks to verify the plausibility of data received from any source on the aircraft. Thus, the crew can be alerted automatically of a parameter that is out of the ordinary. Change to an alternate data source can also be automatic so accurate flight deck and systems operations are continuously maintained. In general, solid-state technology is more reliable and modern units are small and lightweight. *Figure 10-29* shows a schematic of how a DADC is connected into the aircraft's pitot-static and other systems.

Pitot-Static Pressure-Sensing Flight Instruments

The basic flight instruments are directly connected to the pitot-static system on many aircraft. Analog flight instruments primarily use mechanical means to measure and indicate various flight parameters. Digital flight instrument systems use electricity and electronics to do the same. Discussion of the basic pitot-static flight instruments begins with analog instruments to which further information about modern digital instrumentation is added.

Altimeters and Altitude

An altimeter is an instrument that is used to indicate the height of the aircraft above a predetermined level, such as sea level or the terrain beneath the aircraft. The most common way to measure this distance is rooted in discoveries made by scientists centuries ago. Seventeenth century work proving that the air in the atmosphere exerted pressure on the things around us led Evangelista Torricelli to the invention of the barometer. Also in that century, using the concept of this first atmospheric air pressure measuring instrument, Blaise Pascal was able to show that a relationship exists between altitude and air pressure. As altitude increases, air pressure decreases. The amount that it decreases is measurable and consistent for any given altitude change. Therefore, by measuring air pressure, altitude can be determined. *[Figure 10-30]*

Altimeters that measure the aircraft's altitude by measuring the pressure of the atmospheric air are known as pressure altimeters. A pressure altimeter is made to measure the ambient air pressure at any given location and altitude. In aircraft, it is connected to the static vent(s) via tubing in the pitot-static system. The relationship between the measured pressure and the altitude is indicated on the instrument face, which is calibrated in feet. These devises are direct-reading instruments that measure absolute pressure. An aneroid or aneroid bellows is at the core of the pressure altimeter's inner workings. Attached to this sealed diaphragm are the linkages and gears that connect it to the indicating pointer. Static air pressure enters the airtight instrument case and surrounds the aneroid. At sea level, the altimeter indicates zero when this pressure is exerted by the ambient air on the aneroid. As air pressure is reduced by moving the altimeter higher in the atmosphere, the aneroid expands and displays altitude on the instrument by rotating the pointer. As the altimeter is lowered in the atmosphere, the air pressure around the aneroid increases and the pointer moves in the opposite direction. *[Figure 10-31]*

The face, or dial, of an analog altimeter is read similarly to a clock. As the longest pointer moves around the dial, it is registering the altitude in hundreds of feet. One complete revolution of this pointer indicates 1,000 feet of altitude.

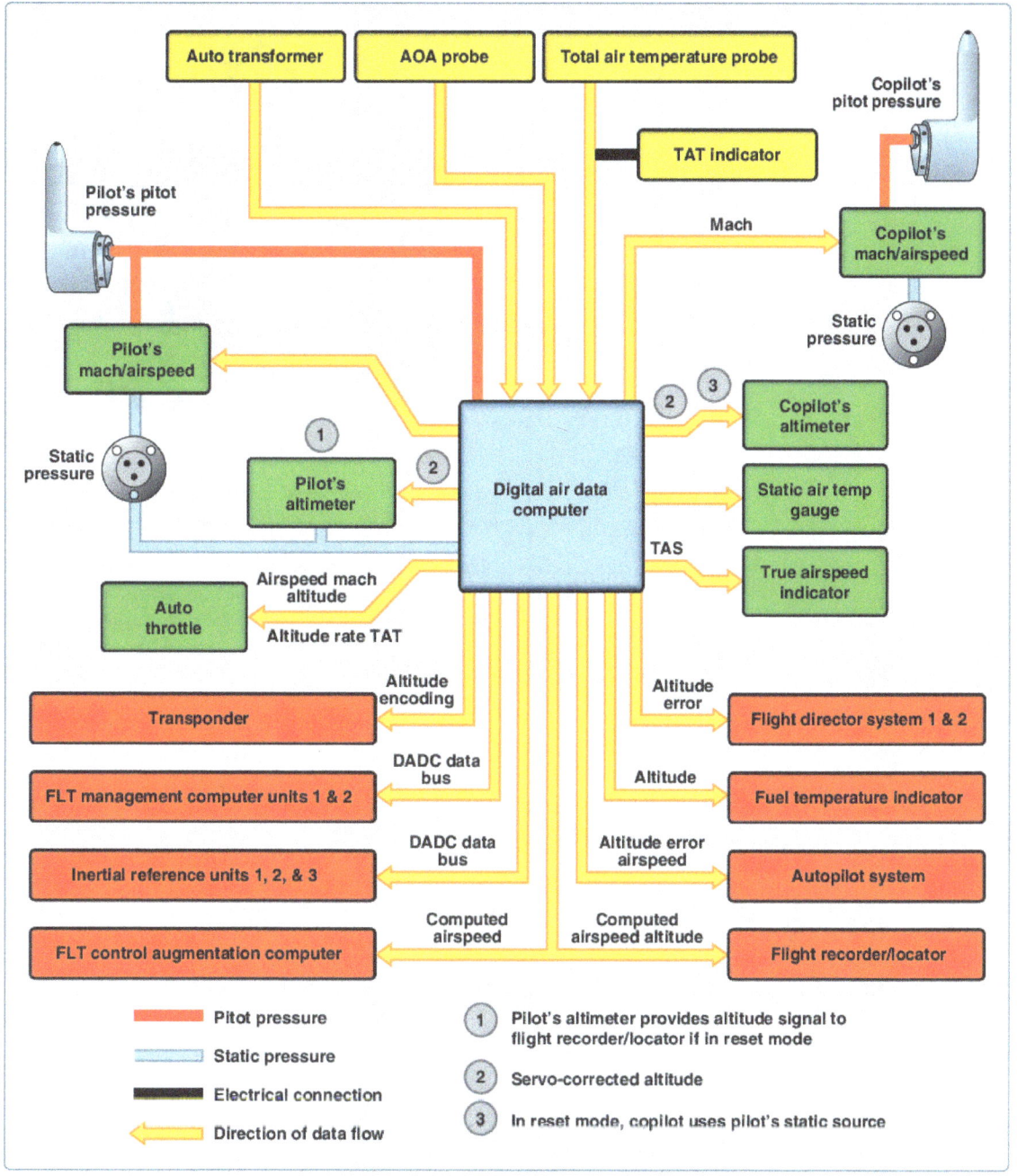

Figure 10-29. *ADCs receive input from the pitot-static sensing devices and process them for use by numerous aircraft systems.*

The second-longest point moves more slowly. Each time it reaches a numeral, it indicates 1,000 feet of altitude. Once around the dial for this pointer is equal to 10,000 feet. When the longest pointer travels completely around the dial one time, the second-longest point moves only the distance between two numerals—indicating 1,000 feet of altitude has been attained. If so equipped, a third, shortest or thinnest pointer registers altitude in 10,000 foot increments. When this pointer reaches a numeral, 10,000 feet of altitude has been attained. Sometimes a black-and-white or red-and-white cross-hatched area is shown on the face on the instrument until the 10,000 foot level has been reached. *[Figure 10-32]*

10-17

| Atmosphere pressure ||
Altitude (ft)	Pressure (psi)
Sea level	14.69
2,000	13.66
4,000	12.69
6,000	11.77
8,000	10.91
10,000	10.10
12,000	9.34
14,000	8.63
16,000	7.96
18,000	7.34
20,000	6.75
22,000	6.20
24,000	5.69
26,000	5.22
28,000	4.77
30,000	4.36
32,000	3.98
34,000	3.62
36,000	3.29
38,000	2.99
40,000	2.72
42,000	2.47
44,000	2.24
46,000	2.04
48,000	1.85
50,000	1.68

Figure 10-30. *Air pressure is inversely related to altitude. This consistent relationship is used to calibrate the pressure altimeter.*

Figure 10-32. *A sensitive altimeter with three pointers and a cross-hatched area displayed during operation below 10,000 feet.*

Many altimeters also contain linkages that rotate a numerical counter in addition to moving pointers around the dial. This quick reference window allows the pilot to simply read the numerical altitude in feet. The motion of the rotating digits or drum-type counter during rapid climb or descent makes it difficult or impossible to read the numbers. Reference can then be directed to the classic clock-style indication. *Figure 10-33* illustrates the inner workings behind this type of mechanical digital display of pressure altitude.

Figure 10-31. *The internal arrangement of a sealed diaphragm pressure altimeter. At sea level and standard atmospheric conditions, the linkage attached to the expandable diaphragm produces an indication of zero. When altitude increases, static pressure on the outside of the diaphragm decreases and the aneroid expands, producing a positive indication of altitude. When altitude decreases, atmospheric pressure increases. The static air pressure on the outside of the diaphragm increases and the pointer moves in the opposite direction, indicating a decrease in altitude.*

Figure 10-33. *A drum-type counter can be driven by the altimeter's aneroid for numerical display of altitude. Drums can also be used for the altimeter's setting indications.*

True digital instrument displays can show altitude in numerous ways. Use of a numerical display rather than a reproduction of the clock-type dial is most common. Often a digital numeric display of altitude is given on the electronic primary flight display near the artificial horizon depiction. A linear vertical scale may also be presented to put this hard numerical value in perspective. An example of this type of display of altitude information is shown in *Figure 10-34*.

Accurate measurement of altitude is important for numerous reasons. The importance is magnified in instrument flight rules (IFR) conditions. For example, avoidance of tall obstacles and rising terrain relies on precise altitude indication, as does flying at a prescribed altitude assigned by air traffic control (ATC) to avoid colliding with other aircraft. Measuring altitude with a pressure measuring device is fraught with complications. Steps are taken to refine pressure altitude indication to compensate for factors that may cause an inaccurate display.

A major factor that affects pressure altitude measurements is the naturally occurring pressure variations throughout the atmosphere due to weather conditions. Different air masses develop and move over the earth's surface, each with inherent pressure characteristics. These air masses cause the weather we experience, especially at the boundary areas between air masses known as fronts. Accordingly, at sea level, even if the temperature remains constant, air pressure rises and falls as weather system air masses come and go. The values in *Figure 10-30*, therefore, are averages for theoretical purposes.

To maintain altimeter accuracy despite varying atmospheric pressure, a means for setting the altimeter was devised. An adjustable pressure scale visible on the face of an analog altimeter known as a barometric or Kollsman window is set to read the existing atmospheric pressure when the pilot rotates the knob on the front of the instrument. This adjustment is linked through gears inside the altimeter to move the altitude indicating pointers on the dial as well. By putting the current known air pressure (also known as the altimeter setting) in the window, the instrument indicates the actual altitude. This altitude, adjusted for atmospheric pressure changes due to weather and air mass pressure inconsistency, is known as the indicated altitude.

It must be noted that in flight the altimeter setting is changed to match that of the closest available weather reporting station or airport. This keeps the altimeter accurate as the flight progresses.

While there was little need for exact altitude measurement in early fixed wing aviation, knowing one's altitude provided the pilot with useful references while navigating in the three dimensions of the atmosphere. As air traffic grew

Figure 10-34. *This primary flight display unit of a Garmin 1000 series glass cockpit instrumentation package for light aircraft indicates altitude using a vertical linear scale and a numerical counter. As the aircraft climbs or descends, the scale behind the black numerical altitude readout changes.*

and the desire to fly in any weather conditions increased, exact altitude measurement became more important and the altimeter was refined. In 1928, Paul Kollsman invented the means for adjusting an altimeter to reflect variations in air pressure from standard atmospheric pressure. The very next year, Jimmy Doolittle made his successful flight demonstrating the feasibility of instrument flight with no visual references outside of the cockpit using a Kollsman sensitive altimeter.

The term pressure altitude is used to describe the indication an altimeter gives when 29.92 is set in the Kollsman window. When flying in U.S. airspace above 18,000 feet mean sea level (MSL), pilots are required to set their altimeters to 29.92. With all aircraft referencing this standard pressure level, vertical separation between aircraft assigned to different altitudes by ATC should be assured. This is the case if all altimeters are functioning properly and pilots hold their assigned altitudes. Note that the true altitude or actual height of an aircraft above sea level is only the same as the pressure altitude when standard day conditions exist. Otherwise, all aircraft with altimeters set to 29.92 "Hg could have true altitudes higher or lower than the pressure altitude indicated. This is due to the pressure within the air mass in which they are flying being above or below standard day pressure (29.92). The actual or true altitude is less important than keeping aircraft from colliding, which is accomplished by all aircraft above 18,000 feet referencing the same pressure level (29.92 "Hg). *[Figure 10-35]*

Temperature also affects the accuracy of an altimeter. The aneroid diaphragms used in altimeters are usually made of metal. Their elasticity changes as their temperature changes. This can lead to a false indication, especially at high altitudes when the ambient air is very cold. A bimetallic compensating device is built into many sensitive altimeters to correct for varying temperature. *Figure 10-33* shows one such device on a drum-type altimeter.

Temperature also affects air density, which has great impact on the performance of an aircraft. Although this does not cause the altimeter to produce an errant reading, flight crews must be aware that performance changes with temperature variations in the atmosphere. The term density altitude describes altitude corrected for nonstandard temperature. That is, the density altitude is the standard day altitude (pressure altitude) at which an aircraft would experience similar performance as it would on the non-standard day

Figure 10-35. *Above 18,000 feet MSL, all aircraft are required to set 29.92 as the reference pressure in the Kollsman window. The altimeter then reads pressure altitude. Depending on the atmospheric pressure that day, the true or actual altitude of the aircraft may be above or below what is indicated (pressure altitude).*

currently being experienced. For example, on a very cold day, the air is denser than on a standard day, so an aircraft performs as though it is at a lower altitude. The density altitude is lower that day. On a very hot day, the reverse is true, and an aircraft performs as though it were at a higher elevation where the air is less dense. The density altitude is higher that day.

Conversion factors and charts have been produced so pilots can calculate the density altitude on any particular day. Inclusion of nonstandard air pressure due to weather systems and humidity can also be factored. So, while the effects of temperature on aircraft performance do not cause an altimeter to indicate falsely, an altimeter indication can be misleading in terms of aircraft performance if these effects are not considered. *[Figure 10-36]*

Other factors can cause an inaccurate altimeter indication. Scale error is a mechanical error whereby the scale of the instrument is not aligned so the altimeter pointers indicate correctly. Periodic testing and adjustment by trained technicians using calibrated equipment ensures scale error is kept to a minimum.

The pressure altimeter is connected to the pitot-static system and must receive an accurate sample of ambient air pressure to indicate the correct altitude. Position error, or installation error, is that inaccuracy caused by the location of the static vent that supplies the altimeter. While every effort is made to place static vents in undisturbed air, airflow over the airframe changes with the speed and attitude of the aircraft. The amount of this air pressure collection error is measured in test flights, and a correction table showing the variances can be included with the altimeter for the pilot's use. Normally, location of the static vents is adjusted during these test flights so that the position error is minimal. *[Figure 10-37]* Position error can be removed by the ADC in modern aircraft, so the pilot need not be concerned about this inaccuracy.

Static system leaks can affect the static air input to the altimeter or ADC resulting in inaccurate altimeter indications. It is for this reason that static system maintenance includes leak checks every 24 months, regardless of whether any discrepancy has been noticed. See the instrument maintenance section toward the end of this chapter for further information on this mandatory check. It should also be understood that analog mechanical altimeters are mechanical devices that often reside in a hostile environment. The significant vibration and temperature range swings encountered by the instruments and the pitot static system (i.e., the tubing connections and fittings) can sometime create damage or a leak, leading to instrument malfunction. Proper care upon installation is the best preventive action. Periodic inspection and testing can also insure integrity.

The mechanical nature of the analog altimeter's diaphragm pressure measuring apparatus has limitations. The diaphragm itself is only so elastic when responding to static air pressure changes. Hysteresis is the term for when the material from which the diaphragm is made takes a set during long periods of level flight. If followed by an abrupt altitude change, the indication lags or responds slowly while expanding or contracting during a rapid altitude change. While temporary, this limitation does cause an inaccurate altitude indication.

It should be noted that many modern altimeters are constructed to integrate into flight control systems, autopilots, and altitude monitoring systems, such as those used by ATC. The basic pressure-sensing operation of these altimeters is the same, but a means for transmitting the information is added.

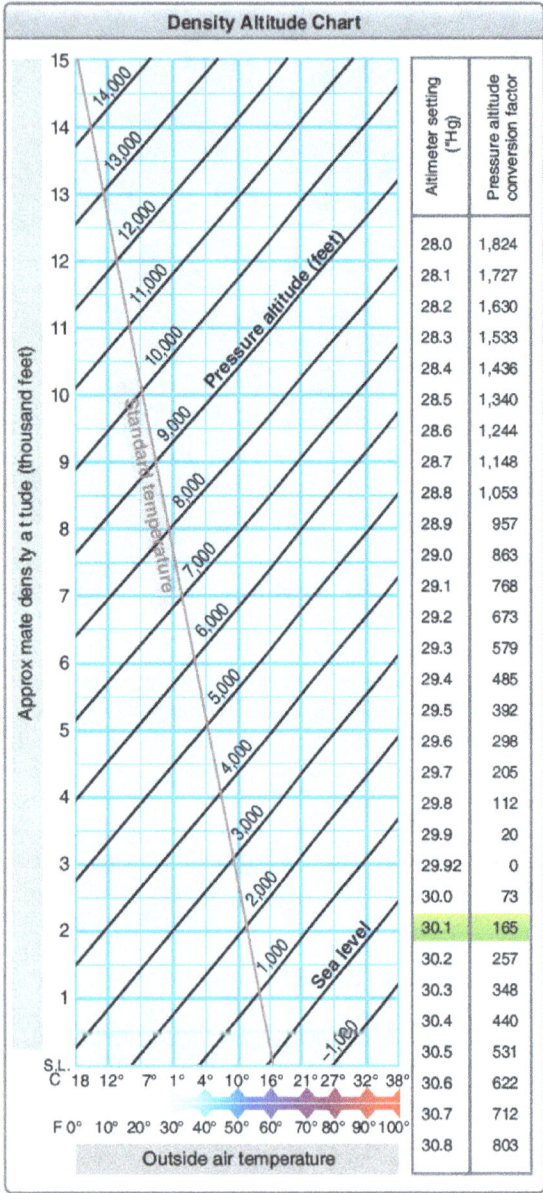

Figure 10-36. *The effect of air temperature on aircraft performance is expressed as density altitude.*

Figure 10-37. *The location of the static vent is selected to keep altimeter position error to a minimum.*

Vertical Speed Indicator

An analog vertical speed indicator (VSI) may also be referred to as a vertical velocity indicator (VVI), or rate-of-climb indicator. It is a direct reading, differential pressure gauge that compares static pressure from the aircraft's static system directed into a diaphragm with static pressure surrounding the diaphragm in the instrument case. Air is free to flow unrestricted in and out of the diaphragm but is made to flow in and out of the case through a calibrated orifice. A pointer attached to the diaphragm indicates zero vertical speed when the pressure inside and outside the diaphragm are the same. The dial is usually graduated in 100s of feet per minute. A zeroing adjustment screw, or knob, on the face of the instrument is used to center the pointer exactly on zero while the aircraft is on the ground. *[Figure 10-38]*

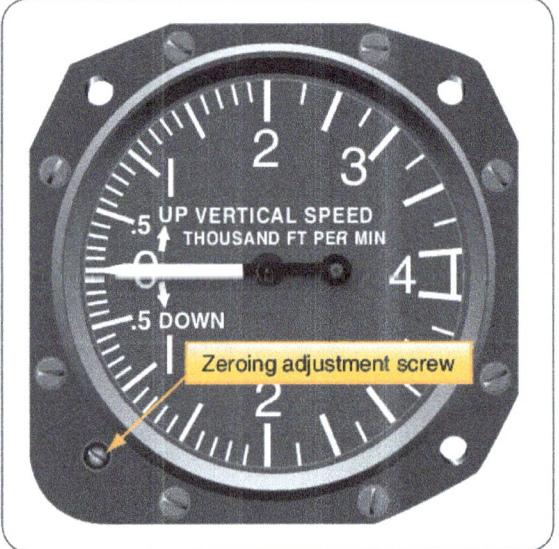

Figure 10-38. *A typical vertical speed indicator.*

As the aircraft climbs, the unrestricted air pressure in the diaphragm lowers as the air becomes less dense. The case air pressure surrounding the diaphragm lowers more slowly, having to pass through the restriction created by the orifice. This causes unequal pressure inside and outside the diaphragm, which in turn causes the diaphragm to contract a bit and the pointer indicates a climb. The process works in reverse for an aircraft in a descent. If a steady climb or descent is maintained, a steady pressure differential is established between the diaphragm and case pressure surrounding it, resulting in an accurate indication of the rate of climb via graduations on the instrument face. *[Figure 10-39]*

A shortcoming of the rate-of-climb mechanism as described is that there is a lag of six to nine seconds before a stable differential pressure can be established that indicates the actual climb or descent rate of the aircraft. An instantaneous vertical speed indicator (IVSI) has a built-in mechanism to reduce this lag. A small, lightly sprung dashpot, or piston, reacts to the direction change of an abrupt climb or descent. As this small accelerometer does so, it pumps air into or out of the diaphragm, hastening the establishment of the pressure differential that causes the appropriate indication. *[Figure 10-40]*

Gliders and lighter-than-air aircraft often make use of a variometer. This is a differential VSI that compares static pressure with a known pressure. It is very sensitive and gives an instantaneous indication. It uses a rotating vane with a pointer attached to it. The vane separates two chambers. One is connected to the aircraft's static vent or is open to the atmosphere. The other is connected to a small reservoir inside the instrument that is filled to a known pressure. As static air pressure increases, the pressure in the static air chamber increases and pushes against the vane. This rotates the vane and pointer, indicating a descent since the static pressure is now greater than the set amount in the chamber with reservoir pressure. During a climb, the reservoir pressure is greater than the static pressure; the vane is pushed in the

Figure 10-40. *The small dashpot in this IVSI reacts abruptly to a climb or descent pumping air into or out of the diaphragm causing an instantaneously vertical speed indication.*

opposite direction, causing the pointer to rotate and indicate a climb. *[Figure 10-41]*

The rate-of-climb indication in a digitally displayed instrument system is computed from static air input to the ADC. An aneroid, or solid-state pressure sensor, continuously reacts to changes in static pressure. The digital clock within the computer replaces the calibrated orifice found on an analog instrument. As the static pressure changes, the computer's clock can be used to develop a rate for the change. Using the known lapse rate conversion for air pressure as altitude increases or decreases, a figure for climb or descent in fpm can be calculated and sent to the cockpit. The vertical

Figure 10-39. *The VSI is a differential pressure gauge that compares free-flowing static air pressure in the diaphragm with restricted static air pressure around the diaphragm in the instrument case.*

10-23

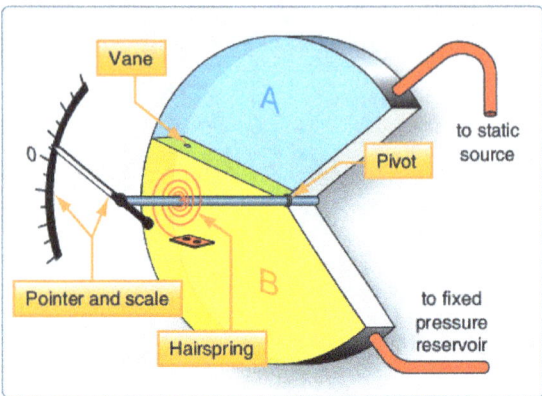

Figure 10-41. *A variometer uses differential pressure to indicate vertical speed. A rotating vane separating two chambers (one with static pressure, the other with a fixed pressure reservoir), moves the pointer as static pressure changes.*

speed is often displayed near the altimeter information on the primary flight display. *[Figure 10-34]*

Airspeed Indicators

The airspeed indicator is another primary flight instrument that is also a differential pressure gauge. Ram air pressure from the aircraft's pitot tube is directed into a diaphragm in an analog airspeed instrument case. Static air pressure from the aircraft static vent(s) is directed into the case surrounding the diaphragm. As the speed of the aircraft varies, the ram air pressure varies, expanding or contracting the diaphragm. Linkage attached to the diaphragm causes a pointer to move over the instrument face, which is calibrated in knots or miles per hour (mph). *[Figure 10-42]*

Figure 10-42. *An airspeed indicator is a differential pressure gauge that compares ram air pressure with static pressure.*

The relationship between the ram air pressure and static air pressure produces the indication known as indicated airspeed. As with the altimeter, there are other factors that must be considered in measuring airspeed throughout all phases of flight. These can cause inaccurate readings or indications that are not useful to the pilot in a particular situation. In analog airspeed indicators, the factors are often compensated for with ingenious mechanisms inside the case and on the instrument dial face. Digital flight instruments can have calculations performed in the ADC so the desired accurate indication is displayed.

While the relationship between ram air pressure and static air pressure is the basis for most airspeed indications, it can be more accurate. Calibrated airspeed takes into account errors due to position error of the pitot static pickups. It also corrects for the nonlinear nature of the pitot static pressure differential when it is displayed on a linear scale. Analog airspeed indicators come with a correction chart that allows cross-referencing of indicated airspeed to calibrated airspeed for various flight conditions. These differences are typically very small and often are ignored. Digital instruments have these corrections performed in the ADC.

More importantly, indicated airspeed does not take into account temperature and air pressure differences needed to indicate true airspeed. These factors greatly affect airspeed indication. True airspeed, therefore, is the same as indicated airspeed when standard day conditions exist. But when atmospheric temperature or pressure varies, the relationship between the ram air pressure and static pressure alters. Analog airspeed instruments often include bimetallic temperature compensating devices that can alter the linkage movement between the diaphragm and the pointer movement. There can also be an aneroid inside the airspeed indicator case that can compensate for non-standard pressures. Alternatively, true airspeed indicators exist that allow the pilot to set temperature and pressure variables manually with external knobs on the instrument dial. The knobs rotate the dial face and internal linkages to present an indication that compensates for non-standard temperature and pressure, resulting in a true airspeed indication. *[Figure 10-43]*

Digital flight instrument systems perform all of the calculations for true airspeed in the ADC. Ram air from the pitot tube and static air from the static vent(s) are run into the sensing portion of the computer. Temperature information is also input. This information can be manipulated and calculations performed so a true airspeed value can be digitally sent to the cockpit for display. Refer to *Figure 10-34* for the display of airspeed information on the primary flight display on a light aircraft. Note that similar to its position in the standard T configuration of an analog cockpit, the airspeed indication is just left of the artificial horizon display.

Figure 10-43. *An analog true airspeed indicator. The pilot manually aligns the outside air temperature with the pressure altitude scale, resulting in an indication of true airspeed.*

Complications continue when considering airspeed indications and operating limitations. It is very important to keep high-speed aircraft from traveling faster than the speed of sound if they are not designed to do so. Even as an aircraft approaches the speed of sound, certain parts on the airframe may experience airflows that exceed it. The problem with this is that near the speed of sound, shock waves can develop that can affect flight controls and, in some cases, can literally tear the aircraft apart if not designed for supersonic airflow. A further complication is that the speed of sound changes with altitude and temperature. So a safe true airspeed at sea level could put the aircraft in danger at altitude due to the lower speed of sound. *[Figure 10-44]*

In order to safeguard against these dangers, pilots monitor airspeed closely. A maximum allowable speed is established for the aircraft during certification flight testing. This speed is known the critical Mach number or Mcrit. Mach is a term for the speed of sound. The critical Mach number is expressed as a decimal of Mach such as 0.8 Mach. This means 8/10 of the speed of sound, regardless of what the actual speed of sound is at any particular altitude.

Many high performance aircraft are equipped with a Machmeter for monitoring Mcrit. The Machmeter is essentially an airspeed instrument that is calibrated in relation to Mach on the dial. Various scales exist for subsonic and supersonic aircraft. *[Figure 10-45]* In addition to the ram air/static air diaphragm arrangement, Machmeters also contain an altitude sensing diaphragm. It adjusts the input to the pointer so changes in the speed of sound due to altitude are incorporated into the indication. Some aircraft use a Mach/

Standard Altitude, Temperature, and the Speed of Sound		
Altitude (feet)	Temperature (°F)	Speed of sound (knots)
Sea level	59	661
2,000	52	657
4,000	48	652
6,000	38	648
8,000	30	643
10,000	23	638
12,000	16	633
14,000	9	629
16,000	2	624
18,000	−5	619
20,000	−12	614
22,000	−19	609
24,000	−27	604
26,000	−34	599
28,000	−41	594
30,000	−48	589
32,000	−55	584
34,000	−62	579
36,000	−69	574
38,000	−70	574
40,000	−70	574
42,000	−70	574
44,000	−70	574
46,000	−70	574
48,000	−70	574
50,000	−70	574

Figure 10-44. *As temperatures fall at higher altitudes, the speed of sound is reduced.*

Figure 10-45. *A Machmeter indicates aircraft speed relative to the speed of sound.*

airspeed indicator as shown in *Figure 10-46*. This two-in-one instrument contains separate mechanisms to display the airspeed and Mach number. A standard white pointer is used to indicate airspeed in knots against one scale. A red and white

Figure 10-46. *A combination Mach/airspeed indicator shows airspeed with a white pointer and Mach number with a red and white striped pointer. Each pointer is driven by separate internal mechanisms.*

striped pointer is driven independently and is read against the Mach number scale to monitor maximum allowable speed.

Remote Sensing and Indication

It is often impractical or impossible to utilize direct reading gauges for information needed to be conveyed in the cockpit. Placing sensors at the most suitable location on the airframe or engine and transmitting the collected data electrically through wires to the displays in the cockpit is a widely used method of remote-sensing and indicating on aircraft. Many remote sensing instrument systems consist simply of the sensing and transmitter unit and the cockpit indicator unit connected to each other by wires. For pressure flight instruments, the ADC and pickup devices (pitot tubes, static vents, etc.) comprise the sensing and transmitter unit. Many aircraft collect sensed data in dedicated engine and airframe computers. There, the information can be processed. An output section of the computer then transmits it electrically or digitally to the cockpit for display. Remote-sensing instrument systems operate with high reliability and accuracy. They are powered by the aircraft's electrical system.

Small electric motors inside the instrument housings are used to position the pointers, instead of direct-operating mechanical linkages. They receive electric current from the output section of the ADC or other computers. They also receive input from sensing transmitters or transducers that are remotely located on the aircraft. By varying the electric signal, the motors are turned to the precise location needed to reflect the correct indication. Direct electric transmission of information from different types of sensors is accomplished with a few reliable and relatively simple techniques. Note that digital cockpit displays receive all of their input from a DADC and other computers, via a digital data bus and do not use electric motors. The data packages transmitted via the bus contain the instructions on how to illuminate the display screen.

Synchro-Type Remote-Indicating Instruments

A synchro system is an electric system used for transmitting information from one point to another. The word "synchro" is a shortened form of the word "synchronous," and refers to any one of a number of similarly operating two-unit electrical systems capable of measuring, transmitting, and indicating a certain parameter on the aircraft. Most position-indicating instruments are designed around a synchro system, such as the flap position indicator. Fluid pressure indicators also commonly use synchro systems. Synchro systems are used as remote position indicators for landing gear, autopilot systems, radar, and many other remote-indicating applications. The most common types of synchro system are the autosyn, selsyn, and magnesyn synchro systems.

These systems are similar in construction, and all operate by exploiting the consistent relationship between electricity and magnetism. The fact that electricity can be used to create magnetic fields that have definite direction, and that magnetic fields can interact with magnets and other electromagnetic fields, is the basis of their operation.

DC Selsyn Systems

On aircraft with direct current (DC) electrical systems, the DC selsyn system is widely used. As mentioned, the selsyn system consists of a transmitter, an indicator, and connecting wires. The transmitter consists of a circular resistance winding and a rotatable contact arm. The rotatable contact arm turns on a shaft in the center of the resistance winding. The two ends of the arm are brushes and always touch the winding on opposite sides. *[Figure 10-47]* On position

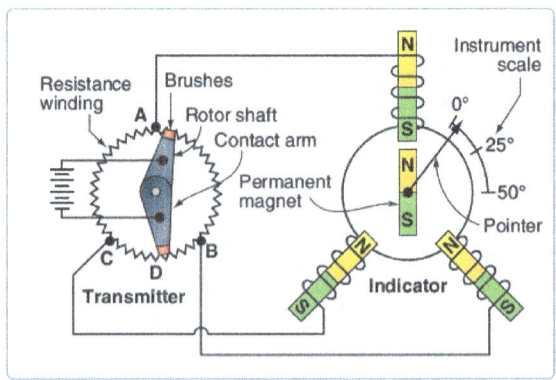

Figure 10-47. *A schematic of a DC selsyn synchro remote indicating system.*

indicating systems, the shaft to which the contact arm is fastened protrudes through the end of transmitter housing and is attached to the unit whose position is to be transmitted (e.g., flaps, landing gear). The transmitter is often connected to the moving unit through a mechanical linkage. As the unit moves, it causes the transmitter shaft to turn. The arm is turned so that voltage is applied through the brushes to any two points around the circumference of the resistance winding. The rotor shaft of DC selsyn systems, measuring other kinds of data, operates the same way, but may not protrude outside of the housing. The sensing device, which imparts rotary motion to the shaft, could be located inside the transmitter housing.

Referring to *Figure 10-47*, note that the resistance winding of the transmitter is tapped off in three fixed places, usually 120° apart. These taps distribute current through the toroidal windings of the indicator motor. When current flows through these windings, a magnetic field is created. Like all magnetic fields, a definite north and south direction to the field exists. As the transmitter rotor shaft is turned, the voltage-supplying contact arm moves. Because it contacts the transmitter resistance winding in different positions, the resistance between the supply arm and the various tapoffs changes. This causes the voltage flowing through the tapoffs to change as the resistance of sections of the winding become longer or shorter. The result is that varied current is sent via the tapoffs to the three windings in the indicator motor.

The resultant magnetic field created by current flowing through the indicator coils changes as each receives varied current from the tapoffs. The direction of the magnetic field also changes. Thus, the direction of the magnetic field across the indicating element corresponds in position to the moving arm in the transmitter. A permanent magnet is attached to the centered rotor shaft in the indicator, as is the indicator pointer. The magnet aligns itself with the direction of the magnetic field and the pointer does as well. Whenever the magnetic field changes direction, the permanent magnet and pointer realign with the new position of the field. Thus, the position of the aircraft device is indicated.

Landing gear contain mechanical devices that lock the gear up, called an up-lock, or down, called a down-lock. When the DC selsyn system is used to indicate the position of the landing gear, the indicator can also show that the up-lock or down-lock is engaged. This is done by again varying the current flowing through the indicator's coils. Switches located on the actual locking devices close when the locks engage. Current from the selsyn system described above flows through the switch and a small additional circuit. The circuit adds an additional resistor to one of the transmitter winding sections created by the rotor arm and a tapoff. This changes the total resistance of that section. The result is a change in the current flowing through one of the indicator's motor coils. This, in turn, changes the magnetic field around that coil. Therefore, the combined magnetic field created by all three motor coils is also affected, causing a shift in the direction of the indicator's magnetic field. The permanent magnet and pointer align with the new direction and shift to the locked position on the indicator dial. *Figure 10-48* shows a simplified diagram of a lock switch in a three-wire selsyn system and an indicator dial.

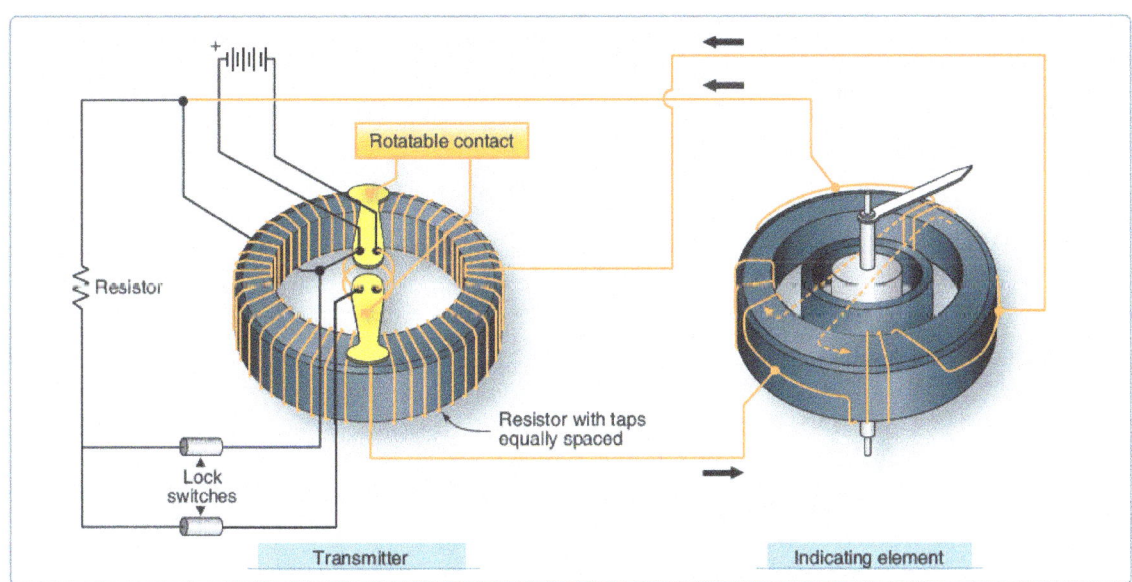

Figure 10-48. *A lock switch circuit can be added to the basic DC selsyn synchro system when used to indicate landing gear position and up- and down-locked conditions on the same indicator.*

AC Synchro Systems

Aircraft with alternating current (AC) electrical power systems make use of autosyn or magnasysn synchro remote indicating systems. Both operate in a similar way to the DC selsyn system, except that AC power is used. Thus, they make use of electric induction, rather than resistance current flows defined by the rotor brushes. Magnasyn systems use permanent magnet rotors such a those found in the DC selsyn system. Usually, the transmitter magnet is larger than the indicator magnet, but the electromagnetic response of the indicator rotor magnet and pointer remains the same. It aligns with the magnetic field set up by the coils, adopting the same angle of deflection as the transmitter rotor. *[Figure 10-49]*

Figure 10-50. *An autosyn remote-indicating system utilizes the interaction between magnetic fields set up by electric current flow to position the indicator pointer.*

Figure 10-49. *A magnasysn synchro remote-indicating system uses AC. It has permanent magnet rotors in the transmitter and indictor.*

Autosyn systems are further distinguished by the fact that the transmitter and indicator rotors used are electro-magnets rather than permanent magnets. Nonetheless, like a permanent magnet, an electro-magnet aligns with the direction of the magnetic field created by current flowing through the stator coils in the indicator. Thus, the indicator pointer position mirrors the transmitter rotor position. *[Figure 10-50]*

AC synchro systems are wired differently than DC systems. The varying current flows through the transmitter and indicator stator coils are induced as the AC cycles through zero and the rotor magnetic field flux is allowed to flow. The important characteristic of all synchro systems is maintained by both the autosyn and magnasyn systems. That is, the position of the transmitter rotor is mirrored by the rotor in the indicator. These systems are used in many of the same applications as the DC systems and more. Since they are usually part of instrumentation for high performance aircraft, adaptations of autosyn and magnasyn synchro systems are frequently used in directional indicators and in autopilot systems.

Remote Indicating Fuel and Oil Pressure Gauges

Fuel and oil pressure indications can be conveniently obtained through the use of synchro systems. As stated previously, running fuel and oil lines into the cabin to direct reading gauges is not desirable. Increased risk of fire in the cabin and the additional weight of the lines are two primary deterrents.

By locating the transmitter of a synchro system remotely, fluid pressure can be directed into it without a long tubing run. Inside the transmitter, the motion of a pressure bellows can be geared to the transmitter rotor in such a way as to make the rotor turn. *[Figure 10-51]* As in all synchros, the transmitter rotor turns proportional to the pressure sensed, which varies the voltages set up in the resistor windings of the synchro stator. These voltages are transmitted to the indicator coils that develop the magnetic field that positions the pointer.

Often on twin-engine aircraft, synchro mechanisms for each engine can be used to drive separate pointers on the same indicator. By placing the coils one behind the other, the pointer shaft from the rear indicator motor can be sent through the hollow shaft of the forward indicator motor. Thus, each pointer responds with the magnet's alignment in its own motor's magnetic field while sharing the same gauge housing. Labeling the pointer's engine 1 or 2 removes any doubt about which indicator pointer is being observed. A similar principle is employed in an indicator that has side-by-side indications for different parameters, such as oil pressure and fuel pressure in the same indicator housing. Each parameter has its own synchro motor for positioning its pointer.

Figure 10-51. *Remote pressure sensing indicators change linear motion to rotary motion in the sensing mechanism part of the synchro transmitter.*

Aircraft with digital instrumentation make use of pressure-sensitive solid-state sensors that output digital signals for collection and processing by dedicated engine and airframe computers. Others may retain their analog sensors, but may forward this information through an analog to digital converter unit from which the appropriate computer can obtain digital information to process and illuminate the digital display. Many more instruments utilize the synchro remote-indicating systems described in this section or similar synchros. Sometimes simple, more suitable, or less expensive technologies are also employed.

Mechanical Movement Indicators

There are many instruments on an aircraft that indicate the mechanical motion of a component, or even the aircraft itself. Some utilize the synchro remote-sensing and indicating systems described above. Other means for capturing and displaying mechanical movement information are also used. This section discusses some unique mechanical motion indicators and groups instruments by function. All give valuable feedback to the pilot on the condition of the aircraft in flight.

Tachometers

The tachometer, or tach, is an instrument that indicates the speed of the crankshaft of a reciprocating engine. It can be a direct- or remote-indicating instrument, the dial of which is calibrated to indicate revolutions per minutes (rpm). On reciprocating engines, the tach is used to monitor engine power and to ensure the engine is operated within certified limits.

Gas turbine engines also have tachometers. They are used to monitor the speed(s) of the compressor section(s) of the engine. Turbine engine tachometers are calibrated in percentage of rpm with 100 percent corresponding to optimum turbine speed. This allows similar operating procedures despite the varied actual engine rpm of different engines. *[Figure 10-52]*

In addition to the engine tachometer, helicopters use a tachometer to indicator main rotor shaft rpm. It should also be noted that many reciprocating-engine tachometers also have built-in numeric drums that are geared to the rotational mechanism inside. These are hour meters that keep track of the time the engine is operated. There are two types of tachometer system in wide use today: mechanical and electrical.

Mechanical Tachometers

Mechanical tachometer indicating systems are found on small, single-engine light aircraft in which a short distance exists between the engine and the instrument panel. They consist of an indicator connected to the engine by a flexible drive shaft. The drive shaft is geared into the engine so that when the engine turns, so does the shaft. The indicator contains a flyweight assembly coupled to a gear mechanism that drives a pointer. As the drive shaft rotates, centrifugal force acts on the flyweights and moves them to an angular position. This angular position varies with the rpm of the engine. The amount of movement of the flyweights is transmitted through the gear mechanism to the pointer. The pointer rotates to indicate this movement on the tachometer indicator, which is directly related to the rpm of the engine. *[Figure 10-53]*

Figure 10-52. *A tachometer for a reciprocating engine is calibrated in rpm. A tachometer for a turbine engine is calculated in percent of rpm.*

Figure 10-53. *The simplified mechanism of a flyweight type mechanical tachometer.*

A more common variation of this type of mechanical tachometer uses a magnetic drag cup to move the pointer in the indicator. As the drive shaft turns, it rotates a permanent magnet in a close-tolerance aluminum cup. A shaft attached to the indicating point is attached to the exterior center of the cup. As the magnet is rotated by the engine flex drive cable, its magnetic field cuts through the conductor surrounding it, creating eddy currents in the aluminum cup. This current flow creates its own magnetic field, which interacts with the rotating magnet's flux field. The result is that the cup tends to rotate, and with it, the indicating pointer. A calibrated restraining spring limits the cup's rotation to the arc of motion of the pointer across the scale on the instrument face. *[Figure 10-54]*

Electric Tachometers

It is not practical to use a mechanical linkage between the engine and the rpm indicator on aircraft with engines not mounted in the fuselage just forward of the instrument panel. Greater accuracy with lower maintenance is achieved through the use of electric tachometers. A wide variety of electric tachometer systems can be employed, so manufacturer's

Figure 10-54. *A simplified magnetic drag cup tachometer indicating device.*

Figure 10-56. *Different types of tach generators.*

The dual tachometer consists of two tachometer indicator units housed in a single case. The indicator pointers show simultaneously, on one or two scales, the rpm of two engines. A dual tachometer on a helicopter often shows the rpm of the engine and the rpm of the main rotor. A comparison of the voltages produced by the two tach generators of this type of helicopter indicator gives information concerning clutch slippage. A third indication showing this slippage is sometimes included in the helicopter tachometer. [*Figure 10-57*]

instructions should be consulted for details of each specific tachometer system.

A popular electric tachometer system makes use of a small AC generator mounted to a reciprocating engine's gear case or the accessory drive section of a turbine engine. As the engine turns, so does the generator. The frequency output of the generator is directly proportional to the speed of the engine. It is connected via wires to a synchronous motor in the indicator that mirrors this output. A drag cup, or drag disk link, is used to drive the indicator as in a mechanical tachometer. [*Figure 10-55*] Two different types of generator units, distinguished by their type of mounting system, are shown in *Figure 10-56*.

Some turbine engines use tachometer probes for rpm indication, rather than a tach generator system. They provide a great advantage in that there are no moving parts. They are sealed units that are mounted on a flange and protrude into the compressor section of the engine. A magnetic field is set up inside the probe that extends through pole pieces and out the end of the probe. A rotating gear wheel, which moves at the same speed as the engine compressor shaft, alters the magnetic field flux density as it moves past the pole pieces at close proximity. This generates voltage signals in coils inside the probe. The amplitude of the EMF signals vary directly with the speed of the engine.

The tachometer probe's output signals need to be processed in a remotely located module. They must also be amplified to drive a servo motor type indicator in the cockpit. They may

Figure 10-55. *An electric tachometer system with synchronous motors and a drag cup indicator.*

Figure 10-57. *A helicopter tachometer with engine rpm, rotor rpm, and slippage indications.*

also be used as input for an automatic power control system or a flight data acquisition system. *[Figure 10-58]*

Figure 10-58. *A tacho probe has no moving parts. The rate of magnetic flux field density change is directly related to engine speed.*

Synchroscope

The synchroscope is an instrument that indicates whether two or more rotating devices, such as engines, are synchronized. Since synchroscopes compare rpm, they utilize the output from tachometer generators. The instrument consists of a small electric motor that receives electrical current from the generators of both engines. Current from the faster running engine controls the direction in which the synchroscope motor rotates.

If both engines are operating at exactly the same speed, the synchroscope motor does not operate. If one engine operates faster that the other, its tach generator signal causes the synchroscope motor to turn in a given direction. Should the speed of the other engine then become greater than that of the first engine, the signal from its tach generator causes the synchroscope motor to reverse itself and turn in the opposite direction. The pilot makes adjustments to steady the pointer so it does not move.

One use of synchroscope involve designating one of the engines as a master engine. The rpm of the other engine(s) is always compared to the rpm of this master engine. The dial face of the synchroscope indicator looks like *Figure 10-59.* "Slow" and "fast" represent the other engine's rpm relative to the master engine, and the pilot makes adjustments accordingly.

Figure 10-59. *This synchroscope indicates the relative speed of the slave engine to the master.*

Accelerometers

An accelerometer is an instrument that measures acceleration. It is used to monitor the forces acting upon an airframe. Accelerometers are also used in inertial reference navigation systems. The installation of accelerometers is usually limited to high-performance and aerobatic aircraft.

Simple accelerometers are mechanical, direct-reading instruments calibrated to indicate force in Gs. One G is equal to one times the force of gravity. The dial face of an accelerometer is scaled to show positive and negative forces. When an aircraft initiates a rapid climb, positive G force tends to push one back into one's seat. Initiating a rapid decent causes a force in the opposite direction, resulting in a negative G force.

Most accelerometers have three pointers. One is continuously indicating the acceleration force experienced. The other two contain ratcheting devices. The positive G pointer follows the continuous pointer and stay at the location on the dial where the maximum positive force is indicated. The negative G pointer does the same for negative forces experienced. Both max force pointers can be reset with a knob on the instrument face.

The accelerometer operates on the principle of inertia. A mass, or weight, inside is free to slide along a shaft in response to the slightest acceleration force. When a maneuver creates an accelerating force, the aircraft and instrument move, but inertia causes the weight to stay at rest in space. As the shaft slides through the weight, the relative position of the weight on the shaft changes. This position corresponds to the force experienced. Through a series of pulleys, springs, and shafts, the pointers are moved on the dial to indicate the relative strength of the acceleration force. [*Figure 10-60*] Forces can act upon an airframe along the three axes of flight. Single and multi-axis accelerometers are available, although most cockpit gauges are of the single-axis type. Inertial reference navigation systems make use of multi-axis accelerometers to continuously, mathematically calculate the location of the aircraft in a three dimensional plane.

Electric and digital accelerometers also exist. Solid-state sensors are employed, such as piezoelectric crystalline devices. In these instruments, when an accelerating force is applied, the amount of resistance, current flow, or capacitance changes in direct relationship to the size of the force. Micro-electric signals integrate well with digital computers designed to process and display information in the cockpit.

Figure 10-60. *The inner workings of a mass-type accelerometer.*

Stall Warning and Angle of Attack (AOA) Indicators

An aircraft's angle of attack (AOA) is the angle formed between the wing cord centerline and the relative wind. At a certain angle, airflow over the wing surfaces is insufficient to create enough lift to keep the aircraft flying, and a stall occurs. An instrument that monitors the AOA allows the pilot to avoid such a condition.

The simplest form of AOA indicator is a stall warning device that does not have a gauge located in the cockpit. It uses an aural tone to warn of an impending stall due to an increase in AOA. This is done by placing a reed in a cavity just aft of the leading edge of the wing. The cavity has an open passage to a precise point on the leading edge.

In flight, air flows over and under a wing. The point on the wing leading edge where the oncoming air diverges is known as the point of stagnation. As the AOA of the wing increases, the point of stagnation moves down below the open passage that leads inside the wing to the reed. Air flowing over the curved leading edge speeds up and causes a low pressure. This causes air to be sucked out of the inside of the wing through the passage. The reed vibrates as the air rushes by making a sound audible in the cockpit. *[Figure 10-61]*

Another common device makes use of an audible tone as the AOA increases to near the point where the aircraft will stall. This stall warning device includes an electric switch that opens and closes a circuit to a warning horn audible in the cockpit. It may also be wired into a warning light circuit.

Figure 10-61. *A reed-type stall warning device is located behind this opening in the leading edge of the wing. When the angle of attack increases to near the point of a stall, low-pressure air flowing over the opening causes a suction, which audibly vibrates the reed.*

The switch is located near the point of stagnation on the wing leading edge. A small lightly sprung tab activates the switch. At normal AOA, the tab is held down by air that diverges at the point of stagnation and flows under the wing. This holds the switch open so the horn does not sound nor the warning light illuminate. As the AOA increases, the point of stagnation moves down. The divergent air that flows up and over the wing now pushes the tab upward to close the switch and complete the circuit to the horn or light. *[Figure 10-62]*

A true AOA indicating system detects the local AOA of the aircraft and displays the information on a cockpit indicator. It also may be designed to furnish reference information to other systems on high-performance aircraft. The sensing

Figure 10-62. *A popular stall warning switch located in the wing leading edge.*

mechanism and transmitter are usually located on the forward side of the fuselage. It typically contains a heating element to ensure ice-free operation. Signals are sent from the sensor to the cockpit or computer(s) as required. An AOA indicator may be calibrated in actual angle degrees, arbitrary units, percentage of lift used, symbols, or even fast/slow. *[Figure 10-63]*

Figure 10-64. *A slotted AOA probe and an alpha vane.*

Figure 10-63. *Angle of attack indicator.*

Figure 10-65. *The internal structure of a slotted probe airstream direction detector.*

There are two main types of AOA sensors in common use. Both detect the angular difference between the relative wind and the fuselage, which is used as a reference plane. One uses a vane, known as an alpha vane, externally mounted to the outside of the fuselage. It is free to rotate in the wind. As the AOA changes, air flowing over the vane changes its angle. The other uses two slots in a probe that extends out of the side of the fuselage into the airflow. The slots lead to different sides of movable paddles in a chamber of the unit just inside the fuselage skin. As the AOA varies, the air pressure ported by each of the slots changes and the paddles rotate to neutralize the pressures. The shaft upon which the paddles rotate connects to a potentiometer wiper contact that is part of the unit. The same is true of the shaft of the alpha vane. The changing resistance of the potentiometer is used in a balanced bridge circuit to signal a motor in the indicator to move the pointer proportional to the AOA. *[Figures 10-64 and 10-65]*

Modern aircraft AOA sensor units send output signals to the ADC. There, the AOA data is used to create an AOA indication, usually on the primary flight display. AOA information can also be integrated with flap and slat position information to better determine the point of stall. Additionally, AOA sensors of the type described are subject to position error since airflow around the alpha vane and slotted probe changes somewhat with airspeed and aircraft attitude. The errors are small, but can be corrected in the ADC.

To incorporate a warning of an impending stall, many AOA systems signal a stick shaker motor that literally shakes the control column to warn the pilot as the aircraft approaches a stall condition. Electrical switches are actuated in the AOA indicator at various preset AOA to activate the motor that drives an unbalanced weighted ring, causing the column to shake. Some systems include a stick pusher actuator that pushes the control yoke forward, lowering the nose of the aircraft when the critical AOA is approached. Regardless of the many existing variations for warning of an impending stall, the AOA system triggers all stall warnings in high performance aircraft.

Temperature Measuring Instruments

The temperature of numerous items must be known for an aircraft to be operated properly. Engine oil, carburetor mixture, inlet air, free air, engine cylinder heads, heater ducts, and exhaust gas temperature of turbine engines are all items requiring temperature monitoring. Many other temperatures must also be known. Different types of thermometers are used to collect and present temperature information.

Non-Electric Temperature Indicators

The physical characteristics of most materials change when exposed to changes in temperature. The changes are consistent, such as the expansion or contraction of solids, liquids, and gases. The coefficient of expansion of different materials varies and it is unique to each material. Most everyone is familiar with the liquid mercury thermometer. As the temperature of the mercury increases, it expands up a narrow passage that has a graduated scale upon it to read the temperature associated with that expansion. The mercury thermometer has no application in aviation.

A bimetallic thermometer is very useful in aviation. The temperature sensing element of a bimetallic thermometer is made of two dissimilar metals strips bonded together. Each metal expands and contracts at a different rate when temperature changes. One end of the bimetallic strip is fixed, the other end is coiled. A pointer is attached to the coiled end which is set in the instrument housing. When the bimetallic strip is heated, the two metals expand. Since their expansion rates differ and they are attached to each other, the effect is that the coiled end tries to uncoil as the one metal expands faster than the other. This moves the pointer across the dial face of the instrument. When the temperature drops, the metals contract at different rates, which tends to tighten the coil and move the pointer in the opposite direction.

Direct reading bimetallic temperature gauges are often used in light aircraft to measure free air temperature or outside air temperature (OAT). In this application, a collecting probe protrudes through the windshield of the aircraft to be exposed to the atmospheric air. The coiled end of the bimetallic strip in the instrument head is just inside the windshield where it can be read by the pilot. *[Figures 10-66 and 10-67]*

A bourdon tube is also used as a direct reading non-electric temperature gauge in simple, light aircraft. By calibrating the dial face of a bourdon tube gauge with a temperature scale, it can indicate temperature. The basis for operation is the consistent expansion of the vapor produced by a volatile liquid in an enclosed area. This vapor pressure changes directly with temperature. By filling a sensing bulb with such a volatile liquid and connecting it to a bourdon tube, the tube causes an indication of the rising and falling vapor pressure due to temperature change. Calibration of the dial face in degrees Fahrenheit or Celsius, rather than psi, provides a temperature reading. In this type of gauge, the sensing bulb is placed in the area needing to have temperature measured. A long capillary tube connects the bulb to the bourdon tube in the instrument housing. The narrow diameter of the capillary tube ensures that the volatile liquid is lightweight and stays primarily in the sensor bulb. Oil temperature is sometimes measured this way.

Figure 10-66. *A bimetallic temperature gauge works because of the dissimilar coefficients of expansion of two metals bonded together. When bent into a coil, cooling or heating causes the dissimilar metal coil to tighten, or unwind, moving the pointer across the temperature scale on the instrument dial face.*

Electrical Temperature Measuring Indication

The use of electricity in measuring temperature is very common in aviation. The following measuring and indication systems can be found on many types of aircraft. Certain temperature ranges are more suitably measured by one or another type of system.

Electrical Resistance Thermometer

The principle parts of the electrical resistance thermometer are the indicating instrument, the temperature-sensitive element (or bulb), and the connecting wires and plug connectors. Electrical resistance thermometers are used widely in many types of aircraft to measure carburetor air, oil, free air temperatures, and more. They are used to measure low and medium temperatures in the –70 °C to 150 °C range.

range. The temperature-sensitive resistor element is a length or winding made of a nickel/manganese wire or other suitable alloy in an insulating material. The resistor is protected by a closed-end metal tube attached to a threaded plug with a hexagonal head. *[Figure 10-68]* The two ends of the winding are brazed, or welded, to an electrical receptacle designed to receive the prongs of the connector plug.

Figure 10-68. *An electric resistance thermometer sensing bulb.*

The indicator contains a resistance-measuring instrument. Sometimes it uses a modified form of the Wheatstone-bridge circuit. The Wheatstone-bridge meter operates on the principle of balancing one unknown resistor against other known resistances. A simplified form of a Wheatstone-bridge circuit is shown in *Figure 10-69*. Three equal values of resistance *[Figure 10-69A, B, and C]* are connected into a diamond shaped bridge circuit. A resistor with an unknown value *[Figure 10-69D]* is also part of the circuit. The unknown resistance represents the resistance of the temperature bulb of the electrical resistance thermometer system. A galvanometer is attached across the circuit at points X and Y.

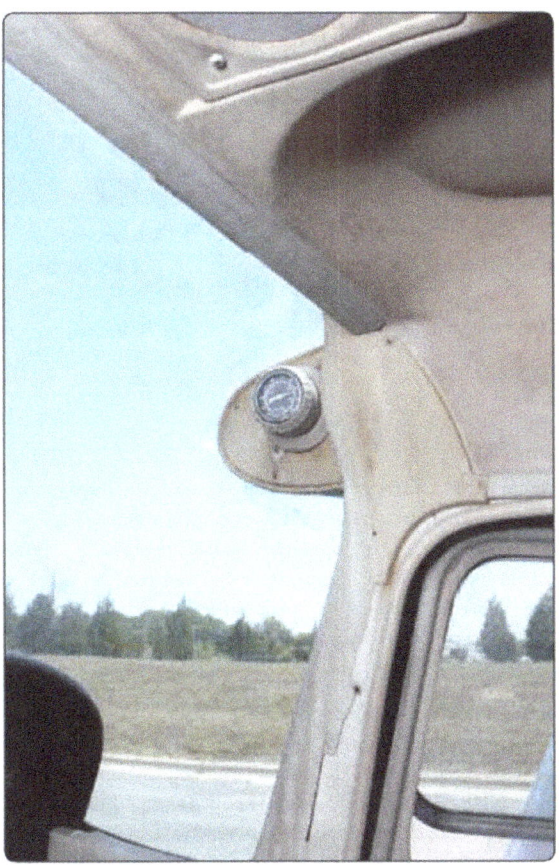

Figure 10-67. *A bimetallic outside air temperature gauge and its installation on a light aircraft.*

For most metals, electrical resistance changes as the temperature of the metal changes. This is the principle upon which a resistance thermometer operates. Typically, the electrical resistance of a metal increases as the temperature rises. Various alloys have a high temperature-resistance coefficient, meaning their resistance varies significantly with temperature. This can make them suitable for use in temperature sensing devices. The metal resistor is subjected to the fluid or area in which temperature needs to be measured. It is connected by wires to a resistance measuring device inside the cockpit indicator. The instrument dial is calibrated in degrees Fahrenheit or Celsius as desired rather than in ohms. As the temperature to be measured changes, the resistance of the metal changes and the resistance measuring indicator shows to what extent.

A typical electrical resistance thermometer looks like any other temperature gauge. Indicators are available in dual form for use in multiengine aircraft. Most indicators are self-compensating for changes in cockpit temperature. The heat-sensitive resistor is manufactured so that it has a definite resistance for each temperature value within its working

Figure 10-69. *The internal structure of an electric resistance thermometer indicator features a bridge circuit, galvanometer, and variable resistor, which is outside the indicator in the form of the temperature sensor.*

10-37

When the temperature causes the resistance of the bulb to equal that of the other resistances, no potential difference exists between points X and Y in the circuit. Therefore, no current flows in the galvanometer leg of the circuit. If the temperature of the bulb changes, its resistance also changes, and the bridge becomes unbalanced, causing current to flow through the galvanometer in one direction or the other. The galvanometer pointer is actually the temperature gauge pointer. As it moves against the dial face calibrated in degrees, it indicates temperature. Many indicators are provided with a zero adjustment screw on the face of the instrument. This adjusts the zeroing spring tension of the pointer when the bridge is at the balance point (the position at which the bridge circuit is balanced and no current flows through the meter).

Ratiometer Electrical Resistance Thermometers

Another way of indicating temperature when employing an electric resistance thermometer is by using a ratiometer. The Wheatstone-bridge indicator is subject to errors from line voltage fluctuation. The ratiometer is more stable and can deliver higher accuracy. As its name suggests, the ratiometer electrical resistance thermometer measures a ratio of current flows.

The resistance bulb sensing portion of the ratiometer electric resistance thermometer is essentially the same as described above. The circuit contains a variable resistance and a fixed resistance to provide the indication. It contains two branches for current flow. Each has a coil mounted on either side of the pointer assembly that is mounted within the magnetic field of a large permanent magnet. Varying current flow through the coils causes different magnetic fields to form, which react with the larger magnetic field of the permanent magnet. This interaction rotates the pointer against the dial face that is calibrated in degrees Fahrenheit or Celsius, giving a temperature indication. *[Figure 10-70]*

The magnetic pole ends of the permanent magnet are closer at the top than they are at the bottom. This causes the magnetic field lines of flux between the poles to be more concentrated at the top. As the two coils produce their magnetic fields, the stronger field interacts and pivots downward into the weaker, less concentrated part of the permanent magnet field, while the weaker coil magnetic field shifts upward toward the more concentrated flux field of the large magnet. This provides a balancing effect that changes but stays in balance as the coil field strengths vary with temperature and the resultant current flowing through the coils.

For example, if the resistance of the temperature bulb is equal to the value of the fixed resistance (R), equal values of current flow through the coils. The torques, caused by the magnetic field each coil creates, are the same and cancel

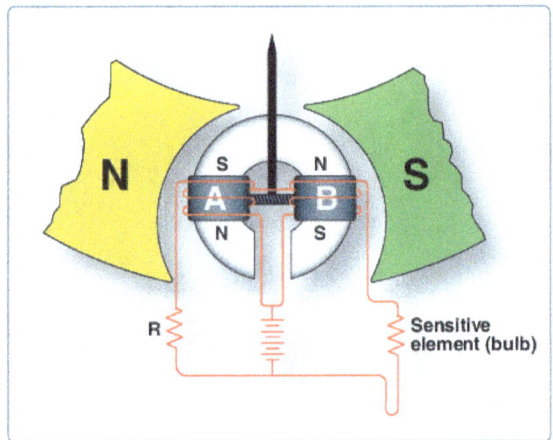

Figure 10-70. *A ratiometer temperature measuring indicator has two coils. As the sensor bulb resistance varies with temperature, different amounts of current flow through the coils. This produces varying magnetic fields. These fields interact with the magnetic field of a large permanent magnet, resulting in an indication of temperature.*

any movement in the larger magnetic field. The indicator pointer will be in the vertical position. If the bulb temperature increases, its resistance also increases. This causes the current flow through coil A circuit branch to increase. This creates a stronger magnetic field at coil A than at coil B. Consequently, the torque on coil A increases, and it is pulled downward into the weaker part of the large magnetic field. At the same time, less current flows through the sensor bulb resistor and coil B, causing coil B to form a weaker magnetic field that is pulled upward into the stronger flux area of the permanent magnet's magnetic field. The pointer stops rotating when the fields reach a new balance point that is directly related to the resistance in the sensing bulb. The opposite of this action would take place if the temperature of the heat-sensitive bulb should decrease.

Ratiometer temperature measuring systems are used to measure engine oil, outside air, carburetor air, and other temperatures in many types of aircraft. They are especially in demand to measure temperature conditions where accuracy is important, or large variations of supply voltages are encountered.

Thermocouple Temperature Indicators

A thermocouple is a circuit or connection of two unlike metals. The metals are touching at two separate junctions. If one of the junctions is heated to a higher temperature than the other, an electromotive force is produced in the circuit. This voltage is directly proportional to the temperature. So, by measuring the amount of electromotive force, temperature can be determined. A voltmeter is placed across the colder of the two junctions of the thermocouple. It is calibrated in degrees Fahrenheit or Celsius, as needed. The hotter the high-temperature junction (hot junction) becomes, the greater the electromotive force produced, and the higher the temperature indication on the meter. *[Figure 10-71]*

Thermocouples are used to measure high temperatures. Two common applications are the measurement of cylinder head temperature (CHT) in reciprocating engines and exhaust gas temperature (EGT) in turbine engines. Thermocouple leads are made from a variety of metals, depending on the maximum temperature to which they are exposed. Iron and constantan, or copper and constantan, are common for CHT measurement. Chromel and alumel are used for turbine EGT thermocouples.

The amount of voltage produced by the dissimilar metals when heated is measured in millivolts. Therefore, thermocouple leads are designed to provide a specific amount of resistance in the thermocouple circuit (usually very little). Their material, length, or cross-sectional size cannot be altered without compensation for the change in total resistance that would result. Each lead that makes a connection back to the voltmeter must be made of the same metal as the part of the thermocouple to which it is connected. For example, a copper wire is connected to the copper portion of the hot junction and a constantan wire is connected to the constantan part.

The hot junction of a thermocouple varies in shape depending on its application. Two common types are the gasket and the bayonet. In the gasket type, two rings of the dissimilar metals are pressed together to form a gasket that can be installed under a spark plug or cylinder hold down nut. In the bayonet type, the metals come together inside a perforated protective sheath. Bayonet thermocouples fit into a hole or well in a cylinder head. On turbine engines, they are found mounted on the turbine inlet or outlet case and extend through the case into the gas stream. Note that for CHT indication, the cylinder chosen for the thermocouple installation is the one that runs the hottest under most operating conditions. The location of this cylinder varies with different engines. *[Figure 10-72]*

The cold junction of the thermocouple circuit is inside the instrument case. Since the electromotive force set up in the circuit varies with the difference in temperature between the hot and cold junctions, it is necessary to compensate the indicator mechanism for changes in cockpit temperature which affect the cold junction. This is accomplished by using a bimetallic spring connected to the indicator mechanism. This actually works the same as the bimetallic thermometer described previously. When the leads are disconnected from the indicator, the temperature of the cockpit area around the instrument panel can be read on the indicator dial. *[Figure 10-73]* Numeric LED indictors for CHT are also common in modern aircraft.

Turbine Gas Temperature Indicating Systems

EGT is a critical variable of turbine engine operation. The EGT indicating system provides a visual temperature indication in the cockpit of the turbine exhaust gases as

Figure 10-71. *Thermocouples combine two unlike metals that cause current flow when heated.*

Figure 10-72. *A cylinder head temperature thermocouple with a gasket type hot junction is made to be installed under the spark plug or a cylinder hold down nut of the hottest cylinder (A). A bayonet type thermocouple is installed in a bore in the cylinder wall (B).*

they leave the turbine unit. In certain turbine engines, the temperature of the exhaust gases is measured at the entrance to the turbine unit. This is referred to as a turbine inlet temperature (TIT) indicating system.

Several thermocouples are used to measure EGT or TIT. They are spaced at intervals around the perimeter of the engine turbine casing or exhaust duct. The tiny thermocouple voltages are typically amplified and used to energize a servomotor that drives the indicator pointer. Gearing a digital drum indication off of the pointer motion is common. *[Figure 10-74]* The EGT indicator shown is a hermetically sealed unit. The instrument's scale ranges from 0 °C to 1,200 °C, with a vernier dial in the upper right-hand corner and a power off warning flag located in the lower portion of the dial.

A TIT indicating system provides a visual indication at the instrument panel of the temperature of gases entering the turbine. Numerous thermocouples can be used with the average voltage representing the TIT. Dual thermocouples exist containing two electrically independent junctions within a single probe. One set of these thermocouples is paralleled to transmit signals to the cockpit indicator. The other set of parallel thermocouples provides temperature signals to engine monitoring and control systems. Each circuit is electrically independent, providing dual system reliability.

Figure 10-73. *Typical thermocouple temperature indicators.*

A schematic for the turbine inlet temperature system for one engine of a four-engine turbine aircraft is shown in *Figure 10-75*. Circuits for the other three engines are identical to this system. The indicator contains a bridge circuit, a chopper circuit, a two-phase motor to drive the pointer, and a feedback potentiometer. Also included are a voltage reference circuit, an amplifier, a power-off flag, a power supply, and an over temperature warning light. Output of the amplifier energizes the variable field of the two-phase motor that positions the indicator main pointer and a digital indicator. The motor also drives the feedback potentiometer to provide a humming signal to stop the drive motor when the correct pointer position, relative to the temperature signal, has been reached. The voltage reference circuit provides a closely regulated reference voltage in the bridge circuit to preclude error from input voltage variation to the indicator power supply.

Figure 10-74. *A typical exhaust gas temperature thermocouple system.*

Figure 10-75. *A typical analog turbine inlet temperature indicating system.*

10-41

The overtemperature warning light in the indicator illuminates when the TIT reaches a predetermined limit. An external test switch is usually installed so that over temperature warning lights for all the engines can be tested at the same time. When the test switch is operated, an overtemperature signal is simulated in each indicator temperature control bridge circuit.

Digital cockpit instrumentation systems need not employ resistance-type indicators and adjusted servo-driven thermocouple gauges to provide the pilot with temperature information. Sensor resistance and voltage values are input to the appropriate computer, where they are adjusted, processed, monitored, and output for display on cockpit display panels. They are also sent for use by other computers requiring temperature information for the control and monitoring of various integrated systems.

Total Air Temperature Measurement

Air temperature is a valuable parameter that many performance monitoring and control variables depend on. During flight, static air temperature changes continuously and accurate measurement presents challenges. Below 0.2 Mach, a simple resistance-type or bimetallic temperature gauge can provide relatively accurate air temperature information. At faster speeds, friction, the air's compressibility, and boundary layer behavior make accurate temperature capture more complex. Total air temperature (TAT) is the static air temperature plus any rise in temperature caused by the high-speed movement of the aircraft through the air. The increase in temperature is known as ram rise. TAT-sensing probes are constructed specifically to accurately capture this value and transmit signals for cockpit indication, as well as for use in various engine and aircraft systems.

Simple TAT systems include a sensor and an indicator with a built-in resistance balance circuit. Air flow through the sensor is designed so that air with the precise temperature impacts a platinum alloy resistance element. The sensor is engineered to capture temperature variations in terms of varying the resistance of the element. When placed in the bridge circuit, the indicator pointer moves in response to the imbalance caused by the variable resistor.

More complex systems use signal correction technology and amplified signals sent to a servo motor to adjust the indicator in the cockpit. These systems include closely regulated power supply and failure monitoring. They often use numeric drum type readouts, but can also be sent to an LCD driver to illuminate LCD displays. Many LCD displays are multifunctional, capable of displaying static air temperature and true airspeed. In fully digital systems, the correction signals are input into the ADC. There, they can be manipulated appropriately for cockpit display or for whichever system requires temperature information. *[Figure 10-76]*

Figure 10-76. *Different cockpit TAT displays.*

TAT sensor/probe design is complicated by the potential of ice forming during icing conditions. Left unheated, a probe may cease to function properly. The inclusion of a heating element threatens accurate data collection. Heating the probe must not affect the resistance of the sensor element. *[Figure 10-77]*

Close attention is paid to airflow and materials conductivity during the design phase. Some TAT sensors channel bleed air through the units to affect the flow of outside air, so that it flows directly onto the platinum sensor without gaining added energy from the probe heater.

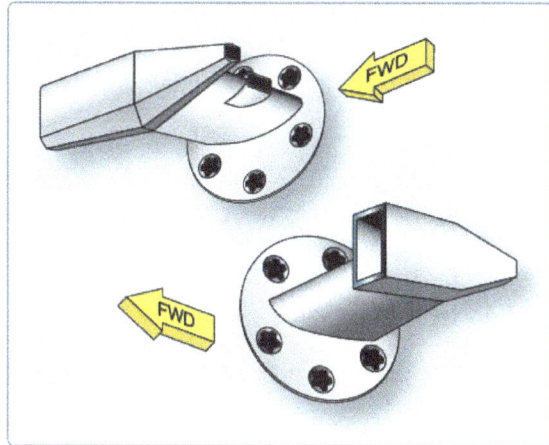

Figure 10-77. *Total air temperature (TAT) probes.*

Direction Indicating Instruments

A myriad of techniques and instruments exist to aid the pilot in navigation of the aircraft. An indication of direction is part of this navigation. While the next chapter deals with communication and navigation, this section discusses some of the magnetic direction indicating instruments. Additionally, a common, reliable gyroscopic direction indicator is discussed in the gyroscopic instrument section of this chapter.

Magnetic Compass

Having an instrument on board an aircraft that indicates direction can be invaluable to the pilot. In fact, it is a requirement that all certified aircraft have some sort of magnetic direction indicator. The magnetic compass is a direction finding instrument that has been used for navigation for hundreds of years. It is a simple instrument that takes advantage of the earth's magnetic field.

Figure 10-78 shows the earth and the magnetic field that surrounds it. The magnetic north pole is very close to the geographic North Pole of the globe, but they are not the same. An ordinary permanent magnet that is free to do so, aligns itself with the direction of the earth's magnetic field. Upon this principle, an instrument is constructed that the pilot can reference for directional orientation. Permanent magnets are attached under a float that is mounted on a pivot so it is free to rotate in the horizontal plane. As such, the magnets align with the earth's magnetic field. A numerical compass card, usually graduated in 5° increments, is constructed around the perimeter of the float. It serves as the instrument dial. The entire assembly is enclosed in a sealed case that is filled with a liquid similar to kerosene. This dampens vibration and oscillation of the moving float assembly and decreases friction.

On the front of the case, a glass face allows the numerical compass card to be referenced against a vertical lubber line.

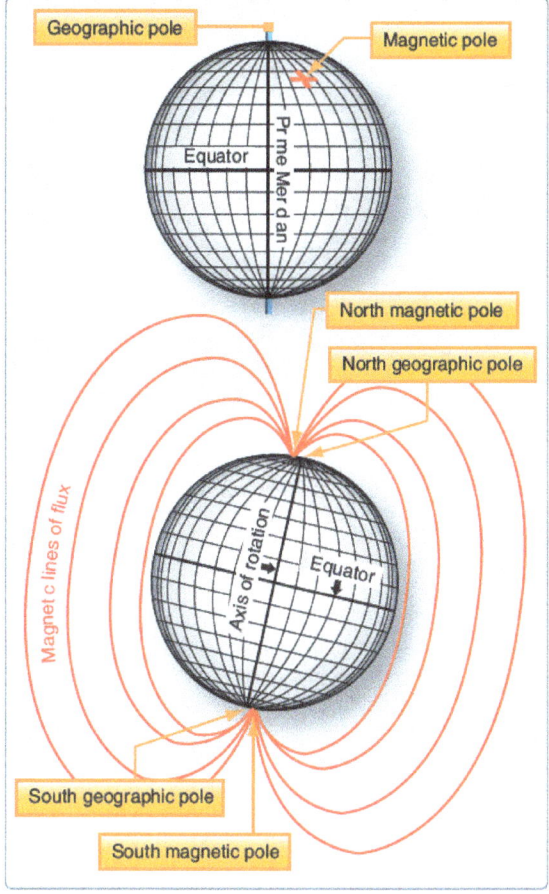

Figure 10-78. *The earth and its magnetic field.*

The magnetic heading of the aircraft is read by noting the graduation on which the lubber line falls. Thus, direction in any of 360° can be read off the dial as the magnetic float compass card assembly holds its alignment with magnetic north, while the aircraft changes direction.

The liquid that fills the compass case expands and contracts as altitude changes and temperature fluctuates. A bellows diaphragm expands and contracts to adjust the volume of the space inside the case so it remains full. *[Figure 10-79]*

There are accuracy issues associated with using a magnetic compass. The main magnets of a compass align not only with the earth's magnetic field, they actually align with the composite field made up of all magnetic influences around them, meaning local electromagnetic influence from metallic structures near the compass and operation aircraft's electrical system. This is called magnetic deviation. It causes a magnet's alignment with the earth's magnetic field to be altered. Compensating screws are turned, which move small permanent magnets in the compass case to correct for this

10-43

Figure 10-79. *The parts of a typical magnetic compass.*

magnetic deviation. The two set-screws are on the face of the instrument and are labeled N-S and E-W. They position the small magnets to counterbalance the local magnetic influences acting on the main compass magnets.

The process for knowing how to adjust for deviation is known as swinging the compass. It is described in the instrument maintenance pages near the end of this chapter. Magnetic deviation cannot be overlooked. It should never be more than 10°. Using nonferrous mounting screws and shielding or twisting the wire running to the compass illuminating lamp are additional steps taken to keep deviation to a minimum.

Another compass error is called magnetic variation. It is caused by the difference in location between the earth's magnetic poles and the geographic poles. There are only a few places on the planet where a compass pointing to magnetic north is also pointing to geographic North. A line drawn through these locations is called the Agonic line. At all other points, there is some variation between that which a magnetic compass indicates is north and geographic (true) North. Isogonic lines drawn on aeronautical charts indicate points of equal variation. Depending on the location of the aircraft, airmen must add or subtract degrees from the magnetic indication to obtain true geographic location information. *[Figure 10-80]*

The earth's magnetic field exits the poles vertically and arches around to extend past the equator horizontally or parallel to the earth's surface. *[Figure 10-78]* Operating an aircraft near the magnetic poles causes what is known as dip error. The compass magnets pull downward toward the pole, rather than horizontally, as is the case near the equator. This downward

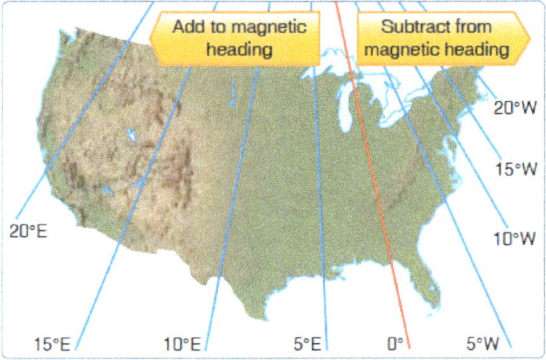

Figure 10-80. *Aircraft located along the agonic line have 0° of variation between magnetic north and true north. Locations on and between the isogonic lines require addition or subtraction, as shown, to magnetic indications to arrive at a true geographic direction.*

motion causes inaccuracy in the indication. Although the compass float mechanism is weighted to compensate, the closer the aircraft is to the north or south magnetic poles, the more pronounced the errors.

Dip errors manifest themselves in two ways. The first is called acceleration error. If an aircraft is flying on an east-west path and simply accelerates, the inertia of the float mechanism causes the compass to swing to the north. Rapid deceleration causes it to swing southward. Second, if flying toward the North Pole and a banked turn is made, the downward pull of the magnetic field initially pulls the card away from the direction of the turn. The opposite is true if flying south from the North Pole and a banked turn is initiated. In this case, there is initially a pull of the compass indicator toward the direction of the turn. These kinds of movements are called turning errors.

Another peculiarity exists with the magnetic compass that is not dip error. Look again at the magnetic compass in *Figure 10-79.* If flying north or toward any indicated heading, turning the aircraft to the left causes a steady decrease in the heading numbers. But, before the turn is made, the numbers to the left on the compass card are actually increasing. The numbers to the right of the lubber line rotate behind it on a left turn. So, the compass card rotates opposite to the direction of the intended turn. This is because, from the pilot's seat, you are actually looking at the back of the compass card. While not a major problem, it is more intuitive to see the 360° of direction oriented as they are on an aeronautical chart or a hand-held compass.

Vertical Magnetic Compass

Solutions to the shortcomings of the simple magnetic compass described above have been engineered. The vertical magnetic compass is a variation of the magnetic compass that eliminates the reverse rotation of the compass card just described. By mounting the main indicating magnets of the compass on a shaft rather than a float, through a series of gears, a compass card can be made to turn about a horizontal axis. This allows the numbers for a heading, towards which the pilot wants to turn, to be oriented correctly on the indicating card. In other words, when turning right, increasing numbers are to the right; when turning left, decreasing numbers rotate in from the left. *[Figure 10-81]* Many vertical magnetic compasses have also replaced the liquid-filled instrument housing with a dampening cup that uses eddy currents to dampen oscillations. Note that a vertical magnetic compass and a directional gyro look very similar and are often in the lower center position of the instrument panel basic T. Both use the nose of an aircraft as the lubber line against which a rotating compass card is read. Vertical magnetic compasses are characterized by the absence of the hand adjustment knob found on DGs, which is used to align the gyro with a magnetic indication.

Remote Indicating Compass

Magnetic deviation is compensated for by swinging the compass and adjusting compensating magnets in the instrument housing. A better solution to deviation is to remotely locate the magnetic compass in a wing tip or vertical stabilizer where there is very little interference with the earth's magnetic field. By using a synchro remote indicating system, the magnetic compass float assembly can act as the rotor of the synchro system. As the float mechanism rotates to align with magnetic north in the remotely located compass, a varied electric current can be produced in the transmitter. This alters the magnetic field produced by the coils of the indicator in the cockpit, and a magnetic indication relatively free from deviation is displayed. Many of these systems are of the magnesyn type.

Figure 10-81. *A vertical magnetic direction indicator provides a realistic reference of headings.*

Remote Indicating Slaved Gyro Compass (Flux Gate Compass)

An elaborate and very accurate method of direction indication has been developed that combines the use of a gyro, a magnetic compass, and a remote indicating system. It is called the slaved gyro compass or flux gate compass system. A study of the gyroscopic instruments section of this chapter assists in understanding this device.

A gyroscopic direction indicator is augmented by magnetic direction information from a remotely located compass. The type of compass used is called a flux valve or flux gate compass. It consists of a very magnetically permeable circular segmented core frame or spider. The earth's magnetic field flows through this iron core and varies its distribution through segments of the core as the flux valve is rotated via the movement of the aircraft. Pickup coil windings are located on each of the core's spider legs that are positioned 120° apart. *[Figure 10-82]*

The distribution of earth's magnetic field flowing through the legs is unique for every directional orientation of the aircraft. A coil is placed in the center of the core and is energized by AC current. As the AC flow passes through zero while changing direction, the earth's magnetic field is allowed to flow through the core. Then, it is blocked or gated as the magnetic field of the core current flow builds to its peak again. The cycle is repeated at the frequency of

Figure 10-82. *As the aircraft turns in the earth's magnetic field, the lines of flux flow lines vary through the permeable core of flux gate, creating variable voltages at the three pickoffs.*

the AC supplied to the excitation coil. The result is repeated flow and nonflow of the earth's flux across the pickup coils. During each cycle, a unique voltage is induced in each of the pickup coils reflecting the orientation of the aircraft in the earth's magnetic field.

The electricity that flows from each of the pickup coils is transmitted out of the flux valve via wires into a second unit. It contains an autosyn transmitter, directional gyro, an amplifier, and a triple wound stator that is similar to that found in the indicator of a synchro system. Unique voltage is induced in the center rotor of this stator which reflects the voltage received from the flux valve pickup coils sent through the stator coils. It is amplified and used to augment the position of the DG. The gyro is wired to be the rotor of an autosyn synchro system, which transmits the position of the gyro into an indicator unit located in the cockpit. In the indicator, a vertical compass card is rotated against a small airplane type lubber line like that in a vertical magnetic compass. *[Figure 10-83 and 84]*

Further enhancements to direction finding systems of this type involving the integration of radio navigation aids are common. The radio magnetic indicator (RMI) is one such variation. *[Figure 10-85]* In addition to the rotating direction indicator of the slaved gyro compass, it contains two pointers. One indicates the bearing to a very high frequency (VHF) omnidirectional range (VOR) station and the other indicates the bearing to a nondirectional automatic direction finder (ADF) beacon. These and other radio navigation aids are discussed further in the communications and navigation chapter of this handbook. It should also be noted that integration of slaved gyro direction indicating system information into auto-pilot systems is also possible.

Solid State Magnetometers

Solid state magnetometers are used on many modern aircraft. They have no moving parts and are extremely accurate. Tiny layered structures react to magnetism on a molecular level resulting in variations in electron activity. These low power consuming devices can sense not only the direction to the earth's magnetic poles, but also the angle of the flux field. They are free from oscillation that plagues a standard magnetic compass. They feature integrated processing algorithms and easy integration with digital systems. *[Figure 10-86]*

Sources of Power for Gyroscopic Instruments

Gyroscopic instruments are essential instruments used on all aircraft. They provide the pilot with critical attitude and directional information and are particularly important while flying under IFR. The sources of power for these instruments can vary. The main requirement is to spin the gyroscopes at a high rate of speed. Originally, gyroscopic instruments were strictly vacuum driven. A vacuum source pulled air across the gyro inside the instruments to make the gyros spin. Later, electricity was added as a source of power. The turning armature of an electric motor doubles as the gyro rotor. In some aircraft, pressure, rather than vacuum, is used to induce the gyro to spin. Various systems and powering configurations have been developed to provide reliable operation of the gyroscopic instruments.

Figure 10-83. *A simplified schematic of a flux gate, or slaved gyro, compass system.*

Figure 10-84. *Solid state magnetometer units.*

Figure 10-85. *A radio magnetic indicator (RMI) combines a slaved gyro heading indication (red triangle at top of gauge) with magnetic bearing information to a VOR station (solid pointer) and an ADF station (hollow pointer).*

Vacuum Systems

Vacuum systems are very common for driving gyro instruments. In a vacuum system, a stream of air directed against the rotor vanes turns the rotor at high speed. The action is similar to a water wheel. Air at atmospheric pressure is first drawn through a filter(s). It is then routed into the instrument and directed at vanes on the gyro rotor. A suction line leads from the instrument case to the vacuum source. From there, the air is vented overboard. Either a venturi or a vacuum pump can be used to provide the vacuum required to spin the rotors of the gyro instruments.

The vacuum value required for instrument operation is usually between 3½ inches to 4½ inches of mercury. It is usually adjusted by a vacuum relief valve located in the supply line. Some turn-and-bank indicators require a lower vacuum setting. This can be obtained through the use of an additional regulating valve in the turn and bank vacuum supply line.

Venturi Tube Systems

The velocity of the air rushing through a venturi can create sufficient suction to spin instrument gyros. A line is run from the gyro instruments to the throat of the venturi mounted on the outside of the airframe. The low pressure in the venturi tube pulls air through the instruments, spins the gyros, and expels the air overboard through the venturi. This source of gyro power is used on many simple, early aircraft.

A light, single-engine aircraft can be equipped with a 2-inch venturi (2 inches of mercury vacuum capacity) to operate the turn and bank indicator. It can also have a larger 8-inch venturi to power the attitude and heading indicators. Simplified illustrations of these venturi vacuum systems are shown in *Figure 10-87*. Normally, air going into the instruments is filtered.

The advantages of a venturi as a suction source are its relatively low cost and its simplicity of installation and operation. It also requires no electric power. But there are serious limitations. A venturi is designed to produce the desired vacuum at approximately 100 mph at standard sea level conditions. Wide variations in airspeed or air density cause the suction developed to fluctuate. Airflow can also be hampered by ice that can form on the venturi tube. Additionally, since the rotor does not reach normal operating speed until after takeoff, preflight operational checks of venturi powered gyro instruments cannot be made. For these reasons, alternate sources of vacuum power were developed.

Engine-Driven Vacuum Pump

The vane-type engine-driven pump is the most common source of vacuum for gyros installed in general aviation,

Figure 10-86. *Solid state magnetometers.*

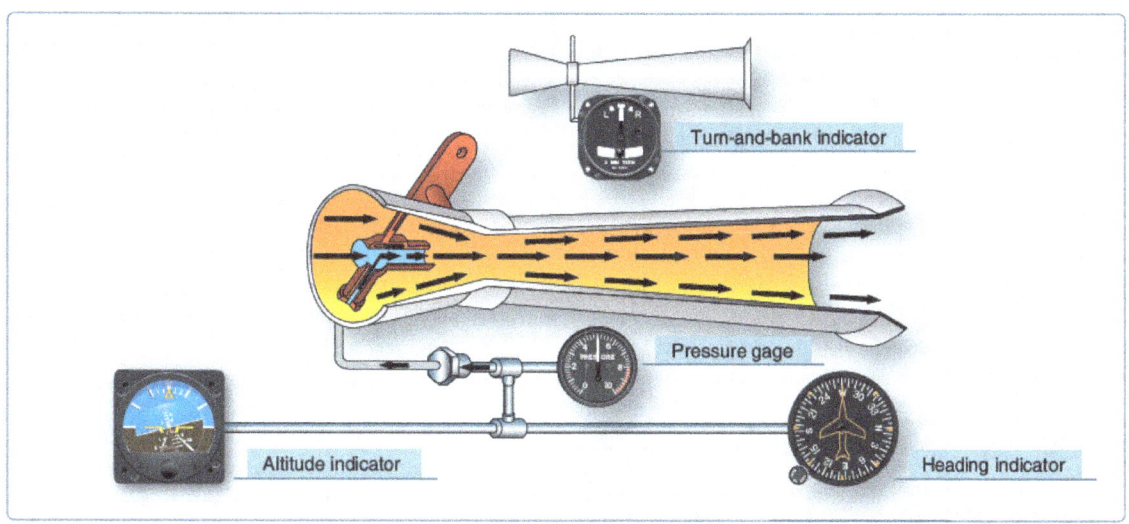

Figure 10-87. *Simple venturi tube systems for powering gyroscopic instruments.*

light aircraft. One type of engine-driven pump is geared to the engine and is connected to the lubricating system to seal, cool, and lubricate the pump. Another commonly used pump is a dry vacuum pump. It operates without external lubrication and installation requires no connection to the engine oil supply. It also does not need the air oil separator or gate check valve found in wet pump systems. In many other respects, the dry pump system and oil lubricated system are the same. *[Figure 10-88]*

Figure 10-88. *Cutaway view of a vane-type engine-driven vacuum pump used to power gyroscopic instruments.*

When a vacuum pump develops a vacuum (negative pressure), it also creates a positive pressure at the outlet of the pump. This pressure is compressed air. Sometimes, it is utilized to operate pressure gyro instruments. The components for pressure systems are much the same as those for a vacuum system as listed below. Other times, the pressure developed by the vacuum pump is used to inflate de-ice boots or inflatable seals or it is vented overboard.

An advantage of engine-driven pumps is their consistent performance on the ground and in flight. Even at low engine rpm, they can produce more than enough vacuum so that a regulator in the system is needed to continuously provide the correct suction to the vacuum instruments. As long as the engine operates, the relatively simple vacuum system adequately spins the instrument gyros for accurate indications. However, engine failure, especially on single-engine aircraft, could leave the pilot without attitude and directional information at a critical time. To thwart this shortcoming, often the turn and bank indicator operates with an electrically driven gyro that can be driven by the battery for a short time. Thus, when combined with the aircraft's magnetic compass, sufficient attitude and directional information is still available.

Multiengine aircraft typically contain independent vacuum systems for the pilot and copilot instruments driven by separate vacuum pumps on each of the engines. Should an engine fail, the vacuum system driven by the still operating engine supplies a full complement of gyro instruments. An interconnect valve may also be installed to connect the failed instruments to the still operational pump.

Typical Pump-Driven System

The following components are found in a typical vacuum system for gyroscopic power supply. A brief description is given of each. Refer to the figures for detailed illustrations.

Air-oil separator—oil and air in the vacuum pump are exhausted through the separator, which separates the oil from the air; the air is vented overboard and the oil is returned to the engine sump. This component is not present when a dry-type vacuum pump is used. The self-lubricating nature of the pump vanes requires no oil.

Vacuum regulator or suction relief valve—since the system capacity is more than is needed for operation of the instruments, the adjustable vacuum regulator is set for the vacuum desired for the instruments. Excess suction in the instrument lines is reduced when the spring-loaded valve opens to atmospheric pressure. *[Figure 10-89]*

Figure 10-89. *A vacuum regulator, also known as a suction relief valve, includes a foam filter. To relieve vacuum, outside air of a higher pressure must be drawn into the system. This air must be clean to prevent damage to the pump.*

Gate check valve—prevents possible damage to the instruments by engine backfire that would reverse the flow of air and oil from the pump. *[Figure 10-90]*

Pressure relief valve—since a reverse flow of air from the pump would close both the gate check valve and the suction relief valve, the resulting pressure could rupture the lines. The pressure relief valve vents positive pressure into the atmosphere.

Figure 10-90. *Gate check valve used to prevent vacuum system damage from engine backfire.*

Selector valve—In twin-engine aircraft having vacuum pumps driven by both engines, the alternate pump can be selected to provide vacuum in the event of either engine or pump failure, with a check valve incorporated to seal off the failed pump.

Restrictor valve—Since the turn needle of the turn and bank indicator operates on less vacuum than that required by the other instruments, the vacuum in the main line must be reduced for use by this instrument. An in-line restrictor valve performs this function. This valve is either a needle valve or a spring-loaded regulating valve that maintains a constant, reduced vacuum for the turn-and-bank indicator.

Air filter—A master air filter screens foreign matter from the air flowing through all the gyro instruments. It is an extremely import filter requiring regular maintenance. Clogging of the master filter reduces airflow and causes a lower reading on the suction gauge. Each instrument is also provided with individual filters. In systems with no master filter that rely only upon individual filters, clogging of a filter does not necessarily show on the suction gauge.

Suction gauge—a pressure gauge which indicates the difference between the pressure inside the system and atmospheric or cockpit pressure. It is usually calibrated in inches of mercury. The desired vacuum and the minimum and maximum limits vary with gyro system design. If the desired vacuum for the attitude and heading indicators is 5 inches and the minimum is 4.6 inches, a reading below the latter value indicates that the airflow is not spinning the gyros fast enough for reliable operation. In many aircraft, the system provides a suction gauge selector valve permitting the pilot to check the vacuum at several points in the system.

Suction/vacuum pressures discussed in conjunction with the operation of vacuum systems are actually negative pressures, indicated as inches of mercury below that of atmospheric pressure. The minus sign is usually not presented, as the importance is placed on the magnitude of the vacuum developed. In relation to an absolute vacuum (0 psi or 0 "Hg), instrument vacuum systems have positive pressure.

Figure 10-91 shows a typical engine-driven pump vacuum system containing the above components. A pump capacity of approximately 10"Hg at engine speeds above 1,000 rpm is normal. Pump capacity and pump size vary in different aircraft, depending on the number of gyros to be operated.

Twin-Engine Aircraft Vacuum System Operation
Twin-engine aircraft vacuum systems are more complicated. They contain an engine-driven vacuum pump on each engine. The associated lines and components for each pump are

Figure 10-91. *A typical pump-driven vacuum system for powering gyroscopic instruments.*

isolated from each other and act as two independent vacuum systems. The vacuum lines are routed from each vacuum pump through a vacuum relief valve and through a check valve to the vacuum four-way selector valve. The four-way valve permits either pump to supply a vacuum manifold. From the manifold, flexible hoses connect the vacuum-operated instruments into the system. To reduce the vacuum for the turn and bank indicators, needle valves are included in both lines to these units. Lines to the artificial horizons and the directional gyro receive full vacuum. From the instruments, lines are routed to the vacuum gauge through a turn and bank selector valve. This valve has three positions: main, left turn and bank (T&B), and right T&B. In the main position, the vacuum gauge indicates the vacuum in the lines of the artificial horizons and directional gyro. In the other positions, the lower value of vacuum for the turn and bank indicators can be read.

A schematic of this twin-engine aircraft vacuum system is shown in *Figure 10-92*. Note the following components: two engine-driven pumps, two vacuum relief valves, two flapper type check valves, a vacuum manifold, a vacuum restrictor for each turn and bank indicator, an engine four-way selector valve, one vacuum gauge, and a turn-and-bank selector valve. Not shown are system and individual instrument filters. A drain line may also be installed at the low point in the system.

Pressure-Driven Gyroscopic Instrument Systems

Gyroscopic instruments are finely balanced devices with jeweled bearings that must be kept clean to perform properly. When early vacuum systems were developed, only oil-lubricated pumps were available. Even with the use of air-oil separators, the pressure outputs of these pumps contain traces of oil and dirt. As a result, it was preferred to draw clean air through the gyro instruments with a vacuum system, rather than using pump output pressure that presented the risk of contamination. The development of self-lubricated dry pumps greatly reduced pressure output contaminates. This made pressure gyro systems possible.

At high altitudes, the use of pressure-driven gyros is more efficient. Pressure systems are similar to vacuum systems and make use of the same components, but they are designed for pressure instead of vacuum. Thus, a pressure regulator is used instead of a suction relief valve. Filters are still extremely important to prevent damage to the gyros. Normally, air is filtered at the inlet and outlet of the pump in a pressure gyro system.

Electrically-Driven Gyroscopic Instrument Systems

A spinning motor armature can act as a gyroscope. This is the basis for electrically driven gyroscopic instruments in which the gyro rotor spin is powered by an electric motor.

Figure 10-92. *An example of a twin-engine instrument vacuum system.*

Electric gyros have the advantage of being powered by battery for a limited time if a generator fails or an engine is lost. Since air is not sent through the gyro to spin the rotor, contamination worries are also reduced. Also, elimination of vacuum pumps, plumbing, and vacuum system components saves weight.

On many small, single-engine aircraft, electric turn-and-bank or turn coordinators are combined with vacuum-powered attitude and directional gyro instruments as a means for redundancy. The reverse is also possible. By combining both types of instruments in the instrument panel, the pilot has more options. On more complex multiengine aircraft, reliable, redundant electrical systems make use of all electric-powered gyro instruments possible.

It should be noted that electric gyro instruments have some sort of indicator on the face of the dial to show when the instrument is not receiving power. Usually, this is in the form of a red flag or mark of some sort often with the word "off" written on it.

Principles of Gyroscopic Instruments
Mechanical Gyros

Three of the most common flight instruments, the attitude indicator, heading indicator, and turn needle of the turn-and-bank indicator, are controlled by gyroscopes. To understand how these instruments operate, knowledge of gyroscopic principles and instrument power systems is required.

A mechanical gyroscope, or gyro, is comprised of a wheel or rotor with its mass concentrated around its perimeter. The rotor has bearings to enable it to spin at high speeds. *[Figure 10-93A]*

Different mounting configurations are available for the rotor and axle, which allow the rotor assembly to rotate about one or two axes perpendicular to its axis of spin. To suspend the rotor for rotation, the axle is first mounted in a supporting ring. *[Figure 10-93B]* If brackets are attached 90° around the supporting ring from where the spin axle attached, the supporting ring and rotor can both move freely 360°. When in this configuration, the gyro is said to be a captive gyro. It can rotate about only one axis that is perpendicular to the axis of spin. *[Figure 10-93C]*

The supporting ring can also be mounted inside an outer ring. The bearing points are the same as the bracket just described, 90° around the supporting ring from where the spin axle attached. Attachment of a bracket to this outer ring allows the rotor to rotate in two planes while spinning. Both of these are perpendicular to the spin axis of the rotor. The plane that the rotor spins in due to its rotation about its axle is not counted as a plane of rotation.

A gyroscope with this configuration, two rings plus the mounting bracket, is said to be a free gyro because it is free to rotate about two axes that are both perpendicular to the rotor's spin axis. *[Figure 10-93D]* As a result, the supporting ring with spinning gyro mounted inside is free to turn 360° inside the outer ring.

Unless the rotor of a gyro is spinning, it has no unusual properties: it is simply a wheel universally mounted. When the rotor is rotated at a high speed, the gyro exhibits a couple of unique characteristics. The first is called gyroscopic rigidity, or rigidity in space. This means that the rotor of a free gyro always points in the same direction no matter which way the base of the gyro is positioned. *[Figure 10-94]*

Figure 10-94. *Once spinning, a free gyro rotor stays oriented in the same position in space despite the position or location of its base.*

Gyroscopic rigidity depends upon several design factors:

1. Weight—for a given size, a heavy mass is more resistant to disturbing forces than a light mass.

2. Angular velocity—the higher the rotational speed, the greater the rigidity or resistance is to deflection.

3. Radius at which the weight is concentrated—maximum effect is obtained from a mass when its principal weight is concentrated near the rim, rotating at high speed.

4. Bearing friction—any friction applies a deflecting force to a gyro. Minimum bearing friction keeps deflecting forces at a minimum.

Figure 10-93. *Gyroscopes.*

This characteristic of gyros to remain rigid in space is exploited in the attitude-indicating instruments and the directional indicators that use gyros.

Precession is a second important characteristic of gyroscopes. By applying a force to the horizontal axis of the gyro, a unique phenomenon occurs. The applied force is resisted. Instead of responding to the force by moving about the horizontal axis, the gyro moves in response about its vertical axis. Stated another way, an applied force to the axis of the spinning gyro does not cause the axis to tilt. Rather, the gyro responds as though the force was applied 90° around in the direction of rotation of the gyro rotor. The gyro rotates rather than tilts. *[Figure 10-95]* This predictable controlled precession of a gyroscope is utilized in a turn and bank instrument.

Figure 10-95. *When a force is applied to a spinning gyroscope, it reacts as though the force came from 90° further around the rotor in the direction it is spinning. The plane of the applied force, the plane of the rotation, and the plane in which the gyro responds (known as the plane of precession), are all perpendicular to each other.*

Solid State Gyros and Related Systems

Improved attitude and direction information is always a goal in aviation. Modern aircraft make use of highly accurate solid-state attitude and directional devices with no moving parts. This results in very high reliability and low maintenance.

Ring Laser Gyros (RLG)

The ring laser gyro (RLG) is widely used in commercial aviation. The basis for RLG operation is that it takes time for light to travel around a stationary, nonrotating circular path. Light takes longer to complete the journey if the path is rotating in the same direction as the light is traveling. And, it takes less time for the light to complete the loop if the path is rotating in the direction opposite to that of the light. Essentially, the path is made longer or shorter by the rotation of the path. *[Figure 10-96]* This is known as the Sagnac effect.

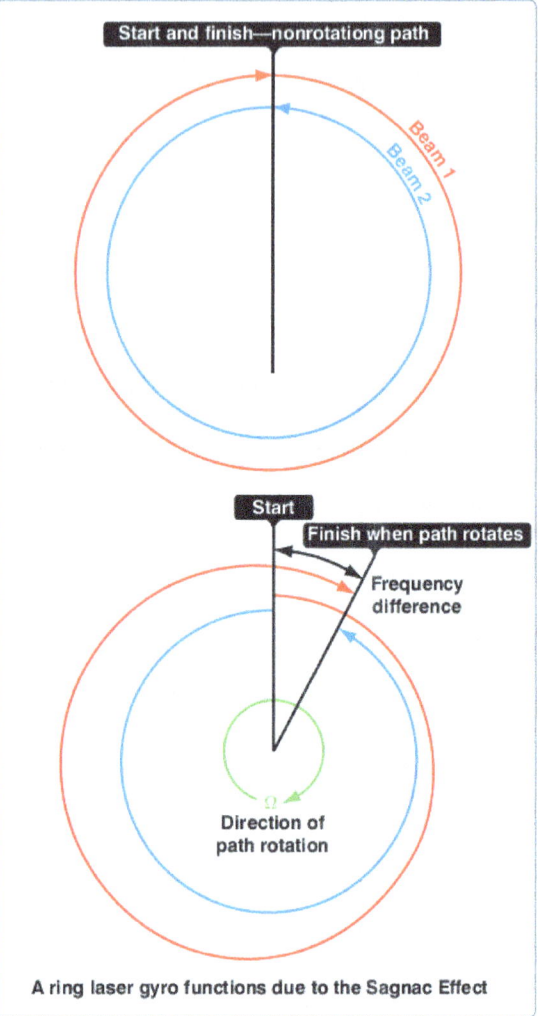

Figure 10-96. *Light traveling in opposite directions around a non-rotating path arrives at the end of the loop at the same time (top). When the path rotates, light traveling with the rotation must travel farther to complete one loop. Light traveling against the rotation completes the loop sooner (bottom).*

A laser is light amplification by stimulated emission of radiation. A laser operates by exciting atoms in plasma to release electromagnetic energy, or photons. A ring laser gyro produces laser beams that travel in opposite directions around a closed triangular cavity. The wavelength of the light traveling around the loop is fixed. As the loop rotates, the path the lasers must travel lengthens or shortens. The light wavelengths compress or expand to complete travel around the loop as the loop changes its effective length. As the wavelengths change, the frequencies also change.

By examining the difference in the frequencies of the two counterrotating beams of light, the rate at which the path is rotating can be measured. A piezoelectric dithering motor in the center of the unit vibrates to prevent lock-in of the output signal at low rotational speeds. It causes units installed on aircraft to hum when operating. *[Figure 10-97]*

Figure 10-97. *The ring laser gyro is rugged, accurate, and free of friction.*

An RLG is remotely mounted so the cavity path rotates around one of the axes of flight. The rate of frequency phase shift detected between the counterrotating lasers is proportional to the rate that the aircraft is moving about that axis. On aircraft, an RLG is installed for each axis of flight. Output can be used in analog instrumentation and autopilot systems. It is also easily made compatible for use by digital display computers and for digital autopilot computers.

RLGs are very rugged and have a long service life with virtually no maintenance due to their lack of moving parts. They measure movement about an axis extremely quickly and provide continuous output. They are extremely accurate and generally are considered superior to mechanical gyroscopes.

Microelectromechanical Based Attitude and Directional Systems

On aircraft, microelectromechanical systems (MEMS) devices save space and weight. Through the use of solid-state MEMS devices, reliability is increased primarily due to the lack of moving parts. The development of MEMS technology for use in aviation instrumentation integrates with the use of ADCs. This newest improvement in technology is low cost and promises to proliferate through all forms of aviation.

MEMS for gyroscopic applications are used in small, general aviation aircraft, as well as larger commercial aircraft. Tiny vibration-based units with resistance and capacitance measuring pick-offs are accurate and reliable and only a few millimeters in length and width. They are normally integrated into a complete micro-electronic solid-state chip designed to yield an output after various conditioning processes are performed. The chips, which are analogous to tiny circuit boards, can be packaged for installation inside a dedicated computer or module that is installed on the aircraft.

While a large mechanical gyroscope spins in a plane, its rigidity in space is used to observe and measure the movement of the aircraft. The basis of operation of many MEMS gyroscopes is the same despite their tiny size. The difference is that a vibrating or oscillating piezoelectric device replaces the spinning, weighted ring of the mechanical gyro. Still, once set in motion, any out-of-plane motion is detectable by varying microvoltages or capacitances detected through geometrically arranged pickups. Since piezoelectric substances have a relationship between movement and electricity, microelectrical stimulation can set a piezoelectric gyro in motion and the tiny voltages produced via the movement in the piezo can be extracted. They can be input as the required variables needed to compute attitude or direction information. *[Figure 10-98]*

Figure 10-98. *The relative scale size of a MEMS gyro.*

Other Attitude and Directional Systems

In modern aircraft, attitude heading and reference systems (AHRS) have taken the place of the gyroscope and other individual instruments. While MEMS devices provide part of the attitude information for the system, GPS, solid state magnetometers, solid state accelerometers, and digital air data signals are all combined in an AHRS to compute and output highly reliable information for display on a cockpit panel. *[Figure 10-99]*

Figure 10-99. *Instrumentation displayed within a glass cockpit using an attitude heading and reference system (AHRS) computer.*

Common Gyroscopic Instruments

Vacuum-Driven Attitude Gyros

The attitude indicator, or artificial horizon, is one of the most essential flight instruments. It gives the pilot pitch and roll information that is especially important when flying without outside visual references. The attitude indicator operates with a gyroscope rotating in the horizontal plane. Thus, it mimics the actual horizon through its rigidity in space. As the aircraft pitches and rolls in relation to the actual horizon, the gyro gimbals allow the aircraft and instrument housing to pitch and roll around the gyro rotor that remains parallel to the ground. A horizontal representation of the airplane in miniature is fixed to the instrument housing. A painted semisphere simulating the horizon, the sky, and the ground is attached to the gyro gimbals. The sky and ground meet at what is called the horizon bar. The relationship between the horizon bar and the miniature airplane are the same as those of the aircraft and the actual horizon. Graduated scales reference the degrees of pitch and roll. Often, an adjustment knob allows pilots of varying heights to place the horizon bar at an appropriate level. *[Figure 10-100]*

In a typical vacuum-driven attitude gyro system, air is sucked through a filter and then through the attitude indicator in a manner that spins the gyro rotor inside. An erecting mechanism is built into the instrument to assist in keeping the gyro rotor rotating in the intended plane. Precession caused by bearing friction makes this necessary. After air engages the scalloped drive on the rotor, it flows from the instrument to the vacuum pump through four ports. These ports all exhaust the same amount of air when the gyro is rotating in plane. When the gyro rotates out of plane, air tends to port out of one side more than another. Vanes close to prevent this, causing more air to flow out of the opposite side. The force from this unequal venting of the air re-erects the gyro rotor. *[Figure 10-101]*

Early vacuum-driven attitude indicators were limited in how far the aircraft could pitch or roll before the gyro gimbals contacted stops, causing abrupt precession and tumbling of the gyro. Many of these gyros include a caging device. It is used to erect the rotor to its normal operating position prior to flight or after tumbling. A flag indicates that the gyro must be uncaged before use. More modern gyroscopic instruments are built so they do not tumble, regardless of the angular movement of the aircraft about its axes.

In addition to the contamination potential introduced by the air-drive system, other shortcomings exist in the performance of vacuum-driven attitude indicators. Some are induced by the erection mechanism. The pendulous vanes that move to direct airflow out of the gyro respond not only to forces caused by a deviation from the intended plane of rotation, but centrifugal force experienced during turns also causes the vanes to allow asymmetric porting of the gyro vacuum air. The result is inaccurate display of the aircraft's attitude, especially in skids and steep banked turns. Also, abrupt acceleration and deceleration imposes forces on the gyro rotor. Suspended in its gimbals, it acts similar to an accelerometer, resulting in a false nose-up or nose-down indication. Pilots must learn to recognize these errors and adjust accordingly.

Figure 10-100. *A typical vacuum-driven attitude indicator shown with the aircraft in level flight (left) and in a climbing right turn (right).*

Figure 10-101. *The erecting mechanism of a vacuum-driven attitude indicator.*

Electric Attitude Indicators

Electric attitude indicators are very similar to vacuum-driven gyro indicators. The main difference is in the drive mechanism. Inside the gimbals of an electric gyro, a small squirrel cage electric motor is the rotor. It is typically driven by 115 volt, 400-cycle AC. It turns at approximately 21,000 rpm.

Other characteristics of the vacuum-driven gyro are shared by the electric gyro. The rotor is still oriented in the horizontal plane. The free gyro gimbals allow the aircraft and instrument case to rotate around the gyro rotor that remains rigid in space. A miniature airplane fixed to the instrument case indicates the aircraft's attitude against the moving horizon bar behind it.

Electric attitude indicators address some of the shortcomings of vacuum-driven attitude indicators. Since there is no air flowing through an electric attitude indicator, air filters, regulators, plumbing lines and vacuum pump(s) are not needed. Contamination from dirt in the air is not an issue, resulting in the potential for longer bearing life and less precession. Erection mechanism ports are not employed, so pendulous vanes responsive to centrifugal forces are eliminated.

It is still possible that the gyro may experience precession and need to be erected. This is done with magnets rather than vent ports. A magnet attached to the top of the gyro shaft spins at approximately 21,000 rpm. Around this magnet, but not attached to it, is a sleeve that is rotated by magnetic attraction at approximately 44 to 48 rpm. Steel balls are free to move around the sleeve. If the pull of gravity is not aligned with the axis of the gyro, the balls fall to the low side. The resulting precession re-aligns the axis of rotation vertically.

10-57

Typically, electric attitude indicator gyros can be caged manually by a lever and cam mechanism to provide rapid erection. When the instrument is not getting sufficient power for normal operation, an off flag appears in the upper right hand face of the instrument. *[Figure 10-102]*

Gyroscopic Direction Indicator or Directional Gyro (DG)

The gyroscopic direction indicator or directional gyro (DG) is often the primary instrument for direction. Because a magnetic compass fluctuates so much, a gyro aligned with the magnetic compass gives a much more stable heading indication. Gyroscopic direction indicators are located at the center base of the instrument panel basic T.

A vacuum-powered DG is common on many light aircraft. Its basis for operation is the gyro's rigidity in space. The gyro rotor spins in the vertical plane and stays aligned with the direction to which it is set. The aircraft and instrument case moves around the rigid gyro. This causes a vertical compass card that is geared to the rotor gimbal to move. It is calibrated in degrees, usually with every 30 degrees labeled. The nose of a small, fixed airplane on the instrument glass indicates the aircraft's heading. *[Figure 10-103]*

Vacuum-driven direction indicators have many of the same basic gyroscopic instrument issues as attitude indicators. Built-in compensation for precession varies and a caging device is usually found. Periodic manual realignment with the magnetic compass by the pilot is required during flight.

Turn Coordinators

Many aircraft make use of a turn coordinator. The rotor of the gyro in a turn coordinator is canted upwards 30°. As such, it responds not only to movement about the vertical axis, but also to roll movements about the longitudinal axis. This is useful because it is necessary to roll an aircraft to

Figure 10-103. *A typical vacuum-powered gyroscopic direction indicator, also known as a directional gyro.*

turn it about the vertical axis. Instrument indication of roll, therefore, is the earliest possible warning of a departure from straight-and-level flight.

Typically, the face of the turn coordinator has a small airplane symbol. The wing tips of the airplane provide the indication of level flight and the rate at which the aircraft is turning. *[Figure 10-104]*

Turn-and-Slip Indicator

The turn-and-slip indicator may also be referred to as the turn-and-bank indicator, or needle-and-ball indicator. Regardless, it shows the correct execution of a turn while banking the aircraft and indicates movement about the vertical axis of the aircraft (yaw). Most turn-and-slip indicators are located below the airspeed indicator of the instrument panel basic T, just to the left of the direction indicator.

Figure 10-102. *Erecting and caging mechanisms of an electric attitude indicator.*

Figure 10-104. *A turn coordinator senses and indicates the rate of both roll and yaw.*

The turn-and-slip indicator is actually two separate devices built into the same instrument housing: a turn indicator pointer and slip indicator ball. The turn pointer is operated by a gyro that can be driven by a vacuum, air pressure, or by electricity. The ball is a completely independent device. It is a round agate, or steel ball, in a glass tube filled with dampening fluid. It moves in response to gravity and centrifugal force experienced in a turn.

Turn indicators vary. They all indicate the rate at which the aircraft is turning. Three degrees of turn per second cause an aircraft to turn 360° in 2 minutes. This is considered a standard turn. This rate can be indicated with marks right and left of the pointer, which normally rests in the vertical position. Sometimes, no marks are present and the width of the pointer is used as the calibration device. In this case, one pointer width deflection from vertical is equal to the 3° per second standard 2-minute turn rate. Faster aircraft tend to turn more slowly and have graduations or labels that indicate 4-minute turns. In other words, a pointer's width or alignment with a graduation mark on this instrument indicates that the aircraft is turning a 1½° per second and completes a 360° turn in 4 minutes. It is customary to placard the instrument face with words indicating whether it is a 2-or 4-minute turn indicator. *[Figure 10-105]*

The turn pointer indicates the rate at which an aircraft is turning about its vertical axis. It does so by using the precession of a gyro to tilt a pointer. The gyro spins in a vertical plane aligned with the longitudinal axis of the aircraft. When the aircraft rotates about its vertical axis during a turn,

Figure 10-105. *Turn-and-slip indicator.*

the force experienced by the spinning gyro is exerted about the vertical axis. Due to precession, the reaction of the gyro rotor is 90° further around the gyro in the direction of spin. This means the reaction to the force around the vertical axis is movement around the longitudinal axis of the aircraft. This causes the top of the rotor to tilt to the left or right. The pointer is attached with linkage that makes the pointer deflect in the opposite direction, which matches the direction of turn. So, the aircraft's turn around the vertical axis is indicated around the longitudinal axis on the gauge. This is intuitive to the pilot when regarding the instrument, since the pointer indicates in the same direction as the turn. *[Figure 10-106]*

The slip indicator (ball) part of the instrument is an inclinometer. The ball responds only to gravity during coordinated straight-and-level flight. Thus, it rests in the lowest part of the curved glass between the reference wires. When a turn is initiated and the aircraft is banked, both gravity and the centrifugal force of the turn act upon the ball. If the turn is coordinated, the ball remains in place. Should a skidding turn exist, the centrifugal force exceeds the force of gravity on the ball and it moves in the direction of the outside of the turn. During a slipping turn, there is more bank than needed, and gravity is greater than the centrifugal force acting on the ball. The ball moves in the curved glass toward the inside of the turn.

As mentioned previously, often power for the turn-and-slip indicator gyro is electrical if the attitude and direction indicators are vacuum powered. This allows limited operation off battery power should the vacuum system and the electric generator fail. The directional and attitude information from the turn-and-slip indicator, combined with information from the pitot static instruments, allow continued safe emergency operation of the aircraft.

Electrically powered turn-and-slip indicators are usually DC powered. Vacuum-powered turn-and-slip indicators are usually run on less vacuum (approximately 2 "Hg) than fully gimbaled attitude and direction indicators. Regardless, proper vacuum must be maintained for accurate turn rate information to be displayed.

Figure 10-106. *The turn-and-slip indicator's gyro reaction to the turning force in a right hand turn. The yaw force results in a force on the gyro 90° around the rotor in the direction it is turning due to precession. This causes the top of the rotor to tilt to the left. Through connecting linkage, the pointer tilts to the right.*

Autopilot Systems

An aircraft automatic pilot system controls the aircraft without the pilot directly maneuvering the controls. The autopilot maintains the aircraft's attitude and/or direction and returns the aircraft to that condition when it is displaced from it. Automatic pilot systems are capable of keeping aircraft stabilized laterally, vertically, and longitudinally.

The primary purpose of an autopilot system is to reduce the work strain and fatigue of controlling the aircraft during long flights. Most autopilots have both manual and automatic modes of operation. In the manual mode, the pilot selects each maneuver and makes small inputs into an autopilot controller. The autopilot system moves the control surfaces of the aircraft to perform the maneuver. In automatic mode, the pilot selects the attitude and direction desired for a flight segment. The autopilot then moves the control surfaces to attain and maintain these parameters.

Autopilot systems provide for one-, two-, or three-axis control of an aircraft. Those that manage the aircraft around only one axis control the ailerons. They are single-axis autopilots, known as wing leveler systems, usually found on light aircraft. *[Figure 10-107]* Other autopilots are two-axis systems that control the ailerons and elevators. Three-axis autopilots control the ailerons, elevators, and the rudder. Two-and three-axis autopilot systems can be found on aircraft of all sizes.

There are many autopilot systems available. They feature a wide range of capabilities and complexity. Light aircraft typically have autopilots with fewer capabilities than high-performance and transport category aircraft. Integration of navigation functions is common, even on light aircraft autopilots. As autopilots increase in complexity, they not only manipulate the flight control surfaces, but other flight parameters as well.

Some modern small aircraft, high-performance, and transport category aircraft have very elaborate autopilot systems known as automatic flight control systems (AFCS). These three-axis systems go far beyond steering the airplane. They control the aircraft during climbs, descents, cruise, and approach to landing. Some even integrate an auto-throttle function that automatically controls engine thrust that makes auto-landings possible.

For further automatic control, flight management systems have been developed. Through the use of computers, an entire flight profile can be programmed ahead of time allowing the pilot to supervise its execution. An FMS computer coordinates nearly every aspect of a flight, including the autopilot and auto throttle systems, navigation route selection, fuel management schemes, and more.

Basis for Autopilot Operation

The basis for autopilot system operation is error correction. When an aircraft fails to meet the conditions selected, an error is said to have occurred. The autopilot system automatically corrects that error and restores the aircraft to the flight attitude desired by the pilot. There are two basic ways modern autopilot systems do this. One is position based and the other is rate based. A position based autopilot manipulates the aircraft's controls so that any deviation from the desired attitude of the aircraft is corrected. This is done by memorizing

Figure 10-107. *The wing leveler system on a small aircraft is a vacuum-operated single-axis autopilot. Only the ailerons are controlled. The aircraft's turn coordinator is the sensing element. Vacuum from the instrument vacuum system is metered to the diaphragm cable actuators to move the ailerons when the turn coordinator senses roll.*

the desired aircraft attitude and moving the control surfaces so that the aircraft returns to that attitude. Rate based autopilots use information about the rate of movement of the aircraft, and move control surfaces to counter the rate of change that causes the error. Most large aircraft use rate-based autopilot systems. Small aircraft may use either.

Autopilot Components

Most autopilot systems consist of four basic components, plus various switches and auxiliary units. The four basic components are: sensing elements, computing element, output elements, and command elements. Many advanced autopilot systems contain a fifth element: feedback or follow-up. This refers to signals sent as corrections are being made by the output elements to advise the autopilot of the progress being made. *[Figure 10-108]*

Sensing Elements

The attitude and directional gyros, the turn coordinator, and an altitude control are the autopilot sensing elements. These units sense the movements of the aircraft. They generate electric signals that are used by the autopilot to automatically take the required corrective action needed to keep the aircraft flying as intended. The sensing gyros can be located in the cockpit mounted instruments. They can also be remotely mounted. Remote gyro sensors drive the servo displays in the cockpit panel, as well as provide the input signals to the autopilot computer.

Modern digital autopilots may use a variety of different sensors. MEMS gyros may be used or accompanied by the use solid state accelerometers and magnetometers. Rate based systems may not use gyros at all. Various input sensors may be located within the same unit or in separate units that transfer information via digital data bus. Navigation information is also integrated via digital data bus connection to avionics computers.

Computer and Amplifier

The computing element of an autopilot may be analog or digital. Its function is to interpret the sensing element data, integrate commands and navigational input, and send signals to the output elements to move the flight controls as required to control the aircraft. An amplifier is used to strengthen the signal for processing, if needed, and for use by the output devices, such as servo motors. The amplifier and associated circuitry is the computer of an analog autopilot system. Information is handled in channels corresponding to the axis of control for which the signals are intended (i.e., pitch channel, roll channel, or yaw channel). Digital systems use solid state microprocessor computer technology and typically only amplify signals sent to the output elements.

Output Elements

The output elements of an autopilot system are the servos that cause actuation of the flight control surfaces. They are independent devices for each of the control channels that

Figure 10-108. *Typical analog autopilot system components.*

integrate into the regular flight control system. Autopilot servo designs vary widely depending on the method of actuation of the flight controls. Cable-actuated systems typically utilize electric servo motors or electro-pneumatic servos. Hydraulic actuated flight control systems use electro-hydraulic autopilot servos. Digital fly-by-wire aircraft utilize the same actuators for carrying out manual and autopilot maneuvers. When the autopilot is engaged, the actuators respond to commands from the autopilot rather than exclusively from the pilot. Regardless, autopilot servos must allow unimpeded control surface movement when the autopilot is not operating.

Aircraft with cable actuated control surfaces use two basic types of electric motor-operated servos. In one, a motor is connected to the servo output shaft through reduction gears. The motor starts, stops, and reverses direction in response to the commands of autopilot computer. The other type of electric servo uses a constantly running motor geared to the output shaft through two magnetic clutches. The clutches are arranged so that energizing one clutch transmits motor torque to turn the output shaft in one direction; energizing the other clutch turns the shaft in the opposite direction. *[Figure 10-109]* Electropneumatic servos can also be used to drive cable flight controls in some autopilot systems. They are controlled by electrical signals from the autopilot amplifier and actuated by an appropriate air pressure source. The source may be a vacuum system pump or turbine engine bleed air. Each servo consists of an electromagnetic valve assembly and an output linkage assembly.

Aircraft with hydraulically actuated flight control systems have autopilot servos that are electro-hydraulic. They are control valves that direct fluid pressure as needed to move the control surfaces via the control surface actuators. They are powered by signals from the autopilot computer. When the autopilot is not engaged, the servos allow hydraulic fluid to flow unrestricted in the flight control system for normal operation. The servo valves can incorporate feedback transducers to update the autopilot of progress during error correction.

Command Elements

The command unit, called a flight controller, is the human interface of the autopilot. It allows the pilot to tell the autopilot what to do. Flight controllers vary with the complexity of the autopilot system. By pressing the desired function buttons, the pilot causes the controller to send instruction signals to the autopilot computer, enabling it to activate the proper servos to carry out the command(s). Level flight, climbs, descents, turning to a heading, or flying a desired heading are some of the choices available on most autopilots. Many aircraft make use of a multitude of radio navigational aids. These can be selected to issue commands directly to the autopilot computer. *[Figure 10-110]*

Figure 10-110. *An autopilot controller of a simple autopilot system.*

In addition to an on/off switch on the autopilot controller, most autopilots have a disconnect switch located on the control wheel(s). This switch, operated by thumb pressure, can be used to disengage the autopilot system should a malfunction occur in the system or any time the pilot wishes to take manual control of the aircraft.

Feedback or Follow-up Element

As an autopilot maneuvers the flight controls to attain a desired flight attitude, it must reduce control surface correction as the desired attitude is nearly attained so the controls and aircraft come to rest on course. Without doing so, the system would continuously overcorrect. Surface deflection would occur until the desired attitude is attained. But movement would still occur as the surface(s) returned to pre-error position. The attitude sensor would once again detect an error and begin the correction process all over again.

Figure 10-109. *A reversible motor with capstan and bridle cable (left), and a single-direction constant motor with clutches that drive the output shafts and control cable in opposite directions (right).*

Various electric feedback, or follow-up signals, are generated to progressively reduce the error message in the autopilot so that continuous over correction does not take place. This is typically done with transducers on the surface actuators or in the autopilot servo units. Feedback completes a loop as illustrated in *Figure 10-111*.

Figure 10-111. *Basic function of an analog autopilot system including follow-up or feedback signal.*

A rate system receives error signals from a rate gyro that are of a certain polarity and magnitude that cause the control surfaces to be moved. As the control surfaces counteract the error and move to correct it, follow-up signals of opposite polarity and increasing magnitude counter the error signal until the aircraft's correct attitude is restored. A displacement follow-up system uses control surface pickups to cancel the error message when the surface has been moved to the correct position.

Autopilot Functions

The following autopilot system description is presented to show the function of a simple analog autopilot. Most autopilots are far more sophisticated; however, many of the operating fundamentals are similar.

The automatic pilot system flies the aircraft by using electrical signals developed in gyro-sensing units. These units are connected to flight instruments that indicate direction, rate of turn, bank, or pitch. If the flight attitude or magnetic heading is changed, electrical signals are developed in the gyros. These signals are sent to the autopilot computer/amplifier and are used to control the operation of servo units.

A servo for each of the three control channels converts electrical signals into mechanical force, which moves the control surface in response to corrective signals or pilot commands. The rudder channel receives two signals that determine when and how much the rudder moves. The first signal is a course signal derived from a compass system. As long as the aircraft remains on the magnetic heading it was on when the autopilot was engaged, no signal develops. But, any deviation causes the compass system to send a signal to the rudder channel that is proportional to the angular displacement of the aircraft from the preset heading.

The second signal received by the rudder channel is the rate signal that provides information anytime the aircraft is turning about the vertical axis. This information is provided by the turn-and-bank indicator gyro. When the aircraft attempts to turn off course, the rate gyro develops a signal proportional to the rate of turn, and the course gyro develops a signal proportional to the amount of displacement. The two signals are sent to the rudder channel of the amplifier, where they are combined and their strength is increased. The amplified signal is then sent to the rudder servo. The servo turns the rudder in the proper direction to return the aircraft to the selected magnetic heading.

As the rudder surface moves, a follow-up signal is developed that opposes the input signal. When the two signals are equal in magnitude, the servo stops moving. As the aircraft arrives on course, the course signal reaches a zero value, and the rudder is returned to the streamline position by the follow-up signal.

The aileron channel receives its input signal from a transmitter located in the gyro horizon indicator. Any movement of the aircraft about its longitudinal axis causes the gyro-sensing unit to develop a signal to correct for the movement. This signal is amplified, phase detected, and sent to the aileron servo, which moves the aileron control surfaces to correct for the error. As the aileron surfaces move, a follow-up signal builds up in opposition to the input signal. When the two signals are equal in magnitude, the servo stops moving. Since the ailerons are displaced from the streamline, the aircraft now starts moving back toward level flight with the input signal becoming smaller and the follow-up signal driving the control surfaces back toward the streamline position. When the aircraft has returned to level flight roll attitude, the input signal is again zero. At the same time, the control surfaces are streamlined, and the follow-up signal is zero.

The elevator channel circuits are similar to those of the aileron channel, with the exception that the elevator channel detects and corrects changes in pitch attitude of the aircraft. For altitude control, a remotely mounted unit containing an altitude pressure diaphragm is used. Similar to the attitude and directional gyros, the altitude unit generates error signals when the aircraft has moved from a preselected altitude. This is known as an altitude hold function. The signals control the pitch servos, which move to correct the error. An altitude select function causes the signals to continuously be sent to the pitch servos until a preselected altitude has been reached. The aircraft then maintains the preselected altitude using altitude hold signals.

Yaw Dampening

Many aircraft have a tendency to oscillate around their vertical axis while flying a fixed heading. Near continuous rudder input is needed to counteract this effect. A yaw damper is used to correct this motion. It can be part of an autopilot system or a completely independent unit. A yaw damper receives error signals from the turn coordinator rate gyro. Oscillating yaw motion is counteracted by rudder movement, which is made automatically by the rudder servo(s) in response to the polarity and magnitude of the error signal.

Automatic Flight Control System (AFCS)

An aircraft autopilot with many features and various autopilot related systems integrated into a single system is called an automatic flight control system (AFCS). These were formerly found only on high-performance aircraft. Currently, due to advances in digital technology for aircraft, modern aircraft of any size may have AFCS.

AFCS capabilities vary from system to system. Some of the advances beyond ordinary autopilot systems are the extent of programmability, the level of integration of navigational aids, the integration of flight director and autothrottle systems, and combining of the command elements of these various systems into a single integrated flight control human interface. *[Figure 10-112]*

It is at the AFCS level of integration that an autothrottle system is integrated into the flight director and autopilot systems with glide scope modes so that auto landings are possible. Small general aviation aircraft being produced with AFCS may lack the throttle-dependent features.

Modern general aviation AFCS are fully integrated with digital attitude heading and reference systems (AHRS) and navigational aids including glideslope. They also contain modern computer architecture for the autopilot (and flight director systems) that is slightly different than described above for analog autopilot systems. Functionality is distributed across a number of interrelated computers and includes the use of intelligent servos that handle some of the error correction calculations. The servos communicate with dedicated avionics computers and display unit computers through a control panel, while no central autopilot computer exists. *[Figure 10-113]*

Flight Director Systems

A flight director system is an instrument system consisting of electronic components that compute and indicate the aircraft attitude required to attain and maintain a preselected flight condition. A command bar on the aircraft's attitude indicator shows the pilot how much and in what direction the attitude of the aircraft must be changed to achieve the desired result. The computed command indications relieve the pilot of many of the mental calculations required for instrument flights, such as interception angles, wind drift correction, and rates of climb and descent.

Essentially, a flight director system is an autopilot system without the servos. All of the same sensing and computations are made, but the pilot controls the airplane and makes maneuvers by following the commands displayed on the instrument panel. Flight director systems can be part of an autopilot system or exist on aircraft that do not possess full autopilot systems. Many autopilot systems allow for the option of engaging or disengaging a flight director display.

Flight director information is displayed on the instrument that displays the aircraft's attitude. The process is accomplished with a visual reference technique. A symbol representing the aircraft is fit into a command bar positioned by the flight director in the proper location for a maneuver to be accomplished. The symbols used to represent the aircraft and the command bar vary by manufacturer. Regardless, the object is always to fly the aircraft symbol into the command bar symbol. *[Figure 10-114]*

Figure 10-112. *The AFCS control panel commands several integrated systems from a single panel including: flight directors, autopilots, autothrottles, autoland, and navigational aids. Mode selections for many features are made from this single interface.*

10-65

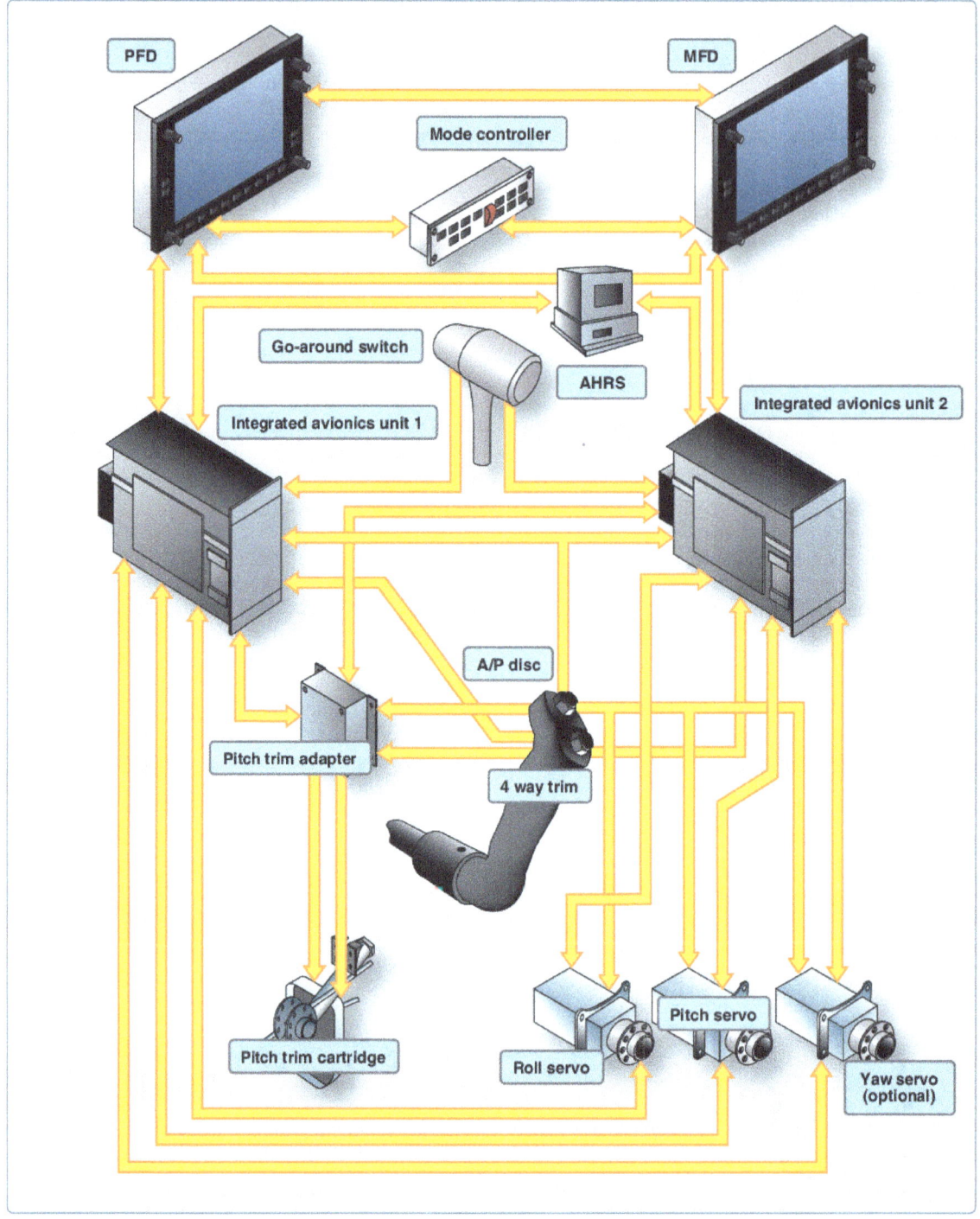

Figure 10-113. *Automatic flight control system (AFCS) of a Garmin G1000 glass cockpit instrument system for a general aviation aircraft.*

Figure 10-114. *The fight director command bar signals the pilot how to steer the aircraft for a maneuver. By flying the aircraft so the triangular airplane symbol fits into the command bar, the pilot performs the maneuver calculated by the flight director. The instrument shown on the left is commanding a climb while the airplane is flying straight and level. The instrument on the right shows that the pilot has accomplished the maneuver.*

The instrument that displays the flight director commands is known as a flight director indicator (FDI), attitude director indicator (ADI), or electronic attitude director indicator (EADI). It may even be referred to as an artificial horizon with flight director. This display element combines with the other primary components of the flight director system. Like an autopilot, these consist of the sensing elements, a computer, and an interface panel.

Integration of navigation features into the attitude indicator is highly useful. The flight director contributes to this usefulness by indicating to the pilot how to maneuver the airplane to navigate a desired course. Selection of the VOR function on the flight director control panel links the computer to the omnirange receiver. The pilot selects a desired course and the flight director displays the bank attitude necessary to intercept and maintain this course. Allocations for wind drift and calculation of the intercept angle is performed automatically.

Flight director systems vary in complexity and features. Many have altitude hold, altitude select, pitch hold, and other features. But flight director systems are designed to offer the greatest assistance during the instrument approach phase of flight. ILS localizer and glideslope signals are transmitted through the receivers to the computer and are presented as command indications. This allows the pilot to fly the airplane down the optimum approach path to the runway using the flight director system.

With the altitude hold function engaged, level flight can be maintained during the maneuvering and procedure turn phase of an approach. Altitude hold automatically disengages when the glideslope is intercepted. Once inbound on the localizer, the command signals of the flight director are maintained in a centered or zero condition. Interception of the glideslope causes a downward indication of the command pitch indicator. Any deviation from the proper glideslope path causes a fly-up or fly-down command indication. The pilot needs only to keep the airplane symbol fit into the command bar.

Electronic Instruments

Electronic Attitude Director Indicator (EADI)

The EADI is an advanced version of attitude and electric attitude indicators previously discussed. In addition to displaying the aircraft's attitude, numerous other situational flight parameters are displayed. Most notable are those that relate to instrument approaches and the flight director command bars. Annunciation of active systems, such as the AFCS and navigation systems, is typical.

The concept behind an EADI is to put all data related to the flight situation in close proximity for easy observation by the pilot. *[Figure 10-115]* Most EADIs can be switched between different display screens depending on the preference of the pilot and the phase of flight. EADIs vary from manufacturer to manufacturer and aircraft to aircraft. However, most of the same information is displayed.

EADIs can be housed in a single instrument housing or can be part of an electronic instrument display system. One such system, the electronic flight instrument system (EFIS), uses a cathode ray tube EADI display driven by a signal generator. Large-screen glass cockpit displays use LCD technology to display EADI information as part of an entire situational display directly in front of the pilot in the middle of the instrument panel. Regardless, the EADI

Figure 10-115. *Some of the many parameters and features of an electronic attitude director indicator (EADI).*

is the primary flight instrument used for aircraft attitude information during instrument flying and especially during instrument approaches. It is almost always accompanied by an electronic horizontal situation indicator (EHSI) located just below it in the display panel.

Electronic Horizontal Situation Indicators (EHSI)

The EHSI is an evolved version of the horizontal situation indicator (HSI), which was born from the gyroscopic direction indicator or directional gyro. The HSI incorporates directional information to two different navigational aids, as well as the heading of the aircraft. The EHSI does this and more. Its primary purpose is to display as much useful navigational information as possible.

In conjunction with a flight management computer and a display controller, an EHSI can display information in PLAN, MAP, VOR, and ILS modes. The PLAN mode shows a fixed map of the input flight plan. This usually includes all selected navigational aids for each flight segment and the destination airport. The MAP mode shows the aircraft against a detailed moving map background. Active and inactive navigational aids are shown, as well as other airports and waypoints. Weather radar information may be selected to be shown in scale as a background. Some HSIs can depict other air traffic when integrated with the TCAS system. Unlike a standard HSI, an EHSI may show only the pertinent portion of the compass rose. Annunciation of active mode and selected features appear with other pertinent information, such as distance and arrival time to the next waypoint, airport designators, wind direction and speed, and more. *[Figure 10-116]* There are many different displays that vary by manufacturer.

The VOR view of an EHSI presents a more traditional focus on a selected VOR, or other navigational station being used, during a particular flight segment. The entire compass rose, the traditional lateral deviation pointer, to/from information, heading, and distance information are standard. Other information may also be displayed. *[Figure 10-117]* The ILS mode of an EHSI shows the aircraft in relation to the ILS approach aids and selected runway with varying degrees of details. With this information displayed, the pilot need not consult printed airport approach information, allowing full attention to flying the aircraft.

Electronic Flight Information Systems

In an effort to increase the safety of operating complicated aircraft, computers and computer systems have been incorporated. Flight instrumentation and engine and airframe monitoring are areas particularly well suited to gain advantages from the use of computers. They contribute by helping to reduce instrument panel clutter and focusing the pilot's attention only on matters of imminent importance.

"Glass cockpit" is a term that refers to the use of flat-panel display screens in cockpit instrumentation. In reality, it also refers to the use of computer-produced images that have replaced individual mechanical gauges. Moreover, computers and computer systems monitor the processes and components of an operating aircraft beyond human ability while relieving the pilot of the stress from having to do so.

Computerized electronic flight instrument systems have additional benefits. The solid-state nature of the components increases reliability. Also, microprocessors, data buses, and

Figure 10-116. *An EHSI presents navigational information for the entire flight. The pilot selects the mode most useful for a particular phase of flight, ranging from navigational planning to instrument approach to landing. The MAP mode is used during most of the flight.*

Figure 10-117. *Approach and VOR mode presentation of an electronic horizontal situation indicator.*

10-69

LCDs all save space and weight. The following systems have been developed and utilized on aircraft for a number of years. New systems and computer architecture are sure to come in the future.

Electronic Flight Instrument System (EFIS)

The flight instruments were the first to adopt computer technology and utilize flat screen, multifunctional displays (MFD). EFIS uses dedicated signal generators to drive two independent displays in the center of the basic T. The attitude indicator and directional gyro are replaced by cathode ray tubes (CRT) used to display EADI and EHSI presentations. These enhanced instruments operate alongside ordinary mechanic and electric instruments with limited integration. Still, EADI and EHSI technology is very desirable, reducing workload and panel scan with the added safety provided by integration of navigation information as described.

Early EFIS systems have analog technology, while newer models may be digital systems. The signal generators receive information from attitude and navigation equipment. Through a display controller, the pilot can select the various mode or screen features wishing to be displayed. Independent dedicated pilot and copilot systems are normal. A third, backup symbol generator is available to assume operation should one of the two primary units fail. *[Figure 10-118]*

Electronic depiction of ADI and HSI information is the core purpose of an EFIS system. Its expanded size and capabilities over traditional gauges allow for integration of even more flight instrument data. A vertical airspeed scale is typically displayed just left of the attitude field. This is in the same relative position as the airspeed indicator in an analog basic T instrument panel. To the right of the attitude field, many EFIS systems display an altitude and vertical speed scale. Since most EFIS EADI depictions include the inclinometer, normally part of the turn coordinator, all of the basic flight instruments are depicted by the EFIS display. *[Figure 10-119]*

Figure 10-119. *An EFIS EADI displays an airspeed scale to the left of the horizon sphere and an altimeter and vertical speed scale to the right. The slip indicator is the small rectangle under the direction triangles at the top. This EFIS display presents all of the flight information in the conventional cockpit basic T.*

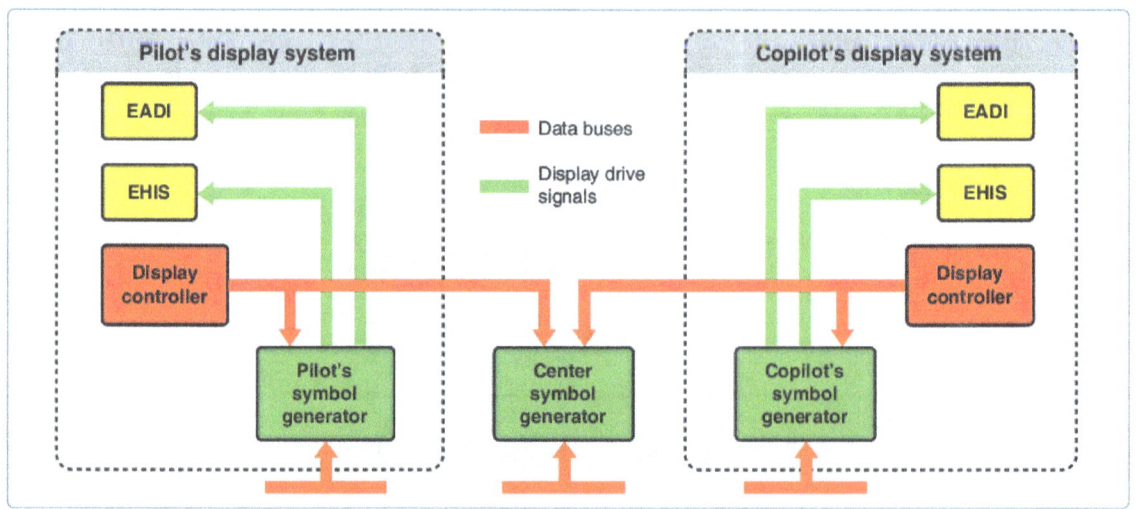

Figure 10-118. *A simplified diagram of an EFIS system. The EADI and EHSI displays are CRT units in earlier systems. Modern systems use digital displays, sometimes with only one multifunctional display unit replacing the two shown. Independent digital processors can also be located in a single unit to replace the three separate symbol generators.*

Electronic Centralized Aircraft Monitor (ECAM)

The pilot's workload on all aircraft includes continuous monitoring of the flight instruments and the sky outside of the aircraft. It also includes vigilant scrutiny for proper operation of the engine and airframe systems. On transport category aircraft, this can mean monitoring numerous gauges in addition to maneuvering the aircraft. The electronic centralized aircraft monitoring (ECAM) system is designed to assist with this duty.

The basic concept behind ECAM (and other monitoring systems) is automatic performance of monitoring duties for the pilot. When a problem is detected or a failure occurs, the primary display, along with an aural and visual cue, alerts the pilot. Corrective action that needs to be taken is displayed, as well as suggested action due to the failure. By performing system monitoring automatically, the pilot is free to fly the aircraft until a problem occurs.

Early ECAM systems only monitor airframe systems. Engine parameters are displayed on traditional full-time cockpit gauges. Later model ECAM systems incorporate engine displays, as well as airframe.

An ECAM system has two CRT monitors. In newer aircraft, these may be LCD. The left or upper monitor, depending on the aircraft panel layout, displays information on system status and any warnings associated corrective actions. This is done in a checklist format. The right or lower monitor displays accompanying system information in a pictorial form, such as a diagram of the system being referred to on the primary monitor.

The ECAM monitors are typically powered by separate signal generators. Aircraft data inputs are fed into two flight warning computers. Analog inputs are first fed through a system data analog converter and then into the warning computers. The warning computers process the information and forward information to the signal generators to illuminate the monitors. *[Figure 10-120]*

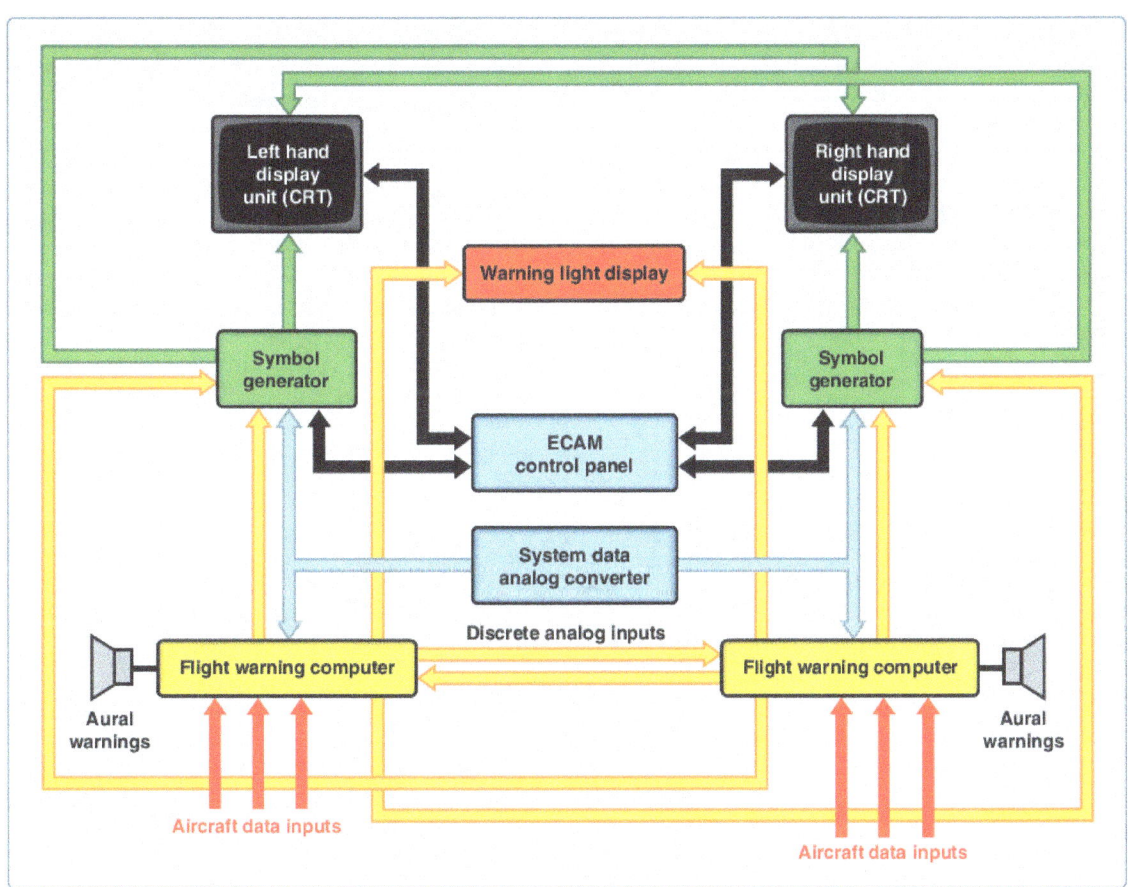

Figure 10-120. *An electronic centralized aircraft monitor (ECAM) system displays aircraft system status, checklists, advisories, and warnings on a pair of controllable monitors.*

There are four basic modes to the ECAM system: flight phase, advisory, failure related, and manual. The flight phase mode is normally used. The phases are: preflight, takeoff, climb, cruise, descent, approach, and post landing. Advisory and failure–related modes will appear automatically as the situation requires. When an advisory is shown on the primary monitor, the secondary monitor will automatically display the system schematic with numerical values. The same is true for the failure-related mode, which takes precedent over all other modes regardless of which mode is selected at the time of the failure. Color coding is used on the displays to draw attention to matters in order of importance. Display modes are selected via a separate ECAM control panel shown in *Figure 10-121*.

The manual mode of an ECAM is set by pressing one of the synoptic display buttons on the control panel. This allows the display of system diagrams. A failure warning or advisory event will cancel this view. *[Figure 10-122]*

ECAM flight warning computers self-test upon startup. The signal generators are also tested. A maintenance panel allows for testing annunciation and further testing upon demand. BITE stands for built-in test equipment. It is standard for monitoring systems to monitor themselves as well as the aircraft systems. All of the system inputs to the flight warning computers can also be tested for continuity from this panel, as well as inputs and outputs of the system data analog converter. Any individual system faults will be listed on the primary display as normal. Faults in the flight warning computers and signal generators will annunciate on the maintenance panel. *[Figure 10-123]* Follow the manufacturer's guidelines when testing ECAM and related systems.

Engine Indicating and Crew Alerting System (EICAS)

An engine indicating and crew alerting system (EICAS) performs many of the same functions as an ECAM system. The objective is still to monitor the aircraft systems for the pilot. All EICAS display engine, as well as airframe, parameters. Traditional gauges are not utilized, other than a standby combination engine gauge in case of total system failure.

EICAS is also a two-monitor, two-computer system with a display select panel. Both monitors receive information from the same computer. The second computer serves as a standby. Digital and analog inputs from the engine and airframe systems are continuously monitored. Caution and warning lights, as well as aural tones, are incorporated. *[Figure 10-124]*

EICAS provides full time primary engine parameters (EPR, N_1, EGT) on the top, primary monitor. Advisories and warning are also shown there. Secondary engine parameters and nonengine system status are displayed on the bottom screen. The lower screen is also used for maintenance diagnosis when the aircraft is on the ground. Color coding is used, as well as message prioritizing.

The display select panel allows the pilot to choose which computer is actively supplying information. It also controls the display of secondary engine information and system status displays on the lower monitor. EICAS has a unique feature that automatically records the parameters of a failure event to be regarded afterwards by maintenance personnel. Pilots that suspect a problem may be occurring during flight can press the event record button on the display select panel. This also records the parameters for that flight period to be studied later by maintenance. Hydraulic, electrical, environmental, performance, and APU data are examples of what may be recorded.

Figure 10-121. *An ECAM display control panel.*

Figure 10-122. *Nine of the 12 available system diagrams from the ECAM manual mode.*

EICAS uses BITE for systems and components. A maintenance panel is included for technicians. From this panel, when the aircraft is on the ground, push-button switches display information pertinent to various systems for analysis. *[Figure 10-125]*

Flight Management System (FMS)

The highest level of automated flight system is the flight FMS. Companies flying aircraft for hire have special results they wish to achieve. On-time performance, fuel conservation, and long engine and component life all contribute to profitability. An FMS helps achieve these results by operating the aircraft with greater precision than possible by a human pilot alone.

A FMS can be thought of as a master computer system that has control over all other systems, computerized and otherwise. As such, it coordinates the adjustment of flight, engine, and airframe parameters either automatically or by instructing the pilot how to do so. Literally, all aspects of the flight are considered, from preflight planning to pulling up to the jet-way upon landing, including in-flight amendments to planned courses of action.

The main component of an FMS is the flight management computer (FMC). It communicates with the EICAS or ECAM, the ADC, the thrust management computer that controls the autothrottle functions, the EIFIS symbol generators, the automatic flight control system, the inertial reference system, collision avoidance systems, and all of the radio navigational aids via data busses. *[Figure 10-126]*

Figure 10-123. *An ECAM maintenance panel used for testing and annunciating faults in the ECAM system.*

The interface to the system is a control display unit (CDU) that is normally located forward on the center pedestal in the cockpit. It contains a full alphanumeric keypad, a CRT or LCD display/work screen, status and condition annunciators, and specialized function keys. *[Figure 10-127]*

The typical FMS uses two FMS FMCs that operate independently as the pilot's unit and the copilot's unit. However, they do crosstalk through the data busses. In normal operation, the pilot and copilot divide the workload, with the pilot's CDU set to supervise and interface with operational parameters and the copilot's CDU handling navigational chores. This is optional at the flightcrew's discretion. If a main component fails (e.g., an FMC or a CDU), the remaining operational units continue to operate with full control and without system compromise.

Each flight of an aircraft has vertical, horizontal, and navigational components, which are maintained by manipulating the engine and airframe controls. While doing so, numerous options are available to the pilot. Rate of climb, thrust settings, EPR levels, airspeed, descent rates, and other terms can be varied. Commercial air carriers use the FMC to establish guidelines by which flights can be flown. Usually, these promote the company's goals for fuel and equipment conservation. The pilot need only enter variables as requested and respond to suggested alternatives as the FMC presents them.

The FMC has stored in its database literally hundreds of flight plans with predetermined operational parameters that can be selected and implemented. Integration with NAV-COM aids allows the FMS to change radio frequencies as the flight plan is enacted. Internal computations using direct input from fuel flow and fuel quantity systems allow the FMC to carry out lean operations or pursue other objectives, such as high performance operations if making up time is paramount on a particular flight. Weather and traffic considerations are also integrated. The FMS can handle all variables automatically, but communicates via the CDU screen to present its planned action, gain consensus, or ask for an input or decision.

As with the monitoring systems, FMS includes BITE. The FMC continuously monitors its entire systems and inputs for faults during operation. Maintenance personal can retrieve system generated and pilot recorded fault messages. They may also access maintenance pages that call out line replaceable units (LRUs) to which faults have been traced by the BITE system. Follow manufacturers' procedures for interfacing with maintenance data information.

Warnings and Cautions

Annunciator Systems

Instruments are installed for two purposes: to display current conditions and to notify of unsatisfactory conditions. Standardized colors are used to differentiate between visual messages. For example, the color green indicates a satisfactory condition. Yellow is used to caution of a serious condition that requires further monitoring. Red is the color for an unsatisfactory condition. Whether part of the instrument face or of a visual warning system, these colors give quick-reference information to the pilot.

Most aircraft include annunciator lights that illuminate when an event demanding attention occurs. These use the aforementioned colors in a variety of presentations. Individual lights near the associated cockpit instrument or a collective display of lights for various systems in a central location are common. Words label each light or are part of the light itself to identify any problem quickly and plainly.

On complex aircraft, the status of numerous systems and components must be known and maintained. Centralized warning systems have been developed to annunciate critical messages concerning a multitude of systems and components in a simplified, organized manner. Often, this will be done by locating a single annunciator panel somewhere on the instrument panel. These analog aircraft warning systems may look different in various aircraft, and depend on manufacturer preference and the systems installed. *[Figure 10-128]* EFIS provide for annunciation of advisory and warning messages as part of its flight control and monitoring capabilities, as previously described. Usually, the primary display unit is designated as the location to display annunciations.

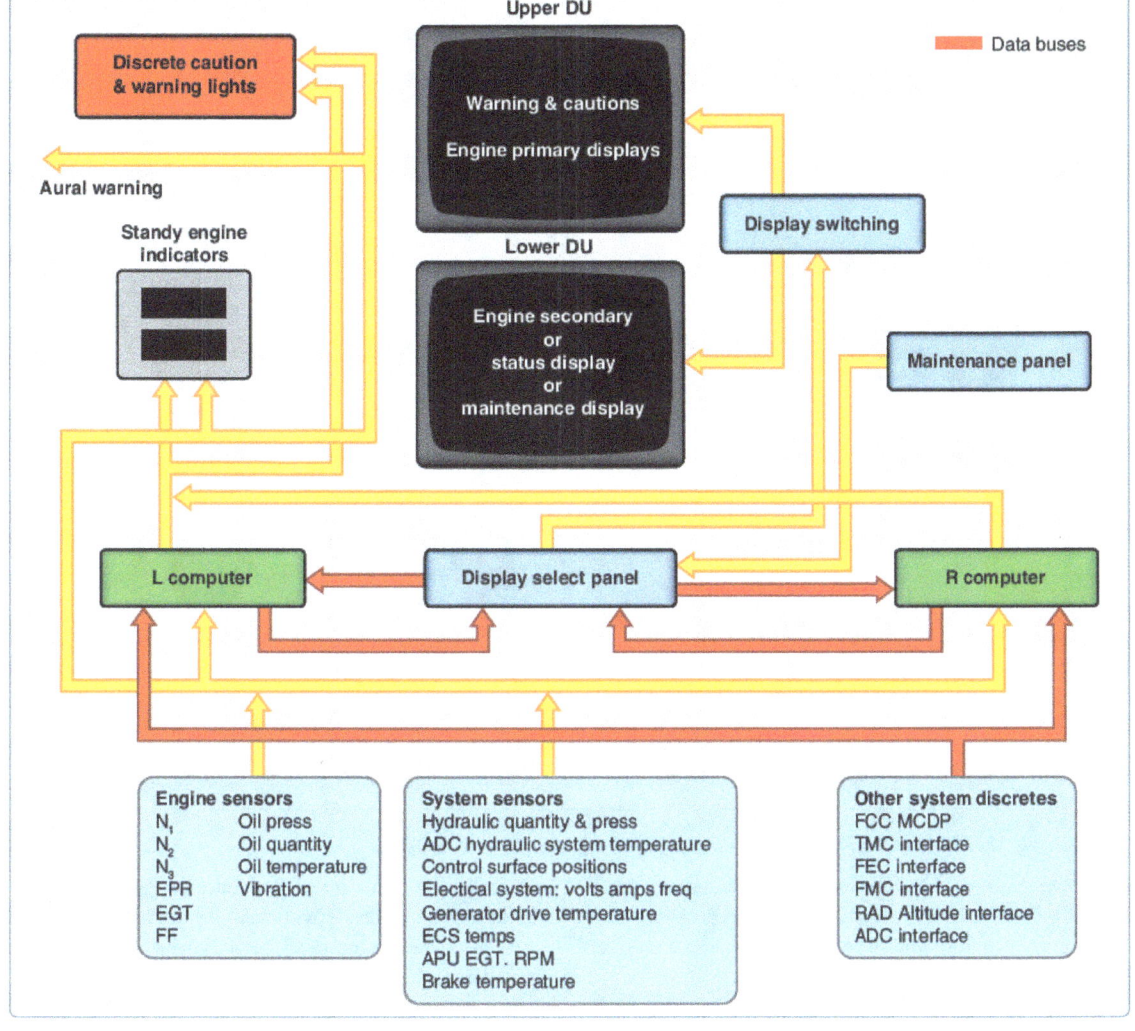

Figure 10-124. *Schematic of an engine indicating and crew alerting system (EICAS).*

Master caution lights are used to draw the attention of the crew to a critical situation in addition to an annunciator that describes the problem. These master caution lights are centrally wired and illuminate whenever any of the participating systems or components require attention. Once notified, the pilot may cancel the master caution, but a dedicated system or component annunciator light stays illuminated until the situation that caused the warning is rectified. Cancelling resets the master caution lights to warn of a subsequent fault event even before the initial fault is corrected. *[Figure 10-129]* Press to test is available for the entire annunciator system, which energizes all warning circuitry and lights to confirm readiness. Often, this test exposes the need to replace the tiny light bulbs that are used in the system.

Aural Warning Systems

Aircraft aural warning systems work in conjunction with illuminated annunciator systems. They audibly inform the pilot of a situation requiring attention. Various tones and phrases sound in the cockpit to alert the crew when certain conditions exist. For example, an aircraft with retractable landing gear uses an aural warning system to alert the crew to an unsafe condition. A bell sounds if the throttle is retarded and the landing gear is not in a down and locked condition.

A typical transport category aircraft has an aural warning system that alerts the pilot with audio signals for the following: abnormal takeoff, landing, pressurization, mach airspeed conditions, an engine or wheel well fire, calls from

Figure 10-125. *The EICAS maintenance control panel is for the exclusive use of technicians.*

the crew call system, collision avoidance recommendations, and more. *Figure 10-130* shows some of the problems that trigger aural warnings and the action to be taken to correct the situation.

Clocks

Whether called a clock or a chronometer, an FAA-approved time indicator is required in the cockpit of IFR-certified aircraft. Pilots use a clock during flight to time maneuvers and for navigational purposes. The clock is usually mounted near the flight instrument group, often near the turn coordinator. It indicates hours, minutes, and seconds.

For many years, the mechanical 8-day clock was the standard aircraft timekeeping device largely because it continues to run without electrical power as long as it has been hand wound. The mechanical 8-day clock is reliable and accurate enough for its intended use. Some mechanical aircraft clocks feature a push-button elapsed time feature. *[Figure 10-131]*

As electrical systems developed into the reliable, highly redundant systems that exist today, use of an electric clock to replace the mechanical clock began. An electric clock is an analog devise that may also have an elapsed time feature. It can be wired to the battery or battery bus. Thus, it continues to operate in the event of a power failure. Electric aircraft clocks are often used in multiengine aircraft where complete loss of electrical power is unlikely.

Many modern aircraft have a digital electronic clock with LED readout. This device comes with the advantages of low power consumption and high reliability due to the lack of moving parts. It is also very accurate. Solid-state electronics allow for expanded features, such as elapsed time, flight time that starts automatically upon takeoff, a stop watch, and memories for all functions. Some even have temperature and date readouts. Although wired into the aircraft's electrical system, electronic digital clocks may include a small independent battery inside the unit that operates the device should aircraft electrical power fail. *[Figure 10-132]*

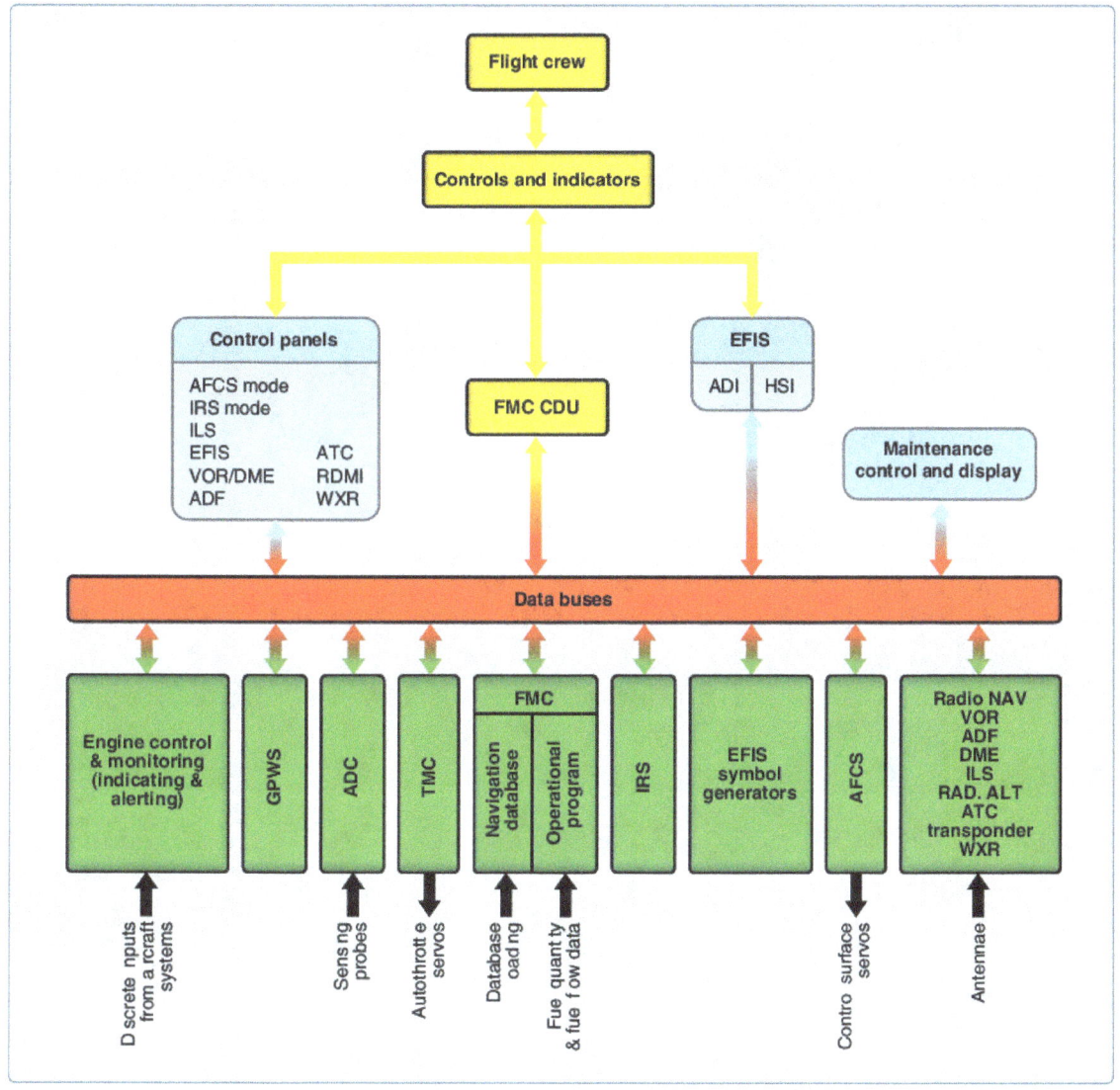

Figure 10-126. *A flight management system (FMS) integrates numerous engine, aircraft, and navigational systems to provide overall management of the flight.*

On aircraft with fully digital computerized instrument systems utilizing flat panel displays, the computer's internal clock, or a GPS clock, can be used with a digital time readout usually located somewhere on the primary flight display.

Instrument Housings and Handling

Various materials are used to protect the inner workings of aircraft instruments, as well as to enhance the performance of the instrument and other equipment mounted in the immediate vicinity. Instrument cases can be one piece or multipiece. Aluminum alloy, magnesium alloy, steel, iron, and plastic are all common materials for case construction.

Electric instruments usually have a steel or iron alloy case to contain electromagnetic flux caused by current flow inside.

Despite their rugged outward appearance, all instruments, especially analog mechanical instruments, should be handled with special care and should never be dropped. A crack in an airtight instrument case renders it unairworthy. Ports should never be blown into and should be plugged until the instrument is installed. Cage all gyro instruments until mounted in the instrument panel. Observe all cautions written on the instrument housing and follow the manufacturer's instruction for proper handling and shipping, as well as installation.

Figure 10-127. *The control display unit (CDU) of an FMS.*

Figure 10-129. *A master caution switch removed from the instrument panel.*

Figure 10-128. *The centralized analog annunciator panel has indicator lights from systems and components throughout the aircraft. It is supported by the master caution system.*

Instrument Installations and Markings

Instrument Panels

Instrument panels are usually made from sheet aluminum alloy and are painted a dark, nonglare color. They sometimes contain subpanels for easier access to the backs of instruments during maintenance. Instrument panels are usually shock-mounted to absorb low-frequency, high-amplitude shocks. The mounts absorb most of the vertical and horizontal vibration, but permit the instruments to operate under conditions of minor vibration. Bonding straps are used to ensure electrical continuity from the panel to the airframe. [Figure 10-133]

The type and number of shock mounts to be used for instrument panels are determined by the weight of the unit. Shock-mounted instrument panels should be free to move in all directions and have sufficient clearance to avoid striking the supporting structure. When a panel does not have

Examples of Aircraft Aural Warnings

Stage of Operation	Warning System	Warning Signal	Cause of Warning Signal Activation	Corrective action
Takeoff	Flight control	Intermittent horn	Throttles are advanced and any of the following conditions exist: 1. Speed brakes are not down 2. Flaps are not in takeoff range 3. Auxiliary power exhaust door is open 4. Stabilizer is not in the takeoff setting	Correct the aircraft to proper takeoff conditions
In flight	Mach warning	Clacker	Equivalent airspeed or mach number exceeds limits	Decrease aircraft speed
In flight	Pressurization	Intermittent horn	If cabin pressure becomes equal to atmospheric pressure at the specific altitude (altitude at time of occurrence)	Correct the condition
Landing	Landing gear	Continuous horn	Landing gear is not down and locked when flaps are less than full up and throttle is retarded to idle	Raise flaps; advance throttle
Any stage	Fire warning	Continuous bell	Any overheat condition or fire in any engine or nacelle, or main wheel or nose wheel well, APU engine, or any compartment having fire warning system installed Whenever the fire warning system is tested	1. Lower the heat in the the area where in the F/W was activated 2. Signal may be silenced pushing the F/W bell cutout switch or the APU cutout switch
Any stage	Communications ATA 2300	High chime	Any time captain's call button is pressed at external power panel forward or rearward cabin attendant's panel	Release button; if button remains locked in, pull button out

Figure 10-130. *Aircraft aural warnings.*

Figure 10-131. *A typical mechanical 8-day aircraft clock.*

Figure 10-132. *A typical aircraft electronic clock.*

adequate clearance, inspect the shock mounts for looseness, cracks, or deterioration.

Instrument panel layout is seemingly random on older aircraft. The advent of instrument flight made the flight instruments of critical importance when flying without outside reference to the horizon or ground. As a result, the basic T arrangement for flight instruments was adopted, as mentioned in the beginning of this chapter. *[Figure 10-4]* Electronic flight instrument systems and digital cockpit displays have kept the same basic T arrangement for flight instrument and data presentations. The flight instruments and basic T are located directly in front of the pilot and copilot's seats. Some light

Figure 10-133. *Instrument panel shock mounts.*

On modern aircraft, EFIS and digital flight information systems reduce panel clutter and allow easier access to all instruments by both crewmembers. Controllable display panels provide the ability to select from pages of information that, when not displayed, are completely gone from view and use no instrument panel space.

Instrument Mounting

The method of mounting instruments in their respective panels depends on the design of the instrument case. In one design, the bezel is flanged in such a manner that the instrument can be flush mounted in its cutout from the rear of the panel. Integral, self-locking nuts are provided at the rear faces of the flange corners to receive mounting screws from the front of the panel. The flanged-type instrument can also be mounted to the front of the panel. In this case, nut-plates are usually installed in the panel itself. Nonferrous screws are usually used to mount the instruments.

aircraft have only one full set of flight instruments that are located in front of the left seat.

The location of engine instruments and navigation instruments varies. Ideally, they should be accessible to both the pilot and copilot. Numerous variations exist to utilize the limited space in the center of the instrument panel and still provide accessibility by the flight crew to all pertinent instruments. On large aircraft, a center pedestal and overhead panels help create more space. On small aircraft, the engine instruments are often moved to allow navigation instruments and radios to occupy the center of the instrument panel. *[Figure 10-134]*

There are also instrument mounting systems where the instruments are flangeless. A special clamp, shaped and dimensioned to fit the instrument case, is permanently secured to the rear face of the panel. The instrument is slid into the panel from the front and into the clamp. The clamp's tightening screw is accessible from the front side of the panel. *[Figure 10-135]* Regardless of how an instrument is mounted, it should not be touching or be so close as to touch another instrument during the shock of landing.

Figure 10-134. *Flight instruments directly in front of the pilot, engine instruments to the left and right, and navigation instruments and radios primarily to the right, which is the center of the instrument panel. This arrangement is commonly on light aircraft to be flown by a single pilot.*

Figure 10-135. *Instrument mounts—flanged (top and middle) and flangeless (bottom).*

Instrument Power Requirements

Many aircraft instruments require electric power for operation. Even nonelectric instruments may include electric lighting. Only a limited amount of electricity is produced by the aircraft's electric generator(s). It is imperative that the electric load of the instruments, radios, and other equipment on board the aircraft does not exceed this amount.

Electric devices, including instruments, have power ratings. These show what voltage is required to correctly operate the unit and the amount of amperage it draws when operating to capacity. The rating must be checked before installing any component. Replacement of a component with one that has the same power rating is recommended to ensure the potential electric load of the installed equipment remains within the limits the aircraft manufacturer intended. Adding a component with a different rating or installing a completely new component may require a load check be performed. This is essentially an on the ground operational check to ensure the electrical system can supply all of the electricity consuming devices installed on the aircraft. Follow the manufacturer's instructions on how to perform this check.

Instrument Range Markings

Many instruments contain colored markings on the dial face to indicate, at a glance, whether a particular system or component is within a range of operation that is safe and desirable or if an undesirable condition exists. These markings are put on the instrument by the original equipment manufacturer in accordance with the Aircraft Specifications in the Type Certificate Data Sheet. Data describing these limitations can also sometimes be found in the aircraft manufacturer's operating and maintenance manuals.

Occasionally, the aircraft technician may find it necessary to apply these marking to an approved replacement instrument on which they do not appear. It is crucial that the instrument be marked correctly and only in accordance with approved data. The marking may be placed on the cover glass of the instrument with paint or decals. A white slippage mark is made to extend from the glass to the instrument case. Should the glass rotate in the bezel, the marking will no longer be aligned properly with the calibrated instrument dial. The broken slippage mark indicates this to the pilot or technician.

The colors used as range markings are red, yellow, green, blue, or white. The markings can be in the form of an arc or a radial line. Red is used to indicate maximum and minimum ranges; operations beyond these markings are dangerous and should be avoided. Green indicates the normal operating range. Yellow is used to indicate caution. Blue and white are used on airspeed indicators to define specific conditions. *[Figures 10-136 and 10-137]*

Maintenance of Instruments and Instrument Systems

An FAA airframe and powerplant (A&P) technician is not qualified to do internal maintenance on instruments and related line replaceable units discussed in this chapter. This must be carried out at facilities equipped with the specialized equipment needed to perform the maintenance properly. Qualified technicians with specialized training and intimate knowledge of instruments perform this type of work, usually under repair station certification.

However, licensed airframe technicians and A&P technicians are charged with a wide variety of maintenance functions related to instruments and instrument systems. Installation, removal, inspection, troubleshooting, and functional checks

Instrument	Range marking
Airspeed indicator	
White arc	Flap operating range
bottom	Flaps-down stall speed
Top	Maximum airspeed for flaps-down flight
Green arc	Normal operating range
bottom	Flaps-up stall speed
Top	Maximum airspeed for rough air
Blue radial line	Best single-engine rate-of-climb airspeed
Yellow arc	Structural warning area
bottom	Maximum airspeed for rough air
top	Never-exceed airspeed
Red radial line	Never-exceed airspeed
Carburetor air temperature	
Green arc	Normal operating range
Yellow arc	Range in which carburetor ice is most likely to form
Red radial line	Maximum allowable inlet air temperature
Cylinder head temperature	
Green arc	Normal operating range
Yellow arc	Operation approved for limited time
Red radial line	Never-exceed temperature
Manifold pressure gauge	
Green arc	Normal operating range
Yellow arc	Precautionary range
Red radial line	Maximum permissible manifold absolute pressure
Fuel pressure gauge	
Green arc	Normal operating range
Yellow arc	Precautionary range
Red radial line	Maximum and/or minimum permissible fuel pressure
Oil pressure gauge	
Green arc	Normal operating range
Yellow arc	Precautionary range
Red radial line	Maximum and/or minimum permissible oil pressure

Instrument	Range marking
Oil temperature gauge	
Green arc	Normal operating range
Yellow arc	Precautionary range
Red radial line	Maximum and/or minimum permissible oil temperature
Tachometer (reciprocating engine)	
Green arc	Normal operating range
Yellow arc	Precautionary range
Red arc	Restricted operating range
Red radial line	Maximum permissible rotational speed
Tachometer (turbine engine)	
Green arc	Normal operating range
Yellow arc	Precautionary range
Red radial line	Maximum permissible rotational speed
Tachometer (helicopter)	
Engine tachometer	
Green arc	Normal operating range
Yellow arc	Precautionary range
Red radial line	Maximum permissible rotational speed
Rotor tachometer	
Green arc	Normal operating range
Red radial line	Maximum and minimum rotor speed for power-off operational conditions
Torque indicator	
Green arc	Normal operating range
Yellow arc	Precautionary range
Red radial line	Maximum permissible torque pressure
Exhaust gas temperature indicator (turbine engine)	
Green arc	Normal operating range
Yellow arc	Precautionary range
Red radial line	Maximum permissible gas temperature
Gas producer N1 tachometer (turboshaft helicopter)	
Green arc	Normal operating range
Yellow arc	Precautionary range
Red radial line	Maximum permissible rotational speed

Figure 10-136. *Instrument range markings.*

are all performed in the field by licensed personnel. It is also a responsibility of the licensed technician holding an airframe rating to know what maintenance is required and to access the approved procedures for meeting those requirements.

In the following paragraphs, various maintenance and servicing procedures and suggestions are given. The discussion follows the order in which the various instruments and instrument systems were presented throughout this chapter. This is not meant to represent all of the maintenance required by any of the instruments or instruments systems. The aircraft manufacturer's and instrument manufacturer's approved maintenance documents should always be consulted for required maintenance and servicing instructions. FAA regulations must also be observed.

Altimeter Tests

When an aircraft is to be operated under IFR, an altimeter test must have been performed within the previous 24 months. Title 14 of the Code of Federal Regulations (14 CFR) part 91, section 91.411, requires this test, as well as tests on the pitot static system and on the automatic pressure altitude reporting system. The licensed airframe or A&P mechanic is not qualified to perform the altimeter inspections. They must be conducted by either the manufacturer or a certified repair station. 14 CFR part 43, Appendixes E and F detail the requirements for these tests.

Figure 10-137. *An airspeed indicator makes extensive use of range markings.*

Pitot-Static System Maintenance and Tests

Water trapped in a pitot static system may cause inaccurate or intermittent indications on the pitot-static flight instruments. This is especially a problem if the water freezes in flight. Many systems are fitted with drains at the low points in the system to remove any moisture during maintenance. Lacking this, dry compressed air or nitrogen may be blown through the lines of the system. Always disconnect all pitot-static instruments before doing so and always blow from the instrument end of the system towards the pitot and static ports. This procedure must be followed by a leak check described below. Systems with drains can be drained without requiring a leak check. Upon completion, the technician must ensure that the drains are closed and made secure in accordance with approved maintenance procedures.

Aircraft pitot-static systems must be tested for leaks after the installation of any component parts or when system malfunction is suspected. It must also be tested every 24 months if on an IFR certified aircraft intended to be flown as such as called out in 14 CFR section 91.411. Licensed airframe and A&P technicians may perform this test.

The method of leak testing depends on the type of aircraft, its pitot-static system, and the testing equipment available. *[Figure 10-138]* Essentially, a testing device is connected into the static system at the static vent end, and pressure is reduced in the system by the amount required to indicate 1,000 feet on the altimeter. Then, the system is sealed and observed for 1 minute. A loss of altitude of more than 100 feet is not permissible. If a leak exists, a systematic check of portions of the system is conducted until the leak is isolated. Most leaks occur at fittings. The pitot portion of the pitot-static system is checked in a similar fashion. Follow the manufacturer's instructions when performing all pitot-static system checks.

In all cases, pressure and suction must be applied and released slowly to avoid damage to the aircraft instruments. Pitot-static system leak check units usually have their own built-in altimeters. This allows a functional cross-check of the aircraft's altimeter with the calibrated test unit's altimeter while performing the static system check. However, this does not meet the requirements of 14 CFR section 91.411 for altimeter tests.

Upon completion of the leak test, be sure that the system is returned to the normal flight configuration. If it is necessary to block off various portions of a system, check to be sure that all blanking plugs, adaptors, or pieces of adhesive tape have been removed.

Figure 10-138. *An analog pitot-static system test unit (left) and a digital pitot static test unit (right).*

Tachometer Maintenance

Tachometer indicators should be checked for loose glass, chipped scale markings, or loose pointers. The difference in indications between readings taken before and after lightly tapping the instrument should not exceed approximately 15 rpm. This value may vary, depending on the tolerance established by the indicator manufacturer. Both tachometer generator and indicator should be inspected for tightness of mechanical and electrical connections, security of mounting, and general condition. For detailed maintenance procedures, the manufacturer's instructions should always be consulted.

When an engine equipped with an electrical tachometer is running at idle rpm, the tachometer indicator pointers may fluctuate and read low. This is an indication that the synchronous motor is not synchronized with the generator output. As the engine speed is increased, the motor should synchronize and register the rpm correctly. The rpm at which synchronization occurs varies with the design of the tachometer system. If the instrument pointer(s) oscillate(s) at speeds above the synchronizing value, determine that the total oscillation does not exceed the allowable tolerance.

Pointer oscillation can also occur with a mechanical indication system if the flexible drive is permitted to whip. The drive shaft should be secured at frequent intervals to prevent it from whipping. When installing mechanical type indicators, be sure that the flexible drive has adequate clearance behind the panel. Any bends necessary to route the drive should not cause strain on the instrument when it is secured to the panel. Avoid sharp bends in the drive. An improperly installed drive can cause the indicator to fail to read or to read incorrectly.

Magnetic Compass Maintenance and Compensation

The magnetic compass is a simple instrument that does not require setting or a source of power. A minimum of maintenance is necessary, but the instrument is delicate and should be handled carefully during inspection. The following items are usually included in an inspection:

1. The compass indicator should be checked for correct readings on various cardinal headings and re-compensated if necessary.
2. Moving parts of the compass should work easily.
3. The compass bowl should be correctly suspended on an antivibration device and should not touch any part of the metal container.
4. The compass bowl should be filled with liquid. The liquid should not contain any bubbles or have any discoloration.
5. The scale should be readable and be well lit.

Compass magnetic deviation is caused by electromagnetic interference from ferrous materials and operating electrical components in the cockpit. Deviation can be reduced by swinging the compass and adjusting its compensating magnets. An example of how to perform this calibration process is given below. The results are recorded on a compass correction card which is placed near the compass in the cockpit. *[Figure 10-139]*

Figure 10-139. *A magnetic compass with a deviation correction card attached, on which the results of swinging the compass should be recorded.*

There are various ways to swing a compass. The following is meant as a representative method. Follow the aircraft manufacturer's instructions for method and frequency of swinging the magnetic compass. This is usually accomplished at flight hour or calendar intervals. Compass calibration is also performed when a new electric component is added to the cockpit, such as a new radio. A complete list of conditions requiring a compass swing and procedure can be found in FAA Advisory Circular (AC) 43.13-1 (as revised), Chapter 12-37.

To swing a compass, a compass rose is required. Most airports have one painted on the tarmac in a low-traffic area where maintenance personnel can work. One can also be made with chalk and a good compass. The area where the compass rose is laid out should be far from any possible electromagnetic disturbances, including those underground, and should remain clear of any ferrous vehicles or large equipment while the procedure takes place. *[Figure 10-140]*

Figure 10-140. *The compass rose on this airport ramp can be used to swing an aircraft magnetic compass.*

The aircraft should be in level flight attitude for the compass swing procedure. Tail draggers need to have the aft end of the fuselage propped up, preferably with wood, aluminum, or some other nonferrous material. The aircraft interior and baggage compartments should be free from miscellaneous items that might interfere with the compass. All normal equipment should be on board and turned on to simulate a flight condition. The engine(s) should be running.

The basic idea when swinging a compass is to note the deviation along the north-south radial and the east-west radial. Then, adjust the compensating magnets of the compass to eliminate as much deviation as possible. Begin by centering or zeroing the compass' compensating magnets with a non-ferrous screw driver. Align the longitudinal axis of the aircraft on the N-S radial facing north. Adjust the N-S compensating screw so the indication is 0°. Next, align the longitudinal axis of the aircraft on the E-W radial facing east. Adjust the E-W compensating screw so that the compass indicates 90°. Now, move the aircraft to be aligned with the N-S radial facing south. If the compass indicates 180°, there is no deviation while the aircraft is heading due north or due south. However, this is unlikely. Whatever the south-facing indication is, adjust the N-S compensating screw to eliminate half of the deviation from 180°. Continue around to face the aircraft west on the E-W radial, and use the E-W compensating screw to eliminate half of the west-facing deviation from 270°.

Once this is done, return the aircraft to alignment with the N-S radial facing north and record the indication. Up to 10° deviation is allowed. Align the aircraft with the radials every 30° around the compass rose and record each indication on the compass compensation card. Date and sign the card and place it in full view of the pilot near the compass in the cockpit.

Vacuum System Maintenance

Errors in the indication presented on a vacuum gyroscopic instrument could be the result of any factor that prevents the vacuum system from operating within the design suction limits. Errors can also be caused by problems within the instrument, such as friction, worn parts, or broken parts. Any source that disturbs the free rotation of the gyro at design speed is undesirable resulting in excessive precession and failure of the instruments to maintain accurate indication.

The aircraft technician is responsible for the prevention or correction of vacuum system malfunctions. Usually this consists of cleaning or replacing filters, checking and correcting insufficient vacuum, or removing and replacing the vacuum pump or instruments. A list of the most common malfunctions, together with their correction, is included in *Figure 10-141*.

Autopilot System Maintenance

The information in this section does not apply to any particular autopilot system, but gives general information that relates to all autopilot systems. Maintenance of an autopilot system consists of visual inspection, replacement of components, cleaning, lubrication, and an operational checkout of the system. Consult the manufacturer's maintenance manual for all of these procedures.

With the autopilot disengaged, the flight controls should function smoothly. The resistance offered by the autopilot servos should not affect the control of the aircraft. The interconnecting mechanisms between the autopilot system and the flight control system should be correctly aligned and smooth in operation. When applicable, the operating cables should be checked for tension.

An operational check is important to assure that every circuit is functioning properly. An autopilot operational check should be performed on new installations, after replacement of an autopilot component, or whenever a malfunction in the autopilot is suspected.

After the aircraft's main power switch has been turned on, allow the gyros to come up to speed and the amplifier to warm up before engaging the autopilot. Some systems are designed with safeguards that prevent premature autopilot engagement. While holding the control column in the normal flight position, engage the autopilot system using the switch on the autopilot controller.

Problem and Potential Causes	Isolation Procedure	Correction
1. No vacuum pressure or insufficient pressure		
Defective vacuum gauge	Check opposite engine system on the gauge	Replace faulty vacuum gauge
Vacuum relief valve incorrectly adjusted	Change valve adjustment	Make final adjustment to correct setting
Vacuum relief valve installed backward	Visually inspect	Install lines properly
Broken lines	Visually inspect	Replace line
Lines crossed	Visually inspect	Install lines properly
Obstruction in vacuum line	Check for collapsed line	Clean & test line; replace defective part(s)
Vacuum pump failure	Remove and inspect	Replace faulty pump
Vacuum regulator valve incorrectly adjusted	Make valve adjustment and note pressure	Adjust to proper pressure
Vacuum relief valve dirty	Clean and adjust relief valve	Replace valve if adjustment fails
2. Excessive vacuum		
Relief valve improperly adjusted		Adjust relief valve to proper setting
Inaccurate vacuum gauge	Check calibration of gauge	Replace faulty gauge
3. Gyro horizon bar fails to respond		
Instrument caged	Visually inspect	Uncage instrument
Instrument filter dirty	Check filter	Replace or clean as necessary
Insufficient vacuum	Check vacuum setting	Adjust relief valve to proper setting
Instrument assembly worn or dirty		Replace instrument
4. Turn-and-bank indicator fails to respond		
No vacuum supplied to instrument	Check lines and vacuum system	Clean and replace lines and components
Instrument filter clogged	Visually inspect	Replace filter
Defective instrument	Test with properly functioning instrument	Replace faulty instrument
5. Turn-and-bank pointer vibrates		
Defective instrument	Test with properly functioning instrument	Replace defective instrument

Figure 10-141. *Vacuum system troubleshooting guide.*

After the system is engaged, perform the operational checks specified for the particular aircraft. In general, the checks are as follows:

1. Rotate the turn knob to the left; the left rudder pedal should move forward, and the control column wheel should move to the left and slightly aft.

2. Rotate the turn knob to the right; the right rudder pedal should move forward, and the control column wheel should move to the right and slightly aft. Return the turn knob to the center position; the flight controls should return to the level-flight position.

3. Rotate the pitch-trim knob forward; the control column should move forward.

4. Rotate the pitch-trim knob aft; the control column should move aft.

If the aircraft has a pitch-trim system installed, it should function to add down-trim as the control column moves forward and add up-trim as the column moves aft. Many pitch-trim systems have an automatic and a manual mode of operation. The above action occurs only in the automatic mode.

Check to see if it is possible to manually override or overpower the autopilot system in all control positions. Center all the controls when the operational checks have been completed.

Disengage the autopilot system and check for freedom of the control surfaces by moving the control columns and rudder pedals. Then, reengage the system and check the emergency disconnect release circuit. The autopilot should disengage each time the release button on the control yoke is actuated.

When performing maintenance and operational checks on a specific autopilot system, always follow the procedure recommended by the aircraft or equipment manufacturer.

LCD Display Screens

Electronic and digital instrument systems utilizing LCD technology may have special considerations for the care of the display screens. Antireflective coatings are sometimes used to reduce glare and make the displays more visible. These treatments can be degraded by human skin oils and certain cleaning agents, such as those containing ammonia. It is very important to clean the display lens using a clean, lint-free cloth and a cleaner that is specified as safe for antireflective coatings, preferable one recommended by the aircraft manufacturer.

Chapter 11
Communication and Navigation

Introduction

With the mechanics of flight secured, early aviators began the tasks of improving operational safety and functionality of flight. These were developed in large part through the use of reliable communication and navigation systems. Today, with thousands of aircraft aloft at any one time, communication and navigation systems are essential to safe, successful flight. Continuing development is occurring. Smaller, lighter, and more powerful communication and navigation devices increase situational awareness on the flight deck. Coupled with improved displays and management control systems, the advancement of aviation electronics is relied upon to increase aviation safety.

Clear radio voice communication was one of the first developments in the use of electronics in aviation. Navigational radios soon followed. Today, numerous electronic navigation and landing aids exist. Electronic devices also exist to assist with weather, collision avoidance, automatic flight control, flight recording, flight management, public address, and entertainment systems.

Avionics in Aviation Maintenance

Avionics is a conjunction of the words aviation and electronics. It is used to describe the electronic equipment found in modern aircraft. The term "avionics" was not used until the 1970s. For many years, aircraft had electrical devices, but true solid-state electronic devices were only introduced in large numbers in the 1960s.

Airframe and engine maintenance is required on all aircraft and is not likely to ever go away. Aircraft instrument maintenance and repair also has an inevitable part in aviation maintenance. The increased use of avionics in aircraft over the past 50 years has increased the role of avionics maintenance in aviation. However, modern, solid-state, digital avionics are highly reliable. Mean times between failures are high, and maintenance rates of avionics systems compared to mechanical systems are likely to be lower.

The first decade of avionics proliferation saw a greater increase in the percent of cost of avionics compared to the overall cost of an aircraft. In some military aircraft with highly refined navigation, weapons targeting, and monitoring systems, it hit a high estimate of 80 percent of the total cost of the aircraft. Currently, the ratio of the cost of avionics to the cost of the total aircraft is beginning to decline. This is due to advances in digital electronics and numerous manufacturers offering highly refined instrumentation, communication, and navigation systems that can be fitted to nearly any aircraft. New aircraft of all sizes are manufactured with digital glass cockpits, and many owners of older aircraft are retrofitting digital avionics to replace analog instrumentation and radio navigation equipment.

The airframe and powerplant (A&P) maintenance technician needs to be familiar with the general workings of various avionics. Maintenance of the actual avionics devices is often reserved for the avionics manufacturers or certified repair stations. However, the installation and proper operation of these devices and systems remains the responsibility of the field technician. This chapter discusses some internal components used in avionics devices. It also discusses a wide range of common communication and navigational aids found on aircraft. The breadth of avionics is so wide that discussion of all avionics devices is not possible.

History of Avionics

The history of avionics is the history of the use of electronics in aviation. Both military and civil aviation requirements contributed to the development. The First World War brought about an urgent need for communications. Voice communications from ground-to-air and from aircraft to aircraft were established. *[Figure 11-1]* The development of aircraft reliability and use for civilian purposes in the 1920s

Figure 11-1. *Early voice communication radio tests in 1917. Courtesy of AT&T Archives and History Center.*

led to increased instrumentation and set in motion the need to conquer blind flight—flight without the ground being visible. Radio beacon direction finding was developed for en route navigation. Toward the end of the decade, instrument navigation combined with rudimentary radio use to produce the first safe blind landing of an aircraft.

In the 1930s, the first all radio-controlled blind-landing was accomplished. At the same time, radio navigation using ground-based beacons expanded. Instrument navigation certification for airline pilots began. Low and medium frequency radio waves were found to be problematic at night and in weather. By the end of the decade, use of high-frequency radio waves was explored and included the advent of high-frequency radar.

In the 1940s, after two decades of development driven by mail carrier and passenger airline requirements, World War II injected urgency into the development of aircraft radio communication and navigation. Communication radios, despite their size, were essential on board aircraft. *[Figure 11-2]* Very high frequencies were developed for communication and navigational purposes. Installation of the first instrument landing systems for blind landings began mid-decade and, by the end of the decade, the very high frequency omni-directional range (VOR) navigational network was instituted. It was also in the 1940s that the first transistor was developed, paving the way for modern, solid-state electronics.

Civilian air transportation increased over the ensuing decades. Communication and navigation equipment was refined. Solid-state radio development, especially in the

It uses the latest technologies to provide a more efficient and effective system of air traffic management. Heavily reliant on global satellite positioning of aircraft in flight and on the ground, NextGen combines GPS technology with automatic dependant surveillance broadcast technology (ADS-B) for traffic separation. A large increase in air system capacity is the planned result. Overhauled ground facilities accompany the technology upgrades mandated for aircraft. NextGen implementation has started and is currently scheduled through the year 2025.

For the past few decades, avionics development has increased at a faster pace than that of airframe and powerplant development. This is likely to continue in the near future. Improvements to solid-state electronics in the form of micro- and nano-technologies continue to this day. Trends are toward lighter, smaller devices with remarkable capability and reliability. Integration of the wide range of communication and navigational aids is a focus.

Fundamentals of Electronics
Analog Versus Digital Electronics
Electronic devices represent and manipulate real world phenomenon through the use of electrical signals. Electronic circuits are designed to perform a wide array of manipulations. Analog representations are continuous. Some aspect of an electric signal is modified proportionally to the real world item that is being represented. For example, a microphone has electricity flowing through it that is altered when sound is applied. The type and strength of the modification to the electric signal is characteristic of the sound that is made into the microphone. The result is that sound, a real world phenomenon, is represented electronically. It can then be moved, amplified, and reconverted from an electrical signal back into sound and broadcast from a speaker across the room or across the globe.

Figure 11-2. *Bomber onboard radio station.*

1960s, produced a wide range of small, rugged radio and navigational equipment for aircraft. The space program began and added a higher level of communication and navigational necessity. Communication satellites were also launched. The Cold War military build-up caused developments in guidance and navigation and gave birth to the concept of using satellites for positioning.

In the 1970s, concept-validation of satellite navigation was introduced for the military and Block I global positioning system (GPS) satellites were launched well into the 1980s. Back on earth, the long range navigation system (LORAN) was constructed. Block II GPS satellites were commissioned in the mid-80s and GPS became operational in 1990 with the full 24-satellite system operational in 1994.

In the new millennium, the Federal Aviation Administration (FAA) assessed the national airspace system (NAS) and traffic projections for the future. Gridlock is predicted by 2022. Therefore, a complete overhaul of the NAS, including communication and navigational systems, has been developed and undertaken. The program is called NextGen.

Since the flow of electricity through the microphone is continuous, the sound continuously modifies the electric signal. On an oscilloscope, an analog signal is a continuous curve. *[Figure 11-3]* An analog electric signal can be modified by changing the signal's amplitude, frequency, or phase.

A digital electronic representation of a real world event is discontinuous. The essential characteristics of the continuous event are captured as a series of discrete incremental values. Electronically, these representative samplings are successive chains of voltage and non-voltage signals. They can be transported and manipulated in electronic circuits. When the samples are sufficiently small and occur with high frequency, real world phenomenon can be represented to appear continuous.

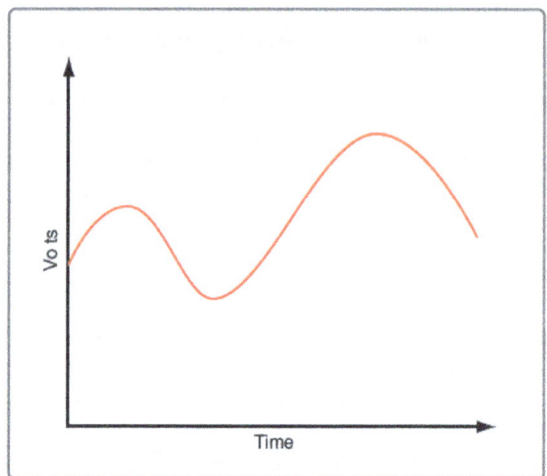

Figure 11-3. *An analog signal displayed on an oscilloscope is a continuous curve.*

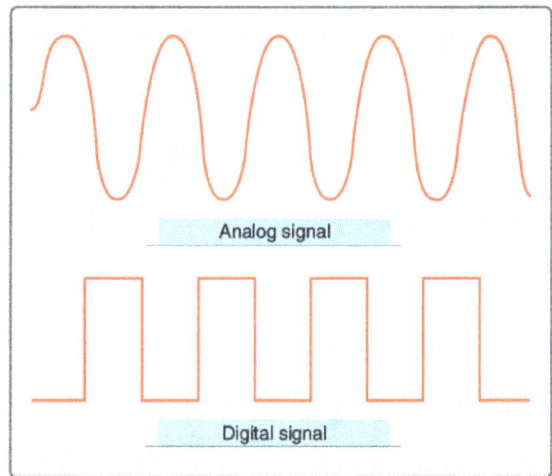

Figure 11-4. *Analog signals are continuous voltage modified by all external events including those that are not desired called noise. Digital signals are a series of voltage or no voltage that represent a desired event.*

Noise

A significant advantage of digital electronics over analog electronics is the control of noise. Noise is any alteration of the represented real world phenomenon that is not intended or desired. Consider the operation of a microphone when understanding noise. A continuous analog voltage is modified by a voice signal that results in the continuous voltage varying in proportion to the volume and tone of the input sound. However, the voltage responds and modifies to any input. Thus, background sounds also modify the continuous voltage as will electrostatic activity and circuitry imperfections. This alteration by phenomenon that are not the intended modifier is noise.

During the processing of digitized data, there is little or no signal degradation. The real world phenomenon is represented in a string of binary code. A series of ones and zeros are electronically created as a sequence of voltage or no voltage and carried through processing stages. It is relatively immune to outside alteration once established. If a signal is close to the set value of the voltage, it is considered to be that voltage. If the signal is close to zero, it is considered to be no voltage. Small variations or modifications from undesired phenomenon are ignored. *Figure 11-4* illustrates an analog sine wave and a digital sine wave. Any unwanted voltage will modify the analog curve. The digital steps are not modified by small foreign inputs. There is either voltage or no voltage.

Analog Electronics

Early aircraft were equipped with radio communication and navigational devices that were constructed with analog electronic circuits. They used vacuum tubes that functioned as electron control valves. These were later replaced by solid-state devices. Today, digital electronic circuits dominate modern avionics. A brief look at various electron control valves used on aircraft follows.

Electron Control Valves

Electron control valves are an essential part of an electronic circuit. Control of electron flow enables the circuit to produce the desired outcome. Early aircraft made use of vacuum tubes to control electron flow. Later, transistors replaced vacuum tubes. Semiconductors used in transistors and integrated circuits have enabled the solid-state digital electronics found in aircraft today.

Vacuum Tubes

Electron control valves found in the analog circuits of early aircraft electronics are constructed of vacuum tubes. Only antique aircraft retain radios with these devices due to their size and inability to withstand the harsh vibration and shock of the aircraft operating environment. However, they do function, and a description is included here as a foundation for the study of more modern electronic circuits and components.

Diodes

A diode acts as a check valve in an alternating current (AC) circuit. It allows current to flow during half of the AC cycle but not the other half. In this manner, it creates a pulsating direct current (DC) with current that drops to zero in between pulses. A diode tube has two active electrodes: the cathode and the plate. It also contains a heater. All of this is housed in a vacuum environment inside the tube. *[Figure 11-5]* The

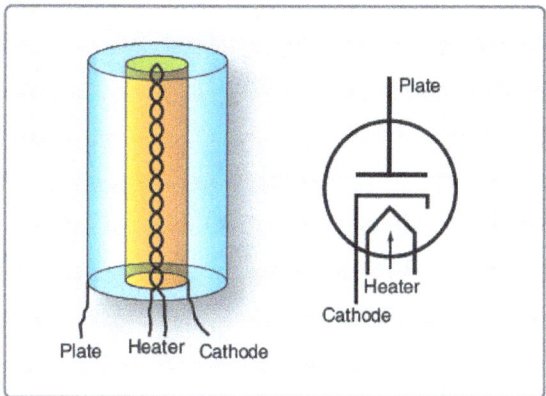

Figure 11-5. *A vacuum tube diode contains a cathode, heater, and plate. Note that the arrow formed in the symbol for the heater points to the direction of electron flow.*

heater glows red hot while heating the cathode. The cathode is coated with a material whose electrons are excited by the heat. The excited electrons expand their orbit when heated. They move close enough to the plate, which is constructed around the cathode and heater arrangement, that they are attracted to the positively-charged plate. When the AC current cycles, the plate becomes negatively charged and the excited cathode electrons do not flow to the plate. In a circuit, this causes a check valve effect that allows current to only flow in one direction, which is the definition of a diode. *[Figure 11-6]* The various symbols used to depict diodes are shown in *Figure 11-7*.

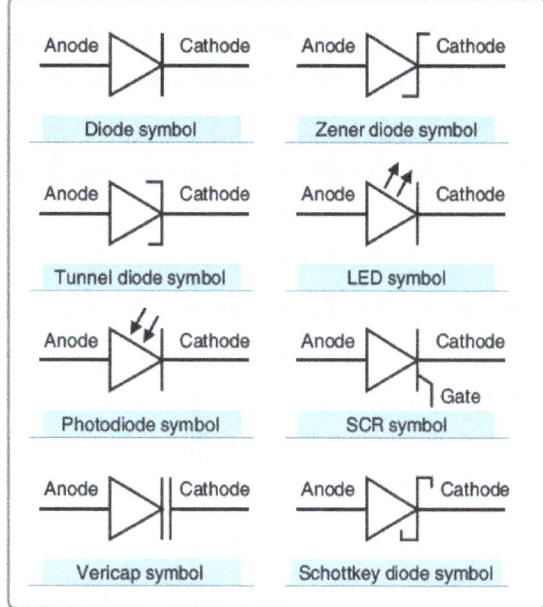

Figure 11-7. *Diode symbols.*

cathode and the plate but closer to the cathode. Applying voltage to the grid can influence the cathode's electrons, which normally flow to the plate when the cathode is heated. Changes in the relatively small amount of current that flows through the grid can greatly impact the flow of electrons from the cathode to the plate. *[Figure 11-8]*

Figure 11-6. *A vacuum tube diode in a circuit allows current to flow in one direction only. The output waveform illustrates the lack of current flow as the AC cycles.*

Triodes

A triode is an electron control valve containing three elements. It is often used to control a large amount of current with a smaller current flow. In addition to the cathode, plate, and heater present in the diode, a triode also contains a grid. The grid is composed of fine wire spiraled between the

Figure 11-8. *A triode has three elements: the cathode, plate, and a grid.*

Figure 11-9 illustrates a triode in a simple circuit. AC voltage input is applied to the grid. A high-resistance resistor is used so that only minimum voltage passes through to the grid. As this small AC input voltage varies, the amount of DC output in the cathode-plate circuit also varies. When the input signal is positive, the grid is positive. This aids in drawing electrons from the cathode to the plate. However, when the AC input signal cycles to negative, the grid becomes negatively

Figure 11-9. *Varying AC input voltage to the grid circuit in a triode produces a varying DC output.*

Figure 11-11. *To enable a triode to be used at high frequencies, a screen grid is constructed between the plate and the control grid.*

charged and flow from the cathode to the plate is cut off with the help of the negatively charged grid that repels the electrons on the cathode.

Tetrodes

A tetrode vacuum tube electron control valve has four elements. In addition to the cathode, plate, and grid found in a tridode, a tetrode also contains a screen grid. The cathode and plate of a vacuum tube electron control valve can act as a capacitor. At high frequencies, the capacitance is so low that feedback occurs. The output in the plate circuit feeds back into the control grid circuit. This causes an oscillation generating AC voltage that is unwanted. By placing a screen grid between the anode and the control grid windings, this feedback and the inter-electrode capacitive effect of the anode and cathode are neutralized. *[Figure 11-10]*

Pentodes

The plate in a vacuum tube can have a secondary emission that must be controlled. When electrons flow from the cathode through the control grid and screen grid to the plate, they can arrive at such high velocity that some bounce off. Therefore, the tendency is for those electrons to be attracted to the positively charged screen grid. The screen grid is not capable of handling large amounts of current without burning up. To solve this problem, a third grid is constructed between the plate and the screen grid. Called a suppression grid, it is charged negatively so that secondary electron flow from the plate is repelled by the negative charge back toward the plate and is not allowed to reach the screen grid. The five element pentode is especially useful in high power circuits where secondary emissions from the plate are high. *[Figure 11-12]*

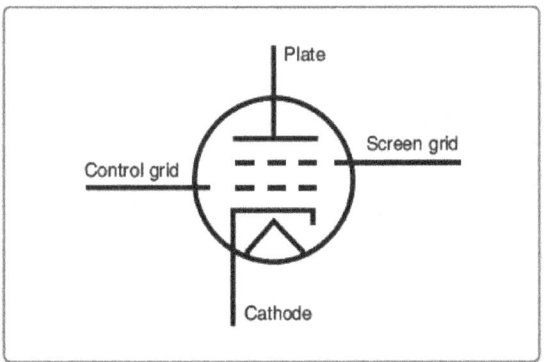

Figure 11-10. *A tetrode is a four element electron control valve vacuum tube including a cathode, a plate, a control grid, and a screen grid.*

Figure 11-11 illustrates a tetrode in a circuit. The screen grid is powered by positive DC voltage. The inter-electrode capacitance is now between the screen grid and the plate. A capacitor is located between the screen grid and ground. AC feedback generated in the screen grid goes to ground and does not oscillate. This allows use of the tetrode at higher frequencies than a triode.

Figure 11-12. *A pentode contains a suppression grid that controls secondary electron emissions from the plate at high power. This keeps the current in the screen grid from becoming too high.*

Solid-State Devices

Solid-state devices began replacing vacuum tube electron control valves in the late 1950s. Their long life, reliability, and resilience in harsh environments make them ideal for use in avionics.

Semiconductors

The key to solid-state electronic devices is the electrical behavior of semiconductors. To understand semiconductors, a review of what makes a material an insulator or a conductor follows. Then, an explanation for how materials of limited conductivity are constructed and some of their many uses is explained. Semiconductor devices are the building blocks of modern electronics and avionics.

An atom of any material has a characteristic number of electrons orbiting the nucleus of the atom. The arrangement of the electrons occurs in somewhat orderly orbits called rings or shells. The closest shell to the nucleus can only contain two electrons. If the atom has more than two electrons, they are found in the next orbital shell away from the nucleus. This second shell can only hold eight electrons. If the atom has more than eight electrons, they orbit in a third shell farther out from the nucleus. This third shell is filled with eight electrons and then a fourth shell starts to fill if the element still has more electrons. However, when the fourth shell contains eight electrons, the number of electrons in the third shell begins to increase again until a maximum of 18 is reached. *[Figure 11-13]*

Shell or Orbit Number	1	2	3	4	5
Maximum number of electrons	2	8	18	32	50

Figure 11-13. *Maximum number of electrons in each orbital shell of an atom.*

The outer most orbital shell of any atom's electrons is called the valence shell. The number of electrons in the valence shell determines the chemical properties of the material. When the valence shell has the maximum number of electrons, it is complete and the electrons tend to be bound strongly to the nucleus. Materials with this characteristic are chemically stable. It takes a large amount of force to move the electrons in this situation from one atom valence shell to that of another. Since the movement of electrons is called electric current, substances with complete valence shells are known as good insulators because they resist the flow of electrons (electricity). *[Figure 11-14]*

In atoms with an incomplete valence shell, that is, those without the maximum number of electrons in their valence shell, the electrons are bound less strongly to the nucleus. The material is chemically disposed to combine with other materials or other identical atoms to fill in the unstable valence configuration and bring the number of electrons in the valence shell to maximum. Two or more substances may share the electrons in their valence shells and form a covalent bond. A covalent bond is the method by which atoms

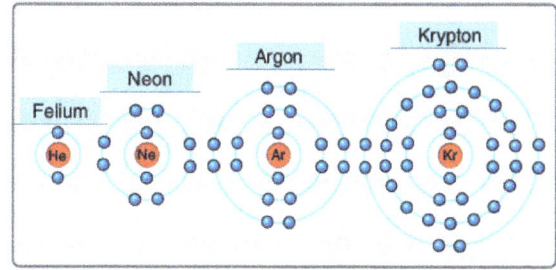

Figure 11-14. *Elements with full valence shells are good insulators. Most insulators used in aviation are compounds of two or more elements that share electrons to fill their valence shells.*

complete their valence shells by sharing valence electrons with other atoms.

Electrons in incomplete valence shells may also move freely from valence shell to valence shell of different atoms or compounds. In this case, these are known as free electrons. As stated, the movement of electrons is known as electric current or current flow. When electrons move freely from atom to atom or compound to compound, the substance is known as a conductor. *[Figure 11-15]*

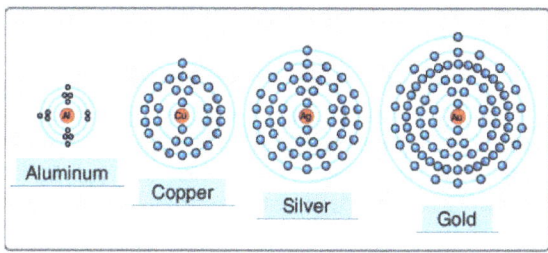

Figure 11-15. *The valence shells of elements that are common conductors have one (or three) electrons.*

Not all materials are pure elements, that is, substances made up of one kind of atom. Compounds occur when two or more different types of atoms combine. They create a new substance with different characteristics than any of the component elements. When compounds form, valence shells and their maximum number of electrons remain the rule of physics. The new compound molecule may either share electrons to fill the valence shell or free electrons may exist to make it a good conductor.

Silicon is an atomic element that contains four electrons in its valence shell. It tends to combine readily with itself and form a lattice of silicon atoms in which adjacent atoms share electrons to fill out the valance shell of each to the maximum of eight electrons. *[Figure 11-16]* This unique symmetric alignment of silicon atoms results in a crystalline structure.

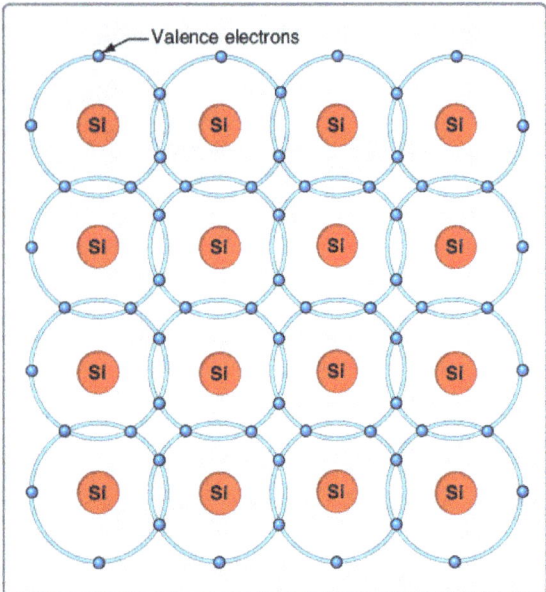

Since silicon is an insulator, it must be modified to become a semiconductor. The process often used is called doping. Starting with ultra-pure silicon crystal, arsenic, phosphorus, or some other element with five valence electrons in each atom is mixed into the silicon. The result is a silicon lattice with flaws. *[Figure 11-17]* The elements bond, but numerous free electrons are present in the material from the 5th electron that is part of the valence shell of the doping element atoms. These free electrons can now flow under certain conditions. Thus, the silicon becomes semiconductive. The conditions required for electron flow in a semiconductor are discussed in the following paragraphs.

When silicon is doped with an element or compound containing five electrons in its valence shell, the result is a negatively charged material due to the excess free electrons, and the fact that electrons are negatively charged. This is known as an N-type semiconductor material. It is also known as a donor material because, when it is used in electronics, it donates the extra electrons to current flow.

Figure 11-16. *The silicon atoms with just the valence shell electrons share these valence electrons with each other. By sharing with four other silicon atoms, the number of electrons in each silicon atom valence shell becomes eight, which is the maximum number. This makes the substance stable and it resists any flow of electrons.*

Once bound together, the valence shells of each silicon atom are complete. In this state, movement of electrons does not occur easily. There are no free electrons to move to another atom and no space in the valence shells to accept a free electron. Therefore, silicon in this form is a good insulator.

Silicon is a primary material used in the manufacture of semiconductors. Germanium and a few other materials are also used.

Doping silicon can also be performed with an element that has only three valence electrons, such as boron, gallium, or indium. Valence electron sharing still occurs, and the silicon atoms with interspersed doping element atoms form a lattice molecular structure. However, in this case, there are many valence shells where there are only seven electrons and not eight. This greatly changes the properties of the material. The absence of the electrons, called holes, encourages electron flow due to the preference to have eight electrons in all valence shells. Therefore, this type of doped silicon is also semiconductive. It is known as P-type material or as an acceptor since it accepts electrons in the holes under certain conditions. *[Figure 11-18]*

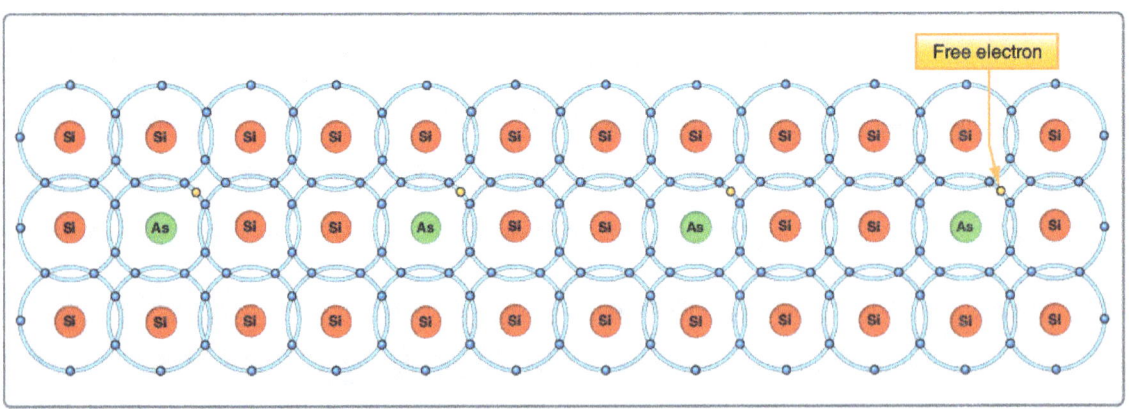

Figure 11-17. *Silicon atoms doped with arsenic form a lattice work of covalent bonds. Free electrons exist in the material from the arsenic atom's 5th valence electron. These are the electrons that flow when the semiconductor material, known as N-type or donor material, is conducting.*

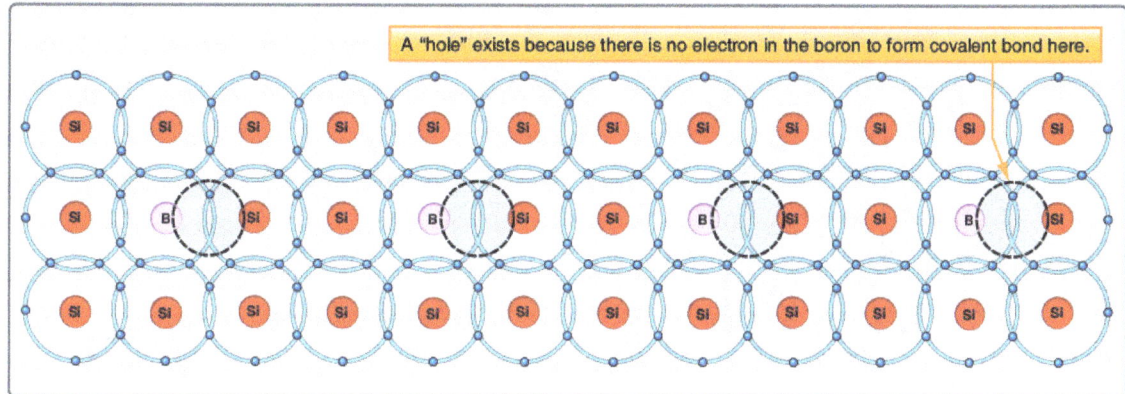

Figure 11-18. *The lattice of boron doped silicon contains holes where the three boron valence shell electrons fail to fill in the combined valence shells to the maximum of eight electrons. This is known as P-type semiconductor material or acceptor material.*

Combining N- and P-type semiconductor material in certain ways can produce very useful results. A look at various semiconductor devices follows.

Semiconductor Diodes

A diode is an electrical device that allows current to flow in one direction through the device but not the other. A simple device that can be made from N- and P-type semiconductors is a semiconductor diode. When joined, the junction of these two materials exhibits unique properties. Since there are holes in the P-type material, free electrons from the N-type material are attracted to fill these holes. Once combined, the area at the junction of the two materials where this happens is said to be depleted. There are no longer free electrons or holes. However, having given up some electrons, the N-type material next to the junction becomes slightly positively charged, and having received electrons, the P-type material next to the junction becomes slightly negatively charged.

The depletion area at the junction of the two semiconductor materials constitutes a barrier or potential hill. The intensity of the potential hill is proportional to the width of the depletion area (where the electrons from the N-type material have filled holes in the P-type material). *[Figure 11-19]*

The two semiconductors joined in this manner form a diode that can be used in an electrical circuit. A voltage source is attached to the diode. When the negative terminal of the battery is attached to the N-type semiconductor material and the positive terminal is attached to the P-type material, electricity can flow in the circuit. The negative potential of the battery forces free electrons in the N-type material toward the junction. The positive potential of the battery forces holes in the P-type material toward the other side of the junction. The holes move by the rebinding of the doping agent ions closer to the junction. At the junction, free electrons continuously

Figure 11-19. *A potential hill.*

arrive and fill the holes in the lattice. As this occurs, more room is available for electrons and holes to move into the area. Pushed by the potential of the battery, electrons and holes continue to combine. The depletion area becomes extremely narrow under these conditions. The potential hill or barrier is, therefore, very small. The flow of current in the electrical circuit is in the direction of electron movement shown in *Figure 11-20*.

In similar circuits where the negative battery terminal is attached to the N-type semiconductor material and the positive terminal is attached to the P-type material, current flows from N-type, or donor material, to P-type receptor material. This is known as a forward biased semiconductor. A voltage of approximately 0.7 volts is needed to begin the current flow over the potential hill. Thereafter, current flow is linear with the voltage. However, temperature affects the ease at which electrons and holes combine given a specific voltage.

Figure 11-20. *The flow of current and the P-N junction of a semiconductor diode attached to a battery in a circuit.*

If the battery terminals are reversed, the semiconductor diode circuit is said to be reversed biased. *[Figure 11-21]* Attaching the negative terminal of the battery to the P-type material attracts the holes in the P-type material away from the junction in the diode. The positive battery terminal attached to the N-type material attracts the free electrons from the junction in the opposite direction. In this way, the width of the area of depletion at the junction of the two materials increases. The potential hill is greater. Current cannot climb the hill; therefore, no current flows in the circuit. The semiconductors do not conduct.

Figure 11-21. *A reversed biased condition.*

Semiconductor diodes are used often in electronic circuits. When AC current is applied to a semiconductor diode, current flows during one cycle of the AC but not during the other cycle. The diode, therefore, becomes a rectifier. When it is forward biased, electrons flow; when the AC cycles, electrons do not flow. A simple AC rectifier circuit containing a semiconductor diode and a load resistor is illustrated in *Figure 11-22*. Semiconductor diode symbols and examples of semiconductor diodes are shown in *Figure 11-23*.

Figure 11-22. *A semiconductor diode acts as a check valve in an AC circuit resulting in a pulsating DC output.*

Figure 11-23. *Symbols and drawings of semiconductor diodes.*

NOTE: Electron flow is typically discussed in this text. The conventional current flow concept where electricity is thought to flow from the positive terminal of the battery through a circuit to the negative terminal is sometimes used in the field.

Semiconductor diodes have limitations. They are rated for a range of current flow. Above a certain level, the diode overheats and burns up. The amount of current that passes through the diode when forward biased is directly proportional to the amount of voltage applied. But, as mentioned, it is affected by temperature.

Figure 11-24 indicates the actual behavior of a semiconductor diode. In practice, a small amount of current does flow

Figure 11-24. *A semiconductor diode.*

through a semiconductor diode when reversed biased. This is known as leakage current and it is in the micro amperage range. However, at a certain voltage, the blockage of current flow in a reversed biased diode breaks down completely. This voltage is known as the avalanche voltage because the diode can no longer hold back the current and the diode fails.

Zener Diodes

Diodes can be designed with a zener voltage. This is similar to avalanche flow. When reversed biased, only leakage current flows through the diode. However, as the voltage is increased, the zener voltage is reached. The diode lets current flow freely through the diode in the direction in which it is normally blocked. The diode is constructed to be able to handle the zener voltage and the resulting current, whereas avalanche voltage burns out a diode. A zener diode can be used as means of dropping voltage or voltage regulation. It can be used to step down circuit voltage for a particular application but only when certain input conditions exist. Zener diodes are constructed to handle a wide range of voltages. *[Figure 11-25]*

Transistors

While diodes are very useful in electronic circuits, semiconductors can be used to construct true control valves known as transistors. A transistor is little more than a sandwich of N-type semiconductor material between two pieces of P-type semiconductor material or vice versa. However, a transistor exhibits some remarkable properties and is the building block of all things electronic. *[Figure 11-26]* As with any union of dissimilar types of semiconductor materials, the junctions of the P- and N- materials in a transistor have depletion areas that create potential hills for the flow of electrical charges.

Figure 11-25. *A zener diode, when reversed biased, will break down and allow a prescribed voltage to flow in the direction normally blocked by the diode.*

Like a vacuum tube triode, the transistor has three electrodes or terminals, one each for the three layers of semiconductor material. The emitter and the collector are on the outside of the sandwiched semiconductor material. The center material is known as the base. A change in a relatively small amount of voltage applied to the base of the transistor allows a relatively large amount of current to flow from the collector to the emitter. In this way, the transistor acts as a switch with a small input voltage controlling a large amount of current.

If a transistor is put into a simple battery circuit, such as the one shown in *Figure 11-27*, voltage from the battery (EB) forces free electrons and holes toward the junction between the base and the emitter just as it does in the junction of a semiconductor diode. The emitter-base depletion area becomes narrow as free electrons combine with the holes at the junction. Current (IB) (solid arrows) flows through the junction in the emitter-base battery circuit. At the same time, an emitter-collector circuit is constructed with a battery (EC) of much higher voltage in its circuit. Because of the narrow depletion area at the emitter-base junction, current IC is able to cross the collector base junction, flow through emitter-base junction, and complete the collector-emitter battery circuit (hollow arrows).

To some extent, varying the voltage to the base material can increase or decrease the current flow through the transistor as the emitter-base depletion area changes width in response to the base voltage. If base voltage is removed, the emitter-

Figure 11-26. *Typical transistors, diagrams of a PNP and NPN transistor, and the symbol for those transistors when depicted in an electronic circuit diagram.*

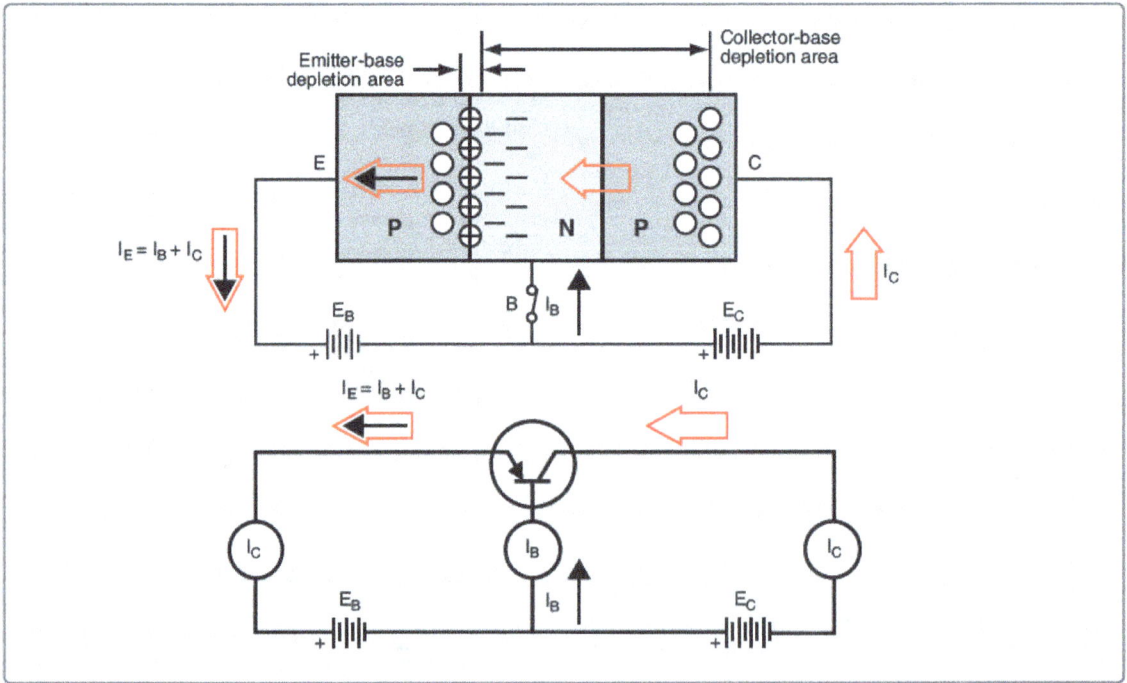

Figure 11-27. *The effect of applying a small voltage to bias the emitter-base junction of a transistor (top). A circuit diagram for this same transistor (bottom).*

11-12

base depletion area becomes too wide and all current flow through the transistor ceases.

Current in the transistor circuit illustrated has a relationship as follows: IE = IB + IC. It should be remembered that it is the voltage applied to the base that turns the collector-emitter transistor current on or off.

Controlling a large amount of current flow with a small independent input voltage is very useful when building electronic circuits. Transistors are the building blocks from which all electronic devices are made, including Boolean gates that are used to create micro processor chips. As production techniques have developed, the size of reliable transistors has shrunk. Now, hundreds of millions and even billions of transistors may be used to construct a single chip such as the one that powers your computer and various avionic devices.

Silicon Controlled Rectifiers

Combination of semiconductor materials is not limited to a two-type, three-layer sandwich transistor. By creating a four-layer sandwich of alternating types of semiconductor material (i.e., **PNPN** or **NPNP**), a slightly different semiconductor diode is created. As is the case in a two-layer diode, circuit current is either blocked or permitted to flow through the diode in a single direction.

Within a four-layer diode, sometimes known as a Shockley diode, there are three junctions. The behavior of the junctions and the entire four-layer diode can be understood by considering it to be two interconnected three-layer transistors. *[Figure 11-28]* Transistor behavior includes no current flow until the base material receives an applied voltage to narrow the depletion area at the base-emitter junction. The base materials in the four-layer diode transistor model receive charge from the other transistor's collector. With no other means of reducing any of the depletion areas at the junctions, it appears that current does not flow in either direction in this device. However, if a large voltage is applied to forward bias the anode or cathode, at some point the ability to block flow breaks down. Current flows through whichever transistor is charged. Collector current then charges the base of the other transistor and current flows through the entire device.

Some caveats are necessary with this explanation. The transistors that comprise this four-layer diode must be constructed of material similar to that described in a zener diode. That is, it must be able to endure the current flow without burning out. In this case, the voltage that causes the diode to conduct is known as breakover voltage rather than breakdown voltage. Additionally, this diode has the unique characteristic of allowing current flow to continue until the applied voltage is reduced significantly, in most cases, until it is reduced to zero. In AC circuits, this would occur when the AC cycles.

While the four-layer, Shockley diode is useful as a switching device, a slight modification to its design creates a silicon controlled rectifier (SCR). To construct a SCR, an additional terminal known as a gate is added. It provides more control and utility. In the four-layer semiconductor construction, there are always two junctions forward biased and one junction reversed biased. The added terminal allows the momentary application of voltage to the reversed biased junction. All three junctions then become forward biased and

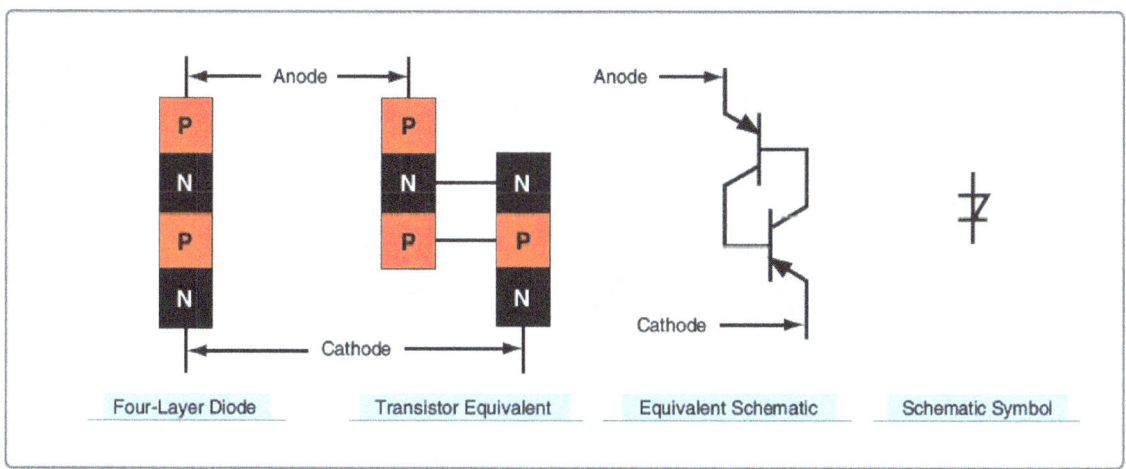

Figure 11-28. *A four-layer semiconductor diode behaves like two transistors. When breakover voltage is reached, the device conducts current until the voltage is removed.*

current at the anode flows through the device. Once voltage is applied to the gate, the SCR become latched or locked on. Current continues to flow through it until the level drops off significantly, usually to zero. Then, another applied voltage through the gate is needed to reactivate the current flow. *[Figures 11-29 and 11-30]*

SCRs are often used in high voltage situations, such as power switching, phase controls, battery chargers, and inverter circuits. They can be used to produce variable DC voltages for motors and are found in welding power supplies. Often, lighting dimmer systems use SCRs to reduce the average voltage applied to the lights by only allowing current flow during part of the AC cycle. This is controlled by controlling the pulses to the SCR gate and eliminating the massive heat dissipation caused when using resistors to reduce voltage. *Figure 11-31* graphically depicts the timing of the gate pulse that limits full cycle voltage to the load. By controlling the phase during which time the SCR is latched, a reduced average voltage is applied.

Triacs

SCRs are limited to allowing current flow in one direction only. In AC circuitry, this means only half of the voltage cycle can be used and controlled. To access the voltage in the reverse cycle from an AC power source, a triac can be used. A triac is also a four-layer semiconductor device. It differs from an SCR in that it allows current flow in both directions. A triac has a gate that works the same way as in a SCR; however, a positive or negative pulse to the gate triggers current flow in a triac. The pulse polarity determines the direction of the current flow through the device.

Figure 11-30. *Cross-section of a medium-power SCR.*

Figure 11-32 illustrates a triac and shows a triac in a simple circuit. It can be triggered with a pulse of either polarity and remains latched until the voltage declines, such as when the AC cycles. Then, it needs to be triggered again. In many ways, the triac acts as though it is two SCRs connected side by side only in opposite directions. Like an SCR, the timing of gate pulses determines the amount of the total voltage that is allowed to pass. The output waveform if triggered at 90° is shown in *Figure 11-32*. Because a triac allows current to flow in both directions, the reverse cycle of AC voltage can also be used and controlled.

When used in actual circuits, triacs do not always maintain the same phase firing point in reverse as they do when fired with a positive pulse. This problem can be regulated

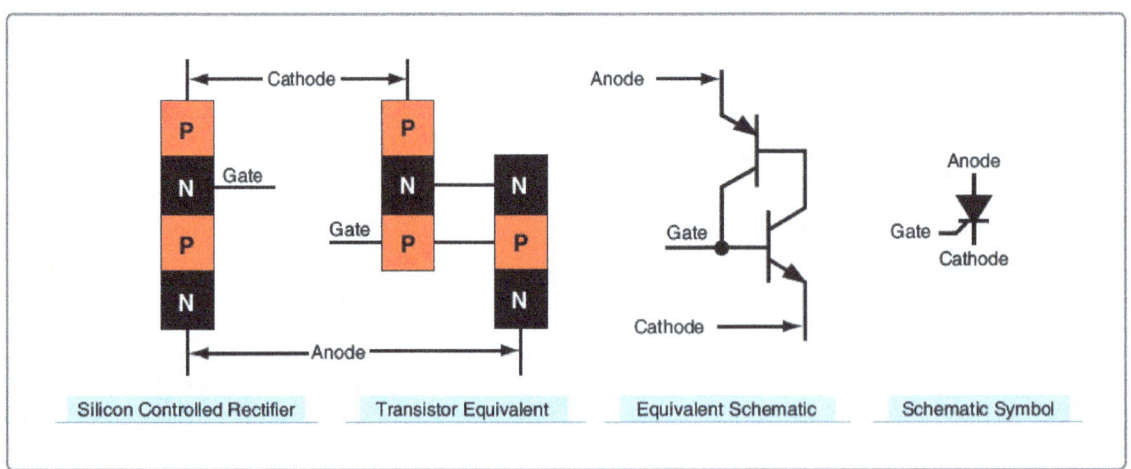

Figure 11-29. *A silicon controlled rectifier (SCR) allows current to pass in one direction when the gate receives a positive pulse to latch the device in the on position. Current ceases to flow when it drops below holding current, such as when AC current reverses cycle.*

Figure 11-31. *Phase control is a key application for SCR. By limiting the percentage of a full cycle of AC voltage that is applied to a load, a reduced voltage results. The firing angle or timing of a positive voltage pulse through the SCR's gate latches the device open allowing current flow until it drops below the holding current, which is usually at or near zero voltage as the AC cycle reverses.*

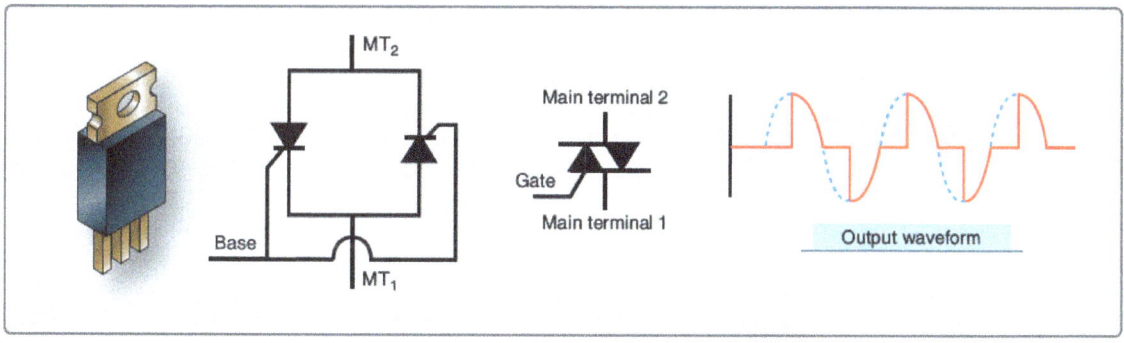

Figure 11-32. *A triac is a controlled semiconductor device that allows current flow in both directions.*

somewhat through the use of a capacitor and a diac in the gate circuit. However, as a result, where precise control is required, two SCRs in reverse of each other are often used instead of the triac. Triacs do perform well in lower voltage circuits. *Figure 11-33* illustrates the semiconductor layering in a triac.

NOTE: The four layers of N- and P-type materials are not uniform as they were in previously described semiconductor devices. None the less, gate pulses affect the depletion areas at the junctions of the materials in the same way allowing current to flow when the areas are narrowed.

Unijunction Transistors (UJT)

The behavior of semiconductor materials is exploited through the construction of numerous transistor devices containing various configurations of N-type and P-type materials. The physical arrangement of the materials in relation to each other yields devices with unique behaviors and applications. The transistors described above having two junctions of P-type and N-type materials (PN) are known as bipolar junction transistors. Other more simple transistors can be fashioned with only one junction of the PN semiconductor materials. These are known as unijunction transistors (UJT). [*Figure 11-34*]

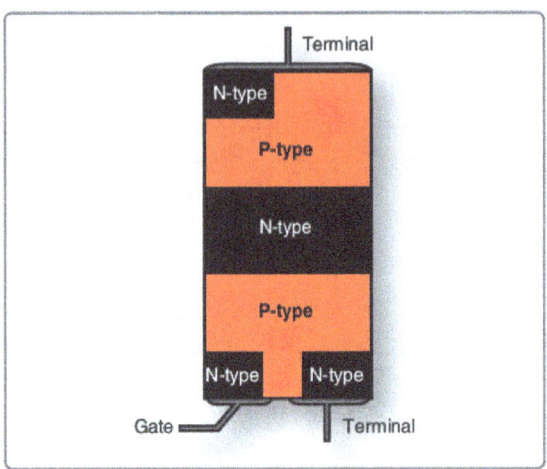

Figure 11-33. *The semiconductor layering in a triac. A positive or negative gate pulse with respect to the upper terminal allows current to flow through the devise in either direction.*

Figure 11-35. *The voltage gradient in a UJT.*

junction is determined. When the applied emitter voltage exceeds the voltage at the gradient point where the emitter is attached, the junction is forward biased and current flows freely from the B1 electrode to the E electrode. Otherwise, the junction is reversed biased and no significant current flows although there is some leakage. By selecting a UJT with the correct bias level for a particular circuit, the applied emitter voltage can control current flow through the device.

UJTs transistors of a wide variety of designs and characteristics exist. A description of all of them is beyond the scope of this discussion. In general, UJTs have some advantages over bipolar transistors. They are stable in a wide range of temperatures. In some circuits, use of UJTs can reduce the overall number of components used, which saves money and potentially increases reliability. They can be found in switching circuits, oscillators, and wave shaping circuits. However, four-layered semiconductor thyristors that function the same as the UJT just described are less expensive and most often used.

Field Effect Transistors (FET)

As shown in the triac and the UJT, creative arrangement of semiconductor material types can yield devices with a variety of characteristics. The field effect transistor (FET) is another such device which is commonly used in electronic circuits. Its N- and P-type material configuration is shown in *Figure 11-36*. A FET contains only one junction of the two types of semiconductor material. It is located at the gate where it contacts the main current carrying portion of the device. Because of this, when an FET has a PN junction, it is known as a junction field effect transistor (JFET). All FETs operate by expanding and contracting the depletion area at the junction of the semiconductor materials.

Figure 11-34. *A unijunction transistor (UJT).*

The UJT contains one base semiconductor material and a different type of emitter semiconductor material. There is no collector material. One electrode is attached to the emitter and two electrodes are attached to the base material at opposite ends. These are known as base 1 (B1) and base 2 (B2). The electrode configuration makes the UJT appear physically the same as a bipolar junction transistor. However, there is only one PN junction in the UJT and it behaves differently.

The base material of a UJT behaves like a resistor between the electrodes. With B2 positive with respect to B1, voltage gradually drops as it flows through the base. *[Figure 11-35]* By placing the emitter at a precise location along the base material gradient, the amount of voltage needed to be applied to the emitter electrode to forward bias the UJT base-emitter

Figure 11-36. *The basic structure of a field effect transistor and its electronic symbol.*

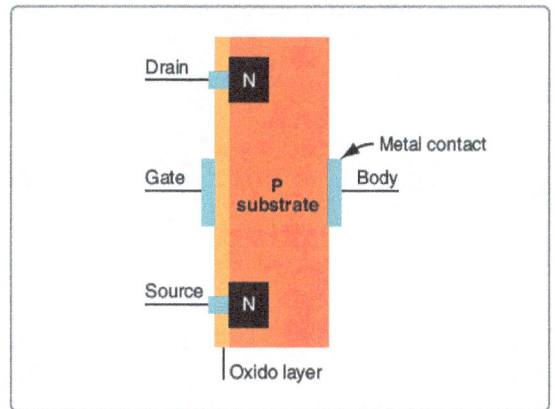

Figure 11-37. *A MOSFET has a metal gate and an oxide layer between it and the semiconductor material to prevent current leakage.*

One of the materials in a FET or JFET is called the channel. It is usually the substrate through which the current needing to be controlled flows from a source terminal to a drain terminal. The other type of material intrudes into the channel and acts as the gate. The polarity and amount of voltage applied to the gate can widen or narrow the channel due to expansion or shrinking of the depletion area at the junction of the semiconductors. This increases or decreases the amount of current that can flow through the channel. Enough reversed biased voltage can be applied to the gate to prevent the flow of current through the channel. This allows the FET to act as a switch. It can also be used as a voltage controlled resistance.

FETs are easier to manufacture than bipolar transistors and have the advantage of staying on once current flow begins without continuous gate voltage applied. They have higher impedance than bipolar transistors and operate cooler. This makes their use ideal for integrated circuits where millions of FETs may be in use on the same chip. FETs come in N-channel and P-channel varieties.

Metal Oxide Semiconductor Field Effect Transistors (MOSFETs) and Complementary Metal Oxide Semiconductor (CMOS)

The basic FET has been modified in numerous ways and continues to be at the center of faster and smaller electronic component development. A version of the FET widely used is the metal oxide semiconductor field effect transistor (MOSFET). The MOSFET uses a metal gate with a thin insulating material between the gate and the semiconductor material. This essentially creates a capacitor at the gate and eliminates current leakage in this area. Modern versions of the MOSFET have a silicon dioxide insulating layer and many have poly-crystalline silicon gates rather than metal, but the MOSFET name remains and the basic behavioral characteristic are the same. *[Figure 11-37]*

As with FETs, MOSFETs come with N-channels or P-channels. They can also be constructed as depletion mode or enhancement mode devices. This is analogous to a switch being normally open or normally closed. Depletion mode MOSFETs have an open channel that is restricted or closed when voltage is applied to the gate (i.e., normally open). Enhancement mode MOSFETs allow no current to flow at zero bias but create a channel for current flow when voltage is applied to the gate (normally closed). No voltage is used when the MOSFETs are at zero bias. Millions of enhancement mode MOSFETs are used in the construction of integrated circuits. They are installed in complimentary pairs such that when one is open, the other is closed. This basic design is known as complementary MOSFET (CMOS), which is the basis for integrated circuit design in nearly all modern electronics. Through the use of these transistors, digital logic gates can be formed and digital circuitry is constructed.

Other more specialized FETs exist. Some of their unique characteristics are owed to design alterations and others to material variations. The transistor devices discussed above use silicon-based semiconductors. But the use of other semiconductor materials can yield variations in performance. Metal semiconductor FETs (MESFETS) for example, are often used in microwave applications. They have a combined metal and semiconductor material at the gate and are typically made from gallium arsenide or indium phosphide. MESFETs are used for their quickness when starting and stopping current flows especially in opposite directions. High electron mobility transistors (HEMT) and pseudomorphic high electron mobility transistors (PHEMT) are also constructed from gallium arsenide semiconductor material and are used for high frequency applications.

Photodiodes and Phototransistors

Light contains electromagnetic energy that is carried by photons. The amount of energy depends on the frequency of light of the photon. This energy can be very useful in the operation of electronic devices since all semiconductors are affected by light energy. When a photon strikes a semiconductor atom, it raises the energy level above what is needed to hold its electrons in orbit. The extra energy frees an electron enabling it to flow as current. The vacated position of the electron becomes a hole. In photodiodes, this occurs in the depletion area of the reversed biased PN junction turning on the device and allowing current to flow.

Figure 11-38 illustrates a photodiode in a coil circuit. In this case, the light striking the photodiode causes current to flow in the circuit whereas the diode would have otherwise blocked it. The result is the coil energizes and closes another circuit enabling its operation.

Figure 11-39. *A photo transistor in a simple coil circuit (bottom) and the symbol for a phototransistor (top).*

Figure 11-00. *The symbol for a photodiode and a photodiode in a simple coil circuit.*

Figure 11-40. *Phototransistors.*

A photon activated transistor could be used to carry even more current than a photodiode. In this case, the light energy is focused on a collector-base junction. This frees electrons in the depletion area and starts a flow of electrons from the base that turns on the transistor. Once on, heavier current flows from the emitter to the collector. *[Figure 11-39]* In practice, engineers have developed numerous ways to use the energy in light photons to trigger semiconductor devices in electronic circuits. *[Figure 11-40]*

Light Emitting Diodes

Light emitting diodes (LEDs) have become so commonly used in electronics that their importance may tend to be overlooked. Numerous avionics displays and indicators use LEDs for indicator lights, digital readouts, and backlighting of liquid crystal display (LCD) screens.

LEDs are simple and reliable. They are constructed of semiconductor material. When a free electron from a semiconductor drops into a semiconductor hole, energy is given off. This is true in all semiconductor materials. However, the energy released when this happens in certain materials is in the frequency range of visible light. *Figure 11-41* is a table that illustrates common LED colors and the semiconductor material that is used in the construction of the diode.

NOTE: When the diode is reversed biased, no light is given off. When the diode is forward biased, the energy given off is visible in the color characteristic for the material being used. *Figure 11-42* illustrates the anatomy of a single LED, the symbol of an LED, and a graphic depiction of the LED process.

Color	Wavelength (nm)	Voltage (V)	Semiconductor Material
Infrared	$\lambda > 760$	$\Delta V < 1.9$	Gallium arsenide (GaAs) Aluminium gallium arsenide (AlGaAs)
Red	$610 < \lambda < 760$	$1.63 < \Delta V < 2.03$	Aluminium gallium arsenide (AlGaAs) Gallium arsenide phosphide (GaAsP) Aluminium gallium indium phosphide (AlGaInP) Gallium(III) phosphide (GaP)
Orange	$590 < \lambda < 610$	$2.03 < \Delta V < 2.10$	Gallium arsenide phosphide (GaAsP) Aluminium gallium indium phosphide (AlGaInP) Gallium(III) phosphide (GaP)
Yellow	$570 < \lambda < 590$	$2.10 < \Delta V < 2.18$	Gallium arsenide phosphide (GaAsP) Aluminium gallium indium phosphide (AlGaInP) Gallium(III) phosphide (GaP)
Green	$500 < \lambda < 570$	$1.9[32] < \Delta V < 4.0$	Indium gallium nitride (InGaN) / Gallium(III) nitride (GaN) Gallium(III) phosphide (GaP) Aluminium gallium indium phosphide (AlGaInP) Aluminium gallium phosphide (AlGaP)
Blue	$450 < \lambda < 500$	$2.48 < \Delta V < 3.7$	Zinc selenide (ZnSe) Indium gallium nitride (InGaN) Silicon carbide (SiC) as substrate Silicon (Si) as substrate — (under development)
Violet	$400 < \lambda < 450$	$2.76 < \Delta V < 4.0$	Indium gallium nitride (InGaN)
Purple	multiple types	$2.48 < \Delta V < 3.7$	Dual blue/red LEDs, blue with red phosphor, or white with purple plastic
Ultraviolet	$\lambda < 400$	$3.1 < \Delta V < 4.4$	diamond (235 nm)[33] Boron nitride (215 nm)[34][35] Aluminium nitride (AlN) (210 nm)[36] Aluminium gallium nitride (AlGaN) Aluminium gallium indium nitride (AlGaInN) — (down to 210 nm)[37]
White	Broad spectrum	$\Delta V = 3.5$	Blue/UV diode with yellow phosphor

Figure 11-41. *LED colors and the materials used to construct them as well as their wavelength and voltages.*

Figure 11-42. *A close up of a single LED (left) and the process of a semi-conductor producing light by electrons dropping into holes and giving off energy (right). The symbol for a light emitting diode is the diode symbol with two arrows pointing away from the junction.*

Basic Analog Circuits

The solid-state semiconductor devices described in the previous section of this chapter can be found in both analog and digital electronic circuits. As digital electronics evolve, analog circuitry is being replaced. However, many aircraft still make use of analog electronics in radio and navigation equipment, as well as in other aircraft systems. A brief look at some of the basic analog circuits follows.

Rectifiers

Rectifier circuits change AC voltage into DC voltage and are one of the most commonly used type of circuits in aircraft electronics. *[Figure 11-43]* The resulting DC waveform output is also shown. The circuit has a single semiconductor diode and a load resistor. When the AC voltage cycles below zero, the diode shuts off and does not allow current flow until the AC cycles through zero voltage again. The result is pronounced pulsating DC. While this can be useful, half of the original AC voltage is not being used.

Figure 11-44. *A full wave rectifier can be built by center tapping the secondary coil of the transformer and using two diodes in separate circuits. This rectifies the entire AC input into a pulsating DC with twice the frequency of a half wave rectifier.*

Diode 1 is blocked. This arrangement yields positive DC from cycling AC with no wasted current.

Another way to construct a full wave rectifier uses four semiconductor diodes in a bridge circuit. Because the secondary coil of the transformer is not tapped at the center, the resultant DC voltage output is twice that of the two-diode full wave rectifier. *[Figure 11-45]* During the first half of the AC cycle, the bottom of the secondary coil is negative.

Figure 11-43. *A half wave rectifier uses one diode to produce pulsating DC current from AC. Half of the AC cycle is wasted when the diode blocks the current flow as the AC cycles below zero.*

A full wave rectifier creates pulsating DC from AC while using the full AC cycle. One way to do this is to tap the secondary coil at its midpoint and construct two circuits with the load resistor and a diode in each circuit. *[Figure 11-44]* The diodes are arranged so that when current is flowing through one, the other blocks current.

When the AC cycles so the top of the secondary coil of the transformer is positive, current flows from ground, through the load resistor (V_{RL}), Diode 1, and the upper half of the coil. Current cannot flow through Diode 2 because it is blocked. *[Figure 11-44A]* As the AC cycles through zero, the polarity of the secondary coil changes. *[Figure 11-44B]* Current then flows from ground, through the load resistor, Diode 2, and the bottom half of the secondary coil. Current flow through

Figure 11-45. *The bridge-type four-diode full wave rectifier circuit is most commonly used to rectify single-phase AC into DC.*

Current flows from it through diode (D1), then through the load resistor, and through diode (D2) on its way back to the top of the secondary coil. When the AC reverses its cycle, the polarity of the secondary coil changes. Current flows from the top of the coil through diode (D3), then through the load resistor, and through diode (D4) on its way back to the bottom of the secondary coil. The output waveform reflects the higher voltage achieved by rectifying the full AC cycle through the entire length of the secondary coil.

Use and rectification of three-phase AC is also possible on aircraft with a specific benefit. The output DC is very smooth and does not drop to zero. A six diode circuit is built to rectify the typical three-phase AC produced by an aircraft alternator. *[Figure 11-46]*

Figure 11-46. *A six-diode three-phase AC rectifier.*

Each stator coil corresponds to a phase of AC and becomes negative for 120° of rotation of the rotor. When stator 1 or the first phase is negative, current flows from it through diode (D1), then through the load resistor and through diode (D2) on its way back to the third phase coil. Next, the second phase coil becomes negative and current flows through diode (D3). It continues to flow through the load resistor and diode (D4) on its way back to the first phase coil. Finally, the third stage coil becomes negative causing current to flow through diode (D5), then the load resistor and diode (D6) on its way back to the second phase coil. The output waveform of this three-phase rectifier depicts the DC produced. It is a relatively steady, non-pulsing flow equivalent to just the tops of the individual curves. The phase overlap prevents voltage from falling to zero producing smooth DC from AC.

Amplifiers

An amplifier is a circuit that changes the amplitude of an electric signal. This is done through the use of transistors. As mentioned, a transistor that is forward biased at the base-emitter junction and reversed biased at the collector-base junction is turned on. It can conduct current from the collector to the emitter. Because a small signal at the base can cause a large current to flow from collector to emitter, a transistor in itself can be said to be an amplifier. However, a transistor properly wired into a circuit with resistors, power sources, and other electronic components, such as capacitors, can precisely control more than signal amplitude. Phase and impedance can also be manipulated.

Since the typical bi-polar junction transistor requires a based circuit and a collector-emitter circuit, there should be four terminals, two for each circuit. However, the transistor only has three terminals (i.e., the base, the collector, and the emitter). Therefore, one of the terminals must be common to both transistor circuits. The selection of the common terminal affects the output of the amplifier.

Since the typical bipolar junction transistor requires a base circuit and a collector-emitter circuit, there should be four terminals—two for each circuit. However, the transistor only has three terminals: the base, the collector, and the emitter. Therefore, one of the terminals must be common to both transistor circuits. The selection of the common terminal affects the output of the amplifier.

The three basic amplifier types, named for which terminal of the transistor is the common terminal to both transistor circuits, include:

1. Common-emitter amplifier
2. Common-collector amplifier
3. Common-base amplifier

Common-Emitter Amplifier

The common-emitter amplifier controls the amplitude of an electric signal and inverts the phase of the input signal. *Figure 11-47* illustrates a common-emitter amplifier for AC using a NPN transistor and its output signal graph. Common emitter circuits are characterized by high current gain and a 180° voltage phase shift from input to output. It is for the amplification of a microphone signal to drive a speaker. As always, adequate voltage of the correct polarity to the base puts the transistor in the active mode, or turns it on. Then, as the base input current fluctuates, the current through the transistor fluctuates proportionally. However, AC cycles through positive and negative polarity. Every 180°, the transistor shuts

Figure 11-47. *A common-emitter amplifier circuit for amplifying an AC microphone signal to drive a speaker (top) and the graph of the output signal showing a 180 degree shift in phase (bottom).*

off because the polarity to the base-emitter junction of the transistor is not correct to forward bias the junction. To keep the transistor on, a DC biasing voltage of the correct polarity (shown as a 2.3 volts (V) battery) is placed in series with the input signal in the base circuit to hold the transistor in the active mode as the AC polarity changes. This way the transistor stays in the active mode to amplify an entire AC signal.

Transistors are rated by ratio of the collector current to the base current, or Beta (β). This is established during the manufacture of the unit and cannot be changed. A 100 β transistor can handle 100 times more current through a collector-emitter circuit than the base input signal. This current in *Figure 11-47* is provided from the 15V battery, V_1. So, the amplitude of amplification is a factor of the beta of the transistor and any in-line resistors used in the circuits. The fluctuations of the output signal, however, are entirely controlled by the fluctuations of current input to the transistor base.

If measurements of input and output voltages are made, it is shown that as the input voltage increases, the output voltage decreases. This accounts for the inverted phase produced by a common-emitter circuit. *[Figure 11-47]*

Common-Collector Amplifier

Another basic type of amplifier circuit is the common-collector amplifier. Common-collector circuits are characterized by high current gain, but vertically no voltage gain. The input circuit and the load circuit in this amplifier share the collector terminal of the transistor used. Because the load is in series with the emitter, both the input current and output current run through it. This causes a directly proportional relationship between the input and the output. The current gain in this circuit configuration is high. A small amount of input current can control a large amount of current to flow from the collector to the emitter. A common collector amplifier circuit is illustrated in *Figure 11-48*. The base current needs to flow through the PN junction of the transistor, which has about a 0.7V threshold to be turned on. The output current of the amplifier is the beta value of the transistor plus 1.

Figure 11-48. *A basic common-collector amplifier circuit. Both the input and output circuits share a path through the load and the emitter. This causes a direct relationship of the output current to the input current.*

During AC amplification, the common-collector amplifier has the same problem that exists in the common-emitter amplifier. The transistor must stay on or in the active mode regardless of input signal polarity. When the AC cycles through zero, the transistor turns off because the minimum amount of current to forward bias the transistor is not available. The addition of a DC biasing source (battery) in series with the AC signal in the input circuit keeps the transistor in the active mode throughout the full AC cycle. *[Figure 11-49]*

A common-collector amplifier can also be built with a PNP transistor. *[Figure 11-50]* It has the same characteristics as the NPN common-collector amplifier shown in *Figure 11-50*. When arranged with a high resistance in the input circuit and a small resistance in the load circuit, the common-collector amplifier can be used to step down the impedance of a signal. *[Figure 11-51]*

Common-Base Amplifier

A third type of amplifier circuit using a bipolar transistor is the common-base amplifier. In this circuit, the shared transistor terminal is the base terminal. *[Figure 11-52]* This causes a unique situation in which the base current is actually larger than the collector or emitter current. As such, the common base amplifier does not boost current as the other amplifiers do. It attenuates current but causes a high gain in voltage. A very small fluctuation in base voltage in the input circuit causes a large variation in output voltage. The effect

Figure 11-49. *A DC biasing current is used to keep the transistor of a common-collector amplifier in the active mode when amplifying AC (top). The output of this amplifier is in phase and directly proportional to the input (bottom). The difference in amplitude between the two is the 0.7V used to bias the PN junction of the transistor in the input circuit.*

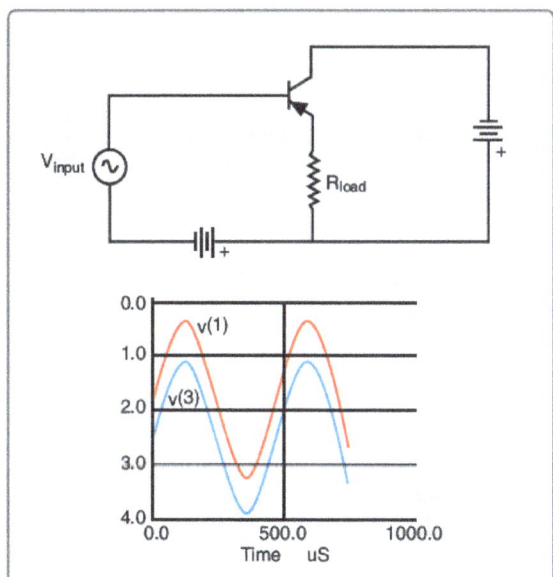

Figure 11-50. *A common-collector amplifier circuit with a PNP transistor has the same characteristics as that of a common-collector amplifier with a NPN transistor except for reversed voltage polarities and current direction.*

Figure 11-51. *This common-collector circuit has high input impedance and low output impedance.*

Figure 11-52. *A common-base amplifier circuit for DC current.*

on the circuit output is direct, so the output voltage phase is the same as the input signal but much greater in amplitude.

As with the other amplifier circuits, when amplifying an AC signal with a common-base amplifier circuit, the input signal to the base must include a DC source to forward bias the transistor's base-emitter junction. This allows current to flow from the collector to the emitter during both cycles of the AC. A circuit for AC amplification is illustrated in *Figure 11-53* with a graph of the output voltage showing the large increase produced. The common-base amplifier is limited in its use since it does not increase current flow. This makes it the least used configuration. However, it is used in radio frequency amplification because of the low input Z. *Figure 11-54* summarizes the characteristics of the bipolar amplifier circuits discussed above.

NOTE: There are many variations in circuit design. JFETs and MOSFETS are also used in amplifier circuits, usually in small signal amplifiers due to their low noise outputs.

Figure 11-53. *In a common-base amplification circuit for AC (top), output voltage amplitude is greatly increased in phase with the input signal (bottom).*

Oscillator Circuits

Oscillators function to make AC from DC. They can produce various waveforms as required by electronic circuits. There are many different types of oscillators and oscillator circuits. Some of the most common types are discussed below.

A sine wave is produced by generators when a conductor is rotated in a uniform magnetic field. The typical AC sine wave is characterized by a gradual build-up and decline of voltage in one direction, followed by a similar smooth build-up to peak voltage and decline to zero again in the opposite direction. The value of the voltage at any given time in the cycle can be calculated by taking the peak voltage and multiplying it by the sine of the angle through which the conductor has rotated. *[Figure 11-55]*

A square wave is produce when there is a flow of electrons for a set period that stops for a set amount of time and

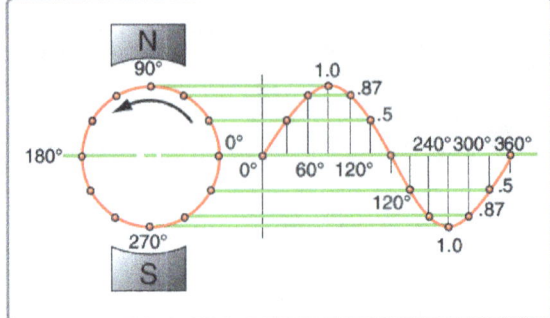

Figure 11-55. *Voltage over time of sine waveform electricity created when a conductor is rotated through a uniform magnetic field, such as in a generator.*

then repeats. In DC current, this is simply pulsing DC. *[Figure 11-56]* This same wave form can be of opposite polarities when passed through a transformer to produce AC. Certain oscillators produce square waves.

Figure 11-56. *The waveform of pulsing DC is a square wave.*

An oscillator known as a relaxation oscillator produces another kind of wave form, a sawtooth wave. A slow rise from zero to peak voltage is followed by a rapid drop-off of voltage back to almost zero. Then it repeats. *[Figure 11-57]* In the circuit, a capacitor slowly charges through a resistor. A neon bulb is wired across the capacitor. When its ignition voltage is reached, the bulb conducts. This short-circuits the charged capacitor, which causes the voltage to drop to nearly zero and the bulb goes out. Then, the voltage rises again as the cycle repeats.

Type of Amplifier	Impedance	Voltage Gain	Current Gain	Power Gain	Phase
Common-emitter	Input: fairly high Output: fairly high	Relatively large	Relatively large	Large	Inverts phase
Common-collector	Input: high Output: low	Always less than one	Relatively large	Relatively large	Output same as input
Common-base	Input: low Output: high	Large	Always less than one	Relatively large	Output same as input

Figure 11-54. *PN junction transistor amplifier characteristics.*

Figure 11-57. *A relaxation oscillator produces a sawtooth wave output.*

Electronic Oscillation

Oscillation in electronic circuits is accomplished by combining a transistor and a tank circuit. A tank circuit is comprised of a capacitor and coil parallel to each other. *[Figure 11-58]* When attached to a power source by closing switch A, the capacitor charges to a voltage equal to the battery voltage. It stays charged, even when the circuit to the battery is open (switch in position B). When the switch is put in position C, the capacitor and coil are in a closed circuit. The capacitor discharges through the coil. While receiving the energy from the capacitor, the coil stores it by building up an electromagnetic field. When the capacitor is fully discharged, the coil stops conducting. The magnetic field collapses, which induces current flow. The current charges the opposite plate of the capacitor. When completely charged, the capacitor discharges into the coil again. The magnetic field builds again and stops when the capacitor is fully discharged. The magnetic field collapses again, which induces current that charges the original plate of the capacitor and the cycle repeats.

Figure 11-58. *A tank circuit alternately charges opposite plates of a capacitor through a coil in a closed circuit. The oscillation is an alternating current that diminishes due to resistance in the circuit.*

This oscillation of charging and discharging the capacitor through the coil would continue indefinitely if a circuit could be built with no resistance. This is not possible. However, a circuit can be built using a transistor that restores losses due to resistance. There are various ways to accomplish this. The Hartley oscillator circuit in *Figure 11-59* is one. The circuit can oscillate indefinitely as long as it is connected to power.

Figure 11-59. *A Hartley oscillator uses a tank circuit and a transistor to maintain oscillation whenever power is applied.*

When the switch is closed, current begins to flow in the oscillator circuit. The transistor base is supplied with biasing current through the voltage divider RA and RB. This allows current to flow through the transistor from the collector to the emitter, through RE and through the lower portion of the center tapped coil that is labeled L1. The current increasing through this coil builds a magnetic field that induces current in the upper half of the coil labeled L2. The current from L2 charges capacitor C2, which increases the forward bias of the transistor. This allows an increasing flow of current through the transistor, RE, and L1 until the transistor is saturated and capacitor C1 is fully charged. Without force to add electrons to capacitor C1, it discharges and begins the oscillation in the tank circuit described in the previous section. As C1 becomes fully charged, current to charge C2 reduces and C2 also discharges. This adds the energy needed to the tank circuit to compensate for resistance losses. As C2 is discharging, it reduces forward biasing and eventually the transistor becomes reversed biased and cuts off. When the opposite plate of capacitor C1 is fully charged, it discharges and the oscillation is in progress. The transistor base becomes forward biased again, allowing for current flow through the resistor RE, coil L1, etc.

The frequency of the AC oscillating in the Hartley oscillator circuit depends on the inductance and capacitance values of the components used. Use of a crystal in an oscillator circuit can control the frequency more accurately. A crystal vibrates at a single, consistent frequency. When flexed, a small pulse of current is produced through the piezoelectric effect. Placed in the feedback loop, the pulses from the crystal control the frequency of the oscillator circuit. The tank circuit component values are tuned to match the frequency of the crystal. Oscillation is maintained as long as power is supplied. *[Figure 11-60]*

Figure 11-60. *A crystal in an electronic oscillator circuit is used to tune the frequency of oscillation.*

Other types of oscillator circuits used in electronics and computers have two transistors that alternate being in the active mode. They are called multi-vibrators. The choice of oscillator in an electronic device depends on the exact type of manipulation of electricity required to permit the device to function as desired.

Digital Electronics

The above discussion of semiconductors, semiconductor devices, and circuitry is only an introduction to the electronics found in communications and navigation avionics. In-depth maintenance of the interior electronics on most avionics devices is performed only by certified repair stations and trained avionics technicians. The airframe technician is responsible for installation, maintenance, inspection, and proper performance of avionics in the aircraft.

Modern aircraft increasingly employs digital electronics in avionics rather than analog electronics. Transistors are used in digital electronics to construct circuits that act as digital logic gates. The purpose and task of a device is achieved by manipulating electric signals through the logic gates. Thousands, and even millions, of tiny transistors can be placed on a chip to create the digital logic landscape through which a component's signals are processed.

Digital Building Blocks

Digital logic is based on the binary number system. There are two conditions than may exist, 1 or 0. In a digital circuit, these are equivalent to voltage or no voltage. Within the binary system, these two conditions are called Logic 1 and Logic 0. Using just these two conditions, gates can be constructed to manipulate information. There are a handful of common logic gates that are used. By combining any number of these tiny solid-state gates, significant memorization, manipulation, and calculation of information can be performed.

The NOT Gate

The NOT gate is the simplest of all gates. If the input to the gate is Logic 1, then the output is NOT Logic 1. This means that it is Logic 0, since there are only two conditions in the binary world. In an electronic circuit, a NOT gate would invert the input signal. In other words, if there was voltage at the input to the gate, there would be no output voltage. The gate can be constructed with transistors and resistors to yield this electrical logic every time. (The gate or circuit would also have to invert an input of Logic 0 into an output of Logic 1.)

To understand logic gates, truth tables are often used. A truth table gives all of the possibilities in binary terms for each gate containing a characteristic logic function. For example, a truth table for a NOT gate is illustrated in *Figure 11-61*. Any input (A) is NOT present at the output (B). This is simple, but it defines this logic situation. A tiny NOT gate circuit can be built using transistors that produce these results. In other words, a circuit can be built such that if voltage arrives at the gate, no voltage is output or vice-versa.

Figure 11-61. *A NOT logic gate symbol and a NOT gate truth table.*

When using transistors to build logic gates, the primary concern is to operate them within the circuits so the transistors are either OFF (not conducting) or fully ON (saturated). In this manner, reliable logic functions can be performed. The variable voltage and current situations present during the active mode of the transistor are of less importance.

Figure 11-62 illustrates an electronic circuit diagram that performs the logic NOT gate function. Any input, either a no voltage or voltage condition, yields the opposite output. This gate is built with bipolar junction transistors, resistors, and a few diodes. Other designs exist that may have different components.

Figure 11-63. *A buffer or amplifier symbol and the truth table of the buffer, which is actually two consecutive NOT gates.*

Most common logic gates have two inputs. Three or more inputs are possible on some gates. When considering the characteristics of any logic gate, an output of Logic 1 is sought and a condition for the inputs is stated or examined. For example, *Figure 11-64* illustrates an AND gate. For an AND gate to have a Logic 1 output, both inputs have to be Logic 1. In an actual electronic circuit, this means that for a voltage to be present at the output, the AND gate circuit has to receive voltage at both of its inputs. As pointed out, there are different arrangements of electronic components that yield this result. Whichever is used is summarized and presented as the AND gate symbol. The truth table in *Figure 11-64* illustrates that there is only one way to have an output of Logic 1 or voltage when using an AND gate.

OR Gate

Figure 11-62. *An electronic circuit that reliably performs the NOT logic function.*

When examining and discussing digital electronic circuits, the electronic circuit design of a gate is usually not presented. The symbol for the logic gate is most often used. *[Figure 11-61]* The technician can then concentrate on the configuration of the logic gates in relation to each other. A brief discussion of the other logic gates, their symbols, and truth tables follow.

Buffer Gate

Another logic gate with only one input and one output is the buffer. It is a gate with the same output as the input. While this may seem redundant or useless, an amplifier may be considered a buffer in a digital circuit because if there is voltage present at the input, there is an output voltage. If there is no voltage at the input, there is no output voltage. When used as an amplifier, the buffer can change the values of a signal. This is often done to stabilize a weak or varying signal. All gates are amplifiers subject to output fluctuations. The buffer steadies the output of the upstream device while maintaining its basic characteristic. Another application of a buffer that is two NOT gates, is to use it to isolate a portion of a circuit. *[Figure 11-63]*

AND Gate

Figure 11-64. *An AND gate symbol and its truth table.*

Another useful and common logic gate is the OR gate. In an OR gate, to have an output of Logic 1 (voltage present), one of the inputs must be Logic 1. As seen in *Figure 11-65*, only one of the inputs needs to be Logic 1 for there to be an output of Logic 1. When both inputs are Logic 1, the OR gate has a Logic 1 output because it still meets the condition of one of the inputs being Logic 1.

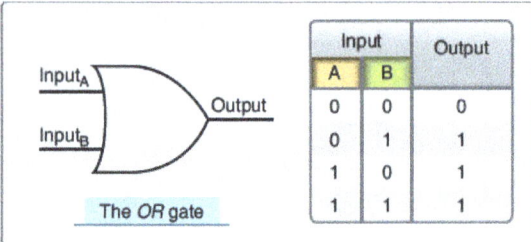

Figure 11-65. *An OR gate symbol and its truth table.*

NAND Gate

The AND, OR, and NOT gates are the basic logic gates. A few other logic gates are also useful. They can be derived from combining the AND, OR, and NOT gates. The NAND gate is a combination of an AND gate and a NOT gate. This means that AND gate conditions must be met and then inverted. So, the NAND gate is an AND gate followed by a NOT gate. The truth table for a NAND gate is shown in *Figure 11-66* along with its symbol. If a Logic 1 output is to exist from a NAND gate, inputs A and B must not both be Logic 1. Or, if a NAND gate has both inputs Logic 1, the output is Logic 0. Stated in electronic terms, if there is to be an output voltage, then the inputs cannot both have voltage or, if both inputs have voltage, there is no output voltage.

NOTE: The values in the output column of the NAND gate table are exactly the opposite of the output values in the AND gate truth table.

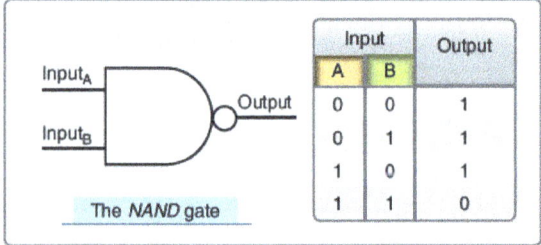

Figure 11-66. *A NAND gate symbol and its truth table illustrating that the NAND gate is an inverted AND gate.*

NOR Gate

A NOR gate is similarly arranged except that it is an inverted OR gate. If there is to be a Logic 1 output, or output voltage, then neither input can be Logic 1 or have input voltage. This is the same as satisfying the OR gate conditions and then putting output through a NOT gate. The NOR gate truth table in *Figure 11-67* shows that the NOR gate output values are exactly the opposite of the OR gate output values.

The NAND gate and the NOR gate have a unique distinction. Each one can be the only gate used in circuitry to produce the same output as any of the other logic gates. While it may

Figure 11-67. *A NOR gate symbol and its truth table illustrating that the NOR gate is an inverted OR gate.*

be inefficient, it is testimonial to the flexibility that designers have when working with logic gates, the NAND and NOR gates in particular.

EXCLUSIVE OR Gate

Another common logic gate is the EXCLUSIVE OR gate. It is the same as an OR gate except for the condition where both inputs are Logic 1. In an OR gate, there would be Logic 1 output when both inputs are Logic 1. This is not allowed in an EXCLUSIVE OR gate. When either of the inputs is Logic 1, the output is Logic 1. But, if both inputs are logic 1, the Logic 1 output is excluded or Logic 0. *[Figure 11-68]*

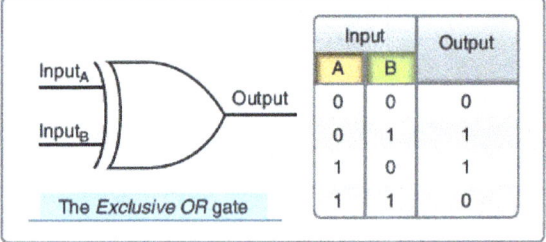

Figure 11-68. *An EXCLUSIVE OR gate symbol and its truth table, which is similar to an OR gate but excludes output when both inputs are the same.*

Negative Logic Gates

There are also negative logic gates. The negative OR and the negative AND gates are gates wherein the inputs are inverted rather than inverting the output. This creates a unique set of outputs as seen in the truth tables in *Figure 11-69*. The negative OR gate is not the same as the NOR gate as is sometimes misunderstood. Neither is the negative AND gate the same as the NAND gate. However, as the truth tables reveal, the output of a negative AND gate is the same as a NOR gate, and the output of a negative OR gate is the same as a NAND gate.

In summary, electronic circuits use transistors to construct logic gates that produce outputs related to the inputs shown in the truth tables for each kind of gate. The gates are then

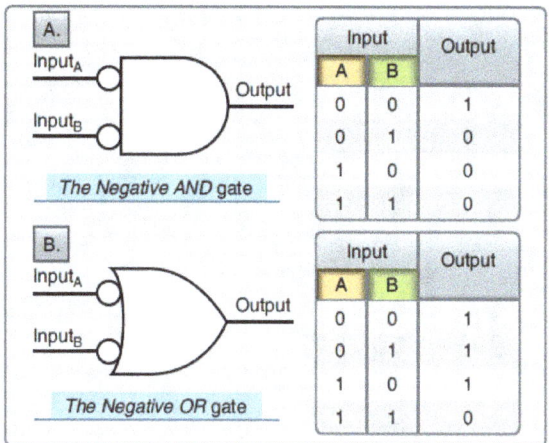

Figure 11-69. *The NEGATIVE AND gate symbol and its truth table (A) and the NEGATIVE OR gate symbol and truth table (B). The inputs are inverted in the NEGATIVE gates.*

assembled with other components to manipulate data in digital circuits. The electronic digital signals used are voltage or no voltage representations of Logic 1 or Logic 0 conditions. By using a series of voltage output or no voltage output gates, manipulation, computation, and storage of data takes place.

Digital Aircraft Systems

Digital aircraft systems are the present and future of aviation. From communication and navigation to engine and flight controls, increased proliferation of digital technology increases reliability and performance. Processing, storing, and transferring vital information for the operation of an aircraft in digital form provides a usable common language for monitoring, control, and safety. Integration of information from different systems is simplified. Self monitoring, built-in test equipment (BITE) and air-to-ground data links increase maintenance efficiency. Digital buss networking allows aircraft system computers to interact for a coordinated comprehensive approach to flight operations.

Digital Data Displays

Modern digital data displays are the most visible features of digital aircraft systems. They extend the functional advantages of state of the art digital communication and navigation avionics and other digital aircraft systems via the use of an enhanced interface with the pilot. The result is an increase in situational awareness and overall safety of flight. Digital data displays are the glass of the glass cockpit. They expand the amount, clarity, and proximity of the information presented to the pilot. *[Figure 11-70]*

Many digital data displays are available from numerous manufacturers as original equipment in new aircraft, or as retrofit components or complete retrofit systems for older aircraft. Approval for retrofit displays is usually accomplished through supplementary type certificate (STC) awarded to the equipment manufacturer.

Early digital displays presented scale indication in digital or integer format readouts. Today's digital data displays are analogous to computer screen presentations. Numerous aircraft and flight instrument readouts and symbolic presentations are combined with communication and navigational information on multifunctional displays (MFD). Often a display has a main function with potential to back-up another display should it fail. Names, such as primary flight display (**PFD**), secondary flight display, navigational display (**ND**), etc., are often used to describe a display by its primary use. The hardware composition of the displays is essentially the same. Avionics components and computers combine to provide the different information portrayed on the displays.

Figure 11-70. *A modern glass cockpit on a general aviation aircraft. Digital data displays replace many older instruments and indicators of the past.*

Controls on the instrument panel or on the display unit itself are used for selection. Some screens have limited display capability because they are not part of a totally integrated system; however, they are extremely power electronic units with wide capability. *[Figure 11-71]*

The basis of the information displayed on what is known as a primary flight display (PFD), is usually an electronic flight instrument system (EFIS) like representation of the aircraft attitude indicator in the upper half of the display, and an electronic horizontal situation indicator display on the lower half. Numerous ancillary readouts are integrated or surround the electronic attitude indicator and the horizontal situation indicator (HSI). On full glass cockpit PFDs, all of the basic T instrument indications are presented and much more, such as communication and navigation information, weather data, terrain features, and approach information. Data displays for engine parameters, hydraulics, fuel, and other airframe systems are often displayed on the secondary flight display or on an independent display made for this purpose. *[Figure 11-72]*

As with other avionics components, repair and maintenance of the internal components of digital data displays is reserved for licensed repair stations only.

Digital Tuners and Audio Panels

Numerous communication and navigation devices are described in the following sections of this chapter. Many of these use radio waves and must be tuned to a desired frequency for operation. As a flight progresses, retuning and changing from one piece of equipment to another can occur frequently. An audio panel or digital tuner consolidates various communication and navigation radio selection controls into a single unit. The pilot can select and use, or select and tune, most of the aircraft's avionics from this one control interface. *[Figure 11-73]*

Radio Communication

Much of aviation communication and navigation is accomplished through the use of radio waves. Communication by radio was the first use of radio frequency transmissions in aviation.

Figure 11-72. *A digital data display dedicated to the depiction of engine and airframe system parameter status.*

Figure 11-71. *A retrofit digital data display.*

Figure 11-73. *An audio panel in a general aviation aircraft integrates the selection of several radio-based communication and navigational aids into a single control panel (left). A digital tuner (right, Image © Rockwell Collins, Inc.) does the same on a business class aircraft and allows the frequency of each device to be tuned from the same panel as well.*

Radio Waves

A radio wave is invisible to the human eye. It is electromagnetic in nature and part of the electronic spectrum of wave activity that includes gamma rays, x-rays, ultraviolet rays, infrared waves, and visible light rays, as well all radio waves. *[Figure 11-74]* The atmosphere is filled with these waves. Each wave occurs at a specific frequency and has a corresponding wavelength. The relationship between frequency and wavelength is inversely proportional. A high frequency wave has a short wave length and a low frequency wave has a long wave length.

In aviation, a variety of radio waves are used for communication. *Figure 11-75* illustrates the radio spectrum that includes the range of common aviation radio frequencies and their applications.

NOTE: A wide range of frequencies are used from low frequency (LF) at 100 kHz (100,000 cycles per second) to super high frequency (SHF) at nearly 10gHz (10,000,000,000 cycles per second). The Federal Communications Commission (FCC) controls the assignment of frequency usage.

AC power of a particular frequency has a characteristic length of conductor that is resonant at that frequency. This length is the wavelength of the frequency that can be seen on an oscilloscope. Fractions of the wavelength also resonate, especially half of a wavelength, which is the same as half of the AC sign wave or cycle.

The frequency of an AC signal is the number of times the AC cycles every second. AC applied to the center of a radio antenna, a conductor half the wavelength of the AC frequency, travels the length of the antenna, collapses, and travels the length of the antenna in the opposite direction. The number of times it does this every second is known as the radio wave signal frequency or radio frequency as shown in *Figure 11-75*. As the current flows through the antenna, corresponding electromagnetic and electric fields build, collapse, build in the opposite direction, and collapse again. *[Figure 11-76]*

To transmit radio waves, an AC generator is placed at the midpoint of an antenna. As AC current builds and collapses in the antenna, a magnetic field also builds and collapses around it. An electric field also builds and subsides as the voltage shifts from one end of the antenna to the other. Both fields, the magnetic and the electric, fluctuate around the antenna at the same time. The antenna is half the wavelength of the AC signal received from the generator. At any one point along the antenna, voltage and current vary inversely to each other.

Figure 11-74. *Radio waves are just some of the electromagnetic waves found in space.*

Figure 11-75. *There is a wide range of radio frequencies. Only the very low frequencies and the extremely high frequencies are not used in aviation.*

Because of the speed of the AC, the electromagnetic fields and electric fields created around the antenna do not have time to completely collapse as the AC cycles. Each new current flow creates new fields around the antenna that force the not-totally-collapsed fields from the previous AC cycle out into space. These are the radio waves. The process is continuous as long as AC is applied to the antenna. Thus, steady radio waves of a frequency determined by the input AC frequency propagate out into space.

Radio waves are directional and propagate out into space at 186,000 miles per second. The distance they travel depends on the frequency and the amplification of the signal AC sent to the antenna. The electric field component and the electromagnetic field component are oriented at 90° to each other, and at 90° to the direction that the wave is traveling. [*Figure 11-77*]

Types of Radio Waves

Radio waves of different frequencies have unique characteristics as they propagate through the atmosphere.

Very low frequency (VLF), LF, and medium frequency (MF) waves have relatively long wavelengths and utilize correspondingly long antennas. Radio waves produced at these frequencies ranging from 3kHz to 3mHz are known as ground waves or surface waves. This is because they follow the curvature of the earth as they travel from the broadcast antenna to the receiving antenna. Ground waves are particularly useful for long distance transmissions. Automatic direction finders (ADF) and LORAN navigational aids use these frequencies. [*Figure 11-78*]

High frequency (HF) radio waves travel in a straight line and do not curve to follow the earth's surface. This would limit transmissions from the broadcast antenna to receiving antennas only in the line-of-sight of the broadcast antenna except for a unique characteristic. HF radio waves bounce off of the ionosphere layer of the atmosphere. This refraction extends the range of HF signals beyond line-of-sight. As a result, transoceanic aircraft often use HF radios for voice communication. The frequency range is between 2 to 25 MHz. These kinds of radio waves are known as sky waves. [*Figure 11-78*]

Above HF transmissions, radio waves are known as space waves. They are only capable of line-of-sight transmission and do not refract off of the ionosphere. [*Figure 11-78*] Most aviation communication and navigational aids operate with space waves. This includes VHF (30-300MHz), UHF (300MHz-3GHz), and super high frequency (SHF) (3Ghz-30Ghz) radio waves.

VHF communication radios are the primary communication radios used in aviation. They operate in the frequency range from 118.0 MHz to 136.975MHz. Seven hundred and twenty separate and distinct channels have been designated in this range with 25 kilohertz spacing between each channel. Further division of the bandwidth is possible, such as in Europe where 8.33 kilohertz separate each VHF communication channel. VHF radios are used for communications between aircraft and air traffic control (ATC), as well as air-to-air communication between aircraft. When using VHF, each party transmits and receives on the same channel. Only one party can transmit at any one time.

Loading Information onto a Radio Wave

The production and broadcast of radio waves does not convey any significant information. The basic radio wave discussed above is known as a carrier wave. To transmit and receive useful information, this wave is altered or modulated by an information signal. The information signal contains the unique voice or data information desired to be conveyed. The modulated carrier wave then carries the information from the transmitting radio to the receiving radio via their respective

Figure 11-76. *Radio waves are produced by applying an AC signal to an antenna. This creates a magnetic and electric field around the antenna. They build and collapse as the AC cycles. The speed at which the AC cycles does not allow the fields to completely collapse before the next fields build. The collapsing fields are then forced out into space as radio waves.*

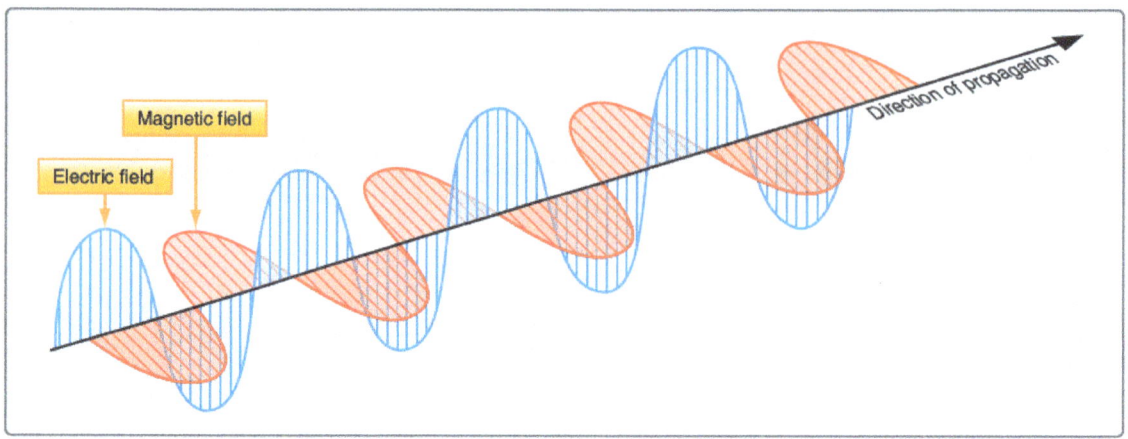

Figure 11-77. *The electric field and the magnetic field of a radio wave are perpendicular to each other and to the direction of propagation of the wave.*

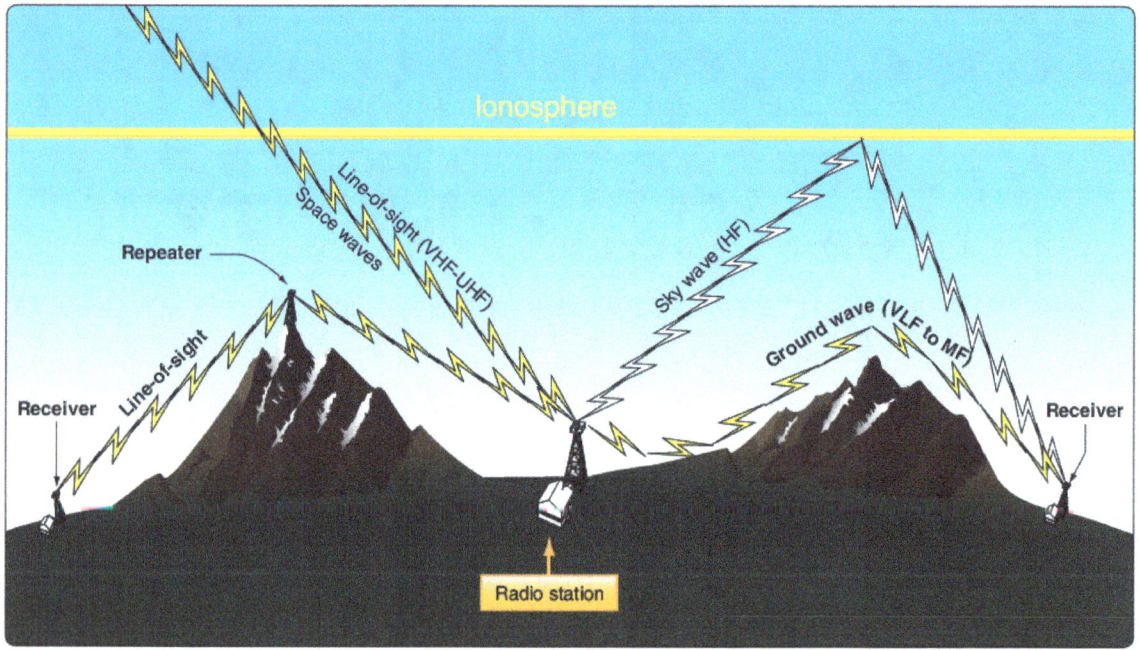

Figure 11-78. *Radio waves behave differently in the atmosphere depending in their frequency.*

antennas. Two common methods of modulating carrier waves are amplitude modulation and frequency modulation.

Amplitude Modulation (AM)

A radio wave can be altered to carry useful information by modulating the amplitude of the wave. A DC signal, for example from a microphone, is amplified and then superimposed over the AC carrier wave signal. As the varying DC information signal is amplified, the amplifier output current varies proportionally. The oscillator that creates the carrier wave does so with this varying current. The oscillator frequency output is consistent because it is built into the oscillator circuit. But the amplitude of the oscillator output varies in relation to the fluctuating current input. *[Figure 11-79]*

When the modulated carrier wave strikes the receiving antenna, voltage is generated that is the same as that which was applied to the transmitter antenna. However, the signal is weaker. It is amplified so that it can be demodulated. Demodulation is the process of removing the original information signal from the carrier wave. Electronic circuits containing capacitors, inductors, diodes, filters, etc., remove

Figure 11-79. *A DC audio signal modifies the 121.5 MHz carrier wave as shown in C. The amplitude of the carrier wave (A) is changed in relation to modifier (B). This is known as amplitude modulation (AM).*

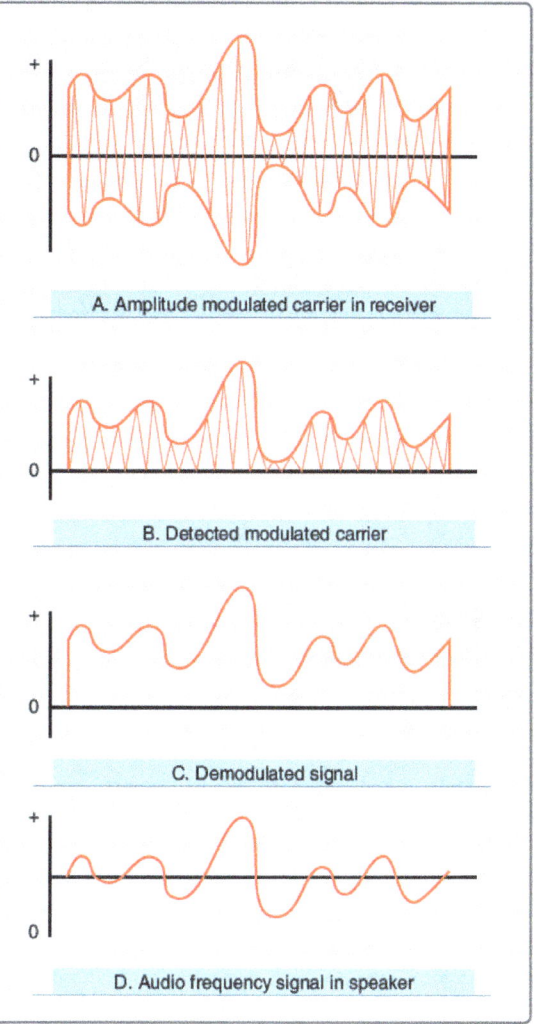

Figure 11-80. *Demodulation of a received radio signal involves separating the carrier wave from the information signal.*

all but the desired information signal identical to the original input signal. Then, the information signal is typically amplified again to drive speakers or other output devices. [Figure 11-80]

AM has limited fidelity. Atmospheric noises or static alter the amplitude of a carrier wave making it difficult to separate the intended amplitude modulation caused by the information signal and that which is caused by static. It is used in aircraft VHF communication radios.

Frequency Modulation (FM)

Frequency modulation (FM) is widely considered superior to AM for carrying and deciphering information on radio waves. A carrier wave modulated by FM retains its constant amplitude. However, the information signal alters the frequency of the carrier wave in proportion to the strength of the signal. Thus, the signal is represented as slight variations to the normally consistent timing of the oscillations of the carrier wave. [Figure 11-81]

Since the transmitter oscillator output fluctuates during modulation to represent the information signal, FM bandwidth is greater than AM bandwidth. This is overshadowed by the ease with which noise and static can be removed from the FM signal. FM has a steady current flow and requires less power to produce since modulating an oscillator producing a carrier wave takes less power than modulating the amplitude of a signal using an amplifier.

Demodulation of an FM signal is similar to that of an AM receiver. The signal captured by the receiving antenna is usually amplified immediately since signal strength is lost as

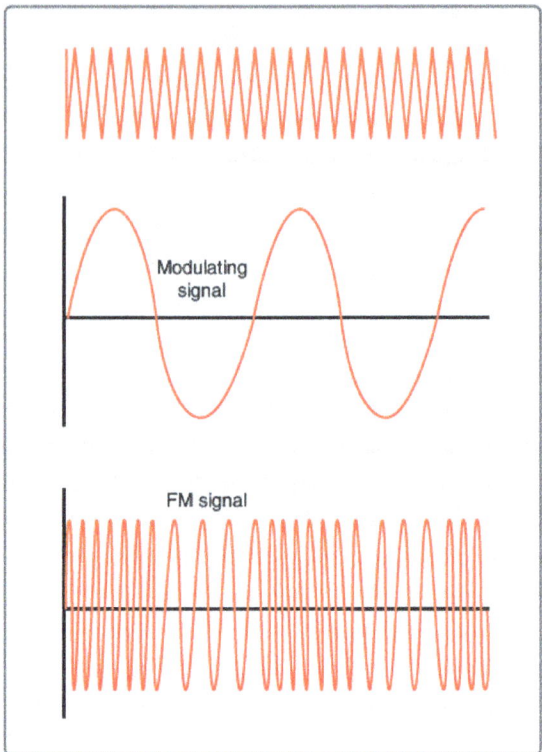

Figure 11-81. *A frequency modulated (FM) carrier wave retains the consistent amplitude of the AC sign wave. It encodes the unique information signal with slight variations to the frequency of the carrier wave. These variations are shown as space variations between the peaks and valleys of the wave on an oscilloscope.*

the wave travels through the atmosphere. Numerous circuits are used to isolate, stabilize, and remove the information from the carrier wave. The result is then amplified to drive the output device.

Single Side Band (SSB)

When two AC signals are mixed together, such as when a carrier wave is modulated by an information signal, three main frequencies result:

1. Original carrier wave frequency;
2. Carrier wave frequency plus the modulating frequency; and
3. Carrier wave frequency minus the modulating frequency.

Due to the fluctuating nature of the information signal, the modulating frequency varies from the carrier wave up or down to the maximum amplitude of the modulating frequency during AM. These additional frequencies on either side of the carrier wave frequency are known as side bands. Each side band contains the unique information signal desired to be conveyed. The entire range of the lower and upper sidebands including the center carrier wave frequency is known as bandwidth. *[Figure 11-82]*

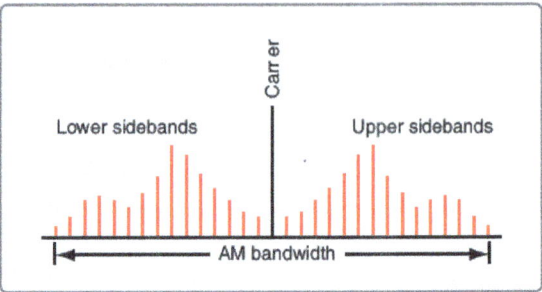

Figure 11-82. *The bandwidth of an AM signal contains the carrier wave, the carrier wave plus the information signal frequencies, and the carrier wave minus the information signal frequencies.*

There are a limited number of frequencies within the usable frequency ranges (i.e., LF, HF, and VHF). If different broadcasts are made on frequencies that are too close together, some of the broadcast from one frequency interfere with the adjacent broadcast due to overlapping side bands. The FCC divides the various frequency bands and issues rules for their use. Much of this allocation is to prevent interference. The spacing between broadcast frequencies is established so that a carrier wave can expand to include the upper and lower side bands and still not interfere with a signal on an adjacent frequency.

As use of the radio frequencies increases, more efficient allocation of bandwidth is imperative. Sending information via radio waves using the narrowest bandwidth possible is the focus of engineering moving forward. At the same time, fully representing all of the desired information or increasing the amount of information conveyed is also desired. Various methods are employed to keep bandwidth to a minimum, many of which restrict the quality or quantity of information able to be transmitted.

In lower frequency ranges, such as those used for ground wave and some sky wave broadcasts, SSB transmissions are a narrow bandwidth solution. Each side band represents the initial information signal in its entirety. Therefore in an SSB broadcast, the carrier wave and either the upper or lower sidebands are filtered out. Only one sideband with its frequencies is broadcast since it contains all of the needed information. This cuts the bandwidth required in half and allows more efficient use of the radio spectrum. SSB transmissions also use less power to transmit the same amount of information over an equal distance. Many HF long-distance aviation communications are SSB. *[Figure 11-83]*

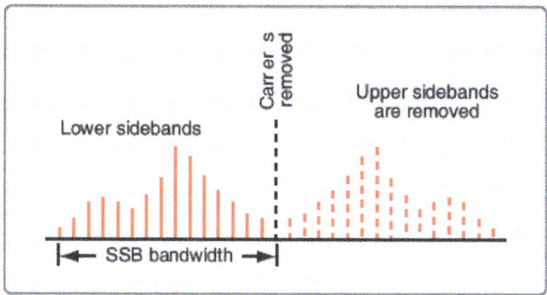

Figure 11-83. *The additional frequencies above and below the carrier wave produced during modulation with the information signal are known as sidebands. Each sideband contains the unique information of the information signal and can be transmitted independent of the carrier wave and the other sideband.*

Radio Transmitters and Receivers

Radio transmitters and receivers are electronic devices that manipulate electricity resulting in the transmission of useful information through the atmosphere or space.

Transmitters

A transmitter consists of a precise oscillating circuit or oscillator that creates an AC carrier wave frequency. This is combined with amplification circuits or amplifiers. The distance a carrier wave travels is directly related to the amplification of the signal sent to the antenna.

Other circuits are used in a transmitter to accept the input information signal and process it for loading onto the carrier wave. Modulator circuits modify the carrier wave with the processed information signal. Essentially, this is all there is to a radio transmitter.

NOTE: Modern transmitters are highly refined devices with extremely precise frequency oscillation and modulation. The circuitry for controlling, filtering, amplifying, modulating, and oscillating electronic signals can be complex.

A transmitter prepares and sends signals to an antenna that, in the process described above, radiates the waves out into the atmosphere. A transmitter with multiple channel (frequency) capability contains tuning circuitry that enables the user to select the frequency upon which to broadcast. This adjusts the oscillator output to the precise frequency desired. It is the oscillator frequency that is being tuned. *[Figure 11-84]* As shown in *Figure 11-84*, most radio transmitters generate a stable oscillating frequency and then use a frequency multiplier to raise the AC to the transmitting frequency. This allows oscillation to occur at frequencies that are controllable and within the physical working limits of the crystal in crystal-controlled oscillators.

Figure 11-84. *Block diagram of a basic radio transmitter.*

Receivers

Antennas are simply conductors of lengths proportional to the wavelength of the oscillated frequency put out by the transmitter. An antenna captures the desired carrier wave as well as many other radio waves that are present in the atmosphere. A receiver is needed to isolate the desired carrier wave with its information. The receiver also has circuitry to separate the information signal from the carrier wave. It prepares it for output to a device, such as speakers or a display screen. The output is the information signal originally introduced into the transmitter.

A common receiver is the super heterodyne receiver. As with any receiver, it must amplify the desired radio frequency captured by the antenna since it is weak from traveling through the atmosphere. An oscillator in the receiver is used to compare and select the desired frequency out of all of the frequencies picked up by the antenna. The undesired frequencies are sent to ground.

A local oscillator in the receiver produces a frequency that is different than the radio frequency of the carrier wave. These two frequencies are mixed in the mixer. Four frequencies result from this mixing. They are the radio frequency, the local oscillator frequency, and the sum and difference of these two frequencies. The sum and difference frequencies contain the information signal.

The frequency that is the difference between the local oscillator frequency and the radio frequency carrier wave frequency is used during the remaining processing. In VHF aircraft communication radios, this frequency is 10.8 MHz. Called the intermediate frequency, it is amplified before it is sent to the detector. The detector, or demodulator, is where the information signal is separated from the carrier wave portion of the signal. In AM, since both sidebands contain the useful information, the signal is rectified leaving just one sideband with a weak version of the original transmitter input signal. In FM receivers, the varying frequency is changed to a varying amplitude signal at this point. Finally, amplification occurs for the output device. *[Figure 11-85]*

Figure 11-85. *The basic stages used in a receiver to produce an output from a radio wave.*

Over the years, with the development of transistors, microtransistors, and integrated circuits, radio transmitters and receivers have become smaller. Electronic bays were established on older aircraft as remote locations to mount radio devices simply because they would not fit in the flight deck. Today, many avionics devices are small enough to be mounted in the instrument panel, which is customary on most light aircraft. Because of the number of communication and navigation aids, as well as the need to present an uncluttered interface to the pilot, most complicated aircraft retain an area away from the flight deck for the mounting of avionics. The control heads of these units remain on the flight deck.

Transceivers

A transceiver is a communication radio that transmits and receives. The same frequency is used for both. When transmitting, the receiver does not function. The push to talk (PTT) switch blocks the receiving circuitry and allows the transmitter circuitry to be active. In a transceiver, some of the circuitry is shared by the transmitting and receiving functions of the device. So is the antenna. This saves space and the number of components used. Transceivers are half duplex systems where communication can occur in both directions but only one party can speak while the other must listen. VHF aircraft communication radios are usually transceivers. *[Figure 11-86]*

Antennas

As stated, antennas are conductors that are used to transmit and receive radio frequency waves. Although the airframe technician has limited duties in relation to maintaining and repairing avionics, it is the responsibility of the technician to install, inspect, repair, and maintain aircraft radio antennas.

Three characteristics are of major concern when considering antennas:

1. Length
2. Polarization
3. Directivity

The exact shape and material from which an antenna is made can alter its transmitting and receiving characteristics. Also note that some non-metallic aircraft have antennas imbedded into the composite material as it is built up.

Length

When an AC signal is applied to an antenna, it has a certain frequency. There is a corresponding wavelength for that frequency. An antenna that is half the length of this wavelength is resonant. During each phase of the applied AC, all voltage and current values experience the full range of their variability. As a result, an antenna that is half the wavelength of the corresponding AC frequency is able to allow full voltage and full current flow for the positive phase of the AC signal in one direction. The negative phase of the full AC sign wave is accommodated by the voltage and current simply changing direction in the conductor. Thus, the applied AC frequency flows through its entire wavelength, first in one direction and then in the other. This produces the strongest signal to be radiated by the transmitting antenna. It also facilitates capture of the wave and maximum induced voltage in the receiving antenna. *[Figure 11-87]*

Figure 11-86. *VHF aircraft communication transceivers.*

Figure 11-87. *An antenna equal to the full length of the applied AC frequency wavelength would have the negative cycle current flow along the antenna as shown by the dotted line. An antenna that is ½ wavelength allows current to reverse its direction in the antenna during the negative cycle. This results in low current at the ends of the ½ wavelength antenna and high current in the center. As energy radiates into space, the field is strongest 90° to the antenna where the current flow is strongest.*

Most radios, especially communication radios, use the same antenna for transmitting and receiving. Multichannel radios could use a different length antenna for each frequency, however, this is impractical. Acceptable performance can exist from a single antenna half the wavelength of a median frequency. This antenna can be made effectively shorter by placing a properly rated capacitor in series with the transmission line from the transmitter or receiver. This electrically shortens the resonant circuit of which the antenna is a part. An antenna may be electrically lengthened by adding an inductor in the circuit. Adjusting antenna length in this fashion allows the use of a single antenna for multiple frequencies in a narrow frequency range.

Many radios use a tuning circuit to adjust the effective length of the antenna to match the wavelength of the desired frequency. It contains a variable capacitor and an inductor connected in parallel in a circuit. Newer radios use a more efficient tuning circuit. It uses switches to combine frequencies from crystal controlled circuits to create a resonant frequency that matches the desired frequency. Either way, the physical antenna length is a compromise when using a multichannel communication or navigation device that must be electronically tuned for the best performance.

A formula can be used to find the ideal length of a half wavelength antenna required for a particular frequency as follows:

$$\text{Antenna Length (feet)} = \frac{468}{F \text{ MHz}}$$

The formula is derived from the speed of propagation of radio waves, which is approximately 300 million meters per second. It takes into account the dielectric effect of the air at the end of an antenna that effectively shortens the length of the conductor required.

VHF radio frequencies used by aircraft communication radios are 118–136.975 MHz. The corresponding half wavelengths of these frequencies are 3.96 – 3.44 feet (47.5–41.2 inches). Therefore, VHF antennas are relatively long. Antennas one-quarter of the wavelength of the transmitted frequency are often used. This is possible because when mounted on a metal fuselage, a ground plane is formed and the fuselage acts as the missing one-quarter length of the half wavelength antenna. This is further discussed in the following antenna types section.

Polarization, Directivity, and Field Pattern

Antennas are polarized. They radiate and receive in certain patterns and directions. The electric field cause by the voltage in the conductor is parallel to the polarization of an antenna. It is caused by the voltage difference between each end of the antenna. The electromagnetic field component of the radio wave is at 90° to the polarization. It is caused by changing current flow in the antenna. These fields were illustrated in *Figure 11-76* and *11-77*. As radio waves radiate out from the antenna they propagate in a specific direction and in a specific pattern. This is the antenna field. The orientation of the electric and electromagnetic fields remains at 90° to each other, but radiate from antenna with varying strength in different directions. The strength of the radiated field varies depending on the type of antenna and the angular proximity to it. All antennas, even those that are omnidirectional, radiate a stronger signal in some direction compared to other directions. This is known as the antenna field directivity.

Receiving antennas with the same polarization as the transmitting antenna generate the strongest signal. A vertically polarized antenna is mounted up and down. It radiates waves out from it in all directions. To receive the strongest signal from these waves, the receiving antenna should also be positioned vertically so the electromagnetic component of the radio wave can cross it at as close to a 90° angle as possible for most of the possible proximities. *[Figure 11-88]*

Horizontally polarized antennas are mounted side to side (horizontally). They radiate in a donut-like field. The strongest signals come from, or are received at, 90° to the length of the antenna. There is no field generated off of the end of the antenna. *Figure 11-89* illustrates the field produced by a horizontally polarized antenna.

Many vertical and horizontal antennas on aircraft are mounted at a slight angle off plane. This allows the antenna to receive a weak signal rather than no signal at all when the

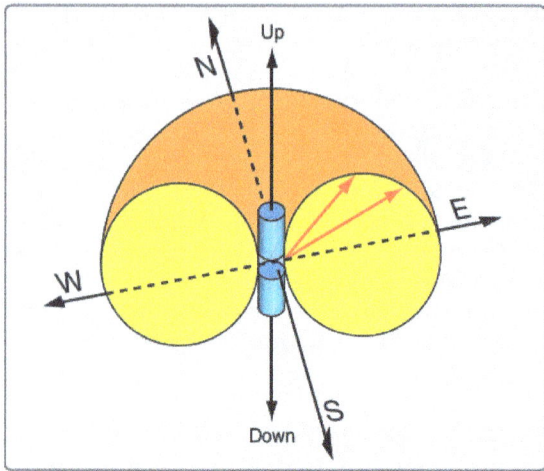

Figure 11-88. *A vertically polarized antenna radiates radio waves in a donut-like pattern in all directions.*

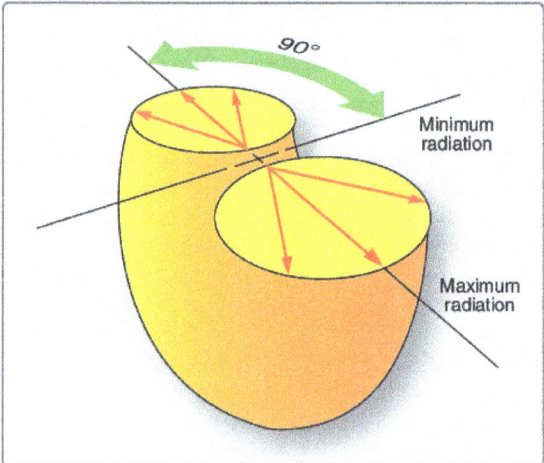

Figure 11-89. *A horizontally polarized antenna radiates in a donut-like pattern. The strongest signal is at 90° to the length of the conductor.*

polarization of the receiving antenna is not identical to the transmitting antenna. *[Figure 11-90]*

Types

There are three basic types of antennas used in aviation:

1. Dipole antenna
2. Marconi antenna
3. Loop antenna.

Dipole Antenna

The dipole antenna is the type of antenna referred to in the discussion of how a radio wave is produced. It is a conductor, the length of which is approximately equal to half the

Figure 11-90. *Many antenna are canted for better reception.*

wavelength of the transmission frequency. This sometimes is referred to as a Hertz antenna. The AC transmission current is fed to a dipole antenna in the center. As the current alternates, current flow is greatest in the middle of the antenna and gradually less as it approaches the ends. Then, it changes direction and flows the other way. The result is that the largest electromagnetic field is in the middle of the antenna and the strongest radio wave field is perpendicular to the length of the antenna. Most dipole antennas in aviation are horizontally polarized.

A common dipole antenna is the V-shaped VHF navigation antenna, known as a VOR antenna, found on numerous aircraft. Each arm of the V is one-fourth wavelength creating a half wave antenna which is fed in the center. This antenna is horizontally polarized. For a dipole receiving antenna, this means it is most sensitive to signals approaching the antenna from the sides rather than head-on in the direction of flight. *[Figure 11-91]*

Marconi Antenna

A Marconi antenna is a one-fourth wave antenna. It achieves the efficiency of a half wave antenna by using the mounting surface of the conductive aircraft skin to create the second one-fourth wavelength. Most aircraft VHF communications antennas are Marconi antennas. They are vertically polarized and create a field that is omnidirectional. On fabric skinned

Figure 11-91. *The V-shaped VOR navigation antenna is a common dipole antenna.*

aircraft, the ground plane that makes up the second one-fourth wavelength of the antenna must be fashioned under the skin where the Marconi antenna is mounted. This can be done with thin aluminum or aluminum foil. Sometimes four or more wires are extended under the skin from the base of the vertical antenna that serve as the ground plane. This is enough to give the antenna the proper conductive length. The same practice is also utilized on ground based antennas. *[Figure 11-92]*

Figure 11-92. *On a metal-skinned aircraft, a ¼ wavelength Marconi antenna is used. The skin is the ground plane that creates the 2nd quarter of the antenna required for resonance (left). On a non-metallic-skinned aircraft, wires, conductive plates or strips equal in length to the antenna must be installed under the skin to create the ground plane (right).*

Loop Antenna

The third type of antenna commonly found on aircraft is the loop antenna. When the length of an antenna conductor is fashioned into a loop, its field characteristics are altered significantly from that of a straight-half wavelength antenna. It also makes the antenna more compact and less prone to damage.

Used as a receiving antenna, the loop antenna's properties are highly direction-sensitive. A radio wave intercepting the loop directly broadside causes equal current flow in both sides of the loop. However, the polarity of the current flows is opposite each other. This causes them to cancel out and produce no signal. When a radio wave strikes the loop antenna in line with the plane of the loop, current is generated first in one side, and then in the other side. This causes the current flows to have different phases and the strongest signal can be generated from this angle. The phase difference (and strength) of the generated current varies proportionally to the angle at which the radio wave strikes the antenna loop. This is useful and is discussed further in the section on automatic direction finder (ADF) navigational aids. *[Figure 11-93]*

Transmission Lines

Transmitters and receivers must be connected to their antenna(s) via conductive wire. These transmission lines are coaxial cable, also known as coax. Coax consists of a center wire conductor surrounded by a semirigid insulator. Surrounding the wire and insulator material is a conductive, braided cover that runs the length of the cable. Finally, a waterproof covering is set around the braided shield to protect the entire assembly from the elements. The braided cover in the coax shields the inner conductor from any external fields. It also prevents the fields generated by the internal conductor from radiating. For optimum performance, the impedance of the transmission line should be equal to the impedance of the antenna. In aviation antenna applications, this is often approximately 50 ohms. *[Figure 11-94]* Special connectors are used for coaxial cable. A variety can be seen in Advisory Circular 43.13-1b. The technician should follow all manufacturer's instructions when installing transmission lines and antenna. Correct installation is critical to radio and antenna performance.

Radio Navigation

In the early years of aviation, a compass, a map, and dead reckoning were the only navigational tools. These were marginally reassuring if weather prevented the pilot from seeing the terrain below. Voice radio transmission from

Figure 11-93. *A loop antenna is highly direction-sensitive. A signal origin perpendicular or broadside to the loop creates a weak signal (A). A signal origin parallel or in the plain of the loop creates a strong signal (B).*

someone on the ground to the pilot indicating that the aircraft could be heard overhead was a preview of what electronic navigational aids could provide. For aviation to reach fruition as a safe, reliable, consistent means of transportation, some sort of navigation system needed to be developed.

Early flight instruments contributed greatly to flying when the ground was obscured by clouds. Navigation aids were needed to indicate where an aircraft was over the earth as it progressed towards its destination. In the 1930s and 1940s, a radio navigation system was used that was a low frequency, four-course radio range system. Airports and selected navigation waypoints broadcast two Morse code signals with finite ranges and patterns. Pilots tuned to the frequency of the broadcasts and flew in an orientation pattern until both signals were received with increasing strength. The signals were received as a blended tone of the highest volume when the aircraft was directly over the broadcast area. From this beginning, numerous refinements to radio navigational aids developed.

Radio navigation aids supply the pilot with intelligence that maintains or enhances the safety of flight. As with communication radios, navigational aids are avionics devices, the repair of which must be carried out by trained technicians at certified repair stations. However, installation, maintenance and proper functioning of the electronic units, as well as their antennas, displays, and any other peripheral devices, are the responsibilities of the airframe technician.

VOR Navigation System

One of the oldest and most useful navigational aids is the VOR system. The system was constructed after WWII and

Figure 11-94. *Coaxial cable is used as the transmission line between an antenna and its transmitters and/or receiver.*

is still in use today. It consists of thousands of land-based transmitter stations, or VORs, that communicate with radio receiving equipment on board aircraft. Many of the VORs are located along airways. The Victor airway system is built around the VOR navigation system. Ground VOR transmitter units are also located at airports where they are known as TVOR (terminal VOR). The U.S. Military has a navigational system known as TACAN that operates similarly to the VOR system. Sometimes VOR and TACAN transmitters share a location. These sites are known as VORTACs.

The position of all VORs, TVORs, and VORTACs are marked on aeronautical charts along with the name of the station, the frequency to which an airborne receiver must be tuned to use the station, and a Morse code designation for the station. Some VORs also broadcast a voice identifier on a separate frequency that is included on the chart. *[Figure 11-95]*

VOR uses VHF radio waves (108–117.95 MHz) with 50 kHz separation between each channel. This keeps atmospheric interference to a minimum but limits the VOR to line-of-sight usage. To receive VOR VHF radio waves, generally a V-shaped, horizontally polarized, bi-pole antenna is used. A typical location for the V dipole is in the vertical fin. Other type antennas are also certified. Follow the manufacturer's instructions for installation location. *[Figure 11-96]*

The signals produced by a VOR transmitter propagate 360° from the unit and are used by aircraft to navigate to and from the station with the help of an onboard VOR receiver and display instruments. A pilot is not required to fly a pattern to intersect the signal from a VOR station since it propagates out in every direction. The radio waves are received as long as the aircraft is in range of the ground unit and regardless of the aircraft's direction of travel. *[Figure 11-97]*

A VOR transmitter produces two signals that a receiver on board an aircraft uses to locate itself in relation to the ground station. One signal is a reference signal. The second is produced by electronically rotating a variable signal. The variable signal is in phase with the reference signal when at magnetic north, but becomes increasingly out of phase as it is rotated to 180°. As it continues to rotate to 360° (0°), the signals become increasingly in phase until they are in phase again at magnetic north. The receiver in the aircraft deciphers the phase difference and determines the aircraft's position in degrees from the VOR ground based unit. *[Figure 11-98]* Most aircraft carry a dual VOR receiver. Sometimes, the VOR receivers are part of the same avionics unit as the VHF communication transceiver(s). These are known as NAV/COM radios. Internal components are shared since frequency bands for each are adjacent. *[Figure 11-99]* Large aircraft may have two dual receivers and even dual antennas. Normally, one receiver is selected for use and the

Figure 11-95. *A VOR ground station.*

Figure 11-96. *V-shaped, horizontally polarized, bi-pole antennas are commonly used for VOR and VOR/glideslope reception. All antenna shown are VOR/glideslope antenna.*

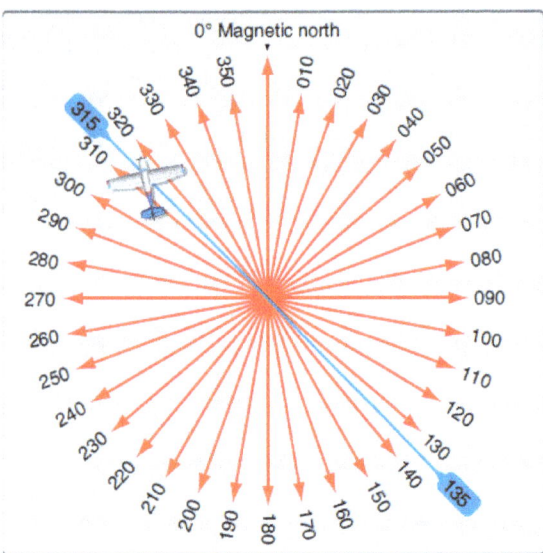

Figure 11-97. *A VOR transmitter produces signals for 360° radials that an airborne receiver uses to indicate the aircraft's location in relation to the VOR station regardless of the aircraft's direction of flight. The aircraft shown is on the 315° radial even though it does not have a heading of 315°.*

second is tuned to the frequency of the next VOR station to be encountered en route. A means for switching between NAV 1 and NAV 2 is provided as is a switch for selecting the active or standby frequency. *[Figure 11-100]* VOR receivers are also found coupled with instrument landing system (ILS) receivers and glideslope receivers.

A VOR receiver interprets the bearing in degrees to (or from) the VOR station where the signals are generated. It also produces DC voltage to drive the display of the deviation from the desired course centerline to (or from) the selected station. Additionally, the receiver decides whether or not the aircraft is flying toward the VOR or away from it. These items can be displayed a number of different ways on various instruments. Older aircraft are often equipped with a VOR gauge dedicated to display only VOR information. This is also called an omni-bearing selector (OBS) or a course deviation indicator (CDI). *[Figure 11-101]*

The CDI linear indicator remains essentially vertical but moves left and right across the graduations on the instrument face to show deviation from being on course. Each graduation represents 2°. The OBS knob rotates the azimuth ring. When in range of a VOR, the pilot rotates the OBS until the course deviation indicator centers. For each location of an aircraft, the OBS can be rotated to two positions where the CDI will center. One produces an arrow in the TO window of the gauge

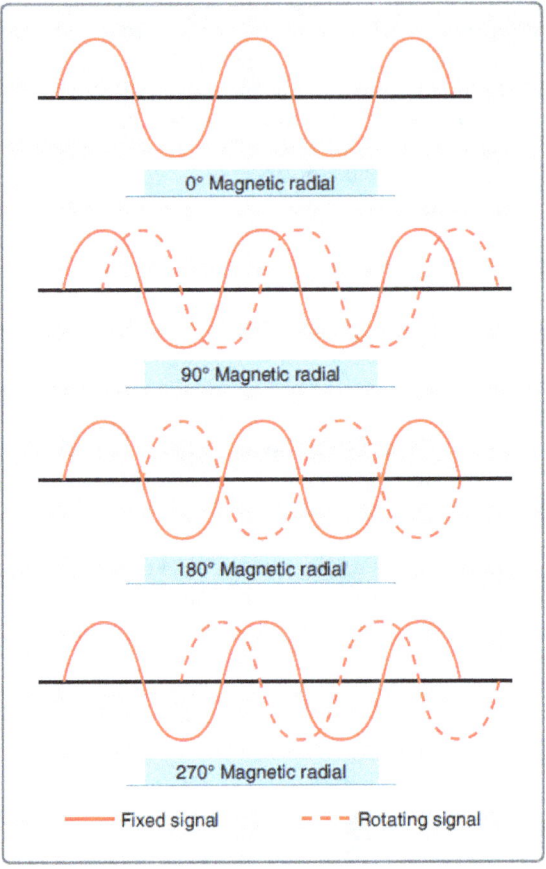

Figure 11-98. *The phase relationship of the two broadcast VOR signals.*

Figure 11-99. *A NAV/COM receiver typically found in light aircraft.*

indicating that the aircraft is traveling toward the VOR station. The other selectable bearing is 180° from this. When chosen, the arrow is displayed in the FROM window indicating the aircraft is moving away from the VOR on the course selected. The pilot must steer the aircraft to the heading with the CDI centered to fly directly to or from the VOR. The displayed VOR information is derived from deciphering the phase relationship between the two simultaneously transmitted signals from the VOR ground station. When power is lost or the VOR signal is weak or interrupted, a NAV warning flag comes into view. *[Figure 11-101]*

Figure 11-100. *An airliner VOR control head with two independent NAV receivers each with an active and standby tuning circuit controlled by a toggle switch.*

Figure 11-101. *A traditional VOR gauge, also known as a course deviation indicator (CDI) or an omni-bearing selector (OBS).*

A separate gauge for the VOR information is not always used. As flight instruments and displays have evolved, VOR navigation information has been integrated into other instruments displays, such as the radio magnetic indicator (RMI), the horizontal situation indicator (HSI), an EFIS display or an electronic attitude director indicator (EADI). Flight management systems and automatic flight control systems are also made to integrate VOR information to automatically control the aircraft on its planned flight segments. Flat panel MFDs integrate VOR information into moving map presentations and other selected displays. The basic information of the radial bearing in degrees, course deviation indication, and to/from information remains unchanged however. *[Figure 11-102]*

Figure 11-102. *A mechanical HSI (left) and an electronic HSI (right) both display VOR information.*

11-45

At large airports, an instrument landing system (ILS) guides the aircraft to the runway while on an instrument landing approach. The aircraft's VOR receiver is used to interpret the radio signals. It produces a more sensitive course deviation indication on the same instrument display as the VOR CDI display. This part of the ILS is known as the localizer and is discussed below. While tuned to the ILS localizer frequency, the VOR circuitry of the VOR/ILS receiver is inactive.

It is common at VOR stations to combine the VOR transmitter with distance measuring equipment (DME) or a nondirectional beacon (NDB) such as an ADF transmitter and antenna. When used with a DME, pilots can gain an exact fix on their location using the VOR and DME together. Since the VOR indicates the aircraft's bearing to the VOR transmitter and a co-located DME indicates how far away the station is, this relieves the pilot from having to fly over the station to know with certainty his or her location. These navigational aids are discussed separately in the following sections.

Functional accuracy of VOR equipment is critical to the safety of flight. VOR receivers are operationally tested using VOR test facilities (VOT). These are located at numerous airports that can be identified in the Airport Facilities Directory for the area concerned. Specific points on the airport surface are given to perform the test. Most VOTs require tuning 108.0 MHz on the VOR receiver and centering the CDI. The OBS should indicate 0° showing FROM on the indicator or 180° when showing TO. If an RMI is used as the indicator, the test heading should always indicate 180°. Some repair stations can also generate signals to test VOR receivers although not on 108.0 MHz. Contact the repair station for the transmission frequency and for their assistance in checking the VOR system. A logbook entry is required.

NOTE: Some airborne testing using VOTs is possible by the pilot.

An error of ±4° should not be exceeded when testing a VOR system with a VOT. An error in excess of this prevents the use of the aircraft for IFR fight until repairs are made. Aircraft having dual VOR systems where only the antenna is shared may be tested by comparing the output of each system to the other. Tune the VOR receivers to the local ground VOR station. A bearing indication difference of no more than ±4° is permissible.

Automatic Direction Finder (ADF)

An automatic direction finder (ADF) operates off of a ground signal transmitted from a NDB. Early radio direction finders (RDF) used the same principle. A vertically polarized antenna was used to transmit LF frequency radio waves in the 190 kHz to 535 kHz range. A receiver on the aircraft was tuned to the transmission frequency of the NDB. Using a loop antenna, the direction to (or from) the antenna could be determined by monitoring the strength of the signal received. This was possible because a radio wave striking a loop antenna broadside induces a null signal. When striking it in the plane of the loop, a much stronger signal is induced. The NDB signals were modulated with unique Morse code pulses that enabled the pilot to identify the beacon to which he or she was navigating.

With RDF systems, a large rigid loop antenna was installed inside the fuselage of the aircraft. The broadside of the antenna was perpendicular to the aircraft's longitudinal axis. The pilot listened for variations in signal strength of the LF broadcast and maneuvered the aircraft so a gradually increasing null signal was maintained. This took them to the transmitting antenna. When over flown, the null signal gradually faded as the aircraft became farther from the station. The increasing or decreasing strength of the null signal was the only way to determine if the aircraft was flying to or from the NDB. A deviation left or right from the course caused the signal strength to sharply increase due to the loop antenna's receiving properties.

The ADF improved on this concept. The broadcast frequency range was expanded to include MF up to about 1800 kHz. The heading of the aircraft no longer needed to be changed to locate the broadcast transmission antenna. In early model ADFs, a rotatable antenna was used instead. The antenna rotated to seek the position in which the signal was null. The direction to the broadcast antenna was shown on an azimuth scale of an ADF indicator in the flight deck. This type of instrument is still found in use today. It has a fixed card with 0° always at the top of a non-rotating dial. A pointer indicates the relative bearing to the station. When the indication is 0°, the aircraft is on course to (or from) the station. *[Figure 11-103]*

As ADF technology progressed, indicators with rotatable azimuth cards became the norm. When an ADF signal is received, the pilot rotates the card so that the present heading is at the top of the scale. This results in the pointer indicating the magnetic bearing to the ADF transmitter. This is more intuitive and consistent with other navigational practices. *[Figure 11-104]*

In modern ADF systems, an additional antenna is used to remove the ambiguity concerning whether the aircraft is heading to or from the transmitter. It is called a sense antenna. The reception field of the sense antenna is omnidirectional. When combined with the fields of the loop antenna, it forms a field with a single significant null reception area on one side. This is used for tuning and produces an indication in the

Figure 11-103. *Older ADF indicators have nonrotating azimuth cards. 0° is fixed at the top of the instrument and the pointer always indicates the relative bearing to the ADF transmission antenna. To fly to the station, the pilot turns the aircraft until the ADF pointer indicates 0°.*

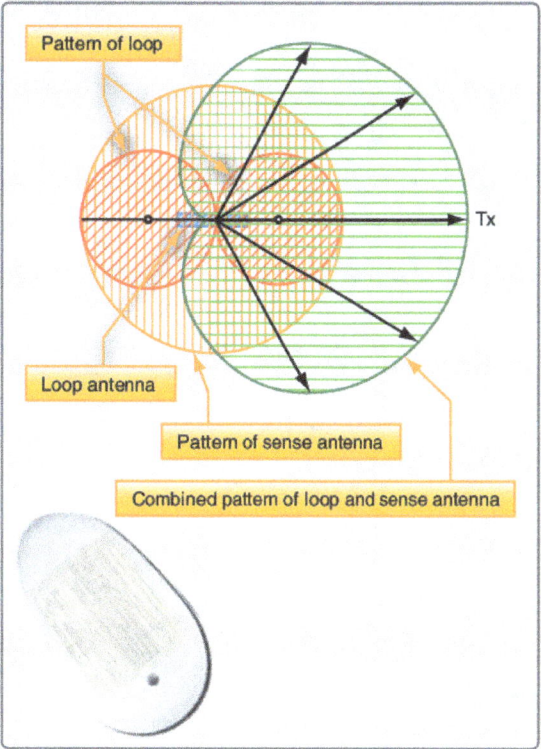

Figure 11-105. *The reception fields of a loop and sense antenna combine to create a field with a sharp null on just one side. This removes directional ambiguity when navigating to an ADF station.*

Any ground antenna transmitting LF or MF radio waves in range of the aircraft receiver's tuning capabilities can be used for ADF. This includes those from AM radio stations. Audible identifier tones are loaded on the NDB carrier waves. Typically a two-character Morse code designator is used. With an AM radio station transmission, the AM broadcast is heard instead of a station identifier code. The frequency for an NDB transmitter is given on an aeronautical chart next to a symbol for the transmitter. The identifying designator is also given. *[Figure 11-106]*

Figure 11-104. *A movable card ADF indicator can be rotated to put the aircraft's heading at the top of the scale. The pointer then points to the magnetic bearing the ADF broadcast antenna.*

direction toward the ADF station at all times. The onboard ADF receiver needs only to be tuned to the correct frequency of the broadcast transmitter for the system to work. The loop and sense antenna are normally housed in a single, low profile antenna housing. *[Figure 11-105]*

ADF receivers can be mounted in the flight deck with the controls accessible to the user. This is found on many general aviation aircraft. Alternately, the ADF receiver is mounted in a remote avionics bay with only the control head in the flight deck. Dual ADF receivers are common. ADF information can be displayed on the ADF indicators mentioned or it can be digital. Modern, flat, multipurpose electronic displays usually display the ADF digitally. *[Figure 11-107]* When ANT is selected on an ADF receiver, the loop antenna is cut out and only the sense antenna is active. This provides better multi-directional reception of broadcasts in the ADF frequency range, such as weather or AWAS broadcasts.

Figure 11-106. *Nondirectional broadcast antenna in the LF and medium frequency range are used for ADF navigation.*

When the best frequency oscillator (BFO) is selected on an ADF receiver/controller, an internal beat frequency oscillator is connected to the IF amplifier inside the ADF receiver. This is used when an NDB does not transmit a modulated signal.

Continued refinements to ADF technology has brought it to its current state. The rotating receiving antenna is replaced by a fixed loop with a ferrite core. This increases sensitivity and allows a smaller antenna to be used. The most modern ADF systems have two loop antennas mounted at 90° to each other. The received signal induces voltage that is sent to two stators in a resolver or goniometer. The goniometer stators induce voltage in a rotor that correlates to the signal of the fixed loops. The rotor is driven by a motor to seek the null. The same motor rotates the pointer in the flight deck indicator to show the relative or magnetic bearing to the station. *[Figure 11-108]*

Figure 11-108. *In modern ADF, a rotor in a goniometer replaces a the rotating loop antenna used in earlier models.*

Technicians should note that the installation of the ADF antenna is critical to a correct indication since it is a directional device. Calibration with the longitudinal axis of the fuselage or nose of the aircraft is important. A single null reception area must exist in the correct direction. The antenna must be oriented so the ADF indicates station location when the aircraft is flying toward it rather than away. Follow all manufacturer's instructions.

Radio Magnetic Indicator (RMI)

To save space in the instrument panel and to consolidate related information into one easy to use location, the radio magnetic indicator (RMI) has been developed. It is widely used. The

Figure 11-107. *A cockpit mountable ADF receiver used on general aviation aircraft.*

RMI combines indications from a magnetic compass, VOR, and ADF into one instrument. *[Figure 11-109]*

Figure 11-109. *A radio magnetic indicator (RMI) combines a magnetic compass, VOR, and ADF indications.*

The azimuth card of the RMI is rotated by a remotely located flux gate compass. Thus, the magnetic heading of the aircraft is always indicated. The lubber line is usually a marker or triangle at the top of the instrument dial. The VOR receiver drives the solid pointer to indicate the magnetic direction TO a tuned VOR station. When the ADF is tuned to an NDB, the double, or hollow pointer, indicates the magnetic bearing to the NDB.

Since the flux gate compass continuously adjusts the azimuth card so that the aircraft heading is at the top of the instrument, pilot workload is reduced. The pointers indicate where the VOR and ADF transmission stations are located in relationship to where the aircraft is currently positioned. Push buttons allow conversion of either pointer to either ADF or VOR for navigation involving two of one type of station and none of the other.

Instrument Landing Systems (ILS)

An ILS is used to land an aircraft when visibility is poor. This radio navigation system guides the aircraft down a slope to the touch down area on the runway. Multiple radio transmissions are used that enable an exact approach to landing with an ILS. A localizer is one of the radio transmissions. It is used to provide horizontal guidance to the center line of the runway. A separate glideslope broadcast provides vertical guidance of the aircraft down the proper slope to the touch down point. Compass locator transmissions for outer and middle approach marker beacons aid the pilot in intercepting the approach navigational aid system. Marker beacons provide distance-from-the-runway information. Together, all of these radio signals make an ILS a very accurate and reliable means for landing aircraft. *[Figure 11-110]*

Localizer

The localizer broadcast is a VHF broadcast in the lower range of the VOR frequencies (108 MHz–111.95 MHz) on odd frequencies only. Two modulated signals are produced from a horizontally polarized antenna complex beyond the far end of the approach runway. They create an expanding field that is 2½° wide (about 1,500 feet) 5 miles from the runway. The field tapers to runway width near the landing threshold. The left side of the approach area is filled with a VHF carrier wave modulated with a 90 Hz signal. The right side of the approach contains a 150 MHz modulated signal. The aircraft's VOR receiver is tuned to the localizer VHF frequency that can be found on published approach plates and aeronautical charts.

The circuitry specific to standard VOR reception is inactive while the receiver uses localizer circuitry and components common to both. The signals received are passed through filters and rectified into DC to drive the course deviation indicator. If the aircraft receives a 150 Hz signal, the CDI of the VOR/ILS display deflects to the left. This indicates that the runway is to the left. The pilot must correct course with a turn to the left. This centers course deviation indicator on the display and centers the aircraft with the centerline of the runway. If the 90 Hz signal is received by the VOR receiver, the CDI deflects to the right. The pilot must turn toward the right to center the CDI and the aircraft with the runway center line. *[Figure 11-111]*

Glideslope

The vertical guidance required for an aircraft to descend for a landing is provided by the glideslope of the ILS. Radio signals funnel the aircraft down to the touchdown point on the runway at an angle of approximately 3°. The transmitting glideslope antenna is located off to the side of the approach runway approximately 1,000 feet from the threshold. It transmits in a wedge-like pattern with the field narrowing as it approaches the runway. *[Figure 11-112]*

The glideslope transmitter antenna is horizontally polarized. The transmitting frequency range is UHF between 329.3 MHz and 335.0 MHz. The frequency is paired to the localizer frequency of the ILS. When the VOR/ILS receiver is tuned for the approach, the glideslope receiver is automatically tuned. Like the localizer, the glideslope transmits two signals, one modulated at 90 Hz and the other modulated at 150

Figure 11-110. *Components of an instrument landing system (ILS).*

Figure 11-111. *An ILS localizer antenna.*

Figure 11-112. *A glideslope antenna broadcasts radio signals to guide an aircraft vertically to the runway.*

Hz. The aircraft's glideslope receiver deciphers the signals similar to the method of the localizer receiver. It drives a vertical course deviation indicator known as the glideslope indicator. The glideslope indicator operates identically to the localizer CDI only 90° to it. The VOR/ILS localizer CDI and the glideslope are displayed together on whichever kind of instrumentation is in the aircraft. *[Figure 11-113]*

The UHF antenna for aircraft reception of the glideslope signals comes in many forms. A single dipole antenna mounted inside the nose of the aircraft is a common option. Antenna manufacturers have also incorporated glideslope reception into the same dipole antenna used for the VHS VOR/ILS localizer reception. Blade type antennas are also used. *[Figures 11-114] Figure 11-115* shows a VOR and a glideslope receiver for a GA aircraft ILS.

Compass Locators

It is imperative that a pilot be able to intercept the ILS to enable its use. A compass locator is a transmitter designed for this purpose. There is typically one located at the outer marker beacon 4-7 miles from the runway threshold. Another may be located at the middle marker beacon about 3,500 feet from the threshold. The outer marker compass locator is a 25 watt **NDB** with a range of about 15 miles. It transmits omnidirectional LF radio waves (190 Hz to 535 Hz) keyed with the first two letters of the ILS identifier. The ADF

Figure 11-113. *A traditional course deviation indicator is shown on the left. The horizontal white line is the deviation indicator for the glideslope. The vertical line is for the localizer. On the right, a Garmin G-1000 PFD illustrates an aircraft during an ILS approach. The narrow vertical scale on the right of the attitude indicator with the "G" at the top is the deviation scale for the glideslope. The green diamond moves up and down to reflect the aircraft being above or below the glidepath. The diamond is shown centered indicating the aircraft is on course vertically. The localizer CDI can be seen at the bottom center of the display. It is the center section of the vertical green course indicator. LOC1 is displayed to the left of it.*

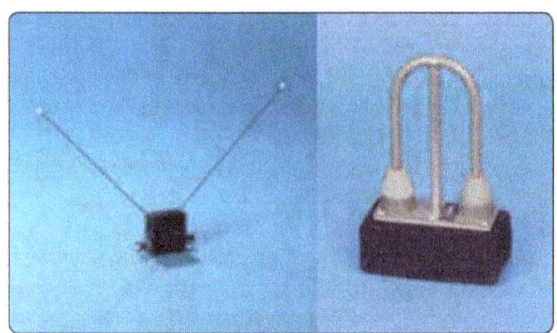

Figure 11-114. *Glideslope antennas—designed to be mounted inside a non-metallic aircraft nose (left), and mounted inside or outside the aircraft (right).*

receiver is used to intercept the locator so no additional equipment is required. If a middle marker compass locator is in place, it is similar but is identified with the last two letters of the ILS identifier. Once located, the pilot maneuvers the aircraft to fly down the glidepath to the runway.

Marker Beacons

Marker beacons are the final radio transmitters used in the ILS. They transmit signals that indicate the position of the aircraft along the glidepath to the runway. As mentioned, an outer marker beacon transmitter is located 4–7 miles from the threshold. It transmits a 75 MHz carrier wave modulated with a 400 Hz audio tone in a series of dashes. The transmission is very narrow and directed straight up. A marker beacon receiver receives the signal and uses it to light a blue light on the instrument panel. This, plus the oral tone in combination with the localizer and the glideslope indicator, positively locates the aircraft on an approach. *[Figure 11-115]*

Figure 11-115. *A localizer and glideslope receiver for a general aviation aircraft ILS.*

A middle marker beacon is also used. It is located on approach approximately 3,500 feet from the runway. It also transmits at 75 MHz. The middle marker transmission is modulated with a 1300 Hz tone that is a series of dots and dashes so as to not be confused with the all dash tone of the outer marker. When the signal is received, it is used in the receiver to illuminate an amber-colored light on the instrument panel. *[Figure 11-116]*

Figure 11-116. *Various marker beacon instrument panel display lights.*

Some ILS approaches have an inner marker beacon that transmits a signal modulated with 3000 Hz in a series of dots only. It is placed at the land-or-go-around decision point of the approach close to the runway threshold. If present, the signal when received is used to illuminate a white light on the instrument panel. The three marker beacon lights are usually incorporated into the audio panel of a general aviation aircraft or may exist independently on a larger aircraft. Electronic display aircraft usually incorporate marker lights or indicators close to the glideslope display near attitude director indicator. *[Figure 11-117]*

ILS radio components can be tested with an ILS test unit. Localizer, glideslope, and marker beacon signals are generated to ensure proper operation of receivers and correct display on flight deck instruments. *[Figure 11-118]*

Distance Measuring Equipment (DME)

Many VOR stations are co-located with the military version of the VOR station, which is known as TACAN. When this occurs, the navigation station is known as a VORTAC station. Civilian aircraft make use of one of the TACAN features not originally installed at civilian VOR stations–distance measuring equipment (DME). A DME system calculates the distance from the aircraft to the DME unit at the VORTAC ground station and displays it on the flight deck. It can also display calculated aircraft speed and elapsed time for arrival when the aircraft is traveling to the station.

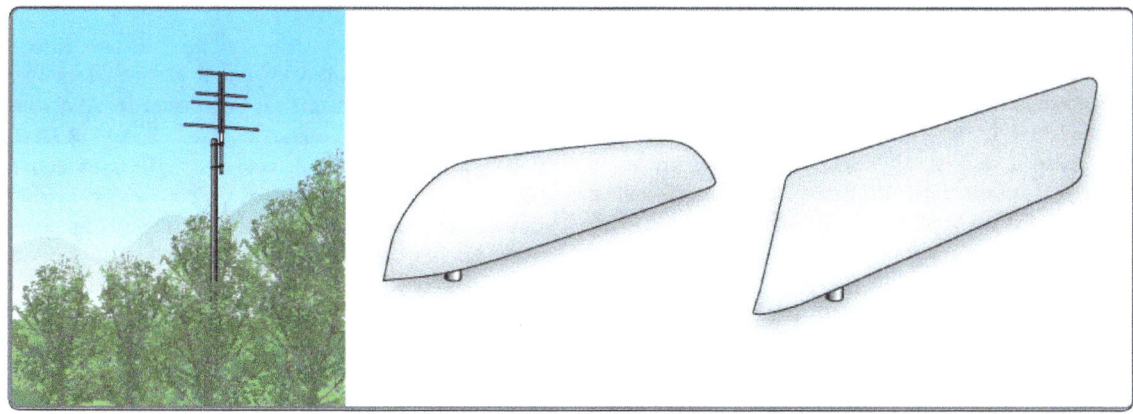

Figure 11-117. *An outer marker transmitter antenna 4–7 miles from the approach runway transmits a 75 MHz signal straight up (left). Aircraft mounted marker beacon receiver antennas are shown (center and right).*

Figure 11-118. *An ILS test unit.*

DME ground stations have subsequently been installed at civilian VORs, as well as in conjunction with ILS localizers. These are known as VOR/DME and ILS/DME or LOC/DME. The latter aid in approach to the runway during landings. The DME system consists of an airborne DME transceiver, display, and antenna, as well as the ground based DME unit and its antenna. *[Figure 11-119]*

Figure 11-119. *A VOR with DME ground station.*

The DME is useful because with the bearing (from the VOR) and the distance to a known point (the DME antenna at the VOR), a pilot can positively identify the location of the aircraft. DME operates in the UHF frequency range from 962 MHz to 1213 MHz. A carrier signal transmitted from the aircraft is modulated with a string of integration pulses. The ground unit receives the pulses and returns a signal to the aircraft. The time that transpires for the signal to be sent and returned is calculated and converted into nautical miles for display. Time to station and speed are also calculated and displayed. DME readout can be on a dedicated DME display or it can be part of an EHSI, EADI, EFIS, or on the primary flight display in a glass cockpit. *[Figure 11-120]*

Figure 11-120. *Distance information from the DME can be displayed on a dedicated DME instrument or integrated into any of the electronic navigational displays found on modern aircraft. A dual display DME is shown with its remote mounted receiver.*

The DME frequency is paired to the co-located VOR or VORTAC frequency. When the correct frequency is tuned for the VOR signal, the DME is tuned automatically. Tones are broadcast for the VOR station identification and then for the DME. The hold selector on a DME panel keeps the DME tuned in while the VOR selector is tuned to a different VOR. In most cases, the UHF of the DME is transmitted and received via a small blade-type antenna mounted to the underside of the fuselage centerline. *[Figure 11-121]*

Figure 11-121. *A typical aircraft mounted DME antenna.*

A traditional DME displays the distance from the DME transmitter antenna to the aircraft. This is called the slant distance. It is very accurate. However, since the aircraft is at altitude, the distance to the DME ground antenna from a point directly beneath the aircraft is shorter. Some modern DMEs are equipped to calculate this ground distance and display it. *[Figure 11-122]*

Figure 11-122. *Many DME's only display the slant distance, which is the actual distance from the aircraft to the DME station. This is different than the ground distance due to the aircraft being at altitude. Some DMEs compute the ground distance for display.*

Area Navigation (RNAV)

Area navigation (RNAV) is a general term used to describe the navigation from point A to point B without direct over flight of navigational aids, such as VOR stations or ADF nondirectional beacons. It includes VORTAC and VOR/DME based systems, as well as systems of RNAV based around LORAN, GPS, INS, and the FMS of transport category aircraft. However, until recently, the term RNAV was most commonly used to describe the area navigation or the process of direct flight from point A to point B using VORTAC and VOR/DME based references which are discussed in this section.

All RNAV systems make use of waypoints. A waypoint is a designated geographical location or point used for route definition or progress-reporting purposes. It can be defined or described by using latitude/longitude grid coordinates or, in the case of VOR based RNAV, described as a point on a VOR radial followed by that point's distance from the VOR station (i.e., 200/25 means a point 25 nautical miles from the VOR station on the 200° radial).

Figure 11-123 illustrates an RNAV route of flight from airport A to airport B. The VOR/DME and VORTAC stations shown are used to create phantom waypoints that are overflown rather than the actual stations. This allows a more direct route to be taken. The phantom waypoints are entered into the RNAV course-line computer (CLC) as a radial and distance number pair. The computer creates the waypoints and causes the aircraft's CDI to operate as though they are actual VOR stations. A mode switch allows the choice between standard VOR navigation and RNAV.

VOR based RNAV uses the VOR receiver, antenna, and VOR display equipment, such as the CDI. The computer in the RNAV unit uses basic geometry and trigonometry calculations to produce heading, speed, and time readouts for each waypoint. VOR stations need to be within line-of-sight and operational range from the aircraft for RNAV use. *[Figure 11-124]*

RNAV has increased in flexibility with the development of GPS. Integration of GPS data into a planned VOR RNAV flight plan is possible as is GPS route planning without the use of any VOR stations.

Radar Beacon Transponder

A radar beacon transponder, or simply, a transponder, provides positive identification and location of an aircraft on the radar screens of ATC. For each aircraft equipped with an altitude encoder, the transponder also provides the pressure altitude of the aircraft to be displayed adjacent to the on-screen blip that represents the aircraft. *[Figure 11-125]*

Figure 11-123. *The pilot uses the aircraft's course deviation indicator to fly to and from RNAV phantom waypoints created by computer. This allows direct routes to be created and flown rather than flying from VOR to VOR.*

Figure 11-124. *RNAV unit from a general aviation aircraft.*

Radar capabilities at airports vary. Generally, two types of radar are used by air traffic control (ATC). The primary radar transmits directional UHF or SHF radio waves sequentially in all directions. When the radio waves encounter an aircraft, part of those waves reflect back to a ground antenna. Calculations are made in a receiver to determine the direction and distance of the aircraft from the transmitter. A blip or target representing the aircraft is displayed on a radar screen also known as a plan position indicator (PPI). The azimuth direction and scaled distance from the tower are presented giving controllers a two dimensional fix on the aircraft. *[Figure 11-126]*

A secondary surveillance radar (SSR) is used by ATC to verify the aircraft's position and to add the third dimension of altitude to its location. SSD radar transmits coded pulse trains that are received by the transponder on board the aircraft. Mode 3/A pulses, as they are known, aid in confirming the location of the aircraft. When verbal communication is established with ATC, a pilot is instructed to select one of 4,096 discrete codes on the transponder. These are digital octal codes. The ground station transmits a pulse of energy at 1030 MHz and the transponder transmits a reply with the assigned code attached at 1090 MHz. This confirms the aircraft's location typically by altering its target symbol on the radar screen. As the screen may be filled with many confirmed aircraft, ATC can also ask the pilot to ident. By pressing the IDENT button on the transponder, it transmits in such a way that the aircraft's target symbol is highlighted on the PPI to be distinguishable.

To gain altitude clarification, the transponder control must be placed in the ALT or Mode C position. The signal transmitted back to ATC in response to pulse interrogation is then modified with a code that places the pressure altitude of the aircraft next to the target symbol on the radar screen. The transponder gets the pressure altitude of the aircraft

Figure 11-125. *A traditional transponder control head (A), a lightweight digital transponder (B), and a remote altitude encoder (C) that connects to a transponder to provide ATC with an aircraft's altitude displayed on a PPI radar screen next to the target that represents the aircraft.*

Figure 11-126. *A plan position indicator (PPI) for ATC primary radar locates target aircraft on a scaled field.*

from an altitude encoder that is electrically connected to the transponder. Typical aircraft transponder antennas are illustrated in *Figure 11-127*.

The ATC/aircraft transponder system described is known as Air Traffic Control Radar Beacon System (ATCRBS). To increase safety, Mode S altitude response has been developed. With Mode S, each aircraft is pre-assigned a unique identity code that displays along with its pressure altitude on ATC radar when the transponder responds to SSR interrogation. Since no other aircraft respond with this code, the chance of two pilots selecting the same response code on the transponder is eliminated. A modern flight data processor computer (FDP) assigns the beacon code and searches flight plan data for useful information to be displayed on screen next to the target in a data block for each aircraft. *[Figure 11-128]*

Mode S is sometimes referred to as mode select. It is a data packet protocol that is also used in onboard collision avoidance systems. When used by ATC, Mode S interrogates one aircraft at a time. Transponder workload is reduced by not having to respond to all interrogations in an airspace. Additionally, location information is more accurate with Mode S. A single reply in which the phase of the transponder reply is used to calculate position, called monopulse, is sufficient to locate the aircraft. Mode S also contains capacity

Figure 11-127. *Aircraft radar beacon transponder antennas transmit and receive UHF and SHF radio waves.*

Figure 11-128. *Air traffic control radar technology and an onboard radar beacon transponder work together to convey and display air traffic information on a PPI radar screen. A modern approach ATC PPI is shown. Targets representing aircraft are shown as little aircraft on the screen. The nose of the aircraft indicates the direction of travel. Most targets shown above are airliners. The data block for each target includes the following information either transmitted by the transponder or matched and loaded from flight plans by a flight data processor computer: call sign, altitude/speed, origination/destination, and aircraft type/ETA (ZULU time). A "C" after the altitude indicates the information came from a Mode C equipped transponder. The absence of a C indicates Mode S is in use. An arrow up indicates the aircraft is climbing. An arrow down indicates a descent. White targets are arrivals, light blue targets are departures, all other colors are for arrivals and departures to different airports in the area.*

for a wider variety of information exchange that is untapped potential for the future. At the same time, compatibility with older radar and transponder technology has been maintained.

Transponder Tests and Inspections

Title 14 of the Code of Federal Regulations (CFR) part 91, section 91.413 states that all transponders on aircraft flown into controlled airspace are required to be inspected and tested in accordance with 14 CFR part 43, Appendix F, every 24 calendar months. Installation or maintenance that may introduce a transponder error is also cause for inspection and test in accordance with Appendix F. Only an appropriately rated repair station, the aircraft manufacturer (if it installed transponder), and holders of a continuous airworthy program are approved to conduct the procedures. As with many radio-electronic devices, test equipment exists to test airworthy operation of a transponder. *[Figure 11-129]*

Figure 11-129. *A handheld transponder test unit.*

Operating a transponder in a hangar or on the ramp does not immunize it from interrogation and reply. Transmission of certain codes reserved for emergencies or military activity must be avoided. The procedure to select a code during ground operation is to do so with the transponder in the OFF or STANDBY mode to avoid inadvertent transmission. Code 0000 is reserved for military use and is a transmittable code. Code 7500 is used in a hijack situation and 7600 and 7700 are also reserved for emergency use. Even the inadvertent transmission of code 1200 reserved for VFR flight not under ATC direction could result in evasion action. All signals received from a radar beacon transponder are taken seriously by ATC.

Altitude Encoders

Altitude encoders convert the aircraft's pressure altitude into a code sent by the transponder to ATC. Increments of 100 feet are usually reported. Encoders have varied over the years. Some are built into the altimeter instrument used in the instrument panel and connected by wires to the transponder. Others are mounted out of sight on an avionics rack or similar out of the way place. These are known as blind encoders. On transport category aircraft, the altitude encoder may be a large black box with a static line connection to an internal aneroid. Modern general aviation encoders are smaller and more lightweight, but still often feature an internal aneroid and static line connection. Some encoders use microtransistors and are completely solid-state including the pressure sensing device from which the altitude is derived. No static port connection is required. Data exchange with GPS and other systems is becoming common. *[Figure 11-130]*

Figure 11-130. *Modern altitude encoders for general aviation aircraft.*

When a transponder selector is set on ALT, the digital pulse message sent in response to the secondary surveillance radar interrogation becomes the digital representation of the pressure altitude of the aircraft. There are 1280 altitude codes, one for each 100 feet of altitude between 1200 feet mean sea level (MSL) and 126,700 feet MSL. Each altitude increment is assigned a code. While these would be 1280 of the same codes used for location and IDENT, the Mode C (or S) interrogation deactivates the 4096 location codes and causes the encoder to become active. The correct altitude code is sent to the transponder that replies to the interrogation. The SSR receiver recognized this as a response to a Mode C (or S) interrogation and interprets the code as altitude code.

Collision Avoidance Systems

The ever increasing volume of air traffic has caused a corresponding increase in concern over collision avoidance. Ground-based radar, traffic control, and visual vigilance are no longer adequate in today's increasingly crowded skies. Onboard collision avoidance equipment, long a staple in larger aircraft, is now common in general aviation aircraft. New applications of electronic technology combined with lower costs make this possible.

Traffic Collision Avoidance Systems (TCAS)

Traffic collision avoidance systems (TCAS) are transponder based air-to-air traffic monitoring and alerting systems. There are two classes of TCAS. TCAS I was developed to accommodate the general aviation community and regional airlines. This system identifies traffic in a 35–40 mile range of the aircraft and issues Traffic Advisories (TA) to assist pilots in visual acquisition of intruder aircraft. TCAS I is mandated on aircraft with 10 to 30 seats.

TCAS II is a more sophisticated system. It is required internationally in aircraft with more than 30 seats or weighing more than 15,000 kg. TCAS II provides the information of TCAS I, but also analyzes the projected flightpath of approaching aircraft. If a collision or near miss is imminent, the TCAS II computer issues a Resolution Advisory (RA). This is an aural command to the pilot to take a specific evasive action (i.e., DESCEND). The computer is programmed such that the pilot in the encroaching aircraft receives an RA for evasive action in the opposite direction (if it is TCAS II equipped). *[Figure 11-131]*

Figure 11-131. *Traffic collision and avoidance system (TCAS) uses an aircraft's transponder to interrogate and receive replies from other aircraft in close proximity. The TCAS computer alerts the pilot as to the presence of an intruder aircraft and displays the aircraft on a screen in the cockpit. Additionally, TCAS II equipped aircraft receive evasive maneuver commands from the computer that calculates trajectories of the aircraft to predict potential collisions or near misses before they become unavoidable.*

The transponder of an aircraft with TCAS is able to interrogate the transponders of other aircraft nearby using SSR technology (Mode C and Mode S). This is done with a 1030 MHz signal. Interrogated aircraft transponders reply with an encoded 1090 MHz signal that allows the TCAS computer to display the position and altitude of each aircraft. Should the aircraft come within the horizontal or vertical distances shown in *Figure 11-131*, an audible TA is announced. The pilot must decide whether to take action and what action to take. TCAS II equipped aircraft use continuous reply information to analyze the speed and trajectory of target aircraft in close proximity. If a collision is calculated to be imminent, an RA is issued.

TCAS target aircraft are displayed on a screen on the flight deck. Different colors and shapes are used to depict approaching aircraft depending on the imminent threat level. Since RAs are currently limited to vertical evasive maneuvers, some stand-alone TCAS displays are electronic vertical speed indicators. Most aircraft use some version of an electronic HSI on a navigational screen or page to display TCAS information. *[Figure 11-132]* A multifunction display may depict TCAS and weather radar information on the same screen. *[Figure 11-133]* A TCAS control panel *[Figure 11-134]* and computer are required to work with a compatible transponder and its antenna(s). Interface with EFIS or other previously installed or selected display(s) is also required.

Figure 11-133. *TCAS information displayed on a multifunction display. An open diamond indicates a target; a solid diamond represents a target that is within 6 nautical miles of 1,2000 feet vertically. A yellow circle represents a target that generates a TA (25-48 seconds before contact). A red square indicates a target that generates an RA in TCAS II (contact within 35 seconds). A (+) indicates the target aircraft is above and a (-) indicates it is below. The arrows show if the target is climbing or descending.*

Figure 11-134. *This control panel from a Boeing 767 controls the transponder for ATC use and TCAS.*

7. The accuracy and reliability of this TCAS information is such that pilots are required to follow a TCAS RA over an ATC command.

ADS-B

Collision avoidance is a significant part of the FAA's NextGen plan for transforming the National Airspace System (NAS). Increasing the number of aircraft using the same quantity of airspace and ground facilities requires the implementation of new technologies to maintain a high level of performance and safety. The successful proliferation of global navigation satellite systems (GNSS), such as GPS, has led to the development of a collision avoidance system

Figure 11-132. *TCAS information displayed on an electronic vertical speed indicator.*

TCAS may be referred to as airborne collision avoidance system (ACAS), which is the international name for the same system. TCAS II with the latest revisions is known as Version known as automatic dependant surveillance broadcast (ADS-B). ADS-B is an integral part of NextGen program. The implementation of its ground and airborne infrastructure is currently underway. ADS-B is active in parts of the United States and around the world. *[Figure 11-135]*

Figure 11-135. *Low power requirements allow remote ADS-B stations with only solar or propane support. This is not possible with ground radar due to high power demands which inhibit remote area radar coverage for air traffic purposes.*

ADS-B is considered in two segments: ADS-B OUT and ADS-B IN. ADS-B OUT combines the positioning information available from a GPS receiver with on-board flight status information, i.e. location including altitude, velocity, and time. It then broadcasts this information to other ADS-B equipped aircraft and ground stations. *[Figure 11-136]*

Two different frequencies are used to carry these broadcasts with data link capability. The first is an expanded use of the 1090 MHz Mode-S transponder protocol known as 1090 ES. The second, largely being introduced as a new broadband solution for general aviation implementation of ADS-B, is at 978 MHz. A 978 universal access transceiver (UAT) is used to accomplish this. An omni-directional antenna is required in addition to the GPS antenna and receiver. Airborne receivers of an ADS-B broadcast use the information to plot the location and movement of the transmitting aircraft on a flight deck display similar to TCAS. *[Figure 11-137]*

Inexpensive ground stations (compared to radar) are constructed in remote and obstructed areas to proliferate ADS-B. Ground stations share information from airborne ADS-B broadcasts with other ground stations that are part of the air traffic management system (ATMS). Data is transferred with no need for human acknowledgement. Microwave and satellite transmissions are used to link the network.

For traffic separation and control, ADS-B has several advantages over conventional ground-based radar. The first is the entire airspace can be covered with a much lower expense. The aging ATC radar system that is in place is expensive to maintain and replace. Additionally, ADS-B provides more accurate information since the vector state is generated from the aircraft with the help of GPS satellites. Weather is

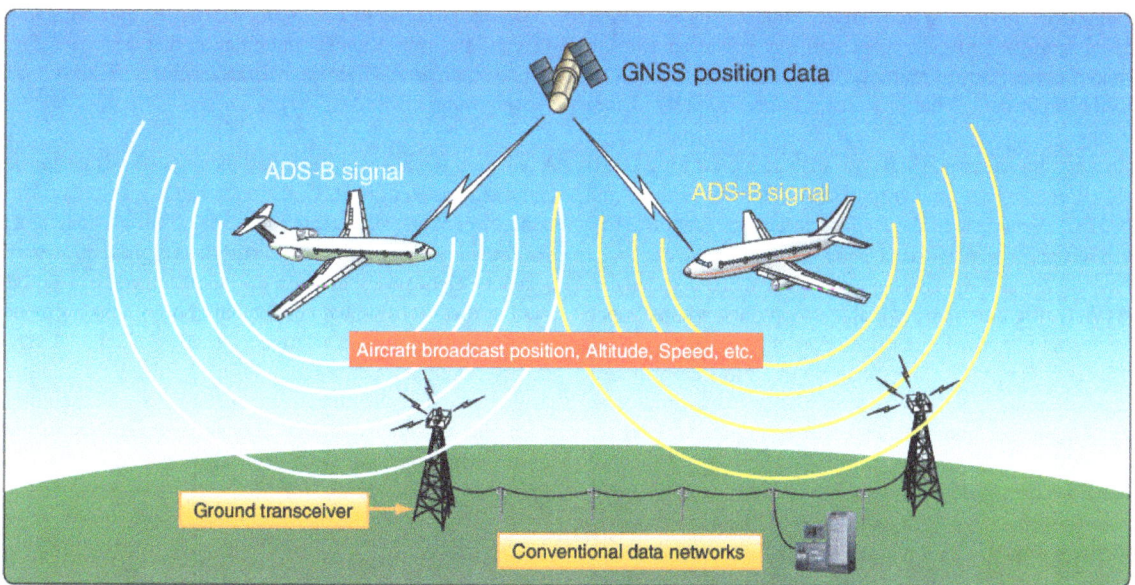

Figure 11-136. *ADS-B OUT uses satellites to identify the position aircraft. This position is then broadcast to other aircraft and to ground stations along with other flight status information.*

Figure 11-137. *A cockpit display of ADS-B generated targets (left) and an ADS-B airborne receiver with antenna (right).*

a greatly reduced factor with ADS-B. Ultra high frequency GPS transmissions are not affected. Increased positioning accuracy allows for higher density traffic flow and landing approaches, an obvious requirement to operate more aircraft in and out of the same number of facilities. The higher degree of control available also enables routing for fewer weather delays and optimal fuel burn rates. Collision avoidance is expanded to include runway incursion from other aircraft and support vehicles on the surface of an airport.

ADS-B IN offers features not available in TCAS. Equipped aircraft are able to receive abundant data to enhance situational awareness. Traffic information services-broadcast (TIS-B) supply traffic information from non-ADS-B aircraft and ADS-B aircraft on a different frequency. Ground radar monitoring of surface targets, and any traffic data in the linked network of ground stations is sent via ADS-B IN to the flight deck. This provides a more complete picture than air-to-air only collision avoidance. Flight information services-broadcast (FIS-B) are also received by ADS-B IN. Weather text and graphics, ATIS information, and NOTAMS are able to be received in aircraft that have 987 UAT capability. *[Figure 11-138]*

ADS-B test units are available for trained maintenance personnel to verify proper operation of ADS-B equipment. This is critical since close tolerance of air traffic separation depends on accurate data from each aircraft and throughout all components of the ADS-B system. *[Figure 11-139]*

Radio Altimeter

A radio altimeter, or radar altimeter, is used to measure the distance from the aircraft to the terrain directly beneath it. It is used primarily during instrument approach and low level or night flight below 2500 feet. The radio altimeter supplies the primary altitude information for landing decision height. It incorporates an adjustable altitude bug that creates a visual or aural warning to the pilot when the aircraft reaches that altitude. Typically, the pilot will abort a landing if the decision height is reached and the runway is not visible.

Using a transceiver and a directional antenna, a radio altimeter broadcasts a carrier wave at 4.3 GHz from the aircraft directly toward the ground. The wave is frequency modulated at 50 MHz and travels at a known speed. It strikes surface features and bounces back toward the aircraft where a second antenna receives the return signal. The transceiver processes the signal by measuring the elapsed time the signal traveled and the frequency modulation that occurred. The display indicates height above the terrain also known as above ground level (AGL). *[Figure 11-140]*

A radar altimeter is more accurate and responsive than an air pressure altimeter for AGL information at low altitudes. The transceiver is usually located remotely from the indicator. Multifunctional and glass cockpit displays typically integrate decision height awareness from the radar altimeter as a digital number displayed on the screen with a bug, light, or color change used to indicate when that altitude is reached. Large aircraft may incorporate radar altimeter information into a ground proximity warning system (GPWS) which aurally alerts the crew of potentially dangerous proximity to the terrain below the aircraft. A decision height window (DH) displays the radar altitude on the EADI in *Figure 11-141*.

Figure 11-138. *ADS-B IN enables weather and traffic information to be sent into the flight deck. In addition to AWOS weather, NWS can also be transmitted.*

Figure 11-139. *An ADS-B test unit.*

Figure 11-140. *A digital display radio altimeter (top), and the two antennas and transceiver for a radio/radar altimeter (bottom).*

11-63

Figure 11-141. *The decision height, DH200, in the lower right corner of this EADI display uses the radar altimeter as the source of altitude information.*

Weather Radar

There are three common types of weather aids used in an aircraft flight deck that are often referred to as weather radar:

1. Actual on-board radar for detecting and displaying weather activity;
2. Lightning detectors; and
3. Satellite or other source weather radar information that is uploaded to the aircraft from an outside source.

On-board weather radar systems can be found in aircraft of all sizes. They function similar to ATC primary radar except the radio waves bounce off of precipitation instead of aircraft. Dense precipitation creates a stronger return than light precipitation. The on-board weather radar receiver is set up to depict heavy returns as red, medium return as yellow and light returns as green on a display in the flight deck. Clouds do not create a return. Magenta is reserved to depict intense or extreme precipitation or turbulence. Some aircraft have a dedicated weather radar screen. Most modern aircraft integrate weather radar display into the navigation display(s). *Figure 11-142* illustrates weather radar displays found on aircraft.

Radio waves used in weather radar systems are in the SHF range such as 5.44 GHz or 9.375 GHz. They are transmitted forward of the aircraft from a directional antenna usually located behind a non-metallic nose cone. Pulses of approximately 1 micro-second in length are transmitted. A duplexer in the radar transceiver switches the antenna to receive for about 2500 micro seconds after a pulse is

Figure 11-142. *A dedicated weather radar display (top) and a multifunctional navigation display with weather radar overlay (bottom).*

transmitted to receive and process any returns. This cycle repeats and the receiver circuitry builds a two dimensional image of precipitation for display. Gain adjustments control the range of the radar. A control panel facilitates this and other adjustments. *[Figure 11-143]*

Severe turbulence, wind shear, and hail are of major concern to the pilot. While hail provides a return on weather radar, wind shear and turbulence must be interpreted from the movement of any precipitation that is detected. An alert is annunciated if this condition occurs on a weather radar system so equipped. Dry air turbulence is not detectable. Ground clutter must also be attenuated when the radar sweep includes any terrain features. The control panel facilitates this.

Special precautions must be followed by the technician during maintenance and operation of weather radar systems. The radome covering the antenna must only be painted with approved paint to allow the radio signals to pass unobstructed. Many radomes also contain grounding strips to conduct lightning strikes and static away from the dome.

Figure 11-143. *A typical on-board weather radar system for a high performance aircraft uses a nose-mounted antenna that gimbals. It is usually controlled by the inertial reference system (IRS) to automatically adjust for attitude changes during maneuvers so that the radar remains aimed at the desired weather target. The pilot may also adjust the angle and sweep manually as well as the gain. A dual mode control panel allows separate control and display on the left or right HSI or navigational display.*

When operating the radar, it is important to follow all manufacturer instructions. Physical harm is possible from the high energy radiation emitted, especially to the eyes and testes. Do not look into the antenna of a transmitting radar. Operation of the radar should not occur in hangars unless special radio wave absorption material is used. Additionally, operation of radar should not take place while the radar is pointed toward a building or when refueling takes place. Radar units should be maintained and operated only by qualified personnel.

Lightning detection is a second reliable means for identifying potentially dangerous weather. Lightning gives off its own electromagnetic signal. The azimuth of a lightning strike can be calculated by a receiver using a loop type antenna such as that used in ADF. *[Figure 11-144]* Some lightning detectors make use of the ADF antenna. The range of the lightning strike is closely associated with its intensity. Intense strikes are plotted as being close to the aircraft.

Stormscope is a proprietary name often associated with lightning detectors. There are others that work in a similar manner. A dedicated display plots the location of each strike within a 200 mile range with a small mark on the screen. As time progresses, the marks may change color to indicate their age. Nonetheless, a number of lightning strikes in a small area indicates a storm cell, and the pilot can navigate around it. Lightning strikes can also be plotted on a multifunctional navigation display. *[Figure 11-145]*

Figure 11-144. *A receiver and antenna from a lightning detector system.*

A third type of weather radar is becoming more common in all classes of aircraft. Through the use of orbiting satellite systems and/or ground up-links, such as described with ADS-B IN, weather information can be sent to an aircraft in flight virtually anywhere in the world. This includes text data as well as real-time radar information for overlay on an aircraft's navigational display(s). Weather radar data produced remotely and sent to the aircraft is refined through consolidation of various radar views from different angles and satellite imagery. This produces more accurate depictions of actual weather conditions. Terrain databases are integrated to eliminate ground clutter. Supplemental data includes the entire range of intelligence available from the National Weather Service (NWS) and the National

Figure 11-145. *A dedicated stormscope lightning detector display (left), and an electronic navigational display with lightning strikes overlaid in the form of green "plus" signs (right).*

Oceanographic and Atmospheric Administration (NOAA). *Figure 11-146* illustrates a plain language weather summary received in an aircraft along with a list of other weather information available through satellite or ground link weather information services.

Figure 11-146. *A plain language METAR weather report received in the cockpit from a satellite weather service for aircraft followed by a list of various weather data that can be radioed to the cockpit from a satellite weather service.*

As mentioned, to receive an ADS-B weather signal, a 1090 ES or 970 UAT transceiver with associated antenna needs to be installed on board the aircraft. Satellite weather services are received by an antenna matched to the frequency of the service. Receivers are typically located remotely and interfaced with existing navigational and multifunction displays. Handheld GPS units also may have satellite weather capability. *[Figure 11-147]*

Emergency Locator Transmitter (ELT)

An emergency locator transmitter (ELT) is an independent battery powered transmitter activated by the excessive G-forces experienced during a crash. It transmits a digital signal every 50 seconds on a frequency of 406.025 MHz at 5 watts for at least 24 hours. The signal is received anywhere in the world by satellites in the COSPAS-SARSAT satellite system. Two types of satellites, low earth orbiting (LEOSATs) and geostationary satellites (GEOSATs) are used with different, complimentary capability. The signal is partially processed and stored in the satellites and then relayed to ground stations known as local user terminals (LUTs). Further deciphering of a signal takes place at the LUTs, and appropriate search and rescue operations are notified through mission control centers (MCCs) set up for this purpose.

NOTE: Maritime vessel emergency locating beacons (EPIRBs) and personal locator beacons (PLBs) use the exact same system. The United States portion of the COSPAS-SARSAT system is maintained and operated by NOAA. *Figure 11-148* illustrates the basic components in the COSPAS-SARSAT system.

Figure 11-147. *A satellite weather receiver and antenna enable display of real-time textual and graphic weather information beyond that of airborne weather radar. A handheld GPS can also be equipped with these capabilities. A built-in multifunctional display with satellite weather overlays and navigation information can be found on many aircraft.*

Figure 11-148. *The basic operating components of the satellite-based COSPAS-SARSAT rescue system of which aircraft ELTs are a part.*

11-67

ELTs are required to be installed in aircraft according to FAR 91.207. This encompasses most general aviation aircraft not operating under Parts 135 or 121. ELTs must be inspected within 12 months of previous inspection for proper installation, battery corrosion, operation of the controls and crash sensor, and the presence of a sufficient signal at the antenna. Built-in test equipment facilitates testing without transmission of an emergency signal. The remainder of the inspection is visual. Technicians are cautioned to not activate the ELT and transmit an emergency distress signal. Inspection must be recorded in maintenance records including the new expiration date of the battery. This must also be recorded on the outside of the ELT.

ELTs are typically installed as far aft in the fuselage of an aircraft as is practicable just forward of the empennage. The built-in G-force sensor is aligned with the longitudinal axis of the aircraft. Helicopter ELTs may be located elsewhere on the airframe. They are equipped with multidirectional activation devices. Follow ELT and airframe manufacturer's instructions for proper installation, inspection, and maintenance of all ELTs. *Figure 11-149* illustrates ELTs mounted locations.

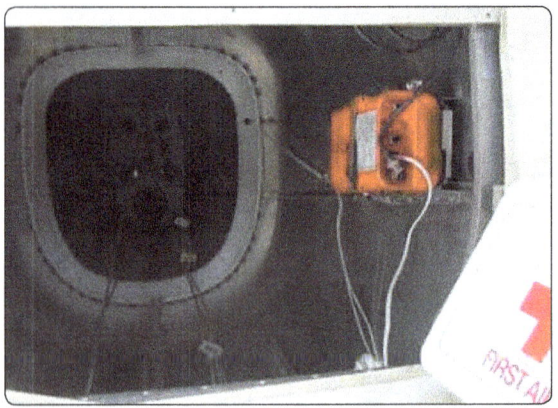

Figure 11-149. *An emergency locator transmitter (ELT) mounting location is generally far aft in a fixed-wing aircraft fuselage in line with the longitudinal axis. Helicopter mounting location and orientation varies.*

Use of Doppler technology enables the origin of the 406 MHz ELT signal to be calculated within 2 to 5 kilometers. Second generation 406 MHz ELT digital signals are loaded with GPS location coordinates from a receiver inside the ELT unit or integrated from an outside unit. This reduces the location accuracy of the crash site to within 100 meters. The digital signal is also loaded with unique registration information. It identifies the aircraft, the owner, and contact information, etc. When a signal is received, this is used to immediately research the validity of the alert to ensure it is a true emergency transmission so that rescue resources are not deployed needlessly.

ELTs with automatic G-force activation mounted in aircraft are easily removable. They often contain a portable antenna so that crash victims may leave the site and carry the operating ELT with them. A flight deck mounted panel is required to alert the pilot if the ELT is activated. It also allows the ELT to be armed, tested, and manually activated if needed. *[Figure 11-150]*

Figure 11-150. *An ELT and its components including a cockpit-mounted panel, the ELT, a permanent mount antenna, and a portable antenna.*

Modern ELTs may also transmit a signal on 121.5 MHz. This is an analog transmission that can be used for homing. Prior to 2009, 121.5 MHz was a worldwide emergency frequency monitored by the CORPAS-SARSAT satellites. However, it has been replaced by the 406 MHz standard. Transmission on 121.5 MHz are no longer received and relayed via satellite.

The use of a 406 MHz ELT has not been mandated by the FAA. An older 121.5 MHz ELT satisfies the requirements of FAR Part 91.207 in all except new aircraft. Thousands of aircraft registered in the United States remain equipped with ELTs that transmit a .75 watt analog 121.5 MHz emergency signal when activated. The 121.5 MHz frequency is still an active emergency frequency and is monitored by over-flying aircraft and control towers.

Technicians are required to perform an inspection/test of 121.5 MHz ELTs within 12 months of the previous one and inspect for the same integrity as required for the 406MHz ELTs mentioned above. However, older ELTs often lack the built-in test circuitry of modern ELTs certified to TSO C-126. Therefore, a true operational test may include activating the signal. This can be done by removing the antenna and installing a dummy load. Any activation of an ELT signal is required to only be done between the top of each hour and 5 minutes after the hour. The duration of activation must be no longer than three audible sweeps. Contact of the local control tower or flight service station before testing is recommended.

It must be noted that older 121.5 MHz analog signal ELTs often also transmit an emergency signal on a frequency of 243.0 MHz. This has long been the military emergency frequency. Its use is being phased out in favor of digital ELT signals and satellite monitoring. Improvements in coverage, location accuracy, identification of false alerts, and shortened response times are so significant with 406 MHz ELTs, they are currently the service standard worldwide.

Long Range Aid to Navigation System (LORAN)

Long range aid to navigation system (LORAN) is a type of RNAV that is no longer available in the United States. It was developed during World War II, and the most recent edition, LORAN-C, has been very useful and accurate to aviators as well as maritime sailors. LORAN uses radio wave pulses from a series of towers and an on-board receiver/computer to positively locate an aircraft amid the tower network. There are twelve LORAN transmitter tower "chains" constructed across North America. Each chain has a master transmitter tower and a handful of secondary towers. All broadcasts from the transmitters are at the same frequency, 100 KHz. Therefore, a LORAN receiver does not need to be tuned. Being in the low frequency range, the LORAN transmissions travel long distances and provide good coverage from a small number of stations.

Precisely-timed, synchronized pulse signals are transmitted from the towers in a chain. The LORAN receiver measures the time to receive the pulses from the master tower and two other towers in the chain. It calculates the aircraft's position based on the intersection of parabolic curves representing elapsed signal times from each of these known points.

The accuracy and proliferation of GPS navigation has caused the U.S. Government to cease support for the LORAN navigation system citing redundancy and expense of operating the towers as reasons. The LORAN chain in the Aleutian Island shared with Russia is the only LORAN chain at the time of printing of this handbook which had not yet been given a date for closure. Panel-mounted LORAN navigation units will likely be removed and replaced by GPS units in aircraft that have not already done so. *[Figure 11-151]*

Figure 11-151. *Panel-mounted LORAN units are now obsolete as LORAN signals are no longer generated from the tower network.*

Global Positioning System (GPS)

Global positioning system navigation (GPS) is the fastest growing type of navigation in aviation. It is accomplished through the use of NAVSTAR satellites set and maintained in orbit around the earth by the U.S. Government. Continuous coded transmissions from the satellites facilitate locating the position of an aircraft equipped with a GPS receiver with extreme accuracy. GPS can be utilized on its own for en route navigation, or it can be integrated into other navigation systems, such as VOR/RNAV, inertial reference, or flight management systems.

There are three segments of GPS: the space segment, the control segment, and the user segment. Aircraft technicians are only involved with user segment equipment such as GPS receivers, displays, and antennas.

Twenty-four satellites (21 active, 3 spares) in six separate plains of orbit 12, 625 feet above the planet comprise what is known as the space segment of the GPS system. The satellites are positioned such that in any place on earth at any one time, at least four will be a minimum of 15° above the horizon. Typically, between 5 and 8 satellites are in view. *[Figure 11-152]*

Two signals loaded with digitally coded information are transmitted from each satellite. The L1 channel transmission on a1575.42 MHz carrier frequency is used in civilian aviation. Satellite identification, position, and time are conveyed to the aircraft GPS receiver on this digitally modulated signal along with status and other information. An L2 channel 1227.60 MHz transmission is used by the military.

The amount of time it takes for signals to reach the aircraft GPS receiver from transmitting satellites is combined with each satellite's exact location to calculate the position of

Figure 11-152. *The space segment of GPS consists of 24 NAVSTAR satellites in six different orbits around the earth.*

an aircraft. The control segment of the GPS monitors each satellite to ensure its location and time are precise. This control is accomplished with five ground-based receiving stations, a master control station, and three transmitting antenna. The receiving stations forward status information received from the satellites to the master control station. Calculations are made and corrective instructions are sent to the satellites via the transmitters.

The user segment of the GPS is comprised of the thousands of receivers installed in aircraft as well as every other receiver that uses the GPS transmissions. Specifically, for the aircraft technician, the user section consists of a control panel/display, the GPS receiver circuitry, and an antenna. The control, display and receiver are usually located in a single unit which also may include VOR/ILS circuitry and a VHF communications transceiver. GPS intelligence is integrated into the multifunctional displays of glass cockpit aircraft. *[Figure 11-153]*

The GPS receiver measures the time it takes for a signal to arrive from three transmitting satellites. Since radio waves travel at 186,000 miles per second, the distance to each satellite can be calculated. The intersection of these ranges provides a two dimensional position of the aircraft. It is expressed in latitude/longitude coordinates. By incorporating the distance to a fourth satellite, the altitude above the surface of the earth can be calculated as well. This results in a three dimensional fix. Additional satellite inputs refine the accuracy of the position.

Figure 11-153. *A GPS unit integrated with NAV/COM circuitry.*

Having deciphered the position of the aircraft, the GPS unit processes many useful navigational outputs such as speed, direction, bearing to a waypoint, distance traveled, time of arrival, and more. These can be selected to display for use. Waypoints can be entered and stored in the unit's memory. Terrain features, airport data, VOR/RNAV and approach information, communication frequencies, and more can also be loaded into a GPS unit. Most modern units come with moving map display capability.

A main benefit of GPS use is immunity from service disruption due to weather. Errors are introduced while the carrier waves travel through the ionosphere; however, these are corrected and kept to a minimum. GPS is also relatively inexpensive. GPS receivers for IFR navigation in aircraft must be built to TSO-129A. This raises the price above that of handheld units used for hiking or in an automobile. But the overall cost of GPS is low due to its small infrastructure. Most of the inherent accuracy is built into the space and control segments permitting reliable positioning with inexpensive user equipment.

The accuracy of current GPS is within 20 meters horizontally and a bit more vertically. This is sufficient for en route navigation with greater accuracy than required. However, departures and approaches require more stringent accuracy. Integration of the wide area augmentation system (WAAS) improves GPS accuracy to within 7.6 meters and is discussed below. The future of GPS calls for additional accuracy by adding two new transmissions from each satellite. An L2C channel will be for general use in non-safety critical application. An aviation dedicated L5 channel will provide the accuracy required for category I, II, and III landings. It will enable the NEXTGEN NAS plan along with ADS-B. The first replacement NAVSTAR satellites with L2C and L5 capability have already been launched. Full implementation is schedule by 2015.

Wide Area Augmentation System (WAAS)

To increase the accuracy of GPS for aircraft navigation, the wide area augmentation system (WAAS) was developed. It consists of approximately 25 precisely surveyed ground stations that receive GPS signals and ultimately transmit correction information to the aircraft. An overview of WAAS components and its operation is shown in *Figure 11-154*.

Figure 11-154. *The wide area augmentation system (WAAS) is used to refine GPS positions to a greater degree of accuracy. A WAAS enabled GPS receiver is required for its use as corrective information is sent from geostationary satellites directly to an aircraft's GPS receiver for use.*

WAAS ground stations receive GPS signals and forward position errors to two master ground stations. Time and location information is analyzed, and correction instructions are sent to communication satellites in geostationary orbit over the NAS. The satellites broadcast GPS-like signals that WAAS enabled GPS receivers use to correct position information received from GPS satellites.

A WAAS enable GPS receiver is required to use the wide area augmentation system. If equipped, an aircraft qualifies to perform precision approaches into thousands of airports without any ground-based approach equipment. Separation minimums are also able to be reduced between aircraft that are WAAS equipped. The WAAS system is known to reduce position errors to 1–3 meters laterally and vertically.

Inertial Navigation System (INS)/Inertial Reference System (IRS)

An inertial navigation system (INS) is used on some large aircraft for long range navigation. This may also be identified as an inertial reference system (IRS), although the IRS designation is generally reserved for more modern systems. An INS/IRS is a self contained system that does not require input radio signals from a ground navigation facility or transmitter. The system derives attitude, velocity, and direction information from measurement of the aircraft's accelerations given a known starting point. The location of the aircraft is continuously updated through calculations based on the forces experienced by INS accelerometers. A minimum of two accelerometers is used, one referenced to north, and the other referenced to east. In older units, they are mounted on a gyro-stabilized platform. This averts the introduction of errors that may result from acceleration due to gravity.

An INS uses complex calculation made by an INS computer to convert applied forces into location information. An interface control head is used to enter starting location position data while the aircraft is stationary on the ground. This is called initializing. *[Figure 11-155]* From then on, all motion of the aircraft is sensed by the built-in accelerometers and run through the computer. Feedback and correction loops are used to correct for accumulated error as flight time progresses. The amount an INS is off in one hour of flight time is a reference point for determining performance. Accumulated error of less than one mile after one hour of flight is possible. Continuous accurate adjustment to the gyro-stabilized platform to keep it parallel to the Earth's surface is a key requirement to reduce accumulated error. A latitude/longitude coordinate system is used when giving the location output.

Figure 11-155. *An interface panel for three air data and inertial reference systems on an Airbus. The keyboard is used to initialize the system. Latitude and longitude position is displayed at the top.*

INS is integrated into an airliner's flight management system and automatic flight control system. Waypoints can be entered for a predetermined flightpath and the INS will guide the aircraft to each waypoint in succession. Integration with other NAV aids is also possible to ensure continuous correction and improved accuracy but is not required.

Modern INS systems are known as IRS. They are completely solid-state units with no moving parts. Three-ring, laser gyros replace the mechanical gyros in the older INS platform systems. This eliminates precession and other mechanical gyro shortcomings. The use of three solid-state accelerometers, one for each plane of movement, also increases accuracy. The accelerometer and gyro output are input to the computer for continuous calculation of the aircraft's position.

The most modern IRS integrate is the satellite GPS. The GPS is extremely accurate in itself. When combined with IRS, it creates one of the most accurate navigation systems available. The GPS is used to initialize the IRS so the pilot no longer needs to do so. GPS also feeds data into the IRS computer to be used for error correction. Occasional service interruptions and altitude inaccuracies of the GPS system pose no problem for IRS/GPS. The IRS functions continuously and is completely self contained within the IRS unit. Should the GPS falter, the IRS portion of the system continues without it. The latest electronic technology has reduced the size and weight of INS/IRS avionics units significantly. *Figure 11-156* shows a modern micro-IRS unit that measures approximately 6-inches on each side.

Figure 11-156. *A modern micro-IRS with built-in GPS.*

Installation of Communication and Navigation Equipment

Approval of New Avionics Equipment Installations

Most of the avionics equipment discussed in this chapter is only repairable by the manufacturer or FAA-certified repair stations that are licensed to perform specific work. The airframe technician: however, must competently remove, install, inspect, maintain, and troubleshoot these ever increasingly complicated electronic devices and systems. It is imperative to follow all equipment and airframe manufacturers' instruction when dealing with an aircraft's avionics.

The revolution to GPS navigation and the pace of modern electronic development results in many aircraft owner operators upgrading flight decks with new avionics. The aircraft technician must only perform airworthy installations. The avionics equipment to be installed must be a TSO'd device that is approved for installation in the aircraft in question. The addition of a new piece of avionics equipment and/or its antenna is a minor alteration if previously approved by the airframe manufacturer. A licensed airframe technician is qualified to perform the installation and return the aircraft to service. The addition of new avionics not on the aircraft's approved equipment list is considered a major alteration and requires an FAA Form 337 to be enacted. A technician with an inspection authorization is required to complete a Form 337.

Most new avionics installations are approved and performed under an STC. The equipment manufacturer supplies a list of aircraft on which the equipment has been approved for installation. The STC includes thorough installation and maintenance instructions which the technician must follow. Regardless, if not on the aircraft's original equipment list, the STC installation is considered a major alteration and an FAA Form 337 must be filed. The STC is referenced as the required approved data.

Occasionally, an owner/operator or technician wishes to install an electronic device in an aircraft that has no STC for the model aircraft in question. A field approval and a Form 337 must be filed on which it must be shown that the installation will be performed in accordance with approved data.

Considerations

There are many factors which the technician must consider prior to altering an aircraft by the addition of avionics equipment. These factors include the space available, the size and weight of the equipment, and previously accomplished alterations. The power consumption of the added equipment must be considered to calculate and determine the maximum continuous electrical load on the aircraft's electrical system.

Each installation should also be planned to allow easy access for inspection, maintenance, and exchange of units.

The installation of avionics equipment is partially mechanical, involving sheet metal work to mount units, racks, antennas, and controls. Routing of the interconnecting wires, cables, antenna leads, etc. is also an important part of the installation process. When selecting a location for the equipment, use the area(s) designated by the airframe manufacturer or the STC. If such information is not available, select a location for installation that will carry the loads imposed by the weight of the equipment, and which is capable of withstanding the additional inertia forces.

If an avionics device is to be mounted in the instrument panel and no provisions have been made for such an installation, ensure that the panel is not a primary structure prior to making any cutouts. To minimize the load on a stationary instrument panel, a support bracket may be installed between the rear of the electronics case or rack and a nearby structural member of the aircraft. *[Figure 11-157]*

Figure 11-157. *An avionics installation in a stationary instrument panel may include a support for the avionics case.*

Avionics radio equipment must be securely mounted to the aircraft. All mounting bolts must be secured by locking devices to prevent loosening from vibration. Adequate clearance between all units and adjacent structure must be provided to prevent mechanical damage to electric wiring or to the avionic equipment from vibration, chafing, or landing shock.

Do not locate avionics equipment and wiring near units containing combustible fluids. When separation is impractical, install baffles or shrouds to prevent contact of the combustible fluids with any electronic equipment in the event of plumbing failure.

Cooling and Moisture

The performance and service life of most avionics equipment is seriously limited by excessive ambient temperatures. High performance aircraft with avionics equipment racks typically route air-conditioned air over the avionics to keep them cool. It is also common for non-air conditioned aircraft to use a blower or scooped ram air to cool avionics installations. When adding a unit to an aircraft, the installation should be planned so that it can dissipate heat readily. In some installations, it may be necessary to produce airflow over the new equipment either with a blower or through the use of routed ram air. Be sure that proper baffling is used to prevent water from reaching any electronics when ducting outside air. The presence of water in avionics equipment areas promotes rapid deterioration of the exposed components and could lead to failure.

Vibration Isolation

Vibration is a continued motion by an oscillating force. The amplitude and frequency of vibration of the aircraft structure will vary considerably with the type of aircraft. Avionics equipment is sensitive to mechanical shock and vibration and is normally shock mounted to provide some protection against in-flight vibration and landing shock.

Special shock mounted racks are often used to isolate avionics equipment from vibrating structure. *[Figure 11-158]* Such mounts should provide adequate isolation over the entire range of expected vibration frequencies. When installing shock mounts, assure that the equipment weight does not exceed the weight-carrying capabilities of the mounts. Radio equipment installed on shock mounts must have sufficient clearance from surrounding equipment and structure to allow for normal swaying of the equipment.

Figure 11-158. *A shock mounted equipment rack is often used to install avionics.*

Radios installed in instrument panels do not ordinarily require vibration protection since the panel itself is usually shock mounted. However, make certain that the added weight of any added equipment can be safely carried by the existing mounts. In some cases, it may be necessary to install larger capacity mounts or to increase the number of mounting points.

Periodic inspection of the shock mounts is required and defective mounts should be replaced with the proper type. The following factors to observe during the inspection are:

1. Deterioration of the shock-absorbing material;
2. Stiffness and resiliency of the material; and
3. Overall rigidity of the mount.

If the mount is too stiff, it may not provide adequate protection against the shock of landing. If the shock mount is not stiff enough, it may allow prolonged vibration following an initial shock.

Shock-absorbing materials commonly used in shock mounts are usually electrical insulators. For this reason, each electronic unit mounted with shock mounts must be electrically bonded to a structural member of the aircraft to provide a current path to ground. This is accomplished by secure attachment of a tinned copper wire braid from the component, across the mount, to the aircraft structure as shown in *Figure 11-159*. Occasional bonding is accomplished with solid aluminum or copper material where a short flexible strap is not possible.

Figure 11-159. *A bonding jumper is used to ground an equipment rack and avionics chassis around the non-conductive shock mount material.*

Reducing Radio Interference

Suppression of unwanted electromagnetic fields and electrostatic interference is essential on all aircraft. In communication radios, this is noticeable as audible noise. In other components, the effects may not be audible but pose a threat to proper operation. Large discharges of static electricity can permanently damage the sensitive solid-state microelectronics found in nearly all modern avionics.

Shielding

Many components of an aircraft are possible sources of electrical interference which can deteriorate the performance and reliability of avionics components. Rotating electrical devices, switching devices, ignition systems, propeller control systems, AC power lines, and voltage regulators all produce potential damaging fields. Shielding wires to electric components and ignition systems dissipates radio frequency noise energy. Instead of radiating into space, the braided conductive shielding guides unwanted current flows to ground. To prevent the build-up of electrical potential, all electrical components should also be bonded to the aircraft structure (ground).

Isolation

Isolation is another practical method of radio frequency suppression to prevent interference. This involves separating the source of the noise from the input circuits of the affected equipment. In some cases, noise in a receiver may be entirely eliminated simply by moving the antenna lead-in wire just a few inches away from a noise source. On other occasions, when shielding and isolation are not effective, a filter may need to be installed in the input circuit of an affected component.

Bonding

The aircraft surface can become highly charged with static electricity while in flight. Measures are required to eliminate the build-up and radiation of unwanted electrical charges. One of the most important measures taken to eliminate unwanted electrical charges which may damage or interfere with avionics equipment is bonding. Charges flowing in paths of variable resistance due to such causes as intermittent contact from vibration or the movement of a control surface produce electrical disturbances (noise) in avionics. Bonding provides the necessary electric connection between metallic parts of an aircraft to prevent variable resistance in the airframe. It provides a low-impedance ground return which minimizes interference from static electricity charges.

All metal parts of the aircraft should be bonded to prevent the development of electrical potential build-up. Bonding also provides the low resistance return path for single-wire electrical systems. Bonding jumpers and clamps are examples of bonding connectors. Jumpers should be as short as possible. Be sure finishes are removed in the contact area of a bonding device so that metal-to-metal contact exists. Resistance should not exceed .003 ohm. When a jumper is used only to reduce radio frequency noise and is not for current carrying purposes, a resistance of 0.01 ohm is satisfactory.

Static Discharge Wicks

Static dischargers, or wicks, are installed on aircraft to reduce radio receiver interference. This interference is caused by corona discharge emitted from the aircraft as a result of precipitation static. Corona occurs in short pulses which produce noise at the radio frequency spectrum. Static dischargers are normally mounted on the trailing edges of the control surfaces, wing tips and the vertical stabilizer. They discharge precipitation static at points a critical distance away from avionics antennas where there is little or no coupling of the static to cause interference or noise.

Flexible and semi-flexible dischargers are attached to the aircraft structure by metal screws, rivets, or epoxy. The connections should be checked periodically for security. A resistance measurement from the mount to the airframe should not exceed 0.1 ohm. Inspect the condition of all static dischargers in accordance with manufacturer's instructions. *Figure 11-160* illustrates examples of static dischargers.

Installation of Aircraft Antenna Systems

Knowledge of antenna installation and maintenance is especially important as these tasks are performed by the aircraft technician. Antennas take many forms and sizes dependent upon the frequency of the transmitter and receiver to which they are connected. Airborne antennas must be mechanically secure. The air loads on an antenna are significant and must be considered. Antennas must be electrically matched to the receiver and transmitter which they serve. They must also be mounted in interference free locations and in areas where signals can be optimally transmitted and received. Antennas must also have the same polarization as the ground station.

The following procedures describe the installation of a typical rigid antenna. They are presented as an example only. Always follow the manufacturer's instructions when installing any antenna. An incorrect antenna installation could cause equipment failure.

1. Place a template similar to that shown in *Figure 11-161* on the fore-and-aft centerline at the desired location. Drill the mounting holes and correct diameter hole for the transmission line cable in the fuselage skin.

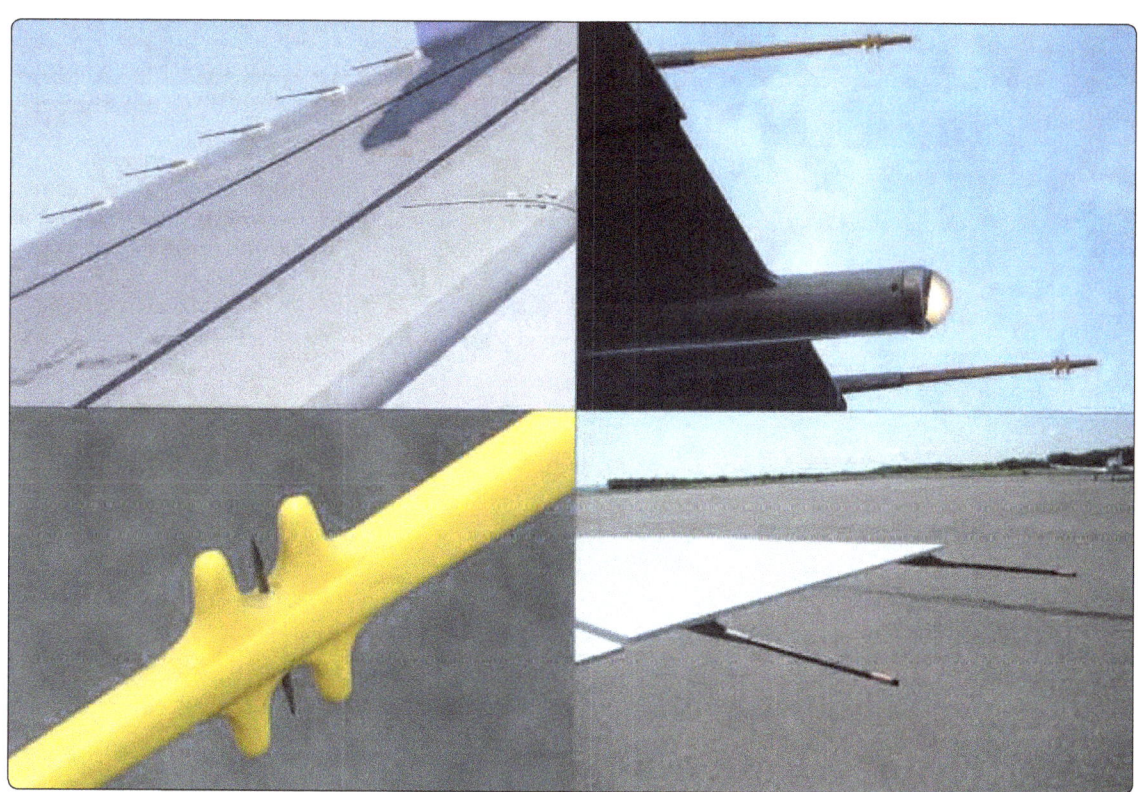

Figure 11-160. *Static dischargers or wicks dissipate built up static energy in flight at points a safe distance from avionics antennas to prevent radio frequency interference.*

Figure 11-161. *A typical antenna mounting template.*

2. Install a reinforcing doubler of sufficient thickness to reinforce the aircraft skin. The length and width of the reinforcing plate should approximate the example shown in *Figure 11-162*.

Figure 11-162. *A typical antenna installation on a skin panel including a doubler.*

3. Install the antenna on the fuselage, making sure that the mounting bolts are tightened firmly against the reinforcing doubler, and the mast is drawn tight against the gasket. If a gasket is not used, seal between the mast and the fuselage with a suitable sealer, such as zinc chromate paste or equivalent.

The mounting bases of antennas vary in shape and sizes; however, the aforementioned installation procedure is typical of mast-type antenna installations.

Transmission Lines

A transmitting or receiving antenna is connected directly to its associated transmitter or receiver by a transmission line. This is a shielded wire also known as coax. Transmission lines may vary from only a few feet to many feet in length. They must transfer energy with minimal loss. Transponders, DME and other pulse type transceivers require transmission lines that are precise in length. The critical length of transmission lines provides minimal attenuation of the transmitted or received signal. Refer to the equipment manufacturer's installation manual for the type and allowable length of transmission lines.

To provide the proper impedance matching for the most efficient power transfer, a balun may be used in some antenna installations. It is formed in the transmission line connection to the antenna. A balun in a dipole antenna installation is illustrated in *Figure 11-163*.

Coax connectors are usually used with coax cable to ensure a secure connection. Many transmission lines are part of the equipment installation kit with connectors previously installed. The aircraft technician is also able to install these connectors on coax. *Figure 11-164* illustrates the basic steps used when installing a coax cable connector.

When installing coaxial cable, secure the cables firmly along their entire length at intervals of approximately 2 feet. To assure optimum operation, coaxial cables should not be routed or tied to other wire bundles. When bending coaxial cable, be sure that the bend is at least 10 times the size of the cable diameter. In all cases, follow the equipment manufacturer's instructions.

Maintenance Procedure

Detailed instructions, procedures, and specifications for the servicing of avionics equipment are contained in the manufacturer's operating manuals. Additional instructions for removal and installation of the units are contained in the maintenance manual for the aircraft in which the equipment is installed. Although an installation may appear to be a simple procedure, many avionics troubles are attributed to

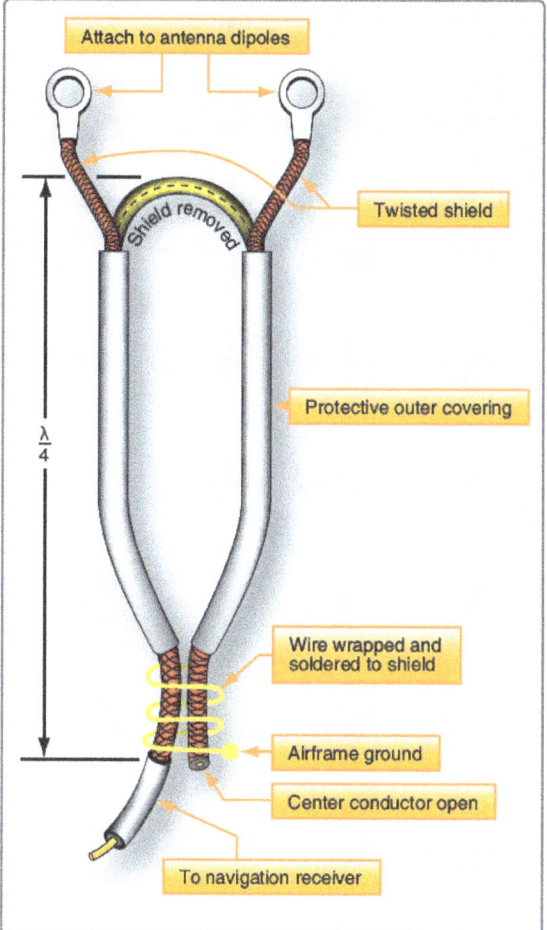

Figure 11-163. *A balun in a dipole antenna installation provides the proper impedance for efficient power transfer.*

careless oversights during equipment replacement. Loose cable connections, switched cable terminations, improper bonding, worn shock mounts, improper safety wiring, and failure to perform an operational check after installation may result in poor performance or inoperative avionics.

Figure 11-164. *Steps in attaching a connector to coax cable used as antenna transmission lines.*

Chapter 12
Hydraulic and Pneumatic Power Systems

Aircraft Hydraulic Systems

The word "hydraulics" is based on the Greek word for water and originally meant the study of the physical behavior of water at rest and in motion. Today, the meaning has been expanded to include the physical behavior of all liquids, including hydraulic fluid. Hydraulic systems are not new to aviation. Early aircraft had hydraulic brake systems. As aircraft became more sophisticated, newer systems with hydraulic power were developed.

Hydraulic systems in aircraft provide a means for the operation of aircraft components. The operation of landing gear, flaps, flight control surfaces, and brakes is largely accomplished with hydraulic power systems. Hydraulic system complexity varies from small aircraft that require fluid only for manual operation of the wheel brakes to large transport aircraft where the systems are large and complex. To achieve the necessary redundancy and reliability, the system may consist of several subsystems. Each subsystem has a power generating device (pump) reservoir, accumulator, heat exchanger, filtering system, etc. System operating pressure may vary from a couple hundred pounds per square inch (psi) in small aircraft and rotorcraft to 5,000 psi in large transports.

Hydraulic systems have many advantages as power sources for operating various aircraft units; they combine the advantages of light weight, ease of installation, simplification of inspection, and minimum maintenance requirements. Hydraulic operations are also almost 100 percent efficient, with only negligible loss due to fluid friction.

Hydraulic Fluid

Hydraulic system liquids are used primarily to transmit and distribute forces to various units to be actuated. Liquids are able to do this because they are almost incompressible. Pascal's Law states that pressure applied to any part of a confined liquid is transmitted with undiminished intensity to every other part. Thus, if a number of passages exist in a system, pressure can be distributed through all of them by means of the liquid.

Manufacturers of hydraulic devices usually specify the type of liquid best suited for use with their equipment in view of the working conditions, the service required, temperatures expected inside and outside the systems, pressures the liquid must withstand, the possibilities of corrosion, and other conditions that must be considered. If incompressibility and fluidity were the only qualities required, any liquid that is not too thick could be used in a hydraulic system. But a satisfactory liquid for a particular installation must possess a number of other properties. Some of the properties and characteristics that must be considered when selecting a satisfactory liquid for a particular system are discussed in the following paragraphs.

Viscosity

One of the most important properties of any hydraulic fluid is its viscosity. Viscosity is internal resistance to flow. A liquid such as gasoline that has a low viscosity flows easily, while a liquid such as tar that has a high viscosity flows slowly. Viscosity increases as temperature decreases. A satisfactory liquid for a given hydraulic system must have enough body to give a good seal at pumps, valves, and pistons, but it must not be so thick that it offers resistance to flow, leading to power loss and higher operating temperatures. These factors add to the load and to excessive wear of parts. A fluid that is too thin also leads to rapid wear of moving parts or of parts that have heavy loads. The instruments used to measure the viscosity of a liquid are known as viscometers or viscosimeters. Several types of viscosimeters are in use today. The Saybolt viscometer measures the time required, in seconds, for 60 milliliters of the tested fluid at 100 °F to pass through a standard orifice. The time measured is used to express the fluid's viscosity, in Saybolt universal seconds or Saybolt furol seconds. *[Figure 12-1]*

Figure 12-1. *Saybolt viscosimeter.*

Chemical Stability

Chemical stability is another property that is exceedingly important in selecting a hydraulic liquid. It is the liquid's ability to resist oxidation and deterioration for long periods. All liquids tend to undergo unfavorable chemical changes under severe operating conditions. This is the case, for example, when a system operates for a considerable period of time at high temperatures. Excessive temperatures have a great effect on the life of a liquid. It should be noted that the temperature of the liquid in the reservoir of an operating hydraulic system does not always represent a true state of operating conditions. Localized hot spots occur on bearings, gear teeth, or at the point where liquid under pressure is forced through a small orifice. Continuous passage of a liquid through these points may produce local temperatures high enough to carbonize or sludge the liquid, yet the liquid in the reservoir may not indicate an excessively high temperature.

Liquids with a high viscosity have a greater resistance to heat than light or low-viscosity liquids that have been derived from the same source. The average hydraulic liquid has a low viscosity. Fortunately, there is a wide choice of liquids available for use within the viscosity range required of hydraulic liquids.

Liquids may break down if exposed to air, water, salt, or other impurities, especially if they are in constant motion or subject to heat. Some metals, such as zinc, lead, brass, and copper, have an undesirable chemical reaction on certain liquids. These chemical processes result in the formation of sludge, gums, and carbon or other deposits that clog openings, cause valves and pistons to stick or leak, and give poor lubrication to moving parts. As soon as small amounts of sludge or other deposits are formed, the rate of formation generally increases more rapidly. As they are formed, certain changes in the physical and chemical properties of the liquid take place. The liquid usually becomes darker in color, higher in viscosity, and acids are formed.

Flash Point

Flash point is the temperature at which a liquid gives off vapor in sufficient quantity to ignite momentarily or flash when a flame is applied. A high flash point is desirable for hydraulic liquids because it indicates good resistance to combustion and a low degree of evaporation at normal temperatures.

Fire Point

Fire point is the temperature at which a substance gives off vapor in sufficient quantity to ignite and continue to burn when exposed to a spark or flame. Like flash point, a high fire point is required of desirable hydraulic liquids.

Types of Hydraulic Fluids

To assure proper system operation and to avoid damage to nonmetallic components of the hydraulic system, the correct fluid must be used. When adding fluid to a system, use the type specified in the aircraft manufacturer's maintenance manual or on the instruction plate affixed to the reservoir or unit being serviced.

The three principal categories of hydraulic fluids are:
1. Minerals
2. Polyalphaolefins
3. Phosphate esters

When servicing a hydraulic system, the technician must be certain to use the correct category of replacement fluid. Hydraulic fluids are not necessarily compatible. For example, contamination of the fire-resistant fluid MIL-H-83282 with MIL-H-5606 may render the MIL-H-83282 non fire-resistant.

Mineral-Based Fluids

Mineral oil-based hydraulic fluid (MIL-H-5606) is the oldest, dating back to the 1940s. It is used in many systems, especially where the fire hazard is comparatively low. MIL-H-6083 is simply a rust-inhibited version of MIL-H-5606. They are completely interchangeable. Suppliers generally ship hydraulic components with MIL-H-6083. Mineral-based hydraulic fluid (MIL–H-5606) is processed from petroleum. It has an odor similar to penetrating oil and is dyed red. Synthetic rubber seals are used with petroleum-based fluids.

Polyalphaolefin-Based Fluids

MIL-H-83282 is a fire-resistant hydrogenated polyalphaolefin-based fluid developed in the 1960s to overcome the flammability characteristics of MIL-H-5606. MIL-H-83282 is significantly more flame resistant than MIL-H-5606, but a disadvantage is the high viscosity at low temperature. It is generally limited to –40 °F. However, it can be used in the same system and with the same seals, gaskets, and hoses as MIL-H-5606. MIL-H-46170 is the rust-inhibited version of MIL-H-83282. Small aircraft predominantly use MIL-H-5606, but some have switched to MIL-H-83282 if they can accommodate the high viscosity at low temperature.

Phosphate Ester-Based Fluid (Skydrol®)

These fluids are used in most commercial transport category aircraft and are extremely fire-resistant. However, they are not fireproof and under certain conditions, they burn. The earliest generation of these fluids was developed after World War II as a result of the growing number of aircraft hydraulic brake fires that drew the collective concern of the commercial aviation industry. Progressive development of these fluids occurred as a result of performance requirements of newer aircraft designs. The airframe manufacturers dubbed these new generations of hydraulic fluid as types based on their performance.

Today, types IV and V fluids are used. Two distinct classes of type IV fluids exist based on their density: class I fluids are low density and class II fluids are standard density. The class I fluids provide weight savings advantages versus class II. In addition to the type IV fluids that are currently in use, type V fluids are being developed in response to industry demands for a more thermally stable fluid at higher operating temperatures. Type V fluids will be more resistant to hydrolytic and oxidative degradation at high temperature than the type IV fluids.

Intermixing of Fluids

Due to the difference in composition, petroleum-based and phosphate ester-based fluids will not mix; neither are the seals for any one fluid usable with or tolerant of any of the other fluids. Should an aircraft hydraulic system be serviced with the wrong type fluid, immediately drain and flush the system and maintain the seals according to the manufacturer's specifications.

Compatibility with Aircraft Materials

Aircraft hydraulic systems designed around Skydrol® fluids should be virtually trouble-free if properly serviced. Skydrol® is a registered trademark of Monsanto Company. Skydrol® does not appreciably affect common aircraft metals—aluminum, silver, zinc, magnesium, cadmium, iron, stainless steel, bronze, chromium, and others—as long as the fluids are kept free of contamination. Due to the phosphate ester base of Skydrol® fluids, thermoplastic resins, including vinyl compositions, nitrocellulose lacquers, oil-based paints, linoleum, and asphalt may be softened chemically by Skydrol® fluids. However, this chemical action usually requires longer than just momentary exposure, and spills that are wiped up with soap and water do not harm most of these materials. Paints that are Skydrol® resistant include epoxies and polyurethanes. Today, polyurethanes are the standard of the aircraft industry because of their ability to keep a bright, shiny finish for long periods of time and for the ease with which they can be removed.

Hydraulic systems require the use of special accessories that are compatible with the hydraulic fluid. Appropriate seals, gaskets, and hoses must be specifically designated for the type of fluid in use. Care must be taken to ensure that the components installed in the system are compatible with the fluid. When gaskets, seals, and hoses are replaced, positive identification should be made to ensure that they are made of the appropriate material. Skydrol® type V fluid is compatible with natural fibers and with a number of synthetics, including nylon and polyester, which are used extensively in most aircraft. Petroleum oil hydraulic system seals of neoprene or Buna-N are not compatible with Skydrol® and must be replaced with seals of butyl rubber or ethylene-propylene elastoiners.

Hydraulic Fluid Contamination

Experience has shown that trouble in a hydraulic system is inevitable whenever the liquid is allowed to become contaminated. The nature of the trouble, whether a simple malfunction or the complete destruction of a component, depends to some extent on the type of contaminant. Two general contaminants are:

- Abrasives, including such particles as core sand, weld spatter, machining chips, and rust.
- Nonabrasives, including those resulting from oil oxidation and soft particles worn or shredded from seals and other organic components.

Contamination Check

Whenever it is suspected that a hydraulic system has become contaminated or the system has been operated at temperatures in excess of the specified maximum, a check of the system should be made. The filters in most hydraulic systems are designed to remove most foreign particles that are visible to the naked eye. Hydraulic liquid that appears clean to the naked eye may be contaminated to the point that it is unfit for use. Thus, visual inspection of the hydraulic liquid does not determine the total amount of contamination in the system. Large particles of impurities in the hydraulic system are indications that one or more components are being subjected to excessive wear. Isolating the defective component requires a systematic process of elimination. Fluid returned to the reservoir may contain impurities from any part of the system. To determine which component is defective, liquid samples should be taken from the reservoir and various other locations in the system. Samples should be taken in accordance with the applicable manufacturer's instructions for a particular hydraulic system. Some hydraulic systems are equipped with permanently installed bleed valves for taking liquid samples, whereas on other systems, lines must be disconnected to provide a place to take a sample.

Hydraulic Sampling Schedule

- Routine sampling—each system should be sampled at least once a year, or every 3,000 flight hours, or whenever the airframe manufacturer suggests.
- Unscheduled maintenance—when malfunctions may have a fluid related cause, samples should be taken.
- Suspicion of contamination—if contamination is suspected, fluids should be drained and replaced, with samples taken before and after the maintenance procedure.

Sampling Procedure

- Pressurize and operate hydraulic system for 10–15 minutes. During this period, operate various flight controls to activate valves and thoroughly mix hydraulic fluid.
- Shut down and depressurize the system.
- Before taking samples, always be sure to wear the proper personal protective equipment that should include, at the minimum, safety glasses and gloves.
- Wipe off sampling port or tube with a lint-free cloth. Do not use shop towels or paper products that could produce lint. Generally speaking, the human eye can see particles down to about 40 microns in size. Since we are concerned with particles down to 5 microns in size, it is easy to contaminate a sample without ever knowing it.
- Place a waste container under the reservoir drain valve and open valve so that a steady, but not forceful, stream is running.
- Allow approximately 1 pint (250 ml) of fluid to drain. This purges any settled particles from the sampling port.
- Insert a precleaned sample bottle under the fluid stream and fill, leaving an air space at the top. Withdraw the bottle and cap immediately.
- Close drain valve.

- Fill out sample identification label supplied in sample kit, making sure to include customer name, aircraft type, aircraft tail number, hydraulic system sampled, and date sampled. Indicate on the sample label under remarks if this is a routine sample or if it is being taken due to a suspected problem.
- Service system reservoirs to replace the fluid that was removed.
- Submit samples for analysis to laboratory.

Contamination Control

Filters provide adequate control of the contamination problem during all normal hydraulic system operations. Control of the size and amount of contamination entering the system from any other source is the responsibility of the people who service and maintain the equipment. Therefore, precautions should be taken to minimize contamination during maintenance, repair, and service operations. If the system becomes contaminated, the filter element should be removed and cleaned or replaced. As an aid in controlling contamination, the following maintenance and servicing procedures should be followed at all times:

- Maintain all tools and the work area (workbenches and test equipment) in a clean, dirt-free condition.
- A suitable container should always be provided to receive the hydraulic liquid that is spilled during component removal or disassembly procedures.
- Before disconnecting hydraulic lines or fittings, clean the affected area with dry cleaning solvent.
- All hydraulic lines and fittings should be capped or plugged immediately after disconnecting.
- Before assembly of any hydraulic components, wash all parts in an approved dry cleaning solvent.
- After cleaning the parts in the dry cleaning solution, dry the parts thoroughly and lubricate them with the recommended preservative or hydraulic liquid before assembly. Use only clean, lint-free cloths to wipe or dry the component parts.
- All seals and gaskets should be replaced during the reassembly procedure. Use only those seals and gaskets recommended by the manufacturer.
- All parts should be connected with care to avoid stripping metal slivers from threaded areas. All fittings and lines should be installed and torqued in accordance with applicable technical instructions.
- All hydraulic servicing equipment should be kept clean and in good operating condition.

Contamination, both particulate and chemical, is detrimental to the performance and life of components in the aircraft hydraulic system. Contamination enters the system through normal wear of components by ingestion through external seals during servicing, or maintenance, when the system is opened to replace/repair components, etc. To control the particulate contamination in the system, filters are installed in the pressure line, in the return line, and in the pump case drain line of each system. The filter rating is given in microns as an indication of the smallest particle size that is filtered out. The replacement interval of these filters is established by the manufacturer and is included in the maintenance manual. In the absence of specific replacement instructions, a recommended service life of the filter elements is:

- Pressure filters—3,000 hours
- Return Filters—1,500 hours
- Case drain filters—600 hours

Hydraulic System Flushing

When inspection of hydraulic filters or hydraulic fluid evaluation indicates that the fluid is contaminated, flushing the system may be necessary. This must be done according to the manufacturer's instructions; however, a typical procedure for flushing is as follows:

1. Connect a ground hydraulic test stand to the inlet and outlet test ports of the system. Verify that the ground unit fluid is clean and contains the same fluid as the aircraft.
2. Change the system filters.
3. Pump clean, filtered fluid through the system, and operate all subsystems until no obvious signs of contamination are found during inspection of the filters. Dispose of contaminated fluid and filter. Note: A visual inspection of hydraulic filters is not always effective.
4. Disconnect the test stand and cap the ports.
5. Ensure that the reservoir is filled to the full line or proper service level.

It is very important to check if the fluid in the hydraulic test stand, or mule, is clean before the flushing operation starts. A contaminated hydraulic test stand can quickly contaminate other aircraft if used for ground maintenance operations.

Health and Handling

Skydrol® fluids are phosphate ester-based fluids blended with performance additives. Phosphate esters are good solvents and dissolve away some of the fatty materials of the skin. Repeated or prolonged exposure may cause drying of the skin, which if unattended, could result in complications, such as dermatitis or even secondary infection from bacteria.

Skydrol® fluids could cause itching of the skin but have not been known to cause allergic-type skin rashes. Always use the proper gloves and eye protection when handling any type of hydraulic fluid. When Skydrol®/Hyjet mist or vapor exposure is possible, a respirator capable of removing organic vapors and mists must be worn. Ingestion of any hydraulic fluid should be avoided. Although small amounts do not appear to be highly hazardous, any significant amount should be tested in accordance with manufacturer's direction, followed with hospital supervised stomach treatment.

Basic Hydraulic Systems

Regardless of its function and design, every hydraulic system has a minimum number of basic components in addition to a means through which the fluid is transmitted. A basic system consists of a pump, reservoir, directional valve, check valve, pressure relieve valve, selector valve, actuator, and filter. *[Figure 12-2]*

Figure 12-3. *Open center hydraulic system.*

Figure 12-2. *Basic hydraulic system.*

Open Center Hydraulic Systems

An open center system is one having fluid flow, but no pressure in the system when the actuating mechanisms are idle. The pump circulates the fluid from the reservoir, through the selector valves, and back to the reservoir. *[Figure 12-3]* The open center system may employ any number of subsystems, with a selector valve for each subsystem. Unlike the closed center system, the selector valves of the open center system are always connected in series with each other. In this arrangement, the system pressure line goes through each selector valve. Fluid is always allowed free passage through each selector valve and back to the reservoir until one of the selector valves is positioned to operate a mechanism.

When one of the selector valves is positioned to operate an actuating device, fluid is directed from the pump through one of the working lines to the actuator. *[Figure 12-3B]* With the selector valve in this position, the flow of fluid through the valve to the reservoir is blocked. The pressure builds up in the system to overcome the resistance and moves the piston of the actuating cylinder; fluid from the opposite end of the actuator returns to the selector valve and flows back to the reservoir. Operation of the system following actuation of the component depends on the type of selector valve being used. Several types of selector valves are used in conjunction with the open center system. One type is both manually engaged and manually disengaged. First, the valve is manually moved to an operating position. Then, the actuating mechanism reaches the end of its operating cycle, and the pump output continues until the system relief valve relieves the pressure. The relief valve unseats and allows the fluid to flow back to the reservoir. The system pressure remains at the relief valve set pressure until the selector valve is manually returned to the neutral position. This action reopens the open center flow and allows the system pressure to drop to line resistance pressure.

The manually engaged and pressure disengaged type of selector valve is similar to the valve previously discussed. When the actuating mechanism reaches the end of its cycle, the pressure continues to rise to a predetermined pressure. The valve automatically returns to the neutral position and to open center flow.

Closed-Center Hydraulic Systems

In the closed-center system, the fluid is under pressure whenever the power pump is operating. The three actuators are arranged in parallel and actuating units B and C are operating at the same time, while actuating unit A is not operating. This system differs from the open-center system in that the selector or directional control valves are arranged in parallel and not in series. The means of controlling pump pressure varies in the closed-center system. If a constant delivery pump is used, the system pressure is regulated by a pressure regulator. A relief valve acts as a backup safety device in case the regulator fails.

If a variable displacement pump is used, system pressure is controlled by the pump's integral pressure mechanism compensator. The compensator automatically varies the volume output. When pressure approaches normal system pressure, the compensator begins to reduce the flow output of the pump. The pump is fully compensated (near zero flow) when normal system pressure is attained. When the pump is in this fully compensated condition, its internal bypass mechanism provides fluid circulation through the pump for cooling and lubrication. A relief valve is installed in the system as a safety backup. *[Figure 12-4]* An advantage of the open-center system over the closed-center system is that the continuous pressurization of the system is eliminated. Since the pressure is built up gradually after the selector valve is moved to an operating position, there is very little shock from pressure surges. This action provides a smoother operation of the actuating mechanisms. The operation is slower than the closed-center system, in which the pressure is available the moment the selector valve is positioned. Since most aircraft applications require instantaneous operation, closed-center systems are the most widely used.

Hydraulic Power Systems

Evolution of Hydraulic Systems

Smaller aircraft have relatively low flight control surface loads, and the pilot can operate the flight controls by hand. Hydraulic systems were utilized for brake systems on early aircraft. When aircraft started to fly faster and got larger in size, the pilot was not able to move the control surfaces by hand anymore, and hydraulic power boost systems were introduced. Power boost systems assist the pilot in overcoming high control forces, but the pilot still actuates the flight controls by cable or push rod.

Many modern aircraft use a power supply system and fly-by-wire flight control. The pilot input is electronically sent to the flight control servos. Cables or push rods are not used. Small power packs are the latest evolution of the hydraulic system. They reduce weight by eliminating hydraulic lines and large quantities of hydraulic fluid. Some manufacturers are reducing hydraulic systems in their aircraft in favor of electrically controlled systems. The Boeing 787 is the first aircraft designed with more electrical systems than hydraulic systems.

Hydraulic Power Pack System

A hydraulic power pack is a small unit that consists of an electric pump, filters, reservoir, valves, and pressure relief valve. *[Figure 12-5]* The advantage of the power pack is that

Figure 12-5. *Hydraulic power pack.*

Figure 12-4. *A basic closed-center hydraulic system with a variable displacement pump.*

there is no need for a centralized hydraulic power supply system and long stretches of hydraulic lines, which reduces weight. Power packs could be driven by either an engine gearbox or electric motor. Integration of essential valves, filters, sensors, and transducers reduces system weight, virtually eliminates any opportunity for external leakage, and simplifies troubleshooting. Some power pack systems have an integrated actuator. These systems are used to control the stabilizer trim, landing gear, or flight control surfaces directly, thus eliminating the need for a centralized hydraulic system.

Hydraulic System Components

Figure 12-6 is a typical example of a hydraulic system in a large commercial aircraft. The following sections discuss the components of such system in more detail.

Reservoirs

The reservoir is a tank in which an adequate supply of fluid for the system is stored. Fluid flows from the reservoir to the pump, where it is forced through the system and eventually returned to the reservoir. The reservoir not only supplies the operating needs of the system, but it also replenishes fluid lost through leakage. Furthermore, the reservoir serves as an overflow basin for excess fluid forced out of the system by thermal expansion (the increase of fluid volume caused by temperature changes), the accumulators, and by piston and rod displacement.

The reservoir also furnishes a place for the fluid to purge itself of air bubbles that may enter the system. Foreign matter picked up in the system may also be separated from the fluid in the reservoir or as it flows through line filters. Reservoirs are either pressurized or nonpressurized.

Baffles and/or fins are incorporated in most reservoirs to keep the fluid within the reservoir from having random movement, such as vortexing (swirling) and surging. These conditions can cause fluid to foam and air to enter the pump along with the fluid. Many reservoirs incorporate strainers in the filler neck to prevent the entry of foreign matter during servicing. These strainers are made of fine mesh screening and are usually referred to as finger strainers because of their shape. Finger strainers should never be removed or punctured as a means of speeding up the pouring of fluid into the reservoir.

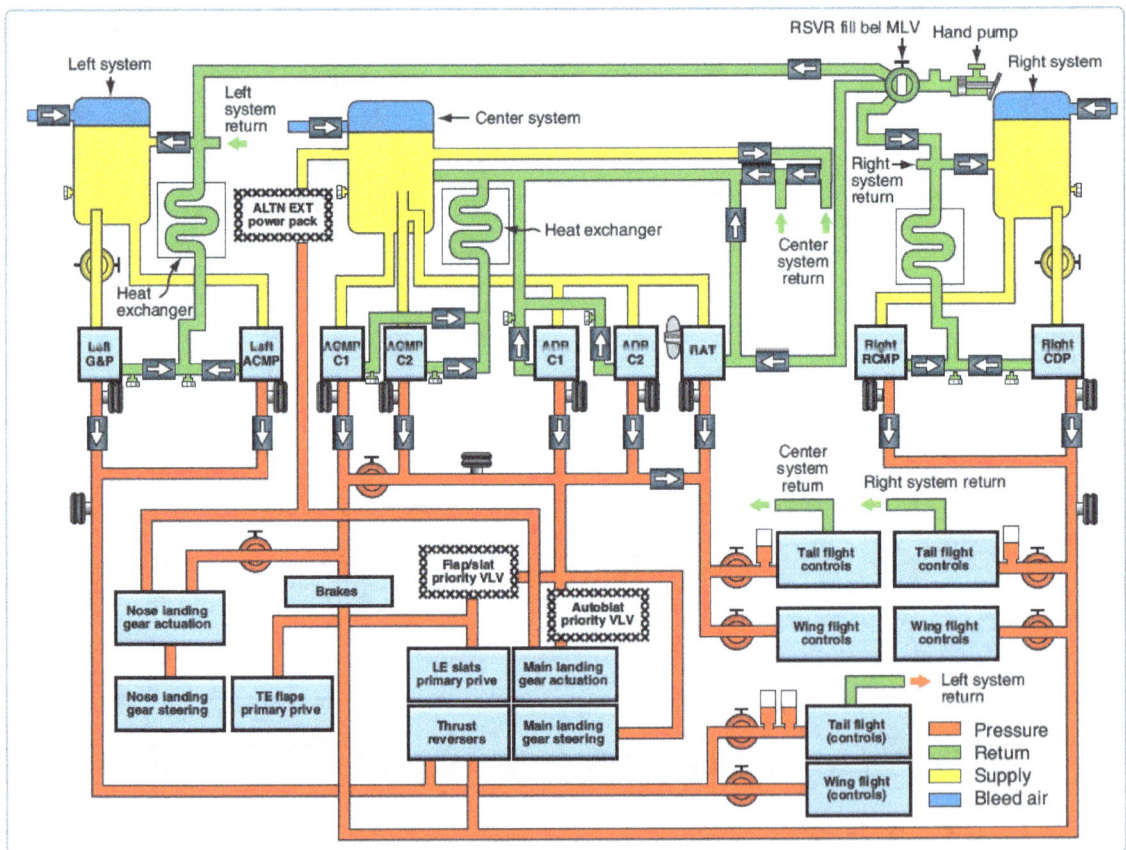

Figure 12-6. *Large commercial aircraft hydraulic system.*

Reservoirs could have an internal trap to make sure fluid goes to the pumps during negative-G conditions.

Most aircraft have emergency hydraulic systems that take over if main systems fail. In many such systems, the pumps of both systems obtain fluid from a single reservoir. Under such circumstances, a supply of fluid for the emergency pump is ensured by drawing the hydraulic fluid from the bottom of the reservoir. The main system draws its fluid through a standpipe located at a higher level. With this arrangement, should the main system's fluid supply become depleted, adequate fluid is left for operation of the emergency system. *Figure 12-7* illustrates that the engine-driven pump (EDP) is not able to draw fluid any more if the reservoir gets depleted below the standpipe. The alternating current motor-driven pump (ACMP) still has a supply of fluid for emergency operations.

Nonpressurized Reservoirs

Nonpressurized reservoirs are used in aircraft that are not designed for violent maneuvers, do not fly at high altitudes, or in which the reservoir is located in the pressurized area of the aircraft. High altitude in this situation means an altitude where atmospheric pressure is inadequate to maintain sufficient flow of fluid to the hydraulic pumps. Most nonpressurized reservoirs are constructed in a cylindrical shape. The outer housing is manufactured from a strong corrosion-resistant metal. Filter elements are normally installed within the reservoir to clean returning system hydraulic fluid.

In some of the older aircraft, a filter bypass valve is incorporated to allow fluid to bypass the filter in the event the filter becomes clogged. Reservoirs can be serviced by pouring fluid directly into the reservoir through a filler strainer (finger strainer) assembly incorporated within the filler well to strain out impurities as the fluid enters the reservoir. Generally, nonpressurized reservoirs use a visual gauge to indicate the fluid quantity. Gauges incorporated on or in the reservoir may be a direct reading glass tube-type or a float-type rod that is visible through a transparent dome. In some cases, the fluid quantity may also be read in the cockpit through the use of quantity transmitters. A typical nonpressurized reservoir is shown in *Figure 12-8*. This reservoir consists of a welded body and cover assembly clamped together. Gaskets are incorporated to seal against leakage between assemblies.

Nonpressurized reservoirs are slightly pressurized due to thermal expansion of fluid and the return of fluid to the reservoir from the main system. This pressure ensures that there is a positive flow of fluids to the inlet ports of the hydraulic pumps. Most reservoirs of this type are vented directly to the atmosphere or cabin with only a check valve and filter to control the outside air source. The reservoir system

Figure 12-7. *Hydraulic reservoir standpipe for emergency operations.*

12-9

Figure 12-8. *Nonpressurized reservoir.*

Figure 12-9. *Air-pressurized reservoir.*

includes a pressure and vacuum relief valve. The purpose of the valve is to maintain a differential pressure range between the reservoir and cabin. A manual air bleed valve is installed on top of the reservoir to vent the reservoir. The valve is connected to the reservoir vent line to allow depressurization of the reservoir. The valve is actuated prior to servicing the reservoir to prevent fluid from being blown out of the filler as the cap is being removed. The manual bleed valve also needs to be actuated if hydraulic components need to be replaced.

Pressurized Reservoirs

Reservoirs on aircraft designed for high-altitude flight are usually pressurized. Pressurizing assures a positive flow of fluid to the pump at high altitudes when low atmospheric pressures are encountered. On some aircraft, the reservoir is pressurized by bleed air taken from the compressor section of the engine. On others, the reservoir may be pressurized by hydraulic system pressure.

Air-Pressurized Reservoirs

Air-pressurized reservoirs are used in many commercial transport-type aircraft. *[Figures 12-9 and 12-10]* Pressurization of the reservoir is required because the reservoirs are often located in wheel wells or other non-pressurized areas of the aircraft and at high altitude there

Figure 12-10. *Components of an air-pressurized reservoir.*

is not enough atmospheric pressure to move the fluid to the pump inlet. Engine bleed air is used to pressurize the reservoir. The reservoirs are typically cylindrical in shape. The following components are installed on a typical reservoir:

- Reservoir pressure relief valve—prevents over pressurization of the reservoir. Valve opens at a preset value.

- Sight glasses (low and overfull)—provides visual indication for flight crews and maintenance personnel that the reservoir needs to be serviced.
- Reservoir sample valve—used to draw a sample of hydraulic fluid for testing.
- Reservoir drain valve—used to drain the fluids out of the reservoir for maintenance operation.
- Reservoir temperature transducer—provides hydraulic fluid temperature information for the flight deck. *[Figure 12-11]*

Figure 12-11. *Temperature and quantity sensors.*

- Reservoir quantity transmitter—transmits fluid quantity to the flight deck so that the flight crew can monitor fluid quantity during flight. *[Figure 12-11]*

A reservoir pressurization module is installed close to the reservoir. *[Figure 12-12]* The reservoir pressurization module supplies airplane bleed air to the reservoirs. The module consists of the following parts:

- Filters (2)
- Check valves (2)
- Test port
- Manual bleed valve
- Gauge port

A manual bleeder valve is incorporated into the module. During hydraulic system maintenance, it is necessary to relieve reservoir air pressure to assist in the installation and removal of components, lines, etc. This type of valve is small in size and has a push button installed in the outer case. When the bleeder valve push button is pushed, pressurized air from the reservoir flows through the valve to an overboard vent until the air pressure is depleted or the button is released. When the button is released, the internal spring causes the poppet to return to its seat. Some hydraulic fluid can escape from the manual bleed valve when the button is depressed.

Caution: Put a rag around the air bleed valve on the reservoir pressurization module to catch hydraulic fluid spray. Hydraulic fluid spray can cause injuries to persons.

Fluid-Pressurized Reservoirs

Some aircraft hydraulic system reservoirs are pressurized by hydraulic system pressure. Regulated hydraulic pump output pressure is applied to a movable piston inside the cylindrical reservoir. This small piston is attached to and moves a larger piston against the reservoir fluid. The reduced force of the small piston when applied by the larger piston is adequate to provide head pressure for high altitude operation. The small piston protrudes out of the body of the reservoir. The amount exposed is used as a reservoir fluid quantity indicator. *Figure 12-13* illustrates the concept behind the fluid-pressurized hydraulic reservoir.

The reservoir has five ports: pump suction, return, pressurizing, overboard drain, and bleed port. Fluid is supplied to the pump through the pump suction port. Fluid returns to the reservoir from the system through the return port. Pressure from the pump enters the pressurizing cylinder in the top of the reservoir through the pressurizing port. The

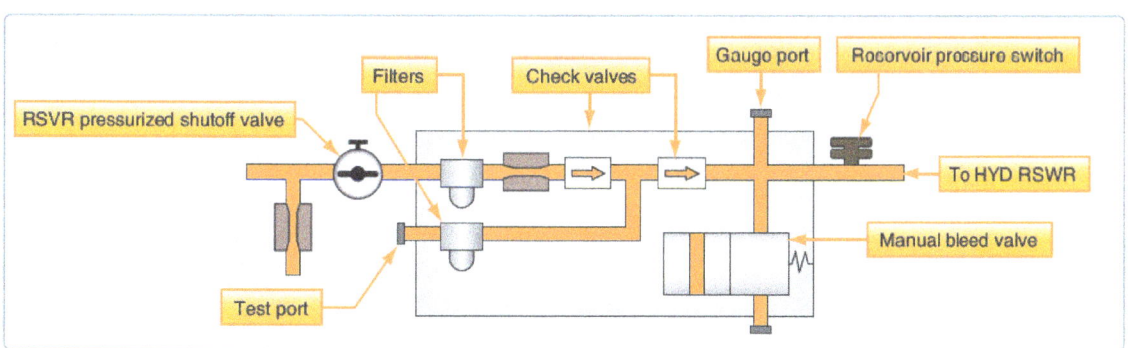

Figure 12-12. *Reservoir pressurization module.*

Figure 12-13. *Operating principle behind a fluid-pressurized hydraulic reservoir.*

overboard drain port drains the reservoir, when necessary, while performing maintenance. The bleed port is used as an aid in servicing the reservoir. When servicing a system equipped with this type of reservoir, place a container under the bleed drain port. The fluid should then be pumped into the reservoir until air-free fluid flows through the bleed drain port.

The reservoir fluid level is indicated by the markings on the part of the pressurizing cylinder that moves through the reservoir dust cover assembly. There are three fluid level markings indicated on the cover: full at zero system pressure (**FULL ZERO PRESS**), full when system is pressurized (**FULL SYS PRESS**), and **REFILL**. When the system is unpressurized and the pointer on the reservoir lies between the two full marks, a marginal reservoir fluid level is indicated. When the system is pressurized and the pointer lies between **REFILL** and **FULL SYS PRESS**, a marginal reservoir fluid level is also indicated.

Reservoir Servicing

Nonpressurized reservoirs can be serviced by pouring fluid directly into the reservoir through a filler strainer (finger strainer) assembly incorporated within the filler well to strain out impurities as the fluid enters the reservoir. Many reservoirs also have a quick disconnect service port at the bottom of the reservoir. A hydraulic filler unit can be connected to the service port to add fluid to the reservoir. This method reduces the chances of contamination of the reservoir. Aircraft that use pressurized reservoirs often have a central filling station in the ground service bay to service all reservoirs from a single point. *[Figure 12-14]*

A built-in hand pump is available to draw fluid from a container through a suction line and pump it into the reservoirs. Additionally, a pressure fill port is available for attachment of a hydraulic mule or serving cart, which uses an external pump to push fluid into the aircraft hydraulic system. A check valve keeps the hand pump output from exiting the pressure fill port. A single filter is located downstream of both the pressure fill port and the hand pump to prevent the introduction of contaminants during fluid servicing.

It is very important to follow the maintenance instructions when servicing the reservoir. To get the correct results when the hydraulic fluid quantities are checked or the reservoirs are to be filled, the airplane should be in the correct configuration. Failure to do so could result in overservicing of the reservoir. This configuration could be different for each aircraft. The following service instructions are an example of a large transport-type aircraft.

Before servicing always make sure that the:

- Spoilers are retracted,
- Landing gear is down,
- Landing gear doors are closed,
- Thrust reversers are retracted, and
- Parking brake accumulator pressure reads at least 2,500 psi.

Filters

A filter is a screening or straining device used to clean the hydraulic fluid, preventing foreign particles and contaminating substances from remaining in the system. *[Figure 12-15]* If such objectionable material were not removed, the entire hydraulic system of the aircraft could fail through the breakdown or malfunctioning of a single unit of the system.

The hydraulic fluid holds in suspension tiny particles of metal that are deposited during the normal wear of selector valves, pumps, and other system components. Such minute particles of metal may damage the units and parts through which they pass if they are not removed by a filter. Since tolerances within the hydraulic system components are quite small, it is apparent that the reliability and efficiency of the entire system depends upon adequate filtering.

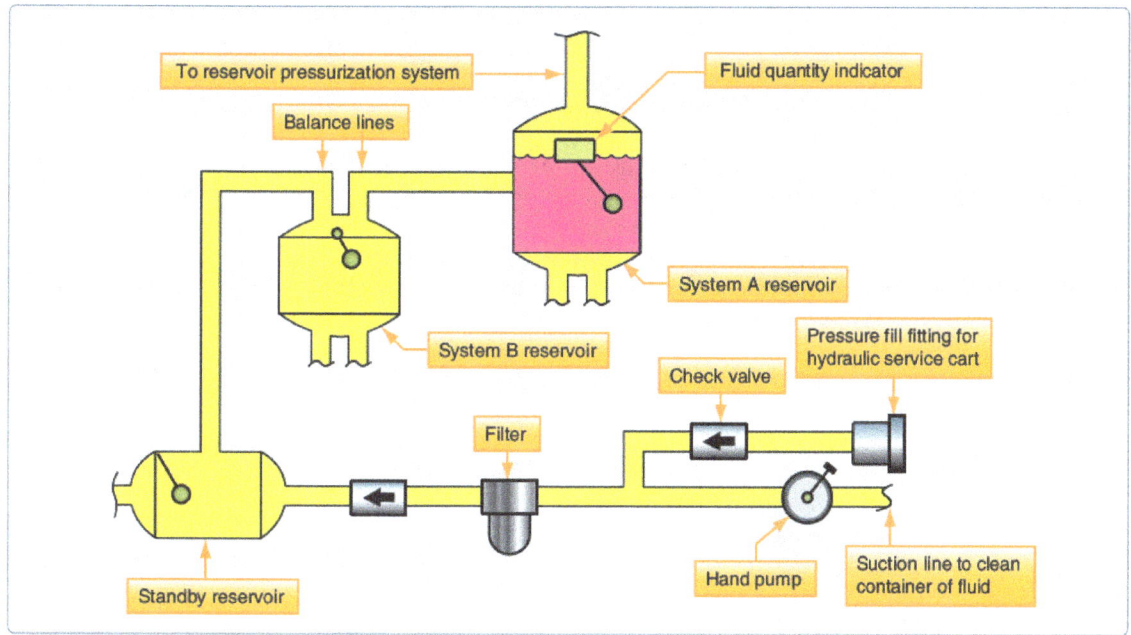

Figure 12-14. *The hydraulic ground serive station on a Boeing 737 provides for hydraulic fluid servicing with a hand pump or via an external pressure fluid source. All three reservoirs are serviced from the same location.*

Figure 12-15. *Filter module components.*

Figure 12-16. *A transport category filter module with two filters.*

Filters may be located within the reservoir, in the pressure line, in the return line, or in any other location the designer of the system decides that they are needed to safeguard the hydraulic system against impurities. Modern design often uses a filter module that contains several filters and other components. *[Figure 12-16]* There are many models and styles of filters. Their position in the aircraft and design requirements determine their shape and size. Most filters used in modern aircraft are of the inline type. The inline filter assembly is comprised of three basic units: head assembly, bowl, and element. The head assembly is secured to the aircraft structure and connecting lines. Within the head, there is a bypass valve that routes the hydraulic fluid directly from the inlet to the outlet port if the filter element becomes clogged with foreign matter. The bowl is the housing that holds the element to the filter head and is removed when element removal is required.

The element may be a micron, porous metal, or magnetic type. The micron element is made of a specially treated paper and is normally thrown away when removed. The porous metal and magnetic filter elements are designed to be cleaned by various methods and replaced in the system.

Micron-Type Filters

A typical micron-type filter assembly utilizes an element made of specially treated paper that is formed in vertical convolutions (wrinkles). An internal spring holds the elements in shape. The micron element is designed to prevent the passage of solids greater than 10 microns (0.000394 inch) in size. *[Figure 12-17]* In the event that the filter element becomes clogged, the spring-loaded relief valve in the filter head bypasses the fluid after a differential pressure of 50 psi has been built up. Hydraulic fluid enters the filter through the inlet port in the filter body and flows around the element inside the bowl. Filtering takes place as the fluid passes through the element into the hollow core, leaving the foreign material on the outside of the element.

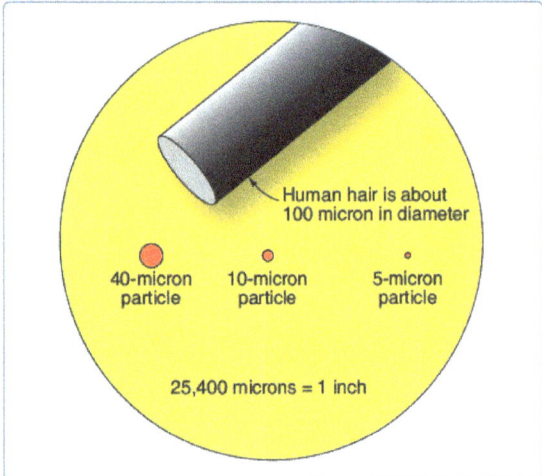

Figure 12-17. *Size comparison in microns.*

Maintenance of Filters

Maintenance of filters is relatively easy. It mainly involves cleaning the filter and element or cleaning the filter and replacing the element. Filters using the micron-type element should have the element replaced periodically according to applicable instructions. Since reservoir filters are of the micron type, they must also be periodically changed or cleaned. For filters using other than the micron-type element, cleaning the filter and element is usually all that is necessary. However, the element should be inspected very closely to ensure that it is completely undamaged. The methods and materials used in cleaning all filters are too numerous to be included in this text. Consult the manufacturer's instructions for this information.

When replacing filter elements, be sure that there is no pressure on the filter bowl. Protective clothing and a face shield must be used to prevent fluid from contacting the eye. Replace the element with one that has the proper rating.

After the filter element has been replaced, the system must be pressure tested to ensure that the sealing element in the filter assembly is intact.

In the event of a major component failure, such as a pump, consideration must be given to replacing the system filter elements, as well as the failed component.

Filter Bypass Valve

Filter modules are often equipped with a bypass relief valve. The bypass relief valve opens if the filter clogs, permitting continued hydraulic flow and operation of aircraft systems. Dirty oil is preferred over no flow at all. *Figure 12-18* shows the principle of operation of a filter bypass valve. Ball valve opens when the filter becomes clogged and the pressure over the filter increases.

Figure 12-18. *Filter bypass valve.*

Filter Differential Pressure Indicators

The extent to which a filter element is loaded can be determined by measuring the drop in hydraulic pressure across the element under rated flow conditions. This drop, or differential pressure, provides a convenient means of monitoring the condition of installed filter elements and is the operating principle used in the differential pressure or loaded-filter indicators found on many filter assemblies.

Differential pressure indicating devices have many configurations, including electrical switches, continuous-reading visual indicators (gauges), and visual indicators with memory. Visual indicators with memory usually take the form of magnetic or mechanically latched buttons or pins that extend when the differential pressure exceeds that allowed for a serviceable element. *[Figure 12-18, top]* When this increased pressure reaches a specific value, inlet pressure forces the spring-loaded magnetic piston downward, breaking the magnetic attachment between the indicator button and the magnetic piston. This allows the red indicator to pop out, signifying that the element must be cleaned. The button or pin, once extended, remains in that position until manually reset and provides a permanent (until reset) warning of a loaded element. This feature is particularly useful where it is impossible for an operator to continuously monitor the visual indicator, such as in a remote location on the aircraft.

Some button indicators have a thermal lockout device incorporated in their design that prevents operation of the indicator below a certain temperature. The lockout prevents the higher differential pressure generated at cold temperatures by high fluid viscosity from causing a false indication of a loaded filter element.

Differential pressure indicators are a component part of the filter assembly in which they are installed and are normally tested and overhauled as part of the complete assembly. With some model filter assemblies, however, it is possible to replace the indicator itself without removal of the filter assembly if it is suspected of being inoperative or out of calibration. It is important that the external surfaces of button-type indicators be kept free of dirt or paint to ensure free movement of the button. Indications of excessive differential pressure, regardless of the type of indicator employed, should never be disregarded. All such indications must be verified and action taken, as required, to replace the loaded filter element. Failure to replace a loaded element can result in system starvation, filter element collapse, or the loss of filtration where bypass assemblies are used. Verification of loaded filter indications is particularly important with button-type indicators as they may have been falsely triggered by mechanical shock, vibration, or cold start of the system. Verification is usually obtained by manually resetting the indicator and operating the system to create a maximum flow demand ensuring that the fluid is at near normal operating temperatures.

Pumps

All aircraft hydraulic systems have one or more power-driven pumps and may have a hand pump as an additional unit when the engine-driven pump is inoperative. Power-driven pumps are the primary source of energy and may be either engine driven, electric motor driven, or air driven. As a general rule, electrical motor pumps are installed for use in emergencies or during ground operations. Some aircraft can deploy a ram air turbine (RAT) to generate hydraulic power.

Hand Pumps

The hydraulic hand pump is used in some older aircraft for the operation of hydraulic subsystems and in a few newer aircraft systems as a backup unit. Hand pumps are generally installed for testing purposes, as well as for use in emergencies. Hand pumps are also installed to service the reservoirs from a single refilling station. The single refilling station reduces the chances for the introduction of fluid contamination.

Several types of hand pumps are used: single action, double action, and rotary. A single action hand pump draws fluid into the pump on one stroke and pumps that fluid out on the next stroke. It is rarely used in aircraft due to this inefficiency.

Double-action hand pumps produce fluid flow and pressure on each stroke of the handle. *[Figure 12-19]* The double-action hand pump consists essentially of a housing that has a cylinder bore and two ports, a piston, two spring-loaded check valves, and an operating handle. An O-ring on the piston seals against leakage between the two chambers of the piston cylinder bore. An O-ring in a groove in the end of the pump housing seals against leakage between the piston rod and housing.

Figure 12-19. *Double action hand pump.*

When the piston is moved to the right, the pressure in the chamber left of the piston is lowered. The inlet port ball check valve opens and hydraulic fluid is drawn into the chamber. At the same time, the rightward movement of the piston forces the piston ball check valve against its seat. Fluid in the chamber to the right of the piston is forced out of the outlet port into the hydraulic system. When the piston is moved to the left, the inlet port ball check valve seats. Pressure in the chamber left of the piston rises, forcing the piston ball check valve off of its seat. Fluid flows from the left chamber through the piston to the right chamber. The volume in the chamber right of the piston is smaller than that of the left chamber due to the displacement created by the piston rod. As the fluid from the left chamber flows into the smaller right chamber, the excess volume of fluid is forced out of the outlet port to the hydraulic system.

A rotary hand pump may also be employed. It produces continuous output while the handle is in motion. *Figure 12-20* shows a rotary hand pump in a hydraulic system.

two hydraulic systems, eight engine-driven pumps, and three electrical driven pumps. The Boeing 777 has three hydraulic systems with two engine driven pumps, four electrical driven pumps, two air driven pumps, and a hydraulic pump motor driven by the RAT. *[Figure 12-21* and *12-22]*

Figure 12-21. *Engine-driven pump.*

Figure 12-22. *Electrically-driven pump.*

Classification of Pumps

All pumps may be classified as either positive displacement or nonpositive displacement. Most pumps used in hydraulic systems are positive displacement. A nonpositive-displacement pump produces a continuous flow. However, because it does not provide a positive internal seal against slippage, its output varies considerably as pressure varies. Centrifugal and propeller pumps are examples of nonpositive-displacement pumps. If the output port of a nonpositive-displacement pump was blocked off, the pressure would rise and output would decrease to zero. Although the pumping element would continue moving, flow would stop because of slippage inside the pump. In a positive-

Figure 12-20. *Rotary hand pump.*

Power-Driven Pumps

Many of the power driven hydraulic pumps of current aircraft are of variable delivery, compensator-controlled type. Constant delivery pumps are also in use. Principles of operation are the same for both types of pumps. Modern aircraft use a combination of engine-driven power pumps, electrical-driven power pumps, air-driven power pumps, power transfer units (PTU), and pumps driven by a RAT. For example, large aircraft, such as the Airbus A380, have displacement pump, slippage is negligible compared to the pump's volumetric output flow. If the output port were plugged, pressure would increase instantaneously to the point that the pump pressure relief valve opens.

Constant-Displacement Pumps

A constant-displacement pump, regardless of pump rotations per minute, forces a fixed or unvarying quantity of fluid through the outlet port during each revolution of the pump. Constant-displacement pumps are sometimes called constant-volume or constant-delivery pumps. They deliver a fixed quantity of fluid per revolution, regardless of the pressure demands. Since the constant-delivery pump provides a fixed quantity of fluid during each revolution of the pump, the quantity of fluid delivered per minute depends upon pump rotations per minute. When a constant-displacement pump is used in a hydraulic system in which the pressure must be kept at a constant value, a pressure regulator is required.

Gear-Type Power Pump

A gear-type power pump is a constant-displacement pump. It consists of two meshed gears that revolve in a housing. *[Figure 12-23]* The driving gear is driven by the aircraft engine or some other power unit. The driven gear meshes with, and is driven by, the driving gear. Clearance between the teeth as they mesh and between the teeth and the housing is very small. The inlet port of the pump is connected to the reservoir, and the outlet port is connected to the pressure line.

Figure 12-23. *Gear-type power pump.*

When the driving gear turns, as shown in *Figure 12-23*, it turns the driven gear. Fluid is captured by the teeth as they pass the inlet, and it travels around the housing and exits at the outlet.

Gerotor Pump

A gerotor-type power pump consists essentially of a housing containing an eccentric-shaped stationary liner, an internal gear rotor having seven wide teeth of short height, a spur driving gear having six narrow teeth, and a pump cover that contains two crescent-shaped openings. *[Figure 12-24]* One opening extends into an inlet port and the other extends into an outlet port. During the operation of the pump, the gears turn clockwise together. As the pockets between the gears

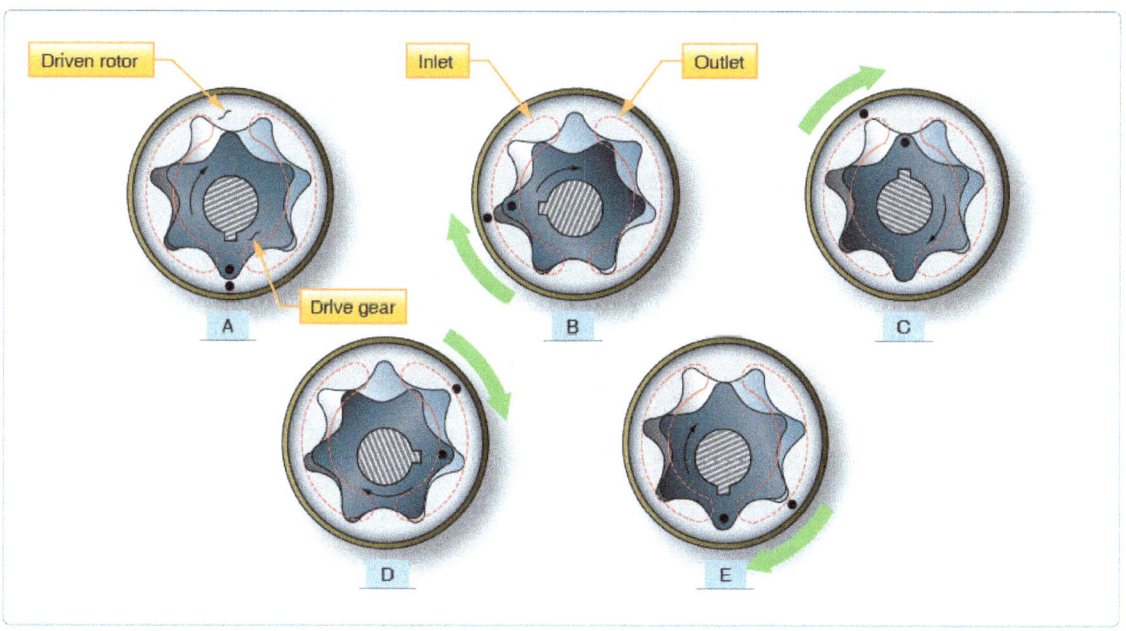

Figure 12-24. *Gerotor pump.*

on the left side of the pump move from a lowermost position toward a topmost position, the pockets increase in size, resulting in the production of a partial vacuum within these pockets. Since the pockets enlarge while over the inlet port crescent, fluid is drawn into them. As these same pockets (now full of fluid) rotate over to the right side of the pump, moving from the topmost position toward the lowermost position, they decrease in size. This results in the fluid being expelled from the pockets through the outlet port crescent.

Piston Pump

Piston pumps can be constant-displacement or variable-displacement pumps. The common features of design and operation that are applicable to all piston-type hydraulic pumps are described in the following paragraphs. Piston-type power-driven pumps have flanged mounting bases for the purpose of mounting the pumps on the accessory drive cases of aircraft engines. A pump drive shaft, which turns the mechanism, extends through the pump housing slightly beyond the mounting base. Torque from the driving unit is transmitted to the pump drive shaft by a drive coupling. The drive coupling is a short shaft with a set of male splines on both ends. The splines on one end engage with female splines in a driving gear: the splines on the other end engage with female splines in the pump drive shaft. Pump drive couplings are designed to serve as safety devices. The shear section of the drive coupling, located midway between the two sets of splines, is smaller in diameter than the splines. If the pump becomes unusually hard to turn or becomes jammed, this section shears, preventing damage to the pump or driving unit. *[Figure 12-25]* The basic pumping mechanism of piston-type pumps consists of a multiple-bore cylinder block, a piston for each bore, and a valve plate with inlet and outlet slots. The purpose of the valve plate slots is to let fluid into and out of the bores as the pump operates. The cylinder bores lie parallel to and symmetrically around the pump axis. All aircraft axial-piston pumps have an odd number of pistons. *[Figure 12-26]*

Figure 12-26. *Hydraulic pump shear shaft.*

Bent Axis Piston Pump

A typical constant-displacement axial-type pump is shown in *Figure 12-27.* The angular housing of the pump causes a corresponding angle to exist between the cylinder block and the drive shaft plate to which the pistons are attached. It is this angular configuration of the pump that causes the pistons to stroke as the pump shaft is turned. When the pump operates, all parts within the pump (except the outer races of the bearings that support the drive shaft, the cylinder bearing pin on which the cylinder block turns, and the oil seal) turn together as a rotating group. At one point of rotation of the rotating group, a minimum distance exists between the top of

Figure 12-25. *Axial inline piston pump.*

Figure 12-27. *Bent axis piston pump.*

the cylinder block and the upper face of the drive shaft plate. Because of the angled housing at a point of rotation 180° away, the distance between the top of the cylinder block and the upper face of the drive shaft plate is at a maximum. At any given moment of operation, three of the pistons are moving away from the top face of the cylinder block, producing a partial vacuum in the bores in which these pistons operate. This occurs over the inlet port, so fluid is drawn into these bores at this time. On the opposite side of the cylinder block, three different pistons are moving toward the top face of the block. This occurs while the rotating group is passing over the outlet port causing fluid to be expelled from the pump by these pistons. The continuous and rapid action of the pistons is overlapping in nature and results in a practically nonpulsating pump output.

Inline Piston Pump

The simplest type of axial piston pump is the swash plate design in which a cylinder block is turned by the drive shaft. Pistons fitted to bores in the cylinder block are connected through piston shoes and a retracting ring so that the shoes bear against an angled swash plate. As the block turns, the piston shoes follow the swash plate, causing the pistons to reciprocate. The ports are arranged in the valve plate so that the pistons pass the inlet as they are pulled out, and pass the outlet as they are forced back in. In these pumps, displacement is determined by the size and number of pistons, as well as their stroke length, which varies with the swash plate angle. This constant-displacement pump is illustrated in *Figure 12-26*.

Vane Pump

The vane-type power pump is also a constant-displacement pump. It consists of a housing containing four vanes (blades), a hollow steel rotor with slots for the vanes, and a coupling to turn the rotor. *[Figure 12-28]* The rotor is positioned off center within the sleeve. The vanes, which are mounted in the slots in the rotor, together with the rotor, divide the bore of the sleeve into four sections. As the rotor turns, each section passes one point where its volume is at a minimum and another point where its volume is at a maximum. The volume gradually increases from minimum to maximum during the first half of a revolution and gradually decreases from maximum to minimum during the second half of the revolution. As the volume of a given section increases, that section is connected to the pump inlet port through a slot in

Figure 12-28. *Vane-type power pump.*

the sleeve. Since a partial vacuum is produced by the increase in volume of the section, fluid is drawn into the section through the pump inlet port and the slot in the sleeve. As the rotor turns through the second half of the revolution and the volume of the given section is decreasing, fluid is displaced out of the section, through the slot in the sleeve aligned with the outlet port, and out of the pump.

Variable-Displacement Pump

A variable-displacement pump has a fluid output that is varied to meet the pressure demands of the system. The pump output is changed automatically by a pump compensator within the pump. The following paragraph discusses a two-stage Vickers variable displacement pump. The first stage of the pump consists of a centrifugal pump that boosts the pressure before the fluid enters the piston pump. *[Figure 12-29]*

Basic Pumping Operation

The aircraft's engine rotates the pump drive shaft, cylinder block, and pistons via a gearbox. Pumping action is generated by piston shoes that are restrained and slide on the shoe bearing plate in the yoke assembly. Because the yoke is at an angle to the drive shaft, the rotary motion of the shaft is converted to piston reciprocating motion.

As the piston begins to withdraw from the cylinder block, system inlet pressure forces fluid through a porting arrangement in the valve plate into the cylinder bore. The piston shoes are restrained in the yoke by a piston shoe retaining plate and a shoe plate during the intake stroke.

Figure 12-29. *Variable displacement pump.*

As the drive shaft continues to turn the cylinder block, the piston shoe continues following the yoke bearing surface. This begins to return the piston into its bore (i.e., toward the valve block).

The fluid contained in the bore is precompressed, then expelled through the outlet port. Discharge pressure holds the piston shoe against the yoke bearing surface during the discharge stroke and also provides the shoe pressure balance and fluid film through an orifice in the piston and shoe subassembly.

With each revolution of the drive shaft and cylinder block, each piston goes through the pumping cycle described above, completing one intake and one discharge stroke. High-pressure fluid is ported out through the valve plate, past the blocking valve, to the pump outlet. The blocking valve is designed to remain open during normal pump operation. Internal leakage keeps the pump housing filled with fluid for lubrication of rotating parts and cooling. The leakage is returned to the system through a case drain port. The case valve relief valve protects the pump against excessive case pressure, relieving it to the pump inlet.

Normal Pumping Mode

The pressure compensator is a spool valve that is held in the closed position by an adjustable spring load. *[Figure 12-30]* When pump outlet pressure (system pressure) exceeds the pressure setting (2,850 psi for full flow), the spool moves to admit fluid from the pump outlet against the yoke actuator piston. In *Figure 12-30,* the pressure compensator is shown at cracking pressure; the pump outlet pressure is just high enough to move the spool to begin admitting fluid to the actuator piston.

The yoke is supported inside the pump housing on two bearings. At pump outlet pressures below 2,850 psi, the yoke is held at its maximum angle relative to the drive shaft centerline by the force of the yoke return spring. Decreasing system flow demand causes outlet pressure to become high enough to crack the compensator valve open and admit fluid to the actuator piston.

Figure 12-30. *Normal pumping mode.*

This control pressure overcomes the yoke return spring force and strokes the pump yoke to a reduced angle. The reduced angle of the yoke results in a shorter stroke for the pistons and reduced displacement. *[Figure 12-31]*

Figure 12-31. *Yoke angle.*

The lower displacement results in a corresponding reduction in pump flow. The pump delivers only that flow required to maintain the desired pressure in the system. When there is no demand for flow from the system, the yoke angle decreases to nearly zero degrees stroke angle. In this mode, the unit pumps only its own internal leakage. Thus, at pump outlet pressures above 2,850 psi, pump displacement decreases as outlet pressure rises. At system pressures below this level, no fluid is admitted through the pressure compensator valve to the actuator piston and the pump remains at full displacement, delivering full flow. Pressure is then determined by the system demand. The unit maintains zero flow at system pressure of 3,025 psi.

Depressurized Mode

When the solenoid valve is energized, the EDV solenoid valve moves up against the spring force and the outlet fluid is ported to the EDV control piston on the top of the compensator (depressurizing piston). *[Figure 12-32]* The high-pressure fluid pushes the compensator spool beyond

Figure 12-32. *Depressurized mode.*

its normal metering position. This removes the compensator valve from the circuit and connects the actuator piston directly to the pump outlet. Outlet fluid is also ported to the blocking valve spring chamber, which equalizes pressure on both sides of its plunger. The blocking valve closes due to the force of the blocking valve spring and isolates the pump from the external hydraulic system. The pump strokes itself to zero delivery at an outlet pressure that is equal to the pressure required on the actuator piston to reduce the yoke angle to nearly zero, approximately 1,100 psi. This depressurization and blocking feature can be used to reduce the load on the engine during startup and, in a multiple pump system, to isolate one pump at a time and check for proper system pressure output.

Valves
Flow Control Valves

Flow control valves control the speed and/or direction of fluid flow in the hydraulic system. They provide for the operation of various components when desired and the speed at which the component operates. Examples of flow control valves include: selector valves, check valves, sequence valves, priority valves, shuttle valves, quick disconnect valves, and hydraulic fuses.

Selector Valves

A selector valve is used to control the direction of movement of a hydraulic actuating cylinder or similar device. It provides for the simultaneous flow of hydraulic fluid both into and out of the unit. Hydraulic system pressure can be routed with the selector valve to operate the unit in either direction and a corresponding return path for the fluid to the reservoir is provided. There are two main types of selector valves: open-center and closed-center. An open center valve allows a continuous flow of system hydraulic fluid through the valve even when the selector is not in a position to actuate a unit. A closed-center selector valve blocks the flow of fluid through the valve when it is in the NEUTRAL or OFF position. *[Figure 12-33A]*

Selector valves may be poppet-type, spool-type, piston-type, rotary-type, or plug-type. *[Figure 12-34]* Regardless, each selector valve has a unique number of ports. The number of ports is determined by the particular requirements of the system in which the valve is used. Closed-centered selector valves with four ports are most common in aircraft hydraulic systems. These are known as four-way valves. *Figure 12-33* illustrates how this valve connects to the pressure and return lines of the hydraulic system, as well as to the two ports on a common actuator. Most selector valves are mechanically controlled by a lever or electrically controlled by solenoid or servo. *[Figure 12-35]*

The four ports on a four-way selector valve always have the same function. One port receives pressurized fluid from the system hydraulic pump. A second port always returns fluid to the reservoir. The third and forth ports are used to connect the selector valve to the actuating unit. There are two ports on the actuating unit. When the selector valve is positioned to connect pressure to one port on the actuator, the other

Figure 12-33. *Operation of a closed-center four-way selector valve, which controls an actuator.*

Figure 12-34. *A poppet-type four-way selector valve.*

Figure 12-35. *Four-way servo control valve.*

actuator port is simultaneously connected to the reservoir return line through selector valve. *[Figure 12-33B]* Thus, the unit operates in a certain direction. When the selector valve is positioned to connect pressure to the other port on the actuating unit, the original port is simultaneously connected to the return line through the selector valve and the unit operates in the opposite direction. *[Figure 12-33C]*

Figure 12-36 illustrates the internal flow paths of a solenoid operated selector valve. The closed center valve is shown in the NEUTRAL or OFF position. Neither solenoid is energized. The pressure port routes fluid to the center lobe on the spool, which blocks the flow. Fluid pressure flows through the pilot valves and applies equal pressure on both ends of the spool. The actuator lines are connected around the spool to the return line.

Figure 12-36. *Servo control valve solenoids not energized.*

When selected via a switch in the cockpit, the right solenoid is energized. The right pilot valve plug shifts left, which blocks pressurized fluid from reaching the right end of the main spool. The spool slides to the right due to greater pressure applied on the left end of the spool. The center lobe of the spool no longer blocks system pressurized fluid, which flows to the actuator through the left actuator line. At the same time, return flow is blocked from the main spool left chamber so the actuator (not shown) moves in the selected direction. Return fluid from the moving actuator flows through the right actuator line past the spool and into the return line. *[Figure 12-37]*

Figure 12-37. *Servo control valve right solenoid energized.*

Typically, the actuator or moving device contacts a limit switch when the desired motion is complete. The switch causes the right solenoid to de-energize and the right pilot valve reopens. Pressurized fluid can once again flow through the pilot valve and into the main spool right end chamber. There, the spring and fluid pressure shift the spool back to the left into the NEUTRAL or OFF position shown in *Figure 12-36*.

To make the actuator move in the opposite direction, the cockpit switch is moved in the opposite direction. All motion inside the selector valve is the same as described above but in the opposite direction. The left solenoid is energized. Pressure is applied to the actuator through the right port and return fluid from the left actuator line is connected to the return port through the motion of the spool to the left.

Check Valve

Another common flow control valve in aircraft hydraulic systems is the check valve. A check valve allows fluid to flow unimpeded in one direction, but prevents or restricts fluid flow in the opposite direction. A check valve may be an independent component situated in-line somewhere in the hydraulic system or it may be built-in to a component. When part of a component, the check valve is said to be an integral check valve.

A typical check valve consists of a spring loaded ball and seat inside a housing. The spring compresses to allow fluid flow in the designed direction. When flow stops, the spring pushes the ball against the seat which prevents fluid from flowing in the opposite direction through the valve. An arrow on the outside of the housing indicated the direction in which fluid flow is permitted. *[Figure 12-38]* A check valve may also be constructed with spring loaded flapper or coned shape piston instead of a ball.

Orifice-Type Check Valve

Some check valves allow full fluid flow in one direction and restricted flow in the opposite direction. These are known as orifice-type check valves, or damping valves. The valve contains the same spring, ball, and seat combination as a normal check valve but the seat area has a calibrated orifice machined into it. Thus fluid flow is unrestricted in the designed direction while the ball is pushed off of its seat. The downstream actuator operates at full speed. When fluid back flows into the valve, the spring forces the ball against the seat which limits fluid flow to the amount that can pass through the orifice. The reduced flow in this opposite direction slows the motion, or dampens, the actuator associated with the check valve. *[Figure 12-38]*

An orifice check valve may be included in a hydraulic landing gear actuator system. When the gear is raised, the check valve allows full fluid flow to lift the heavy gear at maximum speed. When lowering the gear, the orifice in the check valve prevents the gear from violently dropping by restricting fluid flow out of the actuating cylinder.

Sequence Valves

Sequence valves control the sequence of operation between two branches in a circuit: they enable one unit to automatically set another unit into motion. An example of the use of a sequence valve is in an aircraft landing gear actuating system. In a landing gear actuating system, the landing gear doors must open before the landing gear starts to extend. Conversely, the landing gear must be completely retracted before the doors close. A sequence valve installed in each landing gear actuating line performs this function. A sequence valve is somewhat similar to a relief valve except that, after the set pressure has been reached, the sequence valve diverts the fluid to a second actuator or motor to do work in another part of the system. There are various types of sequence valves. Some are controlled by pressure, some are controlled mechanically, and some are controlled by electric switches.

Figure 12-38. *An in-line check valve and orifice type in-line check valve.*

Pressure-Controlled Sequence Valve

The operation of a typical pressure-controlled sequence valve is illustrated in *Figure 12-36*. The opening pressure is obtained by adjusting the tension of the spring that normally holds the piston in the closed position. (Note that the top part of the piston has a larger diameter than the lower part.) Fluid enters the valve through the inlet port, flows around the lower part of the piston and exits the outlet port, where it flows to the primary (first) unit to be operated. *[Figure 12-39A]* This fluid pressure also acts against the lower surface of the piston.

When the primary actuating unit completes its operation, pressure in the line to the actuating unit increases sufficiently to overcome the force of the spring, and the piston rises. The valve is then in the open position. *[Figure 12-39B]* The fluid entering the valve takes the path of least resistance and flows to the secondary unit. A drain passage is provided to allow any fluid leaking past the piston to flow from the top of the valve. In hydraulic systems, this drain line is usually connected to the main return line.

Mechanically Operated Sequence Valve

The mechanically operated sequence valve is operated by a plunger that extends through the body of the valve. *[Figure 12-40]* The valve is mounted so that the plunger is operated by the primary unit. A check valve, either a ball or a poppet, is installed between the fluid ports in the body. It can be unseated by either the plunger or fluid pressure. Port A and the actuator of the primary unit are connected by a common line. Port B is connected by a line to the actuator of the secondary unit. When fluid under pressure flows to the primary unit, it also flows into the sequence valve through port A to the seated check valve in the sequence valve. In order to operate the secondary unit, the fluid must flow through the sequence valve. The valve is located so that the

Figure 12-40. *Mechanically operated sequence valve.*

primary unit moves the plunger as it completes its operation. The plunger unseats the check valve and allows the fluid to flow through the valve, out port B, and to the secondary unit.

Priority Valves

A priority valve gives priority to the critical hydraulic subsystems over noncritical systems when system pressure is low. For instance, if the pressure of the priority valve is set for 2,200 psi, all systems receive pressure when the pressure is above 2,200 psi. If the pressure drops below 2,200 psi, the priority valve closes and no fluid pressure flows to the noncritical systems. *[Figure 12-41]* Some hydraulic designs use pressure switches and electrical shutoff valves to assure that the critical systems have priority over noncritical systems when system pressure is low.

Quick Disconnect Valves

Quick disconnect valves are installed in hydraulic lines to prevent loss of fluid when units are removed. Such valves

Figure 12-39. *A pressure-controlled sequence valve.*

Figure 12-41. *Priority valve.*

are installed in the pressure and suction lines of the system immediately upstream and downstream of the power pump. In addition to pump removal, a power pump can be disconnected from the system and a hydraulic test stand connected in its place. These valve units consist of two interconnecting sections coupled together by a nut when installed in the system. Each valve section has a piston and poppet assembly. These are spring loaded to the closed position when the unit is disconnected. *[Figure 12-42]*

Figure 12-42. *A hydraulic quick-disconnect valve.*

Hydraulic Fuses

A hydraulic fuse is a safety device. Fuses may be installed at strategic locations throughout a hydraulic system. They detect a sudden increase in flow, such as a burst downstream, and shut off the fluid flow. By closing, a fuse preserves hydraulic fluid for the rest of the system. Hydraulic fuses are fitted to the brake system, leading edge flap and slat extend and retract lines, nose landing gear up and down lines, and the thrust reverser pressure and return lines. One type of fuse, referred to as the automatic resetting type, is designed to allow a certain volume of fluid per minute to pass through it. If the volume passing through the fuse becomes excessive, the fuse closes and shuts off the flow. When the pressure is removed from the pressure supply side of the fuse, it automatically resets itself to the open position. Fuses are usually cylindrical in shape, with an inlet and outlet port at opposite ends. *[Figure 12-43]*

Figure 12-43. *Hydraulic fuse.*

Pressure Control Valves

The safe and efficient operation of fluid power systems, system components, and related equipment requires a means of controlling pressure. There are many types of automatic pressure control valves. Some of them are an escape for pressure that exceeds a set pressure; some only reduce the pressure to a lower pressure system or subsystem; and some keep the pressure in a system within a required range.

Relief Valves

Hydraulic pressure must be regulated in order to use it to perform the desired tasks. A pressure relief valve is used to limit the amount of pressure being exerted on a confined liquid. This is necessary to prevent failure of components or rupture of hydraulic lines under excessive pressures. The pressure relief valve is, in effect, a system safety valve.

The design of pressure relief valves incorporates adjustable spring-loaded valves. They are installed in such a manner as to discharge fluid from the pressure line into a reservoir return line when the pressure exceeds the predetermined maximum for which the valve is adjusted. Various makes and designs of pressure relief valves are in use, but, in general, they all employ a spring-loaded valving device operated by hydraulic pressure and spring tension. *[Figure 12-44]* Pressure relief valves are adjusted by increasing or decreasing the tension on the spring to determine the pressure required to open the valve. They may be classified by type of construction or uses in the system. The most common types of valve are:

Figure 12-44. *Pressure relief valve.*

1. Ball type—in pressure relief valves with a ball-type valving device, the ball rests on a contoured seat. Pressure acting on the bottom of the ball pushes it off its seat, allowing the fluid to bypass.

2. Sleeve type—in pressure relief valves with a sleeve-type valving device, the ball remains stationary and a sleeve-type seat is moved up by the fluid pressure. This allows the fluid to bypass between the ball and the sliding sleeve-type seat.

3. Poppet type—in pressure relief valves with a poppet-type valving device, a cone-shaped poppet may have any of several design configurations; however, it is basically a cone and seat machined at matched angles to prevent leakage. As the pressure rises to its predetermined setting, the poppet is lifted off its seat, as in the ball-type device. This allows the fluid to pass through the opening created and out the return port.

Pressure relief valves cannot be used as pressure regulators in large hydraulic systems that depend on engine-driven pumps for the primary source of pressure because the pump is constantly under load and the energy expended in holding the pressure relief valve off its seat is changed into heat. This heat is transferred to the fluid and, in turn, to the packing rings, causing them to deteriorate rapidly. Pressure relief valves, however, may be used as pressure regulators in small, low-pressure systems or when the pump is electrically driven and is used intermittently.

Pressure relief valves may be used as:

1. System relief valve—the most common use of the pressure relief valve is as a safety device against the possible failure of a pump compensator or other pressure regulating device. All hydraulic systems that have hydraulic pumps incorporate pressure relief valves as safety devices.

2. Thermal relief valve—the pressure relief valve is used to relieve excessive pressures that may exist due to thermal expansion of the fluid. They are used where a check valve or selector valve prevents pressure from being relieved through the main system relief valve. Thermal relief valves are usually smaller than system relief valves. As pressurized fluid in the line in which it is installed builds to an excessive amount, the valve poppet is forced off its seat. This allows excessive pressurized fluid to flow through the relief valve to the reservoir return line. When system pressure decreases to a predetermined pressure, spring tension overcomes system pressure and forces the valve poppet to the closed position.

Pressure Regulators

The term pressure regulator is applied to a device used in hydraulic systems that are pressurized by constant-delivery-type pumps. One purpose of the pressure regulator is to manage the output of the pump to maintain system operating pressure within a predetermined range. The other purpose is to permit the pump to turn without resistance (termed unloading the pump) at times when pressure in the system is within normal operating range. The pressure regulator is located in the system so that pump output can get into the system pressure circuit only by passing through the regulator. The combination of a constant-delivery-type pump and the pressure regulator is virtually the equivalent of a compensator-controlled, variable-delivery-type pump. *[Figure 12-45]*

Pressure Reducers

Pressure reducing valves are used in hydraulic systems where it is necessary to lower the normal system operating pressure by a specified amount. Pressure reducing valves provide a steady pressure into a system that operates at a lower pressure

[Figure 12-45 diagram of hydraulic system]

Figure 12-45. *The location of a pressure regulator in a basic hydraulic system. The regulator unloads the constant delivery pump by bypassing fluid to the return line when the predetermined system pressure is reached.*

than the supply system. A reducing valve can normally be set for any desired downstream pressure within the design limits of the valve. Once the valve is set, the reduced pressure is maintained regardless of changes in supply pressure (as long as the supply pressure is at least as high as the reduced pressure desired) and regardless of the system load, if the load does not exceed the designed capacity of the reducer. *[Figure 12-46]*

Shuttle Valves

In certain fluid power systems, the supply of fluid to a subsystem must be from more than one source to meet system requirements. In some systems, an emergency system is provided as a source of pressure in the event of normal system failure. The emergency system usually actuates only essential components. The main purpose of the shuttle valve is to isolate the normal system from an alternate or emergency system. It is small and simple; yet, it is a very important component. *[Figure 12-47]* The housing contains three ports—normal system inlet, alternate or emergency system inlet, and outlet. A shuttle valve used to operate more than one actuating unit may contain additional unit outlet ports.

Figure 12-46. *Operating mechanism of a pressure reducing valve.*

Figure 12-47. *A spring-loaded piston-type shuttle valve in normal configuration (A) and with alternate/emergency supply (B).*

Enclosed in the housing is a sliding part called the shuttle. Its purpose is to seal off one of the inlet ports. There is a shuttle seat at each inlet port. When a shuttle valve is in the normal operation position, fluid has a free flow from the normal system inlet port, through the valve, and out through the outlet port to the actuating unit. The shuttle is seated against the alternate system inlet port and held there by normal system pressure and by the shuttle valve spring. The shuttle remains in this position until the alternate system is activated. This action directs fluid under pressure from the alternate system to the shuttle valve and forces the shuttle from the alternate system inlet port to the normal system inlet port. Fluid from the alternate system then has a free flow to the outlet port, but is prevented from entering the normal system by the shuttle, which seals off the normal system port.

The shuttle may be one of four types:

1. Sliding plunge
2. Spring-loaded piston
3. Spring-loaded ball
4. Spring-loaded poppet

In shuttle valves that are designed with a spring, the shuttle is normally held against the alternate system inlet port by the spring.

Shutoff Valves

Shutoff valves are used to shutoff the flow of fluid to a particular system or component. In general, these types of valves are electrically powered. Shutoff valves are also used to create a priority in a hydraulic system and are controlled by pressure switches. *[Figure 12-48]*

Accumulators

The accumulator is a steel sphere divided into two chambers by a synthetic rubber diaphragm. The upper chamber contains fluid at system pressure, while the lower chamber is charged

Figure 12-48. *Shutoff valves.*

with nitrogen or air. Cylindrical types are also used in high-pressure hydraulic systems. Many aircraft have several accumulators in the hydraulic system. There may be a main system accumulator and an emergency system accumulator. There may also be auxiliary accumulators located in various sub-systems.

The function of an accumulator is to:

- Dampen pressure surges in the hydraulic system caused by actuation of a unit and the effort of the pump to maintain pressure at a preset level.

- Aid or supplement the power pump when several units are operating at once by supplying extra power from its accumulated, or stored, power.

- Store power for the limited operation of a hydraulic unit when the pump is not operating.

- Supply fluid under pressure to compensate for small internal or external (not desired) leaks that would cause the system to cycle continuously by action of the pressure switches continually kicking in.

Types of Accumulators

There are two general types of accumulators used in aircraft hydraulic systems: spherical and cylindrical.

Spherical

The spherical-type accumulator is constructed in two halves that are fastened and threaded, or welded, together. Two threaded openings exist. The top port accepts fittings to connect to the pressurized hydraulic system to the accumulator. The bottom port is fitted with a gas servicing valve, such as a Schrader valve. A synthetic rubber diaphragm, or bladder, is installed in the sphere to create two chambers. Pressurized hydraulic fluid occupies the upper chamber and nitrogen or air charges the lower chamber. A screen at the fluid pressure port keeps the diaphragm, or bladder, from extruding through the port when the lower chamber is charged and hydraulic fluid pressure is zero. A rigid button or disc may also be attached to the diaphragm, or bladder, for this purpose. *[Figure 12-49]* The bladder is installed through a large opening in the bottom of the sphere and is secured with a threaded retainer plug. The gas servicing valve mounts into the retainer plug.

Cylindrical

Cylindrical accumulators consist of a cylinder and piston assembly. End caps are attached to both ends of the cylinder. The internal piston separates the fluid and air/nitrogen chambers. The end caps and piston are sealed with gaskets and packings to prevent external leakage around the end caps and internal leakage between the chambers. In one end cap, a hydraulic fitting is used to attach the fluid chamber to the hydraulic system. In the other end cap, a filler valve is installed to perform the same function as the filler valve installed in the spherical accumulator. *[Figure 12-50]*

Operation

In operation, the compressed-air chamber is charged to a predetermined pressure that is somewhat lower than the system operating pressure. This initial charge is referred to as the accumulator preload. As an example of accumulator operation, let us assume that the cylindrical accumulator is designed for a preload of 1,300 psi in a 3,000-psi system.

Figure 12-50. *Cylindrical accumulator.*

When the initial charge of 1,300 psi is introduced into the unit, hydraulic system pressure is zero. As air pressure is applied through a gas servicing valve, it moves the piston toward the opposite end until it bottoms. If the air behind the piston has a pressure of 1,300 psi, the hydraulic system pump has to create a pressure within the system greater than 1,300 psi before the hydraulic fluid can actuate the piston. At 1,301 psi the piston starts to move within the cylinder, compressing the air as it moves. At 2,000 psi, it has backed up several inches. At 3,000 psi, the piston has backed up to its normal operating position, compressing the air until it

Figure 12-49. *A spherical accumulator with diaphragm (left) and bladder (right). The dotted lines in the right drawing depict the bladder when the accumulator is charged with both hydraulic system fluid and nitrogen preload.*

occupies a space less than one-half the length of the cylinder. When actuation of hydraulic units lowers the system pressure, the compressed air expands against the piston, forcing fluid from the accumulator. This supplies an instantaneous supply of fluid to the hydraulic system component. The charged accumulator may also supply fluid pressure to actuate a component(s) briefly in case of pump failure.

Maintenance of Accumulators

Maintenance consists of inspections, minor repairs, replacement of component parts, and testing. There is an element of danger in maintaining accumulators. Therefore, proper precautions must be strictly observed to prevent injury and damage.

Before disassembling any accumulator, ensure that all preload air (or nitrogen) pressure has been discharged. Failure to release the preload could result in serious injury to the technician. Before making this check, be certain you know the type of high-pressure air valve used. When you know that all air pressure has been removed, you can take the unit apart. Be sure to follow manufacturer's instructions for the specific unit you have.

Heat Exchangers

Transport-type aircraft use heat exchangers in their hydraulic power supply system to cool the hydraulic fluid from the hydraulic pumps. This extends the service life of the fluid and the hydraulic pumps. They are located in the fuel tanks of the aircraft. The heat exchangers use aluminum finned tubes to transfer heat from the fluid to the fuel. The fuel in the tanks that contain the heat exchangers must be maintained at a specific level to ensure adequate cooling of the fluid. *[Figure 12-51]*

Actuators

An actuating cylinder transforms energy in the form of fluid pressure into mechanical force, or action, to perform work. It is used to impart powered linear motion to some movable object or mechanism. A typical actuating cylinder consists of a cylinder housing, one or more pistons and piston rods, and some seals. The cylinder housing contains a polished bore in which the piston operates, and one or more ports through which fluid enters and leaves the bore. The piston and rod form an assembly. The piston moves forward and backward within the cylinder bore, and an attached piston rod moves into and out of the cylinder housing through an opening in one end of the cylinder housing.

Seals are used to prevent leakage between the piston and the cylinder bore and between the piston rod and the end of the

Figure 12-51. *Hydraulic heat exchanger.*

cylinder. Both the cylinder housing and the piston rod have provisions for mounting and for attachment to an object or mechanism that is to be moved by the actuating cylinder.

Actuating cylinders are of two major types: single action and double action. The single-action (single port) actuating cylinder is capable of producing powered movement in one direction only. The double-action (two ports) actuating cylinder is capable of producing powered movement in two directions.

Linear Actuators

A single-action actuating cylinder is illustrated in *Figure 12-52A*. Fluid under pressure enters the port at the left and pushes against the face of the piston, forcing the piston to the right. As the piston moves, air is forced out of the spring chamber through the vent hole, compressing the spring. When pressure on the fluid is released to the point it exerts less force than is present in the compressed spring, the spring pushes the piston toward the left. As the piston moves to the left, fluid is forced out of the fluid port. At the same time, the moving piston pulls air into the spring chamber through the vent hole. A three-way control valve is normally used for controlling the operation of a single-action actuating cylinder.

Figure 12-52. *Linear actuator.*

A double-action (two ports) actuating cylinder is illustrated in *Figure 12-52B*. The operation of a double-action actuating cylinder is usually controlled by a four-way selector valve. *Figure 12-53* shows an actuating cylinder interconnected with a selector valve. Operation of the selector valve and actuating cylinder is discussed below.

Figure 12-53. *Linear actuator operation.*

When the selector valve is placed in the ON or EXTEND position, fluid is admitted under pressure to the left-hand chamber of the actuating cylinder. *[Figure 12-53]* This results in the piston being forced toward the right. As the piston moves toward the right, it pushes return fluid out of the right-hand chamber and through the selector valve to the reservoir. When the selector valve is placed in its RETRACT position, as illustrated in *Figure 12-50*, fluid pressure enters the right chamber, forcing the piston toward the left. As the piston moves toward the left, it pushes return fluid out of the left chamber and through the selector valve to the reservoir.

Besides having the ability to move a load into position, a double-acting cylinder also has the ability to hold a load in position. This capability exists because when the selector valve used to control operation of the actuating cylinder is placed in the off position, fluid is trapped in the chambers on both sides of the actuating cylinder piston. Internal locking actuators also are used in some applications.

Rotary Actuators

Rotary actuators can mount right at the part without taking up the long stroke lengths required of cylinders. Rotary actuators are not limited to the 90° pivot arc typical of cylinders; they can achieve arc lengths of 180°, 360°, or even 720° or more, depending on the configuration. An often used type of rotary actuator is the rack and pinion actuator used for many nose wheel steering mechanisms. In a rack-and-pinion actuator, a long piston with one side machined into a rack engages a

12-33

pinion to turn the output shaft. *[Figure 12-54]* One side of the piston receive fluid pressure while the other side is connected to the return. When the piston moves, it rotates the pinion.

Figure 12-54. *Rack and pinion gear.*

Hydraulic Motor

Piston-type motors are the most commonly used in hydraulic systems. *[Figure 12-55]* They are basically the same as hydraulic pumps except they are used to convert hydraulic energy into mechanical (rotary) energy. Hydraulic motors are either of the axial inline or bent-axis type. The most commonly used hydraulic motor is the fixed-displacement bent-axis type. These types of motors are used for the activation of trailing edge flaps, leading edge slats, and stabilizer trim. Some equipment uses a variable-displacement piston motor where very wide speed ranges are desired. Although some piston-type motors are controlled by directional control valves, they are often used in combination with variable-displacement pumps. This pump-motor combination is used to provide a transfer of power between a driving element and a driven element. Some applications for which hydraulic transmissions may be used are speed reducers, variable speed drives, constant speed or constant torque drives, and torque converters.

Some advantages of hydraulic transmission of power over mechanical transmission of power are as follows:

- Quick, easy speed adjustment over a wide range while the power source is operating at a constant (most efficient) speed
- Rapid, smooth acceleration or deceleration
- Control over maximum torque and power
- Cushioning effect to reduce shock loads
- Smoother reversal of motion

Figure 12-55. *Bent axis piston motor.*

Ram Air Turbine (RAT)

The RAT is installed in the aircraft to provide electrical and hydraulic power if the primary sources of aircraft power are lost. Ram air is used to turn the blades of a turbine that, in turn, operates a hydraulic pump and generator. The turbine and pump assembly is generally installed on the inner surface of a door installed in the fuselage. The door is hinged, allowing the assembly to be extended into the slipstream by pulling a manual release in the flight deck. In some aircraft, the RAT automatically deploys when the main hydraulic pressure system fails and/or electrical system malfunction occurs. *[Figure 12-56]*

Figure 12-56. *Ram air turbine.*

Power Transfer Unit (PTU)

The PTU is able to transfer power but not fluid. It transfers power between two hydraulic systems. Different types of PTUs are in use: some can only transfer power in one direction while others can transfer power both ways. Some PTUs have a fixed displacement, while others use a variable displacement hydraulic pump. The two units, hydraulic pump and hydraulic motor, are connected via a single drive shaft so that power can be transferred between the two systems. Depending on the direction of power transfer, each unit in turn works either as a motor or a pump. *[Figure 12-57]*

Hydraulic Motor-Driven Generator (HMDG)

The HMDG is a servo-controlled variable displacement motor integrated with an AC generator. The HMDG is designed to maintain a desired output frequency of 400 Hz. In case of an electrical failure, the HMDG could provide an alternative source of electrical power.

Seals

Seals are used to prevent fluid from passing a certain point, and to keep air and dirt out of the system in which they are used. The increased use of hydraulics and pneumatics in aircraft systems has created a need for packings and gaskets of varying characteristics and design to meet the many variations of operating speeds and temperatures to which they are subjected. No one style or type of seal is satisfactory for all installations. Some of the reasons for this are:

- Pressure at which the system operates.
- The type fluid used in the system.
- The metal finish and the clearance between adjacent parts.
- The type motion (rotary or reciprocating), if any.

Seals are divided into three main classes: packings, gaskets, and wipers. A seal may consist of more than one component, such as an O-ring and a backup ring, or possibly an O-ring and two backup rings. Hydraulic seals used internally on a sliding or moving assembly are normally called packings. *[Figure 12-58]* Hydraulic seals used between nonmoving fittings and bosses are normally called gaskets.

V-Ring Packings

V-ring packings (AN6225) are one-way seals and are always installed with the open end of the V facing the pressure. V-ring packings must have a male and female adapter to hold them in the proper position after installation. It is also necessary to torque the seal retainer to the value specified by the manufacturer of the component being serviced, or the seal may not give satisfactory service.

U-Ring

U-ring packings (AN6226) and U-cup packings are used in brake assemblies and brake master cylinders. The U-ring and U-cup seals pressure in only one direction; therefore, the lip of the packings must face toward the pressure. U-ring packings are primarily low pressure packings to be used with pressures of less than 1,000 psi.

O-Rings

Most packings and gaskets used in aircraft are manufactured in the form of O-rings. An O-ring is circular in shape, and its cross-section is small in relation to its diameter. The cross-section is truly round and has been molded and trimmed to extremely close tolerances. The O-ring packing seals effectively in both directions. This sealing is done by distortion of its elastic compound.

Advances in aircraft design have made new O-ring composition necessary to meet changing conditions. Hydraulic O-rings were originally established under Air Force-Navy (AN) specification numbers 6227, 6230, and 6290 for use in fluid at operating temperatures ranging from

12-35

Figure 12-57. *Power transfer unit.*

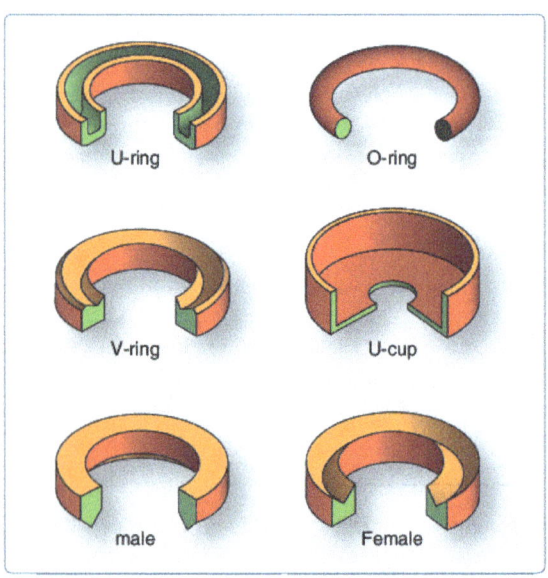

Figure 12-58. *Packings.*

−65 °F to +160 °F. When new designs raised operating temperatures to a possible +275 °F, more compounds were developed and perfected.

Recently, newer compounds were developed under Military Standard (MS) specifications that offered improved low-temperature performance without sacrificing high-temperature performance. These superior materials were adopted in the MS28775 O-ring, which is replacing AN6227 and AN6230 O-rings, and the MS28778 O-ring, which is replacing the AN6290 O-ring. These O-rings are now standard for systems where the operating temperatures may vary from −65 °F to +275 °F.

O-Ring Color Coding

Manufacturers provide color coding on some O-rings, but this is not a reliable or complete means of identification. The color coding system does not identify sizes, but only system fluid or vapor compatibility and, in some cases, the manufacturer. Color codes on O-rings that are compatible with MIL-H-5606

12-36

fluid always contains blue, but may also contain red or other colors. Packings and gaskets suitable for use with Skydrol® fluid are always coded with a green stripe, but may also have a blue, grey, red, green, or yellow dot as a part of the color code. Color codes on O-rings that are compatible with hydrocarbon fluid always contain red, but never contain blue. A colored stripe around the circumference indicates that the O-ring is a boss gasket seal. The color of the stripe indicates fluid compatibility: red for fuel, blue for hydraulic fluid. The coding on some rings is not permanent. On others, it may be omitted due to manufacturing difficulties or interference with operation. Furthermore, the color coding system provides no means to establish the age of the O-ring or its temperature limitations. Because of the difficulties with color coding, O-rings are available in individual hermetically sealed envelopes labeled with all pertinent data. When selecting an O-ring for installation, the basic part number on the sealed envelope provides the most reliable compound identification.

Backup Rings

Backup rings (MS28782) made of Teflon™ do not deteriorate with age, are unaffected by any system fluid or vapor, and can tolerate temperature extremes in excess of those encountered in high pressure hydraulic systems. Their dash numbers indicate not only their size but also relate directly to the dash number of the O-ring for which they are dimensionally suited. They are procurable under a number of basic part numbers, but they are interchangeable: any Teflon™ backup ring may be used to replace any other Teflon™ backup ring if it is of proper overall dimension to support the applicable O-ring. Backup rings are not color coded or otherwise marked and must be identified from package labels. The inspection of backup rings should include a check to ensure that surfaces are free from irregularities, that the edges are clean cut and sharp, and that scarf cuts are parallel. When checking Teflon™ spiral backup rings, make sure that the coils do not separate more than ¼ inch when unrestrained. Be certain that backup rings are installed downstream of the O-ring. *[Figure 12-59]*

Gaskets

Gaskets are used as static (stationary) seals between two flat surfaces. Some of the more common gasket materials are asbestos, copper, cork, and rubber. Asbestos sheeting is used wherever a heat resistant gasket is needed. It is used extensively for exhaust system gaskets. Most asbestos exhaust gaskets have a thin sheet of copper edging to prolong their life.

A solid copper washer is used for spark plug gaskets where it is essential to have a noncompressible, yet semisoft gasket. Cork gaskets can be used as an oil seal between the engine crankcase and accessories, and where a gasket is required

Figure 12-59. *Backup O-rings installed downstream.*

that is capable of occupying an uneven or varying space caused by a rough surface or expansion and contraction. Rubber sheeting can be used where there is a need for a compressible gasket. It should not be used in any place where it may come in contact with gasoline or oil because the rubber deteriorates very rapidly when exposed to these substances. Gaskets are used in fluid systems around the end caps of actuating cylinders, valves, and other units. The gasket generally used for this purpose is in the shape of an O-ring, similar to O-ring packings.

Seal Materials

Most seals are made from synthetic materials that are compatible with the hydraulic fluid used. Seals used for MIL-H-5606 hydraulic fluid are not compatible with Skydrol® and servicing the hydraulic system with the wrong fluid could result in leaks and system malfunctions. Seals for systems that use Mll-H-5606 are made of neoprene or Buna-N. Seals for Skydrol® are made from butyl rubber or ethylene-propylene elastomers.

O-Ring Installation

When removing or installing O-rings, avoid using pointed or sharp-edged tools that might cause scratching or marring of hydraulic component surfaces or cause damage to the O-rings. Special tooling for the installation of O-rings is available. While using the seal removal and the installation tools, contact with cylinder walls, piston heads, and related precision components is not desirable.

After the removal of all O-rings, the parts that receive new O-rings have to be cleaned and inspected to make sure that they are free from all contamination. Each replacement O-ring should be removed from its sealed package and inspected for defects, such as blemishes, abrasions, cuts, or punctures. Although an O-ring may appear perfect at first glance, slight surface flaws may exist. These flaws are often capable of preventing satisfactory O-ring performance under the variable operating pressures of aircraft systems; therefore, O-rings should be rejected for flaws that affect their performance. Such flaws are difficult to detect, and one aircraft manufacturer recommends using a four-power magnifying glass with adequate lighting to inspect each ring before it is installed. By rolling the ring on an inspection cone or dowel, the inner diameter surface can also be checked for small cracks, particles of foreign material, or other irregularities that cause leakage or shorten the life of the O-ring. The slight stretching of the ring when it is rolled inside out helps to reveal some defects not otherwise visible.

After inspection and prior to installation, immerse the O-ring in clean hydraulic fluid. During the installation, avoid rolling and twisting the O-ring to maneuver it into place. If possible, keep the position of the O-ring's mold line constant. When the O-ring installation requires spanning or inserting through sharply threaded areas, ridges, slots, and edges, use protective measures, such as O-ring entering sleeves, as shown in *Figure 12-60A*. After the O-ring is placed in the cavity provided, gently roll the O-ring with the fingers to remove any twist that might have occurred during installation. *[Figure 12-61]*

Wipers

Wipers are used to clean and lubricate the exposed portions of piston shafts. They prevent dirt from entering the system and help protect the piston shaft against scoring. Wipers may be either metallic or felt. They are sometimes used together, a felt wiper installed behind a metallic wiper.

Large Aircraft Hydraulic Systems

Figure 12-62 provides an overview of hydraulic components in large aircraft.

Boeing 737 Next Generation Hydraulic System

The Boeing 737 Next Generation has three 3,000 psi hydraulic systems: system A, system B, and standby. The standby system is used if system A and/or B pressure is lost. The hydraulic systems power the following aircraft systems:

- Flight controls
- Leading edge flaps and slats
- Trailing edge flaps
- Landing gear
- Wheel brakes
- Nose wheel steering
- Thrust reversers
- Autopilots

Reservoirs

The system A, B, and standby reservoirs are located in the wheel well area. The reservoirs are pressurized by bleed air through a pressurization module. The standby reservoir is connected to the system B reservoir for pressurization and servicing. The positive pressure in the reservoir ensures a positive flow of fluid to the pumps. The reservoirs have a standpipe that prevents the loss of all hydraulic fluid if a leak develops in the engine-driven pump or its related lines. The engine-driven pump draws fluid through a standpipe in the reservoir and the AC motor pump draws fluid from the bottom of the reservoir. *[Figure 12-63]*

Pumps

Refer to *Figure 12-64* for the following description. Both A and B hydraulic systems have an engine-driven pump (EDP) and an ACMP. The system A engine-driven pump is installed on the number 1 engine and the system B engine-driven pump is installed on the number 2 engine. The AC pumps are controlled by a switch on the flight deck. The hydraulic case drain fluid that lubricates and cools the pumps return to the reservoir through a heat exchanger. *[Figure 12-65]* The heat exchanger for the A system is installed in the main fuel tank No. 1, and the heat exchanger for the B system is installed in the main fuel tank No. 2. Minimum fuel for ground operation of electric motor-driven pumps is 1,675 pounds in the related main tank. Pressure switches, located in the EDP and ACMP pump output lines, send signals to illuminate the related LOW PRESSURE light if pump output pressure is low. The related system pressure transmitter sends the combined pressure of the EDP and ACMP to the related hydraulic system pressure indicator.

Figure 12-60. *O-ring installation techniques.*

Figure 12-61. *More O-ring installation techniques.*

Filter Units

Filter modules are installed in the pressure, case drain, and return lines to clean the hydraulic fluid. Filters have a differential pressure indicator that pops out when the filter is dirty and needs to be replaced.

Power Transfer Unit (PTU)

The purpose of the PTU is to supply the additional volume of hydraulic fluid needed to operate the autoslats and leading edge flaps and slats at the normal rate when system B EDP malfunctions. The PTU unit consists of a hydraulic motor and hydraulic pump that are connected through a shaft. The PTU uses system A pressure to drive a hydraulic motor. The hydraulic motor of the PTU unit is connected through a shaft with a hydraulic pump that can draw fluid from the system B reservoir. The PTU can only transfer power and cannot transfer fluid. The PTU operates automatically when all of the following conditions are met:

- System B EDP pressure drops below limits.
- Aircraft airborne.
- Flaps are less than 15° but not up.

Stabilizer Trim Motor

Stabilizer trim actuation on the aircraft is provided by two 3,000 psi, constant displacement, nine piston, bent axis hydraulic motors. Each motor produces 77.3 in lb torque at 2,250 psid with a rated speed of 2,700 rpm and an intermittent speed of 4,050 rpm. Displacement is 0.216 in^2/rev; weight is 3.9 lb.

Hydraulic Motor-Driven Generator

The hydraulic motor driven generator (HMDG) is a servo controlled, variable displacement, inline axis piston hydraulic motor integrated with a three stage, brushless generator. The HMDG is designed to maintain a steady state generator output frequency of 400 ±2V (at the point of regulation) over a rated electrical output range of 10kVA.

AC Motor Pump

Auxiliary power is provided by a 3,110 psi, 12 gpm, 8,000 rpm fluid cooled motor pump. Some AC motor pumps feature a ceramic feed through design. This protects the electrical wiring from being exposed to the caustic hydraulic fluid environment.

Leading Edge Slat Drive Motor

Leading edge slat actuation on the aircraft provided by one constant displacement, nine piston, bent axis hydraulic motor. The motor produces 544.3 in lb torque at 2,250 psid with a rated speed of 3,170 rpm and an intermittent speed of 4,755 rpm. Displacement is 1.52 in^2/rev; weight is 13.21 lb.

Emergency Passenger Door Actuator

Plays a critical role in safety; extends to open door when actuated by nitrogen gas pressure. Assembly reaches full extension in 2.75 to 4.16 seconds with output force of 2,507 to 2,830 lb.

Power Transfer Unit

The transfer of hydraulic power (but not fluid) between the left and right independent hydraulic system is accomplished with a nonreversible power transfer unit (PTU) that provides an alternate power source for the leading and trailing edge flaps and the landing gear, including nose gear steering, which are normally driven by the left hydraulic system. The PTU consists of a bent axis hydraulic motor driving a fixed displacement, in line pump. Rated speed is 3,900 rpm. Displacement of the pump is 1.39 in^2/rev and displacement of the motor is 1.52 in^2/rev. The unit weight is 35 lb.

Trailing Edge Flap Drive Motor

Trailing edge flap actuation is provided by one 3,000 psi, constant displacement, nine piston, bent axis hydraulic motor. The motor produces 21.4 in lb torque at 2,250 psid with a rated speed of 3,750 rpm and an intermittent speed of 5,660 rpm. Displacement is 0.596 in^2/rev; weight is 6.5 lb.

Ram Air Turbine Pump

A 3,025 psi in line piston pump provides 20 gpm at 3,920 rpm, delivering hydraulic power for the priority flight control surfaces in the event both engines are lost or a total electrical power failure occurs. Displacement is 1.25 in^2/rev; weight is 15 lb.

Nose Wheel Steering System

Consists of a digital electronic controller, hydro mechanical power unit, mounting collar, tiller, and rudder pedal position sensors. The hydro mechanical power unit (an integrated assembly) includes all the hydraulic valving, power amplification, actuation, and damping components.

Engine-Driven Pump

Hydraulic power for the left and right systems is supplied by two 48 gpm variable displacement, 3,000 psi pressure compensated in line pumps. Displacements 3.0 in^2/rev; weight is 40.1 lb.

Figure 12-62. *Large aircraft hydraulic systems.*

Figure 12-63. *Hydraulic reservoirs on a Boeing 737.*

Landing Gear Transfer Unit

The purpose of the landing gear transfer unit is to supply the volume of hydraulic fluid needed to raise the landing gear at the normal rate when system A EDP is lost. The system B EDP supplies the volume of hydraulic fluid needed to operate the landing gear transfer unit when all of the following conditions are met:

- Aircraft airborne.
- No. 1 engine rpm drops below a limit value.
- Landing gear lever is up.
- Either or both main landing gear not up and locked.

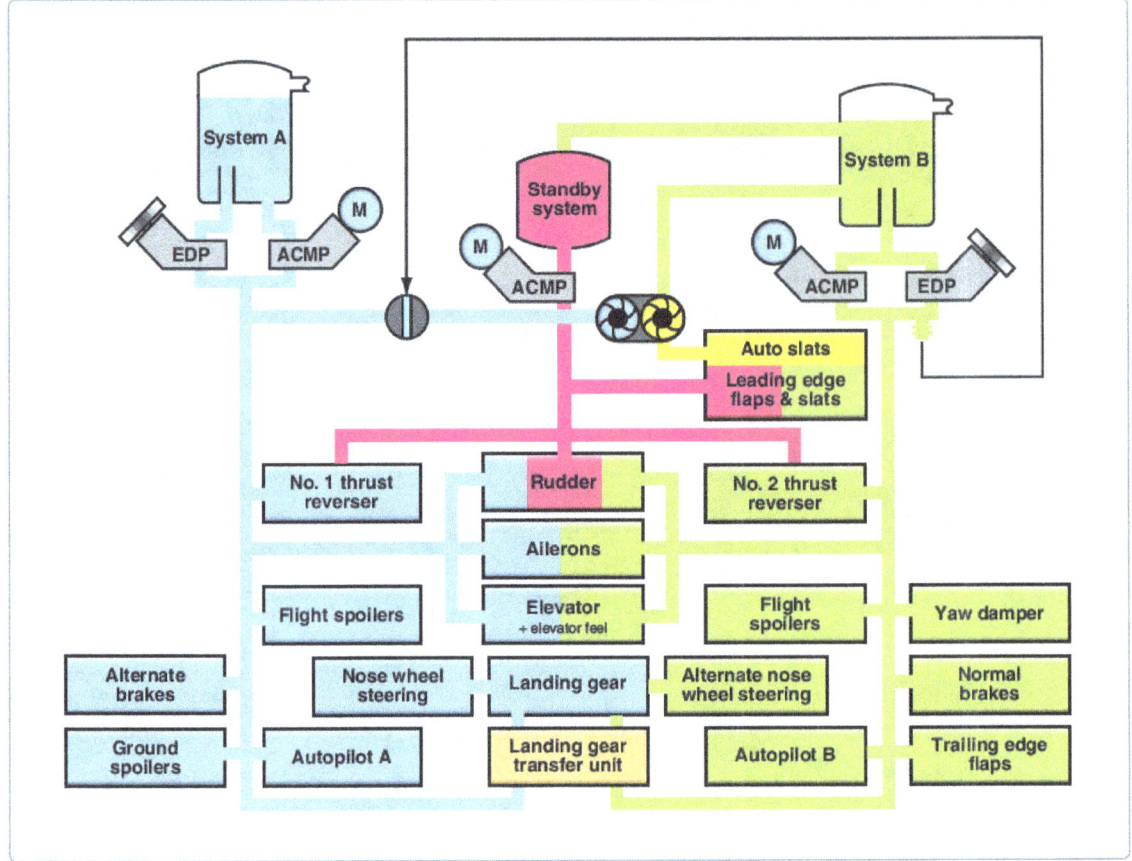

Figure 12-64. *Boeing 737 hydraulic system (simplified).*

Standby Hydraulic System

The standby hydraulic system is provided as a backup if system A and/or B pressure is lost. The standby system can be activated manually or automatically and uses a single electric ACMP to power:

- Thrust reversers
- Rudder
- Leading edge flaps and slats (extend only)
- Standby yaw damper

Indications

A master caution light illuminates if an overheat or low pressure is detected in the hydraulic system. An overheat light on the flight deck illuminates if an overheat is detected in either system A or B and a low-pressure light illuminates if a low pressure is detected in system A and B.

Boeing 777 Hydraulic System

The Boeing 777 is equipped with three hydraulic systems. The left, center, and right systems deliver hydraulic fluid at a rated pressure of 3,000 psi (207 bar) to operate flight controls, flap systems, actuators, landing gear, and brakes. Primary hydraulic power for the left and right systems is provided by two EDPs and supplemented by two on-demand ACMPs. Primary hydraulic power for the center system is provided by two electric motor pumps (ACMP) and supplemented by two on-demand air turbine-driven pumps (ADP). The center system provides hydraulic power for the engine thrust reversers, primary flight controls, landing gear, and flaps/slats. Under emergency conditions, hydraulic power is generated by the ram air turbine (RAT), which is deployed automatically and drives a variable displacement inline pump. The RAT pump provides flow to the center system flight controls. *[Figure 12-66]*

Figure 12-65. *Boeing 737 hydraulic case drain fluid heat exchanger installed in the fuel tank.*

Left and Right System Description

The left and right hydraulic systems are functionally the same. The left hydraulic system supplies pressurized hydraulic fluid to operate the left thrust reverser and the flight control systems. The right hydraulic system supplies pressurized hydraulic fluid to operate the right thrust reverser, flight control systems, and the normal brake system. *[Figure 12-67]*

Figure 12-66 *A Boeing 777 hydraulic system.*

Figure 12-67. *Right hydraulic system of a Boeing 777. A left system is similar.*

Reservoir

The hydraulic system reservoirs of the left and right system contain the hydraulic fluid supply for the hydraulic pumps. The reservoir is pressurized by bleed air through a reservoir pressurization module. The EDP draws fluid through a standpipe. The ACMP draws fluid from the bottom of the reservoir. If the fluid level in the reservoir gets below the standpipe, the EDP cannot draw any fluid any longer, and the ACMP is the only source of hydraulic power. The reservoir can be serviced through a center servicing point in the fuselage of the aircraft. The reservoir has a sample valve for contamination testing purposes, a temperature transmitter for temperature indication on the flight deck, a pressure transducer for reservoir pressure, and a drain valve for reservoir draining.

Pumps

The EDPs are the primary pumps for the left and right hydraulic systems. The EDPs get reservoir fluid through the EDP supply shutoff valves. The EDPs operates whenever the engines operate. A solenoid valve in each EDP controls the pressurization and depressurization of the pump. The pumps are variable displacement inline piston pumps consisting of a first stage impeller pump and a second stage piston pump. The impeller pump delivers fluid under pressure to the piston pump. The ACMPs are the demand pumps for the left and right hydraulic systems. The ACMPs normally operate only when there is high hydraulic system demand.

Filter Module

Pressure and case drain filter modules clean the pressure flows and the case drain flows of the hydraulic pumps. A return filter module cleans the return flow of hydraulic fluid from the user systems. The module can be bypassed if the filter clogs, and a visible indicator pops to indicate a clogged filter. The heat exchanger, which is installed in the wing fuel tanks, cools the hydraulic fluid from ACMP and EDP case drain lines before the fluid goes back to the reservoir.

Indication

The hydraulic system sensors send pressure, temperature, and quantity signals to the flight deck. A reservoir quantity transmitter and temperature transducer are installed on each of the reservoirs, and a hydraulic reservoir pressure switch is located on the pneumatic line between the reservoir pressurization module and the reservoir. The ACMP and EDP filter modules each have a pressure transducer to measure pump output pressure. A temperature transducer is installed in the case drain line of each filter module and measures pump case drain fluid temperature. A system pressure transducer measures hydraulic system pressure. A pressure relief valve on the EDP filter module protects the system against overpressurization. *[Figure 12-67]*

Center Hydraulic System

The center hydraulic system supplies pressurized hydraulic fluid to operate these systems *[Figure 12-68]*:

- Nose landing gear actuation
- Nose landing gear steering
- Alternate brakes
- Main landing gear actuation
- Main landing gear steering
- Trailing edge flaps
- Leading edge slat
- Flight controls

Reservoir

The hydraulic system reservoir of the center system contains the hydraulic fluid supply for the hydraulic pumps. The reservoir is pressurized by bleed air through a reservoir pressurization module. The reservoir supplies fluid to the ADPs, the RAT, and one of the ACMPs through a standpipe. The other ACMP gets fluid from the bottom of the reservoir. The reservoir also supplies hydraulic fluid to the landing gear alternate extension system.

The ACMPs are the primary pumps in the center hydraulic system and are normally turned on. The ADPs are the demand pumps in the center system. They normally operate only when the center system needs more hydraulic flow capacity. The RAT system supplies an emergency source of hydraulic power to the center hydraulic system flight controls. A reservoir quantity transmitter and temperature transducer are installed on the reservoir. A hydraulic reservoir pressure switch is installed on the pneumatic line between the reservoir and the reservoir pressurization module.

Filter

Filter modules clean the pressure and case drain output of the hydraulic pumps. A return filter module cleans the return flow of hydraulic fluid from the user systems. The module can be bypassed. The heat exchanger cools the hydraulic fluid from the ACMP case drains before the fluid goes back to the reservoir. ADP case drain fluid does not go through the heat exchangers.

The ACMP and ADP filter modules each have a pressure transducer to measure pump output pressure. A temperature transducer in each filter module measures the pump case drain temperature. A system pressure transducer measures hydraulic system pressure.

Figure 12-68. *Center hydraulic system.*

Pressure relief valves in each ADP filter module prevent system overpressurization. A pressure relief valve near ACMP C1 supplies overpressure protection for the center hydraulic isolation system (CHIS).

Center Hydraulic Isolation System (CHIS)

The CHIS supplies engine burst protection and a reserve brakes and steering function. CHIS operation is fully automatic. Relays control the electric motors in the reserve and nose gear isolation valves. When the CHIS system is operational, it prevents hydraulic operation of the leading edge slats.

ACMP C1 gets hydraulic fluid from the bottom of the center system reservoir. All other hydraulic pumps in the center system get fluid through a standpipe in the reservoir. This gives ACMP C1 a 1.2 gallon (4.5 liter) reserve supply of hydraulic fluid.

The reserve and nose gear isolation valves are normally open. Both valves close if the quantity in the center system reservoir is low (less than 0.40) and the airspeed is more than 60 knots for more than one second. When CHIS is active, this divides the center hydraulic system into different parts. The NLG actuation and steering and the leading edge slat hydraulic lines are isolated from center system pressure. The output of ACMP C1 goes only to the alternate brake system.

The output of the other center hydraulic system pumps goes to the trailing edge flaps, the MLG actuation and steering, and the flight controls. If there is a leak in the NLG actuation and steering or LE slat lines, there is no further loss of hydraulic fluid. The alternate brakes, the trailing edge flaps, the MLG actuation and steering, and the PFCS continue to operate normally.

If there is a leak in the trailing edge flaps, the MLG actuation and steering, or the flight control lines, the reservoir loses fluid down to the standpipe level (0.00 indication). This causes a loss of these systems but the alternate brake system continues to get hydraulic power from ACMP C1. If there is a leak in the lines between ACMP C1 and the alternate brake system, all center hydraulic system fluid is lost.

Nose Gear Isolation Valve

The nose gear isolation valve opens for any of these conditions:

- Airspeed is less than 60 knots.
- Pump pressures for ACMP C2, ADP C1, ADP C2, and the RAT is less than 1,200 psi for 30 seconds.

- Left and right engine rpm is above idle, left and right EDP pressure is more than 2,400 psi, and the NLG is not up, the NLG doors are not closed, or the landing gear lever is not up for 30 seconds.

The first condition permits the flight crew to operate the NLG steering when airspeed is less than 60 knots (decreased rudder control authority during taxi). The second condition permits operation of the NLG actuation and steering if the hydraulic leak is in the part of the center hydraulic system isolated by the reserve isolation valve. The third condition permits operation of the NLG actuation and steering if there has not been an engine burst and the other hydraulic systems are pressurized. The nose gear isolation valve opens when pressure is necessary at the NLG. If the NLG is not fully retracted or the NLG doors are not closed, the nose gear isolation valve opens to let the NLG complete the retraction. When the landing gear lever is moved to the down position, the nose gear isolation valve opens to let the NLG extend with center system pressure.

Central Hydraulic System Reset

Both valves open again automatically when the center system quantity is more than 0.70 and airspeed is less than 60 knots for 5 seconds. Both valves also reset when the center system quantity is more than 0.70 and both engines and both engine-driven pumps operate normally for 30 seconds. *[Figure 12-69]*

Aircraft Pneumatic Systems

Some aircraft manufacturers have equipped their aircraft with a high pressure pneumatic system (3,000 psi) in the past. The last aircraft to utilize this type of system was the Fokker F27. Such systems operate a great deal like hydraulic systems, except they employ air instead of a liquid for transmitting power. Pneumatic systems are sometimes used for:

- Brakes
- Opening and closing doors
- Driving hydraulic pumps, alternators, starters, water injection pumps, etc.
- Operating emergency devices

Figure 12-69. *Center hydraulic isolation system.*

Both pneumatic and hydraulic systems are similar units and use confined fluids. The word confined means trapped or completely enclosed. The word fluid implies such liquids as water, oil, or anything that flows. Since both liquids and gases flow, they are considered as fluids; however, there is a great deal of difference in the characteristics of the two. Liquids are practically incompressible; a quart of water still occupies about a quart of space regardless of how hard it is compressed. But gases are highly compressible; a quart of air can be compressed into a thimbleful of space. In spite of this difference, gases and liquids are both fluids and can be confined and made to transmit power. The type of unit used to provide pressurized air for pneumatic systems is determined by the system's air pressure requirements.

High-Pressure Systems

For high-pressure systems, air is usually stored in metal bottles at pressures ranging from 1,000 to 3,000 psi, depending on the particular system. *[Figure 12-70]* This type of air bottle has two valves, one of which is a charging valve. A ground-operated compressor can be connected to this valve to add air to the bottle. The other valve is a control valve. It acts as a shutoff valve, keeping air trapped inside the bottle until the system is operated. Although the high-pressure storage cylinder is light in weight, it has a definite disadvantage. Since the system cannot be recharged during flight, operation is limited by the small supply of bottled air. Such an arrangement cannot be used for the continuous operation of a system. Instead, the supply of bottled air is reserved for emergency operation of such systems as the landing gear or brakes. The usefulness of this type of system is increased, however, if other air-pressurizing units are added to the aircraft. *[Figure 12-71]*

Pneumatic System Components

Pneumatic systems are often compared to hydraulic systems, but such comparisons can only hold true in general terms. Pneumatic systems do not utilize reservoirs, hand pumps, accumulators, regulators, or engine-driven or electrically driven power pumps for building normal pressure. But similarities do exist in some components.

Figure 12-70. *High-pressure pneumatic system.*

Figure 12-71. *Pneumatic brake system.*

Air Compressors

On some aircraft, permanently installed air compressors have been added to recharge air bottles whenever pressure is used for operating a unit. Several types of compressors are used for this purpose. Some have two stages of compression, while others have three, depending on the maximum desired operating pressure.

Relief Valves

Relief valves are used in pneumatic systems to prevent damage. They act as pressure limiting units and prevent excessive pressures from bursting lines and blowing out seals.

Control Valves

Control valves are also a necessary part of a typical pneumatic system. *Figure 12-72* illustrates how a valve is used to control emergency air brakes. The control valve consists of a three-port housing, two poppet valves, and a control lever with two lobes.

In *Figure 12-72A*, the control valve is shown in the off position. A spring holds the left poppet closed so that compressed air entering the pressure port cannot flow to the brakes. In *Figure 12-72B*, the control valve has been placed in the on position. One lobe of the lever holds the left poppet

Figure 12-72. *Pneumatic control valve.*

open, and a spring closes the right poppet. Compressed air now flows around the opened left poppet, through a drilled passage, and into a chamber below the right poppet. Since the right poppet is closed, the high-pressure air flows out of the brake port and into the brake line to apply the brakes.

To release the brakes, the control valve is returned to the off position. *[Figure 12-72A]* The left poppet now closes, stopping the flow of high-pressure air to the brakes. At the same time, the right poppet is opened, allowing compressed air in the brake line to exhaust through the vent port and into the atmosphere.

Check Valves

Check valves are used in both hydraulic and pneumatic systems. *Figure 12-73* illustrates a flap-type pneumatic check valve. Air enters the left port of the check valve, compresses a light spring, forcing the check valve open and allowing air

Figure 12-73. *Flap-type pneumatic check valve.*

to flow out the right port. But if air enters from the right, air pressure closes the valve, preventing a flow of air out the left port. Thus, a pneumatic check valve is a one-direction flow control valve.

Restrictors

Restrictors are a type of control valve used in pneumatic systems. *Figure 12-74* illustrates an orifice-type restrictor with a large inlet port and a small outlet port. The small outlet port reduces the rate of airflow and the speed of operation of an actuating unit.

Figure 12-74. *Pneumatic orifice valve.*

Variable Restrictor

Another type of speed-regulating unit is the variable restrictor. *[Figure 12-75]* It contains an adjustable needle valve, which has threads around the top and a point on the lower end. Depending on the direction turned, the needle valve moves the sharp point either into or out of a small opening to decrease or increase the size of the opening. Since air entering the inlet port must pass through this opening before reaching the outlet port, this adjustment also determines the rate of airflow through the restrictor.

Figure 12-75. *Variable pneumatic restrictor.*

Filters

Pneumatic systems are protected against dirt by means of various types of filters. A micronic filter consists of a housing with two ports, a replaceable cartridge, and a relief valve. Normally, air enters the inlet, circulates around the cellulose cartridge, and flows to the center of the cartridge and out the outlet port. If the cartridge becomes clogged with dirt, pressure forces the relief valve open and allows unfiltered air to flow out the outlet port.

A screen-type filter is similar to the micron filter but contains a permanent wire screen instead of a replaceable cartridge. In the screen filter, a handle extends through the top of the housing and can be used to clean the screen by rotating it against metal scrapers.

Desiccant/Moisture Separator

The moisture separator in a pneumatic system is always located downstream of the compressor. Its purpose is to remove any moisture caused by the compressor. A complete moisture separator consists of a reservoir, a pressure switch, a dump valve, and a check valve. It may also include a regulator and a relief valve. The dump valve is energized and deenergized by the pressure switch. When deenergized, it completely purges the separator reservoir and lines up to the compressor. The check valve protects the system against pressure loss during the dumping cycle and prevents reverse flow through the separator.

Chemical Drier

Chemical driers are incorporated at various locations in a pneumatic system. Their purpose is to absorb any moisture that may collect in the lines and other parts of the system. Each drier contains a cartridge that should be blue in color. If otherwise noted, the cartridge is to be considered contaminated with moisture and should be replaced.

Emergency Backup Systems

Many aircraft use a high-pressure pneumatic back-up source of power to extend the landing gear or actuate the brakes, if the main hydraulic braking system fails. The nitrogen is not directly used to actuate the landing gear actuators or brake units but, instead, it applies the pressurized nitrogen to move hydraulic fluid to the actuator. This process is called pneudraulics. The following paragraph discusses the components and operation of an emergency pneumatic landing gear extension system used on a business jet. *[Figure 12-76]*

Nitrogen Bottles

Nitrogen used for emergency landing gear extension is stored in two bottles, one bottle located on each side of the nose wheel well. Nitrogen from the bottles is released by actuation of an outlet valve. Once depleted, the bottles must be recharged by maintenance personnel. Fully serviced pressure is approximately 3,100 psi at 70 °F/21 °C, enough for only one extension of the landing gear.

Gear Emergency Extension Cable and Handle

The outlet valve is connected to a cable and handle assembly. The handle is located on the side of the copilot's console and is labeled EMER LDG GEAR. Pulling the handle fully upward opens the outlet valve, releasing compressed nitrogen into the landing gear extension system. Pushing the handle fully downward closes the outlet valve and allows any nitrogen present in the emergency landing gear extension system to be vented overboard. The venting process takes approximately 30 seconds.

Dump Valve

As compressed nitrogen is released to the landing gear selector/dump valve during emergency extension, the pneudraulic pressure actuates the dump valve portion of the landing gear selector/dump valve to isolate the landing gear system from the remainder of hydraulic system. When activated, a blue DUMP legend is illuminated on the LDG GR DUMP V switch, located on the cockpit overhead panel. A dump valve reset switch is used to reset the dump valve after the system has been used and serviced.

Figure 12-76. *Pneumatic emergency landing gear extension system.*

Emergency Extension Sequence:

1. Landing gear handle is placed in the DOWN position.
2. Red light in the landing gear control handle is illuminated.
3. **EMER LDG GEAR** handle is pulled fully outward.
4. Compressed nitrogen is released to the landing gear selector/dump valve.
5. Pneudraulic pressure actuates the dump valve portion of the landing gear selector/dump valve.
6. Blue DUMP legend is illuminated on the LDG GR DUMP switch.
7. Landing gear system is isolated from the remainder of hydraulic system.
8. Pneudraulic pressure is routed to the OPEN side of the landing gear door actuators, the UNLOCK side of the landing gear uplock actuators, and the EXTEND side of the main landing gear sidebrace actuators and nose landing gear extend/retract actuator.
9. Landing gear doors open.
10. Uplock actuators unlock.
11. Landing gear extends down and locks.
12. Three green DOWN AND LOCKED lights on the landing gear control panel are illuminated.
13. Landing gear doors remain open.

Medium-Pressure Systems

A medium-pressure pneumatic system (50–150 psi) usually does not include an air bottle. Instead, it generally draws air from the compressor section of a turbine engine. This process is often called bleed air and is used to provide pneumatic power for engine starts, engine deicing, wing deicing, and in some cases, it provides hydraulic power to the aircraft systems (if the hydraulic system is equipped with an air-driven hydraulic pump). Engine bleed air is also used to pressurize the reservoirs of the hydraulic system. Bleed air systems are discussed in more detail in the powerplant handbook.

Low-Pressure Systems

Many aircraft equipped with reciprocating engines obtain a supply of low-pressure air from vane-type pumps. These pumps are driven by electric motors or by the aircraft engine. *Figure 12-77* shows a schematic view of one of these pumps, which consists of a housing with two ports, a drive shaft, and two vanes. The drive shaft and the vanes contain slots so the vanes can slide back and forth through the drive shaft. The shaft is eccentrically mounted in the housing, causing the vanes to form four different sizes of chambers (A, B, C, and D). In the position shown, B is the largest chamber and is

Figure 12-77. *Schematic of vane-type air pump.*

connected to the supply port. As depicted in *Figure 12-77*, outside air can enter chamber B of the pump. When the pump begins to operate, the drive shaft rotates and changes positions of the vanes and sizes of the chambers. Vane No. 1 then moves to the right, separating chamber B from the supply port. Chamber B now contains trapped air.

As the shaft continues to turn, chamber B moves downward and becomes increasingly smaller, gradually compressing its air. Near the bottom of the pump, chamber B connects to the pressure port and sends compressed air into the pressure line. Then chamber B moves upward again becoming increasingly larger in area. At the supply port, it receives another supply of air. There are four such chambers in this pump and each goes through this same cycle of operation. Thus, the pump delivers to the pneumatic system a continuous supply of compressed air from 1 to 10 psi. Low-pressure systems are used for wing deicing boot systems.

Pneumatic Power System Maintenance

Maintenance of the pneumatic power system consists of servicing, troubleshooting, removal, and installation of components, and operational testing.

The air compressor's lubricating oil level should be checked daily in accordance with the applicable manufacturer's instructions. The oil level is indicated by means of a sight gauge or dipstick. When refilling the compressor oil tank, the oil (type specified in the applicable instructions manual) is added until the specified level. After the oil is added, ensure that the filler plug is torqued and safety wire is properly installed.

The pneumatic system should be purged periodically to remove the contamination, moisture, or oil from the components and lines. Purging the system is accomplished by pressurizing it and removing the plumbing from various components throughout the system. Removal of the pressurized lines causes a high rate of airflow through the system, causing foreign matter to be exhausted from the system. If an excessive amount of foreign matter, particularly oil, is exhausted from any one system, the lines and components should be removed and cleaned or replaced.

Upon completion of pneumatic system purging and after reconnecting all the system components, the system air bottles should be drained to exhaust any moisture or impurities that may have accumulated there.

After draining the air bottles, service the system with nitrogen or clean, dry compressed air. The system should then be given a thorough operational check and an inspection for leaks and security.

Chapter 13
Aircraft Landing Gear Systems

Landing Gear Types

Aircraft landing gear supports the entire weight of an aircraft during landing and ground operations. They are attached to primary structural members of the aircraft. The type of gear depends on the aircraft design and its intended use. Most landing gear have wheels to facilitate operation to and from hard surfaces, such as airport runways. Other gear feature skids for this purpose, such as those found on helicopters, balloon gondolas, and in the tail area of some tail dragger aircraft. Aircraft that operate to and from frozen lakes and snowy areas may be equipped with landing gear that have skis. Aircraft that operate to and from the surface of water have pontoon-type landing gear. Regardless of the type of landing gear utilized, shock absorbing equipment, brakes, retraction mechanisms, controls, warning devices, cowling, fairings, and structural members necessary to attach the gear to the aircraft are considered parts of the landing gear system. *[Figure 13-1]*

Figure 13-1. *Basic landing gear types include those with wheels (a), skids (b), skis (c), and floats or pontoons (d).*

Numerous configurations of landing gear types can be found. Additionally, combinations of two types of gear are common. Amphibious aircraft are designed with gear that allow landings to be made on water or dry land. The gear features pontoons for water landing with extendable wheels for landings on hard surfaces. A similar system is used to allow the use of skis and wheels on aircraft that operate on both slippery, frozen surfaces and dry runways. Typically, the skis are retractable to allow use of the wheels when needed. *Figure 13-2* illustrates this type of landing gear.

NOTE: References to auxiliary landing gear refer to the nose gear, tail gear, or outrigger-type gear on any particular aircraft. Main landing gear are the two or more large gear located close to the aircraft's center of gravity.

Landing Gear Arrangement

Three basic arrangements of landing gear are used: tail wheel-type landing gear (also known as conventional gear), tandem landing gear, and tricycle-type landing gear.

Figure 13-2. *An amphibious aircraft with retractable wheels (left) and an aircraft with retractable skis (right).*

Tail Wheel-Type Landing Gear

Tail wheel-type landing gear is also known as conventional gear because many early aircraft use this type of arrangement. The main gear are located forward of the center of gravity, causing the tail to require support from a third wheel assembly. A few early aircraft designs use a skid rather than a tail wheel. This helps slow the aircraft upon landing and provides directional stability. The resulting angle of the aircraft fuselage, when fitted with conventional gear, allows the use of a long propeller that compensates for older, underpowered engine design. The increased clearance of the forward fuselage offered by tail wheel-type landing gear is also advantageous when operating in and out of non-paved runways. Today, aircraft are manufactured with conventional gear for this reason and for the weight savings accompanying the relatively light tail wheel assembly. *[Figure 13-3]*

The proliferation of hard surface runways has rendered the tail skid obsolete in favor of the tail wheel. Directional control is maintained through differential braking until the speed of the aircraft enables control with the rudder. A steerable tail wheel, connected by cables to the rudder or rudder pedals, is also a common design. Springs are incorporated for dampening. *[Figure 13-4]*

Tandem Landing Gear

Few aircraft are designed with tandem landing gear. As the name implies, this type of landing gear has the main gear and tail gear aligned on the longitudinal axis of the aircraft. Sailplanes commonly use tandem gear, although many only have one actual gear forward on the fuselage with a skid under the tail. A few military bombers, such as the B-47 and the B-52, have tandem gear, as does the U2 spy plane. The VTOL Harrier has tandem gear but uses small outrigger gear under the wings for support. Generally, placing the gear only under the fuselage facilitates the use of very flexible wings. *[Figure 13-5]*

Tricycle-Type Landing Gear

The most commonly used landing gear arrangement is the tricycle-type landing gear. It is comprised of main gear and nose gear. *[Figure 13-6]*

Tricycle-type landing gear is used on large and small aircraft with the following benefits:

1. Allows more forceful application of the brakes without nosing over when braking, which enables higher landing speeds.

Figure 13-3. *Tail wheel configuration landing gear on a DC-3 (left) and a STOL Maule MX-7-235 Super Rocket.*

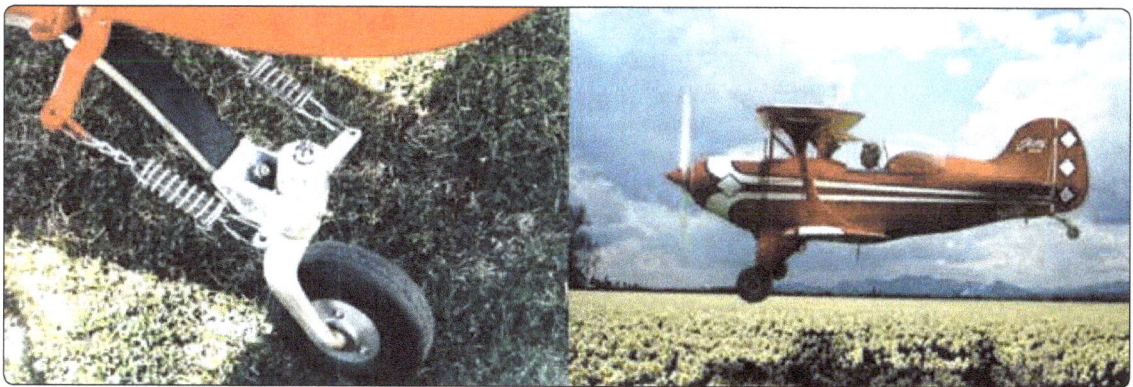

Figure 13-4. *The steerable tail wheel of a Pitts Special.*

Figure 13-5. *Tandem landing gear along the longitudinal axis of the aircraft permits the use of flexible wings on sailplanes (left) and select military aircraft like the B-52 (center). The VTOL Harrier (right) has tandem gear with outrigger-type gear.*

Figure 13-6. *Tricycle-type landing gear with dual main wheels on a Learjet (left) and a Cessna 172, also with tricycle gear (right).*

2. Provides better visibility from the flight deck, especially during landing and ground maneuvering.
3. Prevents ground-looping of the aircraft. Since the aircraft center of gravity is forward of the main gear, forces acting on the center of gravity tend to keep the aircraft moving forward rather than looping, such as with a tail wheel-type landing gear.

The nose gear of a few aircraft with tricycle-type landing gear is not controllable. It simply casters as steering is accomplished with differential braking during taxi. However, nearly all aircraft have steerable nose gear. On light aircraft, the nose gear is directed through mechanical linkage to the rudder pedals. Heavy aircraft typically utilize hydraulic power to steer the nose gear. Control is achieved through an independent tiller in the flight deck. *[Figure 13-7]*

The main gear on a tricycle-type landing gear arrangement is attached to reinforced wing structure or fuselage structure. The number and location of wheels on the main gear vary. Many main gear have two or more wheels. *[Figure 13-8]*

Multiple wheels spread the weight of the aircraft over a larger area. They also provide a safety margin should one tire fail. Heavy aircraft may use four or more wheel assemblies on each main gear. When more than two wheels are attached to a landing gear strut, the attaching mechanism is known as a bogie. The number of wheels included in the bogie is

Figure 13-7. *A nose wheel steering tiller located on the flight deck.*

Figure 13-8. *Dual main gear of a tricycle-type landing gear.*

a function of the gross design weight of the aircraft and the surface type on which the loaded aircraft is required to land. *Figure 13-9* illustrates the triple bogie main gear of a Boeing 777.

Figure 13-9. *Triple bogie main landing gear assembly on a Boeing 777.*

The tricycle-type landing gear arrangement consists of many parts and assemblies. These include air/oil shock struts, gear alignment units, support units, retraction and safety devices, steering systems, wheel and brake assemblies, etc. A main landing gear of a transport category aircraft is illustrated in *Figure 13-10* with many of the parts identified as an introduction to landing gear nomenclature.

Fixed and Retractable Landing Gear

Further classification of aircraft landing gear can be made into two categories: fixed and retractable. Many small, single-engine light aircraft have fixed landing gear, as do a few light twins. This means the gear is attached to the airframe and remains exposed to the slipstream as the aircraft is flown. As discussed in Chapter 2 of this handbook, as the speed of an aircraft increases, so does parasite drag. Mechanisms to retract and stow the landing gear to eliminate parasite drag add weight to the aircraft. On slow aircraft, the penalty of this added weight is not overcome by the reduction of drag, so fixed gear is used. As the speed of the aircraft increases, the drag caused by the landing gear becomes greater and a means to retract the gear to eliminate parasite drag is required, despite the weight of the mechanism.

A great deal of the parasite drag caused by light aircraft landing gear can be reduced by building gear as aerodynamically as possible and by adding fairings or wheel pants to streamline the airflow past the protruding assemblies. A small, smooth profile to the oncoming wind greatly reduces landing gear parasite drag. *Figure 13-11* illustrates a Cessna aircraft landing gear used on many of the manufacturer's light planes. The thin cross section of the spring steel struts combine with the fairings over the wheel and brake assemblies to raise performance of the fixed landing gear by keeping parasite drag to a minimum.

Retractable landing gear stow in fuselage or wing compartments while in flight. Once in these wheel wells, gear are out of the slipstream and do not cause parasite drag. Most retractable gear have a close fitting panel attached to them that fairs with the aircraft skin when the gear is fully retracted. *[Figure 13-12]* Other aircraft have separate doors that open, allowing the gear to enter or leave, and then close again.

NOTE: The parasite drag caused by extended landing gear can be used by the pilot to slow the aircraft. The extension and retraction of most landing gear is usually accomplished with hydraulics. Landing gear retraction systems are discussed later in this chapter.

Shock Absorbing and Non-Shock Absorbing Landing Gear

In addition to supporting the aircraft for taxi, the forces of impact on an aircraft during landing must be controlled by the landing gear. This is done in two ways: 1) the shock energy is altered and transferred throughout the airframe at a different rate and time than the single strong pulse of impact, and 2) the shock is absorbed by converting the energy into heat energy.

Figure 13-10. *Nomenclature of a main landing gear bogie truck.*

Leaf-Type Spring Gear

Many aircraft utilize flexible spring steel, aluminum, or composite struts that receive the impact of landing and return it to the airframe to dissipate at a rate that is not harmful. The gear flexes initially and forces are transferred as it returns to its original position. *[Figure 13-13]* The most common example of this type of non-shock absorbing landing gear are the thousands of single-engine Cessna aircraft that use it. Landing gear struts of this type made from composite materials are lighter in weight with greater flexibility and do not corrode.

Rigid

Before the development of curved spring steel landing struts, many early aircraft were designed with rigid, welded steel landing gear struts. Shock load transfer to the airframe is direct

13-6

Figure 13-11. *Wheel fairings, or pants, and low profile struts reduce parasite drag on fixed gear aircraft.*

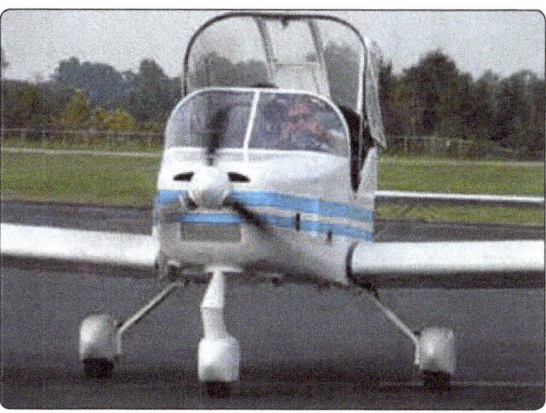

Figure 13-13. *Non-shock absorbing struts made from steel, aluminum, or composite material transfer the impact forces of landing to the airframe at a non-damaging rate.*

with this design. Use of pneumatic tires aids in softening the impact loads. *[Figure 13-14]* Modern aircraft that use skid-type landing gear make use of rigid landing gear with no significant ill effects. Rotorcraft, for example, typically experience low impact landings that are able to be directly absorbed by the airframe through the rigid gear (skids).

Bungee Cord

The use of bungee cords on non-shock absorbing landing gear is common. The geometry of the gear allows the strut assembly to flex upon landing impact. Bungee cords are positioned between the rigid airframe structure and the flexing gear assembly to take up the loads and return them to the airframe at a non-damaging rate. The bungees are made of many individual small strands of elastic rubber that must be inspected for condition. Solid, donut-type rubber cushions are also used on some aircraft landing gear. *[Figure 13-15]*

Shock Struts

True shock absorption occurs when the shock energy of landing impact is converted into heat energy, as in a shock strut landing gear. This is the most common method of landing shock dissipation in aviation. It is used on aircraft

Figure 13-14. *Rigid steel landing gear is used on many early aircraft.*

of all sizes. Shock struts are self-contained hydraulic units that support an aircraft while on the ground and protect the structure during landing. They must be inspected and serviced regularly to ensure proper operation.

Figure 13-12. *The retractable gear of a Boeing 737 fair into recesses in the fuselage. Panels attached to the landing gear provide smooth airflow over the struts. The wheel assemblies mate with seals to provide aerodynamic flow without doors.*

Figure 13-15. *Piper Cub bungee cord landing gear transfer landing loads to the airframe (left and center). Rubber, donut-type shock transfer is used on some Mooney aircraft (right).*

There are many different designs of shock struts, but most operate in a similar manner. The following discussion is general in nature. For information on the construction, operation, and servicing of a specific aircraft shock, consult the manufacturer's maintenance instructions.

A typical pneumatic/hydraulic shock strut uses compressed air or nitrogen combined with hydraulic fluid to absorb and dissipate shock loads. It is sometimes referred to as an air/oil or oleo strut. A shock strut is constructed of two telescoping cylinders or tubes that are closed on the external ends. The upper cylinder is fixed to the aircraft and does not move. The lower cylinder is called the piston and is free to slide in and out of the upper cylinder. Two chambers are formed. The lower chamber is always filled with hydraulic fluid and the upper chamber is filled with compressed air or nitrogen. An orifice located between the two cylinders provides a passage for the fluid from the bottom chamber to enter the top cylinder chamber when the strut is compressed. *[Figure 13-16]*

Most shock struts employ a metering pin similar to that shown in *Figure 13-16* for controlling the rate of fluid flow from the lower chamber into the upper chamber. During the compression stroke, the rate of fluid flow is not constant. It is automatically controlled by the taper of the metering pin in the orifice. When a narrow portion of the pin is in the orifice, more fluid can pass to the upper chamber. As the diameter of the portion of the metering pin in the orifice increases, less fluid passes. Pressure build-up caused by strut compression and the hydraulic fluid being forced through the metered orifice causes heat. This heat is converted impact energy. It is dissipated through the structure of the strut.

On some types of shock struts, a metering tube is used. The operational concept is the same as that in shock struts with metering pins, except the holes in the metering tube control the flow of fluid from the bottom chamber to the top chamber during compression. *[Figure 13-17]*

Upon lift off or rebound from compression, the shock strut tends to extend rapidly. This could result in a sharp impact at the end of the stroke and damage to the strut. It is typical for shock struts to be equipped with a damping or snubbing device to prevent this. A recoil valve on the piston or a recoil tube restricts the flow of fluid during the extension stroke, which slows the motion and prevents damaging impact forces.

Most shock struts are equipped with an axle as part of the lower cylinder to provide installation of the aircraft wheels. Shock struts without an integral axle have provisions on the end of the lower cylinder for installation of the axle assembly. Suitable connections are provided on all shock strut upper cylinders to attach the strut to the airframe. *[Figure 13-18]*

The upper cylinder of a shock strut typically contains a valve fitting assembly. It is located at or near the top of the cylinder. The valve provides a means of filling the strut with hydraulic fluid and inflating it with air or nitrogen as specified by the manufacturer. A packing gland is employed to seal the sliding joint between the upper and lower telescoping cylinders. It is installed in the open end of the outer cylinder. A packing gland wiper ring is also installed in a groove in the lower bearing or gland nut on most shock struts. It is designed to keep the sliding surface of the piston from carrying dirt, mud, ice, and snow into the packing gland and upper cylinder. Regular cleaning of the exposed portion of the strut piston helps the wiper do its job and decreases the possibility of damage to the packing gland, which could cause the strut to a leak.

To keep the piston and wheels aligned, most shock struts are equipped with torque links or torque arms. One end of the links is attached to the fixed upper cylinder. The other end is attached to the lower cylinder (piston) so it cannot rotate. This keeps the wheels aligned. The links also retain the piston in the end of the upper cylinder when the strut is extended, such as after takeoff. *[Figure 13-19]*

Figure 13-16. *A landing gear shock strut with a metering pin to control the flow of hydraulic fluid from the lower chamber to the upper chamber during compression.*

Nose gear shock struts are provided with a locating cam assembly to keep the gear aligned. A cam protrusion is attached to the lower cylinder, and a mating lower cam recess is attached to the upper cylinder. These cams line up the wheel and axle assembly in the straight-ahead position when the shock strut is fully extended. This allows the nose wheel to enter the wheel well when the nose gear is retracted and prevents structural damage to the aircraft. It also aligns the wheels with the longitudinal axis of the aircraft prior to landing when the strut is fully extended. *[Figure 13-20]* Many nose gear shock struts also have attachments for the installation of an external shimmy damper. *[Figure 13-21]*

Nose gear struts are often equipped with a locking or disconnect pin to enable quick turning of the aircraft while towing or positioning the aircraft when on the ramp or in

Figure 13-17. *Some landing gear shock struts use an internal metering tube rather than a metering pin to control the flow of fluid from the bottom cylinder to the top cylinder.*

a hangar. Disengagement of this pin allows the wheel fork spindle on some aircraft to rotate 360°, thus enabling the aircraft to be turned in a tight radius. At no time should the nose wheel of any aircraft be rotated beyond limit lines marked on the airframe.

Nose and main gear shock struts on many aircraft are also equipped with jacking points and towing lugs. Jacks should always be placed under the prescribed points. When towing lugs are provided, the towing bar should be attached only to these lugs. *[Figure 13-22]*

Figure 13-18. *Axles machined out of the same material as the landing gear lower cylinder.*

Figure 13-19. *Torque links align the landing gear and retain the piston in the upper cylinder when the strut is extended.*

Figure 13-20. *An upper locating cam mates into a lower cam recess when the nose landing gear shock strut is extended before landing and before the gear is retracted into the wheel well.*

Shock struts contain an instruction plate that gives directions for filling the strut with fluid and for inflating the strut. The instruction plate is usually attached near filler inlet and air valve assembly. It specifies the correct type of hydraulic fluid to use in the strut and the pressure to which the strut should be inflated. It is of utmost importance to become familiar with these instructions prior to filling a shock strut with hydraulic fluid or inflating it with air or nitrogen.

Shock Strut Operation

Figure 13-23 illustrates the inner construction of a shock strut. Arrows show the movement of the fluid during compression and extension of the strut. The compression stroke of the shock strut begins as the aircraft wheels touch the ground. As the center of mass of the aircraft moves downward, the strut

Figure 13-21. *A shimmy damper helps control oscillations of the nose gear.*

Figure 13-22. *A towing lug on a landing gear is the designed means for attaching a tow bar.*

compresses, and the lower cylinder or piston is forced upward into the upper cylinder. The metering pin is therefore moved up through the orifice. The taper of the pin controls the rate of fluid flow from the bottom cylinder to the top cylinder at all points during the compression stroke. In this manner, the greatest amount of heat is dissipated through the walls of the strut. At the end of the downward stroke, the compressed air in the upper cylinder is further compressed which limits the compression stroke of the strut with minimal impact. During taxi operations, the air in the tires and the strut combine to smooth out bumps.

13-11

Efficient operation of the shock struts requires that proper fluid and air pressure be maintained. To check the fluid level, most struts need to be deflated and compressed into the fully compressed position. Deflating a shock strut can be a dangerous operation. The technician must be thoroughly familiar with the operation of the high-pressure service valve found at the top of the strut's upper cylinder. Refer to the manufacturer's instructions for proper deflating technique of the strut in question and follow all necessary safety precautions.

Two common types of high pressure strut servicing valves are illustrated in *Figure 13-24*. The AN6287-1 valve in *Figure 13-24A* has a valve core assembly and is rated to 3,000 pounds per square inch (psi). However, the core itself is only rated to 2,000 psi. The MS28889-1 valve in *Figure 13-24B* has no valve core. It is rated to 5,000 psi. The swivel nut on the AN6287-1 valve is smaller than the valve body hex. The MS28889-1 swivel nut is the same size as the valve body hex. The swivel nuts on both valves engage threads on an internal stem that loosens or draws tight the valve stem to a metal seat.

Servicing Shock Struts

The following procedures are typical of those used in deflating a shock strut, servicing it with hydraulic fluid, and re-inflating the strut.

1. Position the aircraft so that the shock struts are in the normal ground operating position. Make certain that personnel, work stands, and other obstacles are clear of the aircraft. If the maintenance procedures require, securely jack the aircraft.

2. Remove the cap from the air servicing valve. *[Figure 13-25A]*

3. Check the swivel nut for tightness.

4. If the servicing valve is equipped with a valve core, depress it to release any air pressure that may be trapped under the core in the valve body. *[Figure 13-25B]* Always be positioned to the side of the trajectory of any valve core in case it releases. Propelled by strut air pressure, serious injury could result.

5. Loosen the swivel nut. For a valve with a valve core (AN2687-1), rotate the swivel nut one turn (counter clockwise). Using a tool designed for the purpose, depress the valve core to release all of the air in the strut. For a valve without a valve core (MS28889), rotate the swivel nut sufficiently to allow the air to escape.

6. When all air has escaped from the strut, it should be compressed completely. Aircraft on jacks may need to have the lower strut jacked with an exerciser jack to achieve full compression of the strut. *[Figure 13-26]*

Figure 13-23. *Fluid flow during shock strut operation is controlled by the taper of the metering pin in the shock strut orifice.*

Insufficient fluid, or air in the strut, cause the compression stroke to not be properly limited. The strut could bottom out, resulting in impact forces to be transferred directly to the airframe through the metallic structure of the strut. In a properly serviced strut, the extension stroke of the shock strut operation occurs at the end of the compression stroke. Energy stored in the compressed air in the upper cylinder causes the aircraft to start moving upward in relation to the ground and lower strut cylinder as the strut tries to rebound to its normal position. Fluid is forced back down into the lower cylinder through restrictions and snubbing orifices. The snubbing of fluid flow during the extension stroke dampens the strut rebound and reduces oscillation caused by the spring action of the compressed air. A sleeve, spacer, or bumper ring incorporated into the strut limits the extension stroke.

Figure 13-24. *Valve core-type (A) and core-free valve fittings (B) are used to service landing gear shock struts.*

7. Remove the valve core of an AN6287 valve *[Figure 13-25D]* using a valve core removal tool. *[Figure 13-27]* Then, remove the entire service valve by unscrewing the valve body from the strut. *[Figure 13-25E]*

8. Fill the strut with hydraulic fluid to the level of the service valve port with the approved hydraulic fluid.

9. Re-install the air service valve assembly using a new O-ring packing. Torque according to applicable manufacturer's specifications. If an AN2687-1 valve, install a new valve core.

10. Inflate the strut. A threaded fitting from a controlled source of high pressure air or nitrogen should be screwed onto the servicing valve. Control the flow with the service valve swivel nut. The correct amount of inflation is measured in psi on some struts. Other manufacturers specify struts to be inflated until extension of the lower strut is a certain measurement. Follow manufacturer's instructions. Shock struts should always be inflated slowly to avoid excess heating and over inflation.

11. Once inflated, tighten the swivel nut and torque as specified.

12. Remove the fill hose fitting and finger tighten the valve cap of the valve.

Bleeding Shock Struts

It may be necessary to bleed a shock strut during the service operation or when air becomes trapped in the hydraulic fluid inside the strut. This can be caused by low hydraulic fluid quantity in the strut. Bleeding is normally done with the aircraft on jacks to facilitate repeated extension and compression of the strut to expel the entrapped air. An example procedure for bleeding the shock strut follows.

1. Construct and attach a bleed hose containing a fitting suitable for making an airtight connection at the shock strut service valve port. Ensure a long enough hose to reach the ground while the aircraft is on jacks.

2. Jack the aircraft until the shock struts are fully extended.

3. Release any air pressure in the shock strut.

4. Remove the air service valve assembly.

5. Fill the strut to the level of the service port with approved hydraulic fluid.

6. Attach the bleed hose to the service port and insert the free end of the hose into a container of clean hydraulic fluid. The hose end must remain below the surface of the fluid.

Figure 13-25. *Steps in servicing a landing gear shock strut include releasing the air from the strut and removing the service valve from the top of the strut to permit the introduction of hydraulic fluid. Note that the strut is illustrated horizontally. On an actual aircraft installation, the strut is serviced in the vertical position (landing gear down).*

7. Place an exerciser jack or other suitable jack under the shock strut jacking point. Compress and extend the strut fully by raising and lowering the jack. Continue this process until all air bubbles cease to form in the container of hydraulic fluid. Compress the strut slowly and allow it to extend by its own weight.

8. Remove the exerciser jack. Lower the aircraft and remove all other jacks.

9. Remove the bleed hose assembly and fitting from the service port of the strut.

10. Install the air service valve, torque, and inflate the shock strut to the manufacturer's specifications.

Landing Gear Alignment, Support, and Retraction

Retractable landing gear consist of several components that enable it to function. Typically, these are the torque links, trunnion and bracket arrangements, drag strut linkages, electrical and hydraulic gear retraction devices, as well as locking, sensing, and indicating components. Additionally, nose gear have steering mechanisms attached to the gear.

Alignment

As previously mentioned, a torque arm or torque links assembly keeps the lower strut cylinder from rotating out of alignment with the longitudinal axis of the aircraft. In some strut assemblies, it is the sole means of retaining the piston in

Figure 13-26. *Air trapped in shock strut hydraulic fluid is bled by exercising the strut through its full range of motion while the end of an air-tight bleed hose is submerged in a container of hydraulic fluid.*

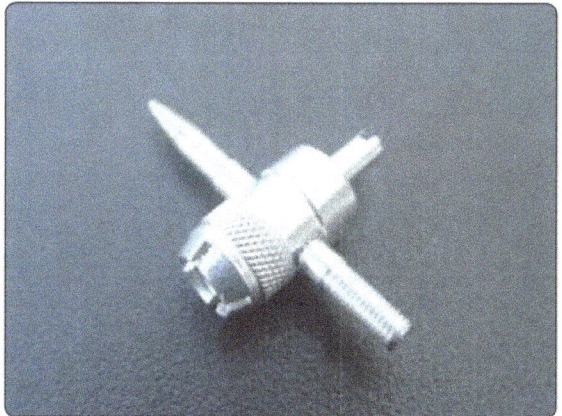

Figure 13-27. *This valve tool features internal and external thread chasers, a notched valve core removal/installation tool, and a tapered end for depressing a valve core or clearing debris.*

the upper strut cylinder. The link ends are attached to the fixed upper cylinder and the moving lower cylinder with a hinge pin in the center to allow the strut to extend and compress.

Alignment of the wheels of an aircraft is also a consideration. Normally, this is set by the manufacturer and only requires occasional attention such as after a hard landing. The aircraft's main wheels must be inspected and adjusted, if necessary, to maintain the proper tow-in or tow-out and the correct camber. Tow-in and tow-out refer to the path a main wheel would take in relation to the airframe longitudinal axis or centerline if the wheel was free to roll forward. Three possibilities exist. The wheel would roll either: 1) parallel to the longitudinal axis (aligned); 2) converge on the longitudinal axis (tow-in); or 3) veer away from the longitudinal axis (tow-out). *[Figure 13-28]*

The manufacturer's maintenance instructions give the procedure for checking and adjusting tow-in or tow-out. A general procedure for checking alignment on a light aircraft follows. To ensure that the landing gear settle properly for a tow-in/tow-out test, especially on spring steel strut aircraft, two aluminum plates separated with grease are put under each wheel. Gently rock the aircraft on the plates to cause the gear to find the at rest position preferred for alignment checks.

A straight edge is held across the front of the main wheel tires just below axle height. A carpenter's square placed against the straight edge creates a perpendicular that is parallel to the longitudinal axis of the aircraft. Slide the square against the wheel assembly to see if the forward and aft sections of the tire touch the square. A gap in front indicates the wheel is towed-in. A gap in the rear indicates the wheel is towed-out. *[Figure 13-29]*

Camber is the alignment of a main wheel in the vertical plain. It can be checked with a bubble protractor held against the wheel assembly. The wheel camber is said to be positive if the top of the wheel tilts outward from vertical. Camber is negative if the top of the wheel tilts inward. *[Figure 13-30]*

Adjustments can be made to correct small amounts of wheel misalignment. On aircraft with spring steel gear, tapered shims can be added or removed between the bolt-on wheel axle and the axle mounting flange on the strut. Aircraft equipped with air/oil struts typically use shims between the two arms of the torque links as a means of aligning tow-in and tow-out. *[Figure 13-31]* Follow all manufacturer's instructions.

Support

Aircraft landing gear are attached to the wing spars or other structural members, many of which are designed for the specific purpose of supporting the landing gear. Retractable gear must be engineered in such a way as to provide strong attachment to the aircraft and still be able to move into a recess or well when stowed. A trunnion arrangement is typical. The trunnion is a fixed structural extension of the upper strut cylinder with bearing surfaces that allow the entire gear assembly to move. It is attached to aircraft structure in such a way that the gear can pivot from the vertical position required for landing and taxi to the stowed position used during flight. *[Figure 13-32]*

Figure 13-28. *Wheel alignment on an aircraft.*

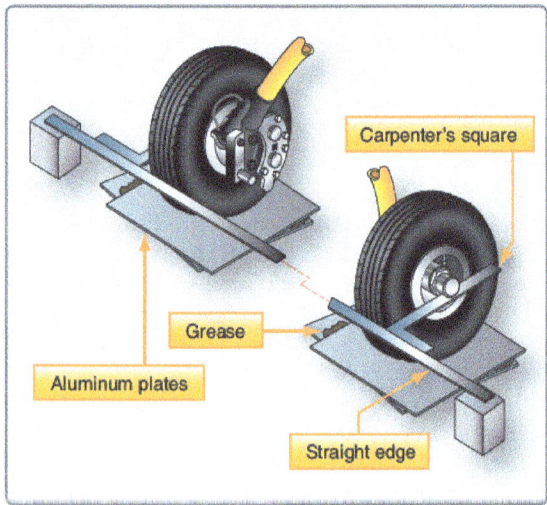

Figure 13-29. *Finding tow-in and tow-out on a light aircraft with spring steel struts.*

Figure 13-30. *Camber of a wheel is the amount the wheel is tilted out of the vertical plain. It can be measured with a bubble protractor.*

While in the vertical gear down position, the trunnion is free to swing or pivot. Alone, it cannot support the aircraft without collapsing. A drag brace is used to restrain against the pivot action built into the trunnion attachment. The upper end of the two-piece drag brace is attached to the aircraft structure and the lower end to the strut. A hinge near the middle of the brace allows the brace to fold and permits the gear to retract. For ground operation, the drag brace is straightened over center to a stop, and locked into position so the gear remains rigid. *[Figure 13-33]* The function of a drag brace on some aircraft is performed by the hydraulic cylinder used to raise and lower the gear. Cylinder internal hydraulic locks replace the over-center action of the drag brace for support during ground maneuvers.

Small Aircraft Retraction Systems

As the speed of a light aircraft increases, there reaches a point where the parasite drag created by the landing gear in the wind is greater than the induced drag caused by the added weight of a retractable landing gear system. Thus, many light aircraft have retractable landing gear. There are many unique designs. The simplest contains a lever in the flight deck mechanically linked to the gear. Through mechanical advantage, the pilot extends and retracts the landing gear by operating the lever. Use of a roller chain, sprockets, and a hand crank to decrease the required force is common.

Figure 13-31. *Tow-in and tow-out adjustments on small aircraft with spring steel landing gear are made with shims behind the axle assembly. On shock strut aircraft, the shims are placed where the torque links couple.*

Electrically operated landing gear systems are also found on light aircraft. An all-electric system uses an electric motor and gear reduction to move the gear. The rotary motion of the motor is converted to linear motion to actuate the gear. This is possible only with the relatively lightweight gear found on smaller aircraft. An all-electric gear retraction system is illustrated in *Figure 13-34*.

Figure 13-32. *The trunnion is a fixed structural support that is part of or attached to the upper strut cylinder of a landing gear strut. It contains bearing surfaces so the gear can retract.*

13-17

Figure 13-33. *A hinged drag strut holds the trunnion and gear firm for landing and ground operation. It folds at the hinge to allow the gear to retract.*

A more common use of electricity in gear retraction systems is that of an electric/hydraulic system found in many Cessna and Piper aircraft. This is also known as a power pack system. A small lightweight hydraulic power pack contains several components required in a hydraulic system. These include the reservoir, a reversible electric motor-driven hydraulic pump, a filter, high-and-low pressure control valves, a thermal relief valve, and a shuttle valve. Some power packs incorporate an emergency hand pump. A hydraulic actuator for each gear is driven to extend or retract the gear by fluid from the power pack. *Figure 13-35* illustrates a power pack system while gear is being lowered. *Figure 13-36* shows the same system while the gear is being raised.

When the flight deck gear selection handle is put in the gear-down position, a switch is made that turns on the electric motor in the power pack. The motor turns in the direction to rotate the hydraulic gear pump so that it pumps fluid to the gear-down side of the actuating cylinders. Pump pressure moves the spring-loaded shuttle valve to the left to allow fluid to reach all three actuators. Restrictors are used in the nose wheel actuator inlet and outlet ports to slow down the motion of this lighter gear. While hydraulic fluid is pumped to extend the gear, fluid from the upside of the actuators returns to the reservoir through the gear-up check valve. When the gear reach the down and locked position, pressure builds in the gear-down line from the pump and the low-pressure control valve unseats to return the fluid to the reservoir. Electric limit switches turn off the pump when all three gear are down and locked.

To raise the gear, the flight deck gear handle is moved to the gear-up position. This sends current to the electric motor, which drives the hydraulic gear pump in the opposite direction causing fluid to be pumped to the gear-up side of the actuators. In this direction, pump inlet fluid flows through the filter. Fluid from the pump flows thought the gear-up check valve to the gear-up sides of the actuating cylinders. As the cylinders begin to move, the pistons release the mechanical down locks that hold the gear rigid for ground operations. Fluid from the gear-down side of the actuators returns to the reservoir through the shuttle valve. When the three gears are fully retracted, pressure builds in the system, and a pressure switch is opened that cuts power to the electric pump motor. The gear are held in the retracted position with hydraulic pressure. If pressure declines, the pressure switch closes to run the pump and raise the pressure until the pressure switch opens again.

Figure 13-34. *A geared electric motor landing gear retraction system.*

Figure 13-35. *A popular light aircraft gear retraction system that uses a hydraulic power pack in the gear down condition.*

Figure 13-36. *A hydraulic power pack gear retraction system in the gear up condition.*

Large Aircraft Retraction Systems

Large aircraft retraction systems are nearly always powered by hydraulics. Typically, the hydraulic pump is driven off of the engine accessory drive. Auxiliary electric hydraulic pumps are also common. Other devices used in a hydraulically-operated retraction system include actuating cylinders, selector valves, uplocks, downlocks, sequence valves, priority valves, tubing, and other conventional hydraulic system components. These units are interconnected so that they permit properly sequenced retraction and extension of the landing gear and the landing gear doors.

The correct operation of any aircraft landing gear retraction system is extremely important. *Figure 13-37* illustrates an example of a simple large aircraft hydraulic landing gear system. The system is on an aircraft that has doors that open before the gear is extended and close after the gear is retracted. The nose gear doors operate via mechanical linkage

Figure 13-37. *A simple large aircraft hydraulic gear retraction system.*

and do not require hydraulic power. There are many gear and gear door arrangements on various aircraft. Some aircraft have gear doors that close to fair the wheel well after the gear is extended. Others have doors mechanically attached to the outside of the gear so that when it stows inward, the door stows with the gear and fairs with the fuselage skin.

In the system illustrated in *Figure 13-37*, when the flight deck gear selector is moved to the gear-up position, it positions a selector valve to allow pump pressure from the hydraulic system manifold to access eight different components. The three downlocks are pressurized and unlocked so the gear can be retracted. At the same time, the actuator cylinder on each gear also receives pressurized fluid to the gear-up side of the piston through an unrestricted orifice check valve. This drives the gear into the wheel well. Two sequence valves (C and D) also receive fluid pressure. Gear door operation must be controlled so that it occurs after the gear is stowed. The sequence valves are closed and delay flow to the door actuators. When the gear cylinders are fully retracted, they mechanically contact the sequence valve plungers that open the valves and allow fluid to flow into the close side of the door actuator cylinders. This closes the doors. Sequence valves A and B act as check valves during retraction. They allow fluid to flow one way from the gear-down side of the main gear cylinders back into the hydraulic system return manifold through the selector valve.

To lower the gear, the selector is put in the gear-down position. Pressurized hydraulic fluid flows from the hydraulic manifold to the nose gear uplock, which unlocks the nose gear. Fluid flows to the gear-down side of the nose gear actuator and extends it. Fluid also flows to the open side of the main gear door actuators. As the doors open, sequence valves A and B block fluid from unlocking the main gear uplocks and prevent fluid from reaching the down side of the main gear actuators. When the doors are fully open, the door actuator engages the plungers of both sequence valves to open the valves. The main gear uplocks, then receives fluid pressure and unlock. The main gear cylinder actuators receive fluid on the down side through the open sequence valves to extend the gear. Fluid from each main gear cylinder up-side flows to the hydraulic system return manifold through restrictors in the orifice check valves. The restrictors slow the extension of the gear to prevent impact damage.

There are numerous hydraulic landing gear retraction system designs. Priority valves are sometimes used instead of mechanically operated sequence valves. This controls some gear component activation timing via hydraulic pressure. Particulars of any gear system are found in the aircraft maintenance manual. The aircraft technician must be thoroughly familiar with the operation and maintenance requirements of this crucial system.

Emergency Extension Systems

The emergency extension system lowers the landing gear if the main power system fails. There are numerous ways in which this is done depending on the size and complexity of the aircraft. Some aircraft have an emergency release handle in the flight deck that is connected through a mechanical linkage to the gear uplocks. When the handle is operated, it releases the uplocks and allows the gear to free-fall to the extended position under the force created by gravity acting upon the gear. Other aircraft use a non-mechanical back-up, such as pneumatic power, to unlatch the gear.

The popular small aircraft retraction system shown in *Figures 13-35* and *13-36* uses a free-fall valve for emergency gear extension. Activated from the flight deck, when the free-fall valve is opened, hydraulic fluid is allowed to flow from the gear-up side of the actuators to the gear-down side of the actuators, independent of the power pack. Pressure holding the gear up is relieved, and the gear extends due to its weight. Air moving past the gear aids in the extension and helps push the gear into the down-and-locked position.

Large and high performance aircraft are equipped with redundant hydraulic systems. This makes emergency extension less common since a different source of hydraulic power can be selected if the gear does not function normally.

If the gear still fails to extend, some sort of unlatching device is used to release the uplocks and allow the gear to free fall. *[Figure 13-38]*

Figure 13-38. *These emergency gear extension handles in a Boeing 737 are located under a floor panel on the flight deck. Each handle releases the gear uplock via a cable system so the gear can freefall into the extended position.*

In some small aircraft, the design configuration makes emergency extension of the gear by gravity and air loads alone impossible or impractical. Force of some kind must therefore be applied. Manual extension systems, wherein the pilot mechanically cranks the gear into position, are common. Consult the aircraft maintenance manual for all emergency landing gear extension system descriptions of operation, performance standards, and emergency extension tests as required.

Landing Gear Safety Devices

There are numerous landing gear safety devices. The most common are those that prevent the gear from retracting or collapsing while on the ground. Gear indicators are another safety device. They are used to communicate to the pilot the position status of each individual landing gear at any time. A further safety device is the nose wheel centering device mentioned previously in this chapter.

Safety Switch

A landing gear squat switch, or safety switch, is found on most aircraft. This is a switch positioned to open and close depending on the extension or compression of the main landing gear strut. *[Figure 13-39]* The squat switch is wired into any number of system operating circuits. One circuit

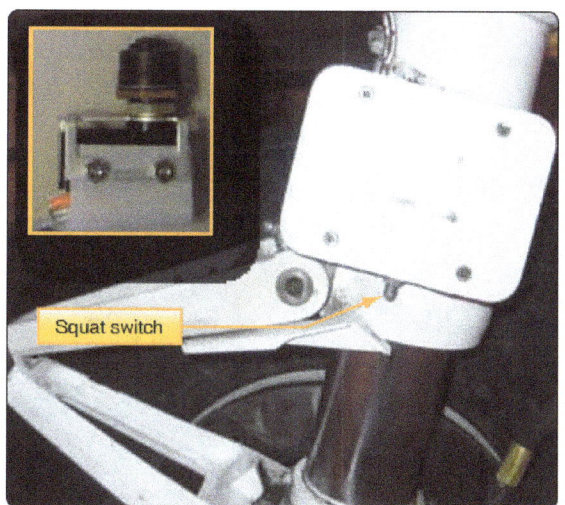

Figure 13-39. *Typical landing gear squat switches.*

The use of proximity sensors for gear position safety switches is common in high-performance aircraft. An electromagnetic sensor returns a different voltage to a gear logic unit depending on the proximity of a conductive target to the switch. No physical contact is made. When the gear is in the designed position, the metallic target is close to the inductor in the sensor which reduces the return voltage. This type of sensing is especially useful in the landing gear environment where switches with moving parts can become contaminated with dirt and moisture from runways and taxi ways. The technician is required to ensure that sensor targets are installed the correct distance away from the sensor. Go–no go gauges are often used to set the distance. *[Figure 13-41]*

Ground Locks

Ground locks are commonly used on aircraft landing gear as extra insurance that the landing gear will remain down and locked while the aircraft is on the ground. They are external devices that are placed in the retraction mechanism to prevent its movement. A ground lock can be as simple as a pin placed into the pre-drilled holes of gear components that keep the gear from collapsing. Another commonly used ground lock clamps onto the exposed piston of the gear retraction cylinder that prevents it from retracting. All ground locks should have a red streamers attached to them so they are visible and removed before flight. Ground locks are typically carried in the aircraft and put into place by the flight crew during the post landing walk-around. *[Figure 13-42]*

prevents the gear from being retracted while the aircraft is on the ground. There are different ways to achieve this lock-out. A solenoid that extends a shaft to physically disable the gear position selector is one such method found on many aircraft. When the landing gear is compressed, the squat safety switch is open, and the center shaft of the solenoid protrudes a hardened lock-pin through the landing gear control handle so that it cannot be moved to the up position. At takeoff, the landing gear strut extends. The safety switch closes and allows current to flow in the safety circuit. The solenoid energizes and retracts the lock-pin from the selector handle. This permits the gear to be raised. *[Figure 13-40]*

Figure 13-40. *A landing gear safety circuit with solenoid that locks the control handle and selector valve from being able to move into the gear up position when the aircraft is on the ground. The safety switch, or squat switch, is located on the aircraft landing gear.*

Figure 13-41. *Proximity sensors are used instead of contact switches on many landing gear.*

Landing Gear Position Indicators

Landing gear position indicators are located on the instrument panel adjacent to the gear selector handle. They are used to inform the pilot of gear position status. There are many arrangements for gear indication. Usually, there is a dedicated light for each gear. The most common display for the landing gear being down and locked is an illuminated green light. Three green lights means it is safe to land. All lights out typically indicates that the gear is up and locked, or there may be gear up indicator lights. Gear in transit lights are used on some aircraft as are barber pole displays when a gear is not up or down and locked. Blinking indicator lights also indicate gear in transit. Some manufacturer's use a gear disagree annunciation when the landing gear is not in the same position as the selector. Many aircraft monitor gear door position in addition to the gear itself. Consult the aircraft manufacturer's maintenance and operating manuals for a complete description of the landing gear indication system. *[Figure 13-43]*

Nose Wheel Centering

Since most aircraft have steerable nose wheel gear assemblies for taxiing, a means for aligning the nose gear before retraction is needed. Centering cams built into the shock strut structure accomplish this. An upper cam is free to mate into a lower cam recess when the gear is fully extended. This aligns the gear for retraction. When weight returns to the wheels after landing, the shock strut is compressed, and the centering cams separate allowing the lower shock strut (piston) to rotate in the upper strut cylinder. This rotation is controlled to steer the aircraft. *[Figure 13-44]* Small aircraft sometimes incorporate an external roller or guide pin on the strut. As the strut is folded into the wheel well during retraction, the roller or guide pin engages a ramp or track mounted to the wheel well structure. The ramp/track guides the roller or pin in such a manner that the nose wheel is straightened as it enters the wheel well.

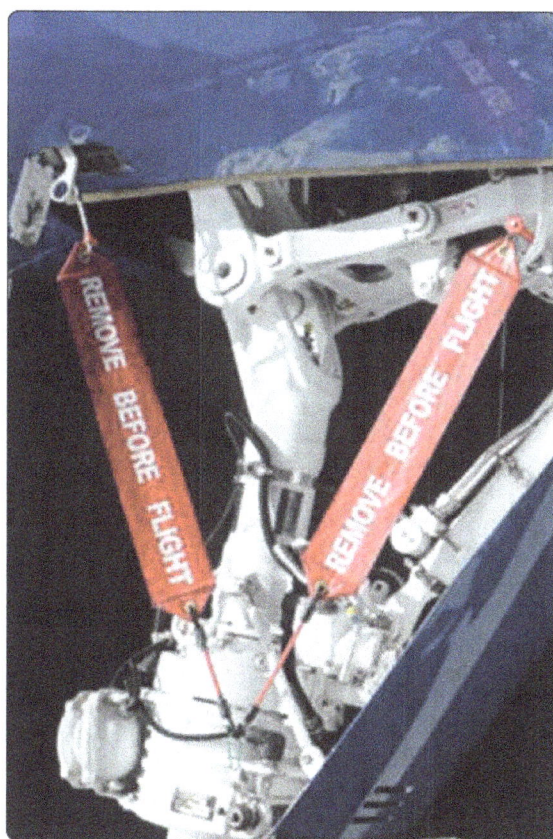

Figure 13-42. *Gear pin ground lock devices.*

Landing Gear System Maintenance

The moving parts and dirty environment of the landing gear make this an area of regular maintenance. Because of the stresses and pressures acting on the landing gear, inspection, servicing, and other maintenance becomes a continuous process. The most important job in the maintenance of the aircraft landing gear system is thorough accurate inspections. To properly perform inspections, all surfaces should be cleaned to ensure that no trouble spots are undetected.

Periodically, it is necessary to inspect shock struts, trunnion and brace assemblies and bearings, shimmy dampers, wheels, wheel bearings, tires, and brakes. Landing gear position indicators, lights, and warning horns must also be checked for proper operation. During all inspections and visits to the wheel wells, ensure all ground safety locks are installed.

Other landing gear inspection items include checking emergency control handles and systems for proper position and condition. Inspect landing gear wheels for cleanliness, corrosion, and cracks. Check wheel tie bolts for looseness. Examine anti-skid wiring for deterioration. Check tires for wear, cuts, deterioration, presence of grease or oil, alignment

Figure 13-43. *Landing gear selector panels with position indicator lights. The Boeing 737 panel illuminates red lights above the green lights when the gear is in transit.*

of slippage marks, and proper inflation. Inspect landing gear mechanism for condition, operation, and proper adjustment. Lubricate the landing gear, including the nose wheel steering. Check steering system cables for wear, broken strands, alignment, and safetying. Inspect landing gear shock struts for such conditions as cracks, corrosion, breaks, and security. Where applicable, check brake clearances and wear.

Various types of lubricant are required to lubricate points of friction and wear on landing gear. Specific products to be used are given by the manufacturer in the maintenance

Figure 13-44. *A cutaway view of a nose gear internal centering cam.*

manual. Lubrication may be accomplished by hand or with a grease gun. Follow manufacturer's instructions. Before applying grease to a pressure grease fitting, be sure the fitting is wiped clean of dirt and debris, as well as old hardened grease. Dust and sand mixed with grease produce a very destructive abrasive compound. Wipe off all excess grease while greasing the gear. The piston rods of all exposed strut cylinders and actuating cylinders should be clean at all times.

Periodically, wheel bearings must be removed, cleaned, inspected, and lubricated. When cleaning a wheel bearing, use the recommended cleaning solvent. Do not use gasoline or jet fuel. Dry the bearing by directing a blast of dry air between the rollers. Do not direct the air so that it spins the bearing as without lubrication, this could cause the bearing to fly apart resulting in injury. When inspecting the bearing, check for defects that would render it unserviceable, such as cracks, flaking, broken bearing surfaces, roughness due to impact pressure or surface wear, corrosion or pitting, discoloration from excessive heat, cracked or broken bearing cages, and scored or loose bearing cups or cones that would affect proper seating on the axle or wheel. If any discrepancies are found, replace the bearing with a serviceable unit. Bearings should be lubricated immediately after cleaning and inspection to prevent corrosion.

To lubricate a tapered roller bearing, use a bearing lubrication tool or place a small amount of the approved grease on the palm of the hand. Grasp the bearing with the other hands and press the larger diameter side of the bearing into the grease to force it completely through the space between the bearing rollers and the cone. Gradually turn the bearing so that all of the rollers have been completely packed with grease. *[Figure 13-45]*

Landing Gear Rigging and Adjustment

Occasionally, it becomes necessary to adjust the landing gear switches, doors, linkages, latches, and locks to ensure proper operation of the landing gear system and doors. When landing gear actuating cylinders are replaced and when length adjustments are made, over-travel must be checked. Over-travel is the action of the cylinder piston beyond the movement necessary for landing gear extension and retraction. The additional action operates the landing gear latch mechanisms.

A wide variety of aircraft types and landing gear system designs result in procedures for rigging and adjustment that vary from aircraft to aircraft. Uplock and downlock clearances, linkage adjustments, limit switch adjustments, and other adjustments must be confirmed by the technician in the manufacturer's maintenance data before taking action. The following examples of various adjustments are given to convey concepts, rather than actual procedures for any particular aircraft.

Figure 13-45. *Packing grease into a clean, dry bearing can be done by hand in the absence of a bearing grease tool. Press the bearing into the grease on the palm of the hand until it passes completely through the gap between the rollers and the inner race all the way around the bearing.*

Figure 13-46. *An example of a main landing gear door latch mechanism.*

Adjusting Landing Gear Latches

The adjustment of various latches is a primary concern to the aircraft technician. Latches are generally used in landing gear systems to hold the gear up or down and/or to hold the gear doors open or closed. Despite numerous variations, all latches are designed to do the same thing. They must operate automatically at the proper time, and they must hold the unit in the desired position. A typical landing gear door latch is examined below. Many gear up latches operate similarly. Clearances and dimensional measurements of rollers, shafts, bushings, pins, bolts, etc., are common.

\On this particular aircraft, the landing gear door is held closed by two latches. To have the door locked securely, both latches must grip and hold the door tightly against the aircraft structure. The principle components of each latch mechanism are shown in *Figure 13-46.* They are a hydraulic latch cylinder, a latch hook, a spring loaded crank-and-lever linkage with sector, and the latch hook.

When hydraulic pressure is applied, the cylinder operates the linkage to engage (or disengage) the hook with (or from) the roller on the gear door. In the gear-down sequence, the hook is disengaged by the spring load on the linkage. In the gear-up sequence, when the closing door is in contact with the latch hook, the cylinder operates the linkage to engage the latch hook with the door roller. Cables on the landing gear emergency extension system are connected to the sector to permit emergency release of the latch rollers. An uplock switch is installed on, and actuated by, each latch to provide a gear up indication in the flight deck.

With the gear up and the door latched, inspect the latch roller for proper clearance as shown in *Figure 13-47A*. On this installation, the required clearance is $1/8 \pm 3/32$-inch. If the roller is not within tolerance, it may be adjusted by loosening its mounting bolts and raising or lowering the latch roller support. This is accomplished via the elongated holes and serrated locking surfaces of the latch roller support and serrated plate. *[Figure 13-47B]*

Figure 13-47. *Main landing gear door latch roller clearance measurement and adjustment.*

Gear Door Clearances

Landing gear doors have specific allowable clearances between the doors and the aircraft structure that must be maintained. Adjustments are typically made at the hinge installations or to the connecting links that support and move the door. On some installations, door hinges are adjusted by placing a serrated hinge with an elongated mounting hole in the proper position in a hinge support fitting. Using serrated washers, the mounting bolt is torqued to hold the position. *Figure 13-48* illustrates this type of mounting, which allows linear adjustments via the elongated hole.

Figure 13-48. *An adjustable door hinge installation for setting door clearance.*

The distance landing gear doors open or close may depend upon the length of the door linkage. Rod end adjustments are common to fit the door. Adjustments to door stops are also a possibility. The manufacturer's maintenance manual specifies the length of the linkages and gives procedure for adjusting the stops. Follow all specified procedures that are accomplished with the aircraft on jacks and the gear retracted. Doors that are too tight can cause structural damage. Doors that are too loose catch wind in flight, which could cause wear and potential failure, as well as parasite drag.

Drag and Side Brace Adjustment

Each landing gear has specific adjustments and tolerances per the manufacturer that permit the gear to function as intended. A common geometry used to lock a landing gear in the down position involves a collapsible side brace that is extended and held in an over-center position through the use of a locking link. Springs and actuators may also contribute to the motion of the linkage. Adjustments and tests are needed to ensure proper operation.

Figure 13-49 illustrates a landing gear on a small aircraft with such a side brace. It consists of an upper and lower link hinged at the center that permits the brace to jackknife during retraction of the gear. The upper end pivots on a trunnion attached to structure in the wheel well overhead. The lower end is attached to the shock strut. A locking

Figure 13-49. *Over-center adjustments on a small aircraft main gear.*

link is incorporated between the upper end of the shock strut and the lower drag link. It is adjustable to provide the correct amount of over-center travel of the side brace links. This locks the gear securely in the down position to prevent collapse of the gear.

To adjust the over-center position of the side brace locking link, the aircraft must be placed on jacks. With the landing gear in the down position, the lock link end fitting is adjusted so that the side brace links are held firmly over-center. When the gear is held inboard six inches from the down and locked position and then released, the gear must free fall into the locked down position.

In addition to the amount the side brace links are adjusted to travel over center, down lock spring tension must also be checked. This is accomplished with a spring scale. The tension on this particular gear is between 40 and 60 pounds. Check the manufacturer's maintenance data for each aircraft to ensure correct tensions exist and proper adjustments are made.

Landing Gear Retraction Test

The proper functioning of a landing gear system and components can be checked by performing a landing gear retraction test. This is also known as swinging the gear. The aircraft is properly supported on jacks for this check, and the landing gear should be cleaned and lubricated if needed. The gear is then raised and lowered as though the aircraft were in flight while a close visual inspection is performed. All parts of the system should be observed for security and proper operation. The emergency back-up extension system should be checked whenever swinging the gear.

Retraction tests are performed at various times, such as during annual inspection. Any time a landing gear component is replaced that could affect the correct functioning of the landing gear system, a retraction test should follow when adjustments to landing gear linkages or components that affect gear system performance are made. It may be necessary to swing the gear after a hard or overweight landing. It is also common to swing the gear while attempting to locate a malfunction within the system. For all required retraction tests and the specific inspection points to check, consult the manufacturer's maintenance manual for the aircraft in question as each landing gear system is unique.

The following is a list of general inspection items to be performed while swinging the gear:

1. Check the landing gear for proper extension and retraction.
2. Check all switches, lights, and warning devices for proper operation.
3. Check the landing gear doors for clearance and freedom from binding.
4. Check landing gear linkage for proper operation, adjustment, and general condition.
5. Check the alternate/emergency extension or retraction systems for proper operation.
6. Investigate any unusual sounds, such as those caused by rubbing, binding, chafing, or vibration.

Nose Wheel Steering Systems

The nose wheel on most aircraft is steerable from the flight deck via a nose wheel steering system. This allows the aircraft to be directed during ground operation. A few simple aircraft have nose wheel assemblies that caster. Such aircraft are steered during taxi by differential braking.

Small Aircraft

Most small aircraft have steering capabilities through the use of a simple system of mechanical linkages connected to the rudder pedals. Push-pull tubes are connected to pedal horns on the lower strut cylinder. As the pedals are depressed, the movement is transferred to the strut piston axle and wheel assembly which rotates to the left or right. *[Figure 13-50]*

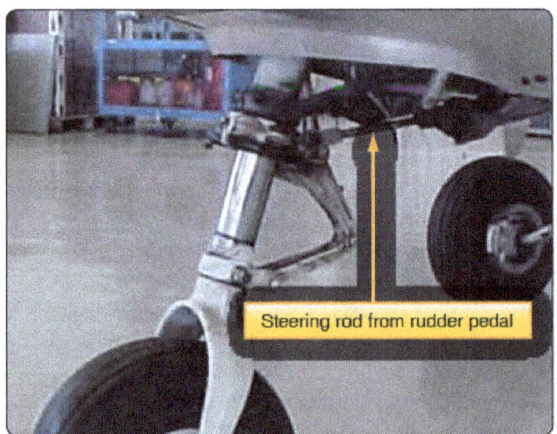

Figure 13-50. *Nose wheel steering on a light aircraft often uses a push-pull rod system connected to the rudder pedals.*

Large Aircraft

Due to their mass and the need for positive control, large aircraft utilize a power source for nose wheel steering. Hydraulic power predominates. There are many different designs for large aircraft nose steering systems. Most share similar characteristics and components. Control of the steering is from the flight deck through the use of a small wheel, tiller, or joystick typically mounted on the left side wall. Switching the system on and off is possible on some aircraft. Mechanical, electrical, or hydraulic connections transmit the controller input movement to a steering control unit. The control unit is a hydraulic metering or control valve. It directs hydraulic fluid under pressure to one or two actuators designed with various linkages to rotate the lower strut. An accumulator and relief valve, or similar pressurizing assembly, keeps fluid in the actuators and system under pressure at all times. This permits the steering actuating cylinders to also act as shimmy dampers. A follow-up mechanism consists of various gears, cables, rods, drums, and/or bell-crank, etc. It returns the metering valve to a neutral position once the steering angle has been reached. Many systems incorporate an input subsystem from the rudder pedals for small degrees of turns made while directing the aircraft at high speed during takeoff and landing. Safety valves are typical in all systems to relieve pressure during hydraulic failure so the nose wheel can swivel.

The following explanation accompanies *Figures 13-51, 13-52,* and *13-53,* which illustrate a large aircraft nose wheel steering system and components. These figures and explanation are for instructional purposes only.

The nose wheel steering wheel connects through a shaft to a steering drum located inside the flight deck control pedestal. The rotation of this drum transmits the steering signal by means of cables and pulleys to the control drum of the differential assembly. Movement of the differential assembly is transmitted by the differential link to the metering valve assembly where it moves the selector valve to the selected position. This provides the hydraulic power for turning the nose gear.

As shown in *Figure 13-52,* pressure from the aircraft hydraulic system is directed through the open safety shutoff valve into a line leading to the metering valve. The metering valve then routes the pressurized fluid out of port A, through the right turn alternating line, and into steering cylinder A. This is a one-port cylinder and pressure forces the piston to begin extension. Since the rod of this piston connects to the nose steering spindle on the nose gear shock strut which pivots at point X, the extension of the piston turns the steering spindle gradually toward the right. As the nose wheel turns, fluid is forced out of steering cylinder B through the left turn alternating line and into port B of the metering valve. The metering valve directs this return fluid into a compensator that routes the fluid into the aircraft hydraulic system return manifold.

Figure 13-51. *Example of a large aircraft hydraulic nose wheel steering system with hydraulic and mechanical units.*

Figure 13-52. Hydraulic system flow diagram of large aircraft nose wheel steering system.

Figure 13-53. Hydraulic system flow diagram of large aircraft nose wheel steering system.

As described, hydraulic pressure starts the nose gear turning. However, the gear should not be turned too far. The nose gear steering system contains devices to stop the gear at the selected angle of turn and hold it there. This is accomplished with follow-up linkage. As stated, the nose gear is turned by the steering spindle as the piston of cylinder A extends. The rear of the spindle contains gear teeth that mesh with a gear on the bottom of the orifice rod. *[Figure 13-51]* As the nose gear and spindle turn, the orifice rod also turns but in the opposite direction. This rotation is transmitted by the two sections of the orifice rod to the scissor follow-up links located at the top of the nose gear strut. As the follow-up links return, they rotate the connected follow-up drum, which transmits the movement by cables and pulleys to the differential assembly. Operation of the differential assembly causes the differential arm and links to move the metering valve back toward the neutral position.

The metering valve and the compensator unit of the nose wheel steering system are illustrated in *Figure 13-53*. The compensator unit system keeps fluid in the steering cylinders pressurized at all times. This hydraulic unit consists of a three-port housing that encloses a spring-loaded piston and poppet. The left port is an air vent that prevents trapped air at the rear of the piston from interfering with the movement of the piston. The second port located at the top of the compensator connects through a line to the metering valve return port. The third port is located at the right side of the compensator. This port connects to the hydraulic system return manifold. It routes the steering system return fluid into the manifold when the poppet valve is open.

The compensator poppet opens when pressure acting on the piston becomes high enough to compress the spring. In this system, 100 psi is required. Therefore, fluid in the metering valve return line is contained under that pressure. The 100 psi pressure also exists throughout the metering valve and back through the cylinder return lines. This pressurizes the steering cylinders at all times and permits them to function as shimmy dampers.

Shimmy Dampers

Torque links attached from the stationary upper cylinder of a nose wheel strut to the bottom moveable cylinder or piston of the strut are not sufficient to prevent most nose gear from the tendency to oscillate rapidly, or shimmy, at certain speeds. This vibration must be controlled through the use of a shimmy damper. A shimmy damper controls nose wheel shimmy through hydraulic damping. The damper can be built integrally within the nose gear, but most often it is an external unit attached between the upper and lower shock struts. It is active during all phases of ground operation while permitting the nose gear steering system to function normally.

Steering Damper

As mentioned above, large aircraft with hydraulic steering hold pressure in the steering cylinders to provide the required damping. This is known as steering damping. Some older transport category aircraft have steering dampers that are vane-type. Nevertheless, they function to steer the nose wheel, as well as to dampen vibration.

Piston-Type

Aircraft not equipped with hydraulic nose wheel steering utilize an additional external shimmy damper unit. The case is attached firmly to the upper shock strut cylinder. The shaft is attached to the lower shock strut cylinder and to a piston inside the shimmy damper. As the lower strut cylinder tries to shimmy, hydraulic fluid is forced through a bleed hole in the piston. The restricted flow through the bleed hole dampens the oscillation. *[Figure 13-54]*

A piston-type shimmy damper may contain a fill port to add fluid or it may be a sealed unit. Regardless, the unit should be checked for leaks regularly. To ensure proper operation, a piston-type hydraulic shimmy damper should be filled to capacity.

Figure 13-54. *A shimmy damper on the nose strut of a small aircraft. The diagram shows the basic internal arrangement of most shimmy dampers. The damper in the photo is essentially the same except the piston shaft extends through both ends of the damper cylinder body.*

Vane-Type

A vane-type shimmy damper is sometime used. *[Figure 13-55]* It uses fluid chambers created by the vanes separated by a valve orifice in a center shaft. As the nose gear tries to oscillate, vanes rotate to change the size of internal chambers filled with fluid. The chamber size can only change as fast as the fluid can be forced through the orifice. Thus, the gear

Figure 13-55. *A typical vane-type shimmy damper.*

13-33

oscillation is dissipated by the rate of fluid flow. An internal spring-loaded replenishing reservoir keeps pressurized fluid in the working chambers and thermal compensation of the orifice size is included. As with the piston type shimmy damper, the vane-type damper should be inspected for leaks and kept serviced. A fluid level indicator protrudes from the reservoir end of the unit.

Non-Hydraulic Shimmy Damper

Non-hydraulic shimmy dampers are currently certified for many aircraft. They look and fit similar to piston-type shimmy dampers but contain no fluid inside. In place of the metal piston, a rubber piston presses out against the inner diameter of the damper housing when the shimmy motion is received through the shaft. The rubber piston rides on a very thin film of grease and the rubbing action between the piston and the housing provides the damping.

This is known as surface-effect damping. The materials use to construct this type of shimmy damper provide a long service life without the need to ever add fluid to the unit. *[Figure 13-56]*

Aircraft Wheels

Aircraft wheels are an important component of a landing gear system. With tires mounted upon them, they support the entire weight of the aircraft during taxi, takeoff, and landing. The typical aircraft wheel is lightweight, strong, and made from aluminum alloy. Some magnesium alloy wheels also exist. Early aircraft wheels were of single piece construction,

Figure 13-56. *A non-hydraulic shimmy damper uses a rubber piston with lubricant that dampens via motion against the inner diameter of the unit housing.*

much the same as the modern automobile wheel. As aircraft tires were improved for the purpose they serve, they were made stiffer to better absorb the forces of landing without blowing out or separating from the rim. Stretching such a tire over a single piece wheel rim was not possible. A two-piece wheel was developed. Early two-piece aircraft wheels were essentially one-piece wheels with a removable rim to allow mounting access for the tire. These are still found on older aircraft. *[Figure 13-57]* Later, wheels with two nearly symmetrical halves were developed. Nearly all modern aircraft wheels are of this two piece construction. *[Figures 13-58 and 13-59]*

Wheel Construction

The typical modern two-piece aircraft wheel is cast or forged from aluminum or magnesium alloy. The halves are bolted together and contain a groove at the mating surface for an o-ring, which seals the rim since most modern aircraft utilize

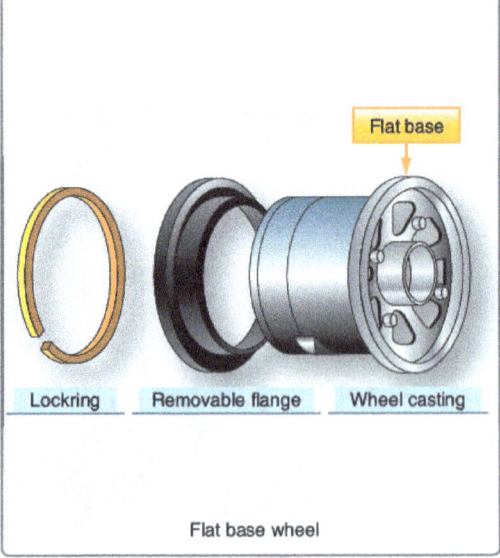

Figure 13-57. *Removable flange wheels found on older aircraft are either drop center or flat base types.*

Figure 13-58. *Two-piece split-wheel aircraft wheels found on modern light aircraft.*

tubeless tires. The bead seat area of a wheel is where the tire actually contacts the wheel. It is the critical area that accepts the significant tensile loads from the tire during landing. To strengthen this area during manufacturing, the bead seat area is typically rolled to prestress it with a compressive stress load.

Inboard Wheel Half

Wheel halves are not identical. The primary reason for this is that the inboard wheel half must have a means for accepting and driving the rotor(s) of the aircraft brakes that are mounted on both main wheels. Tangs on the rotor are fitted into steel reinforced keyways on many wheels. Other wheels have steel keys bolted to the inner wheel halves. These are made to fit slots in the perimeter of the brake rotor. Some small aircraft wheels have provisions for bolting the brake rotor to the inner wheel half. Regardless, the inner wheel half is distinguishable from the outer wheel half by its brake mounting feature. *[Figure 13-60]*

Both wheel halves contain a bearing cavity formed into the center that accepts the polished steel bearing cup, tapered roller bearing, and grease retainer of a typical wheel bearing set-up. A groove may also be machined to accept a retaining clip to hold the bearing assembly in place when the wheel assembly is removed. The wheel bearings are a very important part of the wheel assembly and are discussed in a later section of this chapter.

The inner wheel half of a wheel used on a high performance aircraft is likely to have one or more thermal plugs. *[Figure 13-61]* During heavy braking, temperatures can become so great that tire temperature and pressure rise to a level resulting in explosion of the wheel and tire assembly. The thermal plug core is filled with a low melting point alloy. Before tire and wheel temperatures reach the point of explosion, the core melts and deflates the tire. The tire must be removed from service, and the wheel must be inspected in accordance with the wheel manufacturer's instructions before return to service if a thermal plug melts. Adjacent wheel assemblies should also be inspected for signs of damage. A heat shield is commonly installed under the inserts designed to engage the brake rotor to assist in protecting the wheel and tire assembly from overheating.

An overinflation safety plug may also be installed in the inner wheel half. This is designed to rupture and release all of the air in the tire should it be over inflated. The fill valve is also often installed in the inner wheel half with the stem extending through holes in the outer wheel half to permit access for inflation and deflation.

Outboard Wheel Half

The outboard wheel half bolts to the inboard wheel half to make up the wheel assembly upon which the tire is mounted. The center boss is constructed to receive a bearing cup and bearing assembly as it does on the inboard wheel half. The outer bearing and end of the axle is capped to prevent contaminants from entering this area. Aircraft with anti-skid brake systems typically mount the wheel-spin transducer here. It is sealed and may also serve as a hub cap. The 737 outer wheel half illustrated in *Figure 13-59* also has a hub cap fairing over the entire wheel half. This is to fair it with the wind since the outer wheel half does not close behind a gear door on this aircraft. Hub caps may also be found on fixed gear aircraft.

The outboard wheel half provides a convenient location of the valve stem used to inflate and deflate tubeless tires. Alternately, it may contain a hole through which a valve stem extension may pass from the inner wheel half or the valve stem itself may fit through such a hole if a tube-type tire is used.

Wheel Inspection

An aircraft wheel assembly is inspected while on the aircraft as often as possible. A more detailed inspection and any testing or repairs may be accomplished with the wheel assembly removed from the aircraft.

On Aircraft Inspection

The general condition of the aircraft wheel assemblies can be inspected while on the aircraft. Any signs of suspected damage that may require removal of the wheel assembly from the aircraft should be investigated.

Proper Installation

The landing gear area is such a hostile environment that the technician should inspect the landing gear including the wheels, tires, and brakes whenever possible. Proper installation of the wheels should not be taken for granted.

Figure 13-59. *Features of a two piece aircraft wheel found on a modern airliner.*

All wheel tie bolts and nuts must be in place and secure. A missing bolt is grounds for removal, and a thorough inspection of the wheel halves in accordance with the wheel manufacturer's procedures must be performed due to the stresses that may have occurred. The wheel hub dust cap and anti-skid sensor should also be secure. The inboard wheel half should interface with the brake rotor with no signs of chafing or excessive movement. All brake keys on the wheel must be present and secure.

Examine the wheels for cracks, flaked paint, and any evidence of overheating. Inspect thermal plugs to ensure no sign of the fusible alloy having been melted. Thermal

Figure 13-60. *Keys on the inner wheel half of an aircraft wheel used to engage and rotate the rotors of a disc brake.*

Figure 13-61. *Heavy use of the aircraft brakes can cause tire air temperature and pressure to rise to a level resulting in explosion of the wheel assembly. To alleviate this, thermal plug(s) mounted in the inner wheel half of a high performance aircraft wheels are made with a fusible core that melts and releases the air from the tire before explosion.*

plugs that have permitted pressure loss in the tire require that the wheel assembly be removed for inspection. All other wheels with brakes and thermal plugs should be inspected closely while on the aircraft to determine if they too have overheated. Each wheel should be observed overall to ensure it is not abnormally tilted. Flanges should not be missing any pieces, and there should be no areas on the wheel that show significant impact damage.

Axle Nut Torque

Axle nut torque is of extreme importance on an aircraft wheel installation. If the nut is too loose, the bearing and wheel assembly may have excessive movement. The bearing cup(s) could loosen and spin, which could damage the wheel. There could also be impact damage from the bearing rollers which leads to bearing failure. *[Figure 13-62]* An over-torqued axle nut prevents the bearing from properly accepting the weight load of the aircraft. The bearing spins without sufficient lubrication to absorb the heat caused by the higher friction level. This too leads to bearing failure. All aircraft axle nuts must be installed and torqued in accordance with the airframe manufacturer's maintenance procedures.

Figure 13-62. *Improper loose torque on the axle nut can cause excessive end play leading to bearing race damage known as scalloping. Eventually, this leads to bearing failure.*

Off Aircraft Wheel Inspection

Discrepancies found while inspecting a wheel mounted on the aircraft may require further inspection with the wheel removed from the aircraft. Other items such as bearing condition, can only be performed with the wheel assembly removed. A complete inspection of the wheel requires that the tire be removed from the wheel rim. Observe the following caution when removing a wheel assembly from an aircraft.

Caution: Deflate the tire before starting the procedure of removing the wheel assembly from the aircraft. Wheel assemblies have been known to explode while removing the axle nut, especially when dealing with high pressure, high performance tires. The torque of the nut can be the only force holding together a defective wheel or one with broken tie bolts. When loosened, the high internal pressure of the tire can create a catastrophic failure that could be lethal to the technician. It is also important to let aircraft tires cool before removal. Three hours or more is needed for cool down. Approach the wheel assembly from the front or rear, not broadside. Do not stand in the path of the released air and valve core trajectory when removing air from the tire as it could seriously injure the technician should it release from the valve stem.

NOTE: As a precautionary measure, remove only one tire and wheel assembly from a pair at a time. This leaves a tire and wheel assembly in place should the aircraft fall off its jack, resulting in less chance of damage to the aircraft and injury to personnel.

Loosening the Tire from the Wheel Rim

After inflation and usage, an aircraft tire has a tendency to adhere to the wheel, and the bead must be broken to remove the tire. There are mechanical and hydraulic presses designed for this purpose. In the absence of a device specifically made for the job, an arbor press can be used with patience working sequentially around the wheel as close as possible to the bead. *[Figure 13-63]* As stated above, there should be no air pressure in the tire while it is being pressed off of the wheel. Never pry a tire off of the rim with a screwdriver or other device. The wheels are relatively soft. Any nick or deformation causes a stress concentration that can easily lead to wheel failure.

Disassembly of the Wheel

Disassembly of the wheel should take place in a clean area on a flat surface, such as a table. Remove the wheel bearing first and set aside for cleaning and inspecting. The tie bolts can then be removed. Do not use an impact tool to disassemble the tie bolts. Aircraft wheels are made of relatively soft aluminum and magnesium alloys. They are not designed to receive the repeated hammering of an impact tool and will be damaged if used.

Cleaning the Wheel Assembly

Clean the wheel halves with the solvent recommended by the wheel manufacturer. Use of a soft brush helps this process. Avoid abrasive techniques, materials, and tools, such as scrapers, capable of removing the finish off of the wheel. Corrosion can quickly form and weaken the wheel if the finish is missing in an area. When the wheels are clean, they can be dried with compressed air.

Cleaning the Wheel Bearings

The bearings should be removed from the wheel to be cleaned with the recommended solvent, such as varsol, naptha, or Stoddard® solvent. Soaking the bearings in solvent is acceptable to loosen any dried-on grease. Bearings are brushed clean with a soft bristle brush and dried with compressed air. Never rotate the bearing while drying with compressed air. The high speed metal to metal contact of the bearing rollers with the race causes heat that damages the metal surfaces. The bearing parts could also cause injury should the bearing come apart. Always avoid steam cleaning of bearings. The surface finish of the metals will be compromised leading to early failure.

Wheel Bearing Inspection

Once cleaned, the wheel bearing is inspected. There are many unacceptable conditions of the bearing and bearing cup, which are grounds for rejection. In fact, nearly any flaw detected in a bearing assembly is likely to be grounds for replacement.

Figure 13-63. *Tire beads must be broken from the wheel to remove the tire. A mechanical removal tool designed for breaking the bead is shown in (A); a hydraulic press designed with the capacity for large aircraft wheels is shown in (B); and an arbor press is shown in (C). All are tools available to the technician for this purpose.*

Common conditions of a bearing that are cause for rejection are as follows:

Galling—caused by rubbing of mating surfaces. The metal gets so hot it welds, and the surface metal is destroyed as the motion continues and pulls the metal apart in the direction of motion. *[Figure 13-64]*

Figure 13-64. *Galling is caused by rubbing of mating surfaces. The metal gets so hot it welds, and the surface metal is destroyed as the motion continues and pulls the metal apart in the direction of motion.*

Spalling—a chipped away portion of the hardened surface of a bearing roller or race. *[Figure 13-65]*

Figure 13-65. *Spalling is a chipped away portion of the hardened surface of a bearing roller or race.*

Overheating—caused by lack of sufficient lubrication results in a bluish tint to the metal surface. The ends of the rollers shown were overheated causing the metal to flow and deform, as well as discolor. The bearing cup raceway is usually discolored as well. *[Figure 13-66]*

Figure 13-66. *Overheating caused by lack of sufficient lubrication results in a bluish tint to the metal surface. The ends of the rollers shown were overheated causing the metal to flow and deform, as well as discolor. The bearing cup raceway is usually discolored as well.*

Brinelling—caused by excessive impact. It appears as indentations in the bearing cup raceways. Any static overload or severe impact can cause true brinelling that leads to vibration and premature bearing failure. *[Figure 13-67]*

Figure 13-67. *Brinelling is caused by excessive impact. It appears as indentations in the bearing cup raceways. Any static overload or severe impact can cause true brinelling, which leads to vibration and premature bearing failure.*

False Brinelling—caused by vibration of the bearing while in a static state. Even with a static overload, lubricant can be forced from between the rollers and the raceway. Submicroscopic particles removed at the points of metal-to-metal contact oxidize. They work to remove more particles spreading the damage. This is also known as frictional corrosion. It can be identified by a rusty coloring of the lubricant. *[Figure 13-68]*

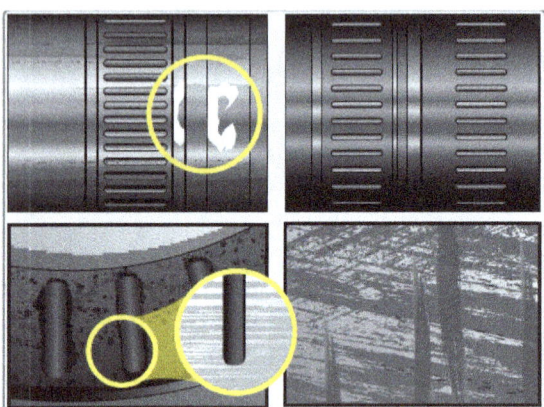

Figure 13-68. *False brinelling is caused by vibration of the bearing while in a static state. Even with a static overload, it can force the lubricant from between the rollers and the raceway. Submicroscopic particles removed at the points of metal-to-metal contact oxidize. They work to remove more particles spreading the damage. This is also known as frictional corrosion. It can be identified by a rusty coloring of the lubricant.*

Staining and surface marks—located on the bearing cup as grayish black streaks with the same spacing as the rollers and caused by water that has gotten into the bearing. It is the first stage of deeper corrosion that follows. *[Figure 13-69]*

Figure 13-69. *Staining and surface marks on the bearing cup that are grayish black streaks with the same spacing as the rollers are caused by water that has gotten into the bearing. It is the first stage of deeper corrosion that will follow.*

Etching and corrosion—caused when water and the damage caused by water penetrates the surface treatment of the bearing element. It appears as a reddish/brown discoloration. *[Figure 13-70]*

Figure 13-70. *Etching and corrosion is caused when water, and the damage caused by water, penetrates the surface treatment of the bearing element. It appears as a reddish/brown discoloration.*

Bruising—caused by fine particle contamination possibly from a bad seal or improper maintenance of bearing cleanliness. It leaves a less than smooth surface on the bearing cup. *[Figure 13-71]*

Figure 13-71. *Bruising is caused by fine particle contamination possibly from a bad seal or improper maintenance of bearing cleanliness. It leaves a less than smooth surface on the bearing cup.*

The bearing cup does not require removal for inspection; however, it must be firmly seated in the wheel half boss. There should be no evidence that a cup is loose or able to spin. *[Figure 13-72]* The cup is usually removed by heating the wheel in a controlled oven and pressing it out or tapping it out with a non-metallic drift. The installation procedure is similar. The wheel is heated and the cup is cooled with dry ice before it is tapped into place with a non-metallic hammer or drift. The outside of the race is often sprayed with primer before insertion. Consult the wheel manufacturer's maintenance manual for specific instructions.

Figure 13-72. *Bearing cups should be tight in the wheel boss and should never rotate. The outside of a bearing cup that was spinning while installed in the wheel is shown.*

Bearing Handling and Lubrication

Handling of bearings is of the utmost importance. Contamination, moisture, and vibration, even while the bearing is in a static state, can ruin a bearing. Avoid conditions where these may affect bearings and be sure to install and torque bearings into place according manufacturer's instructions.

Proper lubrication is a partial deterrent to negative environmental impacts on a bearing. Use the lubricant recommended by the manufacturer. Use of a pressure bearing packing tool or adapter is also recommended as the best method to remove any contaminants from inside the bearing that may have remained after cleaning. *[Figure 13-73]*

Inspection of the Wheel Halves

A thorough visual inspection of each wheel half should be conducted for discrepancies specified in the wheel manufacturer's maintenance data. Use of a magnifying glass is recommended. Corrosion is one of the most common problems encountered while inspecting wheels. Locations where moisture is trapped should be checked closely. It is possible to dress out some corrosion according to the manufacturer's instructions. An approved protective surface treatment and finish must be applied before returning the wheel to service. Corrosion beyond stated limits is cause for rejection of the wheel.

In addition to corrosion, cracks in certain areas of the wheel are particularly prevalent. One such area is the bead seat area. *[Figure 13-74]* The high stress of landing is transferred to the wheel by the tire in this contact area. Hard landings produce distortion or cracks that are very difficult to detect. This is a concern on all wheels and is most problematic in high-pressure, forged wheels. Dye penetrant inspection is generally ineffective when checking for cracks in the bead area. There is a tendency for cracks to close up tightly once the tire is

Figure 13-73. *A pressure bearing lubricating tool.*

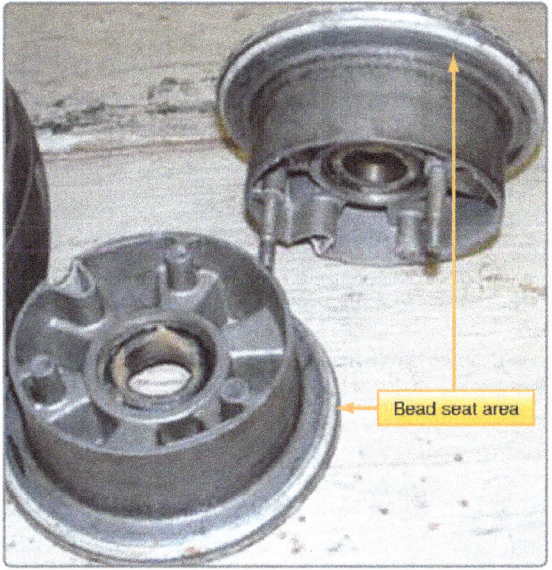

Figure 13-74. *The bead seat areas of a light aircraft wheel set. Eddy current testing for cracks in the bead seat area is common.*

dismounted, and the stress is removed from the metal. Eddy current inspection of the bead seat area is required. Follow the wheel manufacturer's instruction when performing the eddy current check.

The wheel brake disc drive key area is another area in which cracks are common. The forces experienced when the keys drive the disc against the stopping force of the brakes are high. Generally, a dye penetrant test is sufficient to reveal cracks in this area. All drive keys should be secure with no movement possible. No corrosion is permitted in this area. *[Figure 13-75]*

Figure 13-75. *Inspection for cracks in the wheel disc drive key area is performed with dye penetrant on many wheels.*

Wheel Tie Bolt Inspection

Wheel half tie bolts are under great stress while in service and require inspection. The tie bolts stretch and change dimension usually at the threads and under the bolt head. These are areas where cracks are most common. Magnetic particle inspection can reveal these cracks. Follow the maintenance manual procedures for inspecting tie bolts.

Key and Key Screw Inspection

On most aircraft inner wheel halves, keys are screwed or bolted to the wheel to drive the brake disc(s). The drive keys are subject to extreme forces when the brakes are applied. As mentioned, there should be no movement between the wheel and the keys. The bolts should be checked for security, and the area around the keys should be inspected for cracks. There is also a limitation on how worn the keys can be since too much wear allows excessive movement. The wheel manufacturer's maintenance instructions should be used to perform a complete inspection of this critical area.

Fusible Plug Inspection

Fusible plugs or thermal plugs must be inspected visually. These threaded plugs have a core that melts at a lower temperature than the outer part of the plug. This is to release air from the tire should the temperature rise to a dangerous level. A close inspection should reveal whether any core has experienced deformation that might be due to high temperature. If detected, all thermal plugs in the wheel should be replaced with new plugs. *[Figure 13-76]*

Figure 13-76. *Visually inspect the core of a thermal or fusible plug for deformation associated with heat exposure. Replace all of the plugs if any appear to have begun to deform.*

Balance Weights

The balance of an aircraft wheel assembly is important. When manufactured, each wheel set is statically balanced. Weights are added to accomplish this if needed. They are a permanent part of the wheel assembly and must be installed to use the wheel. The balance weights are bolted to the wheel halves and can be removed when cleaning and inspecting the wheel. They must be re-fastened in their original position. When a tire is mounted to a wheel, balancing of the wheel and tire assembly may require that additional weights be added. These are usually installed around the circumference of the outside of the wheel and should not be taken as substitutes for the factory wheel set balance weights. *[Figure 13-77]*

Aircraft Brakes

Very early aircraft have no brake system to slow and stop the aircraft while it is on the ground. Instead, they rely on slow speeds, soft airfield surfaces, and the friction developed by the tail skid to reduce speed during ground operation. Brake systems designed for aircraft became common after World War I as the speed and complexity of aircraft increased and the use of smooth, paved runway surfaces proliferated. All modern aircraft are equipped with brakes. Their proper functioning is relied upon for safe operation of the aircraft on the ground. The brakes slow the aircraft and stop it in a reasonable amount of time. They hold the aircraft stationary during engine run-up and, in many cases, steer the aircraft

Figure 13-77. *Two piece aircraft wheels are statically balanced when manufactured and may include weights attached to each wheel half that must stay with the wheel during its entire serviceable life.*

during taxi. On most aircraft, each of the main wheels is equipped with a brake unit. The nose wheel or tail wheel does not have a brake.

In the typical brake system, mechanical and/or hydraulic linkages to the rudder pedals allow the pilot to control the brakes. Pushing on the top of the right rudder pedal activates the brake on the right main wheel(s) and pushing on the top of the left rudder pedal operates the brake on the left main wheel(s). The basic operation of brakes involves converting the kinetic energy of motion into heat energy through the creation of friction. A great amount of heat is developed and forces on the brake system components are demanding. Proper adjustment, inspection, and maintenance of the brakes is essential for effective operation.

Types and Construction of Aircraft Brakes

Modern aircraft typically use disc brakes. The disc rotates with the turning wheel assembly while a stationary caliper resists the rotation by causing friction against the disc when the brakes are applied. The size, weight, and landing speed of the aircraft influence the design and complexity of the disc brake system. Single, dual, and multiple disc brakes are common types of brakes. Segmented rotor brakes are used on large aircraft. Expander tube brakes are found on older large aircraft. The use of carbon discs is increasing in the modern aviation fleet.

Single Disc Brakes

Small, light aircraft typically achieve effective braking using a single disc keyed or bolted to each wheel. As the wheel turns, so does the disc. Braking is accomplished by applying friction to both sides of the disc from a non-rotating caliper bolted to the landing gear axle flange. Pistons in the caliper housing under hydraulic pressure force wearable brake pads or linings against the disc when the brakes are applied. Hydraulic master cylinders connected to the rudder pedals supply the pressure when the upper halves of the rudder pedals are pressed.

Floating Disc Brakes

A floating disk brake is illustrated in *Figure 13-78*. A more detailed, exploded view of this type of brake is shown in *Figure 13-79*. The caliper straddles the disc. It has three cylinders bored through the housing, but on other brakes this number may vary. Each cylinder accepts an actuating piston assembly comprised mainly of a piston, a return spring, and an automatic adjusting pin. Each brake assembly has six brake linings or pucks. Three are located on the ends of the pistons, which are in the outboard side of the caliper. They are designed to move in and out with the pistons and apply pressure to the outboard side of the disc. Three more linings are located opposite of these pucks on the inboard side of the caliper. These linings are stationary.

Figure 13-78. *A single disc brake is a floating-disc, fixed caliper brake.*

The brake disc is keyed to the wheel. It is free to move laterally in the key slots. This is known as a floating disk. When the brakes are applied, the pistons move out from the outboard cylinders and their pucks contact the disc. The disc slides slightly in the key slots until the inboard stationary pucks also contact the disc. The result is a fairly even amount of friction applied to each side of the disc and thus, the rotating motion is slowed.

When brake pressure is released, the return spring in each piston assembly forces the piston back away from the disc. The spring provides a preset clearance between each puck and the disc. The self adjusting feature of the brake maintains the same clearance, regardless of the amount of wear on the brake pucks. The adjusting pin on the back of each piston

Figure 13-79. *An exploded view of a single-disc brake assembly found on a light aircraft.*

moves with the piston through a frictional pin grip. When brake pressure is relieved, the force of the return spring is sufficient to move the piston back away from the brake disc, but not enough to move the adjusting pin held by the friction of the pin grip. The piston stops when it contacts the head of the adjusting pin. Thus, regardless of the amount of wear, the same travel of the piston is required to apply the brake. The stem of the pin protruding through the cylinder head serves as a wear indicator. The manufacturer's maintenance information states the minimum length of the pin that needs to be protruding for the brakes to be considered airworthy. [Figure 13-80]

The brake caliper has the necessary passages machined into it to facilitate hydraulic fluid movement and the application of pressure when the brakes are utilized. The caliper housing also contains a bleed port used by the technician to remove unwanted air from the system. Brake bleeding, as it is known, should be done in accordance with the manufacturer's maintenance instructions.

Fixed-Disc Brakes

Even pressure must be applied to both sides of the brake disc to generate the required friction and obtain consistent wear properties from the brake linings. The floating disc accomplishes this as described above. It can also be accomplished by bolting the disc rigidly to the wheel and allowing the brake caliper and linings to float laterally when pressure is applied. This is the design of a common fixed-disc brake used on light aircraft. The brake is manufactured by the Cleveland Brake Company and is shown in *Figure 13-81*. An exploded detail view of the same type of brake is shown in *Figure 13-82*.

The fixed-disk, floating-caliper design allows the brake caliper and linings to adjust position in relationship to the disc. Linings are riveted to the pressure plate and backplate. Two anchor bolts that pass through the pressure plate are secured to the cylinder assembly. The other ends of the bolts are free to slide in and out of bushings in the torque plate, which is bolted to the axle flange. The cylinder assembly is bolted to the backplate to secure the assembly around the disc. When pressure is applied, the caliper and linings center on the disc via the sliding action of the anchor bolts in the torque plate bushings. This provides equal pressure to both sides of the disc to slow its rotation.

A unique feature of the Cleveland brake is that the linings can be replaced without removing the wheel. Unbolting the cylinder assembly from the backplate allows the anchor bolts to slide out of the torque plate bushings. The entire caliper assembly is then free and provides access to all of the components.

Maintenance requirements on all single disc brake systems are similar to those on brake systems of any type. Regular inspection for any damage and for wear on the linings and

Figure 13-80. *A cross-sectional view of a Goodyear single-disc brake caliper illustrates the adjusting pin assembly that doubles as a wear indicator.*

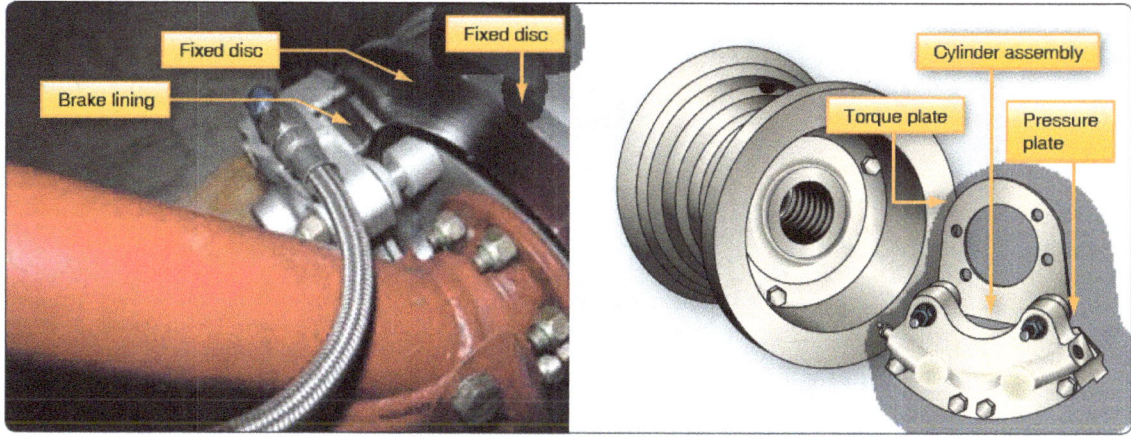

Figure 13-81. *A Cleveland brake on a light aircraft is a fixed-disc brake. It allows the brake caliper to move laterally on anchor bolts to deliver even pressure to each side of the brake disc.*

discs is required. Replacement of parts worn beyond limits is always followed by an operational check. The check is performed while taxiing the aircraft. The braking action for each main wheel should be equal with equal application of pedal pressure. Pedals should be firm, not soft or spongy, when applied. When pedal pressure is released, the brakes should release without any evidence of drag.

Dual-Disc Brakes

Dual-disc brakes are used on aircraft where a single disc on each wheel does not supply sufficient braking friction. Two discs are keyed to the wheel instead of one. A center carrier is located between the two discs. It contains linings on each side that contact each of the discs when the brakes are applied.

13-45

Figure 13-82. *An exploded view of a dual-piston Cleveland brake assembly.*

The caliper mounting bolts are long and mount through the center carrier, as well as the backplate which bolts to the housing assembly. *[Figure 13-83]*

Multiple-Disc Brakes

Large, heavy aircraft require the use of multiple-disc brakes. Multiple-disc brakes are heavy duty brakes designed for

Figure 13-83. *A dual-disc brake is similar to a single-disc brake. It uses a center carrier to hold brake linings against each of the discs.*

use with power brake control valves or power boost master cylinders, which is discussed later in this chapter. The brake assembly consists of an extended bearing carrier similar to a torque tube type unit that bolts to the axle flange. It supports the various brake parts, including an annular cylinder and piston, a series of steel discs alternating with copper or bronze-plated discs, a backplate, and a backplate retainer. The steel stators are keyed to the bearing carrier, and the copper or bronze plated rotors are keyed to the rotating wheel. Hydraulic pressure applied to the piston causes the entire stack of stators and rotors to be compressed. This creates enormous friction and heat and slows the rotation of the wheel. *[Figure 13-84]*

As with the single and dual-disc brakes, retracting springs return the piston into the housing chamber of the bearing carrier when hydraulic pressure is relieved. The hydraulic fluid exits the brake to the return line through an automatic adjuster. The adjuster traps a predetermined amount of fluid in the brakes that is just sufficient to provide the correct clearances between the rotors and stators. *[Figure 13-85]* Brake wear is typically measured with a wear gauge that is not part of the brake assembly. These types of brake are typically found on older transport category aircraft. The rotors and stators are relatively thin, only about ⅛-inch thick. They do not dissipate heat very well and have a tendency to warp.

Segmented Rotor-Disc Brakes

The large amount of heat generated while slowing the rotation of the wheels on large and high performance aircraft is problematic. To better dissipate this heat, segmented rotor-disc brakes have been developed. Segmented rotor-disc brakes are multiple-disc brakes but of more modern design than the type discussed earlier. There are many variations. Most feature numerous elements that aid in the control and dissipation of heat. Segmented rotor-disc brakes are heavy-duty brakes especially adapted for use with the high pressure hydraulic systems of power brake systems. Braking is accomplished by means of several sets of stationary, high friction type brake linings that make contact with rotating segments. The rotors are constructed with slots or in sections with space between them, which helps dissipate heat and give the brake its name. Segmented rotor multiple-disc brakes are the standard brake used on high performance and air carrier aircraft. An exploded view of one type of segmented rotor brake assembly is shown in *Figure 13-86*.

The description of a segmented rotor brake is very similar to the multiple-disc type brake previously described. The brake assembly consists of a carrier, a piston and piston cup seal, a pressure plate, an auxiliary stator plate, rotor segments, stator plates, automatic adjusters, and a backing plate.

The carrier assembly, or brake housing with torque tube, is the basic unit of the segmented rotor brake. It is the part that attaches to the landing gear shock strut flange upon which the other components of the brake are assembled. On some brakes, two grooves or cylinders are machined into the carrier to receive the piston cups and pistons. *[Figure 13-86]* Most segmented rotor-disc brakes have numerous individual cylinders machined into the brake housing into which fit the same number of actuating pistons. Often, these cylinders are supplied by two different hydraulic sources, alternating every other cylinder from a single source. If one source fails, the brake still operates sufficiently on the other. *[Figure 13-87]*

Figure 13-84. *A multiple disc brake with bearing carrier upon which the parts of the brake are assembled including an annular cylinder and piston assembly that apply pressure evenly to a stack of rotors and stators.*

13-47

Figure 13-85. *A multiple-disc brake with details of the automatic adjuster.*

External fittings in the carrier or brake housing admit the hydraulic fluid. A bleed port can also be found.

A pressure plate is a flat, circular, high-strength steel, non-rotating plate notched on the inside circumference to fit over the stator drive sleeves or torque tube spines. The brake actuating pistons contact the pressure plate. Typically, an insulator is used between the piston head and the pressure plate to impede heat conduction from the brake discs. The pressure plate transfers the motion of the pistons to the stack of rotors and stators that compress to slow the rotation of the wheels. On most designs, brake lining material attached directly to the pressure plate contacts the first rotor in the stack to transfer the motion of the piston(s). *[Figure 13-86]* An auxiliary stator plate with brake lining material on the side opposite the pressure plate can also be used.

Any number of alternating rotors and stators are sandwiched under hydraulic pressure against the backing plate of the brake assembly when the brakes are applied. The backing

Figure 13-86. *Exploded and detail views of segmented rotor brakes.*

Figure 13-87. *Many modern segmented rotor disc brakes use a housing machined to fit numerous individual actuating pistons.*

plate is a heavy steel plate bolted to the housing or torque tube at a fixed dimension from the carrier housing. In most cases, it has brake lining material attached to it and contacts the last rotor in the stack. *[Figure 13-86]*

Stators are flat plates notched on the internal circumference to be held stationary by the torque tube spines. They have wearable brake lining material riveted or adhered to each side to make contact with adjacent rotors. The liner is typically constructed of numerous isolated blocks. *[Figure 13-86]* The space between the liner blocks aids in the dissipation of heat. The composition of the lining materials vary. Steel is often used.

Rotors are slit or segmented discs that have notches or tangs in the external circumference that key to the rotating wheel. Slots or spaces between sections of the rotor create segments that allow heat to dissipate faster than it would if the rotor was

13-49

solid. They also allow for expansion and prevent warping. *[Figure 13-86]* Rotors are usually steel to which a frictional surface is bonded to both sides. Typically, sintered metal is used in creating the rotor contact surface.

Segmented multiple-disc brakes use retraction spring assemblies with auto clearance adjusters to pull the backplate away from the rotor and stator stack when brake pressure is removed. This provides clearance so the wheel can turn unimpeded by contact friction between the brake parts, but keeps the units in close proximity for rapid contact and braking when the brakes are applied. The number of retraction devices varies with brake design. *Figure 13-88* illustrates a brake assembly used on a Boeing 737 transport category aircraft. In the cutaway view, the number and locations of the auto adjustment retraction mechanisms can been seen. Details of the mechanisms are also shown.

Instead of using a pin grip assembly for auto adjustment, an adjuster pin, ball, and tube operate in the same manner. They move out when brake pressure is applied, but the ball in the tube limits the amount of the return to that equal to the brake lining wear. Two independent wear indicators are used on the brake illustrated. An indicator pin attached to the backplate protrudes through the carrier. The amount that it protrudes with the brakes applied is measured to ascertain if new linings are required.

NOTE: Other segmented multiple-disc brakes may use slightly different techniques for pressure plate retraction and wear indication. Consult the manufacturer's maintenance information to ensure wear indicators are read correctly.

Carbon Brakes

The segmented multiple-disc brake has given many years of reliable service to the aviation industry. It has evolved through time in an effort to make it lightweight and to dissipate the frictional heat of braking in a quick, safe manner. The latest iteration of the multiple-disc brake is the carbon-disc brake. It is currently found on high performance and air carrier aircraft. Carbon brakes are so named because carbon fiber materials are used to construct the brake rotors. *[Figure 13-89]*

Carbon brakes are approximately forty percent lighter than conventional brakes. On a large transport category aircraft, this alone can save several hundred pounds in aircraft weight. The carbon fiber discs are noticeably thicker than sintered steel rotors but are extremely light. They are able to withstand temperatures fifty percent higher than steel component brakes. The maximum designed operating temperature is limited by the ability of adjacent components to withstand the high temperature. Carbon brakes have been shown to withstand two to three times the heat of a steel brake in non-aircraft applications. Carbon rotors also dissipate heat faster than steel rotors. A carbon rotor maintains its strength and dimensions at high temperatures. Moreover, carbon brakes last twenty to fifty percent longer than steel brakes, which results in reduced maintenance.

The only impediment to carbon brakes being used on all aircraft is the high cost of manufacturing. The price is expected to lower as technology improves and greater numbers of aircraft operators enter the market.

Expander Tube Brakes

An expander tube brake is a different approach to braking that is used on aircraft of all sizes produced in the 1930s–1950s. It is a lightweight, low pressure brake bolted to the axle flange that fits inside an iron brake drum. A flat, fabric-reinforced neoprene tube is fitted around the circumference of a wheel-like torque flange. The exposed flat surface of the expander tube is lined with brake blocks similar to brake lining material. Two flat frames bolt to the sides of the torque flange. Tabs on the frames contain the tube and allow evenly spaced torque bars to be bolted in place across the tube between each brake block. These prevent circumferential movement of the tube on the flange. *[Figure 13-90]*

The expander tube is fitted with a metal nozzle on the inner surface. Hydraulic fluid under pressure is directed through this fitting into the inside of the tube when the brakes are applied. The tube expands outward, and the brake blocks make contact with the wheel drum causing friction that slows the wheel. As hydraulic pressure is increased, greater friction develops. Semi-elliptical springs located under the torque bars return the expander tube to a flat position around the flange when hydraulic pressure is removed. The clearance between the expander tube and the brake drum is adjustable by rotating an adjuster on some expander tube brakes. Consult the manufacturer's maintenance manual for the correct clearance setting. *Figure 13-91* gives an exploded view of an expander tube brake, detailing its components.

Expander tube brakes work well but have some drawbacks. They tend to take a setback when cold. They also have a tendency to swell with temperature and leak. They may drag inside the drum if this occurs. Eventually, expander brakes were abandoned in favor of disc brake systems.

Figure 13-88. *The multiple-disk brake assembly and details from a Boeing 737.*

Figure 13-89. *A carbon brake for a Boeing 737.*

Brake Actuating Systems

The various brake assemblies, described in the previous section, all use hydraulic power to operate. Different means of delivering the required hydraulic fluid pressure to brake assemblies are discussed in this section. There are three basic actuating systems:

1. An independent system not part of the aircraft main hydraulic system;
2. A booster system that uses the aircraft hydraulic system intermittently when needed; and
3. A power brake system that only uses the aircraft main hydraulic system(s) as a source of pressure.

Systems on different aircraft vary, but the general operation is similar to those described.

Independent Master Cylinders

In general, small, light aircraft and aircraft without hydraulic systems use independent braking systems. An independent brake system is not connected in any way to the aircraft hydraulic system. Master cylinders are used to develop the necessary hydraulic pressure to operate the brakes. This is similar to the brake system of an automobile.

In most brake actuating systems, the pilot pushes on the tops of the rudder pedals to apply the brakes. A master cylinder for each brake is mechanically connected to the corresponding rudder pedal (i.e., right main brake to the right rudder pedal, left main brake to the left rudder pedal). *[Figure 13-92]* When the pedal is depressed, a piston inside a sealed fluid-filled chamber in the master cylinder forces hydraulic fluid through a line to the piston(s) in the brake assembly. The brake piston(s) push the brake linings against the brake rotor to create the friction that slows the wheel rotation. Pressure is increased throughout the entire brake systems and against the rotor as the pedal is pushed harder.

Many master cylinders have built-in reservoirs for the brake hydraulic fluid. Others have a single remote reservoir that services both of the aircraft's two master cylinders. *[Figure 13-93]* A few light aircraft with nose wheel steering have only one master cylinder that actuates both main wheel brakes. This is possible because steering the aircraft during taxi does not require differential braking. Regardless of the set-up, it is the master cylinder that builds up the pressure required for braking.

Figure 13-90. *An expander tube brake assembly.*

Figure 13-91. *An exploded view of an expander tube brake.*

Figure 13-92. *Master cylinders on an independent brake system are directly connected to the rudder pedals or are connected through mechanical linkage.*

Figure 13-93. *A remote reservoir services both master cylinders on some independent braking systems.*

A master cylinder used with a remote reservoir is illustrated in *Figure 13-94*. This particular model is a Goodyear master cylinder. The cylinder is always filled with air-free, contaminant-free hydraulic fluid as is the reservoir and the line that connects the two together. When the top of the rudder pedal is depressed, the piston arm is mechanically moved forward into the master cylinder. It pushes the piston against the fluid, which is forced through the line to the brake. When pedal pressure is released, the return springs in the brake assembly retract the brake pistons back into the brake housing. The hydraulic fluid behind the pistons is displaced and must return to the master cylinder. As it does, a return spring in the master cylinder move the piston, piston rod and rudder pedal back to the original position (brake off, pedal not depressed). The fluid behind the master cylinder piston flows back into the reservoir. The brake is ready to be applied again.

Hydraulic fluid expands as temperature increases. Trapped fluid can cause a brake to drag against the rotor(s). Leaks may also result. When the brakes are not applied, fluid must be allowed to expand safely without causing these issues. A compensating port is included in most master cylinders to facilitate this. In the master cylinder in *Figure 13-94*, this port is opened when the piston is fully retracted. Fluid in the brake system is allowed to expand into the reservoir, which has the capacity to accept the extra fluid volume. The typical reservoir is also vented to the atmosphere to provide positive pressure on the fluid.

The forward side of the piston head contains a seal that closes off the compensating port when the brakes are applied so that pressure can build. The seal is only effective in the forward direction. When the piston is returning, or is fully retracted to the off position, fluid behind the piston is free to flow through piston head ports to replenish any fluid that may be lost downstream of the master cylinder. The aft end of the master cylinder contains a seal that prevents leakage at all times. A rubber boot fits over the piston rod and the aft end of the master cylinder to keep out dust.

A parking brake for this remote reservoir master cylinder brake system is a ratcheting mechanical device between the master cylinder and the rudder pedals. With the brakes applied, the ratchet is engaged by pulling the parking brake handle. To release the brakes, the rudder pedals are depressed further allowing the ratchet to disengage. With the parking brake set, any expansion of hydraulic fluid due to temperature is relieved by a spring in the mechanical linkage.

Figure 13-94. *A Goodyear brake master cylinder from an independent braking system with a remote reservoir.*

A common requirement of all braking systems is for there to be no air mixed in with the hydraulic fluid. Since air is compressible and hydraulic fluid essentially is not, any air under pressure when the brakes are applied causes spongy brakes. The pedals do not feel firm when pushed down due to the air compressing. Brake systems must be bled to remove all air from the system. Instructions for bleeding the brakes are in the manufacturer's maintenance information. Brake systems equipped with Goodyear master cylinders must be bled from the top down to ensure any air trapped behind the master cylinder piston is removed.

An alternative common arrangement of independent braking systems incorporates two master cylinders, each with its own integral fluid reservoir. Except for the reservoir location, the brake system is basically the same as just described. The master cylinders are mechanically linked to the rudder pedals as before. Depressing the top of a pedal causes the piston rod to push the piston into the cylinder forcing the fluid out to the brake assembly. The piston rod rides in a compensator sleeve and contains an O-ring that seals the rod to the piston when the rod is moved forward. This blocks the compensating ports. When released, a spring returns the piston to its original position which refills the reservoir as it returns. The rod end seal retracts away from the piston head allowing a free flow of fluid from the cylinder through the compensating ports in the piston to the reservoir. *[Figure 13-95]*

The parking brake mechanism is a ratcheting type that operates as described. A servicing port is supplied at the top of the master cylinder reservoir. Typically, a vented plug is installed in the port to provide positive pressure on the fluid.

Boosted Brakes

In an independent braking system, the pressure applied to the brakes is only as great as the foot pressure applied to the top of the rudder pedal. Boosted brake actuating systems augment the force developed by the pilot with hydraulic system pressure when needed. The boost is only during heavy braking. It results in greater pressure applied to the brakes than the pilot alone can provide. Boosted brakes are used on medium and larger aircraft that do not require a full power brake actuating system.

A boosted brake master cylinder for each brake is mechanically attached to the rudder pedals. However, the boosted brake master cylinder operates differently. *[Figure 13-96]*

When the brakes are applied, the pressure from the pilot's foot through the mechanical linkage moves the master cylinder piston in the direction to force fluid to the brakes. The initial movement closes the compensator poppet used to provide thermal expansion relief when the brakes are not applied. As

Figure 13-95. *A common master cylinder with built-in reservoir is shown. Illustration A depicts the master cylinder when the brakes are off. The compensating port is open to allow fluid to expand into the reservoir should temperature increase. In B, the brakes are applied. The piston rod-end seal covers the compensating port as it contacts the piston head.*

the pilot pushes harder on the pedal, a spring loaded toggle moves a spool valve in the cylinder. Aircraft hydraulic system pressure flows through the valve to the back side of the piston. Pressure is increased, as is the force developed to apply the brakes.

When the pedal is released, the piston rod travels in the opposite direction, and the piston returns to the piston stop. The compensating poppet reopens. The toggle is withdrawn from the spool via linkages, and fluid pushes the spool back

Figure 13-96. *A master cylinder for a boosted brake system augments foot pedal pressure with aircraft system hydraulic pressure during heavy braking.*

to expose the system return manifold port. System hydraulic fluid used to boost brake pressure returns through the port.

Power Brakes

Large and high performance aircraft are equipped with power brakes to slow, stop, and hold the aircraft. Power brake actuating systems use the aircraft hydraulic system as the source of power to apply the brakes. The pilot presses on the top of the rudder pedal for braking as with the other actuating systems. The volume and pressure of hydraulic fluid required cannot be produced by a master cylinder. Instead, a power brake control valve or brake metering valve receives the brake pedal input either directly or through linkages. The valve meters hydraulic fluid to the corresponding brake assembly in direct relation to the pressure applied to the pedal.

Many power brake system designs are in use. Most are similar to the simplified system illustrated in *Figure 13-97A*. Power brake systems are constructed to facilitate graduated brake pressure control, brake pedal feel, and the necessary redundancy required in case of hydraulic system failure. Large aircraft brake systems integrate anti-skid detection and correction devices. These are necessary because wheel skid is difficult to detect on the flight deck without sensors. However, a skid can be quickly controlled automatically through pressure control of the hydraulic fluid to the brakes. Hydraulic fuses are also commonly found in power brake systems. The hostile environment around the landing gear increases the potential for a line to break or sever, a fitting to fail, or other hydraulic system malfunctions to occur where hydraulic fluid is lost en route to the brake assemblies. A fuse stops any excessive flow of fluid when detected by closing to retain the remaining fluid in the hydraulic system. Shuttle valves are used to direct flow from optional sources of fluid, such as in redundant systems or during the use of an emergency brake power source. An airliner power brake system is illustrated in *Figure 13-97B*.

Brake Control Valve/Brake Metering Valve

The key element in a power brake system is the brake control valve, sometimes called a brake metering valve. It responds to brake pedal input by directing aircraft system hydraulic fluid to the brakes. As pressure is increased on the brake pedal, more fluid is directed to the brake causing a higher pressure and greater braking action.

A brake metering valve from a Boeing 737 is illustrated in *Figure 13-98*. The system in which it is installed is diagramed in *Figure 13-99*. Two sources of hydraulic pressure provide redundancy in this brake system. A brake input shaft, connected to the rudder/brake pedal through mechanical linkages, provides the position input to the metering valve. As in most brake control valves, the brake input shaft moves a tapered spool or slide in the valve so that it allows hydraulic system pressure to flow to the brakes. At the same time, the slide covers and uncovers access to the hydraulic system return port as required.

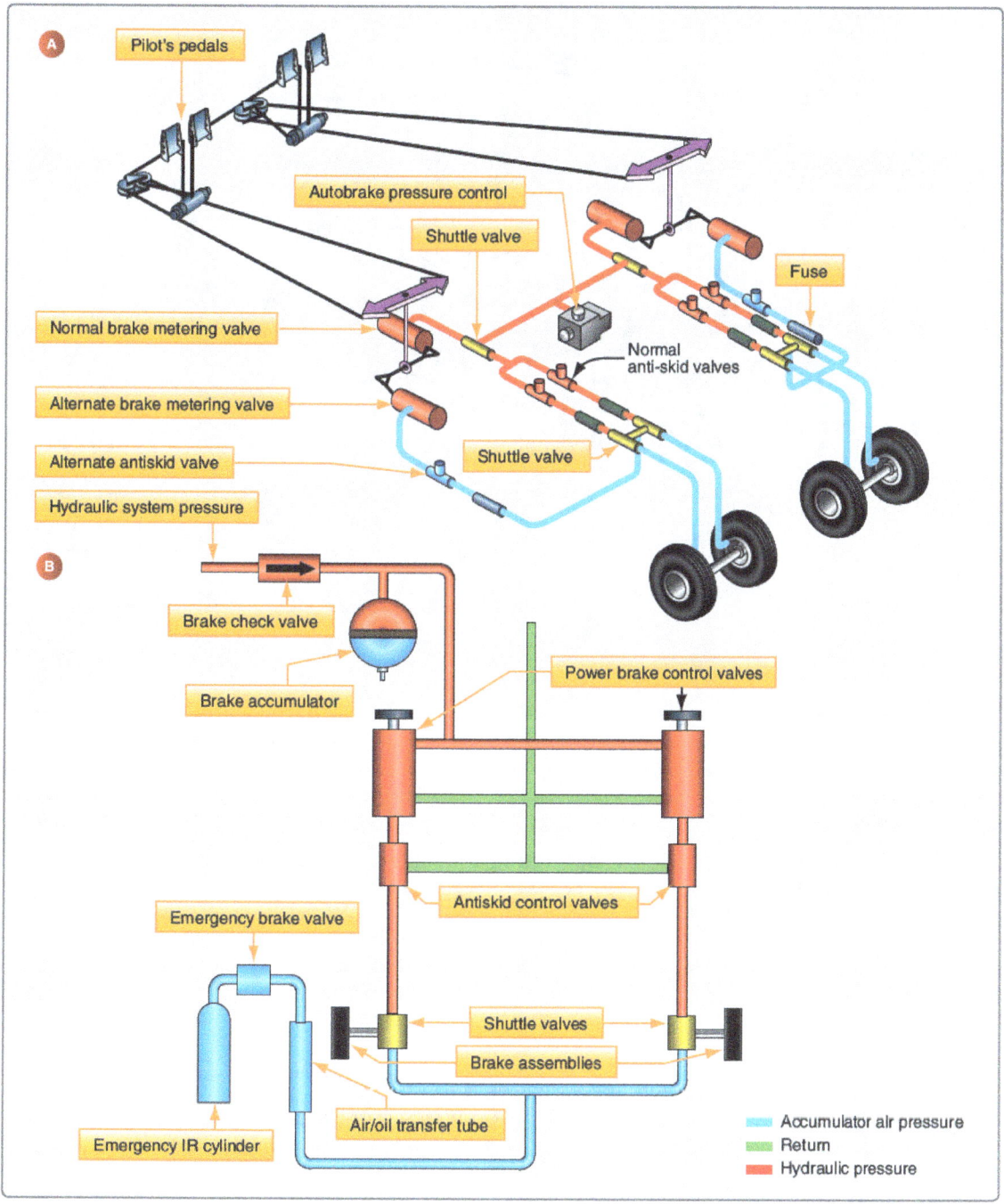

Figure 13-97. *The orientation of components in a basic power brake system is shown in A. The general layout of an airliner power brake system is shown in B.*

Figure 13-98. *A brake metering valve from a Boeing 737. A machined slide or spool moves laterally to admit the correct amount of hydraulic system fluid to the brakes. The pressure developed is in proportion to the amount the rudder/brake pedal is depressed and the amount the slide is displaced. The slide/spool also simultaneously controls the return of fluid to the hydraulic system return manifold when brake pressure is released.*

When the rudder/brake pedal is depressed, the slide in the metering valve moves to the left. *[Figure 13-98]* It covers the return port so pressure can build in the brake system. The hydraulic supply pressure chamber is connected to the brake system pressure chamber by the movement of the slide, which due to its taper, unblocks the passage between these two. As the pedal is depressed further, the valve slide moves farther to the left. This enables more fluid to flow to the brakes due to the narrowing shape of the slide. Brake pressure increases with the additional fluid. A passage in the slide directs brake pressure fluid into a compensating chamber at the end of the slide. This acts on the end of the slide creating a return force that counters the initial slide movement and gives feel to the brake pedal. As a result, the pressure and return ports are closed and pressure proportional to the foot pressure on the pedal is held on the brakes. When the pedal is released, a return spring and compensating chamber pressure drive the slide to the right into its original position (return port open, supply pressure chamber and brake pressure chambers blocked from each other).

The metering valve operates as described simultaneously for the inboard and the outboard brakes. *[Figure 13-98]* The design of the link assembly is such that a single side of the metering valve can operate even if the other fails. Most brake control valves and metering valves function in a similar manner, although many are single units that supply only one brake assembly.

The auto brake, referenced in the metering valve diagram, is connected into the landing gear retraction hydraulic line. Pressurized fluid enters this port and drives the slide slightly to the left to apply the brakes automatically after takeoff. This stops the wheels from rotating when retracted into the wheel wells. Auto brake pressure is withheld from this port when the landing gear is fully stowed since the retraction system is depressurized.

Figure 13-99. *The power brake system on a Boeing 737.*

The majority of the rudder/brake pedal feel is supplied by the brake control or brake metering valve in a power brake system. Many aircraft refine the feel of the pedal with an additional feel unit. The brake valve feel augmentation unit, in the above system, uses a series of internal springs and pistons of various sizes to create a force on the brake input shaft movement. This provides feel back through the mechanical linkages consistent with the amount of rudder/brake pedal applied. The request for light braking with slight pedal depression results in a light feel to the pedal and a harder resistance feel when the pedals are pushed harder during heavy braking. [*Figure 13-100*]

Emergency Brake Systems

As can be seen in *Figure 13-99*, the brake metering valves not only receive hydraulic pressure from two separate hydraulic systems, they also feed two separate brake assemblies. Each main wheel assembly has two wheels. The inboard wheel brake and the outboard wheel brake, located in their respective wheel rims, are independent from each other. In case of hydraulic system failure or brake failure, each is independently supplied to adequately slow and stop the aircraft without the other. More complicated aircraft may involve another hydraulic system for back-up or use a similar alternation of sources and brake assemblies to maintain braking in case of hydraulic system or brake failure.

Figure 13-100. *The power brake system on a Boeing 737.*

NOTE: In the segmented rotor brake section above, a brake assembly was described that had alternating pistons supplied by independent hydraulic sources. This is another method of redundancy particularly suitable on, but not limited to, single main wheel aircraft.

In addition to supply system redundancy, the brake accumulator is also an emergency source of power for the brakes in many power brake systems. The accumulator is pre-charged with air or nitrogen on one side of its internal diaphragm. Enough hydraulic fluid is contained on the other side of the diaphragm to operate the brakes in case of an emergency. It is forced out of the accumulator into the brakes through the system lines under enough stored pressure to slow the aircraft. Typically, the accumulator is located upstream of the brake control/metering valve to capitalize on the control given by the valve. *[Figure 13-101]*

Some simpler power brake systems may use an emergency source of brake power that is delivered directly to the brake assemblies and bypasses the remainder of the brake system completely. A shuttle valve immediately upstream of the brake units shifts to accept this source when pressure is lost from the primary supply sources. Compressed air or nitrogen is sometimes used. A pre-charged fluid source can also be used as an alternate hydraulic source.

Figure 13-101. *Emergency brake hydraulic fluid accumulators are precharged with nitrogen to deliver brake fluid to the brakes in the event normal and alternate hydraulic sources fail.*

Parking Brake

The parking brake system function is a combined operation. The brakes are applied with the rudder pedals and a ratcheting system holds them in place when the parking brake lever on the flight deck is pulled. *[Figure 13-102]* At the same time, a shut-off valve is closed in the common return line from the brakes to the hydraulic system. This traps the fluid in the brakes holding the rotors stationary. Depressing the pedals further releases the pedal ratchet and opens the return line valve.

Figure 13-102. *The parking brake lever on a Boeing 737 center pedestal throttle quadrant.*

Brake Deboosters

Some aircraft brake assemblies that operate on aircraft hydraulic system pressure are not designed for such high pressure. They provide effective braking through a power brake system but require less than maximum hydraulic system pressure. To supply the lower pressure, a brake debooster cylinder is installed downstream of the control valve and anti-skid valve. *[Figure 13-103]* The debooster reduces all pressure from the control valve to within the working range of the brake assembly.

Brake deboosters are simple devices that use the application of force over different sized pistons to reduce pressure. *[Figure 13-104]* Their operation can be understood through the application of the following equation:

Pressure = Force/Area

High-pressure hydraulic system input pressure acts on the small end of a piston. This develops a force proportional to the area of the piston head. The other end of the piston is larger and housed in a separate cylinder. The force from the smaller piston head is transferred to the larger area of the other end of the piston. The amount of pressure conveyed by the larger end of the piston is reduced due to the greater area over which the force is spread. The volume of output fluid increases since a larger piston and cylinder are used. The reduced pressure is delivered to the brake assembly.

The spring in the debooster aids in returning the piston to the ready position. If fluid is lost downstream of the deboost cylinder, the piston travels further down into the cylinder when the brakes are applied. The pin unseats the ball and allows fluid into the lower cylinder to replace what was lost. Once replenished, the piston rises up in the cylinder due to pressure build-up. The ball reseats as the piston travels above the pin and normal braking resumes. This function is not meant to permit leaks in the brake assemblies. Any leak discovered must be repaired by the technician.

A lockout debooster functions as a debooster and a hydraulic fuse. If fluid is not encountered as the piston moves down in the cylinder, the flow of fluid to the brakes is stopped. This prevents the loss of all system hydraulic fluid should a rupture downstream of the debooster occur. Lockout deboosters have a handle to reset the device after it closes as a fuse. If not reset, no braking action is possible.

Anti-Skid

Large aircraft with power brakes require anti-skid systems. It is not possible to immediately ascertain in the flight deck when a wheel stops rotating and begins to skid, especially in aircraft with multiple-wheel main landing gear assemblies. A skid not corrected can quickly lead to a tire blowout, possible damage to the aircraft, and control of the aircraft may be lost.

System Operation

The anti-skid system not only detects wheel skid, it also detects when wheel skid is imminent. It automatically relieves pressure to the brake pistons of the wheel in question by momentarily connecting the pressurized brake fluid area to the hydraulic system return line. This allows the wheel to rotate and avoid a skid. Lower pressure is then maintained to the brake at a level that slows the wheel without causing it to skid.

Maximum braking efficiency exists when the wheels are decelerating at a maximum rate but are not skidding. If a wheel decelerates too fast, it is an indication that the brakes are about to lock and cause a skid. To ensure that this does not happen, each wheel is monitored for a deceleration rate faster

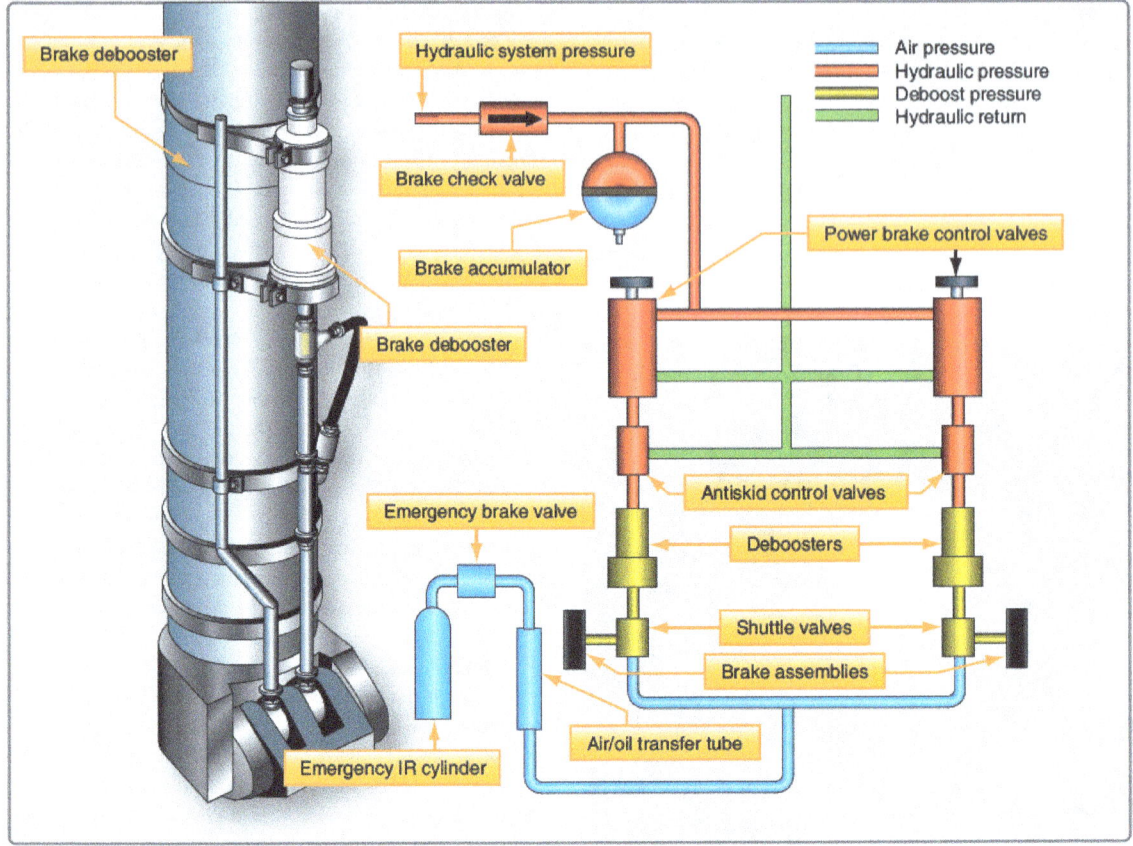

Figure 13-103. *The location of a brake debooster cylinder on a landing gear strut and the debooster's position in relation to other components of a power brake system.*

than a preset rate. When excessive deceleration is detected, hydraulic pressure is reduced to the brake on that wheel. To operate the anti-skid system, flight deck switches must be placed in the ON position. *[Figure 13-105]* After the aircraft touches down, the pilot applies and holds full pressure to the rudder brake pedals. The anti-skid system then functions automatically until the speed of the aircraft has dropped to approximately 20 mph. The system returns to manual braking mode for slow taxi and ground maneuvering.

There are various designs of anti-skid systems. Most contain three main types of components: wheel speed sensors, anti-skid control valves, and a control unit. These units work together without human interference. Some anti-skid systems provide complete automatic braking. The pilot needs only to turn on the auto brake system, and the anti-skid components slow the aircraft without pedal input. *[Figure 13-105]* Ground safety switches are wired into the circuitry for anti-skid and auto brake systems. Wheel speed sensors are located on each wheel equipped with a brake assembly. Each brake also has its own anti-skid control valve. Typically, a single control box contains the anti-skid comparative circuitry for all of the brakes on the aircraft. *[Figure 13-106]*

Wheel Speed Sensors

Wheel speed sensors are transducers. They may be alternating current (AC) or direct current (DC). The typical AC wheel speed sensor has a stator mounted in the wheel axle. A coil around it is connected to a controlled DC source so that when energized, the stator becomes an electromagnet. A rotor that turns inside the stator is connected to the rotating wheel hub assembly through a drive coupling so that it rotates at the speed of the wheel. Lobes on the rotor and stator cause the distance between the two components to constantly change during rotation. This alters the magnetic coupling or reluctance between the rotor and stator. As the electromagnetic field changes, a variable frequency AC is induced in the stator coil. The frequency is directly

Figure 13-104. *Brake deboosters.*

Figure 13-105. *Antiskid switches in the cockpit.*

Figure 13-106. *A wheel sensor (left), a control unit (center), and a control valve (right) are components of an antiskid system. A sensor is located on each wheel equipped with a brake assembly. An antiskid control valve for each brake assembly is controlled from a single central control unit.*

proportional to the speed of rotation of the wheel. The AC signal is fed to the control unit for processing. A DC wheel speed sensor is similar, except that a DC is produced the magnitude of which is directly proportional to wheel speed. *[Figure 13-107]*

Control Units

The control unit can be regarded as the brain of the antiskid system. It receives signals from each of the wheel sensors. Comparative circuits are used to determine if any of the signals indicate a skid is imminent or occurring on a particular wheel. If so, a signal is sent to the control valve of the wheel to relieve hydraulic pressure to that brake which prevents or relieves the skid. The control unit may or may not have external test switches and status indicating lights. It is common for it to be located in the avionics bay of the aircraft. *[Figure 13-108]*

The Boeing anti-skid control valve block diagram in *Figure 13-109* gives further detail on the functions of an antiskid control unit. Other aircraft may have different logic to achieve similar end results. DC systems do not require an input converter since DC is received from the wheel sensors, and the control unit circuitry operates primarily with DC. Only the functions on one circuit card for one wheel brake assembly are shown in *Figure 13-109*. Each wheel has its own identical circuitry card to facilitate simultaneous operation. All cards are housed in a single control unit that Boeing calls a control shield.

The converter shown changes the AC frequency received from the wheel sensor into DC voltage that is proportional to wheel speed. The output is used in a velocity reference loop that contains deceleration and velocity reference circuits. The converter also supplies input for the spoiler system and the locked wheel system, which is discussed at the end of this section. A velocity reference loop output voltage is

13-63

Figure 13-107. *The stator of an antiskid wheel sensor is mounted in the axle, and the rotor is coupled to the wheel hub spider that rotates with the wheel.*

produced, which represents the instantaneous velocity of the aircraft. This is compared to converter output in the velocity comparator. This comparison of voltages is essentially the comparison of the aircraft speed to wheel speed. The output from the velocity comparator is a positive or negative error voltage corresponding to whether the wheel speed is too fast or too slow for optimum braking efficiency for a given aircraft speed.

The error output voltage from the comparator feeds the pressure bias modulator circuit. This is a memory circuit that establishes a threshold where the pressure to the brakes provides optimum braking. The error voltage causes the modulator to either increase or decrease the pressure to the brakes in attempt to hold the modulator threshold. It produces a voltage output that is sent to the summing amplifier to do this. A lead output from the comparator anticipates when the tire is about to skid with a voltage that decreases the pressure to the brake. It sends this voltage to the summing amplifier as well. A transient control output from the comparator designed for rapid pressure dump when a sudden skid has occurred also sends voltage to the summing amp. As the name suggests, the input voltages to the amplifier are summed, and a composite voltage is sent to the valve driver. The driver prepares the current required to be sent to the control valve to adjust the position of the valve. Brake pressure increases, decreases, or holds steady depending on this value.

Anti-Skid Control Valves

Anti-skid control valves are fast-acting, electrically controlled hydraulic valves that respond to the input from the anti-skid control unit. There is one control valve for each brake assembly. A torque motor uses the input from the valve driver to adjust the position of a flapper between

Figure 13-108. *A rack mounted antiskid control unit from an airliner.*

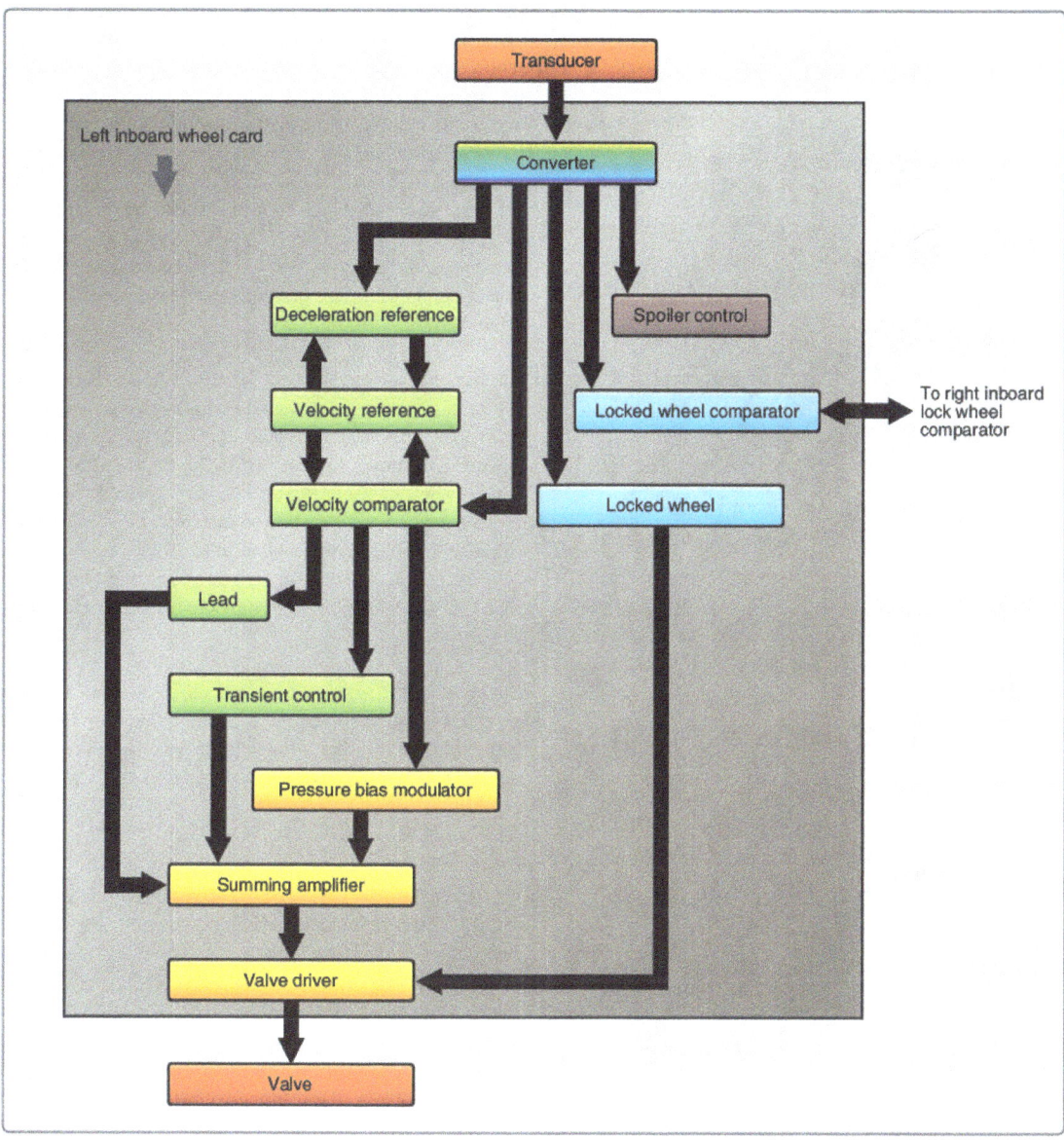

Figure 13-109. *A Boeing 737 antiskid control unit internal block diagram.*

two nozzles. By moving the flapper closer to one nozzle or the other, pressures are developed in the second stage of the valve. These pressures act on a spool that is positioned to build or reduce pressure to the brake by opening and blocking fluid ports. *[Figure 13-110]*

As pressure is adjusted to the brakes, deceleration slows to within the range that provides the most effective braking without skidding. The wheel sensor signal adjusts to the wheel speed, and the control unit processes the change.

Output is altered to the control valve. The control valve flapper position is adjusted and steady braking resumes without correction until needed. Anti-skid control valves are typically located in the main wheel for close access to hydraulic pressure and return manifolds, as well as the brake assemblies. *[Figure 13-111]* Systematically, they are positioned downstream of the power brake control valves but upstream of debooster cylinders if the aircraft is so equipped as was shown in *Figure 13-103*.

Figure 13-110. *An antiskid control valve uses a torque motor controlled flapper in the first stage of the valve to adjust pressure on a spool in the second stage of the valve to build or relieve pressure to the brake.*

Figure 13-111. *Two antiskid control valves with associated plumbing and wiring.*

Touchdown and Lock Wheel Protection

It is essential that the brakes are not applied when the aircraft contacts the runway upon landing. This could cause immediate tire blowout. A touchdown protection mode is built into most aircraft anti-skid systems to prevent this. It typically functions in conjunction with the wheel speed sensor and the air/ground safety switch on the landing gear strut (squat switch). Until the aircraft has weight on wheels, the detector circuitry signals the anti-skid control valve to open the passage between the brakes and the hydraulic system return, thus preventing pressure build-up and application of the brakes. Once the squat switch is open, the anti-skid control unit sends a signal to the control valve to close and permit brake pressure build-up. As a back-up and when the aircraft is on the ground with the strut not compressed enough to open the squat switch, a minimum wheel speed sensor signal can override and allow braking. Wheels are often grouped with one relying on the squat switch and the other on wheel speed sensor output to ensure braking when the aircraft is on the ground, but not before then.

Locked wheel protection recognizes if a wheel is not rotating. When this occurs, the anti-skid control valve is signaled to fully open. Some aircraft anti-skid control logic, such as the Boeing 737 shown in *Figure 13-110*, expands the locked wheel function. Comparator circuitry is used to relieve pressure when one wheel of a paired group of wheels rotates 25 percent slower than the other. Inboard and outboard pairs are used because if one of the pair is rotating at a certain speed, so should the other. If it is not, a skid is beginning or has occurred.

On takeoff, the anti-skid system receives input through a switch located on the gear selector that shuts off the anti-skid system. This allows the brakes to be applied as retraction occurs so that no wheel rotation exists while the gear is stowed.

Auto Brakes

Aircraft equipped with auto brakes typically bypass the brake control valves or brake metering valves and use a separate auto brake control valve to provide this function. In addition to the redundancy provided, auto brakes rely on the anti-skid system to adjust pressure to the brakes if required due to an impending skid. *Figure 13-112* shows a simplified diagram of the Boeing 757 brake system with the auto brake valve in relation to the main metering valve and anti-skid valves in this eight-main wheel system.

Anti-Skid System Tests

It is important to know the status of the anti-skid system prior to attempting to use it during a landing or aborted takeoff. Ground tests and in-flight tests are used. Built-in test circuits and control features allow testing of the system components and provide warnings should a particular component or part of the system become inoperative. An inoperative anti-skid system can be shut off without affecting normal brake operation.

Figure 13-112. *The Boeing 757 normal brake system with auto brake and antiskid.*

Ground Test

Ground tests vary slightly from aircraft to aircraft. Consult the manufacturer's maintenance manual for test procedures specific to the aircraft in question.

Much of the anti-skid system testing originates from testing circuits in the anti-skid control unit. Built-in test circuits continuously monitor the anti-skid system and provide warning if a failure occurs. An operational test can be performed before flight. The anti-skid control switch and/or test switch is used in conjunction with system indicator light(s) to determine system integrity. A test is first done with the aircraft at rest and then in an electrically simulated anti-skid braking condition. Some anti-skid control units contain system and component testing switches and lights for use by the technician. This accomplishes the same operational verification, but allows an additional degree of troubleshooting. Test sets are available for anti-skid systems that produce electric signals that simulate speed outputs of the wheel transducer, deceleration rates, and flight/ground parameters.

In-Flight Test

In-flight testing of the anti-skid system is desirable and part of the pre-landing checklist so that the pilot is aware of system capability before landing. As with ground testing, a combination of switch positions and indicator lights are used according to information in the aircraft operations manual.

Anti-Skid System Maintenance

Anti-skid components require little maintenance. Troubleshooting anti-skid system faults is either performed via test circuitry or can be accomplished through isolation of the fault to one of the three main operating components of the system. Anti-skid components are normally not repaired in the field. They are sent to the manufacturer or a certified repair station when work is required. Reports of anti-skid system malfunction are sometimes malfunctions of the brake system or brake assemblies. Ensure brake assemblies are bled and functioning normally without leaks before attempting to isolate problems in the anti-skid system.

Wheel Speed Sensor

Wheel speed sensors must be securely and correctly mounted in the axle. The means of keeping contamination out of the sensor, such as sealant or a hub cap, should be in place and in good condition. The wiring to the sensor is subject to harsh conditions and should be inspected for integrity and security. It should be repaired or replaced if damaged in accordance with the manufacturer's instructions. Accessing the wheel speed sensor and spinning it by hand or other recommended device to ensure brakes apply and release via the anti-skid system is common practice.

Control Valve

Anti-skid control valve and hydraulic system filters should be cleaned or replaced at the prescribed intervals. Follow all manufacturer's instructions when performing this maintenance. Wiring to the valve must be secure, and there should be no fluid leaks.

Control Unit

Control units should be securely mounted. Test switches and indicators, if any, should be in place and functioning. It is essential that wiring to the control unit is secure. A wide variety of control units are in use. Follow the manufacturer's instructions at all times when inspecting or attempting to perform maintenance on these units.

Brake Inspection and Service

Brake inspection and service is important to keep these critical aircraft components fully functional at all times. There are many different brake systems on aircraft. Brake system maintenance is performed both while the brakes are installed on the aircraft and when the brakes are removed. The manufacturer's instructions must always be followed to ensure proper maintenance.

On Aircraft Servicing

Inspection and servicing of aircraft brakes while installed on the aircraft is required. The entire brake system must be inspected in accordance with manufacturer's instructions. Some common inspection items include: brake lining wear, air in the brake system, fluid quantity level, leaks, and proper bolt torque.

Lining Wear

Brake lining material is made to wear as it causes friction during application of the brakes. This wear must be monitored to ensure it is not worn beyond limits and sufficient lining is available for effective braking. The aircraft manufacturer gives specifications for lining wear in its maintenance information. The amount of wear can be checked while the brakes are installed on the aircraft.

Many brake assemblies contain a built-in wear indicator pin. Typically, the exposed pin length decreases as the linings wear, and a minimum length is used to indicate the linings must be replaced. Caution must be used as different assemblies may vary in how the pin measured. On the Goodyear brake described above, the wear pin is measured where it protrudes through the nut of the automatic adjuster on the back side of the piston cylinder. *[Figure 13-113]*

Figure 13-113. *Brake lining wear on a Goodyear brake is ascertained by measuring the wear pin of the automatic adjuster.*

The Boeing brake illustrated in *Figure 13-88* measures the length of the pin from the back of the pressure plate when the brakes are applied (dimension L). The manufacturer's maintenance information must be consulted to ensure brake wear pin indicators on different aircraft are read correctly.

On many other brake assemblies, lining wear is not measured via a wear pin. The distance between the disc and a portion of the brake housing when the brakes are applied is sometimes used. As the linings wear, this distance increases. The manufacturer specified at what distance the linings should be changed. *[Figure 13-114]*

Figure 13-114. *The distance between the brake disc and the brake housing measured with the brakes applied is a means for determining brake lining wear on some brakes.*

On Cleveland brakes, lining wear can be measured directly, since part of the lining is usually exposed. The diameter of a number 40 twist drill is approximately equal to the minimum lining thickness allowed. *[Figure 13-115]*

Figure 13-115. *A #40 twist drill laid next to the brake lining indicates when the lining needs to be changed on a Cleveland brake.*

Multiple disc brakes typically are checked for lining wear by applying the brakes and measuring the distance between the back of the pressure plate and the brake housing. *[Figure 13-116]* Regardless of the method particular to each brake, regular monitoring and measurement of brake wear ensures linings are replaced as they become unserviceable. Linings worn beyond limits usually require the brake assembly to be removed for replacement.

Figure 13-116. *The distance between the brake housing and the pressure plate indicates lining wear on some multiple disc brakes.*

Air in the Brake System

The presence of air in the brake system fluid causes the brake pedal to feel spongy. The air can be removed by bleeding to restore firm brake pedal feel. Brake systems must be bled according to manufacturers' instructions. The method used is matched to the type of brake system. Brakes are bled by one of two methods: top down, gravity bleeding or bottom up pressure bleeding. Brakes are bled when the pedals feel spongy or whenever the brake system has been opened.

Bleeding Master Cylinder Brake Systems

Brake systems with master cylinders may be bled by gravity or pressure bleeding methods. Follow the instructions in the aircraft maintenance manual. To pressure bleed a brake system from the bottom up, a pressure pot is used. *[Figure 13-117]* This is a portable tank that contains a supply of brake fluid under pressure. When dispersing fluid from the tank, pure air-free fluid is forced from near the bottom of the tank by the air pressure above it. The outlet hose that attaches

Figure 13-117. *A typical brake bleeder pot or tank contains pure brake fluid under pressure. It pushes the fluid through the brake system to displace any air that may be present.*

the bleed port on the brake assembly contains a shut-off valve. Note that a similar source of pure, pressurized fluid can be substituted for a pressure tank, such as a hand-pump type unit found in some hangars.

The typical pressure bleed is accomplished as illustrated in *Figure 13-118*. The hose from the pressure tank is attached to the bleed port on the brake assembly. A clear hose is attached to the vent port on the aircraft brake fluid reservoir or on the master cylinder if it incorporates the reservoir. The other end of this hose is placed in a collection container with a supply of clean brake fluid covering the end of the hose. The brake assembly bleed port is opened. The valve on the pressure tank hose is then opened allowing pure, air-free fluid to enter the brake system. Fluid containing trapped air is expelled through the hose attached to the vent port of the reservoir. The clear hose is monitored for air bubbles. When they cease to exist, the bleed port and pressure tank shutoff are closed and the pressure tank hose is removed. The hose at the reservoir is also removed. Fluid quantity may need to be adjusted to assure the reservoir is not over filled. Note that it is absolutely necessary that the proper fluid be used to service any brake system including when bleeding air from the brake lines.

Brakes with master cylinders may also be gravity bled from the top down. This is a process similar to that used on automobiles. *[Figure 13-119]* Additional fluid is supplied to the aircraft brake reservoir so that the quantity does not exhaust while bleeding, which would cause the reintroduction of more air into the system. A clear hose is connected to the bleed port on the brake assembly. The other end is submersed

Figure 13-118. *Arrangement for bottom-up pressure bleeding of aircraft brakes. Fluid is pushed through the system until no air bubbles are visible in the hose at the top.*

in clean fluid in a container large enough to capture fluid expelled during the bleeding process. Depress the brake pedal and open the brake assembly bleed port. The piston in the master cylinder travels all the way to the end of the cylinder forcing air fluid mixture out of the bleed hose and into the container. With the pedal still depressed, close the bleed port. Pump the brake pedal to introduce more fluid from the reservoir ahead of the piston in the master cylinder. Hold the pedal down, and open the bleed port on the brake assembly. More fluid and air is expelled through the hose into the container. Repeat this process until the fluid exiting the

Figure 13-119. *Arrangement for top down or gravity bleeding of aircraft brakes.*

brake through the hose no longer contains any air. Tighten the bleed port fitting and ensure the reservoir is filled to the proper level.

Whenever bleeding the brakes, ensure that reservoirs and bleed tanks remain full during the process. Use only clean, specified fluid. Always check the brakes for proper operation, any leaks when bleeding is complete, and assure that the fluid quantity level is correct.

Bleeding Power Brake Systems

Top down brake bleeding is used in power brake systems. Power brakes are supplied with fluid from the aircraft hydraulic system. The hydraulic system should operate without air in the fluid as should the brake system. Therefore, bottom up pressure bleeding is not an option for power brakes. The trapped air in the brake system would be forced into the main hydraulic system, which is not acceptable.

Many aircraft with power brake systems accept the connection of an auxiliary hydraulic mule that can be used to establish pressure in the system for bleeding. Regardless, the aircraft system must be pressurized to bleed power brake systems. Attach a clear hose to the brake bleed port fitting on the brake assembly and immerse the other end of the hose in a container of clean hydraulic fluid. With the bleeder valve open, carefully apply the brake to allow aircraft hydraulic fluid to enter the brake system. The fluid expels the fluid contaminated with air out of the bleed hose into the container. When air is no longer visible in the hose, close the bleed valve and restore the hydraulic system to normal operation configuration.

Power brake systems on different aircraft contain many variations and a wide array of components that may affect the proper bleeding technique to be followed. Consult the manufacturer's maintenance information for the correct bleeding procedure for each aircraft. Be sure to bleed auxiliary and emergency brake systems when bleeding the normal brake system to ensure proper operation when needed.

Fluid Quantity and Type

As mentioned, it is imperative that the correct hydraulic fluid is used in each brake system. Seals in the brake system are designed for a particular hydraulic fluid. Deterioration and failure occurs when they are exposed to other fluids. Mineral-based fluid, such as MIL-H-5606 (red oil), should never be mixed with phosphate-ester based synthetic hydraulic fluid such as Skydrol®. Contaminated brake/hydraulic systems must have all of the fluid evacuated and all seals replaced before the aircraft is released for flight.

Fluid quantity is also important. The technician is responsible for determining the method used to ascertain when the brake and hydraulic systems are fully serviced and for the maintenance of the fluid at this level. Consult the manufacturer's specifications for this information.

Inspection for Leaks

Aircraft brake systems should maintain all fluid inside lines and components and should not leak. Any evidence of a leak must be investigated for its cause. It is possible that the leak is a precursor to more significant damage that can be repaired, thus avoiding an incident or accident. *[Figure 13-120]*

Figure 13-120. *The cause of all aircraft brake leaks must be investigated, repaired, and tested before releasing the aircraft for flight.*

Many leaks are found at brake system fittings. While this type of leak may be fixed by tightening an obviously loose connection, the technician is cautioned against over-tightening fittings. Removal of hydraulic pressure from the brake system followed by disconnection and inspection of the connectors is recommended. Over-tightening of fitting can cause damage and make the leak worse. MS flareless fitting are particularly sensitive to over-tightening. Replace all fittings suspected of damage. Once any leak is repaired, the brake system must be re-pressurized and tested for function as well as to ensure the leak no longer exists. Occasionally, a brake housing may seep fluid through the housing body. Consult the manufacturer's maintenance manual for limits, and remove any brake assembly that seeps excessively.

Proper Bolt Torque

The stress experience by the landing gear and brake system requires that all bolts are properly torqued. Bolts used to attach the brakes to the strut typically have the required torque specified in the manufacturer's maintenance manual. Check for torque specifications that may exist for any landing gear and brake bolts, and ensure they are properly tightened. Whenever applying torque to a bolt on an aircraft, use of a calibrated torque wrench is required.

Off Aircraft Brake Servicing and Maintenance

Certain servicing and maintenance of an aircraft brake assembly is performed while it has been removed from the aircraft. A close inspection of the assembly and its many parts should be performed at this time. Some of the inspection items on a typical assembly follow.

Bolt and Threaded Connections

All bolts and threaded connections are inspected. They should be in good condition without signs of wear. Self-locking nuts should still retain their locking feature. The hardware should be what is specified in the brake manufacturer's parts manual. Many aircraft brake bolts, for example, are not standard hardware and may be of closer tolerance or made of a different material. The demands of the high stress environment in which the brakes perform may cause brake failure if improper substitute hardware is used. Be sure to check the condition of all threads and O-ring seating areas machined into the housing. The fittings threaded into the housing must also be checked for condition.

Discs

Brake discs must be inspected for condition. Both rotating and stationary discs in a multiple disc brake can wear. Uneven wear can be an indication that the automatic adjusters may not be pulling the pressure plate back far enough to relieve all pressure on the disc stack.

Stationary discs are inspected for cracks. Cracks usually extend from the relief slots, if so equipped. On multiple disc brakes, the slots that key the disc to the torque tube must also be inspected for wear and widening. The discs should engage the torque tube without binding. The maximum width of the slots is given in the maintenance manual. Cracks or excessive key slot wear are grounds for rejection. Brake wear pads or linings must also be inspected for wear while the brake assembly is removed from the aircraft. Signs of uneven wear should be investigated and the problem corrected. The pads may be replaced if worn beyond limits as long as the stationary disc upon which they mount passes inspection. Follow the manufacturer's procedures for inspections and for pad replacement.

Rotating discs must be similarly inspected. The general condition of the disc must be observed. Glazing can occur when a disc or part of a disc is overheated. It causes brake squeal and chatter. It is possible to resurface a glazed disc if the manufacturer allows it. Rotating discs must also be inspected in the drive key slot or drive tang area for wear and deformation. Little damage is allowed before replacement is required.

The pressure plate and back plate on multiple disc brakes must be inspected for freedom of movement, cracks, general condition, and warping. New linings may be riveted to the plates if the old linings are worn and the condition of the plate is good. Note that replacing brake pads and linings by riveting may require specific tools and technique as described in the maintenance manual to ensure secure attachment. Minor warping can be straightened on some brake assemblies.

Automatic Adjuster Pins

A malfunctioning automatic adjuster assembly can cause the brakes to drag on the rotating disc(s) by not fully releasing and pulling the lining away from the disc. This can lead to excessive, uneven lining wear and disc glazing. The return pin must be straight with no surface damage so it can pass through the grip without binding. Damage under the head can weaken the pin and cause failure. Magnetic inspection is sometimes used to inspect for cracks.

The components of the grip and tube assembly must be in good condition. Clean and inspect in accordance with the manufacturer's maintenance instructions. The grip must move with the force specified and must move through its full range of travel.

Torque Tube

A sound torque tube is necessary to hold the brake assembly stable on the landing gear. General visual inspection should be made for wear, burrs, and scratches. Magnetic particle inspection is used to check for cracks. The key areas should be checked for dimension and wear. All limits of damage are referenced in the manufacturer's maintenance data. The torque tube should be replaced if a limit is exceeded.

Brake Housing and Piston Condition

The brake housing must be inspected thoroughly. Scratches, gouges, corrosion, or other blemishes may be dressed out and the surface treated to prevent corrosion. Minimal material should be removed when doing so. Most important is that there are no cracks in the housing. Fluorescent dye penetrant is typically used to inspect for cracks. If a crack is found, the housing must be replaced. The cylinder area(s) of the housing must be dimensionally checked for wear. Limits are specified in the manufacturer's maintenance manual.

The brake pistons that fit into the cylinders in the housing must also be checked for corrosion, scratches, burrs, etc. Pistons are also dimensionally checked for wear limits specified in the maintenance data. Some pistons have insulators on the bottom. They should not be cracked and should be of a minimal thickness. A file can be used to smooth out minor irregularities.

Seal Condition

Brake seals are very important. Without properly functioning seals, brake operation will be compromised or the brakes will fail. Over time, heat and pressure mold a seal into the seal groove and harden the material. Eventually, resilience is reduced and the seal leaks. New seals should be used to replace all seals in the brake assembly. Acquire seals by part number in a sealed package from a reputable supplier to avoid bogus seals and ensure the correct seals for the brake assembly in question. Check to ensure the new seals have not exceeded their shelf life, which is typically three years from the cure date.

Many brakes use back-up rings in the seal groove to support the O-ring seals and reduce the tendency of the seal to extrude into the space which it is meant to seal. These are often made of Teflon® or similar material. Back-up seals are installed on the side of the O-ring away from the fluid pressure. *[Figure 13-121]* They are often reusable.

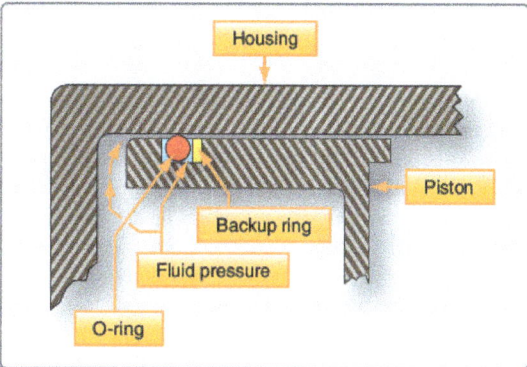

Figure 13-121. *Back-up rings are used to keep O-rings from extruding into the space between the piston and the cylinder. They are positioned on the side of the O-ring away from the fluid pressure.*

Replacement of Brake Linings

In general aviation, replacement of brake linings is commonly done in the hangar. The general procedure used on two common brake assemblies is given. Follow the actual manufacturer's instruction when replacing brake linings on any aircraft brake assembly.

Goodyear Brakes

To replace the linings on a Goodyear single disc brake assembly, the aircraft must be jacked and supported. Detach the anti-rattle clips that help center the disc in the wheel before removing the wheel from the axle. The disc remains between the inner and outer lining when the wheel is removed. Extract the disc to provide access to the old lining pucks. These can be removed from the cavities in the housing and replaced with new pucks. Ensure the smooth braking surface of the puck contacts the disc. Reinsert the disc between the linings. Reinstall the wheel and anti-rattle clips.

Tighten the axle nut in accordance with the manufacturer's instructions. Secure it with a cotter pin and lower the aircraft from the jack. *[Figure 13-122]*

Cleveland Brakes

The popular Cleveland brake uniquely features the ability to change the brake linings without jacking the aircraft or removing the wheel. On these assemblies, the torque plate is bolted to the strut while the remainder of the brake is assembled on the anchor bolts. The disc rides between the pressure plate and back plate. Linings are riveted to both plates. By unbolting the cylinder housing from the backplate, the backplate is freed to drop away from the torque plate. The remainder of the assembly is pulled away, and the pressure plate slides off of the torque bolts. *[Figure 13-123]*

The rivets that hold the linings on the pressure plate and back plate are removed with a knockout punch. After a thorough inspection, new linings are riveted to the pressure plate and backplate using a rivet clinching tool *[Figure 13-124]* Kits are sold that supply everything needed to perform the operation. The brake is reassembled in the reverse order. Be certain to include any shims if required. The bolts holding the backplate to the cylinder assembly must be torqued according to manufacturer specifications and safetied. The manufacturer's data also provides a burn in procedure. The aircraft is taxied at a specified speed, and the brakes are smoothly applied.

After a cooling period, the process is repeated, thus preparing the linings for service.

Brake Malfunctions and Damage

Aircraft brakes operate under extreme stress and varied conditions. They are susceptible to malfunction and damage. A few common brake problems are discussed in this section.

Overheating

While aircraft brakes slow the aircraft by changing kinetic energy into heat energy, overheating of the brakes is not desirable. Excessive heat can damage and distort brake parts weakening them to the point of failure. Protocol for brake usage is designed to prevent overheating. When a brake shows signs of overheating, it must be removed from the aircraft and inspected for damage. When an aircraft is involved in an aborted takeoff, the brakes must be removed and inspected to ensure they withstood this high level of use.

The typical post-overheat brake inspection involves removal of the brake from the aircraft and disassembly of the brakes. All of the seals must be replaced. The brake housing must be checked for cracks, warping, and hardness per the maintenance manual. Any weakness or loss of heat treatment could cause the brake to fail under high-pressure braking. The brake discs must also be inspected. They must not be warped, and the surface treatment must not be damaged or transferred

Figure 13-122. *Goodyear brake lining replacement requires that the wheel be removed from the axle to access the brake assembly. The lining pucks slip into recesses in the brake housing.*

Figure 13-123. *A Cleveland brake disassembles once the four bolts holding the cylinder to the backplate are removed while the aircraft wheel remains in place. The pressure plate slides off the anchor bolts and linings can be replaced by riveting on the pressure plate and back plate.*

Figure 13-124. *Rivet setting tool is used to install brake linings on Cleveland brake pressure plates and back plates.*

to an adjacent disc. Once reassembled, the brake should be bench tested for leaks and pressure tested for operation before being installed on the aircraft.

Dragging

Brake drag is a condition caused by the linings not retracting from the brake disc when the brakes are no longer being applied. It can be caused by several different factors. Brakes that drag are essentially partially on at all times. This can cause excessive lining wear and overheating leading to damage to the disc(s).

A brake may drag when the return mechanism is not functioning properly. This could be due to a weak return spring, the return pin slipping in the auto adjuster pin grip, or similar malfunction. Inspect the auto adjuster(s) and return units on the brake when dragging is reported. An overheated brake that has warped the disc also causes brake drag. Remove the brake and perform a complete inspection as discussed in the previous section. Air in the brake fluid line can also cause brake drag. Heat causes the air to expand, which pushes the brake linings against the disc prematurely. If no damage has been caused when reported, bleed the brakes to remove the air from the system to eliminate the drag.

13-75

At all times, the technician should perform inspections to ensure the proper parts are used in the brake assembly. Improper parts, especially in the retraction/adjuster assemblies, can cause the brakes to drag.

Chattering or Squealing

Brakes may chatter or squeal when the linings do not ride smoothly and evenly along the disc. A warped disc(s) in a multiple brake disc stack produces a condition wherein the brake is actually applied and removed many times per minute. This causes chattering and, at high frequency, it causes squealing. Any misalignment of the disc stack out of parallel causes the same phenomenon. Discs that have been overheated may have damage to the surface layer of the disc. Some of this mix may be transferred to the adjacent disc resulting in uneven disc surfaces that also leads to chatter or squeal. In addition to the noise produced by brake chattering and squealing, vibration is caused that may lead to further damage of the brake and the landing gear system. The technician must investigate all reports of brake chattering and squealing.

Aircraft Tires and Tubes

Aircraft tires may be tube-type or tubeless. They support the weight of the aircraft while it is on the ground and provide the necessary traction for braking and stopping. The tires also help absorb the shock of landing and cushion the roughness of takeoff, rollout, and taxi operations. Aircraft tires must be carefully maintained to perform as required. They accept a variety of static and dynamic stresses and must do so dependably in a wide range of operating conditions.

Tire Classification

Aircraft tires are classified in various ways including by: type, ply rating, whether they are tube-type or tubeless, and whether they are bias ply tires or radials. Identifying a tire by its dimensions is also used. Each of these classifications is discussed as follows.

Types

A common classification of aircraft tires is by type as classified by the United States Tire and Rim Association. While there are nine types of tires, only Types I, III, VII, and VIII, also known as a Three-Part Nomenclature tires, are still in production.

Type I tires are manufactured, but their design is no longer active. They are used on fixed gear aircraft and are designated only by their nominal overall diameter in inches. These are smooth profile tires that are obsolete for use in the modern aviation fleet. They may be found on older aircraft.

Type III tires are common general aviation tires. They are typically used on light aircraft with landing speeds of 160 miles per hour (mph) or less. Type III tires are relatively low-pressure tires that have small rim diameters when compared to the overall width of the tire. They are designed to cushion and provide flotation from a relatively large footprint. Type III tires are designated with a two number system. The first number is the nominal section width of the tire, and the second number is the diameter of the rim the tire is designed to mount upon. *[Figure 13-125]*

Figure 13-125. *Type III aircraft tires are identified via a two-number system with a (-) separating the numbers. The first number is the tire section width in inches. The second number is the rim diameter in inches. For example: 6.00 – 6 is a Cessna 172 tire that is 6.00 inches wide and fits on a rim that has a diameter of 6 inches.*

Type VII tires are high performance tires found on jet aircraft. They are inflated to high-pressure and have exceptional high load carrying capability. The section width of Type VII tires is typically narrower than Type III tires. Identification of Type VII aircraft tires involves a two-number system. An X is used between the two numbers. The first number designates the nominal overall diameter of the tire. The second number designates the section width. *[Figure 13-126]*

Type VIII aircraft tires are also known as three-part nomenclature tires. *[Figure 13-127]* They are inflated to very high-pressure and are used on high-performance jet aircraft. The typical Type VIII tire has relatively low profile and is capable of operating at very high speeds and very high loads. It is the most modern design of all tire types. The three-part nomenclature is a combination of Type III and Type

Figure 13-126. *A Type VII aircraft tire is identified by its two-number designation. The first number represents the tire's overall diameter in inches and the second number represents the section width in inches. Type VII designators separate the first and second number an "X." For example: 26 X 6.6 identifies a tire that is 26 inches in diameter with a 6.6-inch nominal width.*

VII nomenclature where the overall tire diameter, section width, and rim diameter are used to identify the tire. The X and "–" symbols are used in the same respective positions in the designator.

When three part nomenclature is used on a Type VIII tire, dimensions may be represented in inches or in millimeters. Bias tires follow the designation nomenclature and radial tires replace the "–" with the letter R. For example, 30 X 8.8 R 15 designates a Type VIII radial aircraft tire with a 30-inch tire diameter, an 8.8-inch section width to be mounted on a 15-inch wheel rim.

A few special designators may also be found for aircraft tires. When a B appears before the identifier, the tire has a wheel rim to section width ratio of 60 to 70 percent with a bead taper of 15 degrees. When an H appears before the identifier, the tire has a 60 to 70 percent wheel rim to section width ratio but a bead taper of only 5 degrees.

Ply Rating

Tire plies are reinforcing layers of fabric encased in rubber that are laid into the tire to provide strength. In early tires, the number of plies used was directly related to the load the tire could carry. Nowadays, refinements to tire construction techniques and the use of modern materials to build up aircraft tires makes the exact number of plies somewhat irrelevant

Figure 13-127. *A Type VIII or three-part nomenclature tire is identified by 3 parameters: overall diameter, section width, and rim diameter. They are arranged in that order with the first two separated by an "X" and the second two separated by a "–." For example: 18 X 4.25—10 designates a tire that is 18 inches in diameter with a 4.25-inch section width to be mounted on a 10-inch wheel rim.*

when determining the strength of a tire. However, a ply rating is used to convey the relative strength of an aircraft tire. A tire with a high ply rating is a tire with high strength able to carry heavy loads regardless of the actual number of plies used in its construction.

Tube-Type or Tubeless

As stated, aircraft tires can be tube-type or tubeless. This is often used as a means of tire classification. Tires that are made to be used without a tube inserted inside have an

13-77

inner liner specifically designed to hold air. Tube-type tires do not contain this inner liner since the tube holds the air from leaking out of the tire. Tires that are meant to be used without a tube have the word tubeless on the sidewall. If this designation is absent, the tire requires a tube. Consult the aircraft manufacturer's maintenance information for any allowable tire damage and the use of a tube in a tubeless tire.

Bias Ply or Radial

Another means of classifying an aircraft tire is by the direction of the plies used in construction of the tire, either bias or radial. Traditional aircraft tires are bias ply tires. The plies are wrapped to form the tire and give it strength. The angle of the plies in relation to the direction of rotation of the tire varies between 30° and 60°. In this manner, the plies have the bias of the fabric from which they are constructed facing the direction of rotation and across the tire. Hence, they are called bias tires. The result is flexibility as the sidewall can flex with the fabric plies laid on the bias. *[Figure 13-128]*

Figure 13-129. *A radial tire has the fiber strands of the ply fabric oriented with and at 90° to the direction of rotation and the tire sidewall. This restricts flexibility directionally and the flexibility of the sidewall while it strengthens the tire to carry heavy loads.*

landings without being damaged. Only tires designed for an aircraft as specified by the manufacturer should be used.

It is useful to the understanding of tire construction to identify the various components of a tire and the functions contributed to the overall characteristics of a tire. Refer to *Figure 13-130* for tire nomenclature used in this discussion.

Bead

The tire bead is an important part of an aircraft tire. It anchors the tire carcass and provides a dimensioned, firm mounting surface for the tire on the wheel rim. Tire beads are strong. They are typically made from high-strength carbon steel wire bundles encased in rubber. One, two, or three bead bundles may be found on each side of the tire depending on its size and the load it is designed to handle. Radial tires have a single bead bundle on each side of the tire. The bead transfers the impact loads and deflection forces to the wheel rim. The bead toe is closest to the tire centerline and the bead heel fit against the flange of the wheel rim.

Figure 13-128. *A bias ply tire has the fabric bias oriented with and across the direction of rotation and the sidewall. Since fabric can stretch on the bias, the tire is flexible, and can absorb loads. Strength is obtained by adding plies.*

Some modern aircraft tires are radial tires. The plies in radial tires are laid at a 90° angle to the direction of rotation of the tire. This configuration puts the non-stretchable fiber of the plies perpendicular to the sidewall and direction of rotation. This creates strength in the tire allowing it to carry high loads with less deformation. *[Figure 13-129]*

Tire Construction

An aircraft tire is constructed for the purpose it serves. Unlike an automobile or truck tire, it does not have to carry a load for a long period of continuous operation. However, an aircraft tire must absorb the high impact loads of landing and be able to operate at high speeds even if only for a short time. The deflection built into an aircraft tire is more than twice that of an automobile tire. This enables it to handle the forces during

An apex strip is additional rubber formed around the bead to give a contour for anchoring the ply turn-ups. Layers of fabric and rubber called flippers are placed around the beads to insulate the carcass from the beads and improve tire durability. Chafers are also used in this area. Chafer strips made of fabric or rubber are laid over the outer carcass plies after the plies are wrapped around the beads. The chafers protect the carcass from damage during mounting and demounting of the tire. They also help reduce the effects of wear and chafing between the wheel rim and the tire bead especially during dynamic operations.

Figure 13-130. *Construction nomenclature of an aircraft tire.*

Carcass Plies

Carcass plies, or casing plies as they are sometimes called, are used to form the tire. Each ply consists of fabric, usually nylon, sandwiched between two layers of rubber. The plies are applied in layers to give the tire strength and form the carcass body of the tire. The ends of each ply are anchored by wrapping them around the bead on both sides of the tire to form the ply turn-ups. As mentioned, the angle of the fiber in the ply is manipulated to create a bias tire or radial tire as desired. Typically, radial tires require fewer plies than bias tires.

Once the plies are in place, bias tires and radial tires each have their own type of protective layers on top of the plies but under the tread of the running surface of the tire. On bias tires, these single or multiple layers of nylon and rubbers are called tread reinforcing plies. On radial tires, an undertread and a protector ply do the same job. These additional plies stabilize and strengthen the crown area of the tire. They reduce tread distortion under load and increase stability of the tire at high speeds. The reinforcing plies and protector plies also help resist puncture and cutting while protecting the carcass body of the tire.

Tread

The tread is the crown area of the tire designed to come in contact with the ground. It is a rubber compound formulated to resist wear, abrasion, cutting, and cracking. It also is made to resist heat build-up. Most modern aircraft tire tread is formed with circumferential grooves that create tire ribs. The grooves provide cooling and help channel water from under the tire in wet conditions to increase adhesion to the ground surface. Tires designed for aircraft frequently operated from unpaved surfaces may have some type of cross-tread pattern. Older aircraft without brakes or brakes designed only to aid in taxi may not have any grooves in the tread. An all-weather tread may be found on some aircraft tires. This tread has typical circumferential ribs in the center of the tire with a diamond patterned cross tread at the edge of the tire.[*Figure 13-131*]

The tread is designed to stabilize the aircraft on the operating surface and wears with use. Many aircraft tires are designed with protective undertread layers as described above. Extra tread reinforcement is sometimes accomplished with breakers. These are layers of nylon cord fabric under the tread that strengthen the tread while protecting the carcass plies. Tires with reinforced tread are often designed to be re-treaded and used again once the tread has worn beyond limits. Consult the tire manufacturer's data for acceptable tread wear and re-tread capability for a particular tire.

Figure 13-131. *Aircraft tire treads are designed for different uses. A is a rib tread designed for use on paved surfaces. It is the most common aircraft tire tread design. B is a diamond tread designed for unpaved runways. C is an all weather tread that combines a ribbed center tread with a diamond tread pattern of the edges. D is a smooth tread tire found on older, slow aircraft without brakes designed for stopping. E is a chine tire used on the nose gear of aircraft with fuselage mounted jet engines to deflect runway water away from the engine intake(s).*

Sidewall

The sidewall of an aircraft tire is a layer of rubber designed to protect the carcass plies. It may contain compounds designed to resist the negative effects of ozone on the tire. It also is the area where information about the tire is contained. The tire sidewall imparts little strength to the cord body. Its main function is protection.

The inner sidewall of a tire is covered by the tire inner liner. A tube-type tire has a thin rubber liner adhered to the inner surface to prevent the tube from chafing on the carcass plies. Tubeless tires are lined with a thicker, less permeable rubber. This replaces the tube and contains the nitrogen or inflation air within the tire and keeps from seeping through the carcass plies.

The inner liner does not contain 100 percent of the inflation gas. Small amounts of nitrogen or air seep through the liner into the carcass plies. This seepage is released through vent holes in the lower outer sidewall of the tires. These are typically marked with a green or white dot of paint and must be kept unobstructed. Gas trapped in the plies could expand with temperature changes and cause separation of the plies, thus weakening the tire leading to tire failure. Tube-type tires also have seepage holes in the sidewall to allow air trapped between the tube and the tire to escape. *[Figure 13-132]*

Chine

Some tire sidewalls are mounded to form a chine. A chine is a special built-in deflector used on nose wheels of certain aircraft, usually those with fuselage mounted engines. The chine diverts runway water to the side and away from the

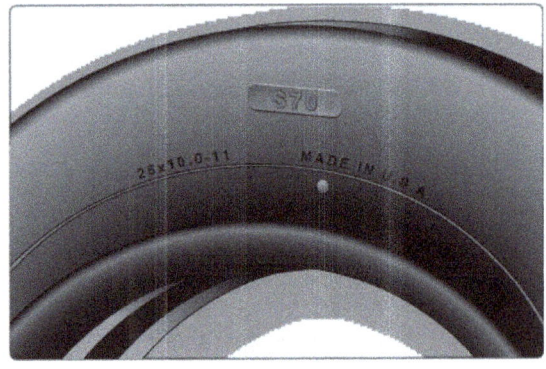

Figure 13-132. *A sidewall vent marked by a colored dot must be kept free from obstruction to allow trapped air or nitrogen to escape from the carcass plies of the tire.*

intake of the engines. *[Figure 13-131E]* Tires with a chine on both sidewalls are produced for aircraft with a single nose wheel.

Tire Inspection on the Aircraft

Tire condition is inspected while mounted on the aircraft on a regular basis. Inflation pressure, tread wear and condition, and sidewall condition are continuously monitored to ensure proper tire performance.

Inflation

To perform as designed, an aircraft tire must be properly inflated. The aircraft manufacturer's maintenance data must be used to ascertain the correct inflation pressure for a tire on a particular aircraft. Do not inflate to a pressure displayed on the sidewall of the tire or by how the tire looks. Tire pressure is checked while under load and is measured with the weight of the aircraft on the wheels. Loaded versus unloaded pressure readings can vary as much as 4 percent. Tire pressure measured with the aircraft on jacks or when the tire is not installed is lower due to the larger volume of the inflation gas space inside of the tire. On a tire designed to be inflated to 160 psi, this can result in a 6.4 psi error. A calibrated pressure gauge should always be used to measure inflation pressure. Digital and dial-type pressure gauges are more consistently accurate and preferred. *[Figure 13-133]*

Aircraft tires disperse the energy from landing, rollout, taxi, and takeoff in the form of heat. As the tire flexes, heat builds and is transferred to the atmosphere, as well as to the wheel rim through the tire bead. Heat from braking also heats the tire externally. A limited amount of heat is able to be handled by any tire beyond which structural damage occurs.

An improperly inflated aircraft tire can sustain internal damage that is not readily visible and that can lead to tire failure. Tire failure upon landing is always dangerous. An aircraft tire is designed to flex and absorb the shock of landing. Temperature rises as a result. However, an underinflated tire may flex beyond design limits of the tire. This causes excessive heat build-up that weakens the carcass construction. To ensure tire temperature is maintained within limits, tire pressure must be checked and maintained within the proper range on a daily basis or before each flight if the aircraft is only flown periodically.

Tire pressure should be measured at ambient temperature. Fluctuations of ambient temperature greatly affect tire pressure and complicate maintenance of pressure within the allowable range for safe operation. Tire pressure typically changes 1 percent for every 5 °F of temperature change. When aircraft are flown from one environment to another, ambient temperature differences can be vast. Maintenance personnel must ensure that tire pressure is adjusted accordingly. For example, an aircraft with the correct tire pressure departing Phoenix, Arizona where the ambient temperature is 100 °F arrives in Vail, Colorado where the temperature is 50 °F. The 50° difference in ambient temperature results in a 10 percent reduction in tire pressure. Therefore the aircraft could land with underinflated tires that may be damaged due to over-temperature from flexing beyond design limits as described above. An increase in tire pressure before takeoff in Phoenix, Arizona prevents this problem as long as the tires are not inflated beyond the allowable limit provided in the maintenance data.

When checking tire pressure, allow 3 hours to elapse after a typical landing to ensure the tire has cooled to ambient

Figure 13-133. *A calibrated bourdon tube dial-type pressure gauge or a digital pressure gauge is recommended for checking tire pressure.*

temperature. The correct tire pressure for each ambient temperature is typically provided by the manufacturer on a table or graph.

In addition to overheating, under inflated aircraft tires wear unevenly, which leads to premature tire replacement. They may also creep or slip on the wheel rim when under stress or when the brakes are applied. Severely under inflated tires can pinch the sidewall between the rim and the runway causing sidewall and rim damage. Damage to the bead and lower sidewall area are also likely. This type of abuse like any over flexing damages the integrity of the tire and it must be replaced. In dual-wheel setups, a severely underinflated tire affects both tires and both should be replaced.

Over inflation of aircraft tires is another undesirable condition. While carcass damage due to overheating does not result, adherence to the landing surface is reduced. Over a long period of time, over inflation leads to premature tread wear. Therefore, over inflation reduces the number of cycles in service before the tire must be replaced. It makes the tire more susceptible to bruises, cutting, shock damage, and blowout. *[Figure 13-134]*

Tread Condition

Condition of an aircraft tire tread is able to be determined while the tire is inflated and mounted on the aircraft. The following is a discussion of some of the tread conditions and damage that the technician may encounter while inspecting tires.

Tread Depth and Wear Pattern

Evenly worn tread is a sign of proper tire maintenance. Uneven tread wear has a cause that should be investigated and corrected. Follow all manufacturer instructions specific to the aircraft when determining the extent and serviceability of a worn tire. In the absence of this information, remove any tire that has been worn to the bottom of a tread groove along more than ⅛ of the circumference of the tire. If either the protector ply on a radial tire or the reinforcing ply on a bias tire is exposed for more than ⅛ of the tire circumference, the tire should also be removed. A properly maintained evenly worn tire usually reaches its wear limits at the centerline of the tire. *[Figure 13-135]*

Asymmetrical tread wear may be caused by the wheels being out of alignment. Follow the manufacturer's instructions while checking caster, camber, tow-in, and tow-out to correct this situation. Occasionally, asymmetrical tire wear is a result of landing gear geometry that cannot, or is not, required to be corrected. It may also be caused by regular taxiing on a single engine or high speed cornering while taxiing. It is acceptable to remove the tire from the wheel rim, turn it around, and remount it to even up tread wear if the tire passes all other criterion of inspection for serviceability.

Removal of a tire before it is worn beyond limits to be eligible for retreading is cost effective and good maintenance practice. Considerable traction is lost when tire tread is severely worn and must also be considered when inspecting a tire for condition. *[Figure 13-136]* Consult airframe manufacturer and tire manufacturer specifications for wear and retread limitations.

Figure 13-134. *Tires that are overinflated lack adherence to the runway and develop excess tread wear in the center of the tread. Tires that are underinflated develop excess tread wear on the tire shoulders. Overheating resulting in internal carcass damage and potential failure are possible from flexing the tire beyond design limits.*

Figure 13-135. *Normal tire wear.*

Figure 13-136. *Tread wear on a bias ply tire (left) and a radial tire (right) show wear beyond limits of serviceability but still eligible to be retreaded.*

Tread Damage

In addition to tread wear, an aircraft tire should be inspected for damage. Cuts, bruises, bulges, imbedded foreign objects, chipping, and other damage must be within limits to continue the tire in service. Some acceptable methods of dealing with this type of damage are described below. All damage, suspected damage, and areas with leaks should be marked with chalk, a wax marker, paint stick, or other device before the tire is deflated or removed. Often, it is impossible to relocate these areas once the tire is deflated. Tires removed for retread should be marked in damaged areas to enable closer inspection of the extent of the damage before the new tread is installed. *[Figure 13-137]*

Foreign objects imbedded in a tire's tread are of concern and should be removed when not imbedded beyond the tread. Objects of questionable depth should only be removed after the tire has been deflated. A blunt awl or appropriately sized screwdriver can be used to pry the object from the tread. Care must be exercised to not enlarge the damaged area with the removal tool. *[Figure 13-138]* Once removed, assess the remaining damage to determine if the tire is serviceable. A round hole caused by a foreign object is acceptable only if it is ⅜-inch or less in diameter. Embedded objects that penetrate

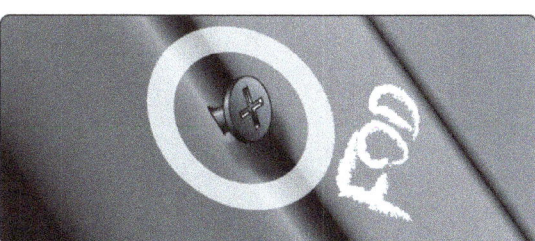

Figure 13-137. *Marking of damaged area to enable closer inspection.*

Figure 13-138. *Deflate a tire before removing or probing any area where a foreign object is lodged.*

or expose the casing cord body of a bias ply tire or the tread belt layer of a radial tire cause the tire to become unairworthy and it must be removed from service.

Cuts and tread undercutting can also render a tire unairworthy. A cut that extends across a tread rib is cause for tire removal. These can sometimes lead to a section of the rib to peel off the tire. *[Figure 13-139]* Consult the aircraft maintenance manual, airline operations manual, or other technical documents applicable to the aircraft tire in question.

A flat spot on a tire is the result of the tire skidding on the runway surface while not rotating. This typically occurs when the brakes lock on while the aircraft is moving. If the flat spot damage does not expose the reinforcing ply of a bias tire or the protector ply of a radial tire, it may remain in service. However, if the flat spot causes vibration, the tire must be removed. Landing with a brake applied can often cause a severe flat spot that exposes the tire under tread. It can also cause a blowout. The tire must be replaced in either case. *[Figure 13-140]*

Figure 13-140. *Landing with the brake on causes a tire flat spot that exposes the under tread and requires replacement of the tire.*

A bulge or separation of the tread from the tire carcass is cause for immediate removal and replacement of the tire. Mark the area before deflation as it could easily become undetectable without air in the tire. *[Figure 13-141]*

Figure 13-139. *Remove an aircraft tire from service when the depth of a cut exposes the casing outer plies of a bias ply tire or the outer belt layer of a radial tire (A); a tread rib has been severed across the entire width (B); or, when undercutting occurs at the base of any cut (C). These conditions may lead to a peeled rib.*

13-84

Figure 13-141. *Bulges and tread separation are cause for removal of a tire from service.*

Operation on a grooved runway can cause an aircraft tire tread to develop shallow chevron shaped cuts. These cuts are allowed for continued service, unless chunks or cuts into the fabric of the tire result. Deep chevrons that cause a chunk of the tread to be removed should not expose more than 1 square inch of the reinforcing or protector ply. Consult the applicable inspection parameters to determine the allowable extent of chevron cutting. *[Figure 13-142]*

Figure 13-143. *Tread chipping and chunking of a tire requires that the tire be removed from service if more than 1 square inch of the reinforcing ply or protector ply is exposed.*

Cracking in a tread groove of an aircraft tire is generally not acceptable if more than ¼-inch of the reinforcing or protector ply is exposed. Groove cracks can lead to undercutting of the tread, which eventually can cause the entire tread to be thrown from the tire. *[Figure 13-144]*

Figure 13-142. *Chevron cuts in a tire are caused by operation on grooved runway surfaces. Shallow chevron cuts are permitted on aircraft tires.*

Tread chipping and chunking sometimes occurs at the edge of the tread rib. Small amounts of rubber lost in this way are permissible. Exposure of more than 1 square inch of the reinforcing or protector ply is cause for removal of the tire. *[Figure 13-143]*

Oil, hydraulic fluid, solvents, and other hydrocarbon substances contaminate tire rubber, soften it, and make it spongy. A contaminated tire must be removed from service. If any volatile fluids come in contact with the tire, it is best to wash the tire or area of the tire with denatured alcohol followed by soap and water. Protect tires from contact with potentially harmful fluids by covering tires during maintenance in the landing gear area.

Figure 13-144. *A thrown tread can result from a groove crack or tread undercutting and must be removed from service.*

Tires are also subject to degradation from ozone and weather. Tires on aircraft parked outside for long periods of times can be covered for protection from the elements. *[Figure 13-145]*

Weather and ozone can cause cracking and checking of the sidewall. If this extends to the sidewall cords, the tire must be removed from service. Otherwise, sidewall checking as show in *Figure 13-146* does not affect the performance of the tire and it may remain in service.

Figure 13-145. *Cover tires to protect from harmful chemicals and from the elements when parked outside for long periods of time.*

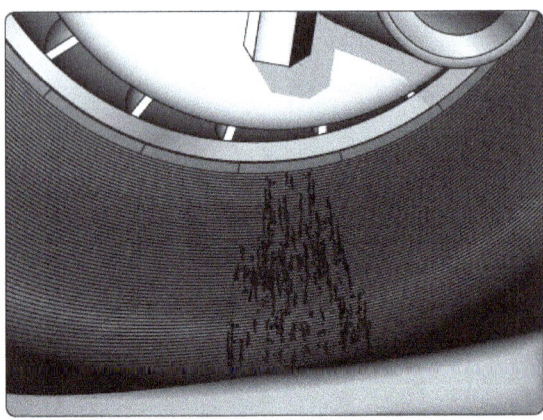

Figure 13-146. *Cracking and checking in the sidewall of a tire is acceptable for service as long as it does not extend to or expose the sidewall carcass plies.*

Sidewall Condition

The primary function of the sidewall of an aircraft tire is protection of the tire carcass. If the sidewall cords are exposed due to a cut, gouge, snag, or other injury, the tire must be replaced. Mark the area of concern before removal of the tire. Damage to the sidewall that does not reach the cords is typically acceptable for service. Circumferential cracks or slits in the sidewall are unacceptable. A bulge in a tire sidewall indicates possible delamination of the sidewall carcass plies. The tire must immediately be removed from service.

Tire Removal

Removal of any tire and wheel assembly should be accomplished following all aircraft manufacturer's instructions for the procedure. Safety procedures are designed for the protection of the technician and the maintenance of aircraft parts in serviceable condition. Follow all safety procedures to prevent personal injury and damage to aircraft parts and assemblies.

An aircraft tire and wheel assembly, especially a high pressure assembly that has been damaged or overheated, should be treated as though it may explode. Never approach such a tire while its temperature is still elevated above ambient temperature. Once cooled, approach a damage tire and wheel assembly from an oblique angle advancing toward the shoulder of the tire. *[Figure 13-147]*

Figure 13-147. *To avoid potential injury, approach a tire/wheel assembly that has damage or has been overheated at an angle toward the tire shoulder only after it has cooled to ambient temperature.*

Deflate all unserviceable and damaged tires before removal from the aircraft. Use a valve core/deflation tool to deflate the tire. Stand to the side—away from the projectile path of the valve core. A dislodged valve core propelled by internal tire pressure can cause serious human injury. When completely deflated, remove the valve core. *[Figure 13-148]* A tire and wheel assembly in airworthy condition may be removed to access other components for maintenance without deflating the tire. This is common practice, such as when accessing the brake when the wheel assembly is immediately reinstalled. For tracking purposes, ensure damaged areas of a tire are marked before deflation. Record all known information about an unserviceable tire and attach it to the tire for use by the retread repair station.

Figure 13-148. *The tire valve core should be removed after the tire is completely deflated and before the tire and wheel assembly is removed from the aircraft.*

Once removed from the aircraft, a tire must be separated from the wheel rim upon which is mounted. Proper equipment and technique should be followed to avoid damage to the tire and wheel. The wheel manufacturer's maintenance information is the primary source for dismounting guidelines.

The bead area of the tire sits firmly against the rim shoulder and must be broken free. Always use proper bead breaking equipment for this purpose. Never pry a tire from a wheel rim as damage to the wheel is inevitable. The wheel tie bolts must remain installed and fully tightened when the bead is broken from the rim to prevent damage to the wheel half mating surfaces.

When the bead breaking press contact surface is applied to the tire, it should be as close to the wheel as possible without touching it during the entire application of pressure. Tires and rims of different sizes require contact pads suitable for the tire. Hand presses and hydraulic presses are available. Apply the pressure and hold it to allow the bead to move on the rim. Gradually progress around the rim until the tire bead is broken free. Ring-type bead breakers apply pressure around the circumference of the entire sidewall so rotation is not required. *[Figure 13-149]* Once the bead is broken free, the wheel halves may be disassembled. *[Figure 13-150]* Radial tires have only one bead bundle on each side of the tire. The sidewall is more flexible in this area than a bias ply tire. The proper tooling should be used, and pressure should be applied slowly to avoid heavy distortion of the sidewall. Lubrication may be applied and allowed to soak into the tire-wheel interface. Only soapy tire solutions should be used. Never apply a hydrocarbon based lubricant to an aircraft tire as this contaminates the rubber compound used to construct the tire. Beads on tube-type and tubeless tires are broken free in a similar manner.

Figure 13-149. *A ring adapter applies pressure around the entire circumference of the lower sidewall of the tire to break the bead free from the wheel rim. The diameter of the adapter must be correct for the tire and the travel limited so as to not injure the tire.*

Figure 13-150. *An electrohydraulic tire bead breaker (left) used on large tires and a manual tire bead breaker (right) used on small tires.*

Tire Inspection Off of the Aircraft

Once a tire has been removed from the wheel rim, it should be inspected for condition. It may be possible to retread the tire at an approved repair station and return it to service. A sequential inspection procedure helps ensure no parts of the tire are overlooked. Mark and record the extent of all damage. Advisory Circular (AC) 43-13-1 gives general guidelines for tire inspection and repair. Tires must only be repaired by those with the experience and equipment to do so. Most tire repairs are accomplished at a certified tire repair facility.

When inspecting a tire removed from the aircraft, pay special attention to the bead area since it must provide an air tight seal to the wheel rim and transfer forces from the tire to the rim. Inspect the bead area closely as it is where the heat is concentrated during tire operation. Surface damage to the chafer is acceptable and can be repaired when the tire is retreaded. Other damage in the bead area is usually cause for rejection. Damage to the turn-ups, ply separation at the bead, or a kinked bead are examples of bead area damage that warrant the tire be discarded. The bead area of the tire may sustain damage or have an altered appearance or texture on a tire that has been overheated. Consult a certified tire repair station or re-tread facility when in doubt about the condition observed. The wheel rim must also be inspected for damage. An effective seal without slippage, especially on tubeless tires, is dependent on the condition and integrity of the wheel in the bead seat area.

Overheating of a tire weakens it even though the damage might not be obvious. Any time a tire is involved in an aborted takeoff, severe braking, or the thermal plug in the wheel has melted to deflate the tire before explosion, the tire must be removed. On a dual installation, both tires must be removed. Even if only one tire shows obvious damage or deflates, the loads experienced by the mate are excessive. Internal damage such as ply separation, is likely. The history of having been through an overheat event is all that is required for the tire to be discarded.

Damaged or suspected damaged areas of the tire should be re-inspected while the tire is off the aircraft. Cuts can be probed to check for depth and extent of damage below the tread. In general, damage that does not exceed 40 percent of the tire plies can be repaired when the tire is retreaded. Small punctures with a diameter on the tire inner surface of less than $\frac{1}{8}$-inch and a diameter on the outer surface of less than $\frac{1}{4}$-inch can also be repaired and retreaded. A bulge caused by ply separation is reason to discard a tire. However, a bulge caused by tread separation from the tire carcass may be repairable during retread. Exposed sidewall cord or sidewall cord damage is unacceptable and the tire cannot be repaired or retreaded. Consult the tire manufacturer or certified retreader for clarification on damage to a tire.

Tire Repair and Retreading

The technician should follow airframe and tire manufacturer instructions to determine if a tire is repairable. Many example guidelines have also been given in this section. Nearly all tire repairs must be made at a certified tire repair facility equipped to perform the approved repair. Bead damage, ply separation, and sidewall cord exposure all require that the tire be scrapped. Inner liner condition on tubeless tires is also critical. Replacing the tube in a tube-type tire is performed by the technician as are mounting and balancing all types of aircraft tires.

Aircraft tires are very expensive. They are also extremely durable. The effective cost of a tire over its life can be reduced by having the tread replaced while the carcass is still sound and injuries are within repairable limits. Federal Aviation Administration (FAA) certified tire retread repair stations, often the original equipment manufacturer (OEM), do this work. The technician inspects a tire to pre-qualify it for retread so that the cost of shipping it to the retread repair facility is not incurred if there is no chance to retread the tire. The tire retreader inspects and tests every tire to a level beyond the capability of the hangar or line technician. Shearography, an optical nondestructive testing method that provides detailed information about the internal integrity of the tire, is used by tire retread repair facilities to ensure a tire carcass is suitable for continued service.

Tires that are retreaded are marked as such. They are not compromised in strength and give the performance of a new tire. No limits are established for the number of times a tire can be retreaded. This is based on the structural integrity of the tire carcass. A well maintained main gear tire may be able to be retreaded a handful of times before fatigue renders the carcass un-airworthy. Some nose tires can be retread nearly a dozen times.

Tire Storage

An aircraft tire can be damaged if stored improperly. A tire should always be stored vertically so that it is resting on its treaded surface. Horizontal stacking of tires is not recommended. Storage of tires on a tire rack with a minimum 3–4-inch flat resting surface for the tread is ideal and avoids tire distortion.

If horizontal stacking of tires is necessary, it should only be done for a short time. The weight of the upper tires on the lower tires cause distortion possibly making it difficult for the bead to seat when mounting tubeless tires. A bulging tread also stresses rib grooves and opens the rubber to ozone attack in this area. *[Figure 13-151]* Never stack aircraft tires horizontally for more than 6 months. Stack no higher than four tires if the tire is less than 40-inches in diameter and no higher than three tires if greater than 40-inches in diameter. The environment in which an aircraft tire is stored is critical. The ideal location in which to store an aircraft tire is cool, dry, and dark, free from air currents and dirt.

An aircraft tire contains natural rubber compounds that are prone to degradation from chemicals and sunlight. Ozone (O_3) and oxygen (O_2) cause degradation of tire compounds. Tires should be stored away from strong air currents that continually present a supply of one or both of these gases. Fluorescent lights, mercury vapor lights, electric motors, battery chargers, electric welding equipment, electric generators, and similar shop equipment produce ozone and should not be operated near aircraft tires. Mounted inflated tires can be stored with up to 25 percent less pressure than operating pressure to reduce vulnerability from ozone attacks. Sodium vapor lighting is acceptable. Storage of an aircraft tire in the dark is preferred to minimize degradation from ultraviolet (UV) light. If this is not possible, wrap the tire in dark polyethylene or paper to form an ozone barrier and to minimize exposure to UV light.

Common hydrocarbon chemicals, such as fuels, oils, and solvents, should not contact a tire. Avoid rolling tires through spills on the hangar or shop floor and be sure to clean any tire immediately if contaminated. Dry the tire and store all tires in a dry place away from any moisture, which has a deteriorating effect on the rubber compounds. Moisture with foreign elements may further damage the rubber and fabric of a tire. Dirty areas must be avoided.

Tires are made to operate in a wide range of temperatures. However, storage should be at cool temperatures to minimize degradation. A general range for safe aircraft tire storage is between 32 °F and 104 °F. Temperatures below this are acceptable but higher temperatures must be avoided.

Aircraft Tubes

Many aircraft tires accept a tube inside to contain the inflation air. Tube-type tires are handled and stored in similar fashion as tubeless tires. A number of issues concerning the tubes themselves must be addressed.

Tube Construction and Selection

Aircraft tire tubes are made of a natural rubber compound. They contain the inflation air with minimal leakage. Unreinforced and special reinforced heavy duty tubes are available. The heavy duty tubes have nylon reinforcing fabric layered into the rubber to provide strength to resist chafing and to protect against heat such as during braking.

Tubes come in a wide range of sizes. Only the tube specified for the applicable tire size must be used. Tubes that are too small stress the tube construction.

Figure 13-151. *Ozone cracking in a tire tread groove is facilitated by horizontal stacking.*

Tube Storage and Inspection

An aircraft tire tube should be kept in the original carton until put into service to avoid deterioration through exposure to environmental elements. If the original carton is not available, the tube can be wrapped in several layers of paper to protect it. Alternately, for short time periods only, a tube may be stored in the correct size tire it is made for while inflated just enough to round out the tube. Application of talc to the inside of the tire and outside of the tube prevents sticking. Remove the tube and inspect it and the tire before permanently mounting the assembly. Regardless of storage method, always store aircraft tubes in a cool, dry, dark place away from ozone producing equipment and moving air.

When handling and storing aircraft tire tubes, creases are to be avoided. These weaken the rubber and eventually cause tube failure. Creases and wrinkles also tend to be chafe points for the tube when mounted inside the tire. Never hang a tube over a nail or peg for storage.

An aircraft tube must be inspected for leaks and damage that may eventually cause a leak or failure. To check for leaks, remove the tube from the tire. Inflate the tube just enough to have it take shape but not stretch. Immerse a small tube in a container of water and look for the source of air bubbles. A large tube may require that water be applied over the tube. Again look for the source of bubbles. The valve core should also be wetted to inspect it for leaks.

There is no mandatory age limit for an aircraft tire tube. It should be elastic without cracks or creases in order to be consider serviceable. The valve area is prone to damage and should be inspected thoroughly. Bend the valve to ensure there are no cracks at the base where it is bonded to the tire or in the area where it passes through the hole in the wheel rim. Inspect the valve core to ensure it is tight and that it does not leak.

If an area of a tube experiences chafing to the point where the rubber is thinned, the tube should be discarded. The inside diameter of the tube should be inspected to ensure it has not been worn by contact with the toe of the tire bead. Tubes that have taken an unnatural set should be discarded. *[Figure 13-152]*

Tire Inspection

It is important to inspect the inside of a tube-type tire before installing a tube for service. Any protrusions or rough areas should be cause for concern, as these tend to abrade the tube and may cause early failure. Follow the tire, tube, and aircraft manufacturer's inspection criterion when inspecting aircraft tires and tubes.

Tire Mounting

A licensed technician is often called upon to mount an aircraft tire onto the wheel rim in preparation for service. In the case of a tube-type tire, the tube must also be mounted. The following section presents general procedures for these operations using tube-type and tubeless tires. Be sure to have the proper equipment and training to perform the work according to manufacturer's instructions.

Tubeless Tires

Aircraft tire and wheel assemblies are subject to enormous stress while in service. Proper mounting ensures tires perform to the limits of their design. Consult and follow all manufacturer's service information including bolt torques, lubrication and balancing requirements, and inflation procedures.

As mentioned, a wheel assembly that is to have a tire mounted upon it must be thoroughly inspected to ensure it is serviceable. Pay close attention to the bead seat area, which should be smooth and free from defects. The wheel half mating surface should be in good condition. The O-ring should be lubricated and in good condition to ensure it seals the wheel for the entire life of the tire. Follow the

Figure 13-152. *During inspection, an aircraft tire tube should retain its natural contour. Tubes with thinned areas or that have taken a set should be discarded and replaced.*

manufacturer's instructions when inspecting wheels and the tips provided earlier in this chapter. *[Figure 13-153]*

Figure 13-153. *The wheel half O-ring for a tubeless tire wheel assembly must be in good condition and lubricated to seal for the entire life of the tire. The mating surfaces of the wheel halves must also be in good condition.*

A final inspection of the tire to be mounted should be made. Most important is to check that the tire is specified for the aircraft application. It should say tubeless on the sidewall. The part number, size, ply rating, speed rating, and technical standard order (TSO) number should also be on the sidewall and be approved for the aircraft installation. Visually check the tire for damage from shipping and handling. There should be no permanent deformation of the tire. It should pass all inspections for cuts and other damage discussed in the previous sections of this chapter. Clean the tire bead area with a clean shop towel and soap and water or denatured alcohol. Inspect the inside of the tire for condition. There should be no debris inside the tire.

Tire beads are sometimes lubricated when mounted on aluminum wheels. Follow the manufacturer's instructions and use only the non-hydrocarbon lubricant specified. Never lubricate any tire bead with grease. Do not use lubricants with magnesium alloy wheels. Most radial tires are mounted without lubricant. The airframe manufacturer may specify lubrication for a radial tire in a few cases.

When the wheel halves and tires are ready to be mounted, thought must be given to tire orientation and the balance marks on the wheel halves and tire. Typically, the tire serial number is mounted to the outboard side of the assembly. The marks indicating the light portion of each wheel half should be opposite each other. The mark indicating the heavy spot of the wheel assembly should be mounted aligned with the light spot on the tire, which is indicated by a red mark. If the wheel lacks a mark indicating the heavy spot, align the red spot on the tire (the light point) with the valve fitting location on the wheel. A properly balanced tire and wheel assembly improves the overall performance of the tire. It promotes smooth operation free from vibration, which results in uniform tread wear and extended tire life.

When assembling the wheel halves, follow manufacturer's instructions for tie bolt tightening sequences and torque specification. Anti-seize lubricants and wet-torque values are common on wheel assemblies. Use a calibrated hand torque wrench. Never use an impact wrench on an aircraft tire assembly.

For the initial inflation of an aircraft tire and wheel assembly, the tire must be placed in a tire inflation safety cage and treated as though it may explode due to wheel or tire failure. The inflation hose should be attached to the tire valve stem, and inflation pressure should be regulated from a safe distance away. A minimum of 30 feet is recommended. Air or nitrogen should be introduced gradually as specified. Dry nitrogen keeps the introduction of water into the tire to a minimum, which helps prevent corrosion. Observe the tire seating progress on the wheel rim while it inflates. Depressurize the tire before approaching it to investigate any observed issue. *[Figure 13-154]*

Aircraft tires are typically inflated to their full specified operating pressure. Then, they are allowed to remain with no load applied for 12-hours. During this time, the tire stretches and tire pressure decreases. A 5-10 percent reduction is normal. Upon bringing the tire up to full pressure again, less than 5 percent loss per day of pressure is allowable. More should be investigated.

Tube-Type Tires

Wheel and tire inspection should precede the mounting of any tire, including tube-type tires. The tube to be installed must also pass inspection and must be the correct size for the tire and tire must be specified for the aircraft. Tire talc is commonly used when installing tube-type tires to ensure easy mounting and free movement between the tube and tire as they inflate. *[Figure 13-155]* The technician should lightly talc the inside of the tire and the outside of the tube. Some tubes come from the factory with a light talc coating over the outside of the tube. Inflate the tube so that it just takes shape with minimal pressure. Install the tube inside the tire. Tubes are typically produced with a mark at the heavy spot of the tube. In the absence of this balance mark, it is assumed that the valve is located at the heaviest part of the tube. For proper balance, align the heavy part of the tube with the red mark on the tire (the light spot on the tire). *[Figure 13-156]*

Figure 13-154. *Modern tire inflation cages have been tested to withstand catastrophic failure of a tire and wheel assembly during inflation. All newly mounted tires should be inflated in such a cage.*

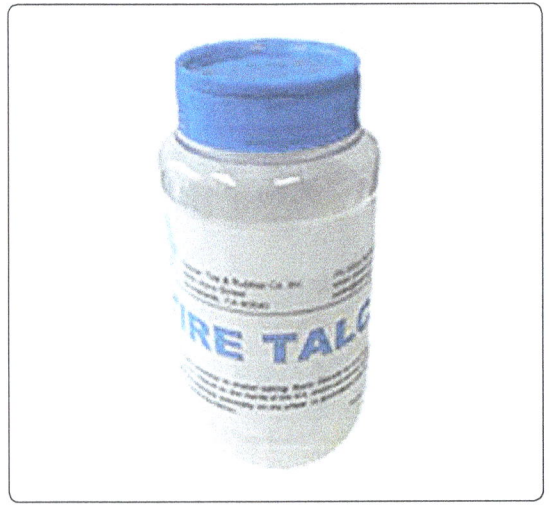

Figure 13-155. *Tire talc is used on the inside of tube-type tires and the outside of aircraft tubes. This prevents binding and allows the tube to expand without stress into place within the tire.*

Figure 13-156. *When assembling a tube into a tire, the heavy balance mark on the tube is aligned with the light balance mark on the tire.*

Once wheel balance is marked and the tube balance mark and the tire balance mark are all positioned correctly, install the outboard wheel half so the valve stem of the tube passes through the valve stem opening. *[Figure 13-157]* Mate the inboard wheel half to it, being careful not to pinch the tube between the wheel rims. Install the tie bolts, tighten, and torque as specified. Inflate the assembly in a tire inflation cage. The inflation procedure for a tube-type tire differs slightly from that of a tubeless tire. The assembly is slowly brought up to full operating pressure. Then, it is completely deflated. Re-inflate the tire/tube assembly a second time to the specified operating pressure and allow it to remain with no load for 12-hours. This allows any wrinkles in the tube to smooth out, helps prevent the tube from being trapped under a bead, and generally evens how the tube lays within the tire to avoid any stretched areas and thinning of the tube. The holding time allows air trapped between the tube and the tire to work its way out of the assembly, typically through the tire sidewall or around the valves stem.

Figure 13-157. *Mounting a tube type tire with the tube valve stem positioned to pass through the outboard wheel half.*

Tire Balancing

Once an aircraft tire is mounted, inflated, and accepted for service, it can be balanced to improve performance. Vibration is the main result of an imbalanced tire and wheel assembly. Nose wheels tend to create the greatest disturbance in the cabin when imbalanced.

Static balance is all that is required for most aircraft tires and wheels. A balance stand typically accepts the assembly on cones. The wheel is free to rotate. The heavy side moves to the bottom. *[Figure 13-158]* Temporary weights are added to eliminate the wheel from rotating and dropping the heavy side down. Once balanced, permanent weights are installed. Many aircraft wheels have provisions for securing the permanent weight to the wheel. Weights with adhesive designed to be glued to the wheel rim are also in use. Occasionally, a weight in the form of a patch glued to the inside of the tire is required. Follow all manufacturer's instructions and use only the weights specified for the wheel assembly. *[Figure 13-159]*

Figure 13-158. *A typical aircraft tire and wheel balancing stand.*

Some aviation facilities offer dynamic balancing of aircraft tire and wheel assemblies. While this is rarely specified by manufacturers, a well balanced tire and wheel assembly helps provide shimmy free operation and reduces wear on brake and landing gear components, such as torque links.

Operation and Handling Tips

Aircraft tires experience longer life if operated in a manner to conserve wear and minimize damage. The most important factor impinging on tire performance and wear, as well as resistance to damage is proper inflation. Always inflate tires to the specified level before flight for maximum performance and minimal damage. An improperly inflated tire has increased potential to fail upon landing due to the high impact loads experienced. The following sections include other suggestions that can extend the life and the investment made in aircraft tires.

Figure 13-159. *A tire balancing patch (left), adhesive wheel weights (center), and a bolted wheel weight (right) are all used to balance aircraft tire and wheel assemblies per the manufacturer's instructions.*

Taxiing

Needless tire damage and excessive wear can be prevented by proper handling of the aircraft during taxi. Most of the gross weight of an aircraft is on the main landing gear wheels. Aircraft tires are designed and inflated to absorb the shock of landing by deflection of the sidewalls two to three times as much as that found on an automobile tire. While this enables the tire to handle heavy loads, it also causes more working of the tread and produces scuffing action along the outer edges of the tread that results in more rapid wear. It also leaves the tire more prone to damage as the tread compound opens during this flexing.

An aircraft tire that strikes a chuck hole, a stone, or some other foreign object is more likely to sustain a cut, snag, or bruise than an automobile tire due to its more flexible nature. There is also increased risk for internal tire injury when a tire leaves the paved surface of the taxi way. These incidents should be avoided. Dual or multiple wheel main gear should be operated so that all tires remain on the paved surface so the weight of the aircraft is evenly distributed between the tires. When backing an aircraft on a ramp for parking, care should be taken to stop the aircraft before the main wheels roll off of the paved surface.

Taxiing for long distances or at high speeds increase the temperature of aircraft tires. This makes them more susceptible to wear and damage. Short taxi distances at moderate speeds are recommended. Caution should also be used to prevent riding the brakes while taxiing, which adds unnecessary heat to the tires.

Braking and Pivoting

Heavy use of aircraft brakes introduces heat into the tires. Sharp radius turns do the same and increase tread abrasion and side loads on the tire. Plan ahead to allow the aircraft to slow without heavy braking and make large radius turns to avoid these conditions. Objects under a tire are ground into the tread during a pivot. Since many aircraft are primarily maneuvered on the ground via differential braking, efforts should be made to always keep the inside wheel moving during a turn rather than pivoting the aircraft with a locked brake around a fixed main wheel tire.

Landing Field and Hangar Floor Condition

One of the main contributions made to the welfare of aircraft tires is good upkeep of airport runway and taxiway surfaces, as well as all ramp areas and hangar floors. While the technician has little input into runway and taxiway surface upkeep, known defects in the paved surfaces can be avoided and rough surfaces can be negotiated at slower than normal speeds to minimize tire damage. Ramps and hangar floors should be kept free of all foreign objects that may cause tire damage. This requires continuous diligence on the part of all aviation personnel. Do not ignore foreign object damage (FOD). When discovered, action must be taken to remove it. While FOD to engines and propellers gains significant attention, much damage to tires is avoidable if ramp areas and hangar floors are kept clean.

Takeoffs and Landings

Aircraft tires are under severe strain during takeoff and landing. Under normal conditions, with proper control and maintenance of the tires, they are able to withstand these stresses and perform as designed.

Most tire failures occur during takeoff which can be extremely dangerous. Tire damage on takeoff is often the result of running over some foreign object. Thorough preflight inspection of the tires and wheels, as well as maintenance of hangar and ramp surfaces free of foreign objects, are keys to prevention of takeoff tire failure. A flat spot caused on the way to the runway may lead to tire failure during takeoff. Heavy braking during aborted takeoffs is also a common cause of takeoff tire failure. *[Figure 13-160]*

Figure 13-160. *Heavy braking during an aborted takeoff caused these tires to fail.*

Tire failure upon landing can have several causes. Landing with the brakes on is one. This is mitigated on aircraft with anti-skid systems, but can occur on other aircraft. Other errors in judgment, such as landing too far down the runway and having to apply the brakes heavily, can cause overheating or skidding. This can lead to flat-spotting the tires or blow out.

Hydroplaning

Skidding on a wet, icy, or dry runway is accompanied by the threat of tire failure due to heat build-up and rapid tire wear damage. Hydroplaning on a wet runway may be overlooked as a damaging condition for a tire. Water building up in front of the tire provides a surface for the tire to run on and contact with the runway surface is lost. This is known as dynamic hydroplaning. Steering ability and braking action is also lost. A skid results if the brakes are applied and held.

Viscous hydroplaning occurs on runways with a thin film of water that mixes with contaminants to cause an extremely slick condition. This can also happen on a very smooth runway surface. A tire with a locked brake during viscous hydroplaning can form an area of reverted rubber or skid burn in the tread. While the tire may continue in service if the damage is not too severe, it can be cause for removal if the reinforcing tread or protector ply is penetrated. The same damage can occur while skidding on ice.

Modern runways are designed to drain water rapidly and provide good traction for tires in wet conditions. A compromise exists in that crosscut runways and textured runway surfaces cause tires to wear at a greater rate than a smooth runway. *[Figure 13-161]* A smooth landing is of great benefit to any tire. Much aircraft tire handling and care is the responsibility of the pilot. However, the technician benefits from knowing the causes of tire failure and communicating this knowledge to the flight crew so that operating procedures can be modified to avoid those causes.

Figure 13-161. *Crosscut runway surfaces drain water rapidly but increase tire wear*

Chapter 14
Aircraft Fuel System

Basic Fuel System Requirements

All powered aircraft require fuel on board to operate the engine(s). A fuel system consisting of storage tanks, pumps, filters, valves, fuel lines, metering devices, and monitoring devices is designed and certified under strict Title 14 of the Code of Federal Regulations (14 CFR) guidelines. Each system must provide an uninterrupted flow of contaminant-free fuel regardless of the aircraft's attitude. Since fuel load can be a significant portion of the aircraft's weight, a sufficiently strong airframe must be designed. Varying fuel loads and shifts in weight during maneuvers must not negatively affect control of the aircraft in flight.

Each Federal Aviation Administration (FAA) certified aircraft is designed and constructed under FARs applicable to that type of aircraft. The certification airworthiness standards are found in 14 CFR as follows:

14 Part 23—Normal, Utility, Acrobatic, and Commuter Category Airplanes

14 Part 25—Transport Category Airplanes

14 Part 27—Normal Category Rotorcraft

14 Part 29—Transport Category Rotorcraft

14 Part 31—Manned Free Balloons

Additional information is found in 14 CFR part 33. It addresses airworthiness standards for engines and pertains mainly to engine fuel filter and intake requirements.

Under each 14 CFR part for a specific aircraft to be certified, paragraphs 951 through 1001 address very specific design criteria required to ensure the fuel system functions properly. These paragraphs from 14 CFR part 23, Normal, Utility, Acrobatic, and Commuter Category Airplanes, are summarized below. Airworthiness standards specified for air carrier and helicopter certification are similar. Although the technician is rarely involved with designing fuel systems, a review of these criteria gives insight into how an aircraft fuel system operates.

Each fuel system must be constructed and arranged to ensure fuel flow at a rate and pressure established for proper engine and auxiliary power unit (APU) functioning under each likely operating condition. This includes any maneuver for which certification is requested and during which the engine or APU may be in operation. *[Figure 14-1]* Each fuel system must be arranged so that no fuel pump can draw fuel from more than one tank at a time. There must also be a means to prevent the introduction of air into the system.

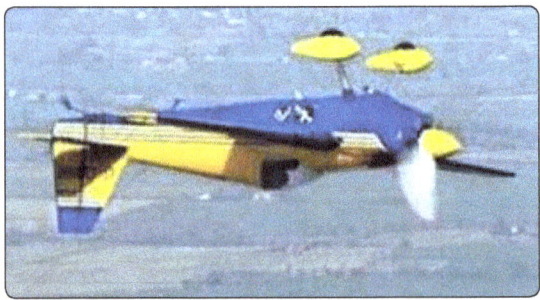

Figure 14-1. *Aircraft fuel systems must deliver fuel during any maneuver for which the aircraft is certified.*

Each fuel system for a turbine engine powered airplane must meet applicable fuel venting requirements. 14 CFR part 34 outlines requirements that fall under the jurisdiction of the Environmental Protection Agency (EPA). A turbine engine fuel system must be capable of sustained operation throughout its flow and pressure range even though the fuel has some water in it. The standard is that the engine continues to run using fuel initially saturated with water at 80 °F having 0.75 cubic centimeters (cm) of free water per gallon added to it and then cooled to the most critical condition for icing likely to be encountered in operation.

Fuel System Independence

Each fuel system for a multiengine airplane must be arranged so that, in at least one system configuration, the failure of any one component (other than a fuel tank) does not result in the loss of power of more than one engine or require immediate action by the pilot to prevent the loss of power of more than one engine.

If a single fuel tank (or series of fuel tanks interconnected to function as a single fuel tank) is used on a multiengine airplane, independent tank outlets for each engine, each incorporating a shut-off valve at the tank, must be provided. The shutoff valves may serve as firewall shutoff valves, which are also required. However, note that if the line between the valve and the engine compartment contains more than one quart of fuel (or any greater amount shown to be safe) that can escape into the engine compartment, an additional firewall shutoff valve is needed. Lines and any components from each tank outlet to each engine must be completely independent of each other.

The fuel tank must have at least two vents arranged to minimize the probability of both vents becoming obstructed simultaneously. The filler caps must be designed to minimize the probability of incorrect installation or in-flight loss.

Fuel System Lightning Protection

The fuel system must be designed and arranged to prevent the ignition of fuel vapor within the system by direct lightning strikes or swept lightning strokes (where highly probable). Swept strokes occur when the lightning strike is deformed by interaction with aerodynamic forces and propagates in a unique manner due to the material and shape of the airframe surfaces. Corona and streamering must also be inhibited at fuel vent outlets since they may ignite the fuel-air mixture. A corona is a luminous discharge that occurs as a result of an electrical potential difference between the aircraft and the surrounding area. Streamering is a branch-like ionized path that occurs in the presence of a direct stroke or under conditions when lightning strokes are imminent. *[Figure 14-2]*

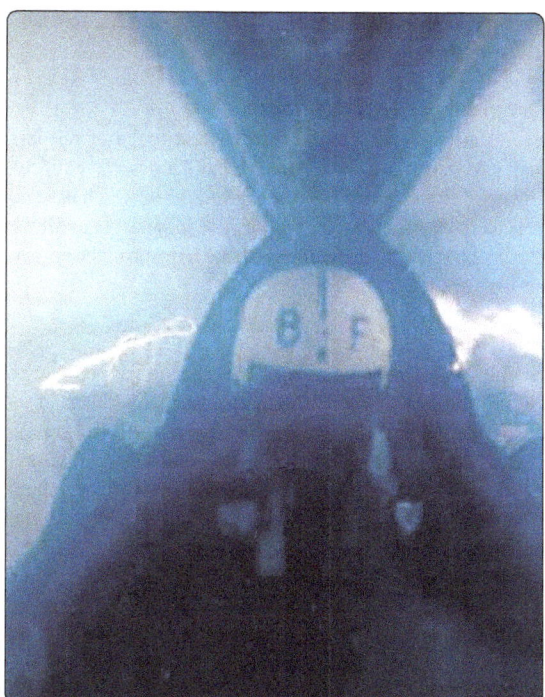

Figure 14-2. *Lightning streamering at the wingtips of a jet fighter.*

Fuel Flow

The ability of the fuel system to provide fuel at a rate of flow and pressure sufficient for proper engine operation is vital in aircraft. Moreover, the fuel system must deliver the fuel at the aircraft attitude that is most critical with respect to fuel feed and quantity of unusable fuel. Tests are performed to demonstrate this performance. Fuel flowmeters are installed on most aircraft. During testing, the flowmeter is blocked and fuel must flow through or bypass the meter and still supply the engine at sufficient rate and pressure.

For gravity-flow fuel systems, the fuel flow rate must be 150 percent of the takeoff fuel consumption of the engine. For fuel pump systems, the fuel flow rate for each pump system (main and reserve supply) for each reciprocating engine must be 125 percent of the fuel flow required by the engine at the maximum takeoff power. However, the fuel pressure, with main and emergency pumps operating simultaneously, must not exceed the fuel inlet pressure limits of the engine. Auxiliary fuel systems and fuel transfer systems may operate under slightly different parameters. Turbine engine fuel systems must provide at least 100 percent required by the engine under each intended operating condition and maneuver.

On aircraft with multiple fuel tanks, performance is monitored when switching to a new tank once fuel has been depleted from a tank. For reciprocating, naturally aspirated, single-engine aircraft in level flight, 75 percent maximum continuous power must be obtainable in not more than 10 seconds. For turbocharged aircraft, 20 seconds is allowed. Twenty seconds is also allowed on multiengine aircraft.

Flow Between Interconnected Tanks

In a gravity feed fuel system with interconnected tank outlets, it must be impossible for enough fuel to flow between the tanks to cause an overflow of fuel from any tank vent under the conditions in 14 CFR part 23, section 23.959. If fuel can be pumped from one tank to another in flight, the fuel tank vents and the fuel transfer system must be designed so that no structural damage to any airplane component can occur because of overfilling of any tank.

Unusable Fuel Supply

The unusable fuel supply for each tank must be established. It cannot be less than that quantity at which the first evidence of malfunctioning appears under the most adverse fuel feed condition occurring under each intended operation and flight maneuver involving that tank. The effect on the usable fuel quantity as a result of a failure of any pump is also determined.

Fuel System Hot Weather Operation

Each fuel system must be free from vapor lock when using fuel at its critical temperature, with respect to vapor formation, when operating the airplane in all critical operating and environmental conditions for which approval is requested. For turbine fuel, the critical temperature must be 110 °F, −0°, +5 °F or the maximum outside air temperature for which approval is requested, whichever is more critical.

Fuel Tanks

Each fuel tank must be able to withstand, without failure, the vibration, inertia, fluid, and structural loads to which it may be subjected in operation. Fuel tanks with flexible liners must demonstrate that the liner is suitable for the particular application. The total usable capacity of any tank(s) must be enough for at least 30 minutes of operation at maximum continuous power. Each integral fuel tank must have adequate facilities for interior inspection and repair. Additionally, each fuel quantity indicator must be adjusted to account for the unusable fuel supply.

Fuel Tank Tests

Aircraft fuel tanks must be able to withstand the forces that are encountered throughout the entire spectrum of operation. Various tank testing standards exist. A main focus is to ensure that tanks are strong enough to remain fully operational and not deform when under various loads. Vibration resistance without leaking is also a concern. Tanks are tested under the most critical condition that may be encountered. Fuel tank supporting structure must be designed for the critical loads that could occur during flight or when landing with fuel pressure loads.

Fuel Tank Installation

Various standards exist for fuel tank installations. No fuel tank may be on the engine side of a firewall, and there must be at least ½-inch of clearance between the fuel tank and the firewall. Each tank must be isolated from personnel compartments of the aircraft by a fume-proof and fuel-proof enclosure that is vented and drained to the exterior of the airplane. Pressurization loads should not affect the tank(s). Each tank compartment must be ventilated and drained to prevent the accumulation of flammable fluids or vapors. Compartments adjacent to tanks must also be ventilated and drained.

Aircraft fuel tanks must be designed, located, and installed to retain fuel when subjected to inertia loads resulting from ultimate static load factors, and under conditions likely to occur when the airplane lands on a paved runway at a normal landing speed with the landing gear retracted. They must also retain fuel if one of the gear collapses or if an engine mount tears away. *[Figure 14-3]*

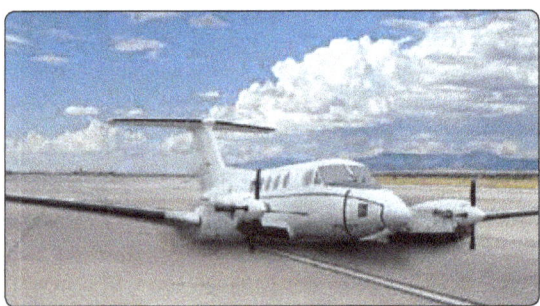

Figure 14-3. *Aircraft fuel tanks must be designed to retain fuel in the event of a gear-up landing. The fuel system drain valve should be located to prevent spillage.*

Many aircraft have fuel tanks that are not metal. Bladder fuel tanks have their own standards of construction and installation. As with metal tanks, there must be pads to prevent any chafing between each tank and its supports. The padding must be nonabsorbent or treated to prevent the absorption of fuel. Bladders must be supported so they are not required to support the entire fuel load. Surfaces adjacent to the liner must be smooth and free from projections that could cause wear. A positive pressure must be maintained within the vapor space of each bladder cell under any condition of operation, or it should be shown not to collapse under zero or negative pressure. Siphoning of fuel or collapse of bladder fuel cells should not result from improper securing or loss of the fuel filler cap. Bladder-type fuel cells must have a retaining shell at least equivalent to a metal fuel tank in structural integrity.

Fuel Tank Expansion Space

Each fuel tank must have an expansion space of not less than two percent of the tank capacity. This is waved if the tank vent discharges clear of the airplane, in which case no expansion space is required. It must be impossible to fill the expansion space inadvertently with the airplane in the normal ground attitude.

Fuel Tank Sump

Keeping contaminants out of the fuel delivered to the engine begins with the proper construction and installation of the fuel tank(s). Each tank must have a drainable sump with an effective capacity, in the normal ground and flight attitudes, of 0.25 percent of the tank capacity, or $^1\!/_{16}$ gallon, whichever is greater. Each fuel tank must allow drainage of any hazardous quantity of water from any part of the tank to its sump with the airplane in the normal ground attitude. Reciprocating engine fuel systems must have a sediment bowl or chamber that is accessible for drainage. Its capacity must be 1 ounce for every 20 gallons of fuel on board. Each fuel tank outlet must be located so that water drains from all parts of the tank, except the sump, to the sediment bowl or chamber in the normal flight attitude.

Fuel Tank Filler Connection

Each fuel tank filler connection must be specifically marked. Aircraft with engines that use only gasoline fuel must have filler openings no larger than 2.36 inches in diameter. Turbine fuel aircraft filler openings must be no smaller than 2.95 inches. Spilled fuel must not enter the fuel tank compartment or any part of the airplane other than the tank itself. Each filler cap must provide a fuel-tight seal for the main filler opening. However, there may be small openings in the fuel tank cap for venting purposes or for the purpose of allowing passage of a fuel gauge through the cap. Fuel filling points must have a provision for electrically bonding the airplane to ground fueling equipment (except pressure fueling connection points).

Fuel Tank Vents and Carburetor Vapor Vents

To allow proper fuel flow, each fuel tank must be vented from the top part of the expansion space. Vent outlets must be located and constructed in a manner that minimizes the possibility of being obstructed by ice or other foreign matter. Siphoning of fuel during normal operation must not occur. Venting capacity must allow the rapid relief of excessive differences of pressure between the interior and exterior of the tank. The airspaces of tanks with interconnected outlets must also be interconnected. There must be no point in any vent line where moisture can accumulate either on the ground or during level flight (unless drainage is provided by an accessible drain valve).

Fuel tank vents may not terminate at a point where the discharge of fuel from the vent outlet constitutes a fire hazard or from which fumes may enter personnel compartments. The vents must be arranged to prevent the loss of fuel when the airplane is parked in any direction on a ramp having a one-percent slope. Fuel discharged because of thermal expansion is allowed.

Each carburetor with vapor elimination connections and each fuel injection engine employing vapor return provisions must have a separate vent line to lead vapors back to the top of one of the fuel tanks. If there is more than one tank and it is necessary to use these tanks in a definite sequence for any reason, the vapor vent line must lead back to the fuel tank to be used first, unless the relative capacities of the tanks are such that return to another tank is preferable.

For acrobatic category airplanes, excessive loss of fuel during acrobatic maneuvers, including short periods of inverted flight, must be prevented. It must be impossible for fuel to siphon from the vent when normal flight has been resumed after any acrobatic maneuver for which certification is requested.

Fuel Tank Outlet

There must be a fuel strainer for the fuel tank outlet or for the booster pump. On reciprocating-engine aircraft, the strainer must have 8 to 16 meshes per inch. The clear area of each fuel tank outlet strainer must be at least five times the area of the outlet line and the strainer diameter must be at least that of the fuel tank outlet. It must also be accessible for inspection and cleaning. Turbine-engine aircraft fuel strainers must prevent the passage of any object that could restrict fuel flow or damage any fuel system component.

Pressure Fueling Systems

Pressure fueling systems are used on many large, high-performance, and air carrier aircraft. Each pressure fueling system fuel manifold connection must have means to prevent the escape of hazardous quantities of fuel from the system if the fuel entry valve fails. A means for automatic shutoff must be provided to prevent the quantity of fuel in each tank from exceeding the maximum quantity approved for that tank. A means must also be provided to prevent damage to the fuel system in the event of failure of the automatic shutoff means prescribed in this section. All parts of the fuel system up to the tank that are subjected to fueling pressures must have a proof pressure of 1.33 times and an ultimate pressure of at least 2.0 times the surge pressure likely to occur during fueling.

Fuel Pumps

Fuel pumps are part of most aircraft fuel systems. Standards exist for main pumps and emergency pumps. Operation of any fuel pump may not affect engine operation by creating a hazard, regardless of the engine power or thrust setting or the functional status of any other fuel pump. On reciprocating engines, one main fuel pump must be engine-driven and there must be at least one for each engine. Turbine engines also require dedicated fuel pumps for each engine. Any pump required for operation is considered a main fuel pump. The power supply for the main pump for each engine must be independent of the power supply for each main pump for any other engine. There must also be a bypass feature for each positive displacement pump.

Emergency pumps are used and must be immediately available to supply fuel to the engine if any main pump fails. The power supply for each emergency pump must be independent of the power supply for each corresponding main pump. If both the main fuel pump and the emergency pump operate continuously, there must be a means to indicate a malfunction of either pump to the appropriate flight crew member.

Fuel System Lines and Fittings

Even aircraft fuel system fluid lines and fittings have standards to ensure proper fuel system operation. Each fuel line must be installed and supported to prevent excessive vibration and to withstand loads due to fuel pressure and accelerated flight conditions. Lines connected to components of the airplane, between which relative motion could exist, must have provisions for flexibility. Flexible hose assemblies are used when lines may be under pressure and subject to axial loads. Any hose that is used must be shown to be suitable for a particular application. Where high temperatures may exist during engine operation or after shutdown, fuel hoses must be capable of withstanding these temperatures.

Fuel System Components

Fuel system components in an engine nacelle or in the fuselage must be protected from damage that could result in spillage of enough fuel to constitute a fire hazard as a result of a wheels-up landing on a paved runway.

Fuel Valves and Controls

There must be a means to allow appropriate flight crew members to rapidly shut off the fuel to each engine individually in flight. No shutoff valve may be on the engine side of any firewall. There must be means to guard against inadvertent operation of each shutoff valve and means to reopen each valve rapidly after it has been closed. Each valve and fuel system control must be supported so that loads resulting from its operation, or from accelerated flight conditions, are not transmitted to the lines connected to the valve. Gravity and vibration should not affect the selected position of any valve.

Fuel valve handles and their connections to valve mechanisms must have design features that minimize the possibility of incorrect installation. Check valves must be constructed to preclude incorrect assembly or connection of the valve. Fuel tank selector valves must require a separate and distinct action to place the selector in the OFF position. The tank selector positions must be located in such a manner that it is impossible for the selector to pass through the OFF position when changing from one tank to another.

Fuel Strainer or Filter

In addition to fuel tank strainers already discussed, there must be a fuel strainer, or filter, between the fuel tank outlet and the inlet of either the fuel metering device or an engine-driven positive displacement pump, whichever is nearer the fuel tank outlet. This fuel strainer, or filter, must be accessible for draining and cleaning and must incorporate a screen or element that is easily removable. The fuel strainer should have a sediment trap and drain, except that it need not have a drain if the strainer or filter is easily removable for drain purposes. The fuel strainer should also be mounted so that its weight is not supported by the connecting lines. It should have the capacity to ensure that engine fuel system function is not impaired when fuel is contaminated to a degree that is greater than that established for the engine during its type certification. Commuter category airplanes must have a means to automatically maintain the fuel flow if ice clogs a filter.

Fuel System Drains

Aircraft fuel systems must be fitted with at least one drain to allow safe drainage of the entire fuel system with the airplane in its normal ground attitude. The drain must discharge the fuel clear of all parts of the aircraft. A readily accessible drain valve that can easily be opened and closed is required. It must have a manual or automatic means for locking in the closed position, and it must be observable that it is closed. Fuel should be collectible from the system drain valve so it can be examined. The location of the valve should be such that spillage is prevented should a gear up landing be made.

Fuel Jettisoning System

If an aircraft's design landing weight is less than that of the maximum takeoff weight, a situation could occur in which a landing is desired before sufficient fuel has burned off to lighten the aircraft. Fuel jettisoning systems are required on these aircraft so that fuel can be jettisoned in flight to avoid structural damage cause by landing the aircraft when it is too heavy. Fuel jettisoning systems are also referred to as fuel dump systems. *[Figure 14-4]*

Figure 14-4. *The fuel jettison panel on a Boeing 767.*

Fuel jettisoning systems must meet several standards. The average rate of fuel jettisoning must be at least 1 percent of the maximum weight per minute, except that the time required to jettison the fuel need not be less than 10 minutes. Fuel jettisoning must be demonstrated at maximum weight with flaps and landing gear up and in a power-off glide at $1.4\,VS_1$. It must also be demonstrated during a climb with a critical engine inoperative and the remaining engines at maximum continuous power. Finally, the fuel jettisoning system must be performed during level flight at $1.4\,VS_1$ if the glide and climb tests show that this condition could be critical.

During the demonstration of the fuel jettisoning system, it must demonstrate that it operates without fire hazard. No fuel or fumes can enter any part of the aircraft. The fuel must discharge clear of any part of the aircraft and the jettisoning operation must not adversely affect the controllability of the airplane. *[Figure 14-5]* The system must be designed so that any reasonably probable single malfunction in the system does not result in a hazardous condition due to unsymmetrical jettisoning of, or inability to jettison, fuel. The fuel jettisoning valve must be designed to allow flight crewmembers to close the valve during any part of the jettisoning operation.

Figure 14-5. *Fuel being jettisoned free of the airframe on a transport category aircraft.*

On reciprocating-engine aircraft, the jettisoning system must be designed so that it is not possible to jettison the fuel in the tanks used for takeoff and landing below the level allowing 45 minutes of flight at 75 percent maximum continuous power. However, if there is an auxiliary control independent of the main jettisoning control, the system may be designed to jettison all the fuel. For turbine engine powered airplanes, the jettisoning system must be designed so that it is not possible to jettison fuel from the tanks used for takeoff and landing below the fuel level that would allow climb from sea level to 10,000 feet plus 45 minutes cruise at a speed for maximum range. If certain flight control configurations negatively affect jettisoning the fuel, a placard stating so must be posted next to the actuation control in the cockpit.

Types of Aviation Fuel

Each aircraft engine is designed to burn a certain fuel. Use only the fuel specified by the manufacturer. Mixing fuels is not permitted. There are two basic types of fuel discussed in this section: reciprocating-engine fuel (also known as gasoline or AVGAS) and turbine-engine fuel (also known as jet fuel or kerosene).

Reciprocating Engine Fuel—AVGAS

Reciprocating engines burn gasoline, also known as AVGAS. It is specially formulated for use in aircraft engines. Combustion releases energy in the fuel, which is converted into the mechanical motion of the engine. AVGAS of any variety is primarily a hydrocarbon compound refined from crude oil by fractional distillation. Aviation gasoline is different from the fuel refined for use in turbine-powered aircraft. AVGAS is very volatile and extremely flammable, with a low flash point. Turbine fuel is a kerosene-type fuel with a much higher flash point so it is less flammable.

Aircraft engines must perform throughout a wide range of demanding conditions. They must be lightweight and produce significant power in a wide range of atmospheric and engine operating temperatures. The gasoline used must support uninterrupted combustion throughout this range and must truly burn rather than explode or detonate. This ensures maximum power derivation and minimal engine wear. Over the years, AVGAS has been available in different formulas. These mostly correlate to how much energy can be produced without the fuel detonating. Larger, high-compression engines require fuel with a greater amount of potential power production without detonation than smaller low-compression engines.

Volatility

One of the most important characteristics of an aircraft fuel is its volatility. Volatility is a term used to describe how readily a substance changes from liquid into a vapor. For reciprocating engines, highly volatile fuel is desired. Liquid gasoline delivered to the engine induction system carburetor must vaporize in the carburetor to burn in the engine. Fuel with low volatility vaporizes slowly. This can cause hard engine starting, slow warm-up, and poor acceleration. It can also cause uneven fuel distribution to the cylinders and excessive dilution of the oil in the crankcase in engines equipped with oil dilution systems. However, fuel can also be too volatile, causing detonation and vapor lock.

AVGAS is a blend of numerous hydrocarbon compounds, each with different boiling points and volatility. A straight chain of volatile compounds creates a fuel that vaporizes easily for starting, but also delivers power through the acceleration and power ranges of the engine.

Vapor Lock

Vapor lock is a condition in which AVGAS vaporizes in the fuel line or other components between the fuel tank and the carburetor. This typically occurs on warm days on aircraft with engine-driven fuel pumps that suck fuel from the tank(s). Vapor lock can be caused by excessively hot fuel, low pressure, or excessive turbulence of the fuel traveling through the fuel system. In each case, liquid fuel vaporizes prematurely and blocks the flow of liquid fuel to the carburetor.

Aircraft gasoline is refined to have a vapor pressure be between 5.5 pounds per square inch (psi) and 7.0 psi at 100 °F. At this pressure, an aircraft fuel system is designed to deliver liquid fuel to the carburetor when drawn out of the tank by an engine-driven fuel pump. But temperatures in the fuel system can exceed 100 °F under the engine cowl on a hot day. Fuel may vaporize before it reaches the carburetor, especially if it is drawn up a line under a low pressure, or if it swirls while navigating a sharp bend in the tubing. To make matters worse, when an aircraft climbs rapidly, the pressure on the fuel in the tank decreases while the fuel is still warm. This causes an increase in fuel vaporization that can also lead to vapor lock.

Various steps can be taken to prevent vapor lock. The use of boost pumps located in the fuel tank that force pressurized liquid fuel to the engine is most common.

Carburetor Icing

As fuel vaporizes, it draws energy from its surroundings to change state from a liquid to a vapor. This can be a problem if water is present. When fuel vaporizes in the carburetor, water in the fuel-air mixture can freeze and deposit inside the carburetor and fuel induction system. The fuel discharge nozzle, throttle valve, venturi, or simply the walls of the induction system all can develop ice. As the ice builds, it restricts the fuel-air flow and causes loss of engine power. In severe cases, the engine stops running. *[Figure 14-6]*

Carburetor icing is most common at ambient temperatures of 30–40 °F but can occur at much higher temperatures, especially in humid conditions. Most aircraft are equipped with carburetor heating to help eliminate this threat caused by the high volatility of the fuel and the presence of moisture. *[Figure 14-7]*

Aromatic Fuels

The aviation gasoline market is a relatively small part of the overall gasoline market. AVGAS producers are few. In years past, when this was less the case, considerable quantities of aromatic hydrocarbons were sometimes added to increase the rich mixture performance of AVGAS. It was used mainly in high horsepower reciprocating engines, such as military and transport category aircraft. Special hoses and seals were required for use of aromatic fuels. These additives are no longer available.

Detonation

Detonation is the rapid, uncontrolled explosion of fuel due to high pressure and temperature in the combustion chamber. The fuel-air charge ignites and explodes before the ignition system spark lights it. Occasionally, detonation occurs when the fuel is ignited via the spark plug but explodes before it is finished burning.

Figure 14-6. *An example of common areas where ice can form on a carburetor. The evaporation of volatile fuel takes energy from its surroundings to change state. As it does, water in the fuel-air mixture condenses and freezes.*

The engine is not designed to withstand the forces caused by detonation. It is made to turn smoothly by having the fuel-air mixture burn in the combustion chamber and propagate directionally across the top of the piston. When it does so, a smooth transfer of the force developed by the burning fuel

Figure 14-7. *To combat carburetor icing, air preheated by the exhaust manifold is directed into the carburetor via a push/pull control in the cockpit. The control changes the position of the air diverter butterfly in the carburetor heat valve box.*

14-8

pushes the piston down. Detonation of fuel instead sends a shock wave of force against the top of the piston, which in turn is transferred through the piston to the piston pin, to the connecting rod, and to the crankshaft. Valve operation is also affected by this shock wave. In short, the explosion of fuel detonating in the combustion chamber transfers the energy contained in the fuel harshly throughout the entire engine, causing damage.

Aviation fuels are refined and blended to avoid detonation. Each has an ignition point and burn speed at specific fuel-air mixture ratios that manufacturers rely on to design engines that can operate without detonation. An engine experiencing detonation in the field should be investigated. A pinging or knocking sound is a sign of detonation. This is often more difficult to detect in an aircraft than in an automobile due to propeller tip noise. Detonation causes an increase in cylinder head temperature.

If ignored or allowed to continue, detonation can eventually lead to engine failure. Causes of detonation include incorrect fuel, already high engine temperature at high power settings, such as takeoff, preignition of the fuel, extended operations with an extremely lean mixture, and operation at high revolutions per minute (rpm) with low airspeed.

Surface Ignition and Preignition

A sharp deposit or incandescent hot spot in the combustion chamber can cause fuel to ignite before the spark plug lights it. Detonation can cause such an area to form as can a cracked spark plug insulator or a sharp valve edge. The result could be ignition of the fuel before the piston is at the proper place during its movement toward top dead center of the compression stroke. The extended burn period of the fuel can increase temperatures and pressure in the combustion chamber to the point at which the fuel detonates. The repeated incorrect flame propagation and detonation can cause serious engine damage and eventual engine failure. *[Figure 14-8]*

Maintenance personnel should ensure that the correct fuel is being used, and that the engine is being operated correctly. Spark plugs and valves should be checked for wear. Signs of deposits and detonation must also be investigated and addressed.

Octane and Performance Number Rating

Octane ratings and performance numbers are given to fuels to describe their resistance to detonation. Fuels with high critical pressure and high octane or performance numbers have the greatest resistance. A referencing system is used to rate the fuel. A mixture of two hydrocarbons, iso-octane (C_8H_{18}) and heptane (C_7H_{16}), is used. Various ratios of the two hydrocarbons in a mixture result in proportional

Figure 14-8. *Preignition can cause detonation and damage to the engine.*

antidetonation properties. The more iso-octane there is in the mixture, the higher its resistance is to detonation.

When a fuel has the same critical pressure as a reference mixture of these two hydrocarbons, it is said to have an octane rating that is the same as the percentage of the iso-octane is this reference mixture. An 80 octane fuel has the same resistance to detonation as an 80 percent iso-octane, 20 percent heptane mixture; a 90 octane fuel has the same resistance to detonation as a 90 percent iso-octane, 10 percent heptane mixture; and a 100 octane fuel has the same resistance to detonation as 100 percent pure iso-octane. So, by comparing a fuel's tendency to detonate to reference mixtures of iso-octane and heptane, octane ratings from 80 to 100 can be established. The highest octane fuel possible with this system of measurement is 100 octane fuel.

To increase antidetonation characteristics of fuel, substances can be added. Tetraethyl lead (TEL) is the most common additive that increases the critical pressure and temperature of a fuel. However, additional additives, such as ethylene dibromide and tricresyl phosphate, must be also be added so that the TEL does not leave solid deposits in the combustion chamber.

The amount of TEL added to a fuel can be increased to raise the antidetonation characteristics from 80 to the 100 octane level and higher. References to octane characteristics above 100 percent iso-octane are made by referencing the antidetonation properties of the fuel to a mixture of pure iso-octane and specific quantities of TEL. The specific mixtures of iso-octane and TEL are assigned arbitrary octane numbers above 100. In addition to increasing the antidetonation characteristics of a fuel, TEL also lubricates the engine valves.

Performance numbers are also used to characterize the antidetonation characteristics of fuel. A performance number consists of two numbers (e.g., 80/87, 100/130, 115/145) in which higher numbers indicate a higher resistance to detonation. The first number indicates the octane rating of the fuel in a lean fuel-air mixture, and the second number indicates the octane rating of the fuel in a rich mixture.

Due to the small size of the worldwide aviation gasoline market, a single 100 octane low-lead fuel (100LL) is desired as the only AVGAS for all aircraft with reciprocating engines. This presents problems in engines originally designed to run on 80/87 fuel; the low lead 100 octane fuel still contains more lead than the 80 octane fuel. Spark plug fouling has been common and lower times between overhaul have occurred. Other engines designed for 91/96 fuel or 100/130 fuel operate satisfactorily on 100LL, which contains 2 milliliters of TEL per gallon (enough to lubricate the valves and control detonation). For environmental purposes, AVGAS with no TEL is sought for the aviation fleet of the future.

Fuel Identification

Aircraft and engine manufacturers designate approved fuels for each aircraft and engine. Consult manufacturer data and use only those fuel specified therein.

The existence of more than one fuel makes it imperative that fuel be positively identified and never introduced into a fuel system that is not designed for it. The use of dyes in fuel helps aviators monitor fuel type. 100LL AVGAS is the AVGAS most readily available and used in the United States. It is dyed blue. Some 100 octane or 100/130 fuel may still be available, but it is dyed green.

80/87 AVGAS is no longer available. It was dyed red. Many supplemental type certificates have been issued to engine and engine/airframe combinations that permit the use of automobile gasoline in engines originally designed for red AVGAS. A relatively new AVGAS fuel, 82UL (unleaded), has been introduced for use by this group of relatively low compression engines. It is dyed purple.

115/145 AVGAS is a fuel designed for large, high performance reciprocating engines from the World War II era. It is available only by special order from refineries, and is also dyed purple in color.

The color of fuel may be referred to in older maintenance manuals. All grades of jet fuel are colorless or straw colored. This distinguishes them from AVGAS of any kind that contains dye of some color. Should AVGAS fuel not be of a recognizable color, the cause should be investigated.

Some color change may not affect the fuel. Other times, a color change may be a signal that fuels have been mixed or contaminated in some way. Do not release an aircraft for flight with unknown fuel onboard.

Identifying fuel and ensuring the correct fuel is delivered into storage tanks, fuel trucks, and aircraft fuel tanks is a process aided by labeling. Decals and markings using the same colors as the AVGAS colors are used. Delivery trucks and hoses are marked as are aircraft tank fuel caps and fill areas. Jet fuel fill hose nozzles are sized too large to fit into an AVGAS tank fill opening. *Figure 14-9* shows examples of color-coded fuel labeling.

Purity

The use of filters in the various stages of transfer and storage of AVGAS removes most foreign sediment from the fuel. Once in the aircraft fuel tanks, debris should settle into the fuel tank drain sumps to be removed before flight. Filters and strainers in the aircraft fuel system can successfully capture any remaining sediment.

The purity of aviation gasoline is compromised most often by water. Water also settles into the sumps given enough time. However, water is not removed by the aircraft's filters and strainers as easily as solid particles. It can enter the fuel even when the aircraft is parked on the ramp with the fuel caps in place. Air in the tank vapor space above the liquid fuel contains water vapor. Temperature fluctuations cause the water vapor to condense on the inner surface of the tanks and settle into the liquid fuel. Eventually, this settles to the sump, but some can remain in the fuel when the aircraft is to be flown.

Proper procedure for minimizing water entering aircraft fuel is to fill the aircraft fuel tanks immediately after each flight. This minimizes the size of the vapor space above the liquid fuel and the amount of air and associated water vapor present in the tank. When excessive water is drawn into the fuel system, it passes through carburetor jets where it can interrupt the smooth operation of the engine(s).

If water is entrained or dissolved in the fuel, it cannot be removed by draining the sump(s) and filter bowls before flight. However, there may be enough water for icing to be a concern. As the aircraft climbs and fuel is drawn out of the tanks, the fuel supply cools. Entrained and dissolved water in the fuel is forced out of solution and becomes free water. If cool enough, ice crystals form rather than liquid water. These can clog filters and disrupt fuel flow to the engines. Both AVGAS and jet fuel have this type of water impurity issue leading to icing that must be monitored and treated.

Fuel Type and Grade	Color of Fuel	Equipment Control Color	Pipe Banding and Marking	Refueler Decal
AVGAS 82UL	Purple	82UL AVGAS	AVGAS 82UL	82UL / AVGAS
AVGAS 100	Green	100 AVGAS	AVGAS 100	100 / AVGAS
AVGAS 100LL	Blue	100LL AVGAS	AVGAS 100LL	100LL / AVGAS
JET A	Colorless or straw	JET A	JET A	JET A
JET A-1	Colorless or straw	JET A 1	JET A-1	JET A-1
JET B	Colorless or straw	JET B	JET B	JET B

Figure 14-9. *Color coded labeling and markings used on fueling equipment.*

Fuel anti-ice additives can be added to the bulk fuel and also directly into the aircraft fuel tank, usually during refueling. These are basically diethylene glycol solutions that work as antifreeze. They dissolve in free water as it comes out of the fuel and lower its freezing point. *[Figure 14-10]*

Turbine Engine Fuels

Aircraft with turbine engines use a type of fuel different from that of reciprocating aircraft engines. Commonly known as jet fuel, turbine engine fuel is designed for use in turbine engines and should never be mixed with aviation gasoline or introduced into the fuel system of a reciprocating aircraft engine fuel system.

The characteristics of turbine engine fuels are significantly different from those of AVGAS. Turbine engine fuels are hydrocarbon compounds of higher viscosity with much lower volatility and higher boiling points than gasoline. In the distillation process from crude oil, the kerosene cut from which jet fuel is made condenses at a higher temperature than the naphtha or gasoline cuts. The hydrocarbon molecules of turbine engine fuels are composed of more carbon than are in AVGAS. *[Figure 14-11]*

Figure 14-10. *Fuel anti-icing products, such as Prist®, act as antifreeze for any free water in aircraft fuel. They dissolve in the water and lower its freezing point to prevent ice crystals from disrupting fuel flow.*

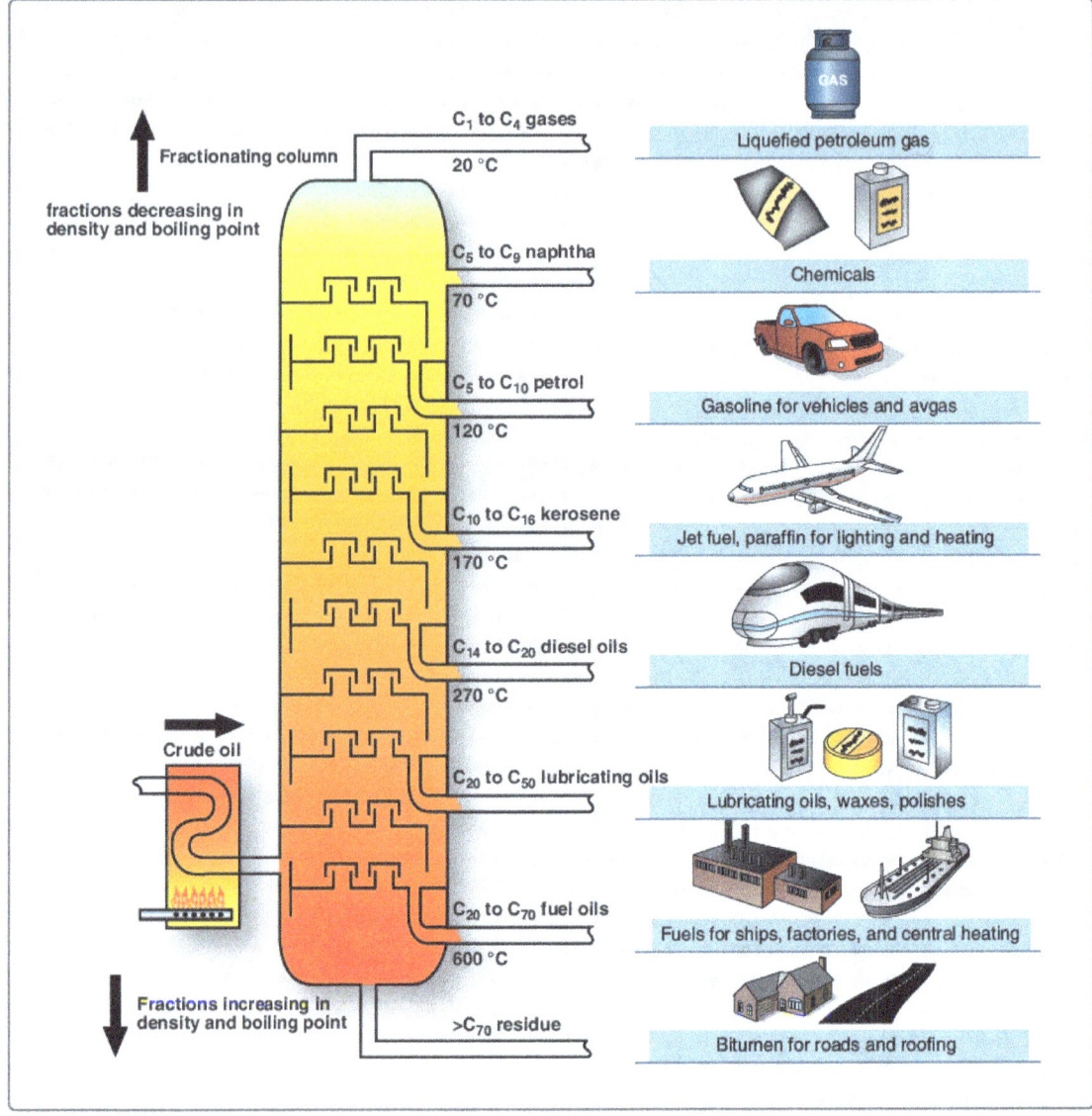

Figure 14-11. *Petroleum products are produced by distillation. Various fractions condense and are collected at different temperatures that correspond to the height of collection in the distillation tower. As can be seen, there are significant differences between turbine engine fuel and ordinary AVGAS.*

Turbine engine fuels sustain a continuous flame inside the engine. They typically have a higher sulfur content than gasoline, and various inhibitors are commonly added them. Used to control corrosion, oxidation, ice, and microbial and bacterial growth, these additives often are already in the fuel when it arrives at the airport for use.

Turbine Fuel Volatility

The choice of turbine engine fuel reflects consideration of conflicting factors. While it is desirable to use a fuel that is low in volatility to resist vapor lock and evaporation while in the aircraft's fuel tanks, turbine engine aircraft operate in cold environments. Turbine engines must start readily, and be able to restart while in flight. Fuel with high volatility makes this easier.

AVGAS has a relatively low maximum vapor pressure compared to automotive gasoline—only 7 psi. But the vapor pressure of Jet A is only 0.125 psi at standard atmospheric conditions. Jet B, a blend of Jet A and gasoline, has higher volatility with a vapor pressure between 2 and 3 psi.

Turbine Engine Fuel Types

Three basic turbine engine fuel types are available worldwide, although some countries have their own unique fuels. The first is Jet A. It is the most common turbine engine fuel available in the continental United States. Globally, Jet A-1 is the most popular. Both Jet A and Jet A-1 are fractionally distilled in the kerosene range. They have low volatility and low vapor pressure. Flashpoints range between 110 °F and 150 °F. Jet A freezes at –40 °F and Jet A-1 freezes at –52.6 °F. Most engine operations manuals permit the use of either Jet A or Jet A-1.

The third basic type of turbine engine fuel available is Jet B. It is a wide-cut fuel that is basically a blend of kerosene and gasoline. Its volatility and vapor pressure reflect this and fall between Jet A and AVGAS. Jet B is primarily available in Alaska and Canada due to its low freezing point of approximately –58 °F, and its higher volatility yields better cold weather performance.

Turbine Engine Fuel Issues

Purity issues related to turbine engine fuels are unique. While AVGAS experiences similar issues of solid particle contamination and icing concerns, the presence of water and fuel-consuming microbes is more prominent in jet fuel, which has different molecular structure and retains water in two principal ways. Some water is dissolved into the fuel. Other water also is entrained in the fuel, which is more viscous than AVGAS. The greater presence of water in jet fuel allows microbes to assemble, grow, and live on the fuel.

Since turbine engine fuels always contain water, microbial contamination is always a threat. The large tanks of many turbine engine aircraft have numerous areas where water can settle and microbes can flourish. Areas between the fuel tank and any water that may come to rest in the bottom of the tanks is where the microbes thrive. These microorganisms form a bio-film that can clog filters, corrode tank coatings, and degrade the fuel. They can be controlled somewhat with the addition of biocides to the fuel. *[Figure 14-12]* Anti-ice additives are also known to inhibit bacterial growth.

Since the microbes are sustained by fuel and water, best practices must be followed to keep the water in fuel to a minimum. Avoid having fuel in a storage tank for a prolonged period of time on or off the aircraft. Drain sumps and monitor the fuel for settled water. Investigate all incidents of water

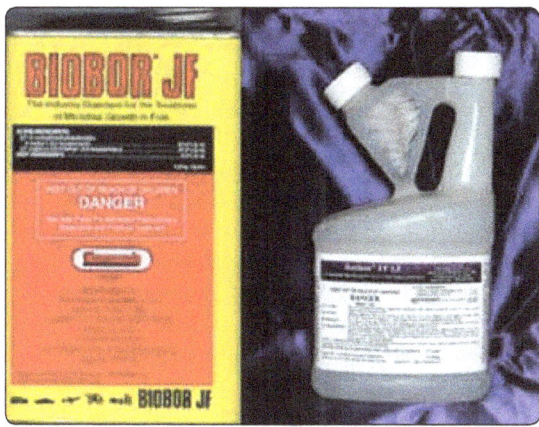

Figure 14-12. *Biocides, such as these, are often added to jet fuel to kill microbes that live on hydrocarbons.*

discovered in the fuel. In addition to water in jet fuel supporting the growth of microorganisms, it also poses a threat of icing. Follow the manufacturer's instructions for fuel handling procedures and fuel system maintenance.

Aircraft Fuel Systems

While each manufacturer designs its own fuel system, the basic fuel system requirements referenced at the beginning of this chapter yield fuel systems of similar design and function in the field. In the following sections are representative examples of various fuel systems in each class of aircraft discussed. Others are similar but not identical. Each aircraft fuel system must store and deliver clean fuel to the engine(s) at a pressure and flow rate able to sustain operations regardless of the operating conditions of the aircraft.

Small Single-Engine Aircraft Fuel Systems

Small single-engine aircraft fuel systems vary depending on factors, such as tank location and method of metering fuel to the engine. A high-wing aircraft fuel system can be designed differently from one on a low-wing aircraft. An aircraft engine with a carburetor has a different fuel system than one with fuel injection.

Gravity Feed Systems

High-wing aircraft with a fuel tank in each wing are common. With the tanks above the engine, gravity is used to deliver the fuel. A simple gravity feed fuel system is shown in *Figure 14-13*. The space above the liquid fuel is vented to maintain atmospheric pressure on the fuel as the tank empties. The two tanks are also vented to each other to ensure equal pressure when both tanks feed the engine. A single screened outlet on each tank feeds lines that connect to either a fuel shutoff valve or multiposition selector valve. The shutoff valve has two positions: fuel ON and fuel OFF. If installed,

Figure 14-13. *The gravity-feed fuel system in a single-engine high-wing aircraft is the simplest aircraft fuel system.*

the selector valve provides four options: fuel shutoff to the engine; fuel feed from the right wing tank only; fuel feed from the left fuel tank only; fuel feed to the engine from both tanks simultaneously.

Downstream of the shutoff valve or selector valve, the fuel passes through a main system strainer. This often has a drain function to remove sediment and water. From there, it flows to the carburetor or to the primer pump for engine starting. Having no fuel pump, the gravity feed system is the simplest aircraft fuel system.

Pump Feed Systems

Low- and mid-wing single reciprocating engine aircraft cannot utilize gravity-feed fuel systems because the fuel tanks are not located above the engine. Instead, one or more pumps are used to move the fuel from the tanks to the engine. A common fuel system of this type is shown in *Figure 14-14*. Each tank has a line from the screened outlet to a selector valve. However, fuel cannot be drawn from both tanks simultaneously; if the fuel is depleted in one tank, the pump would draw air from that tank instead of fuel from the full tank. Since fuel is not drawn from both tanks at the same time, there is no need to connect the tank vent spaces together.

From the selector valve (LEFT, RIGHT, or OFF), fuel flows through the main strainer where it can supply the engine primer. Then, it flows downstream to the fuel pumps. Typically, one electric and one engine-driven fuel pump are arranged in parallel. They draw the fuel from the tank(s) and deliver it to the carburetor. The two pumps provide redundancy. The engine-driven fuel pump acts as the primary pump. The electric pump can supply fuel should the other fail.

Figure 14-14. *A single reciprocating engine aircraft with fuel tanks located in wings below the engine uses pumps to draw fuel from the tanks and deliver it to the engine.*

The electric pump also supplies fuel pressure while starting and is used to prevent vapor lock during flight at high altitude.

High-Wing Aircraft With Fuel Injection System

Some high-wing, high-performance, single-engine general aviation aircraft are equipped with a fuel system that features fuel injection rather than a carburetor. It combines gravity flow with the use of a fuel pump(s). The Teledyne-Continental system is an example. *[Figure 14-15]*

NOTE: Fuel injection systems spray pressurized fuel into the engine intake or directly into the cylinders. Fuel without any air mixed in is required to provide a measured, continuous spray and smooth engine operation.

Fuel pressurized by an engine-driven pump is metered as a function of engine rpm on the Teledyne-Continental system. It is first delivered from the fuel tanks by gravity to two smaller accumulator or reservoir tanks. These tanks, one for each wing tank, consolidate the liquid fuel and have a relatively small airspace. They deliver fuel through a three-way selector valve (LEFT, RIGHT, or OFF). The selector valve also acts simultaneously as a diverter of air that has been separated out of the fuel in the engine-driven fuel pump and returned to the valve. It routes the air to the vent space above the fuel in the selected reservoir tank.

An electric auxiliary fuel pump draws fuel through the selector valve. It forces the fuel through the strainer, making

14-14

The fuel control delivers the fuel to the distribution manifold, which divides it and provides equal, consistent fuel flow for individual fuel injector in each cylinder. *[Figure 14-16]* A fuel flow indicator tapped off of the distribution manifold provides feedback in cockpit. It senses fuel pressure but is displayed on a dial calibrated in gallons per hour.

Figure 14-16. *A fuel distribution manifold for a fuel-injected engine.*

Small Multiengine (Reciprocating) Aircraft Fuel Systems
Low-Wing Twin

The fuel system on a small, multiengine aircraft is more complicated than a single-engine aircraft but contains many of the same elements. An example system used on a low-wing aircraft is illustrated in *Figure 14-17*. It features the main fuel tanks in the wing tips and auxiliary tanks in the wing structure. A boost pump is located at the outlet of each main tank. This pressurizes the entire fuel system from the tank to the injectors eliminating the possibility of vapor lock. An engine can operate with just its boost pump running in the event the engine-driven injection pump fails. Typically, the boost pumps are used to prime and start the engine.

Two selector valves are required on twin-engine aircraft, one for each engine. The right selector valve receives fuel from a main tank on either side of the aircraft and directs it to the right engine. The left selector valve also receives fuel from either main tank and directs it to the left engine. This allows fuel to crossfeed from one side of the aircraft to the opposite engine if desired. The selector valves can also direct fuel from the auxiliary tank to the engine on the same side. Crossfeed of fuel from auxiliary tanks is not possible. From the outlet of the selector valve, fuel flows to the strainer. On some aircraft, the strainer is built into the selector valve unit. From the strainer, fuel flows to the engine-driven fuel pump.

The engine-driven fuel pump is an assembly that also contains a vapor separator and a pressure regulating valve with an adjustment screw. The vapor separator helps

Figure 14-15. *A Teledyne-Continental fuel system featuring fuel injection used on high-wing, high-performance single-engine aircraft.*

it available for the primer pump and the engine-driven fuel pump. This pump is typically used for starting and as a backup should the engine-driven pump fail. It is controlled by a switch in the cockpit and does not need to be operating to allow the engine driven fuel pump access to the fuel.

The engine-driven fuel pump intakes the pressurized fuel from the electrically driven pump or from the reservoir tanks if the electric pump is not operating. It supplies a higher-than-needed volume of fuel under pressure to the fuel control. Excess fuel is returned to the pump, which pumps it through the selector valve into the appropriate reservoir tank. Fuel vapor is also returned to tanks by the pump. The fuel control unit meters the fuel according to engine rpm and mixture control inputs from the cockpit.

Figure 14-17. *A low-wing, twin-engine, light aircraft fuel system.*

eliminate air from the fuel. It returns a small amount of fuel and any vapor present back to the main fuel tank. The pump supplies pressurized fuel to the fuel control. The fuel control, one for each engine, responds to throttle and mixture control settings from the cockpit and supplies the proper amount of fuel to the fuel manifold. The manifold divides the fuel and sends it to an injector in each cylinder. A fuel pressure gauge is placed between the fuel control unit outlet and the manifold to monitor the injector-applied pressure that indicates engine power.

High-Wing Twin

A simplified system on a high-wing, twin-engine aircraft that combines gravity feed with an electric fuel pump is illustrated in *Figure 14-18*. Directly downstream of the selector valves are the fuel strainers and then an electric fuel pump for each engine. This pump draws fuel from the selected tank and sends it under pressure to the inlet side of the fuel injection metering unit. The metering unit for each engine provides the proper flow of fuel to the distribution manifold which feeds the injectors.

Large Reciprocating-Engine Aircraft Fuel Systems

Large, multiengine transport aircraft powered by reciprocating radial engines are no longer produced. However, many are still in operation. They are mostly carbureted and share many features with the light aircraft systems previously discussed.

Figure 14-18. *A simple high-wing fuel injection fuel system for a light twin reciprocating-engine aircraft.*

Figure 14-19 shows the fuel system of a DC-3. A selector valve for each engine allows an engine-driven pump to pull fuel from the main tank or an auxiliary tank. The fuel passes through a strainer before reaching the pump where it is delivered to the engine. The outlet of the pump can feed either engine through the use of a crossfeed line with valves controlled in the cockpit. A hand-operated wobble pump located upstream of the strainer is used to prime the system for starting. Fuel vapor lines run from the pressure carburetor to the vent space in the main and auxilliary tanks. Fuel pressure gauges are tapped off of the carburetor for power indication.

The hand-operated wobble pumps were replaced by electric pumps on later model aircraft. A fuel pressure warning light tapped in downstream of the engine-driven fuel pump alerts the crew should fuel pressure decline.

Not all large, old aircraft have this fuel system. This is merely an example. Others aircraft share similar features and possess unique features of their own. The same is true for small reciprocating-engine aircraft. There are many systems that share features with those described above, but they also differ in some ways. Always consult the manufacturer's data when working on aircraft fuel systems and follow all instructions for service and repair. The fuel system of an aircraft provides the life blood for engine operation and must be maintained with the highest discretion.

Jet Transport Aircraft Fuel Systems

Fuel systems on large transport category jet aircraft are complex with some features and components not found in reciprocating-engine aircraft fuel systems. They typically contain more redundancy and facilitate numerous options from which the crew can choose while managing the aircraft's fuel load. Features like an onboard APU, single point pressure refueling, and fuel jettison systems, which are not needed on smaller aircraft, add to the complexity of an airliner fuel system.

Jet transport fuel systems can be regarded as a handful of fuel subsystems as follows:

1. Storage
2. Vent
3. Distribution
4. Feed
5. Indicating

Most transport category aircraft fuel systems are very much alike. Integral fuel tanks are the norm with much of each wing's structure sealed to enable its use as a fuel tank. Center wing section or fuselage tanks are also common. These may be sealed structure or bladder type. Jet transport aircraft carry tens of thousands of pounds of fuel on board. *Figure 14-20* shows a diagram of a Boeing 777 fuel tank configuration with tank capacities.

Note that there are optional fuel storage configurations available on the same model airliner. For example, airlines expecting to use an aircraft on transoceanic flights may order the aircraft with long-range auxiliary tanks. These

Figure 14-19. *DC-3 fuel system.*

additional tanks, usually located in the fuselage section of the aircraft, can alter fuel management logistics in addition to complicating the fuel system.

In addition to main and auxiliary fuel tanks, surge tanks may also be found on jet transports. These normally empty tanks located in the wing structure outboard of the main wing tanks are used for fuel overflow. A check valve allows the one-way drainage of fuel back into the main tanks. Surge tanks are also use for fuel system venting.

Transport category fuel systems require venting similar to reciprocating engine aircraft fuel systems. A series of vent tubing and channels exists that connects all tanks to vent space in the surge tanks (if present) or vent overboard. Venting must be configured to ensure the fuel is vented regardless of the attitude of the aircraft or the quantity of fuel on board. This sometimes requires the installation of various check valves, float valves, and multiple vent locations in the same tank. *Figure 14-21* shows the fuel vent system of a Boeing 737.

A transport category aircraft fuel distribution subsystem consists of the pressure fueling components, defueling components, transfer system, and fuel jettison or dump system. Single-point pressure fueling at a fueling station

Tank	Gallons	Pounds*
Left main tank	9,560	64,000
Right main tank	9,560	64,000
Center tank	26,100	174,900
Total	45,200	302,900

* Usable fuel at level attitude
Fuel density = 6.7 pounds per U.S. gallon.

Figure 14-20. *Boeing 777 fuel tank locations and capacities.*

Figure 14-21. *A fuel vent system with associated float and check valves that stop fuel and keep the tanks vented regardless of the aircraft attitude.*

14-19

accessible by ramp refueling trucks allows all aircraft fuel tanks to be filled with one connection of the fuel hose. Leading and trailing edge wing locations are common for these stations. *Figure 14-22* shows an airliner fueling station with the fueling rig attached.

Figure 14-22. *A central pressure refueling station on a transport category aircraft allows all fuel tanks to be filled from one position.*

To fuel with pressure refueling, a hose nozzle is attached at the fueling station and valves to the tanks required to be filled are opened. These valves are called fueling valves or refueling valves depending upon the manufacturer's preference. Various automatic shutoff systems have been designed to close tank fueling valves before the tanks overfill or are damaged. Gauges on the refueling panel allow refueling personnel to monitor progress.

Occasionally, defueling the aircraft is required for an inspection or repair. The same fueling station is used, and the hose from the fuel truck is connected to same receptacle used to fuel the aircraft. To allow fuel to exit the aircraft, a defueling valve is opened. Fuel can either be pumped out of the aircraft using the boost pumps located in the tanks that need to be emptied, or the pump in the refueling truck can be used to draw the fuel out of the tanks. Control over the operation is maintained by positioning various shutoff and crossfeed valves, as well as the defuel valve so that fuel travels from the tank to the fueling station and into the truck. The fuel transfer system is a series of plumbing and valves that permits movement of fuel from one tank to another on board the aircraft. In-tank fuel boost pumps move the fuel into a manifold and, by opening the fuel valve (or refueling valve) for the desired tank, the fuel is transferred. Not all jet transports have such fuel transfer capability. Through the use of a fuel feed manifold and crossfeed valves, some aircraft simply allow engines to be run off fuel from any tank as a means for managing fuel location.

Figure 14-23 shows the fuel system diagram for a DC-10. Dedicated transfer boost pumps move fuel into a transfer manifold. Opening the fuel valve on one of the tanks transfers the fuel into that tank. The transfer manifold and boost pumps are also used to jettison fuel overboard by opening the proper dump valves with a transfer boost pump(s) operating. Additionally, the transfer system can function to supply the engines if the normal engine fuel feed malfunctions.

The fuel feed subsystem is sometimes considered part of the fuel distribution system. It is the heart of the fuel system since it delivers fuel to the engines. Jet transport aircraft supply fuel to the engines via in-tank fuel boost pumps, usually two per tank. They pump fuel under pressure through a shutoff valve for each engine. A manifold or connecting tubing typically allows any tank to supply any engine through the use of crossfeed valves. Boost pump bypasses allow fuel flow should a pump fail. Note that the engines are designed to be able to run without any fuel boost pumps operating. But, each engine's shutoff valve must be open to allow flow to the engines from the tanks.

Most jet transport fuel feed systems, or the engine fuel systems, have some means for heating the fuel usually through an exchange with hot air or hot oil taken from the engine. *Figure 14-24* shows the fuel cooled oil cooler (FCOC) on a Rolls Royce RB211 engine, which not only heats the fuel but also cools the engine oil.

Fuel indicating systems on jet transport aircraft monitor a variety of parameters, some not normally found on general aviation aircraft. Business jet aircraft share many of these features. True fuel flow indicators for each engine are used as the primary means for monitoring fuel delivery to the engines. A fuel temperature gauge is common as are fuel filter bypass warning lights. The temperature sensor is usually located in a main fuel tank. The indicator is located on the instrument panel or is displayed on a multifunction display (MFD). These allow the crew to monitor the fuel temperature during high altitude flight in extremely frigid conditions. The fuel filters have bypasses that permit fuel flow around the filters if clogged. Indicator light(s) illuminate in the cockpit when this occurs.

Low fuel pressure warning lights are also common on jet transport aircraft. The sensors for these are located in the boost pump outlet line. They give an indication of possible boost pump failure.

Fuel quantity gauges are important features on all aircraft. Indications exist for all tanks on a transport category aircraft. Often, these use a capacitance type fuel quantity indication system and a fuel totalizer as is discussed later in this chapter.

Figure 14-23. *The fuel distribution systems, components, and cockpit controls of a DC-10 airliner. Note: Fuel transfer system components and lines are used to complete the fuel dump system, the refuel/defuel system, back-up fuel delivery system, and the fuel storage system.*

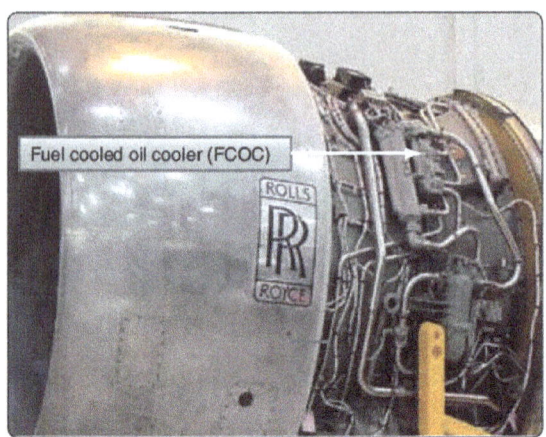

Figure 14-24. *Jet transport aircraft fly at high altitudes where temperatures can reach −50 °F. Most have fuel heaters somewhere in the fuel system to help prevent fuel icing. This fuel-cooled oil cooler on an RB211 turbofan engine simultaneously heats the fuel while cooling the oil.*

The location of fuel instrumentation varies depending on the type of cockpit displays utilized on the aircraft.

Helicopter Fuel Systems

Helicopter fuel systems vary. They can be simple or complex depending on the aircraft. Always consult the manufacturer's manuals for fuel system description, operation, and maintenance instructions.

Typically, a helicopter has only one or two fuel tanks located near the center of gravity (CG) of the aircraft, which is near the main rotor mast. Thus, the tank, or tanks, are usually located in or near the aft fuselage. Some helicopter fuel tanks are mounted above the engine allowing for gravity fuel feed. Others use fuel pumps and pressure feed systems.

Fundamentally, helicopter fuel systems differ little from those on fixed-wing aircraft. Gravity-feed systems have vented fuel tanks with an outlet strainer and shutoff valve. Fuel flows from the tank through a main filter to the carburetor. *[Figure 14-25]*

A slightly more complex system for a light turbine-powered helicopter is shown in *Figure 14-26*. Two in-tank electric boost pumps send fuel through a shutoff valve rather than a selector valve, since there is only one fuel tank. It flows through an airframe filter to an engine filter and then to the engine-driven fuel pump. The fuel tank is vented and contains an electrically operated sump drain valve. A pressure gauge is used to monitor boost pump output pressure and differential pressure switches warn of fuel filter restrictions. Fuel quantity is derived through the use of two in-tank fuel probes with transmitters.

Figure 14-25. *A simple, gravity-feed fuel system on a Robinson helicopter.*

Larger, heavy, multiengine transport helicopters have complex fuel systems similar to jet transport fixed-wing aircraft. They may feature multiple fuel tanks, crossfeed systems, and pressure refueling.

Fuel System Components

To better understand aircraft fuel systems and their operation, the following discussion of various components of aircraft fuel systems is included.

Fuel Tanks

There are three basic types of aircraft fuel tanks: rigid removable tanks, bladder tanks, and integral fuel tanks. The type of aircraft, its design and intended use, as well as the age of the aircraft determine which fuel tank is installed in an aircraft. Most tanks are constructed of noncorrosive material(s). They are typically made to be vented either through a vent cap or a vent line. Aircraft fuel tanks have a low area called a sump that is designed as a place for contaminants and water to settle. The sump is equipped with a drain valve used to remove the impurities during preflight walk-around inspection. *[Figure 14-27]* Most aircraft fuel tanks contain some sort of baffling to subdue the fuel from shifting rapidly during flight maneuvers. Use of a scupper constructed around the fuel fill opening to drain away any spilled fuel is also common.

Figure 14-26. *A pressure-feed fuel system on a light turbine-powered helicopter.*

Figure 14-27. *Sumping a fuel tank with a fuel strainer that is designed to collect the sump drain material in the clear cylinder to be examined for the presence of contaminants.*

Rigid Removable Fuel Tanks

Many aircraft, especially older ones, utilize an obvious choice for fuel tank construction. A rigid tank is made from various materials, and it is strapped into the airframe structure. The tanks are often riveted or welded together and can include baffles, as well as the other fuel tank features described above. They typically are made from 3003 or 5052 aluminum alloy or stainless steel and are riveted and seam welded to prevent leaks. Many early tanks were made of a thin sheet steel coated with a lead/tin alloy called terneplate. The terneplate tanks have folded and soldered seams. *Figure 14-28* shows the parts of a typical rigid removable fuel tank.

Regardless of the actual construction of removable metal tanks, they must be supported by the airframe and held in place with some sort of padded strap arrangement to resist

14-23

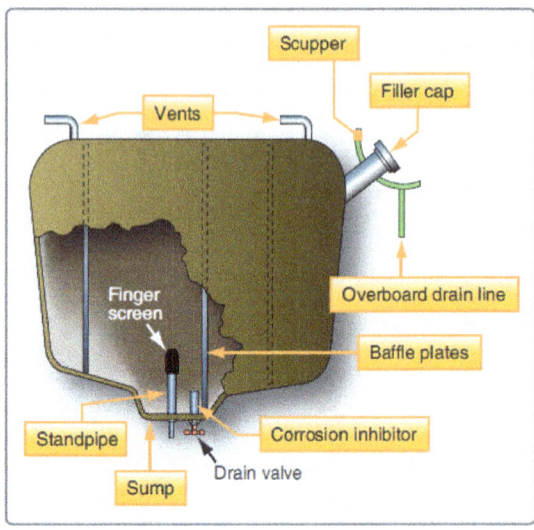

Figure 14-28. *A typical rigid removable aircraft fuel tank and its parts.*

Figure 14-30. *A fuselage tank for a light aircraft.*

shifting in flight. The wings are the most popular location for fuel tanks. *Figure 14-29* shows a fuel tank bay in a wing root with the tank straps. Some tanks are formed to be part of the leading edge of the wing. These are assembled using electric resistance welding and are sealed with a compound that is poured into the tank and allowed to cure. Many fuselage tanks also exist. *[Figure 14-30]* In all cases, the structural integrity of the airframe does not rely on the tank(s) being installed, so the tanks are not considered integral.

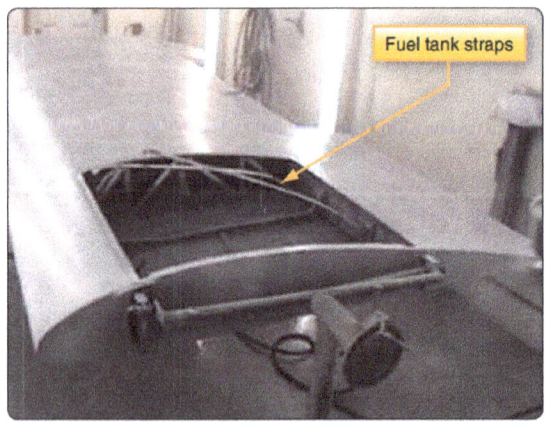

Figure 14-29. *A fuel tank bay in the root of a light aircraft wing on a stand in a paint booth. Padded straps hold the fuel tank securely in the structure.*

Note that as new materials are tested and used in aircraft, fuel tanks are being constructed out of materials other than aluminum, steel, and stainless steel. *Figure 14-31* shows a rigid removable fuel tank

Figure 14-31. *A composite tank from a Challenger ultralight aircraft.*

from an ultralight category aircraft that is constructed from Vipel® isophthalic polyester UL 1316/UL 1746 resin and composite. Its seamless, lightweight construction may lead to the use of this type of tank in other aircraft categories in the future.

Being able to remove and repair, or replace, a fuel tank can be a great convenience if a leak or malfunction with the tank exists. Repairs to fuel tanks must be done in accordance with manufacturer's specifications. It is especially critical to follow all safety procedures when welding repairs are

14-24

performed. Fuel vapors must be removed from the tank to prevent explosion. This typically involves washing out the tank with water and detergent, as well as some number of minutes that steam or water should be run through the tank (time varies by manufacturer). Once repaired, fuel tanks need to be pressure checked, usually while installed in the airframe, to prevent distortion while under pressure.

Bladder Fuel Tanks

A fuel tank made out of a reinforced flexible material called a bladder tank can be used instead of a rigid tank. A bladder tank contains most of the features and components of a rigid tank but does not require as large an opening in the aircraft skin to install. The tank, or fuel cell as it is sometimes called, can be rolled up and put into a specially prepared structural bay or cavity through a small opening, such as an inspection opening. Once inside, it can be unfurled to its full size. Bladder tanks must be attached to the structure with clips or other fastening devices. They should lie smooth and unwrinkled in the bay. It is especially important that no wrinkles exist on the bottom surface so that fuel contaminants are not blocked from settling into the tank sump. *[Figure 14-32]*

Figure 14-32. *A bladder fuel tank for a light aircraft.*

Bladder fuel tanks are used on aircraft of all size. They are strong and have a long life with seams only around installed features, such as the tank vents, sump drain, filler spout, etc. When a bladder tank develops a leak, the technician can patch it following manufacturer's instructions. The cell can also be removed and sent to a fuel tank repair station familiar with and equipped to perform such repairs.

The soft flexible nature of bladder fuel tanks requires that they remain wet. Should it become necessary to store a bladder tank without fuel in it for an extended period of time, it is common to wipe the inside of the tank with a coating of clean engine oil. Follow the manufacturer's instructions for the dry storage procedures for fuel cells.

Integral Fuel Tanks

On many aircraft, especially transport category and high-performance aircraft, part of the structure of the wings or fuselage is sealed with a fuel resistant two-part sealant to form a fuel tank. The sealed skin and structural members provide the highest volume of space available with the lowest weight. This type of tank is called an integral fuel tank since it forms a tank as a unit within the airframe structure.

Integral fuel tanks in the otherwise unused space inside the wings are most common. Aircraft with integral fuel tanks in the wings are said to have wet wings. For fuel management purposes, sometimes a wing is sealed into separate tanks and may include a surge tank or an overflow tank, which is normally empty but sealed to hold fuel when needed.

When an aircraft maneuvers, the long horizontal nature of an integral wing tank requires baffling to keep the fuel from sloshing. The wing ribs and box beam structural members serve as baffles and others may be added specifically for that purpose. Baffle check valves are commonly used. These valves allow fuel to move to the low, inboard sections of the tank but prevent it from moving outboard. They ensure that the fuel boost pumps located in the bottom of the tanks at the lowest points above the sumps always have fuel to pump regardless of aircraft attitude. *[Figure 14-33]*

Integral fuel tanks must have access panels for inspection and repairs of the tanks and other fuel system components. On large aircraft, technicians physically enter the tank for maintenance. Transport category aircraft often have more than a dozen oval access panels or tank plates on the bottom surface of the wing for this purpose. *[Figure 14-34A]* These aluminum panels are each sealed into place with an O-ring and an aluminum gasket for electrostatic bonding. An outer clamp ring is tightened to the inner panel with screws, as shown in *Figure 14-34B.*

When entering and performing maintenance on an integral fuel tank, all fuel must be emptied from the tank and strict safety procedures must be followed. Fuel vapors must be purged from the tank and respiratory equipment must be used by the technician. A full-time spotter must be positioned just outside of the tank to assist if needed.

Aircraft using integral fuel tanks normally have sophisticated fuel systems that include in-tank boost pumps. There are usually at least two pumps in each tank that deliver fuel to the engine(s) under positive pressure. On various aircraft, these in-tank boost pumps are also used to transfer fuel to other tanks, jettison fuel, and defuel the aircraft.

Figure 14-33. *Baffle check valves are installed in the locations shown in the integral tank rib structure of a Boeing 737 airliner. Fuel is prevented from flowing outboard during maneuvers. The tank boost pumps are located inboard of WBL 157.*

Fuel Lines and Fittings

Aircraft fuel lines can be rigid or flexible depending on location and application. Rigid lines are often made of aluminum alloy and are connected with Army/Navy (AN) or military standard (MS) fittings. However, in the engine compartment, wheel wells, and other areas, subject to damage from debris, abrasion, and heat, stainless steel lines are often used.

Flexible fuel hose has a synthetic rubber interior with a reinforcing fiber braid wrap covered by a synthetic exterior. *[Figure 14-35]* The hose is approved for fuel and no other hose should be substituted. Some flexible fuel hose has a braided stainless steel exterior. *[Figure 14-36]* The diameters of all fuel hoses and line are determined by the fuel flow requirements of the aircraft fuel system. Flexible hoses are used in areas where vibration exists between components, such as between the engine and the aircraft structure.

Sometimes manufacturers wrap either flexible or rigid fuel lines to provide even further protection from abrasion and especially from fire. A fire sleeve cover is held over the line with steel clamps at the end fittings. *[Figure 14-37]*

As mentioned, aircraft fuel line fitting are usually either AN or MS fittings. Both flared and flareless fitting are used. Problems with leaks at fittings can occur. Technicians are cautioned to not overtighten a leaky fitting. If the proper torque does not stop a leak, depressurize the line, disconnect the fitting and visually inspect it for a cause. The fitting or line should be replaced if needed. Replace all aircraft fuel lines and fittings with approved replacement parts from the manufacturer. If a line is manufactured in the shop, approved components must be used.

Several installation procedures for fuel hoses and rigid fuel lines exist. Hoses should be installed without twisting. The writing printed on the outside of the hose is used as a lay line to monitor fuel hose twist. Separation should be maintained between all fuel hoses and electrical wiring. Never clamp wires to a fuel line. When separation is not possible, always route the fuel line below any wiring. If a fuel leak develops, it does not drip onto the wires.

Metal fuel lines and all aircraft fuel system components need to be electrically bonded and grounded to the aircraft structure. This is important because fuel flowing through the fuel system generates static electricity that must have a place to flow to ground rather than build up. Special bonded cushion clamps are used to secure rigid fuel lines in place. They are supported at intervals shown in *Figure 14-38*.

All fuel lines should be supported so that there is no strain on the fittings. Clamp lines so that fittings are aligned. Never draw two fittings together by threading. They should thread easily and a wrench should be used only for tightening. Additionally, a straight length of rigid fuel line should not be made between two components or fitting rigidly mounted to the airframe. A small bend is needed to absorb any strain from vibration or expansion and contraction due to temperature changes.

Fuel Valves

There are many fuel valve uses in aircraft fuel systems. They are used to shut off fuel flow or to route the fuel to a desired location. Other than sump drain valves, light aircraft fuel systems may include only one valve, the selector valve. It incorporates the shutoff and selection features into a single valve. Large aircraft fuel systems have numerous valves. Most simply open and close and are know by different names related to their location and function in the fuel system (e.g., shutoff valve, transfer valve, crossfeed valve). Fuel valves can be manually operated, solenoid operated, or operated by electric motor.

A feature of all aircraft fuel valves is a means for positively identifying the position of the valve at all times. Hand-operated valves accomplish this through the use of detents

Figure 14-34. *Fuel tank access panel locations on a Boeing 737 (A), and typical fuel tank access panel seals (B).*

Figure 14-35. *A typical flexible aircraft fuel line with braided reinforcement.*

Figure 14-36. *A braided stainless steel exterior fuel line with fittings.*

Figure 14-37. *Exterior fuel hose wrap that protects from fire, as well as abrasion, shown with the clamps and pliers used to install it.*

into which a spring-loaded pin or similar protrusion locates when the valve is set in each position. Combined with labels and a directional handle, this makes it easy to identify by feel and by sight that the valve is in the desired position. [*Figure 14-39*] Motor- and solenoid-operated valves use position annunciator lights to indicate valve position in addition to the switch position. Flight management system (FMS) fuel pages also display the position of the fuel valves graphically in diagrams called up on the flat screen monitors. [*Figure 14-40*] Note that many valves have an exterior position handle, or lever, that indicates valve position. When maintenance personnel directly observe the valve, it can be manually positioned by the technician using this same lever. [*Figure 14-41*]

Hand-Operated Valves

There are three basic types of hand-operated valves used in aircraft fuel systems. The cone-type valve and the poppet-type valve are commonly used in light general aviation aircraft as fuel selector valves. Gate valves are used on transport category aircraft as shutoff valves. While many are motor operated, there are several applications in which gate valves are hand operated.

Cone Valves

A cone valve, also called a plug valve, consists of a machined valve housing into which a rotatable brass or nylon cone is set. The cone is manually rotated by the pilot with an attached handle. Passageways are machined through the

Tubing OD (inch)	Approximate distance between supports (inches)
1/8 to 3/16	9
1/4 to 5/16	12
3/8 to 1/2	16
5/8 to 3/4	22
7 to 1 1/4	30
1 1/2 to 2	40

Figure 14-38. *Rigid metallic fuel lines are clamped to the airframe with electrically bonded cushion clamps at specified intervals.*

cone so that, as it is rotated, fuel can flow from the selected source to the engine. This occurs when the passageway aligns with the desired fuel input port machined into the housing. *Figure 14-42* shows a cross sectional view of a cone valve. The cone can also be rotated to a position so that the passageway(s) does not align with any fuel input port. This is the fuel OFF position of the valve.

Poppet Valves

Selector valves are also commonly the poppet type. As the handle is rotated in this valve, a cam on the attached shaft lifts the poppet off the seat of the desired port being selected. At the same time, spring-assisted poppets close off the ports that are not selected. Detents lock the valve into position when the cam pushes a poppet fully off of its seat. There is also a positive detent when the cam engages none of the poppets, which is the OFF position of the valve. *[Figure 14-43]* Note that a similar mechanism is use in some selector valves, but balls are used instead of poppets.

Manually-Operated Gate Valves

A single selector valve is not used in complex fuel systems of transport category aircraft. Fuel flow is controlled with a series of ON/OFF, or shutoff, type valves that are plumbed

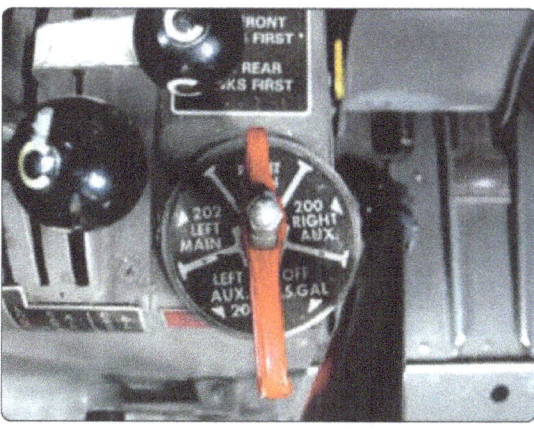

Figure 14-39. *Detents for each position, an indicating handle, and labeling aid the pilot in knowing the position of the fuel valve.*

Figure 14-40. *The graphic depiction of the fuel system on this electronic centralized aircraft monitor (ECAM) fuel page includes valve position information.*

Figure 14-41. *This motor-operated gate valve has a red position indicating lever that can be used by maintenance personnel to identify the position of the valve. The lever can be moved by the technician to position the valve.*

Figure 14-42. *A cone valve is open when the bored cone aligns the inlet and the outlet ports. It shuts off the flow when the un-bored portion of the cone is aligned with the inlet port(s).*

Figure 14-43. *The internal mechanism of a poppet-type fuel selector valve.*

between system components. Hand-operated gate valves can be used, especially as fire control valves, requiring no electrical power to shutoff fuel flow when the emergency fire handle is pulled. The valves are typically positioned in the fuel feed line to each engine. Hand-operated gate valves are also featured as ground-operated defuel valves and boost pump isolation valves, which shut off the fuel to the inlet of the boost pump, allowing it to be changed without emptying the tank.

Gate valves utilize a sealed gate or blade that slides into the path of the fuel, blocking its flow when closed. *Figure 14-44* shows a typical hand-operated gate valve. When the handle is rotated, the actuating arm inside the valve

Figure 14-44. *A hand-operated gate valve used in transport category aircraft fuel systems.*

moves the gate blade down between seals and into the fuel flow path. A thermal relief bypass valve is incorporated to relieve excess pressure buildup against the closed gate due to temperature increases.

Motor-Operated Valves

The use of electric motors to operate fuel system valves is common on large aircraft due to the remote location from the cockpit of fuel system components. The types of valves used are basically the same as the manually operated valves, but electric motors are used to actuate the units. The two most common electric motor operated fuel valves are the gate valve and the plug-type valve.

The motor-operated gate valve uses a geared, reversible electric motor to turn the actuating arm of the valve that moves the fuel gate into or out of the path of the fuel. As with the manually operated gate valve, the gate or blade is sealed. A manual override lever allows the technician to observe the position of the valve or manually position it. *[Figure 14-45]* Less common is the use of a motorized plug-type fuel valve; an electric motor is used to rotate the plug or drum rather than it being rotated manually. Regardless of the type of valve used, large aircraft fuel system valves either allow fuel to flow or shut off flow.

Figure 14-45. *An electric motor-driven gate valve commonly used in large aircraft fuel systems.*

Solenoid-Operated Valves

An additional way to operate a remotely located fuel valve is through the use of electric solenoids. A poppet-type valve is opened via the magnetic pull developed when an opening solenoid is energized. A spring forces a locking stem into a notch in the stem of the poppet to lock the valve in the open position. Fuel then flows through the opening vacated by the poppet. To close the poppet and shut off fuel flow, a closing solenoid is energized. Its magnetic pull overcomes the force of the locking stem spring and pulls the locking stem out of the notch in the poppet stem. A spring behind the poppet forces it back onto its seat. A characteristic of solenoid-operated fuel valves is that they open and close very quickly. *[Figure 14-46]*

Fuel Pumps

Other than aircraft with gravity-feed fuel systems, all aircraft have at least one fuel pump to deliver clean fuel under pressure to the fuel metering device for each engine. Engine-driven pumps are the primary delivery device. Auxiliary pumps are used on many aircraft as well. Sometimes known as booster pumps or boost pumps, auxiliary pumps are used to provide fuel under positive pressure to the engine-driven pump and during starting when the engine-driven pump is not yet up to speed for sufficient fuel delivery. They are also used to back up the engine-driven pump during takeoff and at high altitude to guard against vapor lock. On many large aircraft, boost pumps are used to move fuel from one tank to another.

Figure 14-46. *A solenoid-operated fuel valve uses the magnetic force developed by energized solenoids to open and close a poppet.*

There are many different types of auxiliary fuel pumps in use. Most are electrically operated, but some hand-operated pumps are found on older aircraft. A discussion of the various pump types found in the aviation fleet follows.

Hand-Operated Fuel Pumps

Some older reciprocating engine aircraft have been equipped with hand-operated fuel pumps. They are used to back up the engine-driven pump and to transfer fuel from tank to tank. The wobble pumps, as they are known, are double-acting pumps that deliver fuel with each stroke of the pump handle. They are essentially vane-type pumps that have bored passages in the center of the pump, allowing a back-and-forth motion to pump the fuel rather than a full revolution of the vanes as is common in electrically driven or engine-driven vane-type pumps.

Figure 14-47 illustrates the mechanism found in a wobble pump. As the handle is moved down from where it is shown, the vane on the left side of the pump moves up, and the vane on the right side of the pump moves down. As the left vane moves up, it draws fuel into chamber A. Because chambers A and D are connected through the bored center, fuel is also drawn into chamber D. At the same time, the right vane forces fuel out of chamber B, through the bored passage in the center of the pump, into chamber C and out the fuel outlet through the check valve at the outlet of chamber C. When the handle is moved up again, the left vane moves down, forcing fuel out of chambers A and D because the check valve at the inlet of the A chamber prevents fuel from flowing back through the fuel inlet. The right vane moves up simultaneously and draws fuel into chambers B and C.

Figure 14-47. *A hand-operated wobble pump used for engine starting and fuel transfer on older transport category aircraft.*

While simple with little to go wrong, a hand-operated pump requires fuel lines to be run into the cockpit to the pump, creating a potential hazard that can be avoided by the use of an electrically driven pump. Modern light reciprocating-engine aircraft usually use electric auxiliary pumps, but they often make use of a simple hand pump for priming the engine(s) during starting. These simple devices are single-acting piston pumps that pull fuel into the pump cylinder when the primer knob is pulled aft. When pushed forward, the fuel is pumped through lines to the engine cylinders. *[Figure 14-48]*

Figure 14-48. *This engine primer pump is a hand-operated piston type. It is mounted in the instrument panel and extends through the firewall where fuel intake and delivery lines are attached to the fittings on the left.*

Centrifugal Boost Pumps

The most common type of auxiliary fuel pump used on aircraft, especially large and high-performance aircraft, is the centrifugal pump. It is electric motor driven and most frequently is submerged in the fuel tank or located just outside of the bottom of the tank with the inlet of the pump extending into the tank. If the pump is mounted outside the tank, a pump removal valve is typically installed so the pump can be removed without draining the fuel tank. *[Figure 14-49]*

A centrifugal boost pump is a variable displacement pump. It takes in fuel at the center of an impeller and expels it to the outside as the impeller turns. *[Figure 14-50]* An outlet check valve prevents fuel from flowing back through the pump. A fuel feed line is connected to the pump outlet. A bypass valve may be installed in the fuel feed system to allow the engine-driven pump to pull fuel from the tank if the boost pump is not operating. The centrifugal boost pump is used to supply the engine-driven fuel pump, back up the engine-driven fuel pump, and transfer fuel from tank to tank if the aircraft is so designed.

Some centrifugal fuel pumps operate at more than one speed, as selected by the pilot, depending on the phase of aircraft operation. Single-speed fuel pumps are also common. Centrifugal fuel pumps located in fuel tanks ensure positive pressure throughout the fuel system regardless of temperature, altitude, or flight attitude thus preventing vapor lock. Submerged pumps have fuel proof covers for the electric motor since the motor is in the fuel. Centrifugal pumps mounted on the outside of the tank do not require this but have some sort of inlet that is located in the fuel. This can be a tube in which a shutoff valve is located so the pump can be changed without draining the tank. The inlet of both types of centrifugal pump is covered with a screen to prevent the ingestion of foreign matter. *[Figure 14-51]*

Ejector Pumps

Fuel tanks with in-tank fuel pumps, such as centrifugal pumps, are constructed to maintain a fuel supply to the pump inlet at all times. This ensures that the pump does not cavitate and that the pump is cooled by the fuel. The section of the fuel tank dedicated for the pump installation may be partitioned off with baffles that contain check valves, also known as flapper valves. These allow fuel to flow inboard to the pump during maneuvers but does not allow it to flow outboard.

Some aircraft use ejector pumps to help ensure that liquid fuel is always at the inlet of the pump. A relatively small diameter line circulates pump outflow back into the section of the tank where the pump is located. The fuel is directed through a venturi that is part of the ejector. As the fuel rushes through the venturi, low pressure is formed. An inlet, or line that originates outside of the tank pump area, allows fuel to be drawn into the ejector assembly where it is pumped into the fuel pump tank section. Together, with baffle check valves, ejector pumps keep a positive head of fuel at the inlet of the pump. *[Figure 14-52]*

Figure 14-49. *A centrifugal fuel boost pump can be submersed in the fuel tank (A) or can be attached to the outside of the tank with inlet and outlet plumbing extending into the tank (B). The pump removal valve handle extends below the warning flag clearance panel to indicate the pump inlet is closed.*

Figure 14-50. *The internal workings of a centrifugal fuel boost pump. Fuel is drawn into the center of the impeller through a screen. It is moved to the outside of the case by the impeller and out the fuel outlet tube.*

14-33

Figure 14-51. *A typical fuel boost pump inlet screen installation for a centrifugal pump mounted outside of the bottom of the tank.*

Pulsating Electric Pumps

General aviation aircraft often make use of smaller, less expensive auxiliary fuel pumps. The pulsating electric pump, or plunger-type fuel pump, is common. It is usually used in the same manner as a centrifugal fuel pump on larger aircraft, except it is located downstream of the fuel tank outlets. The pulsating electric fuel pump is plumbed in parallel with the engine-driven pump. During starting, it provides fuel before the engine-driven fuel pump is up to speed, and it can be used during takeoff as a backup. It also can be used at high altitudes to prevent vapor lock.

The pulsating electric pump uses a plunger to draw fuel in and push fuel out of the pump. It is powered by a solenoid that alternates between being energized and de-energized, which moves the plunger back and forth in a pulsating motion. *Figure 14-53* shows the internal workings of the pump. When switched ON, current travels through the solenoid coils, which pull the steel plunger down between the coils. Any fuel in chamber C is forced through the small check valve in the center of the plunger and into chamber D. When positioned between the solenoid, the plunger is far enough away from the magnet that it no longer attracts it, and the pivot allows the contacts to open. This disrupts the current to the solenoid. The calibrated spring shown under the plunger is then strong enough to push the plunger up from between the solenoid coils. As the plunger rises, it pushes fuel in chamber D out the pump outlet port. Also as the plunger rises, it draws fuel into chamber C and through the check valve into chamber C. As the plunger rises, the magnet is attracted to it and the upward motion closes the points. This allows current flow to the solenoid coils, and the process begins again with the plunger pulled down between the coils, the magnet releasing, and the points opening.

Figure 14-52. *An ejector pump uses a venturi to draw fuel into the boost pump sump area of the fuel tank.*

14-34

Figure 14-53. *A pulsating electric auxiliary fuel pump is used on many light reciprocating engine aircraft. In A, the pump is shown with its solenoid coil energized, which draws the plunger down between the coil. This opens the breaker points allowing the calibrated spring to push the plunger upwards, thus pumping fuel out the outlet B. This cycle repeats at a speed related to the fuel pressure buildup at the pump outlet.*

The single-acting pulsating electric fuel pump responds to the pressure of the fuel at its outlet. When fuel is needed, the pump cycles rapidly with little pressure at the pump outlet. As fuel pressure builds, the pump slows because the calibrated spring meets this resistance while attempting to force the piston upwards. A spring in the center of the plunger dampens its motion. A diaphragm between the chamber D fuel and an airspace at the top of the pump dampens the output fuel pulses.

Vane-Type Fuel Pumps

Vane-type fuel pumps are the most common types of fuel pumps found on reciprocating-engine aircraft. They are used as both engine-driven primary fuel pumps and as auxiliary or boost pumps. Regardless, the vane-type pump is a constant displacement pump that moves a constant volume of fuel with each revolution of the pump. When used as an auxiliary pump, an electric motor rotates the pump shaft. On engine-driven applications, the vane pump is typically driven by the accessory gear box.

As with all vane pumps, an eccentric rotor is driven inside a cylinder. Slots on the rotor allow vanes to slide in and out and be held against the cylinder wall by a central floating spacer pin. As the vanes rotate with the eccentric rotor, the volume space created by the cylinder wall, the rotor, and the vanes increases and then decreases. An inlet port is located where the vanes create an increasing volume space, and fuel is drawn into the pump. Further around in the rotation, the space created becomes smaller. An outlet port located there causes fuel to be forced from the cylinder. *[Figure 14-54]*

The fuel metering device for the engine delivers more fuel than it needs to operate. However, the constant volume of a vane pump can be excessive. To regulate flow, most vane pumps have an adjustable pressure relief feature. It uses pressure built up at the outlet of the pump to lift a valve off its seat, which returns excess fuel to the inlet side of the pump. *Figure 14-55* shows a typical vane type fuel pump with this adjustable pressure relief function. By setting the relief at a certain pressure above the engine fuel metering device air intake pressure, the correct volume of fuel is delivered. The relief pressure is set via the pressure adjustment screw which tensions the relief valve spring.

During engine starting, or if the vane pump is inoperative, fuel must be able to flow through the pump to the fuel metering device. This is accomplished with the use of a bypass valve inside the pump. A lightly sprung plate under the relief valve overcomes spring pressure whenever the pump's inlet fuel

Figure 14-54. *The basic mechanism of a vane-type fuel pump.*

Figure 14-56. *The bypass feature in a vane-type fuel pump allows fuel to flow through the pump during starting or when the pump is inoperative.*

Figure 14-55. *The pressure relief valve in a vane-type fuel pump.*

Figure 14-57. *A compensated vane pump is used in engine-driven applications. The fuel metering device inlet air pressure is connected to the vent chamber in the pump. The diaphragm assists or resists the relief valve mechanism depending on the pressure sensed in this chamber.*

pressure is greater than the outlet fuel press. The plate moves down and fuel can flow through the pump. *[Figure 14-56]*

Compensated vane-type fuel pumps are used when the vane pump is the engine-driven primary fuel pump. The relief valve setting varies automatically to provide the correct delivery of fuel as the air inlet pressure of the fuel metering device changes due to altitude or turbocharger outlet pressure. A vent chamber above a diaphragm attached to the relief mechanism is connected to the inlet air pressure source. As air pressure varies, the diaphragm assists or resists the relief valve spring pressure, resulting in proper fuel delivery for the condition at the fuel metering device. *[Figure 14-57]*

Fuel Filters

Two main types of fuel cleaning device are utilized on aircraft. Fuel strainers are usually constructed of relatively coarse wire mesh. They are designed to trap large pieces of debris and prevent their passage through the fuel system. Fuel strainers do not inhibit the flow of water. Fuel filters generally are usually fine mesh. In various applications, they can trap fine sediment that can be only thousands of an inch in diameter and also help trap water. The technician should be aware that the terms "strainer" and "filter" are sometimes used interchangeably. Micronic filters are commonly used on turbine-powered aircraft. This is a type of filter that captures extremely fine particles in the range of 10–25 microns. A micron is $\frac{1}{1,000}$ of a millimeter. *[Figure 14-58]*

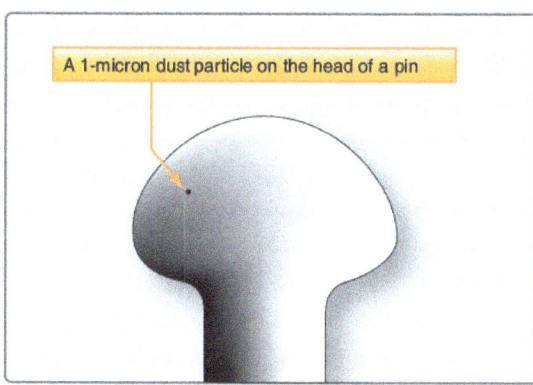

Figure 14-58. *Size comparison of 1-micron dust particle and pin head.*

All aircraft fuel systems have filters and strainers to ensure that the fuel delivered to the engine(s) is free from contaminants. The first of these is encountered at the outlet of the fuel tank. A sump is used to encourage the collection of debris in the lowest part of the tank, which can then be drained off before flight. The actual tank outlet for the fuel is positioned above this sump. Some type of screen is used to trap contaminants attempting to flow out of the tank into the fuel system. Finger screens are common on light aircraft. They effectively increase the area of the fuel tank outlet, allowing a large amount of debris to be trapped while still permitting fuel to flow. *Figure 14-59* illustrates finger screens that are screwed into a fitting welded in the tank outlet.

Figure 14-59. *Fuel tank outlet finger strainers are used in light aircraft.*

Fuel tank outlet screens on aircraft with more complex fuel systems are similarly designed. When in-tank boost pumps are used, the tank outlet strainer is located at the inlet to the boost pump as was shown in *Figure 14-51*. The screen's large area allows debris capture while still permitting sufficient fuel flow for operation. Regularly scheduled inspection and cleaning of these strainers are required.

An additional main strainer for the aircraft fuel system is required between the fuel tank outlet and the fuel metering device (in a carburetor or fuel-injection system). It is normally located between the fuel tank and the engine-driven fuel pump at the low point in the fuel system and is equipped with a drain for preflight sampling and draining. On light aircraft, the main strainer may be in the form of a gascolator. A gascolator is a fuel strainer, or filter, that also incorporates a sediment collection bowl. The bowl is traditionally glass to allow quick visual checks for contaminants; however, many gascolators also have opaque bowls. A gascolator has a drain, or the bowl can be removed to inspect and discard trapped debris and water. *[Figure 14-60]*

Figure 14-60. *A gascolator is the main fuel strainer between the fuel tanks and the fuel metering device on many light aircraft.*

The main fuel strainer is often mounted at a low point on the engine firewall. The drain is accessible through an easy-access panel, or it simply extends through the bottom engine cowling. As with most filters or strainers, fuel is allowed to enter the unit but must travel up through the filtering element to exit. Water, which is heavier than fuel, becomes trapped and collects in the bottom of the bowl. Other debris too large to pass through the element also settles in the strainer bowl.

Higher performance light aircraft may have a main filter/strainer. *[Figure 14-61]* On twin-engine aircraft, there is a main strainer for each engine. As with single-engine aircraft, a strainer is often mounted low on the engine firewall in each nacelle.

up through the cone to get to the filter outlet. The mesh used in this filter assembly prevents water and particles from exiting the filter bowl. The contaminants collect at the bottom to be drained off through a drain valve. *[Figure 14-62]*

8	Arm assembly
9	Bolt
10	Glass bowl
11	Lower gasket
12	Cap
13	Stiffener
14	Drain valve
15	Lid assembly
16	Retainer spring
17	Filter
18	Upper gasket
19	Flat screen
20	Standpipe
22	Filter ring
21	Elbow

1	Bolt
2	Elbow
3	Body assembly
4	Fitting for left engine installation
5	Fitting for right engine installation
6	Mounting bracket nut
7	Nut

Figure 14-61. *A filter assembly on a light twin reciprocating-engine aircraft.*

Other larger fuel filters have double-screen construction. A cylindrical structural screen is wrapped with a fine mesh material through which inlet fuel must pass. Inside the cylinder is an additional cone-shaped screen. Fuel must pass

Figure 14-62. *A large-area double-screen filter passes fuel through the outer cylindrical mesh and the inner conical mesh.*

Turbine engine fuel control units are extremely close tolerance devices. It is imperative that fuel delivered to them is clean and contaminant free. The used of micronic filters makes this possible. The changeable cellulose filter mesh type shown in *Figure 14-63* can block particles 10–200 microns in size and absorbs water if it is present. The small size of the mesh raises the possibility of the filter being blocked by debris or water. Therefore, a relief valve is included in the filter assembly that bypasses fuel through the unit should pressure build up from blockage.

14-38

Indication of a filter blockage may also appear in the cockpit through the use of a bypass-activated switch or a pressure differential switch. The bypass valve physically activates a switch that closes the circuit to the annunciator in the first type. The differential pressure type indicator compares the input pressure of the fuel filter to the output pressure. A circuit is completed when a preset difference occurs. Thus, an indicator is illuminated should a blockage cause the bypass to open or the inlet and outlet pressures to vary significantly. Fuel temperature can also be monitored for the possibility of a blockage caused by frozen water. *[Figure 14-65]*

Fuel Heaters and Ice Prevention

Turbine powered aircraft operate at high altitude where the temperature is very low. As the fuel in the fuel tanks cools, water in the fuel condenses and freezes. It may form ice crystals in the tank or as the fuel/water solution slows and contacts the cool filter element on its way through fuel filter to the engine(s). The formation of ice on the filter element blocks the flow of fuel through the filter. A valve in the filter unit bypasses unfiltered fuel when this occurs. Fuel heaters are used to warm the fuel so that ice does not form. These heat exchanger units also heat the fuel sufficiently to melt any ice that has already formed.

Figure 14-63. *A typical micronic fuel filter with changeable cellulose filter element.*

Fuel filters are often used between the engine-driven fuel pump and the fuel metering device on reciprocating, as well as turbine-engine aircraft. While these are technically part of the engine fuel system, a common type used on turbine engines is discussed here. It is also a micronic filter. It uses finely meshed disks or wafers stacked on a central core. These filters are able to withstand the higher pressure found in the engine fuel system downstream of the engine-driven pump. *[Figure 14-64]*

The most common types of fuel heaters are air/fuel heaters and oil/fuel heaters. An air/fuel heater uses warm compressor bleed air to heat the fuel. An oil/fuel exchanger heats the fuel with hot engine oil. This latter type is often referred to as a fuel-cooled oil cooler (FCOC). *[Figure 14-24]*

Figure 14-64. *A micronic wafer filter uses multiple screen wafers through which fuel must pass to exit the filter through the core. A spring loaded bypass valve in the filter housing unseats when the filter is clogged to continue delivery of fuel.*

14-39

Fuel heaters often operate intermittently as needed. A switch in the cockpit can direct the hot air or oil through the unit or block it. The flight crew uses the information supplied by the filter bypass indicating lights and fuel temperature gauge *[Figure 14-65]* to know when to heat the fuel. Fuel heaters can also be automatic. A built-in thermostatic device opens or closes a valve that permits the hot air or hot oil to flow into the unit to cool the fuel. *[Figure 14-66]*

Figure 14-65. *A Boeing 737 cockpit fuel panel showing illuminated valve position indicators and fuel filter bypass lights. The fuel temperature in tank No.1 is also indicated.*

Note that some aircraft have a hydraulic fluid cooler in one of the aircraft fuel tanks. The fluid helps warm the fuel as it cools in this type of full-time heat exchanger.

Fuel System Indicators

Aircraft fuel systems utilize various indicators. All systems are required to have some sort of fuel quantity indicator. Fuel flow, pressure, and temperature are monitored on many aircraft. Valve position indicators and various warning lights and annunciations are also used.

Fuel Quantity Indicating Systems

All aircraft fuel systems must have some form of fuel quantity indicator. These devices vary widely depending on the complexity of the fuel system and the aircraft on which they are installed. Simple indicators requiring no electrical power were the earliest type of quantity indicators and are still in use today. The use of these direct reading indicators is possible only on light aircraft in which the fuel tanks are in close proximity to the cockpit. Other light aircraft and larger aircraft require electric indicators or electronic capacitance-type indicators.

A sight glass is a clear glass or plastic tube open to the fuel tank that fills with fuel to the same level as the fuel in the tank. It can be calibrated in gallons or fractions of a full tank that can be read by the pilot. Another type of sight gauge makes use of a float with an indicating rod attached to it. As the float moves up and down with the fuel level in the tank, the portion of the rod that extends through the fuel cap indicates the quantity of fuel in the tank. *[Figure 14-67]* These two mechanisms are combined in yet another simple fuel quantity indicator in which the float is attached to a rod that moves up or down in a calibrated cylinder. *[Figure 14-68]*

More sophisticated mechanical fuel quantity gauges are common. A float that follows the fuel level remains the primary sensing element, but a mechanical linkage is connected to move a pointer across the dial face of an instrument. This can be done with a crank and pinion arrangement that drives the pointer with gears, or with a magnetic coupling, to the pointer. *[Figure 14-69]*

Figure 14-66. *An air-fuel heat exchanger uses engine compressor bleed air to warm the fuel on many turbine engine powered aircraft.*

Figure 14-67. *The fuel quantity indicator on this Piper Cub is a float attached to a rod that protrudes through the fuel cap.*

Figure 14-68. *A float-type sight gauge fuel quantity indicator.*

Electric fuel quantity indicators are more common than mechanical indicators in modern aircraft. Most of these units operate with direct current (DC) and use variable resistance in a circuit to drive a ratiometer-type indicator. The movement of a float in the tank moves a connecting arm to the wiper on a variable resistor in the tank unit. This resistor is wired in series with one of the coils of the ratiometer-type fuel gauge in the instrument panel. Changes to the current flowing through the tank unit resistor change the current flowing through one of the coils in the indicator. This alters the magnetic field in which the indicating pointer pivots. The calibrated dial indicates the corresponding fuel quantity. *[Figure 14-70]*

Digital indicators are available that work with the same variable resistance signal from the tank unit. They convert the variable resistance into a digital display in the cockpit instrument head. *[Figure 14-71]* Fully digital instrumentation systems, such as those found in a glass cockpit aircraft, convert the variable resistance into a digital signal to be processed in a computer and displayed on a flat screen panel.

Large and high-performance aircraft typically utilize electronic fuel quantity systems. These more costly systems have the advantage of having no moving parts in the tank sending units. Variable capacitance transmitters are installed in the fuel tanks extending from the top to the bottom of each tank in the usable fuel. Several of these tank units, or fuel probes as they are sometimes called, may be installed in a large tank. *[Figure 14-72]* They are wired in parallel. As the level of the fuel changes, the capacitance of each unit changes. The capacitance transmitted by all of the probes in a tank is totaled and compared in a bridge circuit by a microchip computer in the tank's digital fuel quantity indicator in the cockpit. As the aircraft maneuvers, some probes are in more fuel than others due to the attitude of the aircraft. The indication remains steady, because the total capacitance transmitted by all of the probes remains the same. A trimmer is used to match the capacitance output with the precalibrated quantity indicator.

Figure 14-69. *Simple mechanical fuel indicators used on light aircraft with fuel tanks in close proximity to the pilot.*

14-41

Figure 14-70. *A DC electric fuel quantity indicator uses a variable resistor in the tank unit, which is moved by a float arm.*

Figure 14-71. *Digital fuel quantity gauges that work off of variable resistance from the tank unit are shown in A and B. The fuel quantity indication of a Garmin G-1000 flat screen display is shown in C.*

Figure 14-72. *A fuel tank transmitter for a capacitance-type fuel quantity indicating system.*

A capacitor is a device that stores electricity. The amount it can store depends on three factors: the area of its plates, the distance between the plates, and the dielectric constant of the material separating the plates. A fuel tank unit contains two concentric plates that are a fixed distance apart. Therefore, the capacitance of a unit can change if the dielectric constant of the material separating the plates varies. The units are open at the top and bottom so they can assume the same level of fuel as is in the tanks. Therefore, the material between the plates is either fuel (if the tank is full), air (if the tank is empty), or some ratio of fuel and air depending on how much fuel remains in the tank. *Figure 14-73* shows a simplified illustration of this construction.

Figure 14-74. *A simplified capacitance bridge for a fuel quantity system.*

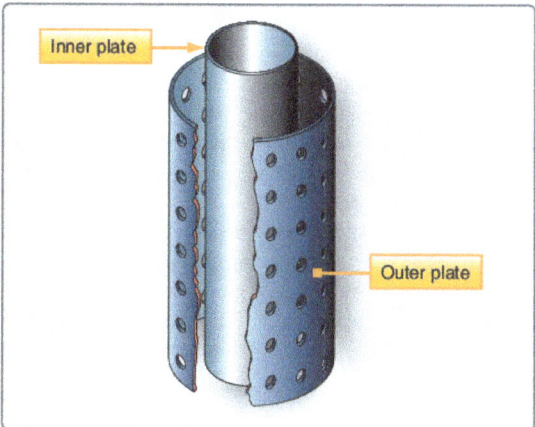

Figure 14-73. *The capacitance of tank probes varies in a capacitance-type fuel tank indicator system as the space between the inner and outer plates is filled with varying quantities of fuel and air depending on the amount of fuel in the tank.*

The bridge circuit that measures the capacitance of the tank units uses a reference capacitor for comparison. When voltage is induced into the bridge, the capacitive reactance of the tank probes and the reference capacitor can be equal or different. The magnitude of the difference is translated into an indication of the fuel quantity in the tank calibrated in pounds. *Figure 14-74* represents the nature of this comparison bridge circuit.

The use of tank unit capacitors, a reference capacitor, and a microchip bridge circuit in the fuel quantity indicators is complicated by the fact that temperature affects the dielectric constant of the fuel. A compensator unit (mounted low in the tank so it is always covered with fuel) is wired into the bridge circuit. It modifies current flow to reflect temperature variations of the fuel, which affect fuel density and thus capacitance of the tank units. *[Figure 14-75]* An amplifier is also needed in older systems. The amplitude of the electric signals must be increased to move the servo

Figure 14-75. *A fuel quantity tank unit and compensator unit installed inside a wing tank.*

motor in the analog indicator. Additionally, the dielectric constant of different turbine-engine fuels approved for a particular aircraft may also vary. Calibration is required to overcome this.

A fuel summation unit is part of the capacitance-type fuel quantity indication system. It is used to add the tank quantities from all indicators. This total aircraft fuel quantity can be used by the crew and by flight management computers for calculating optimum airspeed and engine performance limits for climb, cruise, descent, etc. Capacitance-type fuel quantity system test units are available for troubleshooting and ensuring proper functioning and calibration of the indicating system components.

Many aircraft with capacitance-type fuel indicating systems also use a mechanical indication system to cross-check fuel quantity indications and to ascertain the amount of fuel onboard the aircraft when electrical power is not available. A handful of fuel measuring sticks, or drip sticks, are mounted throughout each tank. When pushed and rotated, the drip stick can be lowered until fuel begins to exit the hole on the bottom of each stick. This is the point at which the top of the stick is equal to the height of the fuel. The sticks have a calibrated scale on them. By adding the indications of all of the drip sticks and converting to pounds or gallons via a chart supplied by the manufacturer, the quantity of the fuel in the tank can be ascertained. *[Figure 14-76]*

Figure 14-76. *A fuel drip stick is lowered from the fuel tank bottom until fuel drips out the hole at the bottom. By reading the calibrated scale and adding readings from all tank drip sticks, a chart can be consulted to arrive at the total fuel quantity on the aircraft by weight or by volume.*

Fuel Flowmeters

A fuel flowmeter indicates an engine's fuel use in real time. This can be useful to the pilot for ascertaining engine performance and for flight planning calculations. The types of fuel flow meter used on an aircraft depends primarily on the powerplant being used and the associated fuel system.

Measuring fuel flow accurately is complicated by the fact that the fuel mass changes with temperature or with the type of fuel used in turbine engines. In light aircraft with reciprocating engines, systems have been devised to measure fuel volume. The actual mass of fuel flowing to the engine is based on an assumption of the average weight of the fuel per unit volume.

The simplest fuel flow sensing device is used in conjunction with fuel injection systems installed on horizontally opposed reciprocating engines. A pressure gauge is used but it is calibrated in gallons per hour or pounds per hour. The amount of fuel that is flowing through the fuel injectors has a direct relationship to the pressure drop across the fuel injector orifices. Therefore, monitoring fuel pressure at the injector(s) closely approximates fuel flow and provides useful flow information for mixture control and flight planning.

There is a major limitation to the use of fuel pressure as a flow indicator. Should an injector become clogged, fuel flow is reduced. However, the pressure gauge indicates a higher fuel pressure (and greater fuel flow) due to the restriction. Operators must be aware of this potential condition and check the flowmeter against EGT to determine the nature of the elevated indication. *[Figure 14-77]*

Large reciprocating engine fuel systems may use a vane-type fuel flow meter that measures the volume of the fuel consumed by the engine. The fuel flow unit is typically located between the engine-driven fuel pump and the carburetor. The entire volume of fuel delivered to the engine is made to pass through the flowmeter. Inside, the fuel pushes against the vane, which counters the force of the fuel flow with a calibrated spring. The vane shaft rotates varying degrees matching the fuel flow rate through the unit. An autosyn transmitter deflects the pointer on the cockpit fuel flow gauge the same amount as the vane deflects. The dial face of the indicator is calibrated in gallons per hour or pounds per hour based on an average weight of fuel.

Since fuel fed to the engine must pass through the flowmeter unit, a relief valve is incorporated to bypass the fuel around the vane should it malfunction and restrict normal fuel flow. The vane chamber is eccentric. As more fuel pushes against the vane, it rotates further around in the chamber. The volume of the chamber gradually increases to permit the greater flow of fuel without restriction or pressure buildup. *[Figure 14-78]*

Turbine-engine aircraft experience the greatest range of fuel density from temperature variation and fuel composition. An elaborate fuel flow device is used on these aircraft. It measures fuel mass for accurate fuel flow indication in the cockpit. The mass flow indicator takes advantage of the direct relationship between fuel mass and viscosity. Fuel is swirled by a cylindrical impeller that rotates at a fixed speed. The outflow deflects a turbine just downstream of the impeller. The turbine is held with calibrated springs. Since the impeller motor swirls the fuel at a fixed rate, any variation of the turbine deflection is caused by the volume and viscosity of the fuel. The viscosity component represents the mass of the fuel. *[Figure 14-79]*

An alternating current (AC) synchro system is part of the mass fuel flowmeter. It is used to position a pointer against the cockpit indicator scale calibrated in pounds per hour.

Figure 14-77. *The pressure drop across the fuel injector nozzles is used to represent fuel flow in light reciprocating-engine aircraft.*

Figure 14-78. *A vane-type fuel flow meter. Greater flow volume increases deflection of the vane against a calibrated spring. An autosyn transmitter replicates the vane shaft rotation on the cockpit indicator that is calibrated in gallons or pounds of fuel flow per hour.*

With accurate fuel flow knowledge, numerous calculations can be performed to aid the pilot's situational awareness and flight planning. Most high-performance aircraft have a fuel totalizer that electronically calculates and displays information, such as total fuel used, total fuel remaining onboard the aircraft, total range and flight time remaining at the present airspeed, rate of fuel consumption, etc. On light aircraft, it is common to replace the original analog fuel indicators with electronic gauges containing similar capabilities and built-in logic. Some of these fuel computers, as they are called, integrate global positioning satellite (GPS) location information. *[Figure 14-80]* Aircraft with fully digital cockpits process fuel flow data in computers and display a wide array of fuel flow related information on demand.

Relatively new types of fuel flow sensors/transmitters are available in new aircraft and for retrofit to older aircraft. One type of device found in home-built and experimental aircraft uses a turbine that rotates in the fuel flow. The higher the flow rate is, the faster the turbine rotates. A Hall effect transducer is used to convert the speed of the turbine to an electrical signal to be used by an advanced fuel gauge similar to a fuel computer to produce a variety of calculated readouts and warnings. The turbine in this unit is in line with the fuel flow, but is fail safe to allow adequate fuel flow without interruption should the unit malfunction. *[Figure 14-81]*

Figure 14-79. *A mass flow fuel flow indicating system used on turbine-engine aircraft uses the direct relationship between viscosity and mass to display fuel flow in pounds per hour.*

Figure 14-80. *A modern fuel management gauge uses a microprocessor to display fuel flow and numerous other fuel consumption related calculations.*

Another fuel flow sensor used primarily on light aircraft also detects the spinning velocity of a turbine in the fuel path. It too has a failsafe design should the turbine malfunction. In this unit, notches in the rotor interrupt an infrared light beam between an LED and phototransistor that creates a signal proportional to the amount fuel flow. *[Figure 14-82]* This type of sensor may be coupled with an electronic indicator.

Increasing use of microprocessors and computers on aircraft enable the integration of fuel temperature and other compensating factors to produce highly accurate fuel flow information. Fuel flow sensing with digital output facilitates this with a high degree of reliability. Thermal dispersion technology provides flow sensing with no moving parts and digital output signals. The sensor consists of two resistance temperature detectors (RTDs). One is a reference RTD that measures the temperature of the fuel. The other is the active RTD. It is heated by an adjacent element to a temperature higher than the fuel. As the fuel flows, the active element cools proportionally to the fuel flow. The temperature difference between the two RTDs is highest at no flow.

The RTDs are connected to an electronic assembly that supplies power to the heater and uses sensing circuitry and a microprocessor to control a constant temperature difference between the heated and unheated RTDs. The electrical current to the heater is proportional to the mass flow of the fuel. As mentioned, the reference RTD is used as a temperature sensor to provide a temperature output and allow for temperature compensation of the flow measurement. *[Figure 14-83]*

Fuel Temperature Gauges

As previously mentioned, monitoring fuel temperature can inform the pilot when fuel temperature approaches that which could cause ice to form in the fuel system, especially at the fuel filter. Many large and high-performance turbine aircraft use a resistance type electric fuel temperature

Figure 14-81. *A transducer and microprocessor for control functions are located in the base of this turbine fuel flow sensor. The gauge is menu driven with numerous display options.*

Figure 14-82. *A turbine flow transducer in this fuel flow sensor produces a current pulse signal from an opto-electronic pickup with a preamplifier.*

Figure 14-83. *Fuel flow sensing units using thermal dispersion technology have no moving parts and output digital signals.*

sender in a main fuel tank for this purpose. It can display on a traditional ratiometer gauge *[Figure 14-65]* or can be input into a computer for processing and digital display. A low fuel temperature can be corrected with the use of a fuel heater if the aircraft is so equipped. Also as mentioned, fuel temperature can be integrated into fuel flow processing calculations. Viscosity differences at varying fuel temperatures that affect fuel flow sensing accuracy can be corrected via microprocessors and computers.

Fuel Pressure Gauges

Monitoring fuel pressure can give the pilot early warning of a fuel system related malfunction. Verification that the fuel system is delivering fuel to the fuel metering device can be critical. Simple light reciprocating-engine aircraft typically utilize a direct reading Bourdon tube pressure gauge. It is connected into the fuel inlet of the fuel metering device with a line extending to the back of the gauge in the cockpit instrument panel. A more complex aircraft may have a sensor with a transducer located at the fuel inlet to the metering device that sends electrical signals to a cockpit gauge. *[Figure 14-84]* In aircraft equipped with an auxiliary pump for starting and to backup the engine-driven pump, the fuel pressure gauge indicates the auxilliary pump pressure until the engine is started. When the auxiliary pump is switched off, the gauge indicates the pressure developed by the engine-driven pump.

14-47

Figure 14-84. *A typical fuel gauge that uses a signal from a sensing transducer to display fuel inlet pressure at the metering device.*

More complex and larger reciprocating engine aircraft may use a differential fuel pressure gauge. It compares fuel inlet pressure to the air inlet pressure at the fuel metering device. A bellows type pressure gauge is normally used. *[Figure 14-85]*

Figure 14-85. *A differential fuel pressure gauge used on complex and high-performance reciprocating-engine aircraft compares the fuel inlet pressure to the air inlet pressure at the fuel metering device.*

Modern aircraft may use a variety of sensors including solid state types and those with digital output signals or signals that are converted to digital output. These can be processed in the instrument gauge microprocessor, if so equipped, or in a computer and sent to the display unit. *[Figure 14-86]*

Pressure Warning Signal

On aircraft of any size, visual and audible warning devices are used in conjunction with gauge indications to draw the pilot's attention to certain conditions. Fuel pressure is an important parameter that merits the use of a warning signal when it falls outside of the normal operating range. Low fuel pressure warning lights can be illuminated through the use of simple pressure sensing switches. *[Figure 14-87]* The contacts of the

Figure 14-86. *An electronic display of fuel parameters, including fuel pressure.*

Figure 14-87. *A fuel pressure warning signal is controlled by a switch that closes when fuel pressure is low.*

switch will close when fuel pressure against the diaphragm is insufficient to hold them open. This allows current to flow to the annunciator or warning light in the cockpit.

Most turbine-powered aircraft utilize a low pressure warning switch at the outlet of each fuel boost pump. The annunciator for each is typically positioned adjacent to the boost pump ON/OFF switch on the fuel panel in the cockpit. *[Figure 14-88]*

Valve-In-Transit Indicator Lights

Aircraft with multiple fuel tanks use valves and pumps to move fuel and to have it flow to desired locations, such as the engines, a certain tank, or overboard during fuel jettison. The functioning of the valves in the fuel system is critical. Some aircraft indicate to the crew when the valve is opening or closing with the use of valve-in-transit lights. Contacts

Figure 14-88. *A transport category aircraft fuel panel with low pressure warning lights for each fuel boost pump.*

in the valve control the lights that go out when the valve is fully open or when it is fully closed. Alternately, annunciator lights that show the valve position as OPEN or CLOSED are also used. Valve-in-transit and valve position indicators, or lights, are located on the fuel panel in the cockpit adjacent to the valve ON/OFF switches. *[Figure 14-89]* Sometimes the switch mechanism has the annunciator light built into it. Digital display systems graphically depict valve positions on screen.

Fuel System Repair

The integrity of an aircraft fuel system is critical and should not be compromised. Any evidence of malfunction or leak should be addressed before the aircraft is released for flight. The danger of fire, explosion, or fuel starvation in flight makes it imperative that fuel system irregularities be given top priority. Each manufacturer's maintenance and operation instructions must be used to guide the technician in maintaining the fuel system in airworthy condition. Follow the manufacturer's instructions at all times. Component manufacturers and STC holder instructions should be used when applicable. Some general instructions for fuel system maintenance and repair are given in the following sections.

Troubleshooting the Fuel System

Knowledge of the fuel system and how it operates is essential when troubleshooting. Manufacturers produce diagrams and descriptions in their maintenance manuals to aid the technician. Study these for insight. Many manuals have troubleshooting charts or flow diagrams that can be followed. As with all troubleshooting, a logical sequence of steps to narrow the problem to a specific component or location should be followed. Defects within the system can often be

Figure 14-89. *Valve-in-transit lights are used on this section of a transport category aircraft fuel panel. Low boost pump pressure lights that look the same are also on the panel.*

located by tracing the fuel flow from the tank through the system to the engine. Each component must be functioning as designed and the cause of the defect symptom must be ruled out sequentially.

Location of Leaks and Defects

Close visual inspection is required whenever a leak or defect is suspected in a fuel system. Leaks can often be traced to the connection point of two fuel lines or a fuel line and a component. Occasionally, the component itself may have an internal leak. Fuel leaks also occur in fuel tanks and are discussed below. Leaking fuel produces a mark where it travels. It can also cause a stronger than normal odor. Gasoline may collect enough of its dye for it to be visible or an area clean of dirt may form. Jet fuel is difficult to detect at first, but it has a slow evaporation rate. Dirt and dust eventually settle into it, which makes it more visible.

When fuel leaks into an area where the vapors can collect, the leak must be repaired before flight due to the potential for fire or explosion. Repair could be deferred for external leaks

14-49

that are not in danger of being ignited. However, the source of the leak should be determined and monitored to ensure it does not become worse. Follow the aircraft manufacturer's instructions on the repair of fuel leaks and the requirements that need to be met for airworthiness. Detailed visual inspection can often reveal a defect.

Fuel Leak Classification

Four basic classifications are used to describe aircraft fuel leaks: stain, seep, heavy seep, and running leak. *[Figure 14-90]* In 30 minutes, the surface area of the collected fuel from a leak is a certain size. This is used as the classification standard. When the area is less than ¾ inch in diameter, the leak is said to be a stain. From ¾ to 1½ inches in diameter, the leak is classified as a seep. Heavy seeps form an area from 1½ inches to 4 inches in diameter. Running leaks pool and actually drip from the aircraft. They may follow the contour of the aircraft for a long distance.

Replacement of Gaskets, Seals, and Packings

A leak can often be repaired by replacing a gasket or seal. When this occurs or a component is replaced or reassembled after a maintenance operation, a new gasket, seal, or packing must be installed. Do not use the old one(s). Always be sure to use the correct replacement as identified by part number. Also, most gaskets, seals, and packings have a limited shelf life. They should be used only if they are within the service life stamped on the package.

Remove the entire old gasket completely, and clean all mating surfaces. Clean surfaces and grooves allow a tight seal. Inspect new gaskets and seals for any flaws. Follow the manufacturer's instructions for replacement, including cleaning procedures and any sealing compound that you may need to apply during replacement. Torque assembly bolts evenly so as to provide even pressure and prevent pinching.

Fuel Tank Repair

Whether rigid removable, bladder-type, or integral, all fuel tanks have the potential to develop leaks. Repair a tank according to the manufacturer's instructions. Some general notes for repair of each tank type follow. Note that at the time a tank is repaired, a thorough inspection should be made. Corrosion, such as that caused by water and microbes, should be identified and treated at this time, even if it is not the cause of the leak.

Rigid removable fuel tanks can be riveted, welded, or soldered together. A leak can develop at any of these types of seams or can be elsewhere on the tank. Generally, the repair must match the construction in technique.

Some metal fuel tanks experiencing minor seepage can be repaired with a sloshing procedure. An approved sloshing compound is poured into the tank, and the tank is moved so that the compound coats the entire inner surface area of the tank. Any excess compound is then poured out and the compound in the tank is allowed to cure for a specified amount

Figure 14-90. *The surface area of collected fuel from a leak is used to classify the leak into the categories shown.*

of time. Minor gaps in the seams of the tank and repairs are filled in this manner. The compound is fuel resistant once dry. Check with the aircraft manufacturer to ensure that sloshing is an airworthy repair for the aircraft fuel tank in question.

Welded Tanks

Welded tank repairs are usually done by welding. These tanks can be constructed from steel or weldable aluminum, such as 3003S or 5052SO. The tank is removed from the aircraft for the repair. It must be treated to remove any fuel vapors that remain in the tank before it is welded. This is critical to avoid serious injury from explosion should the fuel vapor ignite. The manufacturer usually gives a procedure for doing this. Some common methods for purging the tank include steam cleaning, hot water purging, and inert gas purging. Most procedures involve running the steam, water, or gas through the tank for a stated period of time. Adapters may need to be fashioned or purchased for the fill port to enable proper cleaning. Follow the manufacturer's procedure for the proper time to keep the cleaning medium in the tank and for prepping the tank for welding in general.

After a seam or a damaged area is welded, you must clean the tank of any flux or debris that may have fallen into the tank. Water rinsing and acid solutions are commonly used. A leak check to ensure the repair is sound follows a welded repair. This can be done by pressurizing the tank with a specified amount of air pressure and using a soapy solution on all seams and the repaired area. Bubbles form should air escape. The amount of air pressure used for a leak check is very low. One half to 3.5 psi is common. Use an accurate regulator and pressure gauge to prevent overpressurization that could deform or otherwise damage the tank. Tanks ordinarily supported by aircraft structure when installed should be similarly supported or reinstalled in the airframe before pressurization. *Figure 14-91* shows an aircraft fuel tank being welded and the repaired tank installed in the frame of an antique aircraft.

Riveted Tanks

Riveted tanks are often repaired by riveting. The seams and rivets are coated with a fuel resistant compound when assembled to create a leak-free container. This practice is followed during a patch repair, or when repairing a seam, which may require replacing the rivets in the seam. Some minor leak repairs may only require the application of addition compound. Follow manufacturer's instructions. The compound used may be heat sensitive and require inert gas purging to prevent degradation from hot water or steam purging. Again, follow all manufacturer guidance to insure a safe airworthy repair.

Soldered Tanks

Terneplate aircraft fuel tanks that are assembled by soldering are also repaired by soldering. All patches have a minimum amount that must overlap the damaged area. Flux used in soldering must be removed from the tank after the repair with techniques similar to that used on a welded tank. Follow manufacturer's instructions.

Bladder Tanks

Bladder fuel tanks that develop leaks can also be repaired. Most commonly, they are patched using patch material, adhesive, and methods approved by the manufacturer. As with soldered tanks, the patch has a required overlap of the damaged area. Damage that penetrates completely through the bladder is repaired with an external, as well as internal, patch.

Figure 14-91. *A rigid removable fuel tank with welded seams is repaired by welding.*

Synthetic bladder tanks have a limited service life. At some point, they seep fuel beyond acceptable limits and need to be replaced. Bladder tanks are usually required to remain wetted with fuel at all times to prevent drying and cracking of the bladder material. Storage of bladder tanks without fuel can be accomplished by coating the tanks with a substance to prevent drying, such as clean engine oil that can be flushed from the tank when ready to return to service. Follow all manufacturer's instructions for the care and repair of these common tanks. It is important to ensure that bladder tanks are correctly secured in place with the proper fasteners when reinstalling them in the aircraft after a repair.

Integral Tanks

Occasionally, an integral tank develops a leak at an access panel. This can often be repaired by transferring fuel to another tank so the panel can be removed and the seal replaced. Use of the proper sealing compound and bolt torque are required.

Other integral fuel tank leaks can be more challenging and time consuming to repair. They occur when the sealant used to seal the tank seams loses its integrity. To repair, fuel needs to be transferred or defueled out of the tank. You must enter large tanks on transport category aircraft. Preparing the tank for safe entry requires a series of steps outlined by the aircraft manufacturer. These include drying the tank and venting it of dangerous vapors. The tank is then tested with a combustible-gas indicator to be certain it can be entered safely. Clothing that does not cause static electricity and a respirator is worn. An observer is stationed outside of the tank to assist the technician in the tank. *[Figure 14-92]* A continuous flow of ventilating air is made to flow through the tank. A checklist for fuel tank preparation for entry taken from a transport category maintenance manual is shown in *Figure 14-93*. The details of the procedures are also given in the manual.

Once the location of the leak is determined, the tank sealant is removed and new sealant is applied. Remove old sealant with a nonmetallic scraper. Aluminum wool can be used to remove the final traces of the sealant. After cleaning the area with the recommended solvent, apply new sealant as instructed by the manufacturer. Observe cure time and leak checks as recommended before refilling the tank.

Fire Safety

Fuel vapor, air, and a source of ignition are the requirements for a fuel fire. Whenever working with fuel or a fuel system component, the technician must be vigilant to prevent these elements from coming together to cause a fire or explosion. A source of ignition is often the most controllable. In addition to removing all sources of ignition from the work area, care must be exercised to guard against static electricity. Static electricity can easily ignite fuel vapor, and its potential for igniting fuel vapor may not be as obvious as a flame or an operating electrical device. The action of fuel flowing through a fuel line can cause a static buildup as can many other situations in which one object moves past another. Always assess the work area and take steps to remove any potential static electricity ignition sources.

AVGAS is especially volatile. It vaporizes quickly due to its high vapor pressure and can be ignited very easily. Turbine engine fuel is less volatile but still possesses enormous capacity to ignite. This is especially true if atomized, such as when escaping out of a pressurized fuel hose or in a hot engine compartment on a warm day. Treat all fuels as potential fire

Figure 14-92. *Wear a nonstatic protective suit and respirator when entering an integral fuel tank for inspection or repair.*

This checklist must be completed prior to start of wet fuel cell entry and/or at shift change PRIOR to work assignment for the continuation of tank work started by a previous shift.

Wet fuel cell entry location

Area or building: _____ Stall: _____ Airplane: _____ Tank: _____
Shift: _____ Date: _____ Supervisor: _____

○ 1. Airplane and adjacent equipment properly grounded.
○ 2. Area secured and warning signs positioned.
○ 3. Boost pump switches off and circuit breakers pulled and placarded.
○ 4. No power on airplane: battery disconnected, external power cord disconnected from airplane, and external power recepacle placarded.
○ 5. Radio and radar equipment off (see separation distance requirements).
○ 6. Only approved explosion-proof equipment and tools will be used for fuel cell entry (lights, blowers, pressure and test equipment, etc.).
○ 7. Ensure requirements listed on aircraft confined space entry permit are complied with, including appropriate personal protective equipment: OSH class 110 respirator at a minimum, approved coveralls, cotton cap and foot coverings, and eye protection.
○ 8. Trained attendant and confined space logsheet required for all wet fuel cell entries.
○ 9. Aerators checked for cleanliness prior to use.
○ 10. Sponges available for residual fuel mop out.
○ 11. All plugs in use have streamers attached.
○ 12. Mechanical ventilation (venturis or blowers) installed to ventilate all open fuel cells.
   Note: Ventilation system must remain in operation at all times while fuel cells are open. If ventilation system fails or any ill effects, such as dizziness, irriation, or excessive odors, are noted, all work shall stop and fuel cells must be evacuated.
○ 13. Shop personnel entering cells and standby observers have current "fuel cell entry" certification cards. Certification requires the following training:
   • Aircraft confined space entry safety
   • Respirator use and maintenance
   • Wet fuel cell entry
○ 14. Fire department notified.

Meter Reading
○ 15. Oxygen reading (%): _____ By: _____
○ 16. Fuel vapor level reading (ppm): _____ By: _____
○ 17. Combustible gas meter (LEL) reading: _____ By (FD): _____

I confirm that all entry requirements were met prior to any entry.

_____   _____
Signature of supervisor or designee   Date

Figure 14-93. *Fuel tank checklist entry.*

hazards in all situations. As was discussed, empty fuel tanks have an extreme potential for ignition or explosion. Although the liquid fuel has been removed, ignitable fuel vapor can remain for a long period of time. Purging the vapor out of any empty fuel tank is an absolute necessity before any repair is initiated.

A fire extinguisher should be on hand during fuel system maintenance or whenever fuel is being handled. A fuel fire can be put out with a typical carbon dioxide (CO_2) fire extinguisher. Aim the extinguisher nozzle at the base of the flame and spray in a sweeping motion to have the agent fall over the flames to displace the oxygen and smother the fire. Dry chemical fire extinguishers rated for fuel can also be used. These leave behind a residue that requires cleanup that can be extensive and expensive. Do not use a water-type extinguisher. Fuel is lighter than water and could be spread without being extinguished. Additional precautions used to prevent fire are discussed below in the fueling–defueling section of this chapter.

Fuel System Servicing

Maintaining aircraft fuel systems in acceptable condition to deliver clean fuel to the engine(s) is a major safety factor in aviation. Personnel handling fuel or maintaining fuel systems should be properly trained and use best practices to ensure that the fuel, or fuel system, are not the cause of an incident or accident.

Checking for Fuel System Contaminants

Continuous vigilance is required when checking aircraft fuel systems for contaminants. Daily draining of strainers and sumps is combined with periodic filter changes and inspections to ensure fuel is contaminant free. Turbine powered engines have highly refined fuel control systems through which flow hundreds of pounds of fuel per hour of operation. Sumping alone is not sufficient. Particles are suspended longer in jet fuel due to its viscosity. Engineers design a series of filters into the fuel system to trap foreign matter. Technicians must supplement these with cautious procedures and thorough visual inspections to accomplish the overall goal of delivering clean fuel to the engines.

Keeping a fuel system clean begins with an awareness of the common types of contamination. Water is the most common. Solid particles, surfactants, and microorganisms are also common. However, contamination of fuel with another fuel not intended for use on a particular aircraft is possibly the worst type of contamination.

Water

Water can be dissolved into fuel or entrained. Entrained water can be detected by a cloudy appearance to the fuel. Close examination is required. Air in the fuel tends to cause a similar cloudy condition but is near the top of the tank. The cloudiness caused by water in the fuel tends to be more towards the bottom of the tank as the water slowly settles out.

As previously discussed, water can enter a fuel system via condensation. The water vapor in the vapor space above the liquid fuel in a fuel tank condenses when the temperature changes. It normally sinks to the bottom of the fuel tank into the sump where it can be drained off before flight. *[Figure 14-94]* However, time is required for this to happen.

On some aircraft, a large amount of fuel needs to be drained before settled water reaches the drain valve. Awareness of this type of sump idiosyncrasy for a particular aircraft is important. The condition of the fuel and recent fueling practices need to be considered and are equally important. If the aircraft has been flown often and filled immediately after flight, there is little reason to suspect water contamination beyond what would be exposed during a routine sumping.

Figure 14-94. *A sump drain tool used to open and collect fuel and contaminants from the fuel system sumps. Daily sump draining is part of the procedures needed to remove water from fuel that is to be delivered to the engine(s).*

An aircraft that has sat for a long period of time with partially full fuel tanks is a cause of concern.

It is possible that water is introduced into the aircraft fuel load during refueling with fuel that already contains water. Any suspected contamination from refueling or the general handling of the aircraft should be investigated. A change in fuel supplier may be required if water continues to be an issue despite efforts are made to keep the aircraft fuel tanks full and sumps drained on a regular basis. Note that fuel below freezing temperature may contain entrained water in ice form that may not settle into the sump until melted. Use of an anti-icing solution in turbine fuel tanks helps prevent filter blockage from water that condenses out of the fuel as ice during flight.

Note that the fuel anti-ice additive level should be monitored so that recommended quantity for the tank capacity is maintained. After repeated fueling, the level can be obscured. A field hand-held test unit can be used to check the amount of anti-ice additive already in a fuel load. *[Figure 14-95]*

Figure 14-95. *A hand-held refractometer with digital display measures the amount of fuel anti-ice additive contained in a fuel load.*

Strainers and filters are designed with upward flow exits to have water collect at the bottom of the fuel bowl to be drained off. This should not be overlooked. Entrained water in small quantities that makes it to the engine usually poses no problem. Large amounts of water can disrupt engine operation. Settled water in tanks can cause corrosion. This can be magnified by microorganisms that live in the fuel/water interface. High quantities of water in the fuel can also cause discrepancies in fuel quantity probe indications.

Solid Particle Contaminants

Solid particles that do not dissolve in the fuel are common contaminants. Dirt, rust, dust, metal particles, and just about anything that can find its way into an open fuel tank is of concern. Filter elements are designed to trap these contaminants and some fall into the sump to be drained off. Pieces of debris from the inside of the fuel system may also accumulate, such as broken-off sealant, or pieces of filter elements, corrosion, etc.

Preventing solid contaminant introduction into the fuel is critical. Whenever the fuel system is open, care must be taken to keep out foreign matter. Lines should be capped immediately. Fuel tank caps should not be left open for any longer than required to refuel the tanks. Clean the area adjacent to wherever the system is opened before it is opened.

Coarse sediments are those visible to the naked eye. Should they pass beyond system filters, they can clog in fuel metering device orifices, sliding valves, and fuel nozzles. Fine sediments cannot actually be seen as individual particles. They may be detected as a haze in the fuel or they may refract light when examining the fuel. Their presence in fuel controls and metering devices is indicated by dark shellac-like marks on sliding surfaces.

The maximum amount of solid particle contamination allowable is much less in turbine engine fuel systems than in reciprocating-engine fuel systems. It is particularly important to regularly replace filter elements and investigate any unusual solid particles that collect therein. The discovery of significant metal particles in a filter could be a sign of a failing component upstream of the filter. A laboratory analysis is possible to determine the nature and possible source of solid contaminants.

Surfactants

Surfactants are liquid chemical contaminants that naturally occur in fuels. They can also be introduced during the refining or handling processes. These surface active agents usually appear as tan to dark brown liquid when they are present in large quantities. They may even have a soapy consistency. Surfactants in small quantities are unavoidable and pose little threat to fuel system functioning. Larger quantities of surfactants do pose problems. In particular, they reduce the surface tension between water and the fuel and tend to cause water and even small particles in the fuel to remain suspended rather than settling into the sumps. Surfactants also tend to collect in filter elements making them less effective.

Surfactants are usually in the fuel when it is introduced into the aircraft. Discovery of either excessive quantities of dirt and water making their way through the system or a sudsy residue in filters and sumps may indicate their presence. The source of fuel should be investigated and avoided if found to contain a high level of these chemicals. As mentioned, slow settling rates of solids and water into sumps is a key indicator that surfactant levels are high in the fuel. Most quality fuel providers have clay filter elements on their fuel dispensing trucks and in their fixed storage and dispensing systems. These filters, if renewed at the proper intervals, remove most surfactants through adhesion. Surfactants discovered in the aircraft systems should be traced to the fuel supply source and the use and condition of these filters. *[Figure 14-96]*

Figure 14-96. *Clay filter elements remove surfactants. They are used in the fuel dispensing system before fuel enters the aircraft.*

Microorganisms

The presence of microorganisms in turbine engine fuels is a critical problem. There are hundreds of varieties of these life forms that live in free water at the junction of the water and fuel in a fuel tank. They form a visible slime that is dark brown, grey, red, or black in color. This microbial growth can multiply rapidly and can cause interference with the proper functioning of filter elements and fuel quantity indicators. Moreover, the slimy water/microbe layer in contact with the fuel tank surface provides a medium for electrolytic corrosion of the tank. *[Figure 14-97]*

Since the microbes live in free water and feed on fuel, the most powerful remedy for their presence is to keep water from accumulating in the fuel. Fuel 100 percent free of water is not practicable. By following best practices for sump draining and filter changes, combined with care of fuel stock tanks used to refuel aircraft, much of the potential for water to accumulate in the aircraft fuel tanks can be mitigated. The addition of biocides to the fuel when refueling also helps by killing organisms that are present.

Foreign Fuel Contamination

Aircraft engines operate effectively only with the proper fuel. Contamination of an aircraft's fuel with fuel not intended for use in that particular aircraft can have disastrous consequences. It is the responsibility of all aviators to put forth effort continuously to ensure that only the fuel designed for the operation of the aircraft's engine(s) is put into the fuel tanks. Each fuel tank receptacle or fuel cap area is clearly marked to indicate which fuel is required. *[Figure 14-98]*

If the wrong fuel is put into an aircraft, the situation must be rectified before flight. If discovered before the fuel pump is operated and an engine is started, drain all improperly filled tanks. Flush out the tanks and fuel lines with the correct fuel and then refill the tanks with the proper fuel. However, if discovered after an engine has been started or attempted to be started, the procedure is more in depth. The entire fuel system, including all fuel lines, components, metering device(s) and tanks, must be drained and flushed. If the engines have been operated, a compression test should be accomplished and the combustion chamber and pistons should be borescope inspected. Engine oil should be drained and all screens and filters examined for any evidence of damage. Once reassembled and the tanks have been filled with the correct fuel, a full engine run-up check should be performed before releasing the aircraft for flight.

Contaminated fuel caused by the introduction of small quantities of the wrong type of fuel into an aircraft may not look any different when visually inspected, making a dangerous situation more dangerous. Any person recognizing that this error has occurred must ground the aircraft. The lives of the aircraft occupants are at stake.

Detection of Contaminants

Visual inspection of fuel should always reveal a clean, bright looking liquid. Fuel should not be opaque, which could be a sign of contamination and demands further investigation. As mentioned, the technician must always be aware of the fuel's appearance, as well as when and from what sources refueling has taken place. Any suspicion of contamination must be investigated.

In addition to the detection methods mentioned for each type of contamination above, various field and laboratory tests can be performed on aircraft fuel to expose contamination. A common field test for water contamination is performed by adding a dye that dissolves in water but not fuel to a test sample drawn from the fuel tank. The more water present in the fuel, the greater the dye disperses and colors the sample.

Another common test kit commercially available contains a grey chemical powder that changes color to pink or purple when the contents of a fuel sample contains more than 30 parts per million (ppm) of water. A 15 ppm test is available for turbine engine fuel. *[Figure 14-99]* These levels of water are considered generally unacceptable and not safe for operation of the aircraft. If levels are discovered above these amounts, time for the water to settle out of the fuel should be given or the aircraft should be defueled and refueled with acceptable fuel.

Figure 14-97. *This fuel-water sample has microbial growth at the interface of the two liquids.*

Figure 14-98. *All entry points of fuel into the aircraft are marked with the type of fuel to be used. Never introduce any other fuel into the aircraft other than that which is specified.*

Figure 14-99. *This kit allows periodic testing for water in fuel.*

The presence and level of microorganisms in a fuel tank can also be measured with a field device. The test detects the metabolic activity of bacteria, yeast, and molds, including sulfate reducing bacteria, and other anaerobe microorganisms. This could be used to determine the amount of anti-microbial agent to be added to the fuel. The testing unit is shown in *Figure 14-100*.

Figure 14-100. *A capture solution is put into a 1 liter sample of fuel and shaken. The solution is then put into the analyzer shown to determine the level of microorganisms in the fuel.*

Bug test kits test fuel specifically for bacteria and fungus. While other types of microorganisms may exist, this semi-quantitative test is quick and easy to perform. Treat a fuel sample with the product and match the color of the sample to the chart for an indication of the level of bacteria and fungus present. These are some of the most common types of microorganisms that grow in fuel; if growth levels of fungus and bacteria are acceptable, the fuel could be usable. *[Figure 14-101]*

combined with contaminant identification technology and microorganism detection, chances of delivering clean fuel to the aircraft engines are good. *[Figure 14-102]*

Figure 14-102. *This contaminant analyzer is used on fuel supply source outflow, such as that on a refueling truck. Water and solid contaminant levels are detected using laser identification technology. The valve to the fill hose is automatically closed when levels of either are elevated beyond acceptable limits.*

Figure 14-101. *Fuel bug test kits identify the level of bacteria and fungus present in a fuel load by comparing the color of a treated sample with a color chart.*

Fuel trucks and fuel farms may make use of laser contaminant identification technology. All fuel exiting the storage tank going into the servicing hose is passed through the analyzer unit. Laser sensing technology determines the difference between water and solid particle contaminants. When an excessive level of either is detected, the unit automatically shuts off flow to the fueling nozzle. Thus, aircraft are fueled only with clean dry fuel. When surfactant filters are

Before various test kits were developed for use in the field by nonscientific personnel, laboratories provided complete fuel composition analysis to aviators. These services are still available. A sample is sent in a sterilized container to the lab. It can be tested for numerous factors including water, microbial growth, flash point, specific gravity, cetane index (a measure of combustibility and burning characteristics), and more. Tests for microbes involve growing cultures of whatever organisms are present in the fuel. *[Figure 15-103]*

Fuel Contamination Control

A continuous effort must be put forth by all those in the aviation industry to ensure that each aircraft is fueled only with clean fuel of the correct type. Many contaminants, both

Figure 14-103. *Laboratory tests of fuel samples are available.*

soluble and insoluble, can contaminate an aircraft's fuel supply. They can be introduced with the fuel during fueling or the contamination may occur after the fuel is onboard.

Contamination control begins long before the fuel gets pumped into an aircraft fuel tank. Many standard petroleum industry safeguards are in place. Fuel farm and delivery truck fuel handling practices are designed to control contamination. Various filters, testing, and treatments effectively keep fuel contaminant free or remove various contaminants once discovered. However, the correct clean fuel for an aircraft should never be taken for granted. The condition of all storage tanks and fuel trucks should be monitored. All filter changes and treatments should occur regularly and on time. The fuel supplier should take pride in delivering clean, contaminant-free fuel to its customers.

Onboard aircraft fuel systems must be maintained and serviced according to manufacturer's specifications. Samples from all drains should be taken and inspected on a regular basis. Filters should be changed at the specified intervals. The fuel load should be visually inspected and tested from time to time or when there is a potential contamination issue. Particles discovered in filters should be identified and investigated if needed. Inspection of the fuel system during periodic inspections should be treated with highest concern.

Most importantly, the choice of the correct fuel for an aircraft should never be in question. No one should ever put a fuel into an aircraft fuel tank unless absolutely certain it is the correct fuel for that aircraft and its engine(s). Personnel involved in fuel handling should be properly trained. All potential contamination situations should be investigated and remedied.

Fueling and Defueling Procedures

Maintenance technicians are often asked to fuel or defuel aircraft. Fueling procedure can vary from aircraft to aircraft. Tanks may need to be fueled in a prescribed sequence to prevent structural damage to the airframe. The proper procedure should be confirmed before fueling an unfamiliar aircraft.

Fueling

Always fuel aircraft outside, not in a hangar where fuel vapors may accumulate and increase the risk and severity of an accident. Generally, there are two types of fueling process: over-the-wing refueling and pressure refueling. Over-the-wing refueling is accomplished by opening the fuel tank cap on the upper surface of the wing or fuselage, if equipped with fuselage tanks. The fueling nozzle is carefully inserted into the fill opening and fuel is pumped into the tank. This process is similar to the process used to refuel an automobile gas tank. When finished, the cap is secured and subsequent tanks are opened and refilled until the aircraft has the desired fuel load onboard. Pressure refueling occurs at the bottom, front, or rear of the fuel tank. A pressure refueling nozzle locks onto the fueling port at the aircraft fueling station. Fuel is pumped into the aircraft through this secured and sealed connection. Gauges are monitored to ascertain when the tanks are properly loaded. An automatic shutoff system may be part of the aircraft system. It closes the fueling valve when the tanks are full. *[Figure 14-104]*

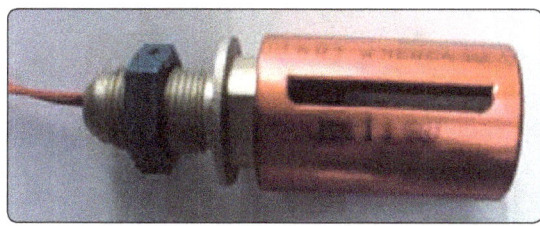

Figure 14-104. *A float switch installed in a fuel tank can close the refueling valve when the tanks are full during pressure fueling of an aircraft. Other more sophisticated automatic shutoff systems exist.*

Precautions should be used with either type of fueling. First and foremost, it is absolutely essential that the correct fuel be put in the aircraft. The type of fuel to be used is placarded near the fill port on over-the-wing systems and at the fueling station on pressure refueled aircraft. If there is any question about which fuel to use, the pilot in command, other knowledgeable personnel, or the manufacturer's maintenance/operations manual should be consulted before proceeding. Note that an over-the-wing refueling nozzle for turbine engine fuel should be too large to fit into the fill opening on an aircraft utilizing gasoline.

Clean the area adjacent to the fill port when refueling over the wing. Ensure the fuel nozzle is also clean. Aviation fuel nozzles are equipped with static bonding wires that must be attached to the aircraft before the fuel cap is opened.

[Figure 14-105] Open the cap only when ready to dispense the fuel. Insert the nozzle into the opening with care. The aircraft structure is much more delicate than the fuel nozzle, which could easily damage the aircraft. Do not insert the neck of the nozzle deeply enough to hit bottom. This could dent the tank, or the aircraft skin, if it is an integral tank. Exercise caution to avoid damage to the surface of the airframe by the heavy fuel hose. Lay the hose over your shoulder or use a refueling mat to protect the paint. *[Figure 14-106]*

Figure 14-105. *An AVGAS fueling nozzle with static bonding grounding wire.*

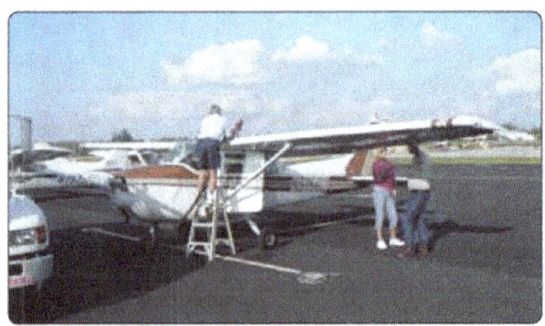

Figure 14-106. *Over-the-wing refueling a Cessna.*

When pressure refueling, the aircraft receptacle is part of a fueling valve assembly. When the fueling nozzle is properly connected and locked, a plunger unlocks the aircraft valve so fuel can be pumped through it. Normally, all tanks can be fueled from a single point. Valves in the aircraft fuel system are controlled at the fueling station to direct the fuel into the proper tank. *[Figure 14-107]* Ensure that the pressure developed by the refueling pump is correct for the aircraft before pumping fuel. Note that, while similar, pressure fueling panels and their operation are different on different aircraft. Refueling personnel should be guided through the correct use of each panel. Do not guess at how the panel and associated valves operate.

Figure 14-107. *This panel at the pressure refueling station has valve position switches and quantity gauges to be used during refueling. Valve open position lights are adjacent to the switches for each tank.*

When fueling from a fuel truck, precautions should be taken. If the truck is not in continuous service, all sumps should be drained before moving the truck, and the fuel should be visually inspected to be sure it is bright and clean. Turbine fuel should be allowed to settle for a few hours if the fuel truck tank has recently been filled or the truck has been jostled, such as when driven over a bumpy service road at the airport. Properly maneuver the fuel truck into position for refueling. The aircraft should be approached slowly. The truck should be parked parallel to the wings and in front of the fuselage if possible. Avoid backing toward the aircraft. Set the parking brake and chock the wheels. Connect a static bonding cable from the truck to the aircraft. This cable is typically stored on a reel mounted on the truck.

There are other miscellaneous good practices that should be employed when refueling an aircraft. A ladder should be used if the refuel point is not accessible while standing on the ground. Climbing on an expensive aircraft to access the fueling ports is possible but does not give the stability of a ladder and may not be appreciated by the aircraft owner. If it is necessary to walk on the wings of the aircraft, do so only in designated areas, which are safe.

Filler nozzles should be treated as the important tools that they are. They should not be dropped or dragged across the apron. Most have attached dust caps that should be removed only for the actual fueling process and then immediately replaced. Nozzles should be clean to avoid contamination of the fuel. They should not leak and should be repaired at the earliest sign of leak or malfunction. Keep the fueling nozzle in constant contact with the filler neck spout when fueling. Never leave the nozzle in the fill spout unattended. When fueling is complete, always doublecheck the security of all fuel caps and ensure that bonding wires have been removed and stowed.

Defueling

Removing the fuel contained in aircraft fuel tanks is sometimes required. This can occur for maintenance, inspection, or due to contamination. Occasionally, a change in flight plan may require defueling. Safety procedures for defueling are the same as those for fueling. Always defuel outside. Fire extinguishers should be on hand. Bonding cables should be attached to guard against static electricity buildup. Defueling should be performed by experienced personnel, and inexperienced personnel must be checked out before doing so without assistance.

Remember that there may be a sequence in defueling an aircraft's fuel tanks just as there is when fueling to avoid structural damage. Consult the manufacturer's maintenance/operations manual(s) if in doubt.

Pressure fueled aircraft normally defuel through the pressure fueling port. The aircraft's in-tank boost pumps can be used to pump the fuel out. The pump on a fuel truck can also be used to draw fuel out. These tanks can also be drained through the tank sump drains, but the large size of the tanks usually makes this impractical. Aircraft fueled over the wing are normally drained through the tank sump drains. Follow the manufacturer's procedure for defueling the aircraft.

What to do with the fuel coming out of a tank depends on a few factors. First, if the tank is being drained due to fuel contamination or suspected contamination, it should not be mixed with any other fuel. It should be stored in a separate container from good fuel, treated if possible, or disposed of properly. Take measures to ensure that contaminated fuel is never placed onboard an aircraft or mixed with good fuel. Second, the manufacturer may have requirements for good fuel that has been defueled from an aircraft, specifying whether it can be reused and the type of storage container in which it must be stored. Above all, fuel removed from an aircraft must not be mixed with any other type of fuel.

Good fuel removed from an aircraft must be handled with all precautions used when handling any fuel. It must only be put into clean tanks and efforts must be made to keep it clean. It may be put back in the aircraft or another aircraft if the manufacturer allows. Large aircraft can often transfer fuel from a tank requiring maintenance to another tank to avoid the defueling process.

Fire Hazards When Fueling or Defueling

Due to the combustible nature of AVGAS and turbine engine fuel, the potential for fire while fueling and defueling aircraft must be addressed. Always fuel and defuel outside, not in a hangar that serves as an enclosed area for vapors to build up to a combustible level. Clothing worn by refueling personnel should not promote static electricity buildup. Synthetics, such as nylon, should be avoided. Cotton has proved to be safe for fuel handling attire.

As previously mentioned, the most controllable of the three ingredients required for fire is the source of ignition. It is absolutely necessary to prevent a source of ignition anywhere near the aircraft during fueling or refueling. Any open flame, such as a lit cigarette, must be extinguished. Operation of any electrical devices must be avoided. Radio and radar use is prohibited. It is important to note that fuel vapors proliferate well beyond the actual fuel tank opening and a simple spark, even one caused by static electricity, could be enough for ignition. Any potential for sparks must be nullified.

Spilled fuel poses an additional fire hazard. A thin layer of fuel vaporizes quickly. Small spills should be wiped up immediately. Larger spills can be flooded with water to dissipate the fuel and the potential for ignition. Do not sweep fuel that has spilled onto the ramp.

Class B fire extinguishers need to be charged and accessible nearby during the fueling and defueling processes. Fueling personnel must know exactly where they are and how to use them. In case of an emergency, the fuel truck, if used, may need to be quickly driven away from the area. For this reason alone, it should be positioned correctly on the ramp relative to the aircraft.

Chapter 15
Ice and Rain Protection

Ice Control Systems

Rain, snow, and ice are transportation's longtime enemies. Flying has added a new dimension, particularly with respect to ice. Under certain atmospheric conditions, ice can build rapidly on airfoils and air inlets. On days when there is visible moisture in the air, ice can form on aircraft leading-edge surfaces at altitudes where freezing temperatures start. Water droplets in the air can be supercooled to below freezing without actually turning into ice unless they are disturbed in some manner. This unusual occurrence is partly due to the surface tension of the water droplet not allowing the droplet to expand and freeze. However, when aircraft surfaces disturb these droplets, they immediately turn to ice on the aircraft surfaces.

The two types of ice encountered during flight are clear and rime. Clear ice forms when the remaining liquid portion of the water drop flows out over the aircraft surface, gradually freezing as a smooth sheet of solid ice. Formation occurs when droplets are large, such as in rain or in cumuliform clouds. Clear ice is hard, heavy, and tenacious. Its removal by deicing equipment is especially difficult.

Rime ice forms when water drops are small, such as those in stratified clouds or light drizzle. The liquid portion remaining after initial impact freezes rapidly before the drop has time to spread over the aircraft surface. The small frozen droplets trap air giving the ice a white appearance. Rime ice is lighter in weight than clear ice and its weight is of little significance. However, its irregular shape and rough surface decrease the effectiveness of the aerodynamic efficiency of airfoils, reducing lift and increasing drag. Rime ice is brittle and more easily removed than clear ice.

Mixed clear and rime icing can form rapidly when water drops vary in size or when liquid drops intermingle with snow or ice particles. Ice particles become imbedded in clear ice, building a very rough accumulation sometimes in a mushroom shape on leading edges. Ice may be expected to form whenever there is visible moisture in the air and temperature is near or below freezing. An exception is carburetor icing, which can occur during warm weather with no visible moisture present.

Ice or frost forming on aircraft creates two basic hazards:

1. The resulting malformation of the airfoil that could decrease the amount of lift.
2. The additional weight and unequal formation of the ice that could cause unbalancing of the aircraft, making it hard to control.

Enough ice to cause an unsafe flight condition can form in a very short period of time, thus some method of ice prevention or removal is necessary. *Figure 15-1* shows the effects of ice on a leading edge.

Icing Effects

Ice buildup increases drag and reduces lift. It causes destructive vibration and hampers true instrument readings. Control surfaces become unbalanced or frozen. Fixed slots are filled and movable slots jammed. Radio reception is hampered and engine performance is affected. Ice, snow, and slush have a direct impact on the safety of flight. Not only because of degraded lift, reduced takeoff performance, and/or maneuverability of the aircraft, but when chunks break off, they can also cause engine failures and structural damage. Fuselage aft-mounted engines are particularly susceptible

Figure 15-1. *Formation of ice on aircraft leading edge.*

to this foreign object damage (FOD) phenomenon. Wing-mounted engines are not excluded however. Ice can be present on any part of the aircraft and, when it breaks off, there is some probability that it could go into an engine. The worst case is that ice on the wing breaks off during takeoff due to the flexing of the wing and goes directly into the engine, leading to surge, vibration, and complete thrust loss. Light snow that is loose on the wing surfaces and the fuselage can also cause engine damage leading to surge, vibration, and thrust loss.

Whenever icing conditions are encountered, the performance characteristics of the airplane deteriorate. *[Figure 15-2]* Increased aerodynamic drag increases fuel consumption, reducing the airplane's range and making it more difficult to maintain speed. Decreased rate of climb must be anticipated, not only because of the decrease in wing and empennage efficiency but also because of the possible reduced efficiency of the propellers and increase in gross weight. Abrupt maneuvering and steep turns at low speeds must be avoided because the airplane stalls at higher-than-published speeds with ice accumulation. On final approach for landing, increased airspeed must be maintained to compensate for this increased stall speed. After touchdown with heavy ice accumulation, landing distances may be as much as twice the normal distance due to the increased landing speeds. In this chapter, ice prevention and ice elimination using pneumatic pressure, application of heat, and the application of fluid is discussed.

The ice and rain protection systems used on aircraft keep ice from forming on the following airplane components:

- Wing leading edges
- Horizontal and vertical stabilizer leading edges
- Engine cowl leading edges
- Propellers

Figure 15-2. *Effects of structural icing.*

- Propeller spinner
- Air data probes
- Flight deck windows
- Water and waste system lines and drains
- Antenna

Figure 15-3 gives an overview of ice and rain protection systems installed in a large transport category aircraft. In modern aircraft, many of these systems are automatically controlled by the ice detection system and onboard computers.

Ice Detector System

Ice can be detected visually, but most modern aircraft have one or more ice detector sensors that warn the flight crew of icing conditions. An annunciator light comes on to alert the flight crew. In some aircraft models, multiple ice detectors are used, and the ice detection system automatically turns on the WAI systems when icing is detected. *[Figure 15-4]*

Ice Prevention

Several means to prevent or control ice formation are used in aircraft today:

1. Heating surfaces with hot air
2. Heating by electrical elements
3. Breaking up ice formations, usually by inflatable boots
4. Chemical application

Equipment is designed for anti-icing or for deicing. Anti-icing equipment is turned on before entering icing conditions and is designed to prevent ice from forming. A surface may be anti-iced by keeping it dry, by heating to a temperature that evaporates water upon impingement, or by heating the surface just enough to prevent freezing, maintaining it running wet. Deicing equipment is designed to remove ice after it begins to accumulate typically on the wings and stabilizer leading edges. Ice may be controlled on aircraft structure by the methods described in *Figure 15-5*.

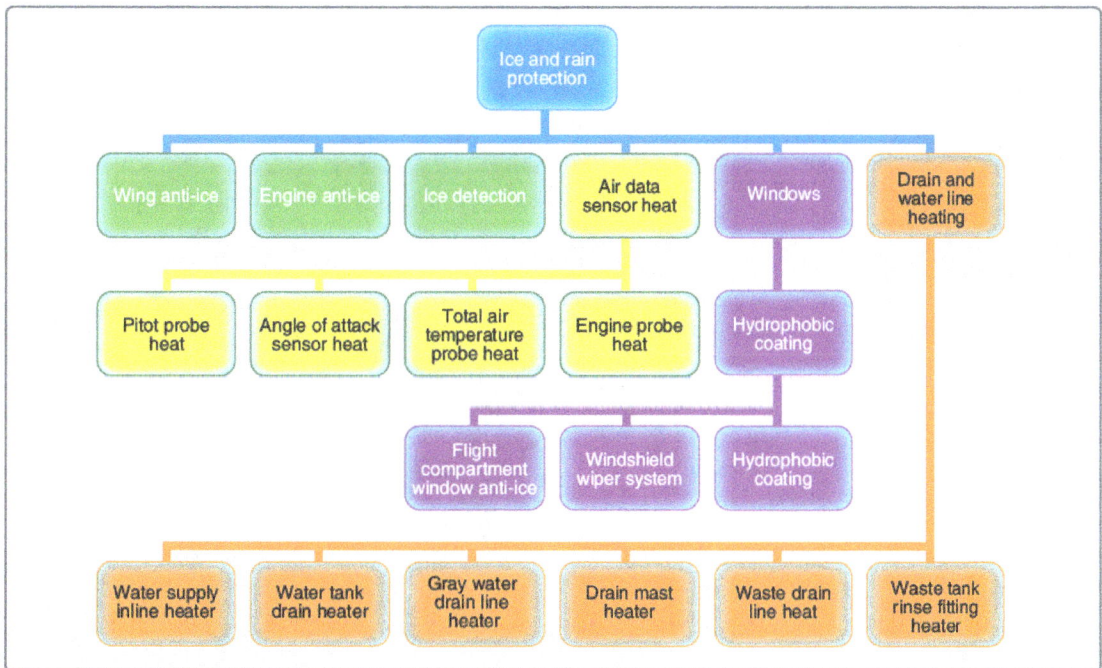

Figure 15-3. *Ice and rain protection systems.*

Figure 15-4. *An ice detector alerts the flight crew of icing conditions and, on some aircraft, automatically activates ice protection systems. One or more detectors are located on the forward fuselage.*

Location of ice	Method of control
Leading edge of the wing	Thermal pneumatic, thermal electric, chemical, and pneumatic (deice)
Leading edges of vertical and horizontal stabilizers	Thermal pneumatic, thermal electric, and pneumatic (deice)
Windshield, windows	Thermal pneumatic, thermal electric, and chemical
Heater and engine air inlets	Thermal pneumatic and thermal electric
Pitot and static air data sensors	Thermal electric
Propeller blade leading edge and spinner	Thermal electric and chemical
Carburetor(s)	Thermal pneumatic and chemical
Lavatory drains and portable water lines	Thermal electric

Figure 15-5. *Typical ice control methods.*

Wing and Horizontal and Vertical Stabilizer Anti-Icing Systems

The wing leading edges, or leading edge slats, and horizontal and vertical stabilizer leading edges of many aircraft make and models have anti-icing systems installed to prevent the formation of ice on these components. The most common anti-icing systems used are thermal pneumatic, thermal electric, and chemical. Most general aviation (GA) aircraft equipped to fly in icing conditions use pneumatic deicing boots, a chemical anti-ice system. High-performance aircraft may have "weeping wings." Large transport-category aircraft are equipped with advanced thermal pneumatic or thermal electric anti-icing systems that are controlled automatically to prevent the formation of ice.

Thermal Pneumatic Anti-icing

Thermal systems used for the purpose of preventing the formation of ice or for deicing airfoil leading edges usually use heated air ducted spanwise along the inside of the leading edge of the airfoil and distributed around its inner surface. These thermal pneumatic anti-icing systems are used for wings, leading edge slats, horizontal and vertical stabilizers, engine inlets, and more. There are several sources of heated air, including hot air bled from the turbine compressor, engine exhaust heat exchangers, and ram air heated by a combustion heater.

Wing Anti-Ice (WAI) System

Thermal wing anti-ice (WAI or TAI) systems for business jet and large-transport category aircraft typically use hot air bled from the engine compressor. *[Figure 15-6]* Relatively

Figure 15-6. *Aircraft with thermal WAI system.*

large amounts of very hot air can be bled off the compressor, providing a satisfactory source of anti-icing heat. The hot air is routed through ducting, manifolds, and valves to components that need to be anti-iced. *Figure 15-7* shows a typical WAI system schematic for a business jet. The bleed air is routed to each wing leading edge by an ejector in each wing inboard area. The ejector discharges the bleed air into piccolo tubes for distribution along the leading edge. Fresh ambient air is introduced into the wing leading edge by two flush-mounted ram air scoops in each wing leading edge, one at the wing root and one near the wingtip. The ejectors entrain ambient air, reduce the temperature of the bleed air, and increase the mass airflow in the piccolo tubes. The wing leading edge is constructed of two skin layers separated by a narrow passageway. *[Figure 15-8]* The air directed against the leading edge can only escape through the passageway, after which it is vented overboard through a vent in the bottom of the wingtip.

When the WAI switch is turned on, the pressure regulator is energized and the shutoff valve opens. When the wing leading edge temperature reaches approximately +140 °F, temperature switches turn on the operation light above the switch. If the temperature in the wing leading edge exceeds approximately +212 °F (outboard) or +350 °F (inboard), the red WING OV HT warning light on the annunciator panel illuminates.

Figure 15-8. *Heated wing leading edge.*

Figure 15-7. *Thermal WAI system.*

The ducting of WAI systems usually consists of aluminum alloy, titanium, stainless steel, or molded fiberglass tubes. The tube, or duct, sections are attached to each other by bolted end flanges or by band-type V-clamps. The ducting is lagged with a fire-resistant, heat-insulating material, such as fiberglass. In some installations, thin stainless steel expansion bellows are used. Bellows are located at strategic positions to absorb any distortion or expansion of the ducting that may occur due to temperature variations. The joined sections of ducting are hermetically sealed by sealing rings. These seals are fitted into annular recesses in the duct joint faces.

When installing a section of duct, make certain that the seal bears evenly against and is compressed by the adjacent joint's flange. When specified, the ducts should be pressure tested at the pressure recommended by the manufacturer of the aircraft concerned. Leak checks are made to detect defects in the duct that would permit the escape of heated air. The rate of leakage at a given pressure should not exceed that recommended in the aircraft maintenance manual.

Air leaks can often be detected audibly and are sometimes revealed by holes in the lagging or thermal insulation material. However, if difficulty arises in locating leaks, a soap-and-water solution may be used. All ducting should be inspected for security, general condition, or distortion. Lagging or insulating blankets must be checked for security and must be free of flammable fluids, such as oil or hydraulic fluid.

Leading Edge Slat Anti-Ice System

Aircraft that utilize leading edge slats often use bleed air from the engine compressor to prevent the formation of frost on these surfaces. On a modern transport category aircraft, the pneumatic system supplies bleed air for this purpose. WAI valves control the air flow from the pneumatic system to WAI ducts. The WAI ducts carry the air to the slats. Holes in the bottom of each slat let the air out.

The airfoil and cowl ice protection system (ACIPS) computer card controls the WAI valves, and pressure sensors send duct air pressure data to the computer. The aircrew can select an auto or manual mode with the WAI selector. In the auto mode, the system turns on when the ice detection system detects ice. The off and on positions are used for manual control of the WAI system. The WAI system is only used in the air, except for ground tests. The weight on wheels system and/or airspeed data disarms the system when the aircraft is on the ground. *[Figure 15-9]*

WAI Valve

The WAI valve controls the flow of bleed air from the pneumatic system to the WAI ducts. The valve is electrically controlled and pneumatically actuated. The torque motor controls operation of the valve. With no electrical power to the torque motor, air pressure on one side of the actuator holds the valve closed. Electrical current through the torque motor allows air pressure to open the valve. As the torque motor current increases, the valve opening increases. *[Figure 15-10]*

WAI Pressure Sensor

The WAI pressure sensor senses the air pressure in the WAI duct after the WAI valve. The ACIPS system card uses the pressure information to control the WAI system.

WAI Ducts

The WAI ducts move air from the pneumatic system through the wing leading edge to the leading edge slats. *Figure 15-9* shows that only leading edge slat sections 3, 4, and 5 on the left wing and 10, 11, and 12 on the right wing receive bleed air for WAI. Sections of the WAI ducting are perforated. The holes allow air to flow into the space inside the leading edge slats. The air leaves the slats through holes in the bottom of each slat. Some WAI ducts have connecting "T" ducts that telescope to direct air into the slats while extended. The telescoping section attached to the slat on one end, slides over the narrow diameter "T" section that is connected into the WAI duct. A seal prevents any loss of air. This arrangement allows warm air delivery to the slats while retracted, in transit, and fully deployed. *[Figure 15-11]*

WAI Control System

Modern aircraft use several onboard computers to control aircraft systems. The WAI system is controlled by the ACIPS computer card. The ACIPS computer card controls both WAI valves. The required positions of the WAI valves change as bleed air temperature and altitude change. The left and right valves operate at the same time to heat both wings equally. This keeps the airplane aerodynamically stable in icing conditions. The WAI pressure sensors supply feedback information to the WAI ACIPS computer card for WAI valve control and position indication. If either pressure sensor fails, the WAI ACIPS computer card sets the related WAI valve to either fully open or fully closed. If either valve fails closed, the WAI computer card keeps the other valve closed.

There is one selector for the WAI system. The selector has three positions: auto, on, and off. With the selector in auto and no operational mode inhibits, the WAI ACIPS computer card sends a signal to open the WAI valves when either ice detector detects ice. The valves close after a 3-minute delay when the ice detector no longer detects ice. The time delay prevents frequent on/off cycles during intermittent icing conditions. With the selector on and no operational mode inhibits, the WAI valves open. With the selector off, the WAI valves close. The operational mode for the WAI valves can be inhibited by many different sets of conditions. *[Figure 15-12]*

Figure 15-9. *Wing leading edge slat anti-ice system.*

Figure 15-10. *A wing anti-ice valve.*

The operational mode is inhibited if all of these conditions occur:

- Auto mode is selected
- Takeoff mode is selected
- Airplane has been in the air less than 10 minutes

With auto or on selected, the operational mode is inhibited if any of these conditions occur:

- Airplane on the ground (except during an initiated or periodic built-in test equipment (BITE) test)
- Total Air Temperature (TAT) is more than 50 °F (10 °C) and the time since takeoff is less than 5 minutes
- Auto slat operation
- Air-driven hydraulic pump operation
- Engine start
- Bleed air temperature less than 200 °F (93 °C).

15-7

Figure 15-11. *WAI ducting.*

Figure 15-12. *WAI inhibit logic schematic.*

The WAI valves stay closed as long as the operational mode inhibit is active. If the valves are already open, the operational mode inhibit causes the valves to close.

WAI Indication System

The aircrew can monitor the WAI system on the onboard computer maintenance page. *[Figure 15-13]* The following information is shown:

- WING MANIFOLD PRESS—pneumatic duct pressure in PSIG
- VALVE—WAI valve open, closed, or regulating
- AIR PRESS—pressure downstream of the WAI valves in PSIG
- AIR FLOW—air flow through the WAI valves in pounds per minute

WAI System (BITE) Test

BITE circuits in the WAI ACIPS computer card continuously monitor the WAI system. Faults that affect the dispatch of the aircraft cause status messages. Other faults cause central maintenance computer system (CMCS) maintenance

Figure 15-13. *Ice protection onboard computer maintenance page.*

messages. The BITE in the WAI ACIPS computer card also performs automatic power-up and periodic tests. Faults found during these tests that affect dispatch cause status messages. Other faults cause CMCS maintenance messages. The power-up test occurs when the card gets power. BITE does a test of the card hardware and software functions and the valve and pressure sensor interfaces. The valves do not move during this test.

The periodic test occurs when all these conditions are true:
- The airplane has been on the ground between 1 and 5 minutes.
- The WAI selector is set to auto or on.
- Air-driven hydraulic pumps are not in intermittent operation.
- Bleed pressure is sufficient to open the WAI valves.
- The time since the last periodic test is more than 24 hours.
- During this test, the WAI valves cycle open and closed. This test makes sure that valve malfunctions are detected.

Thermal Electric Anti-Icing

Electricity is used to heat various components on an aircraft so that ice does not form. This type of anti-ice is typically limited to small components due to high amperage draw. Effective thermal electric anti-ice is used on most air data probes, such as pitot tubes, static air ports, TAT and AOA probes, ice detectors, and engine P2/T2 sensors. Water lines, waste water drains, and some turboprop inlet cowls are also heated with electricity to prevent ice from forming. Transport category and high performance aircraft use thermal electric anti-icing in windshields.

In devices that use thermal electric anti-ice, current flows through an integral conductive element that produces heat. The temperature of the component is elevated above the freezing point of water so ice cannot form. Various schemes are used, such as an internal coil wire, externally wrapped blankets or tapes, as well as conductive films and heated gaskets. A basic discussion of probe heat follows. Windshield heat and portable water heat anti-ice are discussed later in this chapter. Propeller deice boots, which also are used for anti-ice, are also thermal electric and discussed in this chapter. Data probes that protrude into the ambient airstream are particularly susceptible to ice formation in flight. *Figure 15-14* illustrates the types and location probes that use thermal electric heat on one airliner. A pitot tube, for example, contains an internal electric element that is controlled by a switch in the cockpit. Use caution checking the function of the pitot heat when the aircraft is on the ground. The tube gets extremely hot since it must keep ice from forming at altitude in temperatures near -50 °F at speeds possibly over 500 miles per hour. An ammeter or load meter in the circuit can be used as a substitute to touching the probe, if so equipped.

Simple probe heat circuits exist on GA aircraft with a switch and a circuit breaker to activate and protect the device. Advanced aircraft may have more complex circuitry in which control is by computer and flight condition of the aircraft is considered before thermal electric heaters are activated automatically. *Figure 15-15* shows such a circuit for a pitot tube. The primary flight computer (PFC) supplies signals for the air data card (ADC) to energize ground and air heat control relays to activate probe heat. Information concerning speed of the aircraft, whether it is in the air or on the ground, and if the engines are running are factors considered by the ADC logic. Similar control is use for other probe heaters.

Chemical Anti-Icing

Chemical anti-icing is used in some aircraft to anti-ice the leading edges of the wing, stabilizers, windshields, and propellers. The wing and stabilizer systems are often called weeping wing systems or are known by their trade name of TKS™ systems. Ice protection is based upon the freezing point depressant concept. An antifreeze solution is pumped from a reservoir through a mesh screen embedded in the leading edges of the wings and stabilizers. Activated by a switch in the cockpit, the liquid flows over the wing and tail surfaces, preventing the formation of ice as it flows. The solution mixes with the supercooled water in the cloud, depresses its freezing point, and allows the mixture to flow off of the aircraft without freezing. The system is designed to anti-ice, but it is also capable of deicing an aircraft as well. When ice has accumulated on the leading edges, the antifreeze solution chemically breaks down the bond between the ice and airframe. This allows aerodynamic forces to carry the ice away. Thus, the system clears the airframe of accumulated ice before transitioning to anti-ice protection. *Figure 15-16* shows a chemical anti-ice system.

The TKS™ weeping wing system contains formed titanium panels that are laser drilled with over 800 tiny holes (.0025 inch diameter) per square inch. These are mated with non-perforated stainless steel rear panels and bonded to wing and stabilizer leading edges. As fluid is delivered from a central reservoir and pump, it seeps through the holes. Aerodynamic forces cause the fluid to coat the upper and lower surfaces of the airfoil. The glycol based fluid prevents ice from adhering to the aircraft structure.

Some aircraft with weeping wing systems are certified to fly into known icing conditions. Others use it as a hedge against unexpected ice encountered in flight. The systems are basically the same. Reservoir capacity permits 1- 2 hours of operation. TKS™ weeping wings are used primarily on reciprocating aircraft that lack a supply of warm bleed air for the installation of a thermal anti-ice system. However, the system is simple and effective leading to its use on some turbine powered corporate aircraft as well.

Figure 15-14. *Probes with thermal electric anti-icing on one commercial airliner.*

Figure 15-15. *Pitot probe heat system.*

Figure 15-16. *Chemical deicing system.*

Wing and Stabilizer Deicing Systems

GA aircraft and turboprop commuter-type aircraft often use a pneumatic deicing system to break off ice after it has formed on the leading edge surfaces. The leading edges of the wings and stabilizers have inflatable boots attached to them. The boots expand when inflated by pneumatic pressure, which breaks away ice accumulated on the boot. Most boots are inflated for 6 to 8 seconds. They are deflated by vacuum suction. The vacuum is continuously applied to hold the boots tightly against the aircraft while not in use.

Sources of Operating Air

The source of operating air for deice boot systems varies with the type of powerplant installed on the aircraft. Reciprocating engine aircraft typically use a dedicated engine-driven air pump mounted on the accessory drive gear box of the engine. The suction side of the pump is used to operate the gyroscopic instruments installed on the aircraft. It is also used to hold the deice boots tight to the aircraft when they are not inflated. The pressure side of the pump supplies air to inflate the deice boots, which breaks up ice that has formed on the wing and stabilizer leading edges. The pump operates continuously. Valves, regulators, and switches in the cockpit are used to control the flow of source air to the system.

Turbine Engine Bleed Air

The source of deice boot operating air on turbine engine aircraft is typically bleed air from the engine compressor(s). A relatively low volume of air on an intermittent basis is required to operate the boots. This has little effect on engine power enabling use of bleed air instead of adding a separate engine-driven air pump. Valves controlled by switches in the cockpit deliver air to the boots when requested.

Pneumatic Deice Boot System for GA Aircraft

GA aircraft, especially twin-engine models, are commonly equipped with pneumatic deicer systems. Rubber boots are attached with glue to the leading edges of the wings and stabilizers. These boots have a series of inflatable tubes. During operation, the tubes are inflated and deflated in an alternating cycle. *[Figure 15-17]* This inflation and deflation causes the ice to crack and break off. The ice is then carried away by the airstream. Boots used in GA aircraft typically inflate and deflate along the length of the wing. In larger turbo prop aircraft, the boots are installed in sections along the wing with the different sections operating alternately and symmetrically about the fuselage. This is done so that any disturbance to airflow caused by an inflated tube is kept to a minimum by inflating only short sections on each wing at a time.

GA System Operation

Figure 15-18 shows a deice system used on a GA twin-engine aircraft with reciprocating engines. In normal flight, all of the components in the deice system are de-energized. Discharge air from the dry air pumps is dumped overboard through the deice control valves. The deflate valve is open connecting the deice boots to the suction side of the pump through the check valve manifold and the vacuum regulator. The gyroscopic instruments are also connected to the vacuum side of the dry air pump. The vacuum regulator is set to supply the optimum suction for the gyros, which is sufficient to hold the boots tightly against the airfoil surfaces.

When the switch shown in *Figure 15-19* is pushed ON, the solenoid-operated deice control valves in each nacelle open and the deflate valve energizes and closes. Pressurized air from the discharge side of the pumps is routed through the control valves to the deice boot. When the system reaches 17 psi, pressure switches located on the deflate valve de-energize the deice control valve solenoids. The valves close and route pump air output overboard. The deflate valve opens and the boots are again connected to vacuum.

Figure 15-17. *Cross-section of a pneumatic deicing boot uninflated (top) and inflated (bottom).*

Figure 15-18. *Pneumatic deicing system for a twin engine GA aircraft with reciprocating engines.*

Figure 15-19. *Wing deice switch.*

On this simple system, the pilot must manually start this inflation/deflation cycle by pushing the switch each time deice is required. Larger aircraft with more complex systems may include a timer, which will cycle the system automatically until turned OFF. The use of distributor valves is also common. A distributor valve is a multi-position control valve controlled by the timer. It routes air to different deice boots in a sequence that minimizes aerodynamic disturbances as the ice breaks of the aircraft. Boots are inflated symmetrically on each side of the fuselage to maintain control in flight while deicing occurs. Distributor valves are solenoid operated and incorporate the deflate valve function to reconnect the deice boots with the vacuum side of the pump after all have been inflated.

Combining functional components of a deice system into a single unit is fairly common. *Figure 15-20* illustrates the right side of a large aircraft deice boot system. The left side is the same. In addition to the distributor valves, which combine functions of a control valve and deflate valve, the system also uses a combination unit. This unit combines the functions of a shutoff control valve for all pump supply air, as well as a pressure regulator for the system. It also contains a secondary air filter.

Deice System for Turboprop Aircraft

Figure 15-21 shows a pneumatic deice system used on a turboprop aircraft. The source of pneumatic air is engine bleed air, which is used to inflate two inboard wing boots, two outboard boots, and horizontal stabilizer boots. Additional bleed air is routed through the brake deice valve to the brakes. A three-position switch controls the operation of the boots. This switch is spring loaded to the center OFF position. When ice has accumulated, the switch should be selected to the single-cycle (up) position and released. *[Figure 15-22]* Pressure-regulated bleed air from the engine compressors supply air through bleed air flow control units and pneumatic shutoff valves to a pneumatic control assembly that inflates the wing boots. After an inflation period of 6 seconds, an electronic timer switches the distributor in the control assembly to deflate the wing boots, and a 4-second inflation

begins in the horizontal stabilizer boots. After these boots have been inflated and deflated, the cycle is complete, and all boots are again held down tightly against the wings and horizontal stabilizer by vacuum. The spring-loaded switch must be selected up again for another cycle to occur.

Each engine supplies a common bleed air manifold. To ensure the operation of the system, if one engine is inoperative, a flow control unit with check valve is incorporated in the bleed air line from each engine to prevent the loss of pressure through the compressor of the inoperative engine. If the boots fail to function sequentially, they may be operated manually by selecting the DOWN position of the same deice cycle switch. Depressing and holding it in the manual DOWN position inflates all the boots simultaneously. When the switch is released, it returns to the (spring-loaded) off position, and each boot is deflated and held by vacuum. When operated manually, the boot should not be left inflated for more than 7 to 10 seconds, as a new layer of ice may begin to form on the expanded boots and become un-removable. If one engine is inoperative, the loss of its pneumatic pressure does not affect boot operation. Electric power to the boot system is required to inflate the boots in either single-cycle or manual operation. When electric power is lost, the vacuum holds the boots tightly against the leading edge.

Deicing System Components

Several components are used to construct all deice boot systems. The components may differ slightly in name and location within the system depending on the aircraft. Components may also combine functions to save space and weight. The basic functions of filtering, pressure regulation, distribution, and attachment to a vacuum when boots are not in use must all be present. Check valves must also be installed to prevent back flow in the system. Manifolds are common on multiengine aircraft to allow sourcing of low pressure air from both engine pumps. Note that air-pump pressure is typically expelled overboard when not needed. Bleed air is shut off by a valve when not needed for deice boot operation on turbine engine aircraft. A timer, or control unit with an automatic mode, exists on many aircraft to repeat the deice cycle periodically.

Wet-Type Engine-Driven Air Pump

To provide pressure for the deice boots, older aircraft may use a wet-type engine-driven air pump mounted on the accessory drive gear case of the engine. Some modern aircraft may also use a wet-type air pump because of its durability. The pump is typically a four vane, positive displacement pump. Engine oil passes from the accessory case through the pump mounting base flange to lubricate the pump. Some of the oil is entrained in the output air and must be removed by an oil separator before it is sent through other components

Figure 15-20. *Right-side deice boot system on a large aircraft (left side similar).*

Figure 15-21. *Wing deice system for turboprop aircraft.*

Figure 15-22. *Ice protection panel on a turboprop aircraft with deice boots.*

in the deice system. When installing a wet-type pump, care should be taken to ensure that the oil passage in the gasket, pump, and mounting flange are aligned to ensure lubrication. [Figure 15-23]

Figure 15-23. *A wet-type air pump with engine oil lubricating ports in the mounting flange.*

Dry-Type Engine-Driven Air Pump

Most modern GA aircraft are equipped with a dry-type engine-driven air pump. It is also mounted on the engine accessory drive case; however, it is not lubricated with engine oil. The pump is constructed with carbon rotor vanes and bearings. The carbon material wears at a controlled rate to provide adequate lubrication without the need for oil. This keeps output air oil-free; thus, the use of an oil separator is not required. Caution should be used to prevent oil, grease, or degreasing fluids from entering the pump or the air system to ensure proper pump and system operation. *[Figure 15-24]* Dry-type and wet-type pumps are virtually maintenance free. Mounting bolts should be checked for security as should all hose connections. Wet-type pumps have a longer time before requiring overhaul, but dry-type pumps give the assurance that the deice system will not be contaminated with oil.

Figure 15-25. *An oil separator used with a wet-type engine-driven air pump.*

Figure 15-24. *Dry-type engine-driven air pump.*

Oil Separator

An oil separator is required for each wet-type air pump. Pump output air flows through the separator where most of the oil is removed and sent back to the engine though a drain line. Some systems may include a secondary separator to ensure oil free air is delivered to the deice system. There are no moving parts in an oil separator. A convoluted interior allows the air to pass, while the oil condenses and drains back to the engine. The only maintenance required on the separator is flushing the interior of the unit with a specified solvent. This should be done at intervals prescribed in the applicable maintenance manual. *[Figure 15-25]*

Control Valve

A control valve is a solenoid operated valve that allows air from the pump to enter the deice system. When energized by the deice switch in the cockpit, the valve opens. The control valve dumps pump air overboard when the deice system is not in use. Many control valves are built in combination with pressure relief valves that keeps the deice system safe from over pressure. *[Figure 15-26]*

Figure 15-26. *A solenoid operated deice control valve.*

15-17

Deflate Valve

All deice boot systems require a means for connecting vacuum from the air pump to the boots when the boots are not in use. This ensures the boots are held tightly deflated against the aircraft structure to provide the significant change in size and shape needed to break off accumulated ice when the boots inflate. One single deflate valve is used on simple deice boot systems. The deflate valve is solenoid operated. It is located at a point in the system where when closed, air is delivered to the boots. When open, vacuum is applied. Often, the deflate function is built into another unit, such as a distributor valve discussed next.

Distributor Valve

A distributer valve is a type of control valve used in relatively complex deice boot systems. It is an electrically-operated solenoid valve controlled by the deice boot system timer or control unit. On some systems, a distributor valve is assigned to each set of deice boots it controls. It differs from a control valve in that it has the deflate valve function built into it. Therefore, the distributor valve transfers connection of the boots from the pressure side of the air pump to the vacuum side of the pump once the proper inflation time has elapsed. The valve also dumps the unneeded air from the pump overboard.

Another type of distributor valve exists that handles the inflation and deflation of numerous sets of deice boots in a single unit. It also connects the boots to vacuum and dumps pump air when deice is not needed. A servo motor is used to position the multi-position valve. These centralized units are controlled by a timer or control unit. They inflate and deflate all of the boots on the aircraft. The timer may be built into the unit on some models.

Timer/Control Unit

All but the simplest of deice systems contain a timer or control unit. This device controls the action of the distributor valve(s) to ensure all boots are inflated in the proper sequence and for the correct duration. Six seconds of inflation is common to break off accumulated ice. The boot then must be immediately deflated so that ice does not adhere to the inflated geometry of the boot. This could cause it to fail to deflate or break off ice when the boot is re-inflated. The timer, or control unit, can also be made to cycle through the inflation and deflation of all boots periodically, thus relieving the flight crew of repetitive manual activation of the system. The function and capabilities of timers and control units vary. Consult the manufacturer's maintenance information for the performance characteristics of the timer/control unit on the aircraft in question.

The timer, or control unit, may be an independent device, or it may be built-in as part of another deice system component, such as a central distribution valve.

NOTE: A modern system design may use a pressure switch to signal deflation of the deice boots. When pressure builds in the boots to a preset amount, the switch signals the control valve to close and connect the boots to vacuum. However, this system retains a control unit for automatic cycling of the system at a set time interval.

Regulators and Relief Valves

Both the pressure and vacuum developed by an air pump must be regulated for use in the deice boot system. Typical boot inflation air pressure is between 15 and 20 psi. Vacuum pressure is set for the requirements of the gyroscopic instruments operated by the vacuum side of the air pump. Measured in inches of mercury, normal vacuum pressure (suction) is 4.5 to 5.5 "Hg.

Deice boot system air pressure is controlled by a pressure regulator valve located somewhere in the system downstream of the pump or oil separator, if installed. The regulator may be a stand-alone unit, or it may be combined into another deice system component. Regardless, the spring loaded valve relieves pressure overboard when it exceeds the limit for which the system is designed.

A vacuum regulator is installed in the vacuum manifold on the suction side of the air pump to maintain the vacuum at the designed level. Also known as a suction regulating valve or similar, the spring loaded valve contains a filter for the ambient air drawn through the valve during operation. This filter must be changed or kept clean per manufacturer's instructions. *[Figure 15-27]*

Figure 15-27. *A vacuum regulator.*

Manifold Assembly

In all pneumatic deice boot systems, it is necessary for check valves to be installed to prevent backflow of air in the system. The location(s) depend on system design. Sometimes, the check valve is built into another system component. On twin-engine aircraft, it is common to unite the air supplied from each engine-driven pump to provide redundancy. Check valves are required to guard against backflow should one pump fail. A manifold assemble is commonly used to join both sides of the system. *[Figure 15-28]* It contains the required check valves in a single assembly.

Figure 15-28. *A manifold assembly used in multiengine aircraft deice systems.*

Inlet Filter

The air used in a deice boot system is ambient air drawn in upstream of the gyroscopic instruments on the suction side of the engine-driven air pump. This air must be free of contaminants for use spinning the gyros, as well as for inflation of the deice boots. To ensure clean air, an inlet filter is installed as the air intake point for the system. This filter must be regularly maintained as per manufacturer's instructions. *Figure 15-29* shows a typical inlet air filter. *Figure 15-30* shows the relationship of the vacuum regulator and inlet air filter to other system components.

Construction and Installation of Deice Boots

Deicer boots are made of soft, pliable rubber, or rubberized fabric, and contain tubular air cells. The outer ply of the deicer boot is of conductive neoprene to provide resistance to deterioration by the elements and many chemicals. The neoprene also provides a conductive surface to dissipate static electricity charges. These charges, if allowed to accumulate, would eventually discharge through the boot to the metal skin beneath, causing static interference with the radio equipment. *[Figure 15-31]*

Figure 15-29. *Air filter for vacuum system.*

On modern aircraft, the deicer boots are bonded with an adhesive to the leading edge of wing and tail surfaces. The trailing edges of this type boot are tapered to provide a smooth airfoil. Elimination of fairing strips, screws, and rivnuts used on older types of deicing boots reduces the weight of the deice system. The deicer boot air cells are connected to system pressure and vacuum lines by non-kinking flexible hose.

When gluing the deice boots to the leading edge of wings and stabilizers, the manufacturer's instruction must be strictly followed. The glue is typically a contact cement normally spread on both the airfoil and the boot and allowed to become tacky before mating the surfaces. Clean, paint-free surfaces are required for the glue to adhere properly. Removal of old boots is performed by re-softening the cement with solvent.

Inspection, Maintenance, and Troubleshooting of Rubber Deicer Boot Systems

Maintenance on pneumatic deicing systems varies with each aircraft model. The instructions of the airframe or system components manufacturer should be followed in all cases. Depending on the aircraft, maintenance usually consists of operational checks, adjustments, troubleshooting, and inspection.

Operational Checks

An operational check of the system can be made by operating the aircraft engines or by using an external source of air. Most systems are designed with a test plug to permit ground checking the system without operating the engines. When using an external air source, make certain that the air pressure does not exceed the test pressure established for the system. Before turning the deicing system on, observe the vacuum-operated instruments. If any of the gauges begin to operate, it is an indication that one or more check valves have failed to close and that reverse flow through the instruments is

Figure 15-30. *Location of the inlet air filter in relationship to other components in a gyro instrument/pneumatic deice boot system.*

Figure 15-31. *Deicing boots inflated (left) and deflated (right).*

occurring. Correct the difficulty before continuing the test. If no movement of the instrument pointers occurs, turn on the deicing system. With the deicer system controls in their proper positions, check the suction and pressure gauges for proper indications. The pressure gauge fluctuates as the deicer tubes inflate and deflate. A relatively steady reading should be maintained on the vacuum gauge. It should be noted that not all systems use a vacuum gauge. If the operating pressure and vacuum are satisfactory, observe the deicers for actuation. With an observer stationed outside the aircraft, check the inflation sequence to be certain that it agrees with the sequence indicated in the aircraft maintenance manual. Check the timing of the system through several complete cycles. If the cycle time varies more than is allowable, determine the difficulty and correct it. Inflation of the deicers must be rapid to provide efficient deicing. Deflation of the boot being observed should be completed before the next inflation cycle. *[Figure 15-32]*

Adjustments

Examples of adjustments that may be required include adjusting the deicing system control cable linkages, adjusting system pressure relief valves, and deicing system vacuum (suction) relief valves. A pressure relief valve acts as a safety device to relieve excess pressure in the event of regulator valve failure. To adjust this valve, operate the aircraft engines and adjust a screw on the valve until the deicing pressure gauge indicates the specified pressure at which the valve should relieve. Vacuum relief valves are installed in a system that uses a vacuum pump to maintain constant suction during varying vacuum pump speeds. To adjust a vacuum relief valve, operate the engines. While watching the vacuum (suction) gauge, an assistant should adjust the suction relief valve adjusting screw to obtain the correct suction specified for the system.

Troubleshooting

Not all troubles that occur in a deicer system can be corrected by adjusting system components. Some troubles must be corrected by repair or replacement of system components or by tightening loose connections. Several troubles common to pneumatic deicing systems are shown in the left-hand column of the chart in *Figure 15-33*. Note the probable causes and the remedy of each trouble listed in the chart. In addition to using troubleshooting charts, operational checks are sometimes necessary to determine the possible cause of trouble.

Inspection

During each preflight and scheduled inspection, check the deicer boots for cuts, tears, deterioration, punctures, and security; during periodic inspections, go a little further and check deicer components and lines for cracks. If weather cracking of rubber is noted, apply a coating of conductive cement. The cement, in addition to sealing the boots against weather, dissipates static electricity so that it does not puncture the boots by arcing to the metal surfaces.

Deice Boot Maintenance

The life of the deicers can be greatly extended by storing them when they are not needed and by observing these rules when they are in service:

1. Do not drag gasoline hoses over the deicers.
2. Keep deicers free of gasoline, oil, grease, dirt, and other deteriorating substances.
3. Do not lay tools on or lean maintenance equipment against the deicers.
4. Promptly repair or resurface the deicers when abrasion or deterioration is noted.
5. Wrap deice boots in paper or canvas when storing.

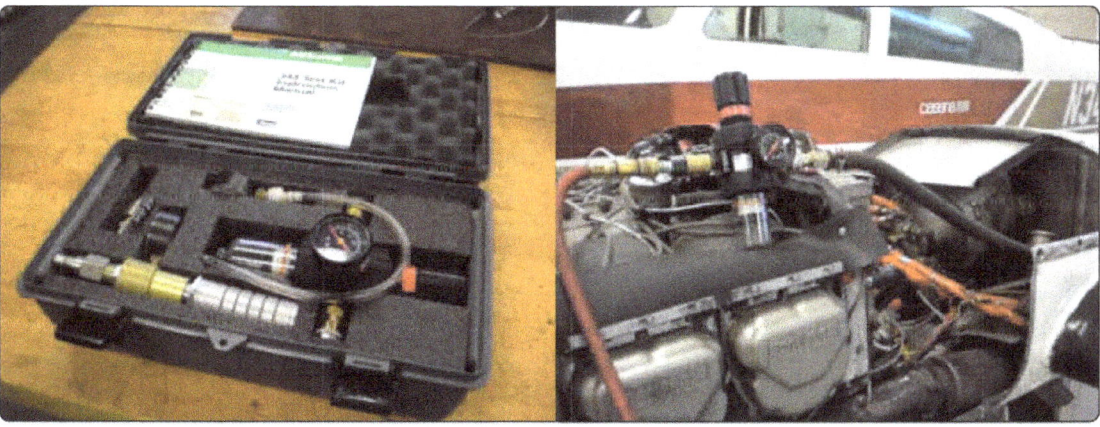

Figure 15-32. *Test equipment used to test a wing deice system (left), and test equipment installed in the aircraft for testing (right).*

15-21

Problem	Causes (most of which can be identified with a 343 Test Kit)	Corrective action(s)

Boots do not inflate	• Open circuit breaker
	• Faulty deflate valve
	Solenoid inoperable:
	  1. Improper voltage at solenoid
	  2. Blocked air vent in solenoid
	  3. Inoperative plunger
	Diaphragm not seated
	  1. Blocked vent orifice located in rivet bottom at center of diaphragm
	  2. Dirty diaphragm seal area
	  3. Diaphragm ruptured
	• Two faulty deice control valves of faulty two stage regulators
	• Faulty check valve
	• Relay not functioning
	• Leak in system boots
		• Reset circuit breaker
		• Check deflate valves as follows:
		Solenoid inoperable:
		  1. Correct electrical system
		  2. Clean with alcohol or replace
		  3. Clean with alcohol or replace
		Diaphragm not seated
		  1. Clean with .010 diameter wire and alcohol
		  2. Clean with blunt instrument and alcohol
		  3. Replace valve
		• Clean or replace valve assembly as noted above
		• Replace check valve
		• Check wiring or replace relay
		• Repair as needed

Slow boot inflation	• Lines blocked or disconnected • Low air pump capacity • One or more deice control valves not functioning properly • Deflate valve not fully closed • Ball check in deflate valve inoperative • Leaks in system or boots	• Check and replace lines • Replace air pump • Clean or replace valve assembly as noted above • Clean or replace valve assembly as noted above • Clean check valve or replace deflate valve • Repair as needed
System will not cycle	• Pressure in system not reaching specified psi to activate pressure switch • Leak in system or boots • Pressure switch on deflate valve inoperative	• Clean or replace deice control valve as noted above • Clean or replace deflate valve, as noted above • Repair as needed, tighten all hose connections • Replace switch
Slow deflation	• Low vacuum • Faulty deflate valve (indicated by temporary reduction in suction gauge reading)	• Repair as needed • Clean or replace valve assembly as noted above
No vacuum for boot hold down	• Malfunctioning deflate valve or deice valve • Leak in system or boots	• Clean or replace valve assembly as noted above • Repair as needed
Boots will not deflate during cycle	• Faulty deflate valve	• Check and replace valve
Boots appear to inflate on aircraft climb	• Vacuum source for boot holddown inoperative • Lines running through pressurized cabin loose or disconnected	• Check operation of ball check in deflate valve • Check for loose or disconnected vacuum lines and repair

Figure 15-33. *Troubleshooting guide for wing deice system.*

Thus far, preventive maintenance has been discussed. The actual work on the deicers consists of cleaning, resurfacing, and repairing. Cleaning should ordinarily be done at the same time the aircraft is washed, using a mild soap and water solution. Grease and oil can be removed with a cleaning agent, such as naptha, followed by soap and water scrubbing. Whenever the degree of wear is such that it indicates that the electrical conductivity of the deicer surface has been destroyed, it may be necessary to resurface the deicer. The resurfacing substance is a black, conductive neoprene cement. Prior to applying the resurfacing material, the deicer must be cleaned thoroughly and the surface roughened. Cold patch repairs can be made on a damaged deicer. The deicer must be relieved of its installed tension before applying the patch. The area to be patched must be clean and buffed to roughen the surface slightly. Patches are glued in place. Follow manufacturer's instructions for all repairs.

Electric Deice Boots

A few modern aircraft are equipped with electric deice boots on wing sections or on the horizontal stabilizer. These boots contain electric heating elements which are bonded to the leading edges similarly to pneumatic deice boots. When activated, the boots heat up and melt the ice off of leading edge surfaces. The elements are controlled by a sequence timer in a deice controller. Ice detector and ram air temperature probe inputs initiate operation when other flight condition parameters exist. The boot elements turn ON and OFF in paired sections to avoid aerodynamic imbalance. The system is inoperative while the aircraft is on the ground.

Figure 15-34 illustrated such a system. A benefit of electric deice boots is the conservation of engine bleed air. Current draw is limited to only those periods when de-ice is required.

Propeller Deice System

The formation of ice on the propeller leading edges, cuffs, and spinner reduces the efficiency of the powerplant system. Deice systems using electrical heating elements and systems using chemical deicing fluid are used.

Electrothermal Propeller Device System

Many propellers are deiced by an electrically heated boot on each blade. The boot, firmly cemented in place, receives current from a slip ring and brush assembly on the spinner bulkhead. The slip ring transmits current to the deice boot. The centrifugal force of the spinning propeller and air blast breaks the ice particles loose from the heated blades. *[Figure 15-35]*

On one aircraft model, the boots are heated in a preset sequence, which is an automatic function controlled by a timer. This sequence is as follows: 30 seconds for the right prop outer elements; 30 seconds for the right prop inner elements; 30 seconds for the left prop outer elements; and, 30 seconds for the left prop inner elements. Once the system is turned on for automatic is activated, it cycles continuously. A manual bypass of the timer is incorporated. *[Figure 15-36]*

Chemical Propeller Deice

Some aircraft models, especially single-engine GA aircraft, use a chemical deicing system for the propellers. Ice usually appears on the propeller before it forms on the wing. The glycol-based fluid is metered from a tank by a small electrically driven pump through a microfilter to the slinger rings on the prop hub. The propeller system can be a stand-alone system, or it can be part of a chemical wing and stabilizer deicing system such as the TKS™ weeping system.

Ground Deicing of Aircraft

The presence of ice on an aircraft may be the result of direct precipitation, formation of frost on integral fuel tanks after prolonged flight at high altitude, or accumulations on the landing gear following taxiing through snow or slush. In accordance with the Federal Aviation Administration (FAA)

Figure 15-34. *Electric stabilizer deice system..*

Figure 15-35. *Electro thermal propeller deice system components.*

Figure 15-36. *Propeller electrical deice system schematic.*

Advisory Circular (AC) 120-60, the aircraft must be free of all frozen contaminants adhering to the wings, control surfaces, propellers, engine inlets, or other critical surfaces before takeoff.

Any deposits of ice, snow, or frost on the external surfaces of an aircraft may drastically affect its performance. This may be due to reduced aerodynamic lift and increased aerodynamic drag resulting from the disturbed airflow over the airfoil surfaces, or it may be due to the weight of the deposit over the whole aircraft. The operation of an aircraft may also be seriously affected by the freezing of moisture in controls, hinges, valves, microswitches, or by the ingestion of ice into the engine. When aircraft are hangared to melt snow or frost, any melted snow or ice may freeze again if the aircraft is subsequently moved into subzero temperatures. Any measures taken to remove frozen deposits while the aircraft is on the ground must also prevent the possible refreezing of the liquid.

Frost Removal

Frost deposits can be removed by placing the aircraft in a warm hangar or by using a frost remover or deicing fluid. These fluids normally contain ethylene glycol and isopropyl alcohol and can be applied either by spray or by hand. It should be applied within 2 hours of flight. Deicing fluids may adversely affect windows or the exterior finish of the aircraft, only the type of fluid recommended by the aircraft manufacturer should be used. Transport category aircraft are often deiced on the ramp or a dedicated deicing location on the airport. Deicing trucks are used to spray the deicing and/or anti-icing fluid on aircraft surfaces. *[Figure 15-37]*

Figure 15-37. *An American Airlines aircraft being deiced at Syracuse Hancock International Airport.*

Deicing and Anti-icing of Transport Type Aircraft

Deicing Fluid

The deicing fluid must be accepted according to its type for holdover times, aerodynamic performance, and material compatibility. The coloring of these fluids is also standardized. In general, glycol is colorless, Type-I fluids are orange, Type-II fluids are white/pale yellow, and Type-IV fluids are green. The color for Type-III fluid has not yet been determined.

When aircraft surfaces are contaminated by frozen moisture, they must be deiced prior to dispatch. When freezing precipitation exists, and there is a risk of contamination of the surface at the time of dispatch, aircraft surfaces must be anti-iced. If both deicing and anti-icing are required, the procedure may be performed in one or two steps. The selection of a one- or two-step process depends upon weather conditions, available equipment, available fluids, and the holdover time to be achieved.

Holdover Time (HOT)

Holdover Time (HOT) is the estimated time that deicing/anti-icing fluid prevents the formation of frost or ice and the accumulation of snow on the critical surfaces of an aircraft.

HOT begins when the final application of deicing/anti-icing fluid commences and expires when the deicing/anti-icing fluid loses its effectiveness. *Figure 15-38* shows a holdover timetable for Type IV fluid.

Critical Surfaces

Basically, all surfaces that have an aerodynamic, control, sensing, movement, or measuring function must be clean. These surfaces cannot necessarily be cleaned and protected in the same conventional deicing/anti-icing manner as the wings. Some areas require only a cleaning operation, while others need protection against freezing. The procedure of deicing may also vary according to aircraft limitations. The use of hot air may be required when deicing (e.g., landing gear or propellers).

Figure 15-39 shows critical areas on an aircraft that should not be sprayed directly. Some critical elements and procedures that are common for most aircraft are:

- Deicing/anti-icing fluids must not be sprayed directly on wiring harnesses and electrical components (e.g., receptacles, junction boxes), onto brakes, wheels, exhausts, or thrust reversers.

- Deicing/anti-icing fluid shall not be directed into the orifices of pitot heads, static ports, or directly onto airstream direction detectors probes/angle of attack airflow sensors.

- All reasonable precautions shall be taken to minimize fluid entry into engines, other intakes/outlets, and control surface cavities.

- Fluids shall not be directed onto flight deck or cabin windows as this can cause crazing of acrylics or penetration of the window seals.

- Any forward area from which fluid can blow back onto windscreens during taxi or subsequent takeoff shall be free of residues prior to departure.

- If Type II, III, or IV fluids are used, all traces of the fluid on flight deck windows should be removed prior to departure, particular attention being paid to windows fitted with wipers.

- Landing gear and wheel bays shall be kept free from buildup of slush, ice, or accumulations of blown snow.

- When removing ice, snow, slush, or frost from aircraft surfaces, care shall be taken to prevent it entering and accumulating in auxiliary intakes or control surface hinge areas (e.g., manually remove snow from wings and stabilizer surfaces forward toward the leading edge and remove from ailerons and elevators back towards the trailing edge)

FAA Type IV Holdover Time Guidelines

Guidelines for holdover times anticipated for SAE type IV fluid mixtures as function of weather conditions and OAT.
CAUTION: This table is for use in departure planning only, and it should be used in conjunction with pretakeoff check procedures.

OAT °C	OAT °F	SAE type IV fluid concentration neat fluid water (vol. %/vol.%)	Frost*	Freezing Fog	Snow◊	Freezing drizzle***	Light free rain	Rain on cold soaked wing	Other*
above 0	above 32	100/0	18:00	1:05 2:15	0:35 1:05	0:40 1:10	0:25 0:40	0:10 0:50	
above 0	above 32	72/25	6:00	1:05 1:45	0:30 1:05	0:35 0:50	0:15 0:30	0:05 0:35	
above 0	above 32	50/50	4:00	0:15 0:35	0:05 0:20	0:10 0:20	0:05 0:10	CAUTION:	CAUTION: no holdover time guidelines exist
0 through 3	32 through 27	100/0	12:00	1:05 2:15	0:30 0:55	0:40 1:10	0:15 0:40	CAUTION: clear ice may require touch for confirmation	
0 through 3	32 through 27	75/25	5:00	1:05 2:15	0:25 0:50	0:35 0:50	0:15 0:30		
0 through 3	32 through 27	50/50	3:00	1:15 0:35	0:05 0:15	0:10 0:20	0:05 0:15		
below 3 through 14	below 27 through 7	100/0	12:00	0:20 0:50	0:20 0:40	**0:20 0:45	**0:10 0:25		
below 3 through 14	below 27 through 7	75/25	5:00	0:25 0:50	0:15 0:25	**0:15 0:30	**0:10 0:20		
below 14 through 25	below 7 through 13	100/0	12:00	0:15 0:40	0:15 0:30				
below 25	below 13	100/0	SAE type IV fluid may be used below 25 °C (13 °F) if the freezing point of the fluid is at least 7 °C (13 °F) below the OAT and the aerodynamic acceptance criteria are met. Consider use of SAE type I when SAE type IV fluid cannot be used.						

°C = degrees Celsius
°F = degrees Fahrenheit
OAT= outside air temperature
VOL = volume

The responsiblity for the application of these data remains with the user.
* During conditions that apply to aircraft protection for ACTIVE FROST
** No holdover time guidelines exist for this condition below 10 °C (14 °F)
*** Use light freezing rain holdover times if positive identification of freezing drizzle is not possible
‡ Snow pellets, ice pellets, heavy snow, moderate and heavy freezing rain, hail.
◊ Snow includes snow grains

CAUTIONS:
- The time of protection will be shortened in heavy weather conditions: heavy precipitation rates or high moisture contents.
- High wind velocity or jet blast may reduce holdover time below the lowest time stated in the range.
- Holdover time may be reduced when aircraft skin temperature is lower than OAT.

Figure 15-38. *FAA deice holdover time guidelines.*

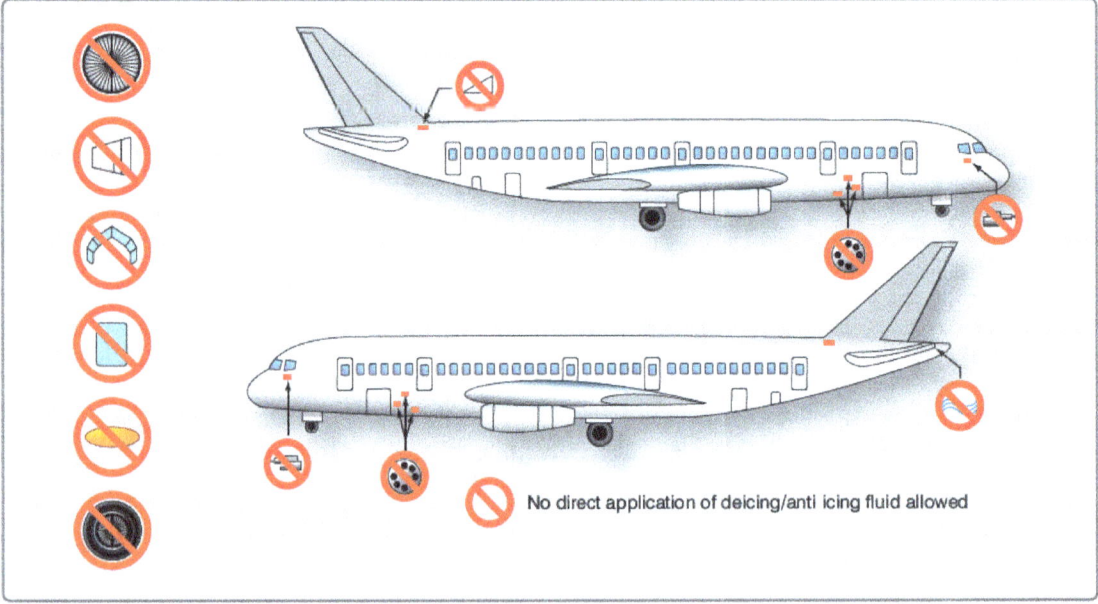

Figure 15-39. *No direct application of deicing/anti-icing fluid allowed.*

Ice and Snow Removal

Probably the most difficult deposit to deal with is deep, wet snow when ambient temperatures are slightly above the freezing point. This type of deposit should be removed with a soft brush or squeegee. Use care to avoid damage to antennas, vents, stall warning devices, vortex generators, etc., that may be concealed by the snow. Light, dry snow in subzero temperatures should be blown off whenever possible; the use of hot air is not recommended, since this would melt the snow, which would then freeze and require further treatment. Moderate or heavy ice and residual snow deposits should be removed with a deicing fluid. No attempt should be made to remove ice deposits or break an ice bond by force.

After completion of deicing operations, inspect the aircraft to ensure that its condition is satisfactory for flight. All external surfaces should be examined for signs of residual snow or ice, particularly in the vicinity of control gaps and hinges. Check the drain and pressure sensing ports for obstructions. When it becomes necessary to physically remove a layer of snow, all protrusions and vents should be examined for signs of damage. Control surfaces should be moved to ascertain that they have full and free movement. The landing gear mechanism, doors and bay, and wheel brakes should be inspected for snow or ice deposits and the operation of uplocks and microswitches checked.

Snow or ice can enter turbine engine intakes and freeze in the compressor. If the compressor cannot be turned by hand for this reason, hot air should be blown through the engine until the rotating parts are free.

Rain Control Systems

There are several different ways to remove the rain from the windshields. Most aircraft use one or a combination of the following systems: windshield wipers, chemical rain repellent, pneumatic rain removal (jet blast), or windshields treated with a hydrophobic surface seal coating.

Windshield Wiper Systems

In an electrical windshield wiper system, the wiper blades are driven by an electric motor(s) that receive(s) power from the aircraft's electrical system. On some aircraft, the pilot's and copilot's windshield wipers are operated by separate systems to ensure that clear vision is maintained through one of the windows should one system fail. Each windshield wiper assembly consists of a wiper, wiper arm, and a wiper motor/converter. Almost all windshield wiper systems use electrical motors. Some older aircraft might be equipped with hydraulic wiper motors. *[Figure 15-40]*

Maintenance performed on windshield wiper systems consists of operational checks, adjustments, and troubleshooting. An operational check should be performed whenever a system component is replaced or whenever the system is suspected of not working properly. During the check, make sure that the windshield area covered by the wipers is free of foreign matter and is kept wet with water. Adjustment of a windshield wiper system consists of adjusting the wiper blade tension, the angle at which the blade sweeps across the windshield, and proper parking of the wiper blades.

Chemical Rain Repellant

Water poured onto clean glass spreads out evenly. Even when the glass is held at a steep angle or subjected to air velocity, the glass remains wetted by a thin film of water. However, when glass is treated with certain chemicals, a transparent film is formed that causes the water to behave very much like mercury on glass. The water draws up into beads that cover only a portion of the glass and the area between beads is dry. The water is readily removed from the glass. This principle lends itself quite naturally to removing rain from aircraft windshields. The high-velocity slipstream continually removes the water beads, leaving a large part of the window dry.

A rain repellant system permits application of the chemical repellant by a switch or push button in the cockpit. The proper amount of repellant is applied regardless of how long the switch is held. On some systems, a solenoid valve controlled by a time delay module meters the repellent to a nozzle which sprays it on the outside of the windshield. Two such units exist — one each for the forward glass of the pilot and copilot. *[Figure 15-41]*

This system should only be used in very wet conditions. The rain repellant system should not be operated on dry windows because heavy undiluted repellant restricts window visibility. Should the system be operated inadvertently, do not operate the windshield wipers or rain clearing system as this tends to increase smearing. Also, the rain repellant residues caused by application in dry weather or very light rain can cause staining or minor corrosion of the aircraft skin. To prevent this, any concentrated repellant or residue should be removed by a thorough fresh water rinse at the earliest opportunity. After application, the repellant film slowly deteriorates with continuing rain impingement. This makes periodic reapplication necessary. The length of time between applications depends upon rain intensity, the type of repellant used, and whether windshield wipers are used.

Figure 15-40. *Windshield wiper assembly/installation on a transport catgory aircraft. The motor-converter is mountd under the aircraft skin.*

Windshield Surface Seal Coating

Some aircraft models use a surface seal coating, also called hydrophobic coating that is on the outside of the pilot's/copilot's windshield. *[Figure 15-42]* The word hydrophobic means to repel or not absorb water. The windshield hydrophobic coating is on the external surface of the windows (windshields). The coatings cause raindrops to bead up and roll off, allowing the flight crew to see through the windshield with very little distortion. The hydrophobic windshield coating reduces the need for wipers and gives the flight crew better visibility during heavy rain.

Most new aircraft windshields are treated with surface seal coating. The manufacturer's coating process deeply penetrates the windshield surface providing hydrophobic action for quite some time. When effectiveness declines, products made to be applied in the field are used. These liquid treatments rubbed onto the surface of the windshield maintain the beading action of rain water. They must be applied periodically or as needed.

Pneumatic Rain Removal Systems

Windshield wipers characteristically have two basic problem areas. One is the tendency of the slipstream aerodynamic forces to reduce the wiper blade loading pressure on the window, causing ineffective wiping or streaking. The other is in achieving fast enough wiper oscillation to keep up with high rain impingement rates during heavy rain falls. As a result, most aircraft wiper systems fail to provide satisfactory vision in heavy rain.

The rain removal system shown in *Figure 15-43* controls windshield icing and removes rain by directing a flow of heated air over the windshield. This heated air serves two purposes. First, the air breaks the rain drops into small particles that are then blown away. Secondly, the air heats the windshield to prevent the moisture from freezing. The air can be supplied by an electric blower or by bleed air.

Windshield Frost, Fog, and Ice Control Systems

In order to keep windshield areas free of ice, frost, and fog, window anti-icing, deicing, and defogging systems are used. These can be electric, pneumatic, or chemical depending on the type and complexity of the aircraft. A few of these systems are discussed in this section.

Electric

High performance and transport category aircraft windshields are typically made of laminated glass, polycarbonate, or similar ply material. Typically clear vinyl plies are also included to improve performance characteristics. The

Figure 15-41. *Cockpit rain repellant canister and reservoir.*

Figure 15-42. *Hydrophobic coating on windshield.*

laminations create the strength and impact resistance of the windshield assembly. These are critical feature for windshields as they are subject to a wide range of temperatures and pressures. They must also withstand the force of a 4 pound bird strike at cruising speed to be certified. The laminated construction facilitates the inclusion of electric heating elements into the glass layers, which are used to keep the windshield clear of ice, frost, and fog. The elements can be in the form of resistance wires or a transparent conductive material may be used as one of the window plies. To ensure enough heating is applied to the outside of the windshield, heating elements are placed on the inside of the outer glass ply. Windshields are typically bonded together by the application of pressure and heat without the use of cement. *Figure 15-44* illustrates the plies in one transport category aircraft windshield.

Whether resistance wires or a laminated conductive film is used, aircraft window heat systems have transformers to supply power and feedback mechanisms, such as thermistors, to provide a window heat control unit with information used to keep operating temperature within acceptable limits. Some systems are automatic while others are controlled by cockpit switches. Separate circuits for pilot and co-pilot are common to ensure visibility in case of a malfunction. Consult the manufacturer's maintenance information for details on the particular window heat system in question.

Some windshield heating systems can be operated at two heat levels. On these aircraft, NORMAL heating supplied heat to the broadest area of windshield. HIGH heating supplies a higher intensity of heat to a smaller but more essential viewing area. Typically, this window heating system is always on and set in the NORMAL position. *Figure 15-45* illustrates a simplified windshield heat system of this type.

Figure 15-43. *Windshield rain and frost removal system.*

Pneumatic

Some laminated windshields on older aircraft have a space between the plies that allows the flow of hot air to be directed between the glass to keep it warm and fog free. The source of air is bleed air or conditioned air from the environmental control system. Small aircraft may utilize ducted warm air, which is release to flow over the windshield inner surface to defrost and defog. These systems are similar to those used in automobiles. The source of air could be ambient (defog only), the aircraft's heating system, or a combustion heater. While these pneumatic windshield heat systems are effective for the aircraft on which they are installed, they are not approved

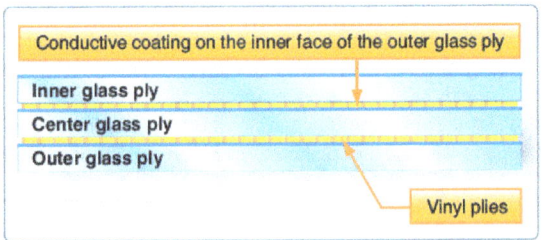

Figure 15-44. *Cross-section of a transport category windshield.*

Figure 15-45. *Electric windshield heat schematic.*

for flying into known icing conditions and, as such, are not effective for anti-ice.

Large aircraft equipped with pneumatic jet blast rain repellant systems achieve some anti-icing effects from operating this system although electric windshield heat is usually used.

Chemical

As previously mentioned in this chapter, chemical anti-ice systems exist generally for small aircraft. This type of anti-ice is also used on windshields. Whether alone or part of a TKS™ system or similar, the liquid chemical is sprayed through a nozzle onto the outside of the windshield which prevents ice from forming. The chemical can also deice the windshield of ice that may have already formed. Systems such as these have a fluid reservoir, pump, control valve, filter, and relief valve. Other components may exist. *Figure 15-46* shows a set of spray tubes for application of chemical anti-ice on an aircraft windshield.

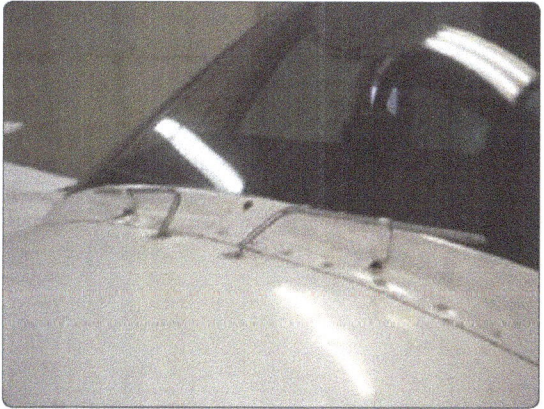

Figure 15-46. *Chemical deicing spray tubes.*

Figure 15-47. *Water supply line heater system.*

Portable Water Tank Ice Prevention

Transport type aircraft have water and waste systems on board, and electrical heaters are often used to prevent the formation of ice in the water lines of these systems. Water lines carry water from the portable tanks to the lavatories and galleys. The waste water tanks collect the gray water from the galleys and lavatories. Heater blankets, in-line heaters, or heater boots are often used to heat the water supply lines, water tank drain hoses, waste drain lines, waste tank rinse fittings, and drain masts. Thermostats in the water lines supply temperature data to the control unit that turns the electrical heaters on and off. When the temperature falls below freezing, the electrical heaters turn on and stay on until the temperature reaches a safe temperature. *Figure 15-47* is a schematic of a water supply line heater system, and *Figure 15-48* shows the location of the waste water tanks and heater blanket.

Figure 15-48. *Waste water tanks and heater blankets.*

Chapter 16
Cabin Environmental Control Systems

Physiology of Flight

Composition of the Atmosphere

The mixture of gases that make up the earth's atmosphere is commonly called air. It is composed principally of 78 percent nitrogen and 21 percent oxygen. The remaining 1 percent is made up of various gases in smaller quantities. Some of these are important to human life, such as carbon dioxide, water vapor, and ozone. *Figure 16-1* indicates the respective percentage of the quantity of each gas in its relation to the total mixture.

As altitude increases, the total quantity of all the atmospheric gases reduces rapidly. However, the relative proportions of nitrogen and oxygen remain unchanged up to about 50 miles above the surface of the earth. The percentage of carbon dioxide is also fairly stable. The amounts of water vapor and ozone vary.

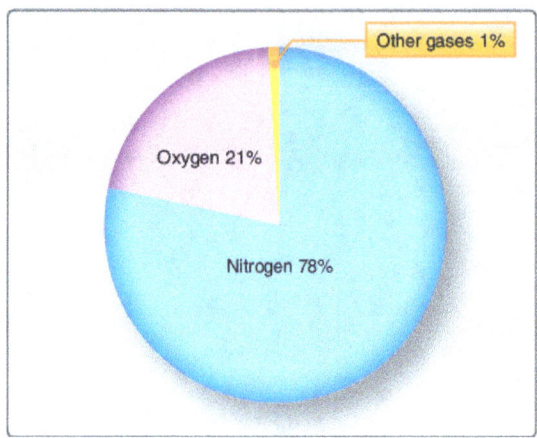

Figure 16-1. *The percentage of the various gases that comprise the atmosphere.*

Nitrogen is an inert gas that is not used directly by man for life processes; however, many compounds containing nitrogen are essential to all living matter.

The small quantity of carbon dioxide in the atmosphere is utilized by plants during photosynthesis. Thus, the food supply for all animals, including man, depends on it. Carbon dioxide also helps control breathing in man and other animals.

The amount of water vapor in the atmosphere is variable but, even under humid conditions at sea level, it rarely exceeds 5 percent. Water also occurs in the atmosphere as ice crystals. All forms of water in the atmosphere absorb far more energy from the sun than do the other gases. Water plays an important role in the formation of weather.

Ozone is a form of oxygen. It contains three oxygen atoms per molecule, rather than the usual two. Most of the atmosphere's ozone is formed by the interaction of oxygen and the sun's rays near the top of the stratosphere in an area called the ozone layer. This is important to living organisms because ozone filters out most of the sun's harmful ultraviolet (UV) radiation. Ozone is also produced by electrical discharges, such as lightning strikes. It has a faint odor, somewhat like that of weak chlorine, that may be detected after a thunderstorm. Auroras and cosmic rays may also produce ozone. Ozone is of great consequence to living creatures on earth and to the circulation of the upper atmosphere.

Human Respiration and Circulation
Oxygen and Hypoxia

The second most prevalent substance in the atmosphere, oxygen, is essential for most living processes. Without oxygen, humans and animals die very rapidly. A reduction in the normal oxygen supply alters the human condition. It causes important changes in body functions, thought processes, and the maintainable degree of consciousness. The resultant sluggish condition of mind and body produced by insufficient oxygen is called hypoxia.

There are several scenarios that can result in hypoxia. During aircraft operations, it is brought about by a decrease in the pressure of oxygen in the lungs at high altitudes. The air contains the typical 21 percent of oxygen, but the rate at which oxygen can be absorbed into the blood depends upon the oxygen pressure. Greater pressure pushes the oxygen from the lung alveoli into the bloodstream. As the pressure is reduced, less oxygen is forced into and absorbed by the blood.

At sea level, oxygen pressure in the lungs is approximately three pounds per square inch (psi). This is sufficient to saturate the blood with oxygen and permit the mind and body to function normally. As altitude is increased, this pressure decreases. Below 7,000 feet above sea level, the available oxygen quantity and pressure remain sufficient for saturation of the blood with oxygen. Above 7,000 feet, however, the oxygen pressure becomes increasingly insufficient to saturate the blood. At 10,000 feet mean sea level (MSL), saturation of the blood with oxygen is only about 90 percent of normal. Long durations at this altitude can result in headache and fatigue, both symptoms of hypoxia. At 15,000 feet MSL, oxygen transfer to the bloodstream drops to 81 percent of saturation. This typically results in sleepiness, headache, blue lips and fingernails, and increased pulse and respiration. Worse yet, vision and judgment become impaired and safe operation of an aircraft becomes compromised. Higher in the atmosphere, decreasing pressure causes even less oxygen to enter the bloodstream; only 68 percent saturation at 22,000 feet MSL. Remaining at 25,000 feet MSL for 5 minutes, where oxygen transfer to the blood is reduced to approximately 50 percent saturation, causes unconsciousness. *[Figure 16-2]*

Altitude MSL (feet)	Oxygen pressure (psi)
0	3.08
5,000	2.57
10,000	2.12
15,000	1.74
20,000	1.42
25,000	1.15
30,000	0.92
35,000	0.76
40,000	0.57

Figure 16-2. *Oxygen pressure in the atmosphere at various altitudes.*

Hyperventilation

Another physiological phenomenon of interest to aviators is hyperventilation. Its symptoms greatly resemble hypoxia. When various cells in the body use oxygen and food delivered to them by the blood, carbon dioxide is a by-product. Blood carries this carbon dioxide to the lungs where it is exhaled.

Carbon dioxide functions in the body to regulate the depth and frequency of breathing. A high level of carbon dioxide in the blood triggers rapid, deep breathing to expel it. This also promotes the intake of a greater amount of oxygen for active cells to use. A low carbon dioxide level causes more relaxed breathing resulting in less oxygen intake. Therefore, an oxygen/carbon dioxide balance exists in the blood.

Occasionally, fear, panic, or pain triggers excessive rapid breathing in a person. With it comes a reduction of carbon dioxide in the blood, even though the body does not need this. The lower carbon dioxide level signals the body that there is enough oxygen available and blood vessels constrict, causing hypoxia-like symptoms because insufficient oxygen is being delivered to the cells. Note that the onset of hypoxia described in the previous section occurs without the rapid breathing that accompanies hyperventilation. Hyperventilation can often be alleviated by having the person calm down and breathe normally, which restores the oxygen/carbon dioxide balance in the bloodstream.

Carbon Monoxide Poisoning

Carbon monoxide is a colorless, odorless gas produced by incomplete combustion of hydrocarbon fuels, such as those used in aviation. The human body does not require this gas to function. Its presence, however, can prevent a sufficient level of oxygen to be maintained in the body, resulting in hypoxia. This is also known as carbon monoxide poisoning. As with all forms of oxygen deprivation, extended exposure to carbon monoxide can result in unconsciousness and even death.

Hemoglobin is the substance in the blood that attaches to oxygen in the lungs and circulates it to cells in the body for use. Carbon monoxide more readily attaches itself to hemoglobin than oxygen. If carbon monoxide is present in the lungs, hemoglobin attaches to it and not oxygen. This results in cells not receiving the amount of oxygen they need. The insufficient oxygen level results in hypoxia-like symptoms.

A real danger of carbon monoxide poisoning is that long exposure to slight traces of carbon monoxide can result in oxygen deprivation just as easily as short-term exposure to a concentrated amount. The onset of its effects can be very subtle.

There are many types of carbon monoxide detectors available to alert aviators of the presence of this gas. Some are made to be permanently installed in the instrument panel, while others are portable. The simplest carbon monoxide detectors are chemical tabs mounted on cardboard that hang on or adhere to something in the cockpit. When carbon monoxide is present, the tab changes color due to a chemical reaction. More sophisticated detectors provide a digital output in parts per million of carbon monoxide present or illuminate a light and/or an audible alarm sounds. *[Figure 16-3]*

Figure 16-3. *An example of a carbon monoxide detector sold in the aviation market.*

Aircraft that utilize exhaust shroud-type heating systems or combustion heaters are more likely to have carbon monoxide introduced into the cabin from these devices. It is very important to discover the source of carbon monoxide if it is detected. Various leak checks and testing for cracks are performed regularly whenever a combustion source is also the source for cabin heat.

Aircraft Oxygen Systems

The negative effects of reduced atmospheric pressure at flight altitudes, forcing less oxygen into the blood, can be overcome. There are two ways this is commonly done: increase the pressure of the oxygen or increase the quantity of oxygen in the air mixture.

Large transport-category and high performance passenger aircraft pressurize the air in the cabin. This serves to push more of the normal 21 percent oxygen found in the air into the blood for saturation. Techniques for pressurization are discussed later in this chapter. When utilized, the percentage of oxygen available for breathing remains the same; only the pressure is increased.

By increasing the quantity of oxygen available in the lungs, less pressure is required to saturate the blood. This is the basic function of an aircraft oxygen system. Increasing the level of oxygen above the 21 percent found in the atmosphere can offset the reduced pressure encountered as altitude increases. Oxygen may be regulated into the air that is breathed so as to maintain a sufficient amount for blood saturation. Normal mental and physical activity can be maintained at indicated altitudes of up to about 40,000 feet with the sole use of supplemental oxygen.

Oxygen systems that increase the quantity of oxygen in breathing air are most commonly used as primary systems in small and medium size aircraft designed without cabin pressurization. Pressurized aircraft utilize oxygen systems as a means of redundancy should pressurization fail. Portable oxygen equipment may also be aboard for first aid purposes.

Forms of Oxygen and Characteristics
Gaseous Oxygen

Oxygen is a colorless, odorless, and tasteless gas at normal atmospheric temperatures and pressures. It transforms into a liquid at –183 °C (its boiling point). Oxygen combines readily with most elements and numerous compounds. This combining is called oxidation. Typically, oxidation produces heat. When something burns, it is actually rapidly combining with oxygen. Oxygen itself does not burn because it does not combine with itself, except to form oxygen or ozone. But, pure oxygen combines violently with petroleum products creating a significant hazard when handling these materials in close proximity to each other. Nevertheless, oxygen and various petroleum fuels combine to create the energy produced in internal combustion engines.

Pure gaseous oxygen, or nearly pure gaseous oxygen, is stored and transported in high-pressure cylinders that are typically painted green. Technicians should be cautious to keep pure oxygen away from fuel, oil, and grease to prevent unwanted combustion. Not all oxygen in containers is the same. Aviator's breathing oxygen is tested for the presence of water. This is done to avoid the possibility of it freezing in the small passage ways of valves and regulators. Ice could prevent delivery of the oxygen when needed. Aircraft often operate in subzero temperatures, increasing the possibility of icing. The water level should be a maximum of .02ml per liter of oxygen. The words "Aviator's Breathing Oxygen" should be marked clearly on any cylinders containing oxygen for this purpose. *[Figure 16-4]*

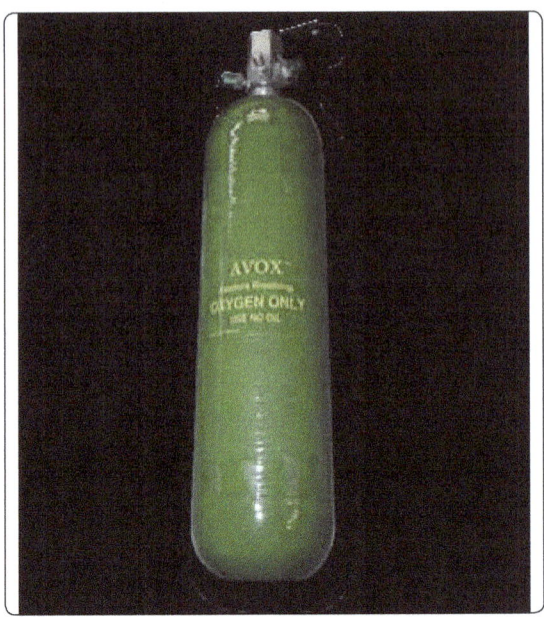

Figure 16-4. *"Aviator's breathing oxygen" is marked on all oxygen cylinders designed for this purpose.*

Production of gaseous oxygen for commercial or aircraft cylinders is often through a process of liquefying air. By controlling temperature and pressure, the nitrogen in the air can be allowed to boil off leaving mostly pure oxygen. Oxygen may also be produced by the electrolysis of water. Passing electric current through water separates the oxygen from the hydrogen. One further method of producing gaseous oxygen is by separating the nitrogen and oxygen in the air through the use of a molecular sieve. This membrane filters out nitrogen and some of the other gases in air, leaving nearly pure oxygen for use. Onboard oxygen sieves, or oxygen concentrators as they are sometimes called, are used on some military aircraft. Their use in civil aviation is expected.

Use of portable pulse oximeters has become more common in aviation. These devices measure the oxygen saturation level of the blood. With this information, adjustments to the oxygen flow rates of onboard oxygen equipment can be made to prevent hypoxia. *Figure 16-5* shows an oximeter into which a finger is inserted to measure oxygen saturation of the blood in percentage. Heart rate is also displayed.

Liquid Oxygen

Liquid oxygen (LOX) is a pale blue, transparent liquid. Oxygen can be made liquid by lowering the temperature to below –183 °C or by placing gaseous oxygen under pressure. A combination of these is accomplished with a Dewar bottle. This special container is used to store and transport liquid

Figure 16-5. *A portable pulse-type oximeter displays percentage of oxygen saturation of the blood and heart rate. Pilots can adjust oxygen supply levels to maintain saturation and avoid hypoxia.*

oxygen. It uses an evacuated, double-walled insulation design to keep the liquid oxygen under pressure at a very low temperature. *[Figure 16-6]* A controlled amount of oxygen is allowed to vaporize and is plumbed into a gaseous oxygen delivery system downstream of a converter that is part of the container assembly.

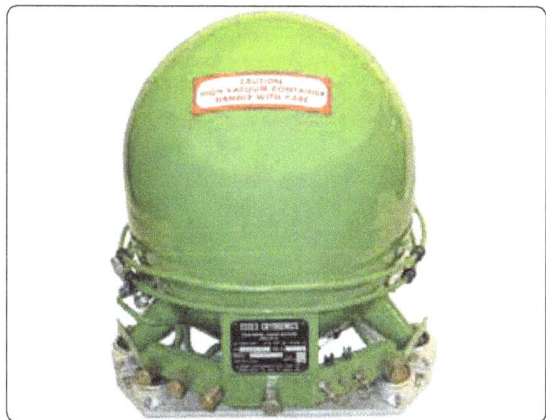

Figure 16-6. *A spherical liquid oxygen onboard container used by the military.*

A small quantity of LOX can be converted to an enormous amount of gaseous oxygen, resulting in the use of very little storage space compared to that needed for high-pressure gaseous oxygen cylinders. However, the difficulty of handling LOX, and the expense of doing so, has resulted in the container system used for gaseous oxygen to proliferate throughout civilian aviation. LOX is used nearly exclusively in military aviation.

Chemical or Solid Oxygen

Sodium chlorate has a unique characteristic. When ignited, it produces oxygen as it burns. This can be filtered and delivered through a hose to a mask that can be worn and breathed directly by the user. Solid oxygen candles, as they are called, are formed chunks of sodium chlorate wrapped inside insulated stainless steel housings to control the heat produced when activated. The chemical oxygen supply is often ignited by a spring-loaded firing pin that when pulled, releases a hammer that smashes a cap creating a spark to light the candle. Electric ignition via a current-induced hot wire also exists. Once lit, a sodium chlorate oxygen generator cannot be extinguished. It produces a steady flow of breathable oxygen until it burns out, typically generating 10–20 minutes of oxygen. *[Figure 16-7]*

Solid oxygen generators are primarily used as backup oxygen devices on pressurized aircraft. They are one-third as heavy as gaseous oxygen systems that use heavy storage tanks for the same quantity of oxygen available. Sodium chlorate chemical oxygen generators also have a long shelf life, making them perfect as a standby form of oxygen. They are inert below 400 °F and can remain stored with little maintenance or inspection until needed, or until their expiration date is reached.

The feature of not extinguishing once lit limits the use of solid oxygen since it becomes an all-or-nothing source. The generators must be replaced if used, which can greatly increase the cost of using them as a source of oxygen for short periods of time. Moreover, chemical oxygen candles must be transported with extreme caution and as hazardous materials. They must be properly packed and their ignition devices deactivated.

Onboard Oxygen Generating Systems (OBOGS)

The molecular sieve method of separating oxygen from the other gases in air has application in flight, as well as on the ground. The sieves are relatively light in weight and relieve the aviator of a need for ground support for the oxygen supply. Onboard oxygen generating systems on military aircraft pass bleed air from turbine engines through a sieve that separates the oxygen for breathing use. Some of the separated oxygen is also used to purge the sieve of the nitrogen and other gases that keep it fresh for use. Use of this type of oxygen production in civilian aircraft is anticipated. *[Figure 16-8]*

Figure 16-7. *A sodium chlorate solid oxygen candle is at the core of a chemical oxygen generator.*

Oxygen Systems and Components

Built-in and portable oxygen systems are used in civilian aviation. They use gaseous or solid oxygen (oxygen generators) as suits the purpose and aircraft. LOX systems and molecular sieve oxygen systems are not discussed, as current applications on civilian aircraft are limited.

Gaseous Oxygen Systems

The use of gaseous oxygen in aviation is common; however, applications vary. On a light aircraft, it may consist of a small carry-on portable cylinder with a single mask attached via a hose to a regulator on the bottle. Larger portable cylinders may be fitted with a regulator that divides the outlet flow for

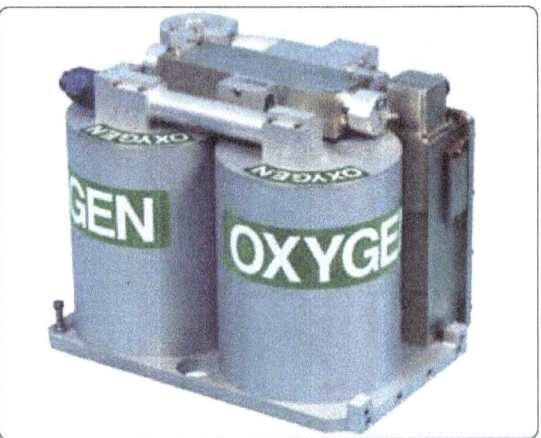

Figure 16-8. *This onboard oxygen generating system uses molecular sieve technology.*

2–4 people. Built-in oxygen systems on high performance and light twin-engine aircraft typically have a location where oxygen cylinders are installed to feed a distribution system via tubing and a regulator. The passenger compartment may have multiple breathing stations plumbed so that each passenger can individually plug in a hose and mask if oxygen is needed. A central regulator is normally controlled by the flight crew who may have their own separate regulator and oxygen cylinder. Transport category aircraft may use an elaborate built-in gaseous oxygen system as a backup system to cabin pressurization. In all of these cases, oxygen is stored as a gas at atmospheric temperature in high-pressure cylinders. It is distributed through a system with various components that are described in this section.

Oxygen Storage Cylinders

Gaseous oxygen is stored and transported in high-pressure cylinders. Traditionally, these have been heavy steel tanks rated for 1800–1850 psi of pressure and capable of maintaining pressure up to 2,400 psi. While these performed adequately, lighter weight tanks were sought. Some newer cylinders are comprised of a lightweight aluminum shell wrapped by Kevlar®. These cylinders are capable of carrying the same amount of oxygen at the same pressure as steel tanks, but weigh much less. Also available are heavy-walled all-aluminum cylinders. These units are common as carry-on portable oxygen used in light aircraft.

Most oxygen storage cylinders are painted green, but yellow and other colors may be used as well. They are certified to Department of Transportation (DOT) specifications. To ensure serviceability, cylinders must be hydrostatically tested periodically. In general, a hydrostatic test consists of filling the container with water and pressurizing it to $\frac{5}{3}$ of its certified rating. It should not leak, rupture, or deform beyond an established limit. *Figure 16-9* shows a hydrostatic cylinder testing apparatus.

Figure 16-9. *This test stand is used for hydrostatic testing of oxygen cylinders. The water-filled cylinder is lowered into the barrel on the left where it is pressurized to the proper level as monitored via gauges mounted on the control panel. A displacement container on the top left of the control board collects water from the barrel to measure the expansion of the cylinder when pressurized to ensure it is within limits.*

Most cylinders also have a limited service life after which they can no longer be used. After a specified number of filling cycles or calendar age, the cylinders must be removed from service. The most common high-pressure steel oxygen cylinders used in aviation are the 3AA and the 3HT. They come in various sizes but are certified to the same specifications. Cylinders certified under DOT-E-8162 are also popular for their extremely light weight. These cylinders typically have an aluminum core around which Kevlar® is wrapped. The DOT-E 8162 approved cylinders are now approved under DOT-SP-8162 specifications. The SP certification has extended the required time between hydrostatic testing to 5 years (previously 3 years). [*Figure 16-10*]

The manufactured date and certification number is stamped on each cylinder near the neck. Subsequent hydrostatic test dates are also stamped there as well. Composite cylinders use placards rather than stamping. The placard must be covered with a coat of clear epoxy when additional information is added, such as a new hydrostatic test date.

Oxygen cylinders are considered empty when the pressure inside drops below 50 psi. This ensures that air containing water vapor has not entered the cylinder. Water vapor could cause corrosion inside the tank, as well as presenting the possibility of ice forming and clogging a narrow passageway in the cylinder valve or oxygen system. Any installed tank allowed to fall below this pressure should be removed from service.

Oxygen Systems and Regulators

The design of the various oxygen systems used in aircraft depends largely on the type of aircraft, its operational requirements, and whether the aircraft has a pressurization system. Systems are often characterized by the type of regulator used to dispense the oxygen: continuous-flow and demand flow. In some aircraft, a continuous-flow oxygen system is installed for both passengers and crew. The pressure demand system is widely used as a crew system, especially on the larger transport aircraft. Many aircraft have a combination of both systems that may be augmented by portable equipment.

Continuous-Flow Systems

In its simplest form, a continuous-flow oxygen system allows oxygen to exit the storage tank through a valve and passes it

Certification Type	Material	Rated pressure (psi)	Required hydrostatic test	Service life (years)	Service life (fillings)
DOT 3AA	Steel	1,800	5	Unlimited	N/A
DOT 3HT	Steel	1,850	3	24	4,380
DOT E 8162	Composite	1,850	3	15	N/A
DOT SP 8162	Composite	1,850	5	15	N/A
DOT 3AL	Aluminum	2,216	5	Unlimited	N/A

Figure 16-10. *Common cylinders used in aviation with some certification and testing specifications.*

through a regulator/reducer attached to the top of the tank. The flow of high-pressure oxygen passes through a section of the regulator that reduces the pressure of the oxygen, which is then fed into a hose attached to a mask worn by the user. Once the valve is opened, the flow of oxygen is continuous. Even when the user is exhaling, or when the mask is not in use, a preset flow of oxygen continues until the tank valve is closed. On some systems, fine adjustment to the flow can be made with an adjustable flow indicator that is installed in the hose in line to the mask. A portable oxygen setup for a light aircraft exemplifies this type of continuous-flow system and is shown in *Figure 16-11*.

Manual continuous-flow regulators are adjusted by the crew as altitude changes. Automatic continuous-flow regulators have a built in aneroid. As the aneroid expands with altitude, a mechanism allows more oxygen to flow though the regulator to the users. [*Figure 16-12*]

Figure 16-12. *A manual continuous flow oxygen system may have a regulator that is adjusted by the pilot as altitude varies. By turning the knob, the left gauge can be made to match the flight altitude thus increasing and decreasing flow as altitude changes.*

Figure 16-11. *A typical portable gaseous oxygen cylinder complete with valve, pressure gauge, regulator/reducer, hose, adjustable flow indicator, and rebreather cannula. A padded carrying case/bag can be strapped to the back of a seat in the cabin to meet certification and testing specifications.*

A more sophisticated continuous-flow oxygen system uses a regulator that is adjustable to provide varying amounts of oxygen flow to match increasing need as altitude increases. These regulators can be manual or automatic in design.

Many continuous-flow systems include a fixed location for the oxygen cylinders with permanent delivery plumbing installed to all passenger and crew stations in the cabin. In large aircraft, separate storage cylinders for crew and passengers are typical. Fully integrated oxygen systems usually have separate, remotely mounted components to reduce pressure and regulate flow. A pressure relief valve is also typically installed in the system, as is some sort of filter and a gauge to indicate the amount of oxygen pressure remaining in the storage cylinder(s). *Figure 16-13* diagrams the type of continuous-flow system that is found on small to medium sized aircraft.

Built-in continuous-flow gaseous oxygen systems accomplish a final flow rate to individual user stations through the use of a calibrated orifice in each mask. Larger diameter orifices are usually used in crew masks to provide greater flow than that for passengers. Special oxygen masks provide even greater flow via larger orifices for passengers traveling with medical conditions requiring full saturation of the blood with oxygen.

Allowing oxygen to continuously flow from the storage cylinder can be wasteful. Lowest sufficient flow rates can

Figure 16-13. *Continuous flow oxygen system found on small to medium size aircraft.*

be accomplished through the use of rebreather apparatus. Oxygen and air that is exhaled still contains usable oxygen. By capturing this oxygen in a bag, or in a cannula with oxygen absorbing reservoirs, it can be inhaled with the next breath, reducing waste. *[Figure 16-14]*

The passenger section of a continuous-flow oxygen system may consist of a series of plug-in supply sockets fitted to the cabin walls adjacent to the passenger seats to which oxygen masks can be connected. Flow is inhibited until a passenger manually plugs in. When used as an emergency system in pressurized aircraft, depressurization automatically triggers the deployment of oxygen ready continuous-flow masks at each passenger station. A lanyard attached to the mask turns on the flow to each mask when it is pulled toward the passenger for use. The masks are normally stowed overhead in the passenger service unit (PSU). *[Figure 16-15]* Deployment of the emergency continuous-flow passenger oxygen masks may also be controlled by the crew. *[Figure 16-16]*

Continuous-flow oxygen masks are simple devices made to direct flow to the nose and mouth of the wearer. They

Figure 16-14. *A rebreather cannula (A) and rebreather bag (B) capture exhaled oxygen to be inhaled on the next breath. This conserves oxygen by permitting lower flow rates in continuous flow systems. The red and green devices are optional flow indicators that allow the user to monitor oxygen flow rate. The type shown also contains needle valves for final regulation of the flow rate to each user.*

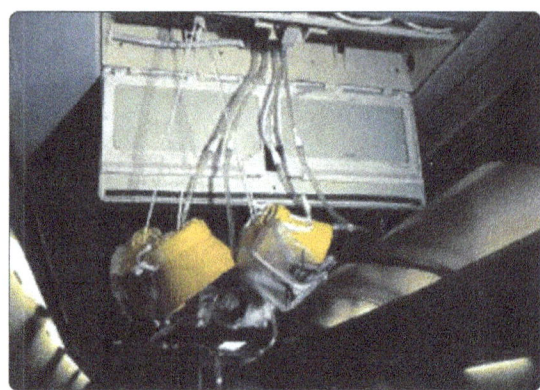

Figure 16-15. *A passenger service unit (psu) is hinged over each row of seats in an airliner. Four yellow continuous flow oxygen masks are shown deployed. They are normally stored behind a separate hinged panel that opens to allow the masks to fall from the PSU for use.*

fit snugly but are not air tight. Vent holes allow cabin air to mix with the oxygen and provide escape for exhalation. In a rebreather mask, the vents allow the exhaled mixture that is not trapped in the rebreather bag to escape. This is appropriate, because this is the air-oxygen mixture that has been in the lungs the longest, so it has less recoverable oxygen to be breathed again. *[Figure 16-17]*

Figure 16-17. *Examples of different continuous-flow oxygen masks.*

Figure 16-16. *The crew can deploy passenger emergency continuous-flow oxygen masks and supply with a switch in the cockpit.*

Demand-Flow Systems

When oxygen is delivered only as the user inhales, or on demand, it is known as a demand-flow system. During the hold and exhalation periods of breathing, the oxygen supply is stopped. Thus, the duration of the oxygen supply is prolonged as none is wasted. Demand-flow systems are used most frequently by the crew on high performance and air transport category aircraft. *[Figure 16-18]*

Figure 16-18. *Location of demand-flow oxygen components on a transport category aircraft.*

Demand-flow systems are similar to continuous-flow systems in that a cylinder delivers oxygen through a valve when opened. The tank pressure gauge, filter(s), pressure relief valve, and any plumbing installed to refill the cylinder while installed on the aircraft are all similar to those in a continuous-flow system. The high-pressure oxygen also passes through a pressure reducer and a regulator to adjust the pressure and flow to the user. But, demand-flow oxygen regulators differ significantly from continuous-flow oxygen regulators. They work in conjunction with close-fitting demand-type masks to control the flow of oxygen. *[Figure 16-19]*

In a demand-flow oxygen system, the system pressure-reducing valve is sometimes called a pressure regulator. This device lowers the oxygen pressure from the storage cylinder(s) to roughly 60–85 psi and delivers it to individual regulators dedicated for each user. A pressure reduction also occurs at the inlet of the individual regulator by limiting the size of the inlet orifice. There are two types of individual regulators: the diluter-demand type and the pressure-demand type. *[Figure 16-20]*

The diluter demand type regulator holds back the flow of oxygen until the user inhales with a demand-type oxygen mask. The regulator dilutes the pure oxygen supply with cabin air each time a breath is drawn. With its control toggle switch set to normal, the amount of dilution depends on the cabin altitude. As altitude increases, an aneroid allows more oxygen and less cabin air to be delivered to the user by adjusting flows through a metering valve. At approximately 34,000 feet, the diluter-demand regulator meters 100 percent oxygen. This should not be needed unless cabin pressurization fails. Additionally, the user may select 100 percent oxygen delivery at any time by positioning the oxygen selection lever on the regulator. A built-in emergency switch also delivers 100 percent oxygen, but in a continuous flow as the demand function is bypassed. *[Figure 16-21]*

Pressure-demand oxygen systems operate similarly to diluter-demand systems, except that oxygen is delivered through the individual pressure regulator(s) under higher pressure. When the demand valve is unseated, oxygen under pressure forces its way into the lungs of the user. The demand function still operates, extending the overall supply of oxygen beyond that of a continuous-flow system. Dilution with cabin air also occurs if cabin altitude is less than 34,000 feet.

Pressure-demand regulators are used on aircraft that regularly fly at 40,000 feet and above. They are also found on many airliners and high-performance aircraft that may not typically fly that high. Forcing oxygen into the lungs under pressure ensures saturation of the blood, regardless of altitude or cabin altitude.

Both diluter-demand and pressure-demand regulators also come in mask-mounted versions. The operation is essentially the same as that of panel-mounted regulators. *[Figure 16-22]*

Flow Indicators

Flow indicators, or flow meters, are common in all oxygen systems. They usually consist of a lightweight object, or apparatus, that is moved by the oxygen stream. When flow exists, this movement signals the user in some way. *[Figure 16-23]* Many flow meters in continuous-flow oxygen systems also double as flow rate adjusters. Needle valves fitted into the flow indicator housing can fine-adjust the

Figure 16-19. *A demand regulator and demand-type mask work together to control flow and conserve oxygen. Demand-flow masks are close fitting so that when the user inhales, low pressure is created in the regulator, which allows oxygen to flow. Exhaled air escapes through ports in the mask, and the regulator ceases the flow of oxygen until the next inhalation.*

Figure 16-20. *The two basic types of regulators used in demand flow oxygen systems. The panel below the diluter demand regulator on the left is available for mask hose plug in (left), lanyard mask hanger (center), and microphone plug in (right). Most high performance demand type masks have a microphone built-in.*

Figure 16-21. *A diluter-demand regulator operates when low pressure caused by inhalation moves the demand diaphragm. A demand valve connected to the diaphragm opens, letting oxygen flow through the metering valve. The metering valve adjusts the mixture of cabin air and pure oxygen via a connecting link to an aneroid that responds to cabin altitude.*

Figure 16-22. *A mask-mounted version of a miniature diluter-demand regulator designed for use in general aviation (left), a mechanical quick-donning diluter-demand mask with the regulator on the mask (center), and an inflatable quick donning mask (right). Squeezing the red grips directs oxygen into the hollow straps.*

oxygen delivery rate. Demand-flow oxygen systems usually have flow indicators built into the individual regulators at each user station. Some contain a blinking device that activates when the user inhales and oxygen is delivered. Others move a colored pith object into a window. Regardless, flow indicators provide a quick verification that an oxygen system is functioning.

Different flow indicators are used to provide verification that the oxygen system is functioning. Other demand-flow indicators are built into the oxygen regulators. *[Figure 16-23]*

A recent development in general aviation oxygen systems is the electronic pulse demand oxygen delivery system (EDS). A small, portable EDS unit is made to connect between the oxygen source and the mask in a continuous-flow oxygen

Figure 16-23. *Different flow indicators are used to provide verification that the oxygen system is functioning: continuous-flow, in-line (left); continuous-flow, in-line with valve adjuster (center); and old style demand flow (right).*

system. It delivers timed pulses of oxygen to the wearer on demand, saving oxygen normally lost during the hold and exhale segments of the breathing cycle. Advanced pressure sensing and processing allows the unit to deliver oxygen only when an inhalation starts. It can also sense differences in users' breathing cycles and physiologies and adjust the flow of oxygen accordingly. A built-in pressure-sensing device adjusts the amount of oxygen released as altitude changes. *[Figure 16-24]*

Permanently mounted EPD systems are also available. They typically integrate with an electronic valve/regulator on the oxygen cylinder and come with an emergency bypass switch to provide continuous-flow oxygen should the system malfunction. A liquid crystal display (LCD) monitor/control panel displays numerous system operating parameters and allows adjustments to the automatic settings. This type of electronic metering of oxygen has also been developed for passenger emergency oxygen use in airliners. *[Figure 16-25]*

Oxygen Plumbing and Valves

Tubing and fittings make up most of the oxygen system plumbing and connect the various components. Most lines are metal in permanent installations. High-pressure lines are usually stainless steel. Tubing in the low-pressure parts of the oxygen system is typically aluminum. Flexible plastic hosing is used deliver oxygen to the masks; its use is increasing in permanent installations to save weight.

Installed oxygen tubing is usually identified with color-coded tape applied to each end of the tubing, and at specified intervals along its length. The tape coding consists of a green band overprinted with the words "BREATHING OXYGEN" and a black rectangular symbol overprinted on a white background border strip. *[Figure 16-26]*

Figure 16-24. *A portable two-person electronic pulse-demand (EPD) oxygen regulating unit.*

Figure 16-25. *The key components of a built-in electronic pulse demand oxygen metering system: (A) electronic regulator, (B) oxygen station distributer unit, (C) command/display unit, (D) emergency bypass switch.*

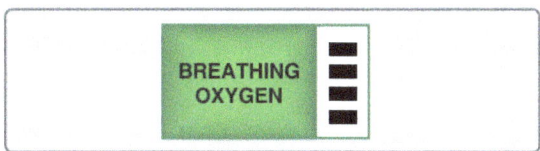

Figure 16-26. *Color-coded tape used to identify oxygen tubing.*

Tubing-to-tubing fittings in oxygen systems are often designed with straight threads to receive flared tube connections. Tubing-to-component fittings usually have straight threads on the tubing end and external pipe threads (tapered) on the other end for attachment to the component. The fittings are typically made of the same material as the tubing (i.e., aluminum or steel). Flared and flareless fittings are both used, depending on the system.

Five types of valves are commonly found in high-pressure gaseous oxygen systems: filler, check, shutoff, pressure reducer, and pressure relief. They function as they would in any other system with one exception: oxygen system shutoff valves are specifically designed to open slowly.

The ignition point for any substances is lower in pure oxygen than it is in air. When high-pressure oxygen is allowed to rush into a low-pressure area, its velocity could reach the speed of sound. If it encounters an obstruction (a valve seat, an elbow, a piece of contaminant, etc.), the oxygen compresses. With this compression, known as adiabatic compression (since it builds so quickly no heat is lost to its surroundings), comes high temperature. Under pressure, this high temperature exceeds the ignition point of the material the oxygen encounters and a fire or explosion results. A stainless steel line, for example, would not normally burn and is used for carrying numerous fluids under high pressure. But under high pressure and temperature in the presence of 100 percent oxygen, even stainless steel can ignite.

To combat this issue, all oxygen shutoff valves are slow, opening valves designed to decrease velocity. *[Figure 16-27]*

Figure 16-27. *This high-pressure oxygen system shutoff valve has fine-pitch threads and a regulating stem to slow the flow of oxygen through the valve. A soft valve seat is also included to assure the valve closes completely.*

Additionally, technicians should always open all oxygen valves slowly. Keeping oxygen from rushing into a low pressure area should be a major concern when working with high-pressure gaseous oxygen systems.

Oxygen cylinder valves and high-pressure systems are often provided with a relief valve should the desired pressure be exceeded. Often, the valve is ported to an indicating or blowout disk. This is located in a conspicuous place, such as the fuselage skin, where it can be seen during walk-around inspection. Most blowout disks are green. The absence of the green disk indicates the relief valve has opened, and the cause should be investigated before flight. *[Figure 16-28]*

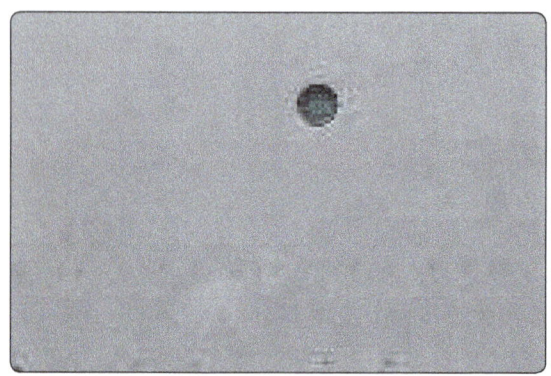

Figure 16-28. *An oxygen blowout plug on the side of the fuselage indicates when pressure relief has occurred and should be investigated.*

Chemical Oxygen Systems

The two primary types of chemical oxygen systems are the portable type, much like a portable carry-on gaseous oxygen cylinder, and the fully integrated supplementary oxygen system used as backup on pressurized aircraft in case of pressurization failure. *[Figure 16-29]* This latter use of solid chemical oxygen generators is most common on airliners. The generators are stored in the overhead PSU attached to hoses and masks for every passenger on board the aircraft. When a depressurization occurs, or the flight crew activates a switch, a compartment door opens and the masks and hoses fall out in front of the passengers. The action of pulling the mask down to a usable position actuates an electric current, or ignition hammer, that ignites the oxygen candle and initiates the flow of oxygen. Typically, 10 to 20 minutes of oxygen is available for each user. This is calculated to be enough time for the aircraft to descend to a safe altitude for unassisted breathing.

Figure 16-29. *An oxygen generator mounted in place in an overhead passenger service unit of an air transport category aircraft.*

Chemical oxygen systems are unique in that they do not produce the oxygen until it is time to be used. This allows safer transportation of the oxygen supply with less maintenance. Chemical oxygen-generating systems also require less space and weigh less than gaseous oxygen systems supplying the same number of people. Long runs of tubing, fittings, regulators, and other components are avoided, as are heavy gaseous oxygen storage cylinders. Each passenger row grouping has its own fully independent chemical oxygen generator. The generators, which often weigh less than a pound, are insulated and can burn completely without getting hot. The size of the orifice opening in the hose-attach nipples regulates the continuous flow of oxygen to the users.

LOX Systems

LOX systems are rarely used in civilian aviation. They may be encountered on former military aircraft now in the civilian fleet. As mentioned, the storage of LOX requires a special container system. The plumbing arrangement to convert the liquid to a usable gas is also unique. It basically consists of a controlled heat exchange assembly of tubing and valves. Overboard pressure relief is provided for excessive temperature situations. Once gaseous, the LOX system is the same as it is in any comparable gaseous oxygen delivery system. Use of pressure-demand regulators and masks is common. Consult the manufacturer's maintenance manual for further information if a LOX system is encountered.

Oxygen System Servicing
Servicing Gaseous Oxygen

Gaseous oxygen systems are prevalent in general, corporate, and airline aviation. The use of light weight aluminum and composite storage cylinders has improved these simple and reliable life support systems. All gaseous oxygen systems require servicing and maintenance. Various procedures and requirements to perform these functions are covered in this section.

Leak Testing Gaseous Oxygen Systems

Leaks in a continuous-flow oxygen system may be difficult to detect because the system is open at the user end. Blocking the flow of oxygen allows pressure to build and leak check procedures can be followed that are similar to those used in the high pressure sections of the systems. Detection of leaks should be performed with oxygen-safe leak check fluid. This is a soapy liquid free from elements that might react with pure oxygen or contaminate the system. As with leak detection on an inflated tire or tube assembly, the oxygen leak detection solution is applied to the outside of fittings and mating surfaces. The formation of bubbles indicates a leak. *[Figure 16-30]*

Figure 16-30. *Oxygen system leak check solution.*

Careful assembly of oxygen components and fittings without overtightening or undertightening is required. If a leak is found at a fitting, it should be checked for the proper torque. Tightening may not always stop the leak. If the fitting is torqued properly and a leak still exists, pressure must be released from the system and the fitting must be examined for flaws or contamination. If necessary, the fitting must be replaced. All system components, lines, and fittings must be replaced with the proper parts, which should be cleaned and inspected thoroughly before installation. Follow the manufacturer's instructions and repeat the leak check when completed.

Use caution when maintaining the high pressure portion of a gaseous oxygen system. An open tank valve pressurizes the lines and components with up to 1,850 pounds per square inch (psi) of oxygen. Identify the high-pressure section of the system as that portion upstream of the reducer or regulator that has stainless steel tubing. Note that no attempt should be made to tighten a leaky oxygen fitting while the system is charging. The oxygen supply should be isolated in the cylinder and the system depressurized to reduce the consequences of a spark or to minimize spillage and injury should a complete fitting failure occur.

Draining an Oxygen System

The biggest factor in draining an oxygen system is safety. The oxygen must be released into the atmosphere without causing a fire, explosion, or hazard. Draining outside is highly recommended. The exact method of draining can vary. The basic procedure involves establishing a continuous flow in a safe area until the system is empty.

If the cylinder valve is operative, close the valve to isolate the oxygen supply in the cylinder. All that remains is to empty the lines and components. This can be done without disassembling the system by letting oxygen flow from the delivery point(s). If the environment is safe to receive the oxygen, positioning a demand-flow regulator to emergency delivers a continuous flow of oxygen to the mask when plugged in. Hang the mask(s) out of a window while the system drains. Plug in all mask(s) to allow oxygen to drain from a continuous-flow oxygen system. Systems without check valves can be drained by opening the refill valve.

Filling an Oxygen System

Filling procedures for oxygen systems vary. Many general aviation aircraft are set up to simply replace an empty cylinder with one that is fully charged. This is also the case with a portable oxygen system. High performance and air transport category aircraft often have built-in oxygen systems that contain plumbing designed to refill gaseous oxygen cylinders while they are in place. A general discussion of the procedure to fill this type of installation follows.

Before charging any oxygen system, consult the aircraft manufacturer's maintenance manual. The type of oxygen to be used, safety precautions, equipment to be used, and the procedures for filling and testing the system must be observed. Several general precautions should also be observed when servicing a gaseous oxygen system. Oxygen valves should be opened slowly and filling should proceed slowly to avoid overheating. The hose from the refill source to the oxygen fill valve on the aircraft should be purged of air before it is used to transfer oxygen into the system. Pressures should also be checked frequently while refilling.

Airline and fixed-base operator maintenance shops often use oxygen filler carts to service oxygen systems. These contain several large oxygen supply cylinders connected to the fill cart manifold. This manifold supplies a fill hose that attaches to the aircraft. Valves and pressure gauges allow awareness and control of the oxygen dispensing process. *[Figure 16-31]* Be sure all cylinders on the cart are aviator's breathing oxygen and that all cylinders contain at least 50 psi of oxygen pressure. Each cylinder should also be within its hydrostatic test date interval. After a cart cylinder has dispensed oxygen, the remaining pressure should be recorded. This is usually written on the outside of the cylinder with chalk or in a cylinder pressure log kept with the cart. As such, the technician can tell at a glance the status of each oxygen bottle.

No pump or mechanical device is used to transfer oxygen from the fill cart manifold to the aircraft system. Objects under pressure flow from high pressure to low pressure. Thus, by connecting the cart to the aircraft and systematically opening oxygen cylinders with increasingly higher pressure, a slow increase in oxygen flow to the aircraft can be managed.

Figure 16-31. *Typical oxygen servicing cart used to fill an aircraft system.*

The following is a list of steps to safely fill an aircraft oxygen system from a typical oxygen refill cart.

1. Check hydrostatic dates on all cylinders, especially those that are to be filled on the aircraft. If a cylinder is out of date, remove and replace it with a specified unit that is serviceable.
2. Check pressures on all cylinders on the cart and in the aircraft. If pressure is below 50 psi, replace the cylinder(s). On the aircraft, this may require purging the system with oxygen when completed. Best practices dictate that any low-pressure or empty cylinder(s) on the cart should also be removed and replaced when discovered.
3. Take all oxygen handling precautions to ensure a safe environment around the aircraft.
4. Ground the refill cart to the aircraft.
5. Connect the cart hose from the cart manifold to the aircraft fill port. Purge the air from the refill hose with oxygen before opening the refill valve on the aircraft. Some hoses are equipped with purge valves to do this while the hose is securely attached to the aircraft. Others hoses need to be purged while attached to the refill fitting but not fully tightened.
6. Observe the pressure on the aircraft bottle to be filled. Open it. On the refill cart, open the cylinder with the closest pressure to the aircraft cylinder that exceeds it.
7. Open the aircraft oxygen system refill valve. Oxygen will flow from cart cylinder (manifold) into the aircraft cylinder.
8. When the cylinder pressures equalize, close the cylinder on the cart, and open the cart cylinder with the next highest pressure. Allow it to flow into the aircraft cylinder until the pressures equalize and flow ceases. Close the cart cylinder, and proceed to the cart cylinder with the next highest pressure.
9. Continue the procedure in step 8 until the desired pressure in the aircraft cylinder is achieved.
10. Close the aircraft refill valve, and close all cylinders on the cart.
11. The aircraft oxygen cylinder valve(s) should be left in the proper position for normal operations. Remotely mounted cylinders are usually left open.
12. Disconnect the refill line from the refill port on the aircraft. Cap or cover both.
13. Remove the grounding strap.

Temperature has a significant effect on the pressure of gaseous oxygen. Manufacturers typically supply a fill chart or a placard at the aircraft oxygen refill station to guide technicians in compensating for temperature/pressure variations. Technicians should consult the chart and fill cylinders to the maximum pressure listed for the prevailing ambient temperature. *[Figure 16-32]*

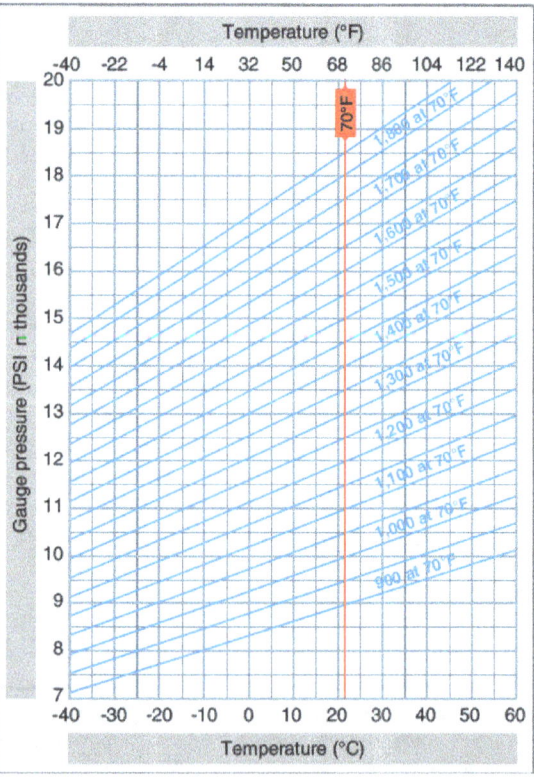

Figure 16-32. *A temperature-compensating pressure refill chart is used by the technician to ensure proper oxygen cylinder pressure in the aircraft system.*

When it is hot, oxygen cylinders are filled to a higher pressure than 1,800 psi or 1,850 psi, the standard maximum pressure ratings of most high-pressure aircraft oxygen cylinders. This is allowable because at altitude the temperature and pressure of the oxygen can decrease significantly. Filling cylinders to temperature-compensated pressure values ensures a full supply of oxygen is available when needed. When filling cylinders on a cold day, compensation for temperature and pressure changes dictates that cylinders be filled to less than the maximum rated capacity to allow for pressure increases as temperature rises. Strict adherence to the temperature/pressure compensation chart values is mandatory to ensure safe storage of aircraft oxygen.

Note that some aircraft have temperature compensation features built into the refill valve. After setting the ambient temperature on the valve dial, the valve closes when the correct amount of oxygen pressure has been established in the aircraft cylinder. A chart can be used to ensure proper servicing.

Purging an Oxygen System

The inside of an oxygen system becomes completely saturated with oxygen during use. This is desirable to deliver clean, odor-free oxygen to the users and to prevent corrosion caused by contamination. An oxygen system needs to be purged if it has been opened or depleted for more than 2 hours, or if it is suspected that the system has been contaminated. Purging is accomplished to evacuate contaminants and to restore oxygen saturation to the inside of the system

The main cause of contamination in an oxygen system is moisture. In very cold weather, the small amount of moisture contained in the breathing oxygen can condense. With repeated charging, a significant amount of moisture may collect. Additionally, systems that are opened contain the moisture from the air that has entered. Damp charging equipment, or poor refill procedures, can also introduce water into the system. Always follow manufacturer's instructions when performing maintenance, refilling, or purging an oxygen system.

Cumulative condensation in an oxygen system cannot be entirely avoided. Purging is needed periodically. The procedure for purging may vary somewhat with each aircraft model. Generally speaking, oxygen is run through a sound oxygen system for a number of minutes at a given pressure to perform the purging. This can be as little as 10 minutes at normal delivery pressure. Other systems may require up to 30 minutes of flow at an elevated pressure. Regardless, the removal of contaminants and the resaturation of the inside of the system with oxygen is the basis for purging. It is acceptable to use nitrogen, or dry air, to blow through lines and components when performing maintenance. However, a final purging with pure oxygen is required before the system is serviceable for use.

It is important to ensure storage cylinders are refilled if they are used during the purging process. Be certain that there are no open lines and all safety caps are installed before returning the aircraft to service.

Filling LOX Systems

The use of LOX in civilian aviation is rare. The most common and safest way to fill a LOX system is to simply exchange the storage unit for one that is full. However, filling LOX on the aircraft is possible.

A portable fill cart is used and all of the same precautions must be observed as when servicing a high pressure gaseous oxygen system. Additionally, protection from cold burns is necessary. Due to the amount of gaseous oxygen released during the process, refilling should be accomplished outside. The servicing cart is attached to the aircraft system through a fill valve. The buildup/vent valve on the LOX container assembly is placed in the vent position. The valve on the service cart is then opened. LOX flows into the aircraft system; some vaporizes and cools the entire setup. This gaseous oxygen flows overboard through the vent valve while the system fills. When a steady stream of LOX flows from the vent valve, the system is filled. The valve is then switched to the buildup position. The aircraft refill valve and cart supply valves are closed and the hose is removed.

Note that back seated valves can freeze in the open position due to the low temperature involved while LOX is being transferred. Valves should be opened completely and then closed slightly so as to not be back seated.

Inspection of Masks and Hoses

The wide varieties of oxygen masks used in aviation require periodic inspection. Mask and hose integrity ensure effective delivery of oxygen to the user when it is needed. Sometimes this is in an emergency situation. Leaks, holes, and tears are not acceptable. Most discrepancies of this type are remedied by replacement of the damaged unit.

Some continuous-flow masks are designed for disposal after use. Be sure there is a mask for each potential user on board the aircraft. Masks designed to be reused should be clean, as well as functional. This reduces the danger of infection and prolongs the life of the mask. Various mild cleaners and antiseptics that are free of petroleum products can be used. A supply of individually wrapped alcohol swabs are often kept in the cockpit.

Built-in microphones should be operational. Donning straps and fittings should be in good condition and function so that the mask is held firm to the user's face. Note that the diameter of mask hoses in a continuous-flow system is quite a bit smaller than those used in a demand-flow system. This is because the inside diameter of the hose aids in controlling flow rate. Masks for each kind of system are made to only connect to the proper hose.

Smoke masks are required on transport aircraft and are used on some other aircraft as well. These cover the eyes, as well as the user's nose and mouth. Smoke masks are usually available within easy grasp of the crew members. They are used when the situation in the cockpit demands the increased level of protection offered. Smoke mask hoses plug into demand regulators in the same port used for regular demand type masks and operate in the same manner. Most include a built-in microphone. *[Figure 16-33]* Some portable oxygen systems are also fitted with smoke masks.

Figure 16-33. *Smoke masks cover the eyes as well as the nose and mouth of the user.*

Replacing Tubing, Valves, and Fittings
The replacement of aircraft oxygen system tubing, valves, and fittings is similar to the replacement of the same components in other aircraft systems. There is, however, an added emphasis on cleanliness and compatible sealant use.

Any oxygen system component should be cleaned thoroughly before installation. Often tubing comes with leftover residue from the bending or flaring processes. Cleaning should be accomplished with nonpetroleum-based cleansers. Trichlorethylene, acetone, and similar cleaners can be used to flush new tubing. Tubing should be blown or baked dry before installation. Follow the manufacturer's procedures for cleaning oxygen system components.

Some oxygen components make use of tapered pipe fittings. This type of connection is usually sealed with the application of thread lubricant/sealant. Typical thread sealers are petroleum based and should not be used; only oxygen compatible thread lubricant/sealers should be used. Alternatively, Teflon® tape is also used on oxygen pipe fitting connections. Be sure to begin wrapping the Teflon® tape at least two threads from the end of the fitting. This prevents any tape from coming loose and entering the oxygen system.

Prevention of Oxygen Fires or Explosions
Precautions must be observed when working with or around pure oxygen. It readily combines with other substances, some in a violent and explosive manner. As mentioned, it is extremely important to keep distance between pure oxygen and petroleum products. When allowed to combine, an explosion can result. Additionally, there are a variety of inspection and maintenance practices that should be followed to ensure safety when working with oxygen and oxygen systems. Care should be used and, as much as possible, maintenance should be done outside.

When working on an oxygen system, it is essential that the warnings and precautions given in the aircraft maintenance manual be carefully observed. Before any work is attempted, an adequate fire extinguisher should be on hand. Cordon off the area and post "NO SMOKING" placards. Ensure that all tools and servicing equipment are clean and avoid power on checks and use of the aircraft electrical system.

Oxygen System Inspection and Maintenance
When working around oxygen and oxygen systems, cleanliness enhances safety. Clean, grease-free hands, clothes, and tools are essential. A good practice is to use only tools dedicated for work on oxygen systems. There should be absolutely no smoking or open flames within a minimum of 50 feet of the work area. Always use protective caps and plugs when working with oxygen cylinders, system components, or plumbing. Do not use any kind of adhesive tape. Oxygen cylinders should be stored in a designated, cool, ventilated area in the hanger away from petroleum products or heat sources.

Oxygen system maintenance should not be accomplished until the valve on the oxygen supply cylinder is closed and pressure is released from the system. Fittings should be unscrewed slowly to allow any residual pressure to dissipate. All oxygen lines should be marked and should have at least 2 inches of clearance from moving parts, electrical wiring, and all fluid lines. Adequate clearance must also be provided from hot ducts and other sources that might heat the oxygen. A pressure and leak check must be performed each time the system is opened for maintenance. Do not use any lubricants, sealers, cleaners, etc., unless specifically approved for oxygen system use.

Aircraft Pressurization Systems
Pressure of the Atmosphere
The gases of the atmosphere (air), although invisible, have weight. A one square inch column of air stretching from sea level into space weighs 14.7 pounds. Therefore, it can be stated that the pressure of the atmosphere, or atmospheric pressure, at sea level is 14.7 psi. *[Figure 16-34]*

Atmospheric pressure is also known as barometric pressure and is measured with a barometer. *[Figure 16-35]* Expressed in various ways, such as in inches of mercury or millimeters of mercury, these measurements come from observing the height of mercury in a column when air pressure is exerted on a reservoir of mercury into which the column is set. The column must be evacuated so air inside does not act against the mercury rising. A column of mercury 29.92 inches high weighs the same as a column of air that extends from sea level to the top of the atmosphere and has the same cross-section as the column of mercury.

Figure 16-35. *The weight of the atmosphere pushes down on the mercury in the reservoir of a barometer, which causes mercury to rise in the column. At sea level, mercury is forced up into the column approximately 29.92 inches. Therefore, it is said that barometric pressure is 29.92 inches of mercury at sea level.*

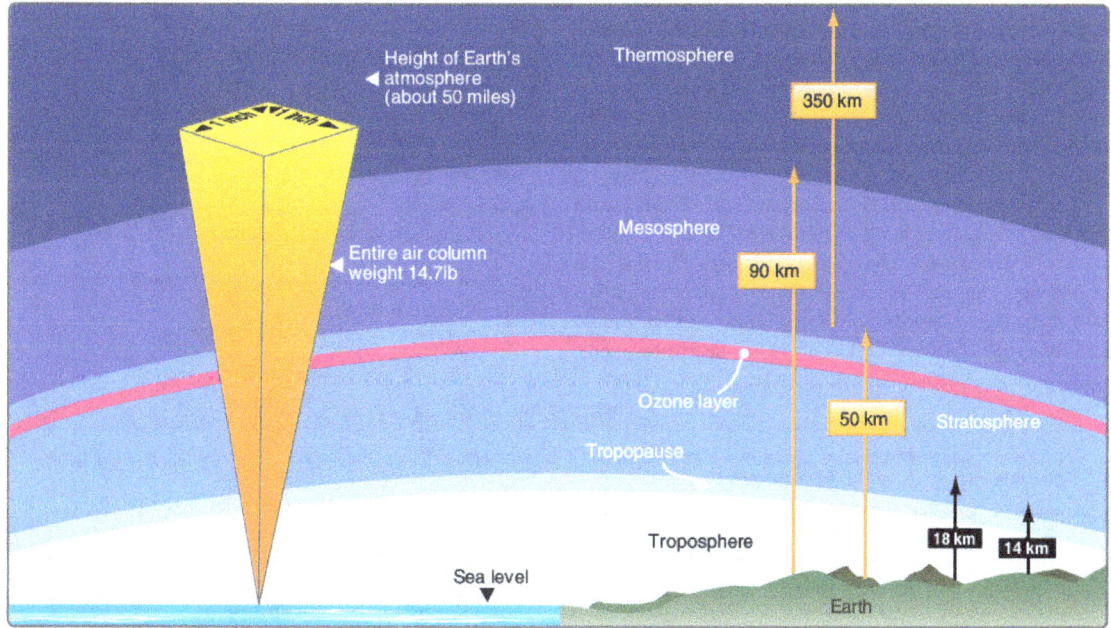

Figure 16-34. *The weight exerted by a 1 square inch column of air stretching from sea level to the top of the atmosphere is what is measured when it is said that atmospheric pressure is equal to 14.7 pounds per square inch.*

Aviators often interchange references to atmospheric pressure between linear displacement (e.g., inches of mercury) and units of force (e.g., psi). Over the years, meteorology has shifted its use of linear displacement representation of atmospheric pressure to units of force. However, the unit of force nearly universally used today to represent atmospheric pressure in meteorology is the hectopascal (hPa). A hectopascal is a metric (SI) unit that expresses force in newtons per square meter. 1,013.2 hPa is equal to 14.7 psi. [Figure 16-36]

Atmospheric pressure decreases with increasing altitude. The simplest explanation for this is that the column of air that is weighed is shorter. How the pressure changes for a given altitude is shown in Figure 16-37. The decrease in pressure is a rapid one and, at 50,000 feet, the atmospheric pressure has dropped to almost one-tenth of the sea level value.

Temperature and Altitude

Temperature variations in the atmosphere are of concern to aviators. Weather systems produce changes in temperature near the earth's surface. Temperature also changes as altitude is increased. The troposphere is the lowest layer of the atmosphere. On average, it ranges from the earth's surface to about 38,000 feet above it. Over the poles, the troposphere extends to only 25,000–30,000 feet and, at the equator, it may extend to around 60,000 feet. This oblong nature of the troposphere is illustrated in Figure 16-38.

Most civilian aviation takes place in the troposphere in which temperature decreases as altitude increases. The rate of change is somewhat constant at about –2 °C or –3.5 °F for every 1,000 feet of increase in altitude. The upper boundary of the troposphere is the tropopause. It is characterized as a zone of relatively constant temperature of –57 °C or –69 °F.

Above the tropopause lies the stratosphere. Temperature increases with altitude in the stratosphere to near 0 °C before decreasing again in the mesosphere, which lies above it. The stratosphere contains the ozone layer that protects the earth's inhabitants from harmful UV rays. Some civilian flights and numerous military flights occur in the stratosphere.

Figure 16-37. *Atmospheric pressure decreasing with altitude. At sea level the pressure is 14.7 psi, while at 40,000 feet, as the dotted lines show, the pressure is only 2.72 psi.*

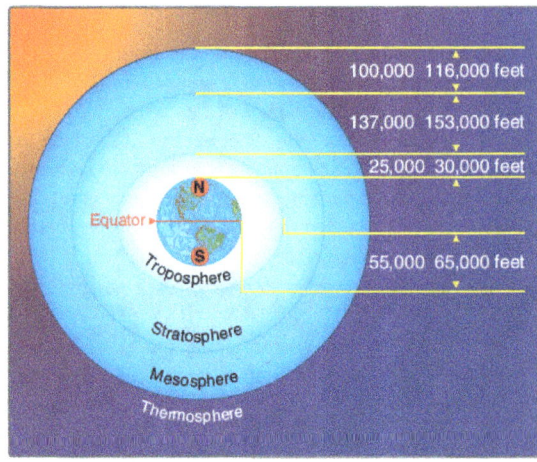

Figure 16-38. *The troposphere extends higher above the earth's surface at the equator than it does at the poles.*

Figure 16-39 diagrams the temperature variations in different layers of the atmosphere.

Figure 16-36. *Various equivalent representations of atmospheric pressure at sea level.*

16-22

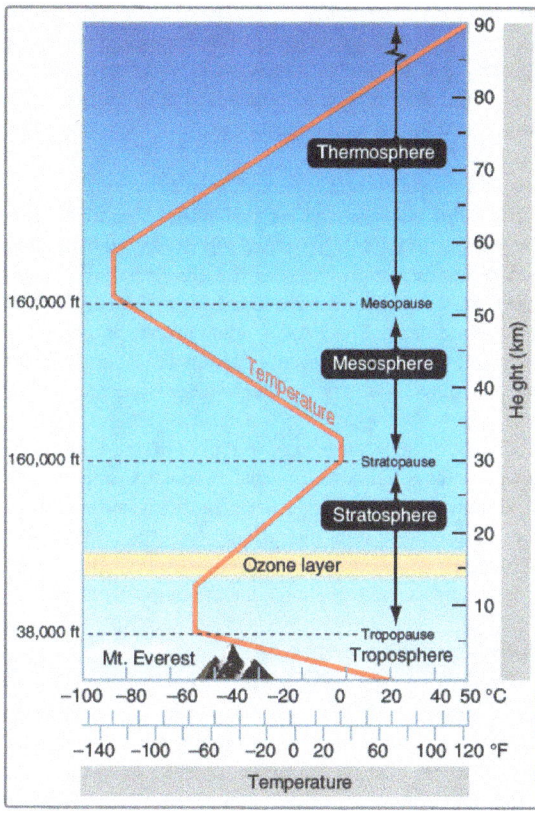

Figure 16-39. *The atmospheric layers with temperature changes depicted by the red line.*

Altitude	Pressure			Temperature	
feet	psi	hPa	in Hg	°F	°C
0	14.69	1013.2	29.92	59.0	15
1,000	14.18	977.2	28.86	55.4	13
2,000	13.66	942.1	27.82	51.9	11
3,000	13.17	908.1	26.82	48.3	9.1
4,000	12.69	875.1	25.84	44.7	7.1
5,000	12.23	843.1	24.90	41.2	5.1
6,000	11.77	812.0	23.98	37.6	3.1
7,000	11.34	781.8	23.09	34.0	1.1
8,000	10.92	752.6	22.23	30.5	−0.8
9,000	10.51	724.3	21.39	26.9	−2.8
10,000	10.10	696.8	20.58	23.3	−4.8
12,000	9.34	644.4	19.03	16.2	−8.8
14,000	8.63	595.2	17.58	9.1	−12.7
16,000	7.96	549.2	16.22	1.9	−16.7
18,000	7.34	506.0	14.94	−5.2	−29.7
20,000	6.76	465.6	13.75	−12.3	−24.6
22,000	6.21	427.9	12.64	−19.5	−28.6
24,000	5.70	392.7	11.60	−26.6	−32.5
26,000	5.22	359.9	10.63	−33.7	−36.5
28,000	4.78	329.3	9.72	−40.9	−40.5
30,000	4.37	300.9	8.89	−48.0	−44.4
32,000	3.99	274.5	8.11	−55.1	−48.4
34,000	3.63	250.0	7.38	−62.2	−52.4
36,000	3.30	227.3	6.71	−69.4	−56.3
38,000	3.00	206.5	6.10	−69.4	−56.5
40,000	2.73	187.5	5.54	−69.4	−56.5
45,000	2.14	147.5	4.35	−69.4	−56.5
50,000	1.70	116.0	3.42	−69.4	−56.5

Figure 16-40. *Cabin environmental systems establish conditions quite different from those found outside the aircraft.*

When an aircraft is flown at high altitude, it burns less fuel for a given airspeed than it does for the same speed at a lower altitude. This is due to decreased drag that results from the reduction in air density. Bad weather and turbulence can also be avoided by flying in the relatively smooth air above storms and convective activity that occur in the lower troposphere. To take advantage of these efficiencies, aircraft are equipped with environmental systems to overcome extreme temperature and pressure levels. While supplemental oxygen and a means of staying warm suffice, aircraft pressurization and air conditioning systems have been developed to make high altitude flight more comfortable. *Figure 16-40* illustrates the temperatures and pressures at various altitudes in the atmosphere.

Pressurization Terms

The following terms should be understood for the discussion of pressurization and cabin environmental systems that follows:

1. Cabin altitude—given the air pressure inside the cabin, the altitude on a standard day that has the same pressure as that in the cabin. Rather than saying the pressure inside the cabin is 10.92 psi, it can be said that the cabin altitude is 8,000 feet (MSL).

2. Cabin differential pressure—the difference between the air pressure inside the cabin and the air pressure outside the cabin. Cabin pressure (psi) − ambient pressure (psi) = cabin differential pressure (psid or Δ psi).

3. Cabin rate of climb—the rate of change of air pressure inside the cabin, expressed in feet per minute (fpm) of cabin altitude change.

Pressurization Issues

Pressurizing an aircraft cabin assists in making flight possible in the hostile environment of the upper atmosphere. The degree of pressurization and the operating altitude of any aircraft are limited by critical design factors. A cabin pressurization system must accomplish several functions if it is to ensure adequate passenger comfort and safety. It must be capable of maintaining a cabin pressure altitude of approximately 8,000 feet or lower regardless of the cruising altitude of the aircraft. This is to ensure that passengers and crew have enough oxygen present at sufficient pressure to facilitate full blood saturation. A pressurization system must also be designed to prevent rapid changes of cabin pressure, which can be uncomfortable or injurious to passengers and crew. Additionally, a pressurization system should circulate air from inside the cabin to the outside at a rate that quickly eliminates odors and to remove stale air. Cabin air must also be heated or cooled on pressurized aircraft. Typically, these functions are incorporated into the pressurization source.

To pressurize, a portion of the aircraft designed to contain air at a pressure higher than outside atmospheric pressure must be sealed. A wide variety of materials facilitate this. Compressible seals around doors combine with various other seals, grommets, and sealants to essentially establish an air tight pressure vessel. This usually includes the cabin, flight compartment, and the baggage compartments. Air is then pumped into this area at a constant rate sufficient to raise the pressure slightly above that which is needed. Control is maintained by adjusting the rate at which the air is allowed to flow out of the aircraft.

A key factor in pressurization is the ability of the fuselage to withstand the forces associated with the increase in pressure inside the structure versus the ambient pressure outside. This differential pressure can range from 3.5 psi for a single-engine reciprocating aircraft, to approximately 9 psi on high performance jet aircraft. *[Figure 16-41]* If the weight of the aircraft structure were of no concern, this would not be a problem. Making an aircraft strong for pressurization, yet also light, has been an engineering challenge met over numerous years beginning in the 1930s. The development of jet aircraft and their ability to exploit low drag flight at higher altitude made the problem even more pronounced. Today, the proliferation of composite materials in aircraft structure continues this engineering challenge.

In addition to being strong enough to withstand the pressure differential between the air inside and the air outside the cabin, metal fatigue from repeated pressurization and depressurization weakens the airframe. Some early pressurized aircraft structures failed due to this and resulted in fatal accidents. The FAA's aging aircraft program was instituted to increase inspection scrutiny of older airframes that may show signs of fatigue due to the pressurization cycle.

Aircraft of any size may be pressurized. Weight considerations when making the fuselage strong enough to endure pressurization usually limit pressurization to high performance light aircraft and larger aircraft. A few pressurized single-engine reciprocating aircraft exist, as well as many pressurized single-engine turboprop aircraft.

Sources of Pressurized Air

The source of air to pressurize an aircraft varies mainly with engine type. Reciprocating aircraft have pressurization sources different from those of turbine-powered aircraft. Note that the compression of air raises its temperature. A means for keeping pressurization air cool enough is built into most pressurization systems. It may be in the form of a heat exchanger, using cold ambient air to modify the temperature of the air from the pressurization source. A full air cycle air conditioning system with expansion turbine may also be used.

Figure 16-41. *Differential pressure (psid) is calculated by subtracting the ambient air pressure from the cabin air pressure.*

The latter provides the advantage of temperature control on the ground and at low altitudes where ambient air temperature may be higher than comfortable for the passengers and crew.

Reciprocating Engine Aircraft

There are three typical sources of air used to pressurize reciprocating aircraft: supercharger, turbocharger, and engine-driven compressor. Superchargers and turbochargers are installed on reciprocating engines to permit better performance at high altitude by increasing the quantity and pressure of the air in the induction system. Some of the air produced by each of these can be routed into the cabin to pressurize it.

A supercharger is mechanically driven by the engine. Despite engine performance increases due to higher induction system pressure, some of the engine output is utilized by the supercharger. Furthermore, superchargers have limited capability to increase engine performance. If supplying both the intake and the cabin with air, the engine performance ceiling is lower than if the aircraft were not pressurized. Superchargers must be located upstream of the fuel delivery to be used for pressurization. They are found on older reciprocating engine aircraft, including those with radial engines. *[Figures 16-42 and 16-43]*

Figure 16-43. *The radial engine supercharger cannot be used since fuel is introduced before the supercharger impeller compresses the air.*

Figure 16-42. *A reciprocating engine supercharger can be used as a source of pressurization if it is upstream of carburetion.*

Turbochargers, sometimes known as turbosuperchargers, are driven by engine exhaust gases. They are the most common source of pressurization on modern reciprocating engine aircraft. The turbocharger impeller shaft extends through the bearing housing to support a compression impeller in a separate housing. By using some of the turbocharger compressed air for cabin pressurization, less is available for the intake charge, resulting in lower overall engine performance. Nonetheless, the otherwise wasted exhaust gases are put to work in the turbocharger compressor, enabling high altitude flight with the benefits of low drag and weather avoidance in relative comfort and without the use of supplemental oxygen. *[Figures 16-44 and 16-45]*

Both superchargers and turbochargers are oil lubricated. The supercharger is part of the fuel intake system and the turbocharger is part of the exhaust system. As such, there is a risk of contamination of cabin air from oil, fuel, or exhaust fumes should a malfunction occur, a shortcoming of these pressurization sources.

A third source of air for pressurizing the cabin in reciprocating aircraft is an engine driven compressor. Either belt driven or gear driven by the accessory drive, an independent, dedicated compressor for pressurization avoids some of the potential contamination issues of superchargers and turbochargers. The compressor device does, however, add significant weight. It also consumes engine output since it is engine driven.

The roots blower is used on older, large reciprocating engine aircraft. *[Figure 16-46]* The two lobes in this compressor do not touch each other or the compressor housing. As they rotate, air enters the space between the lobes and is compressed and delivered to the cabin for pressurization. Independent engine-driven centrifugal compressors can also be found on reciprocating engine aircraft. *[Figure 16-47]* A variable ratio gear drive system is used to maintain a constant rate of airflow during changes of engine rpm.

Figure 16-44. *A turbocharger used for pressurizing cabin air and engine intake air on a reciprocating engine aircraft.*

Figure 16-45. *A turbocharger installation on a reciprocating aircraft engine (top left side).*

Near maximum operating altitude, the performance of any reciprocating engine and the pressurization compressor suffer. This is due to the reduced pressure of the air at altitude that supplies the intake of each. The result is difficulty in maintaining a sufficient volume of air to the engine intake to produce power, as well as to allow enough air to the fuselage for pressurization. These are the limiting factors for determining the design ceiling of most reciprocating aircraft, which typically does not exceed 25,000 feet. Turbine engine aircraft overcome these shortcomings, permitting them to fly at much higher altitudes.

Turbine Engine Aircraft

The main principle of operation of a turbine engine involves the compression of large amounts of air to be mixed with fuel and burned. Bleed air from the compressor section of the engine is relatively free of contaminants. As such, it is a great source of air for cabin pressurization. However, the volume of air for engine power production is reduced. The amount of air bled off for pressurization compared to the overall amount of air compressed for combustion is relatively small but should be minimized. Modern large-cabin turbofan engine aircraft contain recirculation fans to reuse up to 50 percent of the air in the cabin, maintaining high engine output.

There are different ways hot, high-pressure bleed air can be exploited. Smaller turbine aircraft, or sections of a large aircraft, may make use of a jet pump flow multiplier. With this device, bleed air is tapped off of the turbine engine's compressor section. It is ejected into a venturi jet pump mounted in air ducting that has one end open to the ambient air and the other end directed into the compartment to be pressurized. Due to the low pressure established in the

Figure 16-46. *A roots blower found on older pressurized aircraft is gear driven by the engine. It pressurizes air as the rotors rotate very close to each other without touching.*

Figure 16-47. *A centrifugal cabin supercharger.*

venturi by the bleed air flow, air is drawn in from outside the aircraft. It mixes with the bleed air and is delivered to the pressure vessel to pressurize it. An advantage of this type of pressurization is the lack of moving parts. *[Figure 16-48]* A disadvantage is only a relatively small volume of space can be pressurized in this manner.

Another method of pressurizing an aircraft using turbine engine compressor bleed air is to have the bleed air drive a separate compressor that has an ambient air intake. A turbine turned by bleed air rotates a compressor impellor mounted on the same shaft. Outside air is drawn in and compressed. It is mixed with the bleed air outflow from the turbine and is sent to the pressure vessel. Turboprop aircraft often use this device, known as a turbocompressor. *[Figure 16-49]*

The most common method of pressurizing turbine-powered aircraft is with an air cycle air conditioning and pressurization system. Bleed air is used, and through an elaborate system including heat exchangers, a compressor, and an expansion turbine, cabin pressurization and the temperature of the pressurizing air are precisely controlled. This air cycle system is discussed in greater detail in the air conditioning section of this chapter. *[Figure 16-50]*

Control of Cabin Pressure
Pressurization Modes

Aircraft cabin pressurization can be controlled via two different modes of operation. The first is the isobaric mode, which works to maintain cabin altitude at a single pressure despite the changing altitude of the aircraft. For example, the flight crew may select to maintain a cabin altitude of 8,000 feet (10.92 psi). In the isobaric mode, the cabin pressure is established at the 8,000 foot level and remains at this level,

Figure 16-48. *A jet pump flow multiplier ejects bleed air into a venturi which draws air for pressurization from outside the aircraft.*

Figure 16-49. *A turbo compressor used to pressurize cabins mostly in turboprop aircraft.*

even as the altitude of the aircraft fluctuates.

The second mode of pressurization control is the constant differential mode, which controls cabin pressure to maintain a constant pressure difference between the air pressure inside the cabin and the ambient air pressure, regardless of aircraft altitude changes. The constant differential mode pressure differential is lower than the maximum differential pressure for which the airframe is designed, keeping the integrity of the pressure vessel intact.

When in isobaric mode, the pressurization system maintains the cabin altitude selected by the crew. This is the condition for normal operations. But when the aircraft climbs beyond a certain altitude, maintaining the selected cabin altitude may result in a differential pressure above that for which the airframe was designed. In this case, the mode of pressurization automatically switches from isobaric to constant differential mode. This occurs before the cabin's max differential pressure limit is reached. A constant differential pressure is then maintained, regardless of the selected cabin altitude.

In addition to the modes of operation described above, the rate of change of the cabin pressure, also known as the cabin rate of climb or descent, is also controlled. This can be done automatically or manually by the flight crew. Typical rates of change for cabin pressure are 300 to 500 fpm. Also, note that modes of pressurization may also refer to automatic versus standby versus manual operation of the pressurization system.

Cabin Pressure Controller

The cabin pressure controller is the device used to control the cabin air pressure. Older aircraft use strictly pneumatic means for controlling cabin pressure. Selections for the desired cabin altitude, rate of cabin altitude change, and barometric pressure setting are all made directly to the pressure controller from pressurization panel in the cockpit. *[Figure 16-51]*

Figure 16-50. *An air cycle air conditioning system used to pressurize the cabin of a business jet.*

Figure 16-51. *A pressure controller for an all pneumatic cabin pressure control system.*

Adjustments and settings on the pressure controller are the control input parameters for the cabin pressure regulator. The regulator controls the position of the outflow valve(s) normally located at the rear of the aircraft pressure vessel. Valve position determines the pressure level in the cabin.

Modern aircraft often combine pneumatic, electric, and electronic control of pressurization. Cabin altitude, cabin rate of change, and barometric setting are made on the cabin pressure selector of the pressurization panel in the cockpit. Electric signals are sent from the selector to the cabin pressure controller, which functions as the pressure regulator. It is remotely located out of sight near the cockpit but inside the pressurized portion of the aircraft. The signals are converted from electric to digital and are used by the controller. Cabin pressure and ambient pressure are also input to the controller, as well as other inputs. *[Figure 16-52]* Using this information, the controller, which is essentially a computer, supplies pressurization logic for various stages of a flight. On many small transport and business jets, the controller's electric output signal drives a torque motor in the primary outflow valve. This modulates pneumatic airflow through the valve, which positions the valve to maintain the pressurization schedule.

On many transport category aircraft, two cabin pressure controllers, or a single controller with redundant circuitry, are used. Located in the electronics equipment bay, they receive electric input from the panel selector, as well as ambient and cabin pressure input. Flight altitude and landing field altitude information are often the crew selection choices on the pressurization control panel. Cabin altitude, rate of climb, and barometric setting are automatic through built-in logic

Figure 16-52. *The pressurization control system on many small transports and business jets utilizes a combination of electronic, electric, and pneumatic control elements.*

and communication with the ADC and the flight management system (FMS). The controllers process the information and send electric signals to motors that directly position the outflow valve(s). *[Figure 16-53]*

Modern pressurization control is fully automatic once variable selections are made on the pressurization control panel if, in fact, there are any to be made. Entering or selecting a flight plan into the FMS of some aircraft automatically supplies the pressurization controller with the parameters needed to establish the pressurization schedule for the entire flight. No other input is needed from the crew.

All pressurization systems contain a manual mode that can override automatic control. This can be used in flight or on the ground during maintenance. The operator selects the manual mode on the pressurization control panel. A separate switch is used to position the outflow valve open or closed to control cabin pressure. The switch is visible in *Figure 16-53*, as well as a small gauge that indicates the position of the valve.

Cabin Air Pressure Regulator and Outflow Valve

Controlling cabin pressurization is accomplished through regulating the amount of air that flows out of the cabin. A cabin outflow valve opens, closes, or modulates to establish the amount of air pressure maintained in the cabin. Some outflow valves contain the pressure regulating and the valve mechanism in a single unit. They operate pneumatically in response to the settings on the cockpit pressurization panel that influence the balance between cabin and ambient air pressure. *[Figure 16-54]*

Pneumatic operation of outflow valves is common. It is simple, reliable, and eliminates the need to convert air pressure operating variables into some other form. Diaphragms, springs, metered orifices, jet pumps, bellows, and poppet valves are used to sense and manipulate cabin and ambient air pressures to correctly position the outflow valve without the use of electricity. Outflow valves that combine the use of electricity with pneumatic operation have all-pneumatic standby and manual modes, as shown in *Figure 16-52*.

The pressure regulating mechanism can also be found as a separate unit. Many air transport category aircraft have an outflow valve that operates electrically, using signals sent from a remotely located cabin air pressure controller that acts as the pressure regulator. The controller positions the valve(s) to achieve the settings on the cockpit pressurization panel selectors according to predetermined pressurization schedules. Signals are sent to electric motors to move the valve as needed. On transports, often AC motors are used with a redundant DC motor for standby or manual operations. *[Figure 16-55]*

Figure 16-53. *This pressurization panel from an 800 series Boeing 737 has input selections of flight altitude and landing altitude.*

Figure 16-54. *An all-pneumatic cabin pressure regulator and outflow valve.*

Cabin Air Pressure Safety Valve Operation

Aircraft pressurization systems incorporate various features to limit human and structural damage should the system malfunction or become inoperative. A means for preventing overpressurization is incorporated to ensure the structural integrity of the aircraft if control of the pressurization system is lost. A cabin air safety valve is a pressure relief valve set to open at a predetermined pressure differential. It allows air to flow from the cabin to prevent internal pressure from exceeding design limitations. *Figure 16-56* shows cabin air pressure safety valves on a large transport category aircraft. On most aircraft, safety valves are set to open between 8 and 10 psid.

Pressurization safety valves are used to prevent the over pressurization of the aircraft cabin. They open at a preset differential pressure and allow air to flow out of the cabin. Wide-body transport category aircraft cabins may have more than one cabin pressurization safety valve.

16-31

Figure 16-55. *This outflow valve on a transport category aircraft is normally operated by an ac motor controlled by a pressure controller in the electronics equipment bay. A second ac motor on the valve is use when in standby mode. A dc motor also on the valve is used for manual operation.*

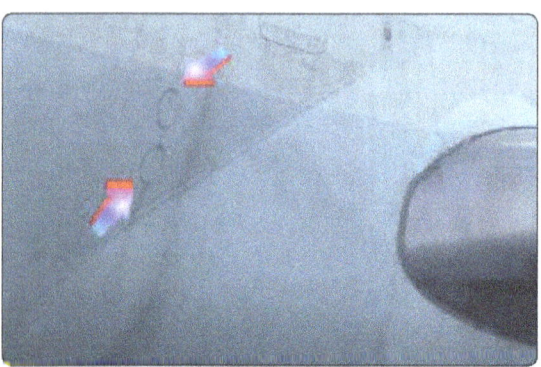

Figure 16-56. *Two pressurization safety valves are shown on a Boeing 747.*

Some outflow valves incorporate the safety valve function into their design. This is common on some corporate jets when two outflow valves are used. One outflow valve operates as the primary and the other as a secondary. Both contain a pilot valve that opens when the pressure differential increases to a preset value. This, in turn, opens the outflow valve(s) to prevent further pressurization. The outflow valves shown in *Figure 16-52* operate in this manner.

Cabin altitude limiters are also used. These close the outflow valves when the pressure in the cabin drops well below the normal cabin altitude range, preventing a further increase in cabin altitude. Some limiter functions are built into the outflow valve(s). An example of this can be seen in *Figure 16-52*. Other limiters are independent bellows units that send input to the outflow valve or are part of the cabin pressurization controller logic.

A negative pressure relief valve is included on pressurized aircraft to ensure that air pressure outside the aircraft does not exceed cabin air pressure. The spring-loaded relief valve opens inward to allow ambient air to enter the cabin when this situation arises. Too much negative pressure can cause difficulty when opening the cabin door. If high enough, it could cause structural damage since the pressure vessel is designed for cabin pressure to be greater than ambient.

Some aircraft are equipped with pressurization dump valves. These essentially are safety valves that are operated automatically or manually by a switch in the cockpit. They are used to quickly remove air and air pressure from the cabin, usually in an abnormal, maintenance, or emergency situation.

Incorporation of an emergency pressurization mode is found on some aircraft. A valve opens when the air conditioning packs fail or emergency pressurization is selected from the cockpit. It directs a mixture of bleed air and ram air into the cabin. This combines with fully closed outflow valves to preserve some pressurization in the aircraft.

Pressurization Gauges

While all pressurization systems differ slightly, usually three cockpit indications, in concert with various warning lights and alerts, advise the crew of pressurization variables. They are the cabin altimeter, the cabin rate of climb or vertical speed indicator, and the cabin differential pressure indicator. These can be separate gauges or combined into one or two gauges. All are typically located on the pressurization panel, although sometimes they are elsewhere on the instrument panel. Outflow valve position indicator(s) are also common. *[Figure 16-57]*

On modern aircraft equipped with digital aircraft monitoring systems with LCD displays, such as Engine Indicating and Crew Alerting System (EICAS) or Electronic Centralized Aircraft Monitor (ECAM), the pressurization panel may contain no gauges. The environmental control system (ECS) page of the monitoring system is selected to display similar information. Increased use of automatic redundancy and advanced operating logic simplifies operation of the pressurization system. It is almost completely automatic. The cabin pressurization panel remains in the cockpit primarily for manual control. *[Figure 16-58]*

Pressurization Operation

The normal mode of operation for most pressurization control systems is the automatic mode. A standby mode can also be selected. This also provides automatic control

Figure 16-57. *This cabin pressurization gauge is a triple combination gauge. The long pointer operates identically to a vertical speed indicator with the same familiar scale on the left side of the gauge. It indicates the rate of change of cabin pressure. The orange PSI pointer indicates the differential pressure on the right side scale. The ALT indicator uses the same scale as the PSI pointer, but it indicates cabin altitude when ALT indicator moves against it.*

of pressurization, usually with different inputs, a standby controller, or standby outflow valve operation. A manual mode is available should the automatic and standby modes fail. This allows the crew to directly position the outflow valve through pneumatic or electric control, depending on the system.

Coordination of all pressurization components during various flight segments is essential. A weight-on-wheels (WOW) switch attached to the landing gear and a throttle position switch are integral parts of many pressurization control systems. During ground operations and prior to takeoff, the WOW switch typically controls the position of the pressurization safety valve, which is held in the open position until the aircraft takes off. In an advanced system, the WOW switch may give input to the pressurization controller, which in turn controls the positions and operation of all pressurization components. In other systems, the WOW switch may directly control the safety valve or a pneumatic source valve that causes the safety valve to be held open until the source is cut at takeoff when the WOW switch opens.

Throttle position switches can be used to cause a smooth transition from an unpressurized cabin to a pressurized cabin. A partial closing of the outflow valve(s) when the WOW switch is closed (on the ground) and the throttles are advanced gradually initiates pressurization during rollout. At takeoff, the rate of climb and the pressurization schedule require the outflow valve(s) to fully close. Passengers do not experience a harsh sensation from the fully closed valves because the cabin has already begun to pressurize slightly.

Once in flight, the pressurization controller automatically controls the sequence of operation of the pressurization components until the aircraft lands. When the WOW switch closes again at landing, it opens the safety valve(s) and, in some aircraft, the outflow valve(s) makes pressurizing impossible on the ground in the automatic pressurization mode. Maintenance testing of the system is done in manual

Figure 16-58. *The pressurization panel and environmental control system page on a Bombardier CRJ200 50 passenger jet have no gauges. Traditional pressurization data is presented in digital format at the bottom of the page.*

mode. This allows the technician to control the position of all valves from the cockpit panel.

Air Distribution

Distribution of cabin air on pressurized aircraft is managed with a system of air ducts leading from the pressurization source into and throughout the cabin. Typically, air is ducted to and released from ceiling vents, where it circulates and flows out floor-level vents. The air then flows aft through the baggage compartments and under the floor area. It exits the pressure vessel through the outflow valve(s) mounted low, on, or near the aft pressure bulkhead. The flow of air is nearly imperceptible. Ducting is hidden below the cabin floor and behind walls and ceiling panels depending on the aircraft and system design. Valves to select pressurization air source, ventilating air, temperature trim air, as well as in line fans and jet pumps to increase flow in certain areas of the cabin, are all components of the air distribution system. Temperature sensors, overheat switches, and check valves are also common.

On turbine powered aircraft, temperature controlled air from the air conditioning system is the air that is used to pressurize the cabin. The final regulation of the temperature of that air is sometimes considered part of the distribution system. Mixing air conditioned air with bleed air in a duct or a mixing chamber allows the crew to select the exact temperature desired for the cabin. The valve for mixing is controlled in the cockpit or cabin by a temperature selector. Centralized manifolds from which air can be distributed are common. *[Figure 16-59]*

Large aircraft may be divided into zones for air distribution. Each zone has its own temperature selector and associated valve to mix conditioned and bleed air so that each zone can be maintain at a temperature independent of the others.

The air distribution system on most aircraft makes provisions for ducting and circulating cooling air to electronics equipment bays. It also contains a gasper air system. This is air ducted from the cold air manifold or duct to an overhead adjustable delivery nozzle at each passenger station. An inline fan controlled from the cockpit supplies a steady stream of gasper air that can be regulated or shut off with the delivery nozzle(s). *[Figure 16-60]*

When an aircraft is on the ground, operating the engines or the APU to provide air for air conditioning is expensive. It increases the time in service of these expensive components and expedites expensive mandatory overhauls that are performed at specified time intervals. Most high-performance, medium size, and larger turbine-powered aircraft are fitted with a receptacle in the air distribution system. To this a ground source of conditioned air can be connected via a ducting hose. The cabin can be heated or cooled through the aircraft's air distribution ducting using air from the ground source. This limits the operating time on the engines and APU. Once preflight checks and passenger boarding are completed, the ducting hose can be disconnected for taxi and flight. A check valve is used to prevent ground source air from flowing upstream into the air conditioning system. *[Figure 16-61]*

Cabin Pressurization Troubleshooting

While pressurization systems on different aircraft operate similarly with similar components, it cannot be assumed that they are the same. Even those systems constructed by a single manufacturer likely have differences when installed on different aircraft. It is important to check the aircraft manufacture's service information when troubleshooting the pressurization system. A fault, such as failure to pressurize or failure to maintain pressurization, can have many different causes. Adherence to the steps in a manufacturer's troubleshooting procedures is highly recommended to sequentially evaluate possible causes. Pressurization system test kits are available, or the aircraft can be pressurized by its normal sources during troubleshooting. A test flight may be required after maintenance.

Air Conditioning Systems

There are two types of air conditioning systems commonly used on aircraft. Air cycle air conditioning is used on most turbine-powered aircraft. It makes use of engine bleed air or APU pneumatic air during the conditioning process. Vapor

Figure 16-59. *Centralized manifolds from which air can be distributed are common.*

Figure 16-60. *The conditioned air distribution system on a Boeing 737. The main distribution manifold is located under the cabin floor. Riser ducts run horizontally then vertically from the manifold to supply ducts, which follow the curvature of the fuselage carrying conditioned air to be released in the cabin.*

cycle air conditioning systems are often used on reciprocating aircraft. This type system is similar to that found in homes and automobiles. Note that some turbine-powered aircraft also use vapor cycle air conditioning.

Air Cycle Air Conditioning

Air cycle air conditioning prepares engine bleed air to pressurize the aircraft cabin. The temperature and quantity of the air must be controlled to maintain a comfortable cabin

Figure 16-61. *A duct hose installed on this airliner distributes hot or cold air from a ground-based source throughout the cabin using the aircraft's own air distribution system ducting.*

environment at all altitudes and on the ground. The air cycle system is often called the air conditioning package or pack. It is usually located in the lower half of the fuselage or in the tail section of turbine-powered aircraft. *[Figure 16-62]*

System Operation

Even with the frigid temperatures experienced at high altitudes, bleed air is too hot to be used in the cabin without being cooled. It is let into the air cycle system and routed through a heat exchanger where ram air cools the bleed air. This cooled bleed air is directed into an air cycle machine. There, it is compressed before flowing through a secondary heat exchange that cools the air again with ram air. The bleed air then flows back into the air cycle machine where it drives an expansion turbine and cools even further. Water is then removed and the air is mixed with bypassed bleed air for final temperature adjustment. It is sent to the cabin through the air distribution system. By examining the operation of each component in the air cycle process, a better understanding can be developed of how bleed air is conditioned for cabin use. Refer to *Figure 16-63*, which diagrams the air cycle air conditioning system of the Boeing 737.

Figure 16-62. *Boeing 737 air cycle system. The photo is taken looking up into the air conditioning bay located in the lower fuselage on each side of the aircraft.*

Pneumatic System Supply

The air cycle air conditioning system is supplied with air by the aircraft pneumatic system. In turn, the pneumatic system is supplied by bleed air tap-offs on each engine compressor section or from the APU pneumatic supply. An external pneumatic air supply source may also be connected while the aircraft is stationary on the ground. In normal flight operations, a pneumatic manifold is supplied by the engine bleed air through the use of valves, regulators, and ducting. The air conditioning packs are supplied by this manifold as are other critical airframe systems, such as the anti-ice and hydraulic pressurization system.

Component Operation

Pack Valve

The pack valve is the valve that regulates bleed air from the pneumatic manifold into the air cycle air conditioning system. It is controlled with a switch from the air conditioning panel in the cockpit. Many pack valves are electrically controlled

Figure 16-63. *The air cycle air conditioning system on a Boeing 737.*

Figure 16-64. *This pack valve drawing illustrates the complexity of the valve, which opens, closes, and modulates. It is manually actuated from the cockpit and automatically responds to supply and air cycle system parameter inputs.*

and pneumatically operated. Also known as the supply shutoff valve, the pack valve opens, closes, and modulates to allow the air cycle air conditioning system to be supplied with a designed volume of hot, pressurized air. *[Figure 16-64]* When an overheat or other abnormal condition requires that the air conditioning package be shut down, a signal is sent to the pack valve to close.

Bleed Air Bypass

A means for bypassing some of the pneumatic air supplied to the air cycle air conditioning system around the system is present on all aircraft. This warm bypassed air must be mixed with the cold air produced by the air cycle system so the air delivered to the cabin is a comfortable temperature. In the system shown in *Figure 16-58*, this is accomplished by the mixing valve. It simultaneously controls the flow of bypassed air and air to be cooled to meet the requirements of the auto temperature controller. It can also be controlled manually with the cabin temperature selector in manual mode. Other air cycle systems may refer to the valve that controls the air bypassed around the air cycle cooling system as a temperature control valve, trim air pressure regulating valve, or something similar.

Primary Heat Exchanger

Generally, the warm air dedicated to pass through the air cycle system first passes through a primary heat exchanger. It acts similarly to the radiator in an automobile. A controlled flow of ram air is ducted over and through the exchanger, which reduces the temperature of the air inside the system.

[Figure 16-65] A fan draws air through the ram air duct when the aircraft is on the ground so that the heat exchange is possible when the aircraft is stationary. In flight, ram air doors are modulated to increase or decrease ram air flow to the exchanger according to the position of the wing flaps. During slow flight, when the flaps are extended, the doors are open. At higher speeds, with the flaps retracted, the doors move toward the closed position reducing the amount of ram

Figure 16-65. *The primary and secondary heat exchangers in an air cycle air conditioning system are of similar construction. They both cool bleed air when ram air passes over the exchanger coils and fins.*

air to the exchanger. Similar operation is accomplished with a valve on smaller aircraft. *[Figure 16-66]*

Figure 16-66. *A ram air door controls the flow of air through the primary and secondary heat exchangers.*

Refrigeration Turbine Unit or Air Cycle Machine and Secondary Heat Exchanger

The heart of the air cycle air conditioning system is the refrigeration turbine unit, also known as the air cycle machine (ACM). It is comprised of a compressor that is driven by a turbine on a common shaft. System air flows from the primary heat exchanger into the compressor side of the ACM. As the air is compressed, its temperature rises. It is then sent to a secondary heat exchanger, similar to the primary heat exchanger located in the ram air duct. The elevated temperature of the ACM compressed air facilitates an easy exchange of heat energy to the ram air. The cooled system air, still under pressure from the continuous system air flow and the ACM compressor, exits the secondary heat exchanger. It is directed into the turbine side of the ACM. The steep blade pitch angle of the ACM turbine extracts more energy from the air as it passes through and drives the turbine. Once through, the air is allowed to expand at the ACM outlet, cooling even further. The combined energy loss from the air first driving the turbine and then expanding at the turbine outlet lowers the system air temperature to near freezing. *[Figure 16-67]*

Water Separator

The cool air from the air cycle machine can no longer hold the quantity of water it could when it was warm. A water separator is used to remove the water from the saturated air before it is sent to the aircraft cabin. The separator operates with no moving parts. Foggy air from the ACM enters and is forced through a fiberglass sock that condenses and coalesces the mist into larger water drops. The convoluted interior structure of the separator swirls the air and water. The water collects on the sides of the separator and drains down and out of the unit, while the dry air passes through. A bypass valve is incorporated in case of a blockage. *[Figure 16-68]*

Refrigeration Bypass Valve

As mentioned, air exiting the ACM turbine expands and cools. It becomes so cold, it could freeze the water in the water separator, thus inhibiting or blocking airflow. A temperature sensor in the separator controls a refrigeration bypass valve designed to keep the air flowing through the water separator above freezing temperature. The valve is also identified by other names such as a temperature control valve, 35° valve, anti-ice valve, and similar. It bypasses warm air around the ACM when opened. The air is introduced into the expansion ducting, just upstream of the water separator, where it heats the air just enough to keep it from freezing. Thus, the refrigeration bypass valve regulates the temperature of the ACM discharge air so it does not freeze when passing through the water separator. This valve is visible in *Figure 16-62* and is diagrammed in the system in *Figure 16-63*.

All air cycle air conditioning systems use at least one ram air heat exchanger and an air cycle machine with expansion turbine to remove heat energy from the bleed air, but variations exist. An example of a system different from that described above is found on the McDonnell Douglas DC-10. Bleed air from the pneumatic manifold is compressed by the air cycle machine compressor before it flows to a single heat exchanger. Condensed water from the water separator is sprayed into the ram air at its entrance to the exchanger to draw additional heat from the compressed bleed air as the water evaporates. A trim air valve for each cabin zone mixes bypassed bleed air with conditioned air in response to individual temperature selectors for each zone. When cooling air demands are low, a turbine bypass valve routes some heat exchanger air directly to the conditioned air manifold. *[Figure 16-69]*

Cabin Temperature Control System

Typical System Operation

Most cabin temperature control systems operate in a similar manner. Temperature is monitored in the cabin, cockpit, conditioned air ducts, and distribution air ducts. These values are input into a temperature controller, or temperature control regulator, normally located in the electronics bay. A temperature selector in the cockpit can be adjusted to input the desired temperature. *[Figure 16-70]* The temperature controller compares the actual temperature signals received from the various sensors with the desired temperature input. Circuit logic for the selected mode processes these input signals. An output signal is sent to a valve in the

Figure 16-67. *A cutaway diagram of an air cycle machine. The main housing supports the single shaft to which the compressor and turbine are attached. Oil lubricates and cools the shaft bearings.*

air cycle air conditioning system. This valve has different names depending on the aircraft manufacturer and design of the environmental control systems (i.e., mixing valve, temperature control valve, trim air valve). It mixes warm bleed air that bypassed the air cycle cooling process with the cold air produced by it. By modulating the valve in response to the signal from the temperature controller, air of the selected temperature is sent to the cabin through the air distribution system.

Cabin temperature pickup units and duct temperature sensors used in the temperature control system are thermistors. Their resistance changes as temperature changes. The temperature selector is a rheostat that varies its resistance as the knob is turned. In the temperature controller, resistances are compared in a bridge circuit. The bridge output feeds a temperature regulating function. An electric signal output is prepared and sent to the valve that mixes hot and cold air. On large aircraft with separate temperature zones, trim air modulating valves for each zone are used. The valves modulate to provide the correct mix required to match the selected temperature. Cabin, flight deck, and duct temperature sensors are strategically located to provide useful information to control cabin temperature. *[Figure 16-71]*

Vapor Cycle Air Conditioning

The absence of a bleed air source on reciprocating engine aircraft makes the use of an air cycle system impractical for conditioning cabin air. Vapor cycle air conditioning is used on most nonturbine aircraft that are equipped with air conditioning. However, it is not a source of pressurizing air as the air cycle system conditioned air is on turbine powered aircraft. The vapor cycle system only cools the cabin. If an aircraft equipped with a vapor cycle air conditioning system is pressurized, it uses one of the sources discussed in the pressurization section above. Vapor cycle air conditioning is a closed system used solely for the transfer of heat from inside the cabin to outside of the cabin. It can operate on the ground and in flight.

Figure 16-68. *A water separator coalesces and removes water by swirling the air/water mixture from ACM expansion turbine. Centrifugal force sends the water to the walls of the collector where it drains from the unit.*

Theory of Refrigeration

Energy can be neither created nor destroyed; however, it can be transformed and moved. This is what occurs during vapor cycle air conditioning. Heat energy is moved from the cabin air into a liquid refrigerant. Due to the additional energy, the liquid changes into a vapor. The vapor is compressed and becomes very hot. It is removed from the cabin where the very hot vapor refrigerant transfers its heat energy to the outside air. In doing so, the refrigerant cools and condenses back into a liquid. The refrigerant returns to the cabin to repeat the cycle of energy transfer. *[Figure 16-72]*

Figure 16-69. *The air cycle air conditioning system of a DC-10 transport category aircraft uses only one heat exchanger per ACM.*

Figure 16-70. *Typical temperature selectors on a transport category aircraft temperature control panel in the cockpit (left) and a business jet (right). On large aircraft, temperature selectors may be located on control panels located in a particular cabin air distribution zone.*

Figure 16-71. *The temperature control system of a Boeing 777 combines the use of zone and duct temperature sensors with trim air modulating valves for each zone. Redundant digital left and right cabin temperature controllers process temperature input signals from the sensors and temperature selectors on the cockpit panel and throughout the aircraft to modulate the valves.*

16-43

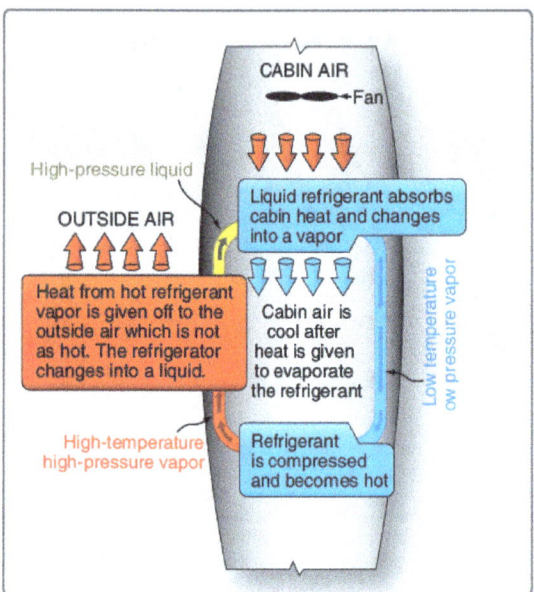

Figure 16-72. *In vapor cycle air conditioning, heat is carried from the cabin to the outside air by a refrigerant which changes from a liquid to a vapor and back again.*

Heat is an expression of energy, typically measured by temperature. The higher the temperature of a substance, the more energy it contains. Heat always flows from hot to cold. These terms express the relative amount of energy present in two substances. They do not measure the absolute amount of heat present. Without a difference in energy levels, there is no transfer of energy (heat).

Adding heat to a substance does not always raise its temperature. When a substance changes state, such as when a liquid changes into a vapor, heat energy is absorbed. This is called latent heat. When a vapor condenses into a liquid, this heat energy is given off. The temperature of a substance remains constant during its change of state. All energy absorbed or given off, the latent heat, is used for the change process. Once the change of state is complete, heat added to a substance raises the temperature of the substance. After a substance changes state into a vapor, the rise in temperature of the vapor caused by the addition of still more heat is called superheat.

The temperature at which a substance changes from a liquid into a vapor when heat is added is known as its boiling point. This is the same temperature at which a vapor condenses into a liquid when heat is removed. The boiling point of any substance varies directly with pressure. When pressure on a liquid is increased, its boiling point increases, and when pressure on a liquid is decreased, its boiling point also decreases. For example, water boils at 212 °F at normal atmospheric temperature (14.7 psi). When pressure on liquid water is increased to 20 psi, it does not boil at 212 °F. More energy is required to overcome the increase in pressure. It boils at approximately 226.4 °F. The converse is also true. Water can also boil at a much lower temperature simply by reducing the pressure upon it. With only 10 psi of pressure upon liquid water, it boils at 194 °F. *[Figure 16-73]*

Figure 16-73. *Boiling point of water changes as pressure changes.*

Vapor pressure is the pressure of the vapor that exists above a liquid that is in an enclosed container at any given temperature. The vapor pressure developed by various substances is unique to each substance. A substance that is said to be volatile, develops high vapor pressure at standard day temperature (59 °F). This is because the boiling point of the substance is much lower. The boiling point of tetrafluoroethane (R134a), the refrigerant used in most aircraft vapor cycle air conditioning systems, is approximately –15 °F. Its vapor pressure at 59 °F is about 71 psi. The vapor pressure of any substance varies directly with temperature.

Basic Vapor Cycle

Vapor cycle air conditioning is a closed system in which a refrigerant is circulated through tubing and a variety of components. The purpose is to remove heat from the aircraft cabin. While circulating, the refrigerant changes state. By manipulating the latent heat required to do so, hot air is replaced with cool air in the aircraft cabin.

To begin, R134a is filtered and stored under pressure in a reservoir known as a receiver dryer. The refrigerant is in liquid form. It flows from the receiver dryer through tubing to an expansion valve. Inside the valve, a restriction in the form of a small orifice blocks most of the refrigerant. Since it is under pressure, some of the refrigerant is forced through the orifice. It emerges as a spray of tiny droplets in the tubing downstream of the valve. The tubing is coiled into a radiator-type assembly known as an evaporator. A fan is positioned to blow cabin air over the surface of the evaporator. As it does, the heat in the cabin air is absorbed by the refrigerant, which uses it to change state from a liquid to a vapor. So much heat is absorbed that the cabin air blown by the fan across the evaporator cools significantly. This is the vapor cycle conditioned air that lowers the temperature in the cabin.

The gaseous refrigerant exiting the evaporator is drawn into a compressor. There, the pressure and the temperature of the refrigerant are increased. The high-pressure high-temperature gaseous refrigerant flows through tubing to a condenser. The condenser is like a radiator comprised of a great length of tubing with fins attached to promote heat transfer. Outside air is directed over the condenser. The temperature of the refrigerant inside is higher than the ambient air temperature, so heat is transferred from the refrigerant to the outside air.

The amount of heat given off is enough to cool the refrigerant and to condense it back to a high-pressure liquid. It flows through tubing and back into the receiver dryer, completing the vapor cycle.

There are two sides to the vapor cycle air conditioning system. One accepts heat and is known as the low side. The other gives up heat and is known as the high side. The low and high refer to the temperature and pressure of the refrigerant. As such, the compressor and the expansion valve are the two components that separate the low side from the high side of the cycle. *[Figure 16-74]* Refrigerant on the low side is characterized as having low pressure and temperature. Refrigerant on the high side has high pressure and temperature.

Figure 16-74. *A basic vapor cycle air conditioning system. The compressor and the expansion valve are the two components that separate the low side from the high side of the cycle. This figure illustrates this division. Refrigerant on the low side is characterized as having low pressure and temperature. Refrigerant on the high side has high pressure and temperature.*

Vapor Cycle Air Conditioning System Components

By examining each component in the vapor cycle air conditioning system, greater insight into its function can be gained.

Refrigerant

For many years, dichlorodifluoromethane (R12) was the standard refrigerant used in aircraft vapor cycle air conditioning systems. Some of these systems remain in use today. R12 was found to have a negative effect on the environment; in particular, it degraded the earth's protective ozone layer. In most cases, it has been replaced by tetrafluoroethane (R134a), which is safer for the environment. R12 and R134a should not be mixed, nor should one be used in a system designed for the other. Possible damage to soft components, such as hoses and seals, could result causing leaks and or malfunction. Use only the specified refrigerant when servicing vapor cycle air conditioning systems. *[Figure 16-75]* R12 and R134a behave so similarly that the descriptions of the R134a vapor cycle air conditioning system and components in the following paragraphs also apply to an R12 system and its components.

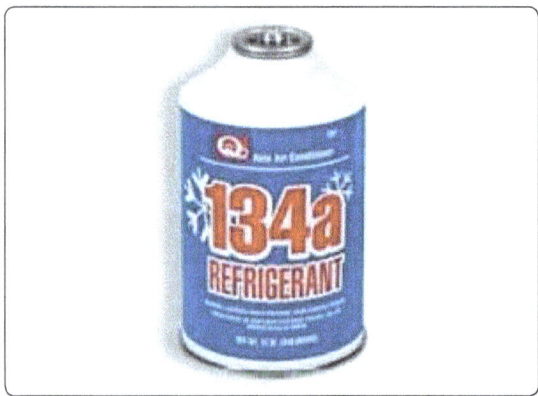

Figure 16-75. *A small can of R134a refrigerant used in vapor cycle air conditioning systems.*

R134a is a halogen compound (CF3CFH2). As mentioned, it has a boiling point of approximately –15 °F. It is not poisonous to inhale in small quantities, but it does displace oxygen. Suffocation is possible if breathed in mass quantity.

Regardless of manufacturer, refrigerants are sometimes called Freon®, which is a trade name owned by the Dupont Company. Caution should be used when handling any refrigerant. Because of the low boiling points, liquid refrigerants boil violently at typical atmospheric temperatures and pressure. They rapidly absorb heat energy from all surrounding matter. If a drop lands on skin, it freezes, resulting in a burn. Similar tissue damage can result if a drop gets in one's eye. Gloves and other skin protection, as well as safety goggles, are required when working with refrigerant.

Receiver Dryer

The receiver dryer acts as the reservoir of the vapor cycle system. It is located downstream of the condenser and upstream of the expansion valve. When it is very hot, more refrigerant is used by the system than when temperatures are moderate. Extra refrigerant is stored in the receiver dryer for this purpose.

Liquid refrigerant from the condenser flows into the receiver dryer. Inside, it passes through filters and a desiccant material. The filters remove any foreign particles that might be in the system. The desiccant captures any water in the refrigerant. Water in the refrigerant causes two major problems. First, the refrigerant and water combine to form an acid. If left in contact with the inside of the components and tubing, the acid deteriorates the materials from which these are made. The second problem with water is that it could form ice and block the flow of refrigerant around the system, rendering it inoperative. Ice is particularly a problem if it forms at the orifice in the expansion valve, which is the coldest point in the cycle.

Occasionally, vapor may find its way into the receiver dryer, such as when the gaseous refrigerant does not completely change state to a liquid in the condenser. A stand tube is used to remove refrigerant from the receiver dryer. It runs to the bottom of the unit to ensure liquid is withdrawn and forwarded to the expansion valve. At the top of the stand tube, a sight glass allows the technician to see the refrigerant. When enough refrigerant is present in the system, liquid flows in the sight glass. If low on refrigerant, any vapor present in the receiver dryer may be sucked up the stand tube causing bubbles to be visible in the sight glass. Therefore, bubbles in the sight glass indicate that the system needs to have more refrigerant added. *[Figure 16-76]*

Expansion Valve

Refrigerant exits the receiver dryer and flows to the expansion valve. The thermostatic expansion valve has an adjustable orifice through which the correct amount of refrigerant is metered to obtain optimal cooling. This is accomplished by monitoring the temperature of the gaseous refrigerant at the outlet of the next component in the cycle, the evaporator. Ideally, the expansion valve should only let the amount of refrigerant spray into the evaporator that can be completely converted to a vapor.

The temperature of the cabin air to be cooled determines the amount of refrigerant the expansion valve should spray into the evaporator. Only so much is needed to completely attempts are made to compress it, the compressor could break, since liquids are essentially incompressible.

The temperature of superheated vapor is higher than liquid refrigerant that has not totally vaporized. A coiled capillary tube with a volatile substance inside is located at the evaporator outlet to sense this difference. Its internal pressure increases and decreases as temperature changes. The coiled end of the tube is closed and attached to the evaporator outlet. The other end terminates in the area above a pressure diaphragm in the expansion valve. When superheated refrigerant vapor reaches the coiled end of the tube, its elevated temperature increases the pressure inside the tube and in the space above the diaphragm. This increase in pressure causes the diaphragm to overcome spring tension in the valve. It positions a needle valve that increases the amount of refrigerant released by the valve. The quantity of refrigerant is increased so that the refrigerant only just evaporates, and the refrigerant vapor does not superheat. When too much liquid refrigerant is released by the expansion valve, low-temperature liquid refrigerant arrives at the outlet of the evaporator. The result is low pressure inside the temperature bulb and above the expansion valve diaphragm. The superheat spring in the valve moves the needle valve toward the closed position, reducing the flow of refrigerant into the evaporator as the spring overcomes the lower pressure above the diaphragm. [*Figure 16-77*]

Figure 16-76. *A receiver dryer acts as reservoir and filter in a vapor cycle system. Bubbles viewed in the sight glass indicate the system is low on refrigerant and needs to be serviced.*

change the state of the refrigerant from a liquid to a vapor. Too little causes the gaseous refrigerant to be superheated by the time it exits the evaporator. This is inefficient. Changing the state of the refrigerant from liquid to vapor absorbs much more heat than adding heat to already converted vapor (superheat). The cabin air blowing over the evaporator will not be cooled sufficiently if superheated vapor is flowing through the evaporator. If too much refrigerant is released by the expansion valve into the evaporator, some of it remains liquid when it exits the evaporator. Since it next flows to the compressor, this could be dangerous. The compressor is designed to compress only vapor. If liquid is drawn in and

Figure 16-77. *An internally equalized expansion valve.*

Vapor cycle air conditioning systems that have large evaporators experience significant pressure drops while refrigerant is flowing through them. Externally equalized expansion valves use a pressure tap from the outlet of the evaporator to help the superheat spring balance the diaphragm. This type of expansion valve is easily recognizable by the additional small-diameter line that comes from the evaporator into the valve (2 total). Better control of the proper amount of refrigerant allowed through the valve is attained by considering both the temperature and pressure of the evaporator refrigerant. [*Figure 16-78*]

Figure 16-78. *An externally equalized expansion valve uses evaporator discharge temperature and pressure to regulate the amount of refrigerant passing through the valve and into the evaporator.*

Evaporator

Most evaporators are constructed of copper or aluminum tubing coiled into a compact unit. Fins are attached to increase surface area, facilitating rapid heat transfer between the cabin air blown over the outside of the evaporator with a fan and the refrigerant inside. The expansion valve located at the evaporator inlet releases high-pressure, high-temperature liquid refrigerant into the evaporator. As the refrigerant absorbs heat from the cabin air, it changes into a low-pressure vapor. This is discharged from the evaporator outlet to the next component in the vapor cycle system, the compressor. The temperature and pressure pickups that regulate the expansion valve are located at the evaporator outlet.

The evaporator is situated in such a way that cabin air is pulled to it by a fan. The fan blows the air over the evaporator and discharges the cooled air back into the cabin. [*Figure 16-79*] This discharge can be direct when the evaporator is located in a cabin wall. A remotely located evaporator may require ducting from the cabin to the evaporator and from the evaporator back into the cabin. Sometimes the cool air produced may be introduced into an air distribution system where it can blow directly on the occupants through individual delivery vents. In this manner, the entire vapor cycle air conditioning system may be located fore or aft of the cabin. A multiposition fan switch controlled by the pilot is usually available. *Figure 16-80* diagrams the vapor cycle air conditioning system in a Cessna Mustang very light jet. It has two evaporators that share in the cooling, with outlets integrated into a distribution system and cockpit mounted switches for the fans, as well as engaging and disengaging the system.

Figure 16-79. *The evaporator of this aircraft's vapor cycle air conditioning system is visible in the forward cabin sidewall behind the right rudder pedal.*

When cabin air is cooled by flowing over the evaporator, it can no longer retain the water that it could at higher temperature. As a result, it condenses on the outside of the evaporator and needs to be collected and drained overboard. Pressurized aircraft may contain a valve in the evaporator drain line that opens only periodically to discharge the water, to maintain pressurization. Fins on the evaporator must be kept from being damaged, which could inhibit airflow. The continuous movement of warm cabin air around the fins keeps condensed water from freezing. Ice on the evaporator reduces the efficiency of the heat exchange to the refrigerant.

Compressor

The compressor is the heart of the vapor cycle air conditioning system. It circulates the refrigerant around the vapor cycle system. It receives low-pressure, low-temperature refrigerant vapor from the outlet of the evaporator and compresses it. As the pressure is increased, the temperature also increases. The refrigerant temperature is raised above that of the outside air temperature. The refrigerant then flows out of the compressor

Figure 16-80. *The vapor cycle air conditioning system on a Cessna Mustang has two evaporators, one for the cockpit and one for the cabin. Each evaporator assembly contains the evaporator, a blower, a thermal expansion valve and the temperature feedback line from the outlet of the evaporator to the expansion valve.*

to the condenser where it gives off the heat to the outside air.

The compressor is the dividing point between the low side and the high side of the vapor cycle system. Often it is incorporated with fittings or has fittings in the connecting lines to it that are designed to service the system with refrigerant. Access to the low and high sides of the system are required for servicing, which can be accomplished with fitting upstream and downstream of the compressor.

Modern compressors are either engine driven or driven by an electric motor. Occasionally, a hydraulically driven compressor is used. A typical engine-driven compressor, similar to that found in an automobile, is located in the engine nacelle and operated by a drive belt off of the engine crankshaft. An electromagnetic clutch engages when cooling is required, which causes the compressor to operate. When cooling is sufficient, power to the clutch is cut, and the drive pulley rotates but the compressor does not. [*Figure 16-81*]

Dedicated electric motor-driven compressors are also used on aircraft. Use of an electric motor allows the compressor to be located nearly anywhere on the aircraft, since wires can be run from the appropriate bus to the control panel and to the compressor. [*Figure 16-82*] Hydraulically driven compressors are also able to be remotely located. Hydraulic lines from the hydraulic manifold are run through a switch-activated solenoid to the compressor. The solenoid allows fluid to the compressor or bypasses it. This controls the operation of the hydraulically driven compressor.

Figure 16-81. *A typical belt drive engine driven compressor. The electromagnetic clutch pulley assembly in the front starts and stops the compressor depending on cooling demand.*

Figure 16-82. *Examples of electric motor driven vapor cycle air conditioning compressors.*

Regardless of how the vapor cycle air conditioning compressor is driven, it is usually a piston type pump. It requires use of a lightweight oil to lubricate and seal the unit. The oil is entrained by the refrigerant and circulates with it around the system. The crankcase of the compressor retains a supply of the oil, the level of which can be checked and adjusted by the technician. Valves exist on some compressor installations that can be closed to isolate the compressor from the remainder of the vapor cycle system while oil servicing takes place.

Condenser

The condenser is the final component in the vapor cycle. It is a radiator-like heat exchanger situated so that outside air flows over it and absorbs heat from the high-pressure, high-temperature refrigerant received from the compressor. A fan is usually included to draw the air through the compressor during ground operation. On some aircraft, outside air is ducted to the compressor. On others, the condenser is lowered into the airstream from the fuselage via a hinged panel. Often, the panel is controlled by a switch on the throttle levers. It is set to retract the compressor and streamline the fuselage when full power is required. *[Figure 16-83]*

Figure 16-83. *A vapor cycle air conditioning condenser assembly with an integral fan used to pull outside air through the unit during ground operation.*

The outside air absorbs heat from the refrigerant flowing through the condenser. The heat loss causes the refrigerant to change state back into a liquid. The high-pressure liquid refrigerant then leaves the condenser and flows to the receiver dryer. A properly engineered system that is functioning normally fully condenses all the refrigerant flowing through the condenser.

Service Valves

All vapor cycle air conditioning systems are closed systems; however, access is required for servicing. This is accomplished through the use of two service valves. One valve is located in the high side of the system and the other in the low side. A common type of valve used on vapor cycle systems that operate with R12 refrigerant is the Schrader valve. It is similar to the valve used to inflate tires. *[Figure 16-84]* A central valve core seats and unseats by depressing a stem attached to it. A pin in the servicing hose fitting is designed to do this when screwed onto the valve's exterior threads. All aircraft service valves should be capped when not in use.

R134a systems use valves that are very similar to the Schrader valve in function, operation, and location. As a safety device to prevent inadvertent mixing of refrigerants, R134a valve fittings are different from Schrader valve fittings and do not attach to Schrader valve threads. The R134a valve fittings are a quick-disconnect type.

Figure 16-84. *Cross-section of an R12 refrigerant service valve.*

Another type of valve called a compressor isolation valve is used on some aircraft. It serves two purposes. Like the Schrader valve, it permits servicing the system with refrigerant. It also can isolate the compressor so the oil level can be checked and replenished without opening the entire system and losing the refrigerant charge. These valves are usually hard mounted to the inlet and outlet of the compressor.

A compressor isolation valve has three positions. When fully open, it back seats and allows the normal flow of refrigerant in the vapor cycle. When fully closed or front seated, the valve isolates the compressor from the rest of the system and servicing with oil, or even replacement of the compressor, is possible without losing the refrigerant charge. When in an intermediate position, the valve allows access to the system for servicing. The system can be operated with the valve in this position, but should be back seated for normal operation. The valve handle and service port should be capped when servicing is complete. *[Figure 16-85]*

Vapor Cycle Air Conditioning Servicing Equipment

Special servicing equipment is used to service vapor cycle air conditioning systems. The U.S. Environmental Protection Agency (EPA) has declared it illegal to release R12 refrigerant into the atmosphere. Equipment has been designed to capture the refrigerant during the servicing process. Although R134a does not have this restriction, it is illegal in some locations to release it to the atmosphere, and it may become universally so in the near future. It is good

Figure 16-85. *Compressor isolation valves isolate the compressor for maintenance or replacement. They also allow normal operation and servicing of the vapor cycle air conditioning system with refrigerant.*

practice to capture all refrigerants for future use, rather than to waste them or to harm the environment by releasing them into the atmosphere. Capturing the refrigerant is a simple process designed into the proper servicing equipment. The technician should always be vigilant to use the approved refrigerant for the system being serviced and should follow all manufacturer's instruction.

Manifold Set, Gauges, Hoses, and Fittings

In the past, the main servicing device for vapor cycle air conditioning systems was the manifold set. It contains three hose fittings, two O-ring sealed valves, and two gauges. It is essentially a manifold into which the gauges, fittings, and valves are attached. The valves are positioned to connect or isolate the center hose with either fitting.

Hoses attach to the right and left manifold set fittings and the other ends of those hoses attach to the service valves in the vapor cycle system. The center fitting also has a hose attached to it. The other end of this hose connects to either a refrigerant supply or a vacuum pump, depending on the servicing function to be performed. All servicing operations are performed by manipulating the valves. *[Figure 16-86]*

Figure 16-86. *A basic manifold set for servicing a vapor cycle air conditioning system.*

The gauges on the manifold set are dedicated—one for the low side of the system and the other for the high side. The low-pressure gauge is a compound gauge that indicates pressures above or below atmospheric pressure (0 gauge pressure). Below atmospheric pressure, the gauge is scaled in inches of mercury down to 30 inches. This is to indicate vacuum. 29.92 inches equals an absolute vacuum (absolute zero air pressure). Above atmospheric pressure, gauge pressure is read in psi. The scale typically ranges from 0 to 60 psi, although some gauges extend up to 150 psi. The high-pressure gauge usually has a range from zero up to about 500 psi gauge pressure. It does not indicate vacuum (pressure lower than atmospheric). These gauges and their scales can be seen in *Figure 16-87*.

The low-pressure gauge is connected on the manifold directly to the low side fitting. The high-pressure gauge connects directly to the high side fitting. The center fitting of the manifold can be isolated from either of the gauges or the high and low service fittings by the hand valves. When these valves are turned fully clockwise, the center fitting is isolated. If the low pressure valve is opened (turned counterclockwise), the

Figure 16-87. *The internal workings of a manifold set with the center fitting isolated (top). Opening a valve connects the center hose to that side of the system and the gauge (bottom).*

center fitting is opened to the low pressure gauge and the low side service line. The same is true for the high side when the high-pressure valve is opened. *[Figure 16-87]*

Special hoses are attached to the fittings of the manifold valve for servicing the system. The high-pressure charging hose is usually red and attaches to the service valve located in the high side of the system. The low-pressure hose, usually blue, attaches to the service valve that is located in the low side of the system. The center hose attaches to the vacuum pump for evacuating the system, or to the refrigerant supply for charging the system. Proper charging hoses for the refrigerant specific service valves must be used. When not using the manifold set, be sure the hoses are capped to prevent moisture from contaminating the valves.

Full Service Refrigerant Recovery, Recycling, Evacuation, and Recharging Units

Regulations that require capture of all vapor cycle refrigerant have limited the use of the manifold set. It can still be used to charge a system. The refrigerant container is attached to the center hose and the manifold set valves are manipulated to allow flow into the low or high side of the system as required. But, emptying a system of refrigerant requires a service unit made to collect it. Allowing the refrigerant to flow into a collection container attached to the center hose will not capture the entire refrigerant charge, as the system and container pressures equalize above atmospheric pressure. An independent compressor and collection system is required.

Modern refrigeration recharging and recovery units are available to perform all of the servicing functions required for vapor cycle air conditioning systems. These all-in-one service carts have the manifold set built into the unit. As such, the logic for using a manifold set still applies. Integral solenoid valves, reservoirs, filters, and smart controls allow the entire servicing procedure to be controlled from the unit panel once the high side and low side services hoses are connected. A built-in compressor enables complete system refrigerant purging. A built-in vacuum pump performs system evacuation. A container and recycling filters for the refrigerant and the lubricating oil allow total recovery and recycling of these fluids. The pressure gauges used on the service unit panel are the same as those on a manifold set. Top-of-the-line units have an automatic function that performs all of the servicing functions sequentially and automatically once the hoses are hooked up to the vapor cycle air conditioning system and the system quantity of refrigerant has been entered. *[Figure 16-88]*

Refrigerant Source

R134a comes in containers measured by the weight of the refrigerant they hold. Small 12-ounce to 2½-pound cans are common for adding refrigerant. Larger 30- and 50-pound cylinders equipped with shutoff valves are often used to charge an evacuated system, and they are used in shops that service vapor cycle systems frequently. *[Figure 16-89]* These larger cylinders are also used in the full servicing carts described above. The amount of refrigerant required for any system is measured in pounds. Check the manufacturer's service data and charge the system to the level specified using only the approved refrigerant from a known source.

Vacuum Pumps

Vacuum pumps used with a manifold set, or as part of a service cart, are connected to the vapor cycle system so that the system pressure can be reduced to a near total vacuum. The reason for doing this is to remove all of the water in the system. As mentioned, water can freeze, causing system

Figure 16-88. *A modern refrigerant recovery/recycle/charging service unit. Electronic control of solenoid activated valves combine with a built-in system for recovering, recycling, and recharging. A built-in vacuum pump and heated refrigerant reservoir are also included.*

Inches of vacuum on low side gauge (inches Hg)	Temperature at which water boils (°F)	Absolute pressure (psi)
0	212	14.696
4.92	204.98	12.279
9.23	194	10.152
15.94	176	6.866
20.72	158	4.519
24.04	140	2.888
26.28	122	1.788
27.75	104	1.066
28.67	86	0.614
28.92	80.06	0.491
29.02	75.92	0.442
29.12	71.96	0.393
29.22	69.08	0.344
29.32	64.04	0.295
29.42	59	0.246
29.52	53.06	0.196
29.62	44.96	0.147
29.74	32	0.088
29.82	21.02	0.0049
29.87	6.08	0.00245
29.91	−23.98	0.00049

Figure 16-89. *A 30 pound R134a refrigerant container with dual fittings. The fitting controlled by the blue valve wheel opens to the vapor space above the liquid refrigerant for connection to the low side of the vapor cycle system. The fitting controlled by the red valve wheel draws liquid refrigerant from the bottom of the cylinder through a stand tube. This fitting is connected to the system high side. On containers without dual fittings, the container must be inverted to deliver liquid refrigerant through a connected hose.*

malfunction and can also combine with the refrigerant to create corrosive compounds.

Once the system has been purged of its refrigerant and it is at atmospheric pressure, the vacuum pump is operated. It gradually reduces the pressure in the system. As it does, the boiling point of any water in the system is also reduced. Water boils off or is vaporized under the reduced pressure and is pulled from the system by the pump, leaving the system moisture free to be recharged with refrigerant. *[Figure 16-90]* The strength and efficiency of vacuum pumps varies as does the amount of time to hold the system at reduced pressure specified by manufacturers. Generally, the best established vacuum is held for 15–30 minutes to ensure all water is removed from the system. Follow the manufacturer's instructions when evacuating a vapor cycle air conditioning system. *[Figure 16-91]*

Leak Detectors

Even the smallest leak in a vapor cycle air conditioning system can cause a loss of refrigerant. When operating normally, little or no refrigerant escapes. A system that requires the addition of refrigerant should be suspected of having a leak. Electronic leak detectors are safe, effective

Figure 16-90. *When the temperature is low, a greater amount of vacuum is needed to boil off and remove any water in the vapor cycle system.*

Figure 16-91. *A vacuum pump is used to lower the pressure in the vapor cycle air conditioning system. This reduces the boiling point of water in the system, which vaporizes and is drawn out by the pump.*

devices used to find leaks. There are many types available that are able to detect extremely small amounts of escaped refrigerant. The detector is held close to component and hose connections where most leaks occur. Audible and visual alarms signal the presence of refrigerant. A detector specified for the type of refrigerant in the system should be chosen. A good leak detector is sensitive enough to detect leaks that would result in less than ½ ounce of refrigerant to be lost per year. *[Figure 16-92]*

Figure 16-92. *This electronic infrared leak detector can detect leaks that would lose less than ¼ ounce of refrigerant per year.*

Other leak detection methods exist. A soapy solution can also be applied to fittings and inspected for the formation of bubbles indicating a leak. Special leak detection dyes compatible for use with refrigerant can be injected into the vapor cycle system and can be seen when they are forced out at a leak. Many of these are made to be visible under UV light. Occasionally, a leak can be detected upon close visual inspection. Oil in the system can be forced out of a leak, leaving a visible residue that is usually on the bottom side of a leaky fitting. Old hoses may become slightly porous and leak a significant amount of refrigerant over time. Because of the length and area through which the refrigerant is lost, this type of leak may be difficult to detect, even with leak detecting methods. Visibly deteriorated hoses should be replaced.

System Servicing

Vapor cycle air conditioning systems can give many hours of reliable, maintenance-free service. Periodic visual inspections, tests, and refrigerant level and oil level checks may be all that is required for some time. Follow the manufacturer's instructions for inspection criteria and intervals.

Visual Inspection

All components of any vapor cycle system should be checked to ensure they are secure. Be vigilant for any damage, misalignment, or visual signs of leakage. The evaporator and condenser fins should be checked to ensure they are clean, unobstructed, and not folded over from an impact. Dirt and inhibited airflow through the fins can prevent effective heat exchange to and from the refrigerant. Occasionally, these units can be washed. Since the condenser often has ram air ducted to it or extends into the airstream, check for the presence of debris that may restrict airflow. Hinged units should be checked for security and wear. The mechanism to extend and retract the unit should function as specified, including the throttle position switch present on many systems. It is designed to cut power to the compressor clutch and retract the condenser at full power settings. Condensers may also have a fan to pull air over them during ground operation. It should be checked to ensure it functions correctly. *[Figure 16-93]*

Figure 16-93. *Damaged fins on a condenser*

Be sure the capillary temperature feedback sensor to the expansion valve is securely attached to the evaporator outlet. Also, check the security of the pressure sensor and thermostat sensor if the system has them. The evaporator should not have ice on the outside. This prevents proper heat exchange to the refrigerant from the warm cabin air blown over the unit. The fan blower should be checked to ensure it rotates freely. Depending on the system, it should run whenever the cooling switch is selected and should change speeds as the selector is rotated to more or less cooling. Sometimes systems low on refrigerant can cause ice on the evaporator, as can a faulty expansion valve or feedback control line. Ice formation anywhere on the outside of a vapor cycle air conditioning system should be investigated for cause and corrected. *[Figure 16-94]*

Security and alignment of the compressor is critical and should be checked during inspection. Belt-driven compressors need to have proper belt tension to function properly. Check the manufacturer's data for information on how to determine the condition and tension of the belt, as well as how to make adjustments. Oil level should be sufficient. Typically, ¼ ounce of oil is added for each pound of refrigerant added to the system. When changing a

Figure 16-94. *Ice on the evaporator coils is cause for investigation. It prevents proper heat exchange to the refrigerant.*

component, additional oil may need to be added to replace that which is trapped in the replaced unit. Always use the oil specified in the manufacturer's maintenance manual.

Leak Test

As mentioned under the leak detector section above, leaks in a vapor cycle air conditioning system must be discovered and repaired. The most obvious sign of a possible leak is a low refrigerant level. Bubbles present in the sight glass of the receiver dryer while the system is operating indicate more refrigerant is needed. A system check for a leak may be in order. Note that vapor cycle systems normally lose a small amount of refrigerant each year. No action is needed if this amount is within limits.

Occasionally, all of the refrigerant escapes from the system. No bubbles are visible in the sight glass, but the complete lack of cooling indicates the refrigerant has leaked out. To locate the leak point, the system needs to be partially charged with refrigerant so leak detection methods can be employed. About 50 psi of refrigerant in the high and low sides should be sufficient for a leak check. By introducing the refrigerant into the high side, pressure indicated on the low side gauge verifies the orifice in the expansion valve is not clogged. When all refrigerant is lost due to a leak, the entire system should be checked. Each fitting and connection should be inspected visually and with a leak detector.

When a vapor cycle air conditioning system loses all of its refrigerant charge, air may enter the system. Water may also enter since it is in the air. This means that a full system evacuation must be performed after the leak is found and repaired. By establishing only a 50 psi charge in a depleted system, the leak(s) becomes detectable, but time and refrigerant are not wasted prior to evacuation. System evacuation is discussed below.

Performance Test

Verification of proper operation of a vapor cycle air conditioning system is often part of a performance test. This involves operating the system and checking parameters to ensure they are in the normal range. A key indication of performance is the temperature of the air that is cooled by the evaporator. This can be measured at the air outflow from the evaporator or at a nearby delivery duct outlet. An ordinary thermometer should read 40–50 °F, with the controls set to full cold after the system has been allowed to operate for a few minutes. Manufacturer's instructions include information on where to place the thermometer and the temperature range that indicates acceptable performance.

Pressures can also be observed to indicate system performance. Typically, low side pressure in a vapor cycle system operating normally is 10–50 psi, depending on ambient temperature. High side pressure is between 125 and 250 psi, again, depending on ambient temperature and the design of the system. All system performance tests are performed at a specified engine rpm (stable compressor speed) and involve a period of time to stabilize the operation of the vapor cycle. Consult the manufacturer's instructions for guidance.

Feel Test

A quick reference field test can be performed on a vapor cycle air conditioning system to gauge its health. In particular, components and lines in the high side (from the compressor to the expansion valve) should be warm or hot to the touch. The lines on both sides of the receiver dryer should be the same temperature. Low side lines and the evaporator should be cool. Ice should not be visible on the outside of the system. If any discrepancies exist, further investigation is needed. On hot, humid days, the cooling output of the vapor cycle system may be slightly compromised due to the volume of water condensing on the evaporator.

Purging the System

Purging the system means emptying it of its refrigerant charge. Since the refrigerant must be captured, a service cart with this capability should be used. By connecting the hoses to the high side and low side service valves and selecting recover, cart solenoid valves position so that a system purging compressor pumps the refrigerant out of the vapor cycle system and into a recovery tank.

Vapor cycle systems must be properly purged before opening for maintenance or component replacement. Once opened, precautions should be taken to prevent contaminants from entering the system. When suspicion exists that the system has been contaminated, such as when a component has catastrophically failed, it can be flushed clean. Special fluid flush formulated for vapor cycle air conditioning systems should be used. The receiver dryer is removed from the system for flushing and a new unit is installed, as it contains fresh filters. Follow the aircraft manufacturer's instructions.

Checking Compressor Oil

The compressor is a sealed unit in the vapor cycle system that is lubricated with oil. Any time the system is purged, it is an opportunity to check the oil quantity in the compressor crankcase. This is often done by removing a filler plug and using a dip stick. Oil quantity should be maintained within the proper range using oil recommended by the manufacturer. Be certain to replace the filler plug after checking or adding oil. *[Figure 16-95]*

Evacuating the System

Only a few drops of moisture can contaminate a vapor cycle air conditioning system. If this moisture freezes in the expansion valve, it could completely block the refrigerant flow. Water is removed from the system by evacuation. Anytime the system refrigerant charge falls below atmospheric pressure, the refrigerant is lost, or the system is opened, it must be evacuated before recharging.

Evacuating a vapor cycle air conditioning system is also known as pumping down the system. A vacuum pump is connected and pressure inside the system is reduced to vaporize any water that may exist. Continued operation of the vacuum pump draws the water vapor from the system. A typical pump used for evacuating an air conditioning system can reduce system pressure to about 29.62 "Hg (gauge

Figure 16-95. *Checking the compressor oil when the system is open.*

pressure). At this pressure, water boils at 45 °F. Operate the vacuum pump to achieve the recommended gauge pressure. Hold this vacuum for as long as the manufacturer specifies.

As long as a vapor cycle air conditioning system retains a charge higher than atmospheric pressure, any leak forces refrigerant out of the system. The system pressure prevents air (and water vapor) from entering. Therefore, it is permissible to recharge or add refrigerant to a system that has not dropped below atmospheric pressure without evacuating the system.

Charging the System

Charging capacity of a vapor cycle air conditioning system is measured by weight. The aircraft manufacturer's maintenance manual specifies this amount and the amount and type of oil to be put into the system when filling. Pre-weighing the refrigerant or setting the refrigerant weight into the servicing cart input ensures the system is filled to capacity.

Charging a vapor cycle air conditioning system should be undertaken immediately after evacuation of the system is completed. With the hoses still connected to the high and low side service valves, selecting charge on the service cart panel positions solenoid operated valves so that the refrigerant supply is available. First, refrigerant is released into the high side of the system. Observe the low side gauge. When the low side gauge begins to indicate pressure, it is known that refrigerant is passing through the tiny orifice in the expansion valve. As pressure builds in the high side, the flow of refrigerant into the system stops.

To complete the charge of the system, refrigerant needs to be drawn in by the compressor. A major concern is to avoid damage to the compressor by having liquid refrigerant enter the compressor inlet. After the initial release of refrigerant into the high side, the high side service valve is closed and the remaining charge is made through the low side service valve. The engine is started and run at a specified rpm, usually a high idle speed. Full cool is selected on the air conditioning control panel in the cockpit. As the compressor operates, it draws vapor into the low side until the correct weighed amount of refrigerant is in the system. Charging is completed with a full performance test.

Charging with a manifold set is accomplished in the same way. The manifold center hose is connected to the refrigerant source that charges the system. After opening the valve on the container (or puncturing the seal on a small can), the center hose connection on the manifold set should be loosened to allow air in the hose to escape. Once the air is bled out of the hose, the refrigerant can enter the system through whichever service valve is opened. The sequence is the same as above and all manufacturer instructions should be followed.

Oil quantity added to the system is specified by the manufacturer. Refrigerant premixed with oil is available and may be permissible for use. This eliminates the need to add oil separately. Alternately, the amount of oil to be put into the system can be selected on the servicing cart. Approximately ¼ ounce of oil for each pound of refrigerant is a standard amount; however, follow the manufacturer's specifications.

Technician Certification
The EPA requires certification of technicians that work with vapor cycle air conditioning refrigerant and equipment to ensure safe compliance with current regulations. Aircraft technicians can obtain certification or can refer vapor cycle air conditioning work to shops that specialize in this work.

Aircraft Heaters
Bleed Air Systems
Temperatures at high altitudes in which aircraft operate can be well below 0 °F. Combined with seasonally cold temperatures, this makes heating the cabin more than just a luxury. Pressurized aircraft that use air cycle air conditioning systems mix bleed air with cold air produced by the air cycle machine expansion turbine to obtain warm air for the cabin. This is discussed in the section that covers air cycle air conditioning in this chapter. Aircraft not equipped with air cycle air conditioning may be heated by one of a few possible methods.

Some turbine-powered aircraft not equipped with air cycle systems still make use of engine compressor bleed air to heat the cabin. Various arrangements exist. The bleed air is mixed with ambient air, or cabin return air, and distributed throughout the aircraft via ducting. The mixing of air can be done in a variety of ways. Mixing air valves, flow control valves, shutoff valves, and other various control valves are controlled by switches in the cockpit. One STC'd bleed air heat system uses mini-ejectors in helicopter cabins to combine bleed air with cabin air. All of these bleed air heating systems are simple and function well, as long as the valves, ducting, and controls are in operational condition.

Electric Heating Systems
Occasionally, an electric heating device is used to heat the aircraft. Electricity flowing through a heating element makes the element warm. A fan to blow air over the elements and into the cabin is used to transfer the heat. Other floor or sidewall elements simply radiate heat to warm the cabin.

Electric heating element heaters require a significant amount of the aircraft's generator output, which is better dedicated to the operation of other electrical devices. For this reason, they are not very common. However, their use on the ground when powered by a ground electrical power source preheats the cabin before passengers board and does not tax the electrical system.

Exhaust Shroud Heaters
Most single-engine light aircraft use exhaust shroud heating systems to heat the cabin. Ambient air is directed into a metal shroud, or jacket, that encases part of the engine's exhaust system. The air is warmed by the exhaust and directed through a firewall heater valve into the cabin. This simple solution requires no electrical or engine power and it makes use of heat that would otherwise be wasted. *[Figures 16-96 and 16-97]*

Figure 16-96. *The basic arrangement of an aircraft exhaust shroud heater.*

Figure 16-97. *The environmental system of a single-engine Piper aircraft with an exhaust shroud heating system.*

A major concern of exhaust shroud heat systems is the possibility that exhaust gases could contaminate the cabin air. Even the slightest crack in an exhaust manifold could send enough carbon monoxide into the cabin to be fatal. Strict inspection procedures are in place to minimize this threat. Most involve pressurizing the exhaust system with air, while inspecting for leaks with a soapy solution. Some require the exhaust to be removed and pressurized while submerged under water to detect any leaks. Frequency of exhaust heat leak detection can be every 100 hours.

Occasionally, the exhaust system is slightly modified in a shroud heat configuration. For example, an exhaust muffler may have numerous welded studs attached, which increase heat transfer to the cabin air. Each weld point is a location for a potential leak. *[Figure 16-98]*

Figure 16-98. *An exhaust manifold with its shroud removed showing numerous welded studs used to increase heat transfer from the exhaust to the ambient air going to the cabin.*

Regardless of age or condition, aircraft with exhaust shroud heating systems should contain a carbon monoxide detection device in the cockpit.

Combustion Heaters

An aircraft combustion heater is used on many small to medium sized aircraft. It is a heat source independent from the aircraft's engine(s), although it does use fuel from the aircraft's main fuel system. Combustion heaters are manufactured by a few different companies that supply the aviation industry. Most are similar to the description that follows. The most up to date units have electronic ignition and temperature control switches.

Combustion heaters are similar to exhaust shroud heaters in that ambient air is heated and sent to the cabin. The source of heat in this case is an independent combustion chamber located inside the cylindrical outer shroud of the heater unit. The correct amount of fuel and air are ignited in the air-tight inner chamber. The exhaust from combustion is funneled overboard. Ambient air is directed between the combustion chamber and the outer shroud. It absorbs the combustion heat by convection and is channeled into the cabin. *[Figure 16-99]* Refer to *Figure 16-100* for the following descriptions of the combustion heater subsystems and heater operation.

Combustion Air System

The air used in the combustion process is ambient air scooped from outside the aircraft, or from the compartment in which the combustion heater is mounted. A blower ensures that the correct quantity and pressure of air are sent into the chamber.

Figure 16-99. *A modern combustion heater.*

Some units have regulators or a relief valve to ensure these parameters. The combustion air is completely separate from the air that is warmed and sent into the cabin.

Ventilating Air System

Ventilating air is the name of the air that is warmed and sent into the cabin. Typically, it comes into the combustion heater through a ram air intake. When the aircraft is on the ground, a ventilating air fan controlled by a landing gear squat switch operates to draw in the air. Once airborne, the fan ceases to operate as the ram air flow is sufficient. Ventilating air passes between the combustion chamber and the outer shroud of the combustion heater where it is warmed and sent to the cabin.

Figure 16-100. *A diagram of a typical combustion heater and its components.*

Fuel System

As mentioned, fuel for the combustion heater is drawn from an aircraft fuel tank. A constant pressure fuel pump with relief valve pulls the fuel through a filter. A main solenoid valve downstream delivers the fuel to the unit. The solenoid is controlled by the cabin heater switch in the cockpit and three safety switches located on the combustion heater. The first safety switch is a duct limit switch that keeps the valve closed should the unit not have enough ventilating airflow to keep it within the correct operating temperature range. The second is a pressure switch that must sense pressure from the combustion air fan to allow the solenoid to open. Fuel is delivered to the combustion chamber only if there is air there with which it can be mixed. Finally, an overheat switch also controls the main fuel supply solenoid. When an over temperature condition occurs, it closes the solenoid to stop the supply of fuel.

A secondary solenoid is located downstream of the main fuel supply solenoid. It is part of a fuel control unit that also houses a pressure regulator and an additional fuel filter. The valve opens and closes on command from the combustion heater thermostat. During normal operation, the heater cycles on and off by opening and closing this solenoid at the entrance to the combustion chamber. When opened, fuel flows through a nozzle that sprays it into the combustion chamber. *[Figure 16-100]*

Ignition System

Most combustion heaters have an ignition unit designed to receive aircraft voltage and step it up to fire a spark plug located in the combustion chamber. Older combustion heaters use vibrator-type ignition units. Modern units have electronic ignition. *[Figure 16-101]* The ignition is continuous when activated. This occurs when the heater switch is placed in the ON position in the cockpit, and the combustion air blower builds sufficient air pressure in the combustion chamber. Use of the proper spark plug for the combustion heater is essential. Check the manufacturer's approved data. *[Figure 16-102]*

Controls

The combustion heater controls consist of a cabin heat switch and a thermostat. The cabin heat switch starts the fuel pump, opens the main fuel supply solenoid, and turns on the combustion air fan, as well as the ventilating air fan if the aircraft is on the ground. When the combustion air fan builds pressure, it allows the ignition unit to start. The thermostat sends power to open the fuel control solenoid when heat is needed. This triggers combustion in the unit and heat is delivered to the cabin. When the preselected temperature is reached, the thermostat cuts power to the fuel control solenoid and combustion stops. Ventilating air continues to

Figure 16-101. *The fuel nozzle located at the end of the combustion chamber sprays aircraft fuel, which is lit by a continuous sparking ignition system spark plug.*

Figure 16-102. *Examples of ignition units used on combustion heaters.*

circulate and carry heat away. When the temperature level falls to that below which the thermostat is set, the combustion heater cycles on again.

Safety Features

Various automatic combustion heater controls prevent operation of the heater when dangerous conditions exist. As stated, a duct limit switch cuts off fuel to the heater when there is not enough airflow to keep the heater duct below a preset temperature. This is usually caused by a lack of ventilating air flow. An overheat switch set at a higher temperature than the duct limit switch guards against overheat of any kind. It is designed to cut fuel to the combustion heater before an unwanted fire occurs. When this switch activates, a light is illuminated in the cockpit and the heater cannot be restarted until maintenance determines the cause. Some heaters contain a circuit to prevent fuel from being delivered to the combustion chamber if the ignition system is not working.

Maintenance and Inspection

Maintenance of combustion heaters consists of routine items, such as cleaning filters, checking spark plug wear, and ensuring inlets are not plugged. All maintenance and inspection of combustion heaters should be accomplished in accordance with the aircraft manufacturer's instructions. Combustion heater manufacturers also produce maintenance guidelines that should be followed. Intervals between the performance of maintenance items and the time between overhauls must be followed to help ensure a properly functioning heater is available when it is needed.

Inspection of the combustion heater should be performed on schedule as provided by the manufacturer or whenever a malfunction is suspected. Inlets and outlets should be clear. All controls should be checked for freedom of operation and function. Close observation for any sign of fuel leaks or cracks in the combustion chamber and/or shroud should be made. All components should be secure. An operational check can also be made. Follow the manufacturer's inspection criteria to ensure the combustion heater is in airworthy condition.

Chapter 17
Fire Protection Systems

Introduction

Because fire is one of the most dangerous threats to an aircraft, the potential fire zones of modern multiengine aircraft are protected by a fixed fire protection system. A fire zone is an area, or region, of an aircraft designed by the manufacturer to require fire detection and/or fire extinguishing equipment and a high degree of inherent fire resistance. The term "fixed" describes a permanently installed system in contrast to any type of portable fire extinguishing equipment, such as a hand-held Halon or water fire extinguisher. A complete fire protection system on modern aircraft, and on many older aircraft, includes a fire detection system and a fire extinguishing system. Typical zones on aircraft that have a fixed fire detection and/or fire extinguisher system are:

1. Engines and auxiliary power unit (APU)
2. Cargo and baggage compartments
3. Lavatories on transport aircraft
4. Electronic bays
5. Wheel wells
6. Bleed air ducts

To detect fires or overheat conditions, detectors are placed in the various zones to be monitored. Fires are detected in reciprocating engine and small turboprop aircraft using one or more of the following:

1. Overheat detectors
2. Rate-of-temperature-rise detectors
3. Flame detectors
4. Observation by crewmembers

In addition to these methods, other types of detectors are used in aircraft fire protection systems but are seldom used to detect engine fires. For example, smoke detectors are better suited to monitor areas where materials burn slowly or smolder, such as cargo and baggage compartments. Other types of detectors in this category include carbon monoxide detectors and chemical sampling equipment capable of detecting combustible mixtures that can lead to accumulations of explosive gases.

The complete aircraft fire protection systems of most large turbine-engine aircraft incorporate several of these different detection methods.

1. Rate-of-temperature-rise detectors
2. Radiation sensing detectors
3. Smoke detectors
4. Overheat detectors
5. Carbon monoxide detectors
6. Combustible mixture detectors
7. Optical detectors
8. Observation of crew or passengers

The types of detectors most commonly used for fast detection of fires are the rate-of-rise, optical sensor, pneumatic loop, and electric resistance systems.

Classes of Fires

The following classes of fires that are likely to occur onboard aircraft, as defined in the U.S. National Fire Protection Association (NFPA) Standard 10, Standard for Portable Fire Extinguishers, 2007 Edition, are:

1. Class A—fires involving ordinary combustible materials, such as wood, cloth, paper, rubber, and plastics.
2. Class B—fires involving flammable liquids, petroleum oils, greases, tars, oil-based paints, lacquers, solvents, alcohols, and flammable gases.
3. Class C—fires involving energized electrical equipment in which the use of an extinguishing media that is electrically nonconductive is important.
4. Class D—fires involving combustible metals, such as magnesium, titanium, zirconium, sodium, lithium, and potassium.

Requirements for Overheat and Fire Protection Systems

Fire protection systems on current-production aircraft do not rely on observation by crew members as a primary method of fire detection. An ideal fire detector system includes as many of the following features as possible:

1. No false warnings under any flight or ground condition.
2. Rapid indication of a fire and accurate location of the fire.
3. Accurate indication that a fire is out.
4. Indication that a fire has re-ignited.
5. Continuous indication for duration of a fire.
6. Means for electrically testing the detector system from the aircraft cockpit.
7. Resists damage from exposure to oil, water, vibration, extreme temperatures, or handling.
8. Light in weight and easily adaptable to any mounting position.
9. Circuitry that operates directly from the aircraft power system without inverters.
10. Minimum electrical current requirements when not indicating a fire.
11. Cockpit light that illuminates, indicating the location of the fire, and with an audible alarm system.
12. A separate detector system for each engine.

Fire Detection/Overheat Systems

A fire detection system should signal the presence of a fire. Units of the system are installed in locations where there are greater possibilities of a fire. Three detector system types in common use are the thermal switch, thermocouple, and the continuous loop.

Thermal Switch System

A number of detectors, or sensing devices, are available. Many older-model aircraft still operating have some type of thermal switch system or thermocouple system. A thermal switch system has one or more lights energized by the aircraft power system and thermal switches that control operation of the light(s). These thermal switches are heat-sensitive units that complete electrical circuits at a certain temperature. They are connected in parallel with each other but in series with the indicator lights. *[Figure 17-1]* If the temperature rises above a set value in any one section of the circuit, the thermal switch closes, completing the light circuit to indicate a fire or overheat condition. No set number of thermal switches is required; the exact number is usually determined by the aircraft manufacturer. On some installations, all the thermal detectors are connected to one light; on others, there may be one thermal switch for each indicator light.

2. Alarm circuit
3. Test circuit

These circuits are shown in *Figure 17-2*. The relay box contains two relays, the sensitive relay and the slave relay, and the thermal test unit. Such a box may contain from one to eight identical circuits, depending on the number of potential fire zones. The relays control the warning lights. In turn, the thermocouples control the operation of the relays. The circuit consists of several thermocouples in series with each other and with the sensitive relay.

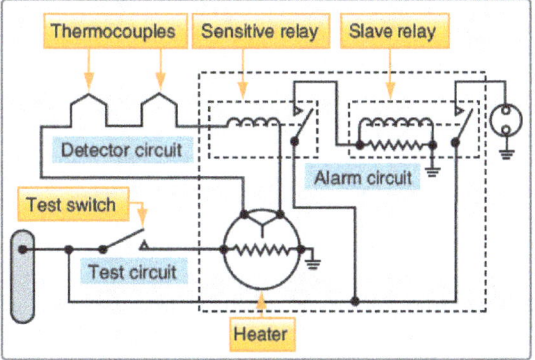

Figure 17-2. *Thermocouple fire warning circuit.*

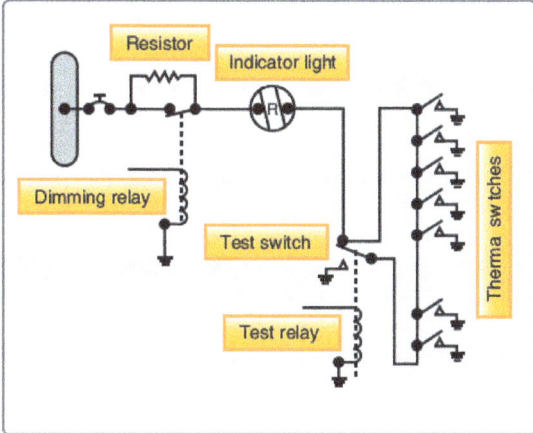

Figure 17-1. *Thermal switch fire circuit.*

Some warning lights are push-to-test lights. The bulb is tested by pushing it in to check an auxiliary test circuit. The circuit shown in *Figure 17-1* includes a test relay. With the relay contact in the position shown, there are two possible paths for current flow from the switches to the light. This is an additional safety feature. Energizing the test relay completes a series circuit and checks all the wiring and the light bulb. Also included in the circuit shown in *Figure 17-1* is a dimming relay. By energizing the dimming relay, the circuit is altered to include a resistor in series with the light. In some installations, several circuits are wired through the dimming relay, and all the warning lights may be dimmed at the same time.

Thermocouple System

The thermocouple fire warning system operates on an entirely different principle from the thermal switch system. A thermocouple depends on the rate of temperature rise and does not give a warning when an engine slowly overheats or a short circuit develops. The system consists of a relay box, warning lights, and thermocouples. The wiring system of these units may be divided into the following circuits:

1. Detector circuit

The thermocouple is constructed of two dissimilar metals, such as chromel and constantan. The point at which these metals are joined and exposed to the heat of a fire is called a hot junction. There is also a reference junction enclosed in a dead air space between two insulation blocks. A metal cage surrounds the thermocouple to give mechanical protection without hindering the free movement of air to the hot junction. If the temperature rises rapidly, the thermocouple produces a voltage because of the temperature difference between the reference junction and the hot junction. If both junctions are heated at the same rate, no voltage results. In the engine compartment, there is a normal, gradual rise in temperature from engine operation; because it is gradual, both junctions heat at the same rate and no warning signal is given. If there is a fire, however, the hot junction heats more rapidly than the reference junction. The ensuing voltage causes a current to flow within the detector circuit. Any time the current is greater than 4 milliamperes (0.004 ampere), the sensitive relay closes. This completes a circuit from the aircraft power system to the coil of the slave relay. The slave relay then closes and completes the circuit to the warning light to give a visual fire warning.

The total number of thermocouples used in individual detector circuits depends on the size of the fire zones and the total circuit resistance, which usually does not exceed 5 ohms.

As shown in *Figure 17-2*, the circuit has two resistors. The resistor connected across the slave relay terminals absorbs the coil's self-induced voltage to prevent arcing across the points of the sensitive relay. The contacts of the sensitive relay are so fragile that they burn, or weld, if arcing is permitted.

When the sensitive relay opens, the circuit to the slave relay is interrupted and the magnetic field around its coil collapses. The coil then gets a voltage through self-induction but, with the resistor across the coil terminals, there is a path for any current flow as a result of this voltage, eliminating arcing at the sensitive relay contacts.

Continuous-Loop Systems

Transport aircraft almost exclusively use continuous thermal sensing elements for powerplant and wheel well protection. These systems offer superior detection performance and coverage, and they have the proven ruggedness to survive in the harsh environment of modern turbofan engines.

A continuous-loop detector or sensing system permits more complete coverage of a fire hazard area than any of the spot-type temperature detectors. Two widely used types of continuous-loop systems are the thermistor type detectors, such as the Kidde and the Fenwal systems, and the pneumatic pressure detector, such as the Lingberg system. (Lindberg system is also known as Systron-Donner and, more recently, Meggitt Safety Systems.)

Fenwal System

The Fenwal system uses a slender Inconel tube packed with thermally sensitive eutectic salt and a nickel wire center conductor. *[Figure 17-3]* Lengths of these sensing elements are connected in series to a control unit. The elements may be of equal or varying length and of the same or different temperature settings. The control unit, operating directly from the power source, impresses a small voltage on the sensing elements. When an overheat condition occurs at any point along the element length, the resistance of the eutectic salt within the sensing element drops sharply, causing current to flow between the outer sheath and the center conductor. This current flow is sensed by the control unit, which produces a signal to actuate the output relay and activate the alarms. When the fire has been extinguished or the critical temperature lowered below the set point, the Fenwal system automatically returns to standby alert, ready to detect any subsequent fire or overheat condition. The Fenwal system may be wired to employ a loop circuit. In this case, should an open circuit occur, the system still signals fire or overheat. If multiple open circuits occur, only that section between breaks becomes inoperative.

Kidde System

In the Kidde continuous-loop system, two wires are imbedded in an inconel tube filled with a thermistor core material. *[Figure 17-4]* Two electrical conductors go through the length of the core. One conductor has a ground connection to the tube, and the other conductor connects to the fire detection control unit. As the temperature of the core increases, electrical resistance to the ground decreases. The fire detection control unit monitors this resistance. If the resistance decreases to the overheat set point, an overheat indication occurs in the flight deck. Typically, a 10-second time delay is incorporated for the overheat indication. If the resistance decreases more to the fire set point, a fire warning occurs. When the fire or overheat condition is gone, the resistance of the core material increases to the reset point and the flight deck indications disappear. The rate of change of resistance identifies an electrical short or a fire. The resistance decreases more quickly with an electrical short than with a fire. In some aircraft, in addition to fire and overheat detection, the Kidde continuous-loop system can supply nacelle temperature data to the airplane condition monitoring function of the aircraft in-flight monitoring system (AIMS).

Sensing Element

The resistance of a sensor varies inversely as it is heated; as sensor temperature is increased, its resistance decreases. Each sensor is composed of two wires embedded in thermistor material that is encased in a heavy wall inconel tube for high strength at elevated temperatures. The electrical connectors at each end of the sensor are ceramic insulated. The inconel tubes are shrouded in a perforated stainless steel tube and supported by Teflon-impregnated asbestos bushings at intervals. The shroud protects the sensor from breakage due to vibration, abrasion against airplane structure, and damage from maintenance activity.

The resistance of a sensor also varies inversely with its length, the increments of length being resistances in parallel. The heating of a short length of sensor out of a given length

Figure 17-3. *Fenwal sensing element.*

Figure 17-4. *Kidde continuous-loop system.*

requires that the short length be heated above the temperature alarm point so the total resistance of the sensor decreases to the alarm point. This characteristic permits integration of all temperatures throughout the length of the installation rather than sensing only the highest local temperature. The two wires encased within the thermistic material of each inconel tube form a variable resistance network between themselves, between the detector wire and the inconel tube, and between each adjacent incremental length of sensor. These variable resistance networks are monitored by the application of 28 volts direct current (DC) to the detector wire from the detector control unit.

Combination Fire and Overheat Warning

The analog signal from the thermistor-sensing element permits the control circuits to be arranged to give a two-level response from the same sensing element loop. The first is an overheat warning at a temperature level below the fire warning indicating a general engine compartment temperature rise, such as would be caused by leakage of hot bleed air or combustion gas into the engine compartment. It could also be an early warning of fire and would alert the crew to appropriate action to reduce the engine compartment temperature. The second-level response is at a level above that attainable by a leaking hot gas and is the fire warning.

Temperature Trend Indication

The analog signal produced by the sensing element loop as its temperature changes is converted to signals suitable for flight deck display to indicate engine bay temperature increases from normal. A comparison of the readings from each loop system also provides a check on the condition of the fire detection system, because the two loops should normally read alike.

System Test

The integrity of the continuous-loop fire detection system may be tested by actuating a test switch in the flight deck that switches one end of the sensing element loop from its control circuit to a test circuit built into the control unit, which simulates the sensing element resistance change due to fire. *[Figure 17-5]* If the sensing element loop is unbroken, the resistance detected by the control circuit is that of the simulated fire, and the alarm is activated. The test demonstrates, in addition to the continuity of the sensing

Figure 17-5. *Continuously loop fire detection system test circuit.*

element loop, the integrity of the alarm indicator circuit and the proper functioning of the control circuits. The thermistic properties of the sensing element remain unchanged for the life of the element (no irreversible changes take place when heated); the element functions properly as long as it is electrically connected to the control unit.

Fault Indication

Provision is made in the control unit to output a fault signal which activates a fault indicator whenever the short discriminator circuit detects a short in the sensing element loop. This is a requirement for transport category aircraft because such a short disables the fire detection system.

Dual-Loop Systems

Dual-loop systems are two complete basic fire detection systems with their output signals connected so that both must signal to result in a fire warning. This arrangement, called AND logic, results in greatly increased reliability against false fire warnings from any cause. Should one of the two loops be found inoperative at the preflight integrity test, a cockpit selector switch disconnects that loop and allows the signal from the other loop alone to activate the fire warning. Since the single operative loop meets all fire detector requirements, the aircraft can be safely dispatched and maintenance deferred to a more convenient time. However, should one of the two loops become inoperative in flight and a fire subsequently occur, the fire signaling loop activates a cockpit fault signal that alerts the flight crew to select single-loop operation to confirm the possible occurrence of fire.

Automatic Self-Interrogation

Dual-loop systems automatically perform the loop switching and decision-making function required of the flight crew upon appearance of the fault indication in the cockpit, a function called automatic self-interrogation. Automatic self-interrogation eliminates the fault indication and assures the immediate appearance of the fire indication should fire occur while at least one loop of the dual-loop system is operative. Should the control circuit from a single-loop signal fire, the self-interrogation circuit automatically tests the functioning of the other loop. If it tests operative, the circuit suppresses the fire signal because the operative loop would have signaled if a fire existed. If, however, the other loop tests inoperative, the circuit outputs a fire signal. The interrogation and decision takes place in milliseconds, so that no delay occurs if a fire actually exists.

Support Tube Mounted Sensing Elements

For those installations where it is desired to mount the sensing elements on the engine, and in some cases, on the aircraft structure, the support tube mounted element solves the problem of providing sufficient element support points and greatly facilitates the removal and reinstallation of the sensing elements for engine or system maintenance.

Most modern installations use the support tube concept of mounting sensing elements for better maintainability, as well as increased reliability. The sensing element is attached to a prebent stainless steel tube by closely spaced clamps and bushings, where it is supported from vibration damage and protected from pinching and excessive bending. The support tube-mounted elements can be furnished with either single or dual sensing elements.

Being prebent to the designed configuration assures its installation in the aircraft precisely in its designed location, where it has the necessary clearance to be free from the possibility of the elements chafing against engine or aircraft structure. The assembly requires only a few attachment points and, should its removal for engine maintenance be necessary, it is quickly and easily accomplished. Should the assembly require repair or maintenance, it is easily replaced with another assembly, leaving the repair for the shop. Should a sensing element be damaged, it is easily replaced in the assembly.

Fire Detection Control Unit (Fire Detection Card)

The control unit for the simplest type of system typically contains the necessary electronic resistance monitoring and alarm output circuits housed in a hermetically sealed aluminum case fitted with a mounting bracket and electrical connector. For more sophisticated systems, control modules are employed that contain removable control cards with circuitry for individual hazard areas and/or unique functions. In the most advanced applications, the detection system circuitry controls all aircraft fire protection functions, including fire detection and extinguishing for engines, APUs, cargo bays, and bleed-air systems.

Pressure Type Sensor Responder Systems

Some smaller turboprop aircraft are outfitted with pneumatic single point detectors. The design of these detectors is based on the principles of gas laws. The sensing element consists of a closed, helium-filled tube connected at one end to a responder assembly. As the element is heated, the gas pressure inside the tube increases until the alarm threshold is reached. At this point, an internal switch closes and reports an alarm to the cockpit. Continuous fault monitoring is included. This type of sensor is designed as a single-sensor detection system and does not require a control unit.

Pneumatic Continuous-Loop Systems

The pneumatic continuous-loop systems are also known by their manufacturers' names Lindberg, Systron-Donner, and Meggitt Safety Systems. These systems are used for engine fire detection of transport type aircraft and have the same function as the Kidde system; however, they work on a different principle. They are typically used in a dual-loop design to increase reliability of the system.

The pneumatic detector has two sensing functions. It responds to an overall average temperature threshold and to a localized discrete temperature increase caused by impinging flame or hot gasses. Both the average and discrete temperature are factory set and are not field adjustable. *[Figure 17-6]*

Figure 17-6. *Pneumatic dual fire/overheat detector assembly.*

Averaging Function

The fire/overheat detector serves as a fixed-volume device filled with helium gas. The helium gas pressure inside the detector increases in proportion to the absolute temperature and operates a pressure diaphragm that closes an electrical contact, actuating the alarm circuit. The pressure diaphragm within the responder assembly serves as one side of the electrical alarm contact and is the only moving part in the detector. The alarm switch is preset at an average temperature. Typical temperature ranges for average temperature settings are 200 °F (93 °C) to 850 °F (454 °C).

Discrete Function

The fire/overheat detector's sensor tube also contains a hydrogen-filled core material. *[Figure 17-7]* Large quantities of hydrogen gas are released from the detector core whenever a small section of the tube is heated to the preset discrete temperature or higher. The core outgassing increases the pressure inside the detector and actuates the alarm switch. Both the averaging and discrete functions are reversible. When the sensor tube is cooled, the average gas pressure is lowered and the discrete hydrogen gas returns to the core material. The reduction of internal pressure allows the alarm switch to return to its normal position, opening the electrical alarm circuit.

Figure 17-8 shows a typical aircraft fire detection system in which a control module monitors two loops of up to four pneumatic detectors each, connected in parallel. The control module responds directly to an alarm condition and continuously monitors the wiring and integrity of each loop. The normally open alarm switch closes upon an overheat or fire condition, causing a short circuit between terminals A and C. During normal operation, a resistance value is maintained across the terminals by a normally closed integrity switch. Loss of sensor gas pressure opens the integrity switch, creating an open circuit across the terminals of the faulted detector. In addition to the pressure-activated alarm switch, there is a second integrity switch in the detector that is held closed by the averaging gas pressure at all temperatures down to −65 °F (−54 °C). If the detector should develop a leak, the loss of gas pressure would allow the integrity switch to open and signal a lack of detector integrity. The system then does not operate during test.

Figure 17-7. *Pneumatic pressure loop detector system.*

Figure 17-8. *Aircraft detection system control module.*

Fire Zones

Powerplant compartments are classified into zones based on the airflow through them.

1. Class A zone—area of heavy airflow past regular arrangements of similarly shaped obstructions. The power section of a reciprocating engine is usually of this type.

2. Class B zone—area of heavy airflow past aerodynamically clean obstructions. Included in this type are heat exchanger ducts, exhaust manifold shrouds, and areas where the inside of the enclosing cowling or other closure is smooth, free of pockets, and adequately drained so leaking flammables cannot puddle. Turbine engine compartments may be considered in this class if engine surfaces are aerodynamically clean and all airframe structural formers are covered by a fireproof liner to produce an aerodynamically clean enclosure surface.

3. Class C zone—area of relatively low airflow. An engine accessory compartment separated from the power section is an example of this type of zone.

4. Class D zone—area of very little or no airflow. These include wing compartments and wheel wells where little ventilation is provided.

5. Class X zone—area of heavy airflow and of unusual construction, making uniform distribution of the extinguishing agent very difficult. Areas containing deeply recessed spaces and pockets between large structural formers are of this type. Tests indicate agent requirements to be double those for Class A zones.

Smoke, Flame, and Carbon Monoxide Detection Systems

Smoke Detectors

A smoke detection system monitors the lavatories and cargo baggage compartments for the presence of smoke, which is indicative of a fire condition. Smoke detection instruments that collect air for sampling are mounted in the compartments in strategic locations. A smoke detection system is used where the type of fire anticipated is expected to generate a substantial amount of smoke before temperature changes are sufficient to actuate a heat detection system. Two common types used are light refraction and ionization.

Light Refraction Type

The light refraction type of smoke detector contains a photoelectric cell that detects light refracted by smoke particles. Smoke particles refract the light to the photoelectric cell and, when it senses enough of this light, it creates an electrical current that sets off a light.

Ionization Type

Some aircraft use an ionization type smoke detector. The system generates an alarm signal (both horn and indicator) by detecting a change in ion density due to smoke in the cabin. The system is connected to the 28 volt DC electrical power supplied from the aircraft. Alarm output and sensor sensitive checks are performed simply with the test switch on the control panel.

Flame Detectors

Optical sensors, often referred to as flame detectors, are designed to alarm when they detect the presence of prominent, specific radiation emissions from hydrocarbon flames. The two types of optical sensors available are infrared (IR) and ultraviolet (UV), based on the specific emission wavelengths that they are designed to detect. IR-based optical flame detectors are used primarily on light turboprop aircraft and helicopter engines. These sensors have proven to be very dependable and economical for these applications.

When radiation emitted by the fire crosses the airspace between the fire and the detector, it impinges on the detector front face and window. The window allows a broad spectrum of radiation to pass into the detector where it strikes the sensing device filter. The filter allows only radiation in a tight waveband centered on 4.3 micrometers in the IR band to pass on to the radiation-sensitive surface of the sensing device. The radiation striking the sensing device minutely raises its temperature causing small thermoelectric voltages to be generated. These voltages are fed to an amplifier whose output is connected to various analytical electronic processing circuits. The processing electronics are tailored exactly to the time signature of all known hydrocarbon flame sources and ignores false alarm sources, such as incandescent lights and sunlight. Alarm sensitivity level is accurately controlled by a digital circuit. *[Figure 17-9]*

Carbon Monoxide Detectors

Carbon monoxide is a colorless, odorless gas that is a byproduct of incomplete combustion. Its presence in the breathing air of human beings can be deadly. To ensure crew and passenger safety, carbon monoxide detectors are used in aircraft cabins and cockpits. They are most often found on reciprocating engine aircraft with exhaust shroud heaters and on aircraft equipped with a combustion heater. Turbine bleed air, when used for heating the cabin, is tapped off of the engine upstream of the combustion chamber. Therefore, no threat of carbon monoxide presence is posed.

Carbon monoxide gas is found in varying degrees in all smoke and fumes of burning carbonaceous substances. Exceedingly small amounts of the gas are dangerous if inhaled. A concentration of as little as 2 parts in 10,000 may produce headache, mental dullness, and physical lethargy within a few hours. Prolonged exposure or higher concentrations may cause death.

There are several types of carbon monoxide detectors. Electronic detectors are common. Some are panel mounted and others are portable. Chemical color-change types are also common. These are mostly portable. Some are simple buttons, cards, or badges that have a chemical applied to the surface. Normally, the color of the chemical is tan. In the presence of carbon monoxide, the chemical darkens to grey or even black. The transition time required to change color is inversely related to the concentration of CO present. At 50 parts per million, the indication is apparent within 15 to 30 minutes. A concentration of 100 parts per million changes the color of the chemical in as little as 2–5 minutes. As concentration increases or duration of exposure is prolonged, the color evolves from grey to dark grey to black.

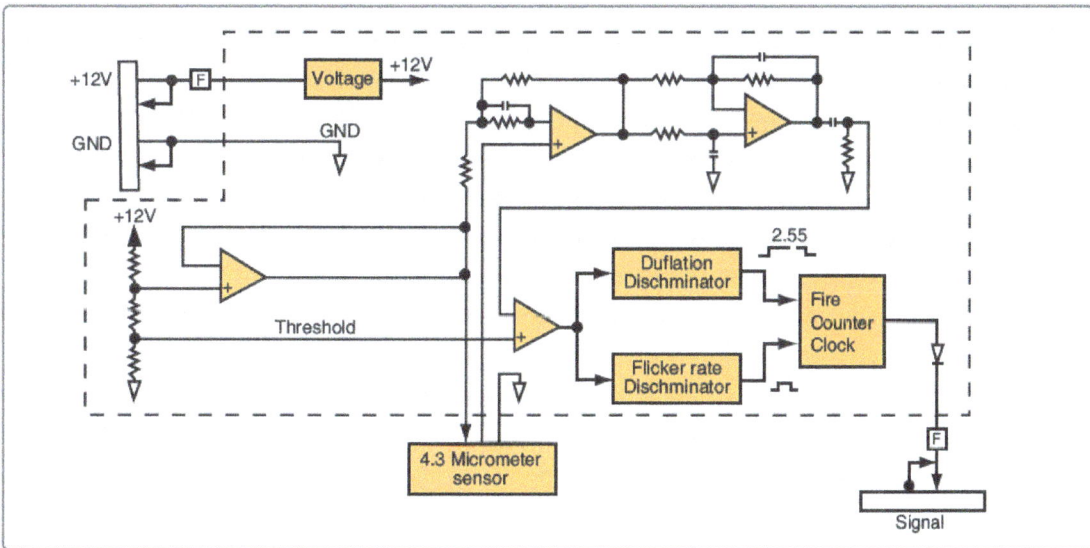

Figure 17-9. *Infrared (IR) based optical flame detector.*

Extinguishing Agents and Portable Fire Extinguishers

There must be at least one hand held, portable fire extinguisher for use in the pilot compartment that is located within easy access of the pilot while seated. There must be at least one hand held fire extinguisher located conveniently in the passenger compartment of each airplane accommodating more than 6 and less than 30 passengers. Each extinguisher for use in a personnel compartment must be designed to minimize the hazard of toxic gas concentrations. The number of portable, hand held fire extinguishers for transport aircraft is shown in *Figure 17-10*.

Passenger capacity	No. of extinguishers
7 through 30	1
31 through 60	2
61 through 200	3
201 through 300	4
301 through 400	5
401 through 500	6
501 through 600	7
601 through 700	8

Figure 17-10. *Hand held fire extinguisher requirement for transport aircraft.*

Halogenated Hydrocarbons

For over 45 years, halogenated hydrocarbons (Halons) have been practically the only fire extinguishing agents used in civil transport aircraft. However, Halon is an ozone depleting and global warming chemical, and its production has been banned by international agreement. Although Halon usage has been banned in some parts of the world, aviation has been granted an exemption because of its unique operational and fire safety requirements. Halon has been the fire extinguishing agent of choice in civil aviation because it is extremely effective on a per unit weight basis over a wide range of aircraft environmental conditions. It is a clean agent (no residue), electrically nonconducting, and has relatively low toxicity.

Two types of Halons are employed in aviation: Halon 1301($CBrF_3$) a total flooding agent, and Halon 1211 ($CBrClF_2$) a streaming agent. Class A, B, or C fires are appropriately controlled with Halons. However, do not use Halons on a class D fire. Halon agents may react vigorously with the burning metal.

NOTE: While Halons are still in service and are appropriate agents for these classes of fires, the production of these ozone depleting agents has been restricted. Although not required, consider replacing Halon extinguishers with Halon replacement extinguishers when discharged. Halon replacement agents found to be compliant to date include the halocarbons HCFC Blend B, HFC-227ea, and HFC-236fa.

Inert Cold Gases

Carbon dioxide (CO_2) is an effective extinguishing agent. It is most often used in fire extinguishers that are available on the ramp to fight fires on the exterior of the aircraft, such as engine or APU fires. CO_2 has been used for many years to extinguish flammable fluid fires and fires involving electrical equipment. It is noncombustible and does not react with most substances. It provides its own pressure for discharge from the storage vessel, except in extremely cold climates where a booster charge of nitrogen may be added to winterize the system. Normally, CO_2 is a gas, but it is easily liquefied by compression and cooling. After liquification, CO_2 remains in a closed container as both liquid and gas. When CO_2 is then discharged to the atmosphere, most of the liquid expands to gas. Heat absorbed by the gas during vaporization cools the remaining liquid to -110 °F, and it becomes a finely divided white solid, dry ice snow.

Carbon dioxide is about 1½ times as heavy as air, which gives it the ability to replace air above burning surfaces and maintain a smothering atmosphere. CO_2 is effective as an extinguishing agent primarily because it dilutes the air and reduces the oxygen content so that combustion is no longer supported. Under certain conditions, some cooling effect is also realized. CO_2 is considered only mildly toxic, but it can cause unconsciousness and death by suffocation if the victim is allowed to breathe CO_2 in fire extinguishing concentrations for 20 to 30 minutes. CO_2 is not effective as an extinguishing agent on fires involving chemicals containing their own oxygen supply, such as cellulose nitrate (used in some aircraft paints). Also, fires involving magnesium and titanium cannot be extinguished by CO_2.

Dry Powders

Class A, B, or C fires can be controlled by dry chemical extinguishing agents. The only all purpose (Class A, B, C rating) dry chemical powder extinguishers contain monoammonium phosphate. All other dry chemical powders have a Class B, C U.S – UL fire rating only. Dry powder chemical extinguishers best control class A, B, and C fire but their use is limited due to residual residue and clean up after deployment.

Water

Class A type fires are best controlled with water by cooling the material below its ignition temperature and soaking the material to prevent re-ignition.

Cockpit and Cabin Interiors

All materials used in the cockpit and cabin must conform to strict standards to prevent fire. In case of a fire, several types of portable fire extinguishers are available to fight the fire. The most common types are Halon 1211 and water.

Extinguisher Types

Portable fire extinguishers are used to extinguish fires in the cabin or flight deck. *Figure 17-11* shows a Halon fire extinguisher used in a general aviation aircraft. The Halon extinguishers are used on electrical and flammable liquid fires. Some transport aircraft also use water fire extinguisher for use on non-electrical fires.

The following is a list of extinguishing agents and the type (class) fires for which each is appropriate.

1. Water—class A. Water cools the material below its ignition temperature and soaks it to prevent reignition.
2. Carbon dioxide—class B or C. CO_2 acts as a blanketing agent. NOTE: CO_2 is not recommended for hand-held extinguishers for internal aircraft use.
3. Dry chemicals—class A, B, or C. Dry chemicals are the best control agents for these types of fires.
4. Halons—only class A, B, or C.
5. Halocarbon clean agents—only class A, B, or C.
6. Specialized dry powder—class D. (Follow the recommendations of the extinguisher's manufacturer because of the possible chemical reaction between the burning metal and the extinguishing agent.)

The following hand-held extinguishers are unsuitable as cabin or cockpit equipment.

- CO_2
- Dry chemicals (due to the potential for corrosion damage to electronic equipment, the possibility of visual obscuration if the agent were discharged into the flight deck area, and the cleanup problems from their use)
- Specialized dry powder (it is suitable for use in ground operations)

Installed Fire Extinguishing Systems

Transport aircraft have fixed fire extinguishing systems installed in:

1. Turbine engine compartments
2. APU compartments
3. Cargo and baggage compartments
4. Lavatories

CO_2 Fire Extinguishing Systems

Older aircraft with reciprocating engines used CO_2 as an extinguishing agent, but all newer aircraft designs with turbine engines use Halon or equivalent extinguishing agent, such as halocarbon clean agents.

Halogenated Hydrocarbons Fire Extinguishing Systems

The fixed fire extinguisher systems used in most engine fire and cargo compartment fire protection systems are designed to dilute the atmosphere with an inert agent that does not support combustion. Many systems use perforated tubing or discharge nozzles to distribute the extinguishing agent. High rate of discharge (HRD) systems use open-end tubes to deliver a quantity of extinguishing agent in 1 to 2 seconds.

Figure 17-11. *Portable fire extinguisher.*

The most common extinguishing agent still used today is Halon 1301 because of its effective firefighting capability and relatively low toxicity (UL classification Group 6). Noncorrosive Halon 1301 does not affect the material it contacts and requires no cleanup when discharged. Halon 1301 is the current extinguishing agent for commercial aircraft but a replacement is under development. Halon 1301 cannot be produced anymore because it depletes the ozone layer. Halon 1301 will be used until a suitable replacement is developed. Some military aircraft use HCL-125 and the Federal Aviation Administration (FAA) is testing HCL-125 for use in commercial aircraft.

Containers

Fire extinguisher containers (HRD bottles) store a liquid halogenated extinguishing agent and pressurized gas (typically nitrogen). They are normally manufactured from stainless steel. Depending upon design considerations, alternate materials are available, including titanium. Containers are also available in a wide range of capacities. They are produced under Department of Transportation (DOT) specifications or exemptions. Most aircraft containers are spherical in design, which provides the lightest weight possible. However, cylindrical shapes are available where space limitations are a factor. Each container incorporates a temperature/pressure sensitive safety relief diaphragm that prevents container pressure from exceeding container test pressure in the event of exposure to excessive temperatures. *[Figures 17-12 and 17-13]*

Figure 17-12. *Built-in non-portable fire extinguisher containers (HRD bottles) on an airliner.*

Figure 17-13. *Diagram of fire extinguisher containers (HRD bottles).*

Discharge Valves

Discharge valves are installed on the containers. A cartridge (squib) and frangible disk-type valve are installed in the outlet of the discharge valve assembly. Special assemblies having solenoid-operated or manually-operated seat-type valves are also available. Two types of cartridge disk-release techniques are used. Standard release-type uses a slug driven by explosive energy to rupture a segmented closure disc. For high temperature or hermetically sealed units, a direct explosive impact-type cartridge is used that applies fragmentation impact to rupture a prestressed corrosion resistant steel diaphragm. Most containers use conventional metallic gasket seals that facilitate refurbishment following discharge. *[Figure 17-14]*

Pressure Indication

A wide range of diagnostics is utilized to verify the fire extinguisher agent charge status. A simple visual indication gauge is available, typically a helical bourdon-type indicator that is vibration resistant. *[Figure 17-13]* A combination gauge switch visually indicates actual container pressure and also provides an electrical signal if container pressure is lost, precluding the need for discharge indicators. A ground checkable diaphragm-type low-pressure switch is commonly used on hermetically sealed containers. The Kidde system has a temperature compensated pressure switch that tracks the container pressure variations with temperatures by using a hermetically sealed reference chamber.

Two-Way Check Valve

Two-way check valves are required in a two-shot system to prevent the extinguisher agent from a reserve container from backing up into the previous emptied main container. Valves are supplied with either MS-33514 or MS-33656 fitting configurations.

Discharge Indicators

Discharge indicators provide immediate visual evidence of container discharge on fire extinguishing systems. Two kinds of indicators can be furnished: thermal and discharge. Both types are designed for aircraft and skin mounting. *[Figure 17-15]*

Figure 17-15. *Discharge indicators.*

Thermal Discharge Indicator (Red Disk)

The thermal discharge indicator is connected to the fire container relief fitting and ejects a red disk to show when container contents have dumped overboard due to excessive heat. The agent discharges through the opening left when the disk blows out. This gives the flight and maintenance crews an indication that the fire extinguisher container needs to be replaced before next flight.

Figure 17-14. *Discharge valve (left) and cartridge, or squib (right).*

17-13

Yellow Disk Discharge Indicator

If the flight crew activates the fire extinguisher system, a yellow disk is ejected from the skin of the aircraft fuselage. This is an indication for the maintenance crew that the fire extinguishing system was activated by the flight crew, and the fire extinguishing container needs to be replaced before next flight.

Fire Switch

The engine and APU fire switches are typically installed on the center overhead panel or center console in the flight deck. *[Figure 17-16]* When an engine fire switch is activated, the following happens: the engine stops because the fuel control shuts off, the engine is isolated from the aircraft systems, and the fire extinguishing system is activated. Some aircraft use fire switches that need to be pulled and turned to activate the system, while others use a push-type switch with a guard. To prevent accidental activation of the fire switch, a lock is installed that releases the fire switch only when a fire has been detected. This lock can be manually released by the flight crew if the fire detection system malfunctions. *[Figure 17-17]*

Cargo Fire Detection

Transport aircraft need to have the following provisions for each cargo or baggage compartment:

Figure 17-16. *Engine and APU fire switches on the cockpit center overhead panel.*

1. The detection system must provide a visual indication to the flight crew within 1 minute after the start of a fire.

Figure 17-17. *Engine fire switch operation.*

2. The system must be capable of detecting a fire at a temperature significantly below that at which the structural integrity of the airplane is substantially decreased.

3. There must be means to allow the crew to check, in flight, the functioning of each fire detector circuit.

Cargo Compartment Classification
Class A
A Class A cargo or baggage compartment, is one in which the presence of a fire would be easily discovered by a crewmember while at his or her station and each part of the compartment is easily accessible in flight.

Class B
A Class B cargo, or baggage compartment, is one in which there is sufficient access in flight to enable a crewmember to effectively reach any part of the compartment with the contents of a hand fire extinguisher. When the access provisions are being used, no hazardous quantity of smoke, flames, or extinguishing agent enters any compartment occupied by the crew or passengers. There is a separate approved smoke detector or fire detector system to give warning at the pilot or flight engineer station.

Class C
A Class C cargo, or baggage compartment, is one not meeting the requirements for either a Class A or B compartment but in which:

1. There is a separate approved smoke detector or fire detector system to give warning at the pilot or flight engineer station.

2. There is an approved built-in fire extinguishing or suppression system controllable from the cockpit.

3. There are means to exclude hazardous quantities of smoke, flames, or extinguishing agent from any compartment occupied by the crew or passengers.

4. There are means to control ventilation and drafts within the compartment so that the extinguishing agent used can control any fire that may start within the compartment.

Class E
Class E cargo compartment is one on airplanes used only for the carriage of cargo and in which:

1. There is a separate approved smoke or fire detector system to give warning at the pilot or flight engineer station.

2. The controls for shutting off the ventilating airflow to, or within, the compartment are accessible to the flight crew in the crew compartment.

3. There are means to exclude hazardous quantities of smoke, flames, or noxious gases from the flight crew compartment.

4. The required crew emergency exits are accessible under any cargo loading condition.

Cargo and Baggage Compartment Fire Detection and Extinguisher System
The cargo compartment smoke detection system gives warnings in the flight deck if there is smoke in a cargo compartment. *[Figure 17-18]* Each compartment is equipped with a smoke detector. The smoke detectors monitor air in the cargo compartments for smoke. The fans bring air from the cargo compartment into the smoke detector. Before the air goes in the smoke detector, in-line water separators remove condensation and heaters increase the air temperature. *[Figure 17-19]*

Figure 17-18. *Cargo fire detection warning.*

Figure 17-19. *Smoke detector installation.*

Smoke Detector System

The optical smoke detector consists of source light emitting diodes (LEDs), intensity monitor photodiodes, and scatter detector photodiodes. Inside the smoke detection chamber, air flows between a source (LED) and a scatter detector photodiode. Usually, only a small amount of light from the LED gets to the scatter detector. If the air has smoke in it, the smoke particles reflect more light on the scatter detector. This causes an alarm signal. The intensity monitor photodiode makes sure that the source LED is on and keeps the output of the source LED constant. This configuration also finds contamination of the LED and photodiodes. A defective diode, or contamination, causes the detector to change to the other set of diodes. The detector sends a fault message.

The smoke detector has multiple sampling ports. The fans draw air from the sampling ports through a water separator and a heater unit to the smoke detector. *[Figure 17-20]*

Cargo Compartment Extinguishing System

The cargo compartment extinguishing system is activated by the flight crew if the smoke detectors detect smoke in the cargo compartment. Some aircraft are outfitted with two types of fire extinguisher containers. The first system is the dump system that releases the extinguishing agent directly when the cargo fire discharge switch is activated. This action extinguishes the fire.

The second system is the metered system. After a time delay, the metered bottles discharge slowly and at a controlled rate through the filter regulator. Halon from the metered bottles replaces the extinguishing agent leakage. This keeps the correct concentration of extinguishing agent in the cargo compartment to keep the fire extinguished for 180 minutes.

The fire extinguishing bottles contain Halon 1301 or equivalent fire extinguishing agent pressurized with nitrogen. Tubing connects the bottles to discharge nozzles in the cargo compartment ceilings.

The extinguishing bottles are outfitted with squibs. The squib is an electrically operated explosive device. It is adjacent to a bottle diaphragm that can break. The diaphragm normally seals the pressurized bottle. When the cargo discharge switch is activated, the squib fires and the explosion breaks the diaphragm. Nitrogen pressure inside the bottle pushes the Halon through the discharge port into the cargo compartment. When the bottle discharges, a pressure switch is activated that sends an indication to the flight deck that a bottle has been discharged. Flow control valves are incorporated if the bottles can be discharged in multiple compartments. The flow control valves direct the extinguishing agent to the selected cargo compartment. *[Figure 17-21]*

The following indications occur in the cockpit if there is smoke in a cargo compartment:

- Master warning lights come on.
- Fire warning aural operates.
- A cargo fire warning message shows.
- Cargo fire warning light comes on.

Figure 17-20. *Smoke detector system.*

Figure 17-21. *Cargo and baggage compartment extinguishing system.*

The master warning lights and fire warning aural are prevented from operating during part of the takeoff operation.

Lavatory Smoke Detectors

Airplanes that have a passenger capacity of 20 or more are equipped with a smoke detector system that monitors the lavatories for smoke. Smoke indications provide a warning light in the cockpit or provide a warning light or audible warning at the lavatory and at flight attendant stations that would be readily detected by a flight attendant. Each lavatory must have a built-in fire extinguisher that discharges automatically. The smoke detector is located in the ceiling of the lavatory. *[Figure 17-22]*

Lavatory Smoke Detector System

Refer to *Figure 17-23*. The lavatory smoke detector is powered by the 28-volt DC left/right main DC bus. If there is smoke in the sensing chamber of the smoke detector, the alarm LED (red) comes on. The timing circuit makes an intermittent ground. The warning horn and lavatory call

Figure 17-22. *Lavatory smoke detector.*

17-17

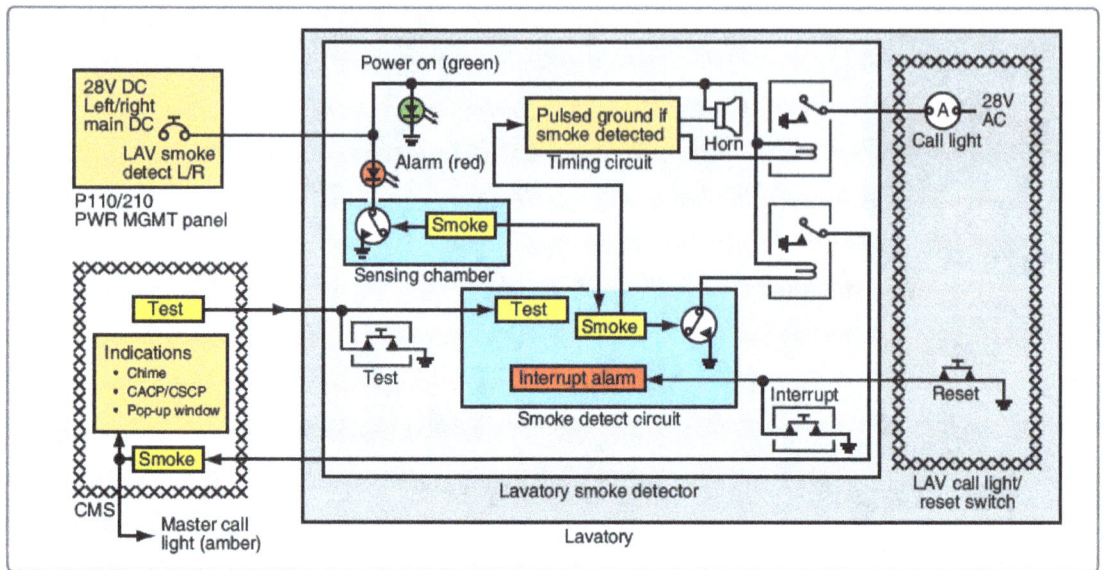

Figure 17-23. *Lavatory smoke detector diagram.*

light operate intermittently. The smoke detection circuit makes a ground for the relay. The energized relay makes a ground signal for the overhead electronics unit (OEU) in the central monitoring systems (CMS). This interface gives these indications: lavatory master call light flashes, cabin system control panel (CSCP) and cabin area control panel (CACP) pop-up window shows, and the lavatory call chime operates. Push the lavatory call reset switch or the smoke detector interrupt switch to cancel the smoke indications. If there is still smoke in the lavatory, the alarm LED (red) stays on. All smoke indications go away automatically when the smoke is gone.

Lavatory Fire Extinguisher System

The lavatory compartment is outfitted with a fire extinguisher bottle to extinguish fires in the waste compartment. The fire extinguisher is a bottle with two nozzles. The bottle contains pressurized Halon 1301 or equivalent fire extinguishing agent. When the temperature in the waste compartment reaches approximately 170 °F, the solder that seals the nozzles melt and the Halon is discharged. Weighing the bottle is often the only way to determine if the bottle is empty or full. *[Figure 17-24]*

Fire Detection System Maintenance

Fire detector sensing elements are located in many high-activity areas around aircraft engines. Their location, together with their small size, increases the chance of damage to the sensing elements during maintenance. An inspection and maintenance program for all types of continuous-loop

Figure 17-24. *Lavatory fire extinguishing bottle.*

systems should include the following visual checks. Note: These procedures are examples and should not be used to replace the applicable manufacturer's instructions.

Sensing elements of a continuous-loop system should be inspected for the following:

1. Cracked or broken sections caused by crushing or squeezing between inspection plates, cowl panels, or engine components.

2. Abrasion caused by rubbing of the element on cowling, accessories, or structural members.
3. Pieces of safety wire, or other metal particles, that may short the spot-detector terminals.
4. Condition of rubber grommets in mounting clamps that may be softened from exposure to oils or hardened from excessive heat.
5. Dents and kinks in sensing element sections. Limits on the element diameter, acceptable dents and kinks, and degree of smoothness of tubing contour are specified by manufacturers. No attempt should be made to straighten any acceptable dent or kink, since stresses may be set up that could cause tubing failure. *[Figure 17-25]*

Figure 17-25. *Sensing element defects.*

6. Nuts at the end of the sensing elements should be inspected for tightness and safety wire. *[Figure 17-26]* Loose nuts should be retorqued to the value specified by the manufacturer's instructions. Some types of sensing element connection joints require the use of copper crush gaskets. These should be replaced any time a connection is separated.

Figure 17-26. *Connector joint fitting attached to the structure.*

7. If shielded flexible leads are used, they should be inspected for fraying of the outer braid. The braided sheath is made up of many fine metal strands woven into a protective covering surrounding the inner insulated wire. Continuous bending of the cable or rough treatment can break these fine wires, especially those near the connectors.
8. Sensing element routing and clamping should be inspected carefully. *[Figure 17-27]* Long, unsupported sections may permit excessive vibration that can cause breakage. The distance between clamps on straight runs, usually about 8 to 10 inches, is specified by each manufacturer. At end connectors, the first support clamp usually is located about 4 to 6 inches from the end connector fittings. In most cases, a straight run of one inch is maintained from all connectors before a bend is started, and an optimum bend radius of 3 inches is normally adhered to.

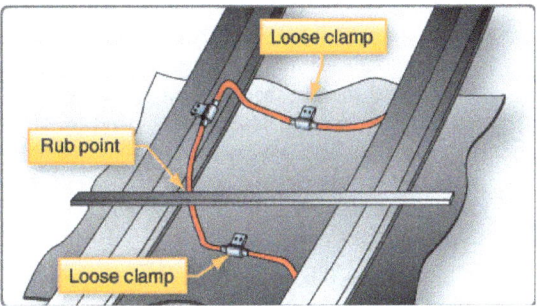

Figure 17-27. *Rubbing interference.*

9. Interference between a cowl brace and a sensing element can cause rubbing. This interference may cause wear and short the sensing element.
10. Grommets should be installed on the sensing element so that both ends are centered on its clamp. The split end of the grommet should face the outside of the nearest bend. Clamps and grommets should fit the element snugly. *[Figure 17-28]*

Fire Detection System Troubleshooting

The following troubleshooting procedures represent the most common difficulties encountered in engine fire detection systems:

1. Intermittent alarms are most often caused by an intermittent short in the detector system wiring. Such shorts may be caused by a loose wire that occasionally touches a nearby terminal, a frayed wire brushing against a structure, or a sensing element rubbing against a structural member long enough to wear

Figure 17-28. *Inspection of fire detector loop clamp.*

through the insulation. Intermittent faults often can be located by moving wires to recreate the short.

2. Fire alarms and warning lights can occur when no engine fire or overheat condition exists. Such false alarms can be most easily located by disconnecting the engine sensing loop connections from the control unit. If the false alarm ceases when the engine sensing loop is disconnected, the fault is in the disconnected sensing loop, which should be examined for areas that have been bent into contact with hot parts of the engine. If no bent element can be found, the shorted section can be located by isolating the connecting elements consecutively around the entire loop.

3. Kinks and sharp bends in the sensing element can cause an internal wire to short intermittently to the outer tubing. The fault can be located by checking the sensing element with an ohm meter while tapping the element in the suspected areas to produce the short.

4. Moisture in the detection system seldom causes a false fire alarm. If, however, moisture does cause an alarm, the warning persists until the contamination is removed, or boils away, and the resistance of the loop returns to its normal value.

5. Failure to obtain an alarm signal when the test switch is actuated may be caused by a defective test switch or control unit, the lack of electrical power, inoperative indicator light, or an opening in the sensing element or connecting wiring. When the test switch fails to provide an alarm, the continuity of a two-wire sensing loop can be determined by opening the loop and measuring the resistance. In a single-wire, continuous-loop system, the center conductor should be grounded.

Fire Extinguisher System Maintenance

Regular maintenance of fire extinguisher systems typically includes such items as the inspection and servicing of fire extinguisher bottles (containers), removal and reinstallation of cartridge and discharge valves, testing of discharge tubing for leakage, and electrical wiring continuity tests. The following paragraphs contain details of some of the most typical maintenance procedures.

Container Pressure Check

Fire extinguisher containers are checked periodically to determine that the pressure is between the prescribed minimum and maximum limits. Changes of pressure with ambient temperatures must also fall within prescribed limits. The graph shown in *Figure 17-29* is typical of the pressure-temperature curve graphs that provide maximum and minimum gauge readings. If the pressure does not fall within the graph limits, the extinguisher container is replaced.

Figure 17-29. *Fire extinguisher container pressure-temperature chart.*

Discharge Cartridges

The service life of fire extinguisher discharge cartridges is calculated from the manufacturer's date stamp, which is usually placed on the face of the cartridge. The cartridge service life recommended by the manufacturer is usually in terms of years. Cartridges are available with a service life of 5 years or more. To determine the unexpired service life of a discharge cartridge, it is usually necessary to remove the electrical leads and discharge line from the plug body, which can then be removed from the extinguisher container.

Agent Containers

Care must be taken in the replacement of cartridge and discharge valves. Most new extinguisher containers are supplied with their cartridge and discharge valve disassembled. Before installation on the aircraft, the cartridge must be assembled properly in the discharge valve and the valve connected to the container, usually by means of a swivel nut that tightens against a packing ring gasket. *[Figure 17-30]*

Figure 17-30. *Components of fire extinguisher container.*

If a cartridge is removed from a discharge valve for any reason, it should not be used in another discharge valve assembly, since the distance the contact point protrudes may vary with each unit. Thus, continuity might not exist if a used plug that had been indented with a long contact point were installed in a discharge valve with a shorter contact point.

Note: The preceding material in this chapter has been largely of a general nature dealing with the principles involved and general procedures to be followed. When actually performing maintenance, always refer to the applicable maintenance manuals and other related publications pertaining to a particular aircraft.

Fire Prevention

Leaking fuel, hydraulic, deicing, or lubricating fluids can be sources of fire in an aircraft. This condition should be noted and corrective action taken when inspecting aircraft systems. Minute pressure leaks of these fluids are particularly dangerous for they quickly produce an explosive atmospheric condition. Carefully inspect fuel tank installations for signs of external leaks. With integral fuel tanks, the external evidence may occur at some distance from where the fuel is actually escaping. Many hydraulic fluids are flammable and should not be permitted to accumulate in the structure. Sound-proofing and lagging materials may become highly flammable if soaked with oil of any kind. Any leakage or spillage of flammable fluid in the vicinity of combustion heaters is a serious fire risk, particularly if any vapor is drawn into the heater and passes over the hot combustion chamber.

Oxygen system equipment must be kept absolutely free from traces of oil or grease, since these substances spontaneously ignite when in contact with oxygen under pressure. Oxygen servicing cylinders should be clearly marked so they cannot be mistaken for cylinders containing air or nitrogen, as explosions have resulted from this error during maintenance operations.

Glossary

Aborted takeoff. A takeoff that is terminated prematurely when it is determined that some condition exists that makes takeoff or further flight dangerous.

Absolute pressure. Pressure measured from zero pressure or a vacuum.

Absolute pressure regulator. A valve used in a pneumatic system at the pump inlet to regulate the compressor inlet air pressure to prevent excessive speed variation and/or overspeeding of the compressor.

Absolute zero. The point at which all molecular motion ceases. Absolute zero is –460 °F and –273 °C.

Accumulator. A hydraulic component that consists of two compartments separated by a movable component, such as a piston, diaphragm, or bladder. One compartment is filled with compressed air or nitrogen, and the other is filled with hydraulic fluid and is connected into the system pressure manifold. An accumulator allows an incompressible fluid to be stored under pressure by the force produced by a compressible fluid. Its primary purposes are to act as a shock absorber in the system, and to provide a source of additional hydraulic power when heavy demands are placed on the system.

Actuator. A fluid power device that changes fluid pressure into mechanical motion.

ADC. Air data computer.

ADF. Automatic direction finder.

ADI. Attitude director indicator.

Advancing blade. The blade on a helicopter rotor whose tip is moving in the same direction the helicopter is moving.

Adverse yaw. A condition of flight at the beginning of a turn in which the nose of an airplane momentarily yaws in the opposite direction from the direction in which the turn is to be made.

Aerodynamic drag. The total resistance to the movement of an object through the air. Aerodynamic drag is composed of both induced drag and parasite drag. See induced drag and parasite drag.

Aerodynamic lift. The force produced by air moving over a specially shaped surface called an airfoil. Aerodynamic lift acts in a direction perpendicular to the direction the air is moving.

Aeroelastic tailoring. The design of an aerodynamic surface whose strength and stiffness are matched to the aerodynamic loads that will be imposed upon it.

Aeronautical Radio Incorporated (ARINC). A corporation whose principal stockholders are the airlines. Its function is to operate certain communication links between airliners in flight and the airline ground facilities. ARINC also sets standards for communication equipment used by the airlines.

Aging. A change in the characteristics of a material with time. Certain aluminum alloys do not have their full strength when they are first removed from the quench bath after they have been heat-treated, but they gain this strength after a few days by the natural process of aging.

Agonic line. A line drawn on an aeronautical chart along which there is no angular difference between the magnetic and geographic north poles.

Air carrier. An organization or person involved in the business of transporting people or cargo by air for compensation or hire.

Air-cycle cooling system. A system for cooling the air in the cabin of a turbojet-powered aircraft. Compressor bleed air passes through two heat exchangers where it gives up some of its heat; then, it drives an expansion turbine where it loses still more of its heat energy as the turbine drives a compressor. When the air leaves the turbine, it expands and its pressure and temperature are both low.

Aircraft communication addressing and reporting system (ACARS). A two-way communication link between an airliner in flight and the airline's main ground facilities. Data is collected in the aircraft by digital sensors and is transmitted to the ground facilities. Replies from the ground may be printed out so the appropriate flight crewmember can have a hard copy of the response.

Airfoil. Any surface designed to obtain a useful reaction, or lift, from air passing over it.

Airspeed indicator. A flight instrument that measures the pressure differential between the pitot, or ram, air pressure, and the static pressure of the air surrounding the aircraft. This differential pressure is shown in units of miles per hour, knots, or kilometers per hour.

Airworthiness Alert. A notice sent by the FAA to certain interested maintenance personnel identifying problems with aircraft that have been gathered from Malfunction and Defect Reports. These problems are being studied at the time the Airworthiness Alert is issued but have not been fully evaluated by the time the material went to press.

Airworthiness Directive (AD note). A notice sent out by the FAA to the registered owner of an aircraft notifying him or her of an unsafe condition that has been found on the aircraft. Compliance with AD notes is mandatory.

Alclad. A registered trade name for clad aluminum alloy.

Alodine. The registered trade name for a popular conversion coating chemical used to produce a hard, airtight, oxide film on aluminum alloy for corrosion protection.

Alphanumeric symbols. Symbols made up of all of the letters in our alphabet, numerals, punctuation marks, and certain other special symbols.

Alternator. An electrical generator that produces alternating current. The popular DC alternator used on light aircraft produces three-phase AC in its stator windings. This AC is changed into DC by a six-diode, solid-state rectifier before it leaves the alternator.

Altimeter setting. The barometric pressure at a given location corrected to mean (average) sea level.

Altitude engine. A reciprocating engine whose rated sea-level takeoff power can be produced to an established higher altitude.

Alumel. An alloy of nickel, aluminum, manganese, and silicon that is the negative element in a thermocouple used to measure exhaust gas temperature.

Ambient pressure. The pressure of the air surrounding a person or an object.

Ambient temperature. The temperature of the air surrounding a person or an object.

American wire gauge. The system of measurement of wire size used in aircraft electrical systems.

Amphibian. An airplane with landing gear that allows it to operate from both water and land surfaces.

Amplifier. An electronic circuit in which a small change in voltage or current controls a much larger change in voltage or current.

Analog electronics. Electronics in which values change in a linear fashion. Output values vary in direct relationship to changes of input values.

Analog-type indicator. An electrical meter that indicates values by the amount a pointer moves across a graduated numerical scale.

Aneroid. The sensitive component in an altimeter or barometer that measures the absolute pressure of the air. The aneroid is a sealed, flat capsule made of thin corrugated disks of metal soldered together and evacuated by pumping all of the air out of it. Evacuating the aneroid allows it to expand or collapse as the air pressure on the outside changes.

Angle of attack. The acute angle formed between the chord line of an airfoil and the direction of the air that strikes the airfoil.

Angle of attack indicator. An instrument that measures the angle between the local airflow around the direction detector and the fuselage reference plane.

Angle of incidence. The acute angle formed between the chord line of an airfoil and the longitudinal axis of the aircraft on which it is mounted.

Annual rings. The rings that appear in the end of a log cut from a tree. The number of annual rings per inch gives an indication of the strength of the wood. The more rings there are and the closer they are together, the stronger the wood. The pattern of alternating light and dark rings is caused by the seasonal variations in the growth rate of the tree. A tree grows quickly in the spring and produces the light-colored, less dense rings. The slower growth during the summer, or latter part of the growing season, produces the dark-colored, denser rings.

Annunciator panel. A panel of warning lights in plain sight of the pilot. These lights are identified by the name of the system they represent and are usually covered with colored lenses to show the meaning of the condition they announce.

Anodizing. The electrolytic process in which a hard, airtight, oxide film is deposited on aluminum alloy for corrosion protection.

Antenna. A special device used with electronic communication and navigation systems to radiate and receive electromagnetic energy.

Anti-icer system. A system that prevents the formation of ice on an aircraft structure.

Anti-icing additive. A chemical added to the turbine-engine fuel used in some aircraft. This additive mixes with water that condenses from the fuel and lowers its freezing temperature so it will not freeze and block the fuel filters. It also acts as a biocidal agent and prevents the formation of microbial contamination in the tanks.

Antidrag wire. A structural wire inside a Pratt truss airplane wing between the spars. Antidrag wires run from the rear spar inboard, to the front spar at the next bay outboard. Antidrag wires oppose the forces that try to pull the wing forward.

Antiservo tab. A tab installed on the trailing edge of a stabilator to make it less sensitive. The tab automatically moves in the same direction as the stabilator to produce an aerodynamic force that tries to bring the surface back to a streamline position. This tab is also called an antibalance tab.

Antiskid brake system. An electrohydraulic system in an airplane's power brake system that senses the deceleration rate of every main landing gear wheel. If any wheel decelerates too rapidly, indicating an impending skid, pressure to that bake is released and the wheel stops decelerating. Pressure is then reapplied at a slightly lower value.

Antitear strip. Strips of aircraft fabric laid under the reinforcing tape before the fabric is stitched to an aircraft wing.

Arbor press. A press with either a mechanically or hydraulically operated ram used in a maintenance shop for a variety of pressing functions.

Arcing. Sparking between a commutator and brush or between switch contacts that is caused by induced current when a circuit is broken.

Area. The number of square units in a surface.

Aspect ratio. The ratio of the length, or span, of an airplane wing to its width, or chord. For a nonrectangular wing, the aspect ratio is found by dividing the square of the span of the wing by its area. Aspect Ratio = $span^2 \div area$.

Asymmetrical airfoil. An airfoil section that is not the same on both sides of the chord line.

Asymmetrical lift. A condition of uneven lift produced by the rotor when a helicopter is in forward flight. Asymmetrical lift is caused by the difference between the airspeed of the advancing blade and that of the retreating blade.

Attenuate. To weaken, or lessen the intensity of, an activity.

Attitude indicator. A gyroscopic flight instrument that gives the pilot an indication of the attitude of the aircraft relative to its pitch and roll axes. The attitude indicator in an autopilot is in the sensing system that detects deviation from a level-flight attitude.

Augmenter tube. A long, stainless steel tube around the discharge of the exhaust pipes of a reciprocating engine. Exhaust gases flow through the augmenter tube and produce a low pressure that pulls additional cooling air through the engine compartment. Heat may be taken from the augmenter tubes and directed through the leading edges of the wings for thermal anti-icing.

Autoclave. A pressure vessel inside of which air can be heated to a high temperature and pressure raised to a high value. Autoclaves are used in the composite manufacturing industry to apply heat and pressure for curing resins.

Autogiro. A heavier-than-air rotor-wing aircraft sustained in the air by rotors turned by aerodynamic forces rather than by engine power. When the name Autogiro is spelled with a capital A, it refers to a specific series of machines built by Juan de la Cierva or his successors.

Autoignition system. A system on a turbine engine that automatically energizes the igniters to provide a relight if the engine should flame out.

Automatic adjuster. A subsystem in an aircraft disk brake that compensates for disk or lining wear. Each time the brakes are applied, the automatic adjuster is reset for zero clearance, and when the brakes are released, the clearance between the disks or the disk and lining is returned to a preset value. A malfunctioning automatic adjuster in a multiple-disk brake can cause sluggish and jerky operation.

Automatic flight control system (AFCS). The full system of automatic flight control that includes the autopilot, flight director, horizontal situation indicator, air data sensors, and other avionics inputs.

Automatic pilot (autopilot). An automatic flight control device that controls an aircraft about one or more of its three axes. The primary purpose of an autopilot is to relieve the pilot of the control of the aircraft during long periods of flight. autorotation. Descent of a helicopter without the use of engine power. An aerodynamic force causes the rotors to rotate.

Autosyn system. A synchro system used in remote indicating instruments. The rotors in an Autosyn system are two-pole electromagnets, and the stators are delta-connected, three-phase, distributed-pole windings in the stator housings. The rotors in the transmitters and indicators are connected in parallel and are excited with 26-volt, 400-Hz AC. The rotor in the indicator follows the movement of the rotor in the transmitter.

Auxiliary power unit (APU). A small turbine or reciprocating engine that drives a generator, hydraulic pump, and air pump. The APU is installed in the aircraft and is used to supply electrical power, compressed air, and hydraulic pressure when the main engines are not running.

Aviation snips. Compound-action hand shears used for cutting sheet metal. Aviation snips come in sets of three. One pair cuts to the left, one pair cuts to the right, and the third pair of snips cuts straight.

Aviator's oxygen. Oxygen that has had almost all of the water and water vapor removed from it.

Avionics. The branch of technology that deals with the design, production, installation, use, and servicing of electronic equipment mounted in aircraft.

Azimuth. A horizontal angular distance, measured clockwise from a fixed reference direction to an object.

Back course. The reciprocal of the localizer course for an ILS (Instrument Landing System). When flying a back-course approach, the aircraft approaches the instrument runway from the end on which the localizer antennas are installed.

Backhand welding. Welding in which the torch is pointed away from the direction the weld is progressing.

Backplate (brake component). A floating plate on which the wheel cylinder and the brake shoes attach on an energizing-type brake.

Backup ring. A flat leather or Teflon ring installed in the groove in which an O-ring or T-seal is placed. The backup ring is on the side of the seal away from the pressure, and it prevents the pressure extruding the seal between the piston and the cylinder wall.

Balance cable. A cable in the aileron system of an airplane that connects to one side of each aileron. When the control wheel is rotated, a cable from the cockpit pulls one aileron down and relaxes the cable going to the other aileron. The balance cable pulls the other aileron up.

Balance panel. A flat panel hinged to the leading edge of some ailerons that produces a force which assists the pilot in holding the ailerons deflected. The balance panel divides a chamber ahead of the aileron in such a way that when the aileron is deflected downward, for example, air flowing over its top surface produces a low pressure that acts on the balance panel and causes it to apply an upward force to the aileron leading edge.

Balance tab. An adjustable tab mounted on the trailing edge of a control surface to produce a force that aids the pilot in moving the surface. The tab is automatically actuated in such a way it moves in the direction opposite to the direction the control surface on which it is mounted moves.

Balanced actuator. A linear hydraulic or pneumatic actuator that has the same area on each side of the piston.

Banana oil. Nitrocellulose dissolved in amyl acetate, so named because it smells like bananas.

Bank (verb). The act of rotating an aircraft about its longitudinal axis.

Barometric scale. A small window in the dial of a sensitive altimeter in which the pilot sets the barometric pressure level from which the altitude shown on the altimeter is measured. This window is sometimes called the "Kollsman" window. base. The electrode of a bipolar transistor between the emitter and the collector. Varying a small flow of electrons moving into or out of the base controls a much larger flow of electron between the emitter and the collector.

Base. The electrode of a bipolar transistor between the emitter and the collector. Varying a small flow of electrons moving into or out of the base controls a much larger flow of electrons between the emitter and the collector.

Bead (tire component). The high-strength carbon-steel wire bundles that give an aircraft tire its strength and stiffness where it mounts on the wheel.

Bead seat area. The flat surface on the inside of the rim of an aircraft wheel on which the bead of the tire seats.

Bearing strength (sheet metal characteristic). The amount of pull needed to cause a piece of sheet metal to tear at the points at which it is held together with rivets. The bearing strength of a material is affected by both its thickness and the diameter of the rivet.

Beehive spring. A hardened-steel, coil-spring retainer used to hold a rivet set in a pneumatic rivet gun. This spring gets its name from its shape. It screws onto the end of the rivet gun and allows the set to move back and forth, but prevents it being driven from the gun.

Bend allowance. The amount of material actually used to make a bend in a piece of sheet metal. Bend allowance depends upon the thickness of the metal and the radius of the bend, and is normally found in a bend allowance chart.

Bend radius. The radius of the inside of a bend.

Bend tangent line. A line made in a sheet metal layout that indicates the point at which the bend starts.

Bernoulli's principle. The basic principle that explains the relation between kinetic energy and potential energy in fluids that are in motion. When the total energy in a column of moving fluid remains constant, any increase in the kinetic energy of the fluid (its velocity) results in a corresponding decrease in its potential energy (its pressure).

Bezel. The rim that holds the glass cover in the case of an aircraft instrument.

Bias-cut surface tape. A fabric tape in which the threads run at an angle of 45° to the length of the tape. Bias-cut tape may be stretched around a compound curve such as a wing tip bow without wrinkling.

Bilge area. A low portion in an aircraft structure in which water and contaminants collect. The area under the cabin floorboards is normally called the bilge.

Bipolar transistor. A solid-state component in which the flow of current between its emitter and collector is controlled by a much smaller flow of current into or out of its base. Bipolar transistors may be of either the NPN or PNP type.

BITE. Built-in test equipment.

Blade track. The condition of a helicopter rotor in which each blade follows the exact same path as the blade ahead of it.

Black box. A term used for any portion of an electrical or electronic system that can be removed as a unit. A black box does not have to be a physical box.

Bladder-type fuel cell. A plastic-impregnated fabric bag supported in a portion of an aircraft structure so that it forms a cell in which fuel is carried.

Bleeder. A material such as glass cloth or mat that is placed over a composite lay-up to absorb the excess resin forced out of the ply fibers when pressure is applied.

Bleeding dope. Dope whose pigments are soluble in the solvents or thinners used in the finishing system. The color will bleed up through the finished coats.

Bleeding of brakes. The maintenance procedure of removing air entrapped in hydraulic fluid in the brakes. Fluid is bled from the brake system until fluid with no bubbles flows out.

Blimp. A cigar-shaped, nonrigid lighter-than-air flying machine.

Blush. A defect in a lacquer or dope finish caused by moisture condensing on the surface before the finish dries. If the humidity of the air is high, the evaporation of the solvents cools the air enough to cause the moisture to condense. The water condensed from the air mixes with the lacquer or dope and forms a dull, porous, chalky-looking finish called blush. A blushed finish is neither attractive nor protective.

Bonding. The process of electrically connecting all isolated components to the aircraft structure. Bonding provides a path for return current from electrical components, and a low-impedance path to ground to minimize static electrical charges. Shock-mounted components have bonding braids connected across the shock mounts.

Boost pump. An electrically driven centrifugal pump mounted in the bottom of the fuel tanks in large aircraft. Boost pumps provide a positive flow of fuel under pressure to the engine for starting and serve as an emergency backup in the event an engine-driven pump should fail. They are also used to transfer fuel from one tank to another and to pump fuel overboard when it is being dumped. Boost pumps prevent vapor locks by holding pressure on the fuel in the line to the engine-driven pump. Centrifugal boost pumps have a small agitator propeller on top of the impeller to force vapors from the fuel before it leaves the tank.

Boundary layer. The layer of air that flows next to an aerodynamic surface. Because of the design of the surface and local surface roughness, the boundary layer often has a random flow pattern, sometimes even flowing in a direction opposite to the direction of flight. A turbulent boundary layer causes a great deal of aerodynamic drag.

Bourdon tube. A pressure-indicating mechanism used in most oil pressure and hydraulic pressure gages. It consists of a sealed, curved tube with an elliptical cross section. Pressure inside the tube tries to straighten it, and as it straightens, it moves a pointer across a calibrated dial. Bourdon-tube pressure gauges are used to measure temperature by measuring the vapor pressure in a sealed container of a volatile liquid, such as methyl chloride, whose vapor pressure varies directly with its temperature.

Brazing. A method of thermally joining metal parts by wetting the surface with a molten nonferrous alloy. When the molten material cools and solidifies, it holds the pieces together. Brazing materials melt at a temperature higher than 800 °F, but lower than the melting temperature of the metal on which they are used.

British thermal unit (BTU). The amount of heat energy needed to raise the temperature of one pound of pure water 1 °F.

Bucking bar. A heavy steel bar with smooth, hardened surfaces, or faces. The bucking bar is held against the end of the rivet shank when it is driven with a pneumatic rivet gun, and the shop head is formed against the bucking bar.

Buffeting. Turbulent movement of the air over an aerodynamic surface.

Bulb angle. An L-shaped metal extrusion having an enlarged, rounded edge that resembles a bulb on one of its legs.

Bulkhead. A structural partition that divides the fuselage of an aircraft into compartments, or bays.

Bungee shock cord. A cushioning material used with the nonshock absorbing landing gears installed on older aircraft. Bungee cord is made up of many small rubber bands encased in a loose-woven cotton braid.

Burnish (verb). To smooth the surface of metal that has been damaged by a deep scratch or gouge. The metal piled up at the edge of the damage is pushed back into the damage with a smooth, hard steel burnishing tool.

Burr. A sharp rough edge of a piece of metal left when the metal was sheared, punched, or drilled.

Bus. A point within an electrical system from which the individual circuits get their power.

Buttock line. A line used to locate a position to the right or left of the center line of an aircraft structure.

Butyl. Trade name for a synthetic rubber product made by the polymerization of isobutylene. Butyl withstands such potent chemicals as phosphate ester-base (Skydrol) hydraulic fluids.

Cage (verb). To lock the gimbals of a gyroscopic instrument so it will not be damaged by abrupt flight maneuvers or rough handling.

Calendar month. A measurement of time used by the FAA for inspection and certification purposes. One calendar month from a given day extends from that day until midnight of the last day of that month.

Calender (fabric treatment). To pass fabric through a series of heated rollers to give it a smooth shiny surface.

Calibrated airspeed (CAS). Indicated airspeed corrected for position error. See position error.

Calorie. The amount of heat energy needed to raise the temperature of one gram of pure water 1 °C.

Canted rate gyro. A rate gyro whose gimbal axis is tilted so it can sense rotation of the aircraft about its roll axis as well as its yaw axis.

Camber (wheel alignment). The amount the wheels of an aircraft are tilted, or inclined, from the vertical. If the top of the wheel tilts outward, the camber is positive. If the top of the wheel tilts inward, the camber is negative.

Canard. A horizontal control surface mounted ahead of the wing to provide longitudinal stability and control.

Cantilever wing. A wing that is supported by its internal structure and requires no external supports. The wing spars are built in such a way that they carry all the bending and torsional loads.

Cap strip. The main top and bottom members of a wing rib. The cap strips give the rib its aerodynamic shape.

Capacitance-type fuel quantity measuring system. A popular type of electronic fuel quantity indicating system that has no moving parts in the fuel tank. The tank units are cylindrical capacitors, called probes, mounted across the tank, from top to bottom. The dielectric between the plates of the probes is either fuel or the air above the fuel, and the capacitance of the probe varies with the amount of fuel in the tank. The indicator is a servo-type instrument driven by the amplified output of a capacitance bridge.

Capillary tube. A soft copper tube with a small inside diameter. The capillary tube used with vapor-pressure thermometer connects the temperature sensing bulb to the Bourdon tube. The capillary tube is protected from physical damage by enclosing it in a braided metal wire jacket.

Carbon monoxide detector. A packet of chemical crystals mounted in the aircraft cockpit or cabin where they are easily visible. The crystals change their color from yellow to green when they are exposed to carbon monoxide.

Carbon-pile voltage regulator. A type of voltage regulator used with high-output DC generators. Field current is controlled by varying the resistance of a stack of thin carbon disks. This resistance is varied by controlling the amount the stack is compressed by a spring whose force is opposed by the pull of an electromagnet. The electromagnet's strength is proportional to the generator's output voltage.

Carburizing flame. An oxyacetylene flame produced by an excess of acetylene. This flame is identified by a feather around the inner cone. A carburizing flame is also called a reducing flame.

Carcass (tire component). The layers of rubberized fabric that make up the body of an aircraft tire.

Case pressure. A low pressure that is maintained inside the case of a hydraulic pump. If a seal becomes damaged, hydraulic fluid will be forced out of the pump rather than allowing air to be drawn into the pump.

Cathode-ray tube (CRT). A display tube used for oscilloscopes and computer video displays. An electron gun emits a stream of electrons that is attracted to a positively charged inner surface of the face of the tube. Acceleration and focusing grids speed the movement of the electrons and shape the beam into a pinpoint size. Electrostatic or electromagnetic forces caused by deflection plates or coils move the beam over the face of the tube. The inside surface of the face of the tube is treated with a phosphor material that emits light when the beam of electrons strikes it.

Cavitation. A condition that exist in a hydraulic pump when there is not enough pressure in the reservoir to force fluid to the inlet of the pump. The pump picks up air instead of fluid.

CDI. Course deviation indicator.

CDU. Control display unit.

Center of gravity. The location on an aircraft about which the force of gravity is concentrated.

Center of lift. The location of the chord line of an airfoil at which all the lift forces produced by the airfoil are considered to be concentrated.

Center of pressure. The point on the chord line of an airfoil where all of the aerodynamic forces are considered to be concentrated.

Centering cam. A cam in the nose-gear shock strut that causes the piston to center when the strut fully extends. When the aircraft takes off and the strut extends, the wheel is straightened in its fore-and-aft position so it can be retracted into the wheel well.

Charging stand (air conditioning service equipment). A handy and compact arrangement of air conditioning servicing equipment. A charging stand contains a vacuum pump, a manifold gauge set, and a method of measuring and dispensing the refrigerant.

Chatter. A type of rapid vibration of a hydraulic pump caused by the pump taking in some air along with the hydraulic fluid.

Check (wood defect). Longitudinal cracks that extend across a log's annual rings.

Check valve. A hydraulic or pneumatic system component that allows full flow of fluid in one direction but blocks all flow in the opposite direction.

Chemical oxygen candle system. An oxygen system used for emergency or backup use. Solid blocks of material that release oxygen when they are burned are carried in special fireproof fixtures. When oxygen is needed, the candles are ignited with an integral igniter, and oxygen flows into the tubing leading to the masks.

Chevron seal. A form of one-way seal used in some fluid-power actuators. A chevron seal is made of a resilient material whose cross section is in the shape of the letter V. The pressure being sealed must be applied to the open side of the V.

Chromel. An alloy of nickel and chromium used as the positive element in a thermocouple for measuring exhaust gas temperature.

Circle. A closed plane figure with every point an equal distance from the center. A circle has the greatest area for its circumference of any enclosed shape.

Circuit breaker. An electrical component that automatically opens a circuit any time excessive current flows through it. A circuit breaker may be reset to restore the circuit after the fault causing the excessive current has been corrected.

Clad aluminum. A sheet of aluminum alloy that has a coating of pure aluminum rolled on one or both of its surfaces for corrosion protection.

Clamp-on ammeter. An electrical instrument used to measure current without opening the circuit through which it is flowing. The jaws of the ammeter are opened, slipped over the current-carrying wire, and then clamped shut. Current flowing through the wire produces a magnetic field which induces a voltage in the ammeter that is proportional to the amount of current.

Cleco fastener. A patented spring-type fastener used to hold metal sheets in position until they can be permanently riveted together.

Close-quarter iron. A small hand-held iron with an accurately calibrated thermostat. This iron is used for heat-shrinking polyester fabrics in areas that would be difficult to work with a large iron.

Closed angle. An angle formed in sheet metal that has been bent more than 90°.

Closed assembly time. The time elapsing between the assembly of glued joints and the application of pressure.

Closed-center hydraulic system. A hydraulic system in which the selector valves are installed in parallel with each other. When no unit is actuated, fluid circulates from the pump back to the reservoir without flowing through any of the selector valves.

Closed-center selector valve. A type of flow-control valve used to direct pressurized fluid into one side of an actuator, and at the same time, direct the return fluid from the other side of the actuator to the fluid reservoir. Closed-center selector valves are connected in parallel between the pressure manifold and the return manifold.

Coaxial. Rotating about the same axis. Coaxial rotors of a helicopter are mounted on concentric shafts in such a way that they turn in opposite directions to cancel torque.

Coaxial cable. A special type of electrical cable that consists of a central conductor held rigidly in the center of a braided outer conductor. Coaxial cable, commonly called coax, is used for attaching radio receivers and transmitters to their antenna.

Coefficient of drag. A dimensionless number used in the formula for determining induced drag as it relates to the angle of attack.

Coefficient of lift. A dimensionless number relating to the angle of attack used in the formula for determining aerodynamic lift.

Coin dimpling. A process of preparing a hole in sheet metal for flush riveting. A coining die is pressed into the rivet hole to form a sharp-edged depression into which the rivet head fits.

Collective pitch control. The helicopter control that changes the pitch of all of the rotor blades at the same time. Movement of the collective pitch control increases or decreases the lift produced by the entire rotor disk.

Collodion. Cellulose nitrate used as a film base for certain aircraft dopes.

Combustion heater. A type of cabin heater used in some aircraft. Gasoline from the aircraft fuel tanks is burned in the heater.

Compass fluid. A highly refined, water-clear petroleum product similar to kerosene. Compass fluid is used to dampen the oscillations of magnetic compasses.

Compass rose. A location on an airport where an aircraft can be taken to have its compasses "swung." Lines are painted on the rose to mark the magnetic directions in 30° increments.

Compass swinging. A maintenance procedure that minimizes deviation error in a magnetic compass. The aircraft is aligned on a compass rose, and the compensating magnets in the compass case are adjusted so the compass card indicates the direction marked on the rose. After the deviation error is minimized on all headings, a compass correction card is completed and mounted on the instrument panel next to the compass.

Compensated fuel pump. A vane-type, engine-driven fuel pump that has a diaphragm connected to the pressure regulating valve. The chamber above the diaphragm is vented to the carburetor upper deck where it senses the pressure of the air as it enters the engine. The diaphragm allows the fuel pump to compensate for altitude changes and keeps the carburetor inlet fuel pressure a constant amount higher than the carburetor inlet air pressure.

Compensator port (brake system component). A small hole between a hydraulic brake master cylinder and the reservoir. When the brakes are released, this port is uncovered and the fluid in the master cylinder is vented to the reservoir. When the brake is applied, the master-cylinder piston covers the compensator port and allows pressure in the line to the brake to build up and apply the brakes. When the brake is released, the piston uncovers the compensator port. If any fluid has been lost from the brake, the reservoir will refill the master cylinder. A restricted compensator port will cause the brakes to drag or will cause them to be slow to release.

Composite. Something made up of different materials combined in such a way that the characteristics of the resulting material are different from those of any of the components.

Compound curve. A curve formed in more than one plane. The surface of a sphere is a compound curve.

Compound gauge (air conditioning servicing equipment). A pressure gauge used to measure the pressure in the low side of an air conditioning system. A compound gauge is calibrated from zero to 30 inches of mercury vacuum, and from zero to about 150-psi positive gauge pressure.

Compressibility effect. The sudden increase in the total drag of an airfoil in transonic flight caused by formation of shock waves on the surface.

Compression failure. A type of structural failure in wood caused by the application of too great a compressive load. A compression failure shows up as a faint line running at right angles to the grain of the wood.

Compression strut. A heavy structural member, often in the form of a steel tube, used to hold the spars of a Pratt truss airplane wing apart. A compression strut opposes the compressive loads between the spars arising from the tensile loads produced by the drag and antidrug wires.

Compression wood. A defect in wood that causes it to have a high specific gravity and the appearance of an excessive growth of summerwood. In most species, there is little difference between the color of the springwood and the summerwood. Any material containing compression wood is unsuited for aircraft structural use and must be rejected.

Compressor (air conditioning system component). The component in a vapor-cycle cooling system in which the low-pressure refrigerant vapors, after they leave the evaporator, are compressed to increase both their temperature and pressure before they pass into the condenser. Some compressors are driven by electric motors, others by hydraulic motors and, in the case of most light airplanes, are belt driven from the engine.

Concave surface. A surface that is curved inward. The outer edges are higher than the center.

Condenser (air conditioning system component). The component in a vapor-cycle cooling system in which the heat taken from the aircraft cabin is given up to the ambient air outside the aircraft.

Conductor (electrical). A material that allows electrons to move freely from one atom to another within the material.

Coning angle. The angle formed between the plane of rotation of a helicopter rotor blade when it is producing lift and a line perpendicular to the rotor shaft. The degree of the coning angle is determined by the relationship between the centrifugal force acting on the blades and the aerodynamic lift produced by the blades.

Constant (mathematical). A value used in a mathematical computation that is the same every time it is used. For example, the relationship between the length of the circumference of a circle and the length of its diameter is a constant, 3.1416. This constant is called by the Greek name of Pi (π).

Constant differential mode (cabin pressurization). The mode of pressurization in which the cabin pressure is maintained a constant amount higher than the outside air pressure. The maximum differential pressure is determined by the structural strength of the aircraft cabin.

Constant-displacement pump. A fluid pump that moves a specific volume of fluid each time it rotates; the faster the pump turns, the more fluid it moves. Some form of pressure regulator or relief valve must be used with a constant-displacement pump when it is driven by an aircraft engine.

Constant-speed drive (CSD). A special drive system used to connect an alternating current generator to an aircraft engine. The drive holds the generator speed (and thus its frequency) constant as the engine speed varies.

Constantan. A copper-nickel alloy used as the negative lead of a thermocouple for measuring the cylinder head temperature of a reciprocating engine.

Contactor (electrical component). A remotely actuated, heavy-duty electrical switch. Contactors are used in an aircraft electrical system to connect the battery to the main bus.

Continuity tester. A troubleshooting tool that consists of a battery, a light bulb, and test leads. The test leads are connected to each end of the conductor under test, and if the bulb lights up, there is continuity. If it does not light up, the conductor is open.

Continuous Airworthiness Inspection Program. An inspection program that is part of a continuous airworthiness maintenance program approved for certain large airplanes (to which 14 CFR Part 125 is not applicable), turbojet multi-engine airplanes, turbopropeller-powered multi-engine airplanes, and turbine-powered rotorcraft.

Continuous-duty solenoid. A solenoid-type switch designed to be kept energized by current flowing through its coil for an indefinite period of time. The battery contactor in an aircraft electrical system is a continuous-duty solenoid. Current flows through its coil all the time the battery is connected to the electrical system.

Continuous-flow oxygen system. A type of oxygen system that allows a metered amount of oxygen to continuously flow into the mask. A rebreather-type mask is used with a continuous-flow system. The simplest form of continuous-flow oxygen system regulates the flow by a calibrated orifice in the outlet to the mask, but most systems use either a manual or automatic regulator to vary the pressure across the orifice proportional to the altitude being flown.

Continuous-loop fire-detection system. A fire-detection system that uses a continuous loop of two conductors separated with a thermistor-type insulation. Under normal temperature conditions, the thermistor material is an insulator; but if it is exposed to a fire, the thermistor changes into a conductor and completes the circuit between the two conductors, initiating a fire warning.

Control horn. The arm on a control surface to which the control cable or push-pull rod attaches to move the surface.

Control stick. The type of control device used in some airplanes. A vertical stick in the flight deck controls the ailerons by side-to-side movement and the elevators by fore-and-aft movement.

Control yoke. The movable column on which an airplane control wheel is mounted. The yoke may be moved in or out to actuate the elevators, and the control wheel may be rotated to actuate the ailerons.

Controllability. The characteristic of an aircraft that allows it to change its flight attitude in response to the pilot's movement of the flight deck controls.

Conventional current. An imaginary flow of electricity that is said to flow from the positive terminal of a power source, through the external circuit to its negative terminal. The arrowheads in semiconductor symbols point in the direction of conventional current flow.

Converging duct. A duct, or passage, whose cross-sectional area decreases in the direction of fluid flow.

Conversion coating. A chemical solution used to form an airtight oxide or phosphate film on the surface of aluminum or magnesium parts. The conversion coating prevents air from reaching the metal and keeps it from corroding.

Convex surface. A surface that is curved outward. The outer edges are lower than the center.

Coriolis effect. The change in rotor blade velocity to compensate for a change in the distance between the center of mass of the rotor blade and the axis rotation of the blade as the blades flap in flight.

Cornice brake. A large shop tool used to make straight bends across a sheet of metal. Cornice brakes are often called leaf brakes.

Corrugated metal. Sheets of metal that have been made more rigid by forming a series of parallel ridges or waves in its surface.

Cotter pin. A split metal pin used to safety a castellated or slotted nut on a bolt. The pin is passed through the hole in the shank of the bolt and the slots in the nut, and the ends of the pin are spread to prevent it backing out of the hole.

Countersinking. Preparation of a rivet hole for a flush rivet by beveling the edges of the holes with a cutter of the correct angle.

Coverite surface thermometer. A small surface-type bimetallic thermometer that calibrates the temperature of an iron used to heat-shrink polyester fabrics.

Crabbing. Pointing the nose of an aircraft into the wind to compensate for wind drift.

Crazing. A form of stress-caused damage that occurs in a transparent thermoplastic material. Crazing appears as a series of tiny, hair-like cracks just below the surface of the plastic.

Critical Mach number. The flight Mach number at which there is the first indication of supersonic airflow over any part of the aircraft structure.

Cross coat. A double coat of aircraft finishing material in which the second coat is sprayed at right angles to the first coat, before the solvents have evaporated from the first coat.

Cross-feed valve (fuel system component). A valve in a fuel system that allows any of the engines of a multi-engine aircraft to draw fuel from any fuel tank. Cross-feed systems are used to allow a multi-engine aircraft to maintain a balanced fuel condition.

Cross-flow valve. An automatic flow-control valve installed between the gear-up and gear-down lines of the landing gear of some large airplanes. When the landing gear is released from its uplocks, its weight causes it to fall faster than the hydraulic system can supply fluid to the gear-down side of the actuation cylinder. The cross-flow valve opens and directs fluid from the gear-up side into the gear-down side. This allows the gear to move down with a smooth motion.

CRT. Cathode-ray tube.

Cryogenic liquid. A liquid which boils at temperatures of less than about 110 °F (–163 °C) at normal atmospheric pressures.

Cuno filter. The registered trade name for a particular style of edge-type fluid filter. Cuno filters are made up of a stack of thin metal disks that are separated by thin scraper blades. Contaminants collect on the edge of the disks, and they are periodically scraped out and allowed to collect in the bottom of the filter case for future removal.

Current. A general term used for electrical flow. See conventional current.

Current limiter. An electrical component used to limit the amount of current a generator can produce. Some current limiters are a type of slow-blow fuse in the generator output. Other current limiters reduce the generator output voltage if the generator tries to put out more than its rated current.

Cusp. A pointed end.

Cyclic pitch control. The helicopter control that allows the pilot to change the pitch of the rotor blades individually, at a specific point in their rotation. The cyclic pitch control allows the pilot to tilt the plane of rotation of the rotor disk to change the direction of lift produced by the rotor.

Dacron. The registered trade name for a cloth woven from polyester fibers.

Damped oscillation. Oscillation whose amplitude decreases with time.

Database. A body of information that is available on any particular subject.

Data bus. A wire or group of wires that are used to move data within a computer system.

Debooster valve. A valve in a power brake system between the power brake control valve and the wheel cylinder. This valve lowers the pressure of the fluid going to the brake and increases its volume. A debooster valve increases the smoothness of brake application and aids in rapid release of the brakes.

Decay. The breakdown of the structure of wood fibers. Wood that shows any indication of decay must be rejected for use in aircraft structure.

Decomposition. The breakdown of the structure of wood fibers. Wood that shows any indication of decay must be rejected for use in aircraft structure.

Deciduous. A type of tree that sheds its foliage at the end of the growing season. Hardwoods come from deciduous trees.

Dedicated computer. A small digital computer, often built into an instrument or control device that contains a built-in program that causes it to perform a specific function.

Deep-vacuum pump. A vacuum pump capable of removing almost all of the air from a refrigeration system. A deep-vacuum pump can reduce the pressure inside the system to a few microns of pressure.

Deflator cap. A cap for a tire, strut, or accumulator air valve that, when screwed onto the valve, depresses the valve stem and allows the air to escape safely through a hole in the side of the cap.

Deicer system. A system that removes ice after it has formed on an aircraft.

Delamination. The separation of the layers of a laminated material.

Delivery air duct check valve. An isolation valve at the discharge side of the air turbine that prevents the loss of pressurization through a disengaged cabin air compressor.

Delta airplane. An airplane with a triangular-shaped wing. This wing has an extreme amount of sweepback on its leading edge, and a trailing edge that is almost perpendicular to the longitudinal axis of the airplane.

Delta connection (electrical connection). A method of connecting three electrical coils into a ring or, as they are drawn on a schematic diagram as a triangle, a delta (D).

Denier. A measure of the fineness of the yarns in a fabric.

Density altitude. The altitude in standard air at which the density is the same as that of the existing air.

Density ratio (σ). The ratio of the density of the air at a given altitude to the density of the air at sea level under standard conditions.

Derated (electrical specification). Reduction in the rated voltage or current of an electrical component. Derating is done to extend the life or reliability of the device.

Desiccant (air conditioning component). A drying agent used in an air conditioning system to remove water from the refrigerant. A desiccant is made of silica-gel or some similar material.

Detent. A spring-loaded pin or tab that enters a hole or groove when the device to which it is attached is in a certain position. Detents are used on a fuel valve to provide a positive means of identifying the fully on and fully off position of the valve.

Detonation. An explosion, or uncontrolled burning of the fuel-air mixture inside the cylinder of a reciprocating engine. Detonation occurs when the pressure and the temperature inside the cylinder become higher than the critical pressure and temperature of the fuel. Detonation is often confused with preignition.

Deviation error. An error in a magnetic compass caused by localized magnetic fields in the aircraft. Deviation error, which is different on each heading, is compensated by the technician "swinging" the compass. A compass must be compensated so the deviation error on any heading is no greater than 10 degrees.

Dewar bottle. A vessel designed to hold liquefied gases. It has double walls with the space between being evacuated to prevent the transfer of heat. The surfaces in the vacuum area are made heat-reflective.

Differential aileron travel. Aileron movement in which the upward-moving aileron deflects a greater distance than the one moving downward. The up aileron produces parasite drag to counteract the induced drag caused by the down aileron. Differential aileron travel is used to counteract adverse yaw.

Differential pressure. The difference between two pressures. An airspeed indicator is a differential-pressure gauge. It measures the difference between static air pressure and pitot air pressure.

Differential-voltage reverse-current cutout. A type of reverse-current cutout switch used with heavy-duty electrical systems. This switch connects the generator to the electrical bus when the generator voltage is a specific amount higher than the battery voltage.

Digital multimeter. An electrical test instrument that can be used to measure voltage, current, and resistance. The indication is in the form of a liquid crystal display in discrete numbers.

Dihedral. The positive angle formed between the lateral axis of an airplane and a line that passes through the center of the wing or horizontal stabilizer. Dihedral increases the lateral stability of an airplane.

Diluter-demand oxygen system. A popular type of oxygen system in which the oxygen is metered to the mask, where it is diluted with cabin air by an airflow-metering aneroid assembly which regulates the amount of air allowed to dilute the oxygen on the basis of cabin altitude. The mixture of oxygen and air flows only when the wearer of the mask inhales. The percentage of oxygen in the air delivered to the mask is regulated, on the basis of altitude, by the regulator. A diluter-demand regulator has an emergency position which allows 100 percent oxygen to flow to the mask, by-passing the regulating mechanism.

Dipole antenna. A half wavelength, center-fed radio antenna. The length of each of the two arms is approximately one fourth of the wavelength of the center frequency for which the antenna is designed.

Dirigible. A large, cigar-shaped, rigid, lighter-than-air flying machine. Dirigibles are made of a rigid truss structure covered with fabric. Gas bags inside the structure contain the lifting gas, which is either helium or hydrogen.

Disc area (helicopter specification). The total area swept by the blades of a helicopter main rotor.

Divergent oscillation. Oscillation whose amplitude increases with time.

Diverging duct. A duct, or passage, whose cross-sectional area increases in the direction of fluid flow.

DME. Distance measuring equipment.

Dope proofing. The treatment of a structure to be covered with fabric to keep the solvents in the dope from softening the protective coating on the structure.

Dope roping. A condition of aircraft dope brushed onto a surface in such a way that it forms a stringy, uneven surface rather than flowing out smoothly.

Double-acting actuator (hydraulic system component). A linear actuator moved in both directions by fluid power.

Double-acting hand pump (hydraulic system component). A hand-operated fluid pump that moves fluid during both strokes of the pump handle.

Doubler. A piece of sheet metal used to strengthen and stiffen a repair in a sheet metal structure.

Downtime. Any time during which an aircraft is out of commission and unable to be operated.

Downwash. Air forced down by aerodynamic action below and behind the wing of an airplane or the rotor of a helicopter. Aerodynamic lift is produced when the air is deflected downward. The upward force on the aircraft is the same as the downward force on the air.

Drag (helicopter rotor blade movement). Fore-and-aft movement of the tip of a helicopter rotor blade in its plane of rotation.

Dragging brakes. Brakes that do not fully release when the brake pedal is released. The brakes are partially applied all the time, which causes excessive lining wear and heat.

Drag wire. A structural wire inside a Pratt truss airplane wing between the spars. Drag wires run from the front spar inboard, to the rear spar at the next bay outboard. Drag wires oppose the forces that try to drag the wing backward.

Drill motor. An electric or pneumatic motor that drives a chuck that holds a twist drill. The best drill motors produce high torque, and their speed can be controlled.

Drip stick. A fuel quantity indicator used to measure the fuel level in the tank when the aircraft is on the ground. The drip stick is pulled down from the bottom of the tank until fuel drips from its opened end. This indicates that the top of the gauge inside the tank is at the level of the fuel. Note the number of inches read on the outside of the gauge at the point it contacts the bottom of the tank, and use a drip stick table to convert this measurement into gallons of fuel in the tank.

Dry air pump. An engine-driven air pump which used carbon vanes. Dry pumps do not use any lubrication, and the vanes are extremely susceptible to damage from the solid airborne particles. These pumps must be operated with filters in their inlet so they will take in only filtered air.

Dry ice. Solidified carbon dioxide. Dry ice sublimates, or changes from a solid directly into a gas, at a temperature of $-110\ °F\ (-78.5\ °C)$.

Dry rot. Decomposition of wood fibers caused by fungi. Dry rot destroys all strength in the wood.

Ductility. The property of a material that allows it to be drawn into a thin section without breaking.

Dummy load (electrical load). A noninductive, high-power, 50-ohm resistor that can be connected to a transmission line in place of the antenna. The transmitter can be operated into the dummy load without transmitting any signal.

Duralumin. The name for the original alloy of aluminum, magnesium, manganese, and copper. Duralumin is the same as the modern 2017 aluminum alloy.

Dutch roll. An undesirable, low-amplitude coupled oscillation about both the yaw and roll axes that affects many swept wing airplanes. Dutch roll is minimized by the use of a yaw damper.

Dutchman shears. A common name for compound-action sheet metal shears.

Dynamic pressure (q). The pressure a moving fluid would have if it were stopped. Dynamic pressure is measured in pounds per square foot.

Dynamic stability. The stability that causes an aircraft to return to a condition of straight and level flight after it has been disturbed from this condition. When an aircraft is disturbed from the straight and level flight, its static stability starts it back in the correct direction; but it overshoots, and the corrective forces are applied in the opposite direction. The aircraft oscillates back and forth on both sides of the correct condition, with each oscillation smaller than the one before it. Dynamic stability is the decreasing of these restorative oscillations.

EADI. Electronic Attitude Director Indicator.

ECAM. Electronic Centralized Aircraft Monitor.

Eccentric brushing. A special bushing used between the rear spar of certain cantilever airplane wings and the wing attachment fitting on the fuselage. The portion of the bushing that fits through the hole in the spar is slightly offset from that which passes through the holes in the fitting. By rotating the bushing, the rear spar may be moved up or down to adjust the root incidence of the wing.

Eddy current damping (electrical instrument damping). Decreasing the amplitude of oscillations by the interaction of magnetic fields. In the case of a vertical-card magnetic compass, flux from the oscillating permanent magnet produces eddy currents in a damping disk or cup. The magnetic flux produced by the eddy currents opposes the flux from the permanent magnet and decreases the oscillations.

Edge distance. The distance between the center of a rivet hole and the edge of the sheet of metal.

EFIS. Electronic Flight Instrument System.

EHSI. Electronic Horizontal Situation Indicator.

EICAS. Engine Indicating and Crew Alerting System.

Ejector. A form of jet pump used to pick up a liquid and move it to another location. Ejectors are used to ensure that the compartment in which the boost pumps are mounted is kept full of fuel. Part of the fuel from the boost pump flowing through the ejector produces a low pressure that pulls fuel from the main tank and forces it into the boostpump sump area.

Elastic limit. The maximum amount of tensile load, in pounds per square inch, a material is able to withstand without being permanently deformed.

Electromotive force (EMF). The force that causes electrons to move from one atom to another within an electrical circuit. Electromotive force is an electrical pressure, and it is measured in volts.

Electron current. The actual flow of electrons in a circuit. Electrons flow from the negative terminal of a power source through the external circuit to its positive terminal. The arrowheads in semiconductor symbols point in the direction opposite to the flow of electron current.

ELT (emergency locator transmitter). A self-contained radio transmitter that automatically begins transmitting on the emergency frequencies any time it is triggered by a severe impact parallel to the longitudinal axis of the aircraft.

Elevator downspring. A spring in the elevator control system that produces a mechanical force that tries to lower the elevator. In normal flight, this spring force is overcome by the aerodynamic force from the elevator trim tab. But in slow flight with an aft CG position, the trim tab loses its effectiveness and the downspring lowers the nose to prevent a stall.

Elevons. Movable control surfaces on the trailing edge of a delta wing or a flying wing airplane. These surfaces operate together to serve as elevators, and differentially to act as ailerons.

EMI. Electromagnetic interference.

Empennage. The tail section of an airplane.

Enamel. A type of finishing material that flows out to form a smooth surface. Enamel is usually made of a pigment suspended in some form of resin. When the resin cures, it leaves a smooth, glossy protective surface.

Energizing brake. A brake that uses the momentum of the aircraft to increase its effectiveness by wedging the shoe against the brake drum. Energizing brakes are also called servo brakes. A single-servo brake is energizing only when moving in the forward direction, and a duo-servo brake is energizing when the aircraft is moving either forward or backward.

Epoxy. A flexible, thermosetting resin that is made by polymerization of an epoxide. Epoxy has wide application as a matrix for composite materials and as an adhesive that bonds many different types of materials. It is noted for its durability and its chemical resistance.

Equalizing resistor. A large resistor in the ground circuit of a heavy-duty aircraft generator through which all of the generator output current flows. The voltage drop across this resistor is used to produce the current in the paralleling circuit that forces the generators to share the electrical load equally.

Ethylene dibromide. A chemical compound added to aviation gasoline to convert some of the deposits left by the tetraethyl lead into lead bromides. These bromides are volatile and will pass out of the engine with the exhaust gases.

Ethylene glycol. A form of alcohol used as a coolant for liquid-cooled engines and as an anti-icing agent.

Eutectic material. An alloy or solution that has the lowest possible melting point.

Evacuation (air conditioning servicing procedure). A procedure in servicing vapor-cycle cooling systems. A vacuum pump removes all the air from the system. Evacuation removes all traces of water vapor that could condense out, freeze, and block the system.

Evaporator (air conditioning component). The component in a vapor-cycle cooling system in which heat from the aircraft cabin is absorbed into the refrigerant. As the heat is absorbed, the refrigerant evaporates, or changes from a liquid into a vapor. The function of the evaporator is to lower the cabin air temperature.

Expander-tube brake. A brake that uses hydraulic fluid inside a synthetic rubber tube around the brake hub to force rectangular blocks of brake-lining material against the rotating brake drum. Friction between the brake drum and the lining material slows the aircraft.

Expansion wave. The change in pressure and velocity of a supersonic flow of air as it passes over a surface which drops away from the flow. As the surface drops away, the air tries to follow it. In changing its direction, the air speeds up to a higher supersonic velocity and its static pressure decreases. There is no change in the total energy as the air passes through an expansion wave, and so there is no sound as there is when air passes through a shock wave.

Extruded angle. A structural angle formed by passing metal heated to its plastic state through specially shaped dies.

FAA Form 337. The FAA form that must be filled in and submitted to the FAA when a major repair or major alteration has been completed.

Federal Aviation Administration Flight Standards District Office (FAA FSDO). An FAA field office serving an assigned geographical area staffed with Flight Standards personnel who serve the aviation industry and the general public on matters relating to certification and operation of air carrier and general aviation aircraft.

Fading of brakes. The decrease in the amount of braking action that occurs with some types of brakes that are applied for a long period of time. True fading occurs with overheated drum-type brakes. As the drum is heated, it expands in a bell-mouthed fashion. This decreases the amount of drum in contact with the brake shoes and decreases the braking action. A condition similar to brake fading occurs when there is an internal leak in the brake master cylinder. The brakes are applied, but as the pedal is held down, fluid leaks past the piston, and the brakes slowly release.

Fairing. A part of a structure whose primary purpose is to produce a smooth surface or a smooth junction where two surfaces join.

Fairlead. A plastic or wooden guide used to prevent a steel control cable rubbing against an aircraft structure.

FCC. Federal Communications Commission.

FCC. Flight Control Computer.

Feather (helicopter rotor blade movement). Rotation of a helicopter rotor blade about its pitch-change axis.

Ferrous metal. Any metal that contains iron and has magnetic characteristics.

Fiber stop nut. A form of a self-locking nut that has a fiber insert crimped into a recess above the threads. The hole in the insert is slightly smaller than the minor diameter of the threads. When the nut is screwed down over the bolt threads, the opposition caused by the fiber insert produces a force that prevents vibration loosening the nut.

File. A hand-held cutting tool used to remove a small amount of metal with each stroke.

Fill threads. Threads in a piece of fabric that run across the width of the fabric, interweaving with the warp threads. Fill threads are often called woof, or weft, threads.

Fillet. A fairing used to give shape but not strength to an object. A fillet produces a smooth junction where two surfaces meet.

Finishing tape. Another name for surface tape. See surface tape.

Fishmouth splice. A type of splice used in a welded tubular structure in which the end of the tube whose inside diameter is the same as the outside diameter of the tube being spliced is cut in the shape of a V, or a fishmouth, and is slipped over the smaller tube welded. A fishmouth splice has more weld area than a butt splice and allows the stresses from one tube to transfer into the other tube gradually.

Fire pull handle. The handle in an aircraft flight deck that is pulled at the first indication of an engine fire. Pulling this handle removes the generator from the electrical system, shuts off the fuel and hydraulic fluid to the engine, and closes the compressor bleed air valve. The fire extinguisher agent discharge switch is uncovered, but it is not automatically closed.

Fire zone. A portion of an aircraft designated by the manufacturer to require fire-detection and/or fire-extinguishing equipment and a high degree of inherent fire resistance.

Fitting. An attachment device that is used to connect components to an aircraft structure.

Fixed fire-extinguishing system. A fire-extinguishing system installed in an aircraft.

Flameout. A condition in the operation of a gas turbine engine in which the fire in the engine unintentionally goes out.

Flap (aircraft control). A secondary control on an airplane wing that changes its camber to increase both its lift and its drag.

Flap (helicopter rotor blade movement). Up-and-down movement of the tip of a helicopter rotor blade.

Flap overload valve. A valve in the flap system of an airplane that prevents the flaps being lowered at an airspeed which could cause structural damage. If the pilot tries to extend the flaps when the airspeed is too high, the opposition caused by the air flow will open the overload valve and return the fluid to the reservoir.

Flash point. The temperature to which a material must be raised for it to ignite, but not continue to burn, when a flame is passed above it.

Flat pattern layout. The pattern for a sheet metal part that has the material used for each flat surface, and for all of the bends, marked out with bend-tangent lines drawn between the flats and bend allowances.

Flight controller. The component in an autopilot system that allows the pilot to maneuver the aircraft manually when the autopilot is engaged.

Fluid. A form of material whose molecules are able to flow past one another without destroying the material. Gases and liquids are both fluids.

Fluid power. The transmission of force by the movement of a fluid. The most familiar examples of fluid power systems are hydraulic and pneumatic systems.

Flutter. Rapid and uncontrolled oscillation of a flight control surface on an aircraft that is caused by a dynamically unbalanced condition.

Fly-by-wire. A method of control used by some modern aircraft in which control movement or pressures exerted by the pilot are directed into a digital computer where they are input into a program tailored to the flight characteristics of the aircraft. The computer output signal is sent to actuators at the control surfaces to move them the optimum amount for the desired maneuver.

Flying boat. An airplane whose fuselage is built in the form of a boat hull to allow it to land and takeoff from water. In the past, flying boats were a popular form of large airplane.

Flying wing. A type of heavier-than-air aircraft that has no fuselage or separate tail surfaces. The engines and useful load are carried inside the wing, and movable control surfaces on the trailing edge provide both pitch and roll control.

Foot-pound. A measure of work accomplished when a force of 1 pound moves an object a distance of 1 foot.

Force. Energy brought to bear on an object that tends to cause motion or to change motion.

Forehand welding. Welding in which the torch is pointed in the direction the weld is progressing.

Form drag. Parasite drag caused by the form of the object passing through the air.

Former. An aircraft structural member used to give a fuselage its shape.

FMC. Flight Management Computer.

Forward bias. A condition of operation of a semiconductor device such as a diode or transistor in which a positive voltage is connected to the P-type material and a negative voltage to the N-type material.

FPD. Freezing point depressant.

Fractional distillation. A method of separating the various components from a physical mixture of liquids. The material to be separated is put into a container and its temperature is increased. The components having the lowest boiling points boil off first and are condensed. Then, as the temperature is further raised, other components are removed. Kerosene, gasoline, and other petroleum products are obtained by fractional distillation of crude oil.

Frangible. Breakable, or easily broken.

Freon. The registered trade name for a refrigerant used in a vapor-cycle air conditioning system.

Frise aileron. An aileron with its hinge line set back from the leading edge so that when it is deflected upward, part of the leading edge projects below the wing and produces parasite drag to help overcome adverse yaw.

Full-bodied. Not thinned.

Fully articulated rotor. A helicopter rotor whose blades are attached to the hub in such a way that they are free to flap, drag, and feather. See each of these terms.

Frost. Ice crystal deposits formed by sublimation when the temperature and dew point are below freezing.

Fuel-flow transmitter. A device in the fuel line between the engine-driven fuel pump and the carburetor that measures the rate of flow of the fuel. It converts this flow rate into an electrical signal and sends it to an indicator in the instrument panel.

Fuel jettison system. A system installed in most large aircraft that allows the flight crew to jettison, or dump, fuel to lower the gross weight of the aircraft to its allowable landing weight. Boost pumps in the fuel tanks move the fuel from the tank into a fuel manifold. From the fuel manifold, it flows away from the aircraft through dump chutes is each wing tip. The fuel jettison system must be so designed and constructed that it is free from fire hazards.

Fuel totalizer. A fuel quantity indicator that gives the total amount of fuel remaining on board the aircraft on one instrument. The totalizer adds the quantities of fuel in all of the tanks.

Fungus (plural: fungi). Any of several types of plant life that include yeasts, molds, and mildew.

Fusible plugs. Plugs in the wheels of high-performance airplanes that use tubeless tires. The centers of the plugs are filled with a metal that melts at a relatively low temperature. If a takeoff is aborted and the pilot uses the brakes excessively, the heat transferred into the wheel will melt the center of the fusible plugs and allow the air to escape from the tire before it builds up enough pressure to cause an explosion.

Gauge (rivet). The distance between rows of rivets in a multirow seam. Gauge is also called transverse pitch.

Gauge pressure. Pressure referenced from the existing atmospheric pressure.

Galling. Fretting or pulling out chunks of a surface by sliding contact with another surface or body.

Gasket. A seal between two parts where there is no relative motion.

Gear-type pump. A constant-displacement fluid pump that contains two meshing large-tooth spur gears. Fluid is drawn into the pump as the teeth separate and is carried around the inside of the housing with teeth and is forced from the pump when the teeth come together.

General Aviation Airworthiness Alerts. Documents published by the FAA that provide an economical interchange of service experience and cooperation in the improvement of aeronautical product durability, reliability, and safety. Alerts include items that have been reported to be significant, but which have not been fully evaluated at the time the material went to press.

Generator. A mechanical device that transforms mechanical energy into electrical energy by rotating a coil inside a magnetic field. As the conductors in the coil cut across the lines of magnetic flux, a voltage is generated that causes current to flow.

Generator series field. A set of heavy field windings in a generator connected in a series with the armature. The magnetic field produced by the series windings is used to change the characteristics of the generator.

Generator shunt field. A set of field windings in a generator connected in parallel with the armature. Varying the amount of current flowing in the shunt field windings controls the voltage output of the generator.

Gerotor pump. A form of constant-displacement gear pump. A gerotor pump uses an external-tooth spur gear that rides inside of and drives an internal-tooth rotor gear. There is one more tooth space inside the rotor than there are teeth on the drive gear. As the gears rotate, the volume of the space between two of the teeth on the inlet side of the pump increases, while the volume of the space between the two teeth on the opposite side of the pump decreases.

GHz (gigahertz). 1,000,000,000 cycles per second.

Gimbal. A support that allows a gyroscope to remain in an upright condition when its base is tilted.

Glass cockpit. An aircraft instrument system that uses a few cathode-ray-tube displays to replace a large number of mechanically actuated instruments.

Glaze ice. Ice that forms when large drops of water strike a surface whose temperature is below freezing. Glaze ice is clear and heavy.

Glide slope. The portion of an ILS (Instrument Landing System) that provides the vertical path along which an aircraft descends on an instrument landing.

Goniometer. Electronic circuitry in an ADF system that uses the output of a fixed loop antenna to sense the angle between a fixed reference, usually the nose of the aircraft, and the direction from which the radio signal is being received.

Gram. The basic unit of weight or mass in the metric system. One gram equals approximately 0.035 ounce.

Graphite. A form of carbon. Structural graphite is used in composite structure because of its strength and stiffness.

Greige (pronounced "gray"). The unshrunk condition of a polyester fabric as it is removed from the loom.

Ground effect. The increased aerodynamic lift produced when an airplane or helicopter is flown nearer than half wing span or rotor span to the ground. This additional lift is caused by an effective increase in angle of attack without the accompanying increase in induced drag, which is caused by the deflection of the downwashed air.

Ground. The voltage reference point in an aircraft electrical system. Ground has zero electrical potential. Voltage values, both positive and negative, are measured from ground. In the United Kingdom, ground is spoken of as "earth."

Ground-power unit (GPU). A service component used to supply electrical power to an aircraft when it is being operated on the ground.

Guncotton. A highly explosive material made by treating cotton fibers with nitric and sulfuric acids. Guncotton is used in making the film base of nitrate dope.

Gusset. A small plate attached to two or more members of a truss structure. A gusset strengthens the truss.

Gyro (gyroscope). The sensing device in an autopilot system. A gyroscope is a rapidly spinning wheel with its weight concentrated around its rim. Gyroscopes have two basic characteristics that make them useful in aircraft instruments: rigidity in space and precession. See rigidity in space and precession.

Gyroscopic precession. The characteristic of a gyroscope that causes it to react to an applied force as though the force were applied at a point 90° in the direction of rotation from the actual point of application. The rotor of a helicopter acts in much the same way as a gyroscope and is affected by gyroscopic precession.

Halon 1211. A halogenated hydrocarbon fire-extinguishing agent used in many HRD fire-extinguishing systems for powerplant protection. The technical name for Halon 1211 is bromochlorodifluoromethane.

Halon 1301. A halogenated hydrocarbon fire-extinguishing agent that is one of the best for extinguishing cabin and powerplant fires. It is highly effective and is the least toxic of the extinguishing agents available. The technical name for Halon 1301 is bromotrifluoromethane.

Hangar rash. Scrapes, bends, and dents in an aircraft structure caused by careless handling.

Hardwood. Wood from a broadleaf tree that sheds its leaves each year.

Heading indicator. A gyroscopic flight instrument that gives the pilot an indication of the heading of the aircraft.

Heat exchanger. A device used to exchange heat from one medium to another. Radiators, condensers, and evaporators are all examples of heat exchangers. Heat always moves from the object or medium having the greatest level of heat energy to a medium or object having a lower level.

Helix. A screw-like, or spiral, curve.

Hertz. One cycle per second.

Holding relay. An electrical relay that is closed by sending a pulse of current through the coil. It remains closed until the current flowing through its contacts is interrupted.

Homebuilt aircraft. Aircraft that are built by individuals as a hobby rather than by factories as commercial products. Homebuilt, or amateur-built, aircraft are not required to meet the stringent requirements imposed on the manufacture of FAA-certified aircraft.

Horsepower. A unit of mechanical power that is equal to 33,000 foot-pounds of work done in 1 minute, or 550 foot-pounds of work done in 1 second.

Hot dimpling. A process used to dimple, or indent, the hole into which a flush rivet is to be installed. Hot dimpling is done by clamping the metal between heating elements and forcing the dies through the holes in the softened metal. Hot dimpling prevents hard metal from cracking when it is dimpled.

Hot-wire cutter. A cutter used to shape blocks of Styrofoam. The wire is stretched tight between the arms of a frame and heated by electrical current. The hot wire melts its way through the foam.

HRD. High-rate-discharge.

HSI. Horizontal situation indicator.

Hydraulic actuator. The component in a hydraulic system that converts hydraulic pressure into mechanical force. The two main types of hydraulic actuators are linear actuators (cylinders and pistons) and rotary actuators (hydraulic motors).

Hydraulic fuse. A type of flow control valve that allows a normal flow of fluid in the system but, if the flow rate is excessive, or if too much fluid flows for normal operation, the fuse will shut off all further flow.

Hydraulic motor. A hydraulic actuator that converts fluid pressure into rotary motion. Hydraulic motors have an advantage in aircraft installations over electric motors, because they can operate in a stalled condition without the danger of a fire.

Hydraulic power pack. A small, self-contained hydraulic system that consists of a reservoir, pump, selector valves, and relief valves. The power pack is removable from the aircraft as a unit to facilitate maintenance and service.

Hydraulics. The system of fluid power which transmits force through an incompressible fluid.

Hydrocarbon. An organic compound that contains only carbon and hydrogen. The vast majority of fossil fuels, such as gasoline and turbine-engine fuel, are hydrocarbons.

Hydroplaning. A condition that exists when a high-speed airplane is landed on a water-covered runway. When the brakes are applied, the wheels lock up and the tires skid on the surface of the water in much the same way a water ski rides on the surface. Hydroplaning develops enough heat in a tire to ruin it.

Hydrostatic test. A pressure test used to determine the serviceability of high-pressure oxygen cylinders. The cylinders are filled with water and pressurized to $5/3$ of their working pressure. Standard-weight cylinders (DOT 3AA) must by hydrostatically tested every five years, and lightweight cylinders (DOT 3HT) must be tested every three years.

Hypersonic speed. Speed of greater than Mach 5 (5 times the speed of sound).

Hyperbolic navigation. Electronic navigation systems that determine aircraft location by the time difference between reception of two signals. Signals from two stations at different locations will be received in the aircraft at different times. A line plotted between two stations along which the time difference is the same forms a hyperbola.

Hypoxia. A physiological condition in which a person is deprived of the needed oxygen. The effects of hypoxia normally disappear as soon as the person is able to breathe air containing sufficient oxygen.

ICAO. The International Civil Aeronautical Organization.

Icebox rivet. A solid rivet made of 2017 or 2024 aluminum alloy. These rivets are too hard to drive in the condition they are received from the factory, and must be heat-treated to soften them. They are heated in a furnace and then quenched in cold water. Immediately after quenching they are soft, but within a few hours at room temperature they become quite hard. The hardening can be delayed for several days by storing them in a subfreezing icebox and holding them at this low temperature until they are to be used.

IFR. Instrument flight rules.

Inch-pound. A measure of work accomplished when a force of 1 pound moves an object a distance of 1 inch.

Indicated airspeed (IAS). The airspeed as shown on an airspeed indicator with no corrections applied.

Induced current. Electrical current produced in a conductor when it is moved through or crossed by a magnetic field.

Induced drag. Aerodynamic drag produced by an airfoil when it is producing lift. Induced drag is affected by the same factors that affect induced lift.

Induction time. The time allowed an epoxy or polyurethane material between its initial mixing and its application. This time allows the materials to begin their cure.

Infrared radiation. Electromagnetic radiation whose wavelengths are longer than those of visible light.

Ingot. A large block of metal that was molded as it was poured from the furnace. Ingots are further processed into sheets, bars, tubes, or structural beams.

INS. Inertial Navigation System.

Inspection Authorization (IA). An authorization that may be issued to an experienced aviation maintenance technician who holds both an Airframe and Powerplant rating. It allows the holder to conduct annual inspections and to approve an aircraft or aircraft engine for return to service after a major repair or major alteration.

Integral fuel tank. A fuel tank which is formed by sealing off part of the aircraft structure and using it as a fuel tank. An integral wing tank is called a "wet wing." Integral tanks are used because of their large weight saving. The only way of repairing an integral fuel tank is by replacing damaged sealant and making riveted repairs, as is done with any other part of the aircraft structure.

Interference drag. Parasite drag caused by air flowing over one portion of the airframe interfering with the smooth flow of air over another portion.

Intermittent-duty solenoid. A solenoid-type switch whose coil is designed for current to flow through it for only a short period of time. The coil will overheat if current flows through it too long.

IRS. Inertial Reference System.

IRU. Inertial Reference Unit.

Iso-octane. A hydrocarbon, C_8H_{18}, which has very high critical pressure and temperature. Iso-octane is used as the high reference for measuring the antidetonation characteristics of a fuel.

Isobaric mode. The mode of pressurization in which the cabin pressure is maintained at a constant value regardless of the outside air pressure.

Isogonic line. A line drawn on an aeronautical chart along which the angular difference between the magnetic and geographic north poles is the same.

Isopropyl alcohol. A colorless liquid used in the manufacture of acetone and its derivatives and as a solvent and anti-icing agent.

Jackscrew. A hardened steel rod with strong threads cut into it. A jackscrew is rotated by hand or with a motor to apply a force or to lift an object.

Jet pump. A special venturi in a line carrying air from certain areas in an aircraft that need an augmented flow of air through them. High-velocity compressor bleed air is blown into the throat of a venturi where it produces a low pressure that pulls air from the area to which it is connected. Jet pumps are often used in the lines that pull air through galleys and toilet areas.

Joggle. A small offset near the edge of a piece of sheet metal. It allows one sheet of metal to overlap another sheet while maintaining a flush surface.

Jointer. A woodworking power tool used to smooth edges of a piece of wood.

K-factor. A factor used in sheet metal work to determine the setback for other than a 90° bend. Setback = K · (bend radius + metal thickness). For bends of less than 90°, the value of K is less than 1; for bends greater than 90°, the value of K is greater than 1.

Kevlar. A patented synthetic aramid fiber noted for its flexibility and light weight. It is to a great extent replacing fiberglass as a reinforcing fabric for composite construction.

Key (verb). To initiate an action by depressing a key or a button.

kHz (kilohertz). 1,000 cycles per second.

Kick-in pressure. The pressure at which an unloading valve causes a hydraulic pump to direct its fluid into the system manifold.

Kick-out pressure. The pressure at which an unloading valve shuts off the flow of fluid into the system pressure manifold and directs it back to the reservoir under a much reduced pressure.

Kilogram. One thousand grams.

Kinetic energy. Energy that exists because of motion.

Knot (wood defect). A hard, usually round section of a tree branch embedded in a board. The grain of the knot is perpendicular to the grain of the board. Knots decrease the strength of the board and should be avoided where strength is needed.

Knot (measure of speed). A speed measurement that is equal to one nautical mile per hour. One knot is equal to 1.15 statute mile per hour.

Kollsman window. The barometric scale window of a sensitive altimeter. See barometric scale.

Koroseal lacing. A plastic lacing material available in round or rectangular cross sections and used for holding wire bundles and tubing together. It holds tension on knots indefinitely and is impervious to petroleum products.

Kraft paper. A tough brown wrapping paper, like that used for paper bags.

Labyrinth seal. A type of seal in a Roots blower cabin supercharger that is made in the form of knife edges riding in step-shaped grooves. Air pressure is dropped in each section of the seal, and any oil in the air is trapped in the grooves.

Lacquer. A finishing material made of a film base, solvents, plasticizers, and thinners. The film base forms a tough film over the surface when it dries. The solvents dissolve the film base so it can be applied as a liquid. The plasticizers give the film base the needed resilience, and the thinners dilute the lacquer so it can be applied with a spray gun. Lacquer is sprayed on the surface as a liquid, and when the solvents and thinners evaporate, the film base remains as a tough decorative and protective coating.

Landing gear warning system. A system of lights used to indicate the condition of the landing gear. A red light illuminates when any of the gears are in an unsafe condition; a green light shows when all of the gears are down and locked, and no light is lit when the gears are all up and locked. An aural warning system is installed that sounds a horn if any of the landing gears are not down and locked when the throttles are retarded for landing.

Laminar flow. Airflow in which the air passes over the surface in smooth layers with a minimum of turbulence.

Laminated wood. A type of wood made by gluing several pieces of thin wood together. The grain of all pieces runs in the same direction.

Latent heat. Heat that is added to a material that causes a change in its state without changing its temperature.

Lateral axis. An imaginary line, passing through the center of gravity of an airplane, and extending across it from wing tip to wing tip.

Lay-up. The placement of the various layers of resin-impregnated fabric in the mold for a piece of laminated composite material.

L/D ratio. A measure of efficiency of an airfoil. It is the ratio of the lift to the total drag at a specified angle of attack.

Left-right indicator. The course-deviation indicator used with a VOR navigation system.

Lightening hole. A hole cut in a piece of structural material to get rid of weight without losing any strength. A hole several inches in diameter may be cut in a piece of metal at a point where the metal is not needed for strength, and the edges of the hole are flanged to give it rigidity. A piece of metal with properly flanged lightening holes is more rigid than the metal before the holes were cut.

Linear actuator. A fluid power actuator that uses a piston moving inside a cylinder to change pressure into linear, or straight-line, motion.

Linear change. A change in which the output is directly proportional to the input.

Loadmeter. A current meter used in some aircraft electrical systems to show the amount of current the generator or alternator is producing. Loadmeters are calibrated in percent of the generator rated output.

Localizer. The portion of an ILS (Instrument Landing System) that directs the pilot along the center line of the instrument runway.

Lodestone. A magnetized piece of natural iron oxide.

Logic flow chart. A type of graphic chart that can be made up for a specific process or procedure to help follow the process through all of its logical steps.

Longitudinal axis. An imaginary line, passing through the center of gravity of an airplane, and extending lengthwise through it from nose to tail.

Longitudinal stability. Stability of an aircraft along its longitudinal axis and about its lateral axis. Longitudinal stability is also called pitch stability.

LORAN A. Long Range Aid to Navigation. A hyperbolic navigation system that operates with frequencies of 1,950 kHz, 1,850 kHz, and 1,900 kHz.

LORAN C. The LORAN system used in aircraft. It operates on a frequency of 100 kHz.

LRU. Line replaceable unit.

Lubber line. A reference on a magnetic compass and directional gyro that represents the nose of the aircraft. The heading of the aircraft is shown on the compass card opposite the lubber line.

Mach number. A measurement of speed based on the ratio of the speed of the aircraft to the speed of sound under the same atmospheric conditions. An airplane flying at Mach 1 is flying at the speed of sound.

Magnetic bearing. The direction to or from a radio transmitting station measured relative to magnetic north.

Major alteration. An alteration not listed in the aircraft, aircraft engine, or propeller specifications. It is one that might appreciably affect weight, balance, structural strength performance, powerplant operation, flight characteristics, or other qualities affecting airworthiness, or that cannot be made with elementary operations.

Major repair. A repair to an aircraft structure or component that if improperly made might appreciably affect weight, balance, structural strength, performance, powerplant operation, flight characteristics, or other qualities affecting airworthiness, or that is not done according to accepted practices, or cannot be made with elementary operation.

Manifold cross-feed fuel system. A type of fuel system commonly used in large transport category aircraft. All fuel tanks feed into a common manifold, and the dump chutes and the single-point fueling valves are connected to the manifold. Fuel lines to each engine are taken from the manifold.

Manifold pressure. The absolute pressure of the air in the induction system of a reciprocating engine.

Manifold pressure gauge. A pressure gauge that measures the absolute pressure inside the induction system of a reciprocating engine. When the engine is not operating, this instrument shows the existing atmospheric pressure.

Master switch. A switch in an aircraft electrical system that can disconnect the battery from the bus and open the generator or alternator field circuit.

Matrix. The material used in composite construction to bond the fibers together and to transmit the forces into the fibers. Resins are the most widely used matrix materials.

Mean camber. A line that is drawn midway between the upper and lower camber of an airfoil section. The mean camber determines the aerodynamic characteristics of the airfoil.

MEK. Methyl-ethyl-ketone is an organic chemical solvent that is soluble in water and is used as a solvent for vinyl and nitrocellulose films. MEK is an efficient cleaner for preparing surfaces for priming or painting.

Mercerize. A treatment given to cotton thread to make it strong and lustrous. The thread is stretched while it is soaked in a solution of caustic soda.

MFD. Multi-function display.

MHz (megahertz). 1,000,000 cycles per second.

Microballoons. Tiny, hollow spheres of glass or phenolic material used to add body to a resin.

Microbial contaminants. The scum that forms inside the fuel tanks of turbine-engine-powered aircraft that is caused by micro-organisms. These micro-organisms live in water that condenses from fuel, and they feed on the fuel. The scum they form clogs fuel filters, lines, and fuel controls and holds water in contact with the aluminum alloy structure, causing corrosion.

Micro-Mesh. A patented graduated series of cloth-backed cushioned seats that contain abrasive crystals. Micro-Mesh is used for polishing and restoring transparency to acrylic plastic windows and windshields.

Micron ("micro meter"). A unit of linear measurement equal to one millionth of a meter, one thousandth of a millimeter, or 0.000039 inch. A micron is also called a micrometer.

Micronic filter. The registered trade name of a type of fluid filter whose filtering element is a specially treated cellulose paper formed into vertical convolutions, or wrinkles. Micronic filters prevent the passage of solids larger than about 10 microns, and are normally replaced with new filters rather than cleaned.

Micro-organism. An organism, normally bacteria or fungus, or microscopic size.

Microswitch. The registered trade name for a precision switch that uses a short throw of the control plunger to actuate the contacts. Microswitches are used primarily as limit switches to control electrical units automatically.

MIG welding. Metal inert gas welding is a form of electric arc welding in which the electrode is an expendable wire. MIG welding is now called GMA (gas metal arc) welding.

Mil. One thousandth of an inch (0.001 inch). Paint film thickness is usually measured in mils.

Mildew. A gray or white fungus growth that forms on organic materials. Mildew forms on cotton and linen aircraft fabric and destroys its strength.

Millivoltmeter. An electrical instrument that measures voltage in units of millivolts (thousandths of a volt).

Mist coat. A very light coat of zinc chromate primer. It is so thin that the metal is still visible, but the primer makes pencil marks easy to see.

Moisture separator. A component in a high-pressure pneumatic system that removes most of the water vapor from the compressed air. When the compressed air is used, its pressure drops, and this pressure drop causes a drop in temperature. If any moisture were allowed to remain in the air, it would freeze and block the system.

Mold line. A line used in the development of a flat pattern for a formed piece of sheet metal. The mold line is an extension of the flat side of a part beyond the radius. The mold line dimension of a part is the dimension made to the intersection of mold lines and is the dimension the part would have if its corners had no radius.

Mold point. The intersection of two mold lines of a part. Mold line dimensions are made between mold points.

Moment. A force that causes or tries to cause an object to rotate. The value of a moment is the product of the weight of an object (or the force), multiplied by the distance between the center of gravity of the object (or the point of application of the force) and the fulcrum about which the object rotates.

Monel. An alloy of nickel, copper, and aluminum or silicon.

Monocoque. A single-shell type of aircraft structure in which all of the flight loads are carried in the outside skin of the structure.

MSDS. Material Safety Data Sheets. MSDS are required by the Federal Government to be available in workplaces to inform workers of the dangers that may exist from contact with certain materials.

MSL. Mean sea level. When the letters MSL are used with an altitude, it means that the altitude is measured from mean, or average, sea level.

MTBF. Mean time between failures.

Multimeter. An electrical test instrument that consists of a single current-measuring meter and all of the needed components to allow the meter to be used to measure voltage, resistance, and current. Multimeters are available with either analog-or digital-type displays.

Multiple-disk brakes. Aircraft brakes in which one set of disks is keyed to the axle and remains stationary. Between each stationary disk there is a rotating disk that is keyed to the inside of the wheel. When the brakes are applied, the stationary disks are forced together, clamping the rotating disks between them. The friction between the disks slows the aircraft.

Nailing strip. A method of applying pressure to the glue in a scarf joint repair in a plywood skin. A strip of thin plywood is nailed over the glued scarf joint with the nails extending into a supporting structure beneath the skin. The strip is installed over vinyl sheeting to prevent it sticking to the skin. When the glue is thoroughly dry, the nailing strip is broken away and the nails removed.

Nap of the fabric. The ends of the fibers in a fabric. The first coat of dope on cotton or linen fabric raises the nap, and the fiber ends stick up. These ends must be carefully removed by sanding to get a smooth finish.

Naphtha. A volatile and flammable hydrocarbon liquid used chiefly as a solvent or as a cleaning fluid.

NDB. Non-directional beacons.

Negative pressure relief valve (pressurization component). A valve that opens anytime the outside air pressure is greater than the cabin pressure. It prevents the cabin altitude from ever becoming greater than the aircraft flight altitude.

Neutral axis (neutral plane). A line through a piece of material that is bent. The material in the outside of the bend is stretched and that on the inside of the bend is shrunk. The material along the neutral plane is neither shrunk nor stretched.

Neutral flame. An oxyacetylene flame produced when the ratio of oxygen and acetylene is chemically correct and there is no excess of oxygen or carbon. A neutral flame has a rounded inner cone and no feather around it.

Noise (electrical). An unwanted electrical signal within a piece of electronic equipment.

Nomex. A patented nylon material used to make the honeycomb core for certain types of sandwich materials.

Nonenergizing brake. A brake that does not use the momentum of the aircraft to increase the friction.

Nonvolatile memory. Memory in a computer that is not lost when power to the computer is lost.

Normal heptane. A hydrocarbon, C_7H_{16}, with a very low critical pressure and temperature. Normal heptane is used as the low reference in measuring the anti-detonation characteristics of a fuel.

Normal shock wave. A shock wave that forms ahead of a blunt object moving through the air at the speed of sound. The shock wave is normal (perpendicular) to the air approaching the object. Air passing through a normal shock wave is slowed to a subsonic speed and its static pressure is increased.

Normalizing. A process of strain-relieving steel that has been welded and left in a strained condition. The steel is heated to a specified temperature, usually red hot, and allowed to cool in still air to room temperature.

Nose-gear centering cam. A cam in the nose-gear shock strut that causes the piston to center when the strut fully extends. When the aircraft takes off and the strut extends, the wheel is straightened in its fore-and-aft position so it can be retracted into the wheel well.

NPN transistor. A bipolar transistor made of a thin base of P-type silicon or geranium sandwiched between a collector and an emitter, both of which are made of N-type material.

Null position. The position of an ADF loop antenna when the signal being received is canceled in the two sides of the loop and the signal strength is the weakest.

Oblique shock wave. A shock wave that forms on a sharp-pointed object moving through air at a speed greater than the speed of sound. Air passing through an oblique shock wave is slowed down, but not to a subsonic speed, and its static pressure is increased.

Oleo shock absorber. A shock absorber used on aircraft landing gear. The initial landing impact is absorbed by oil transferring from one compartment in the shock strut into another compartment through a metering orifice. The shocks of taxiing are taken up by a cushion of compressed air.

Octane rating. A rating of the anti-detonation characteristics of a reciprocating engine fuel. It is based on the performance of the fuel in a special test engine. When a fuel is given a dual rating such as 80/87, the first number is its anti-detonating rating with a lean fuel-air mixture, and the higher number is its rating with a rich mixture.

Open angle. An angle in which sheet metal is bent less than 90°.

Open assembly time. The period of time between the application of the glue and the assembly of the joint components.

Open-hydraulic system. A fluid power system in which the selector valves are arranged in series with each other. Fluid flows from the pump through the center of the selector valves, back into the reservoir when no unit is being actuated.

Open-center selector valve. A type of selector valve that functions as an unloading valve as well as a selector valve. Open-center selector valves are installed in series, and when no unit is actuated, fluid from the pump flows through the centers of all the valves and returns to the reservoir. When a unit is selected for actuation, the center of the selector valve is shut off and the fluid from the pump goes through the selector valve into one side of the actuator. Fluid from the other side of the actuator returns to the valve and goes back to the reservoir through the other selector valves. When the actuation is completed, the selector valve is placed in its neutral position. Its center opens, and fluid from the pump flows straight through the valve.

Open wiring. An electrical wiring installation in which the wires are tied together in bundles and clamped to the aircraft structure rather than being enclosed in conduit.

Orifice check valve. A component in a hydraulic or pneumatic system that allows unrestricted flow in one direction, and restricted flow in the opposite direction.

O-ring. A widely used type of seal made in the form of a rubber ring with a round cross section. An O-ring seals in both directions, and it can be used as a packing or a gasket.

Ornithopter. A heavier-than-air flying machine that produces lift by flapping its wings. No practical ornithopter has been built.

Oscilloscope. An electrical instrument that displays on the face of a cathode-ray tube the waveform of the electrical signal it is measuring.

Outflow valve (pressurization component). A valve in the cabin of a pressurized aircraft that controls the cabin pressure by opening to relieve all pressure above that for which the cabin pressure control is set.

Overvoltage protector. A component in an aircraft electrical system that opens the alternator field circuit any time the alternator output voltage is too high.

Oxidizing flame. An oxyacetylene flame in which there is an excess of oxygen. The inner cone is pointed and often a hissing sound is heard.

Ozone. An unstable form of oxygen produced when an electric spark passes through the air. Ozone is harmful to rubber products.

Packing. A seal between two parts where there is relative motion.

Paint. A covering applied to an object or structure to protect it and improve its appearance. Paint consists of a pigment suspended in a vehicle such as oil or water. When the vehicle dries by evaporation or curing, the pigment is left as a film on the surface.

Parabolic reflector. A reflector whose surface is made in the form of a parabola.

Parallel circuit. A method of connecting electrical components so that each component is in a path between the terminals of the source of electrical energy.

Paralleling circuit. A circuit in a multi-engine aircraft electrical system that controls a flow of control current which is used to keep the generators or alternators sharing the electrical load equally. The relay opens automatically to shut off the flow of paralleling current any time the output of either alternator or generator drops to zero.

Paralleling relay. A relay in multi-engine aircraft electrical system that controls a flow of control current which is used to keep the generators or alternators sharing the electrical load equally. The relay opens automatically to shut off the flow of paralleling current any time the output of either alternator or generator drops to zero.

Parasite drag. A form of aerodynamic drag caused by friction between the air and the surface over which it is flowing.

Parent metal. The metal being welded. This term is used to distinguish between the metal being welded and the welding rod.

Partial pressure. The percentage of the total pressure of a mixture of gases produced by each of the individual gases in the mixture.

Parting film. A layer of thin plastic material placed between a composite lay-up and the heating blanket. It prevents the blanket from sticking to the fabric.

Pascal's Law. A basic law of fluid power which states that the pressure in an enclosed container is transmitted equally and undiminished to all points of the container, and the force acts at right angles to the enclosing walls.

Performance number. The anti-detonation rating of a fuel that has a higher critical pressure and temperature than iso-octane (a rating of 100). Iso-octane that has been treated with varying amounts of tetraethyl lead is used as the reference fuel.

Petrolatum-zinc dust compound. A special abrasive compound used inside an aluminum wire terminal being swaged onto a piece of aluminum electrical wire. When the terminal is compressed, the zinc dust abrades the oxides from the wire, and the petrolatum prevents oxygen reaching the wire so no more oxides can form.

Petroleum fractions. The various components of a hydrocarbon fuel that are separated by boiling them off at different temperatures in the process of fractional distillation.

Phased array antenna. A complex antenna which consists of a number of elements. A beam of energy is formed by the superimposition of the signals radiating from the elements. The direction of the beam can be changed by varying the relative phase of the signals applied to each of the elements.

Phenolic plastic. A plastic material made of a thermosetting phenol-formaldehyde resin, reinforced with cloth or paper. Phenolic plastic materials are used for electrical insulators and for chemical-resistant table tops.

Pilot hole. A small hole punched or drilled in a piece of sheet metal to locate a rivet hole.

Pin knot cluster. A group of knots, all having a diameter of less than approximately $1/16$ inch.

Pinked-edge tape. Cloth tape whose edges have small V-shaped notches cut along their length. The pinked edges prevent the tape from raveling.

Pinking shears. Shears used to cut aircraft fabric with a series of small notches along the cut edge.

Pinion. A small gear that meshes with a larger gear, a sector of a gear, or a toothed rack.

Piston. A sliding plug in an actuating cylinder used to convert pressure into force and then into work.

Pitch (aircraft maneuver). Rotation of an aircraft about its lateral axis.

Pitch (rivet). The distance between the centers of adjacent rivets installed in the small row.

Pitch pocket (wood defect). Pockets of pitch that appear in the growth rings of a piece of wood.

Pitot pressure. Ram air pressure used to measure airspeed. The pitot tube faces directly into the air flowing around the aircraft. It stops the air and measures its pressure.

Plain-weave fabric. Fabric in which each warp thread passes over one fill thread and under the next. Plain-weave fabric typically has the same strength in both warp and fill directions.

Plan position indicator (PPI). A type of radar scope that shows both the direction and distance of the target from the radar antenna. Some radar antenna rotate and their PPI scopes are circular. Other antenna oscillate and their PPI scopes are fan shaped.

Planer. A woodworking power tool used to smooth the surfaces of a piece of wood.

Plasticizer. A constituent in dope or lacquer that gives its film flexibility and resilience.

Plastic media blasting (PMB). A method of removing paint from an aircraft surface by dry-blasting it with tiny plastic beads.

Plastics. The generic name for any of the organic materials produced by polymerization. Plastics can be shaped by molding or drawing.

Plenum. An enclosed chamber in which air can be held at a pressure higher than that of the surrounding air.

Ply rating. The rating of an aircraft tire that indicates its relative strength. The ply rating does not indicate the actual number of plies of fabric in the tire; it indicates the number of piles of cotton fabric needed to produce the same strength as the actual piles.

Plywood. A wood product made by gluing several pieces of thin wood veneer together. The grain of the wood in each layer runs at 90° or 45° to the grain of the layer next to it.

Pneumatics. The system of fluid power which transmits force by the use of a compressible fluid.

PNP transistor. A bipolar transistor made of a thin base of N-type silicon or germanium sandwiched between a collector and an emitter, both of which are made of P-type material.

Polyester fibers. A synthetic fiber made by the polymerization process in which tiny molecules are united to form a long chain of molecules. Polyester fibers are woven into fabrics that are known by their trade names of Dacron, Fortrel, and Kodel. Polyester film and sheet are known as Mylar and Celenar.

Polyester resin. A thermosetting resin used as a matrix for much of the fiberglass used in composite construction.

Polyurethane enamel. A hard, chemically resistant finish used on aircraft. Polyurethane enamel is resistant to damage from all types of hydraulic fluid.

Polyvinyl chloride. A thermoplastic resin used in the manufacture of transparent tubing for electrical insulation and fluid lines which are subject to low pressures.

Position error. The error in pitot-static instruments caused by the static ports not sensing true static air pressure. Position error changes with airspeed and is usually greatest at low airspeeds.

Potential energy. Energy possessed in an object because of its position, chemical composition, shape, or configuration.

Potentiometer. A variable resistor having connections to both ends of the resistance element and to the wiper that moves across the resistance.

Pot life. The length of time a resin will remain workable after the catalyst has been added. If a catalyzed material is not used within its usable pot life, it must be discarded and a new batch mixed up.

Power. The time rate of doing work. Power is force multiplied by distance (work), divided by time.

Power brakes. Aircraft brakes that use the main hydraulic system to supply fluid for the brake actuation. Aircraft that require a large amount of fluid for their brake actuation normally use power brakes, and the volume of fluid sent to the brakes is increased by the use of deboosters.

Power control valve. A hand-operated hydraulic pump unloading valve. When the valve is open, fluid flows from the pump to the reservoir with little opposition. To actuate a unit, turn the selector valve, and manually close the power control valve. Pressurized fluid flows to the unit, and when it is completely actuated, the power control valve automatically opens.

Precession. The characteristic of a gyroscope that causes a force to be felt, not at the point of application, but at a point 90° in the direction of rotation from that point.

Preflight inspection. A required inspection to determine the condition of the aircraft for the flight to be conducted. It is conducted by the pilot-in-command.

Precipitation heat treatment. A method of increasing the strength of heat-treated aluminum alloy. After the aluminum alloy has been solution-heat-treated by heating and quenching, it is returned to the oven and heated to a temperature lower than that used for the initial heat treatment. It is held at this temperature for a specified period of time, and then removed from the oven and allowed to cool slowly.

Prepreg (preimpregnated fabric). A type of composite material in which the reinforcing fibers are encapsulated in an uncured resin. Prepreg materials must be kept refrigerated to prevent them from curing before they are used.

Press-to-test light fixture. An indicator light fixture whose lens can be pressed in to complete a circuit that tests the filament of the light bulb.

Pressure. Force per unit area. Hydraulic and pneumatic pressure are normally given in units of pounds per square inch (psi).

Pressure altitude. The altitude in standard air at which the pressure is the same as that of the existing air. Pressure altitude is read on an altimeter when the barometric scale is set to the standard sea level pressure of 29.92 inches of mercury.

Pressure-demand oxygen system. A type of oxygen system used by aircraft that fly at very high altitude. This system functions as a diluter-demand system until, at about 40,000 feet, the output to the mask is pressurized enough to force the needed oxygen into the lungs, rather than depending on the low pressure produced when the wearer of the mask inhales to pull in the oxygen. (See diluter-demand oxygen system.)

Pressure fueling. The method of fueling used by almost all transport aircraft. The fuel is put into the aircraft through a single underwing fueling port. The fuel tanks are filled to the desired quantity and in the sequence selected by the person conducting the fueling operation. Pressure fueling saves servicing time by using a single point to fuel the entire aircraft, and it reduces the chances for fuel contamination.

Pressure manifold (hydraulic system component). The portion of a fluid power system from which the selector valves receive their pressurized fluid.

Pressure plate (brake component). A strong, heavy plate used in a multiple-disk brake. The pressure plate receives the force from the brake cylinders and transmits this force to the disks.

Pressure reducing valve (oxygen system component). A valve used in an oxygen system to change high cylinder pressure to low system pressure.

Pressure relief valve (oxygen system component). A valve in an oxygen system that relieves the pressure if the pressure reducing valve should fail.

Pressure vessel. The strengthened portion of an aircraft structure that is sealed and pressurized in flight.

Primer (finishing system component). A component in a finishing system that provides a good bond between the surface and the material used for the topcoats.

Profile drag. Aerodynamic drag produced by skin friction. Profile drag is a form of parasite drag.

Progressive inspection. An inspection that may be used in place of an annual or 100-hour inspection. It has the same scope as an annual inspection, but it may be performed in increments so the aircraft will not have to be out of service for a lengthy period of time.

Pump control valve. A control valve in a hydraulic system that allows the pilot to manually direct the output of the hydraulic pump back to the reservoir when no unit is being actuated.

Pureclad. A registered trade name for clad aluminum alloy.

Purge (air conditioning system operation). To remove all of the moisture and air from a cooling system by flushing the system with a dry gaseous refrigerant.

Pusher powerplant. A powerplant whose propeller is mounted at the rear of the airplane and pushes, rather than pulls, the airplane through the air.

PVC (Polyvinylchloride). A thermoplastic resin used to make transparent tubing for insulating electrical wires.

Quartersawed wood. Wood sawed from a tree in such a way that the annual rings cross the plank at an angle greater than 45°.

Quick-disconnect fitting. A hydraulic line fitting that seals the line when the fitting is disconnected. Quick-disconnect fittings are used on the lines connected to the engine-driven hydraulic pump. They allow the pump to be disconnected and an auxiliary hydraulic power system connected to perform checks requiring hydraulic power while the aircraft is in the hangar.

Rack-and-pinion actuator. A form of rotary actuator where the fluid acts on a piston on which a rack of gear teeth is cut. As the piston moves, it rotates a pinion gear which is mated with the teeth cut in the rack.

Radial. A directional line radiating outward from a radio facility, usually a VOR. When an aircraft is flying outbound on the 330° from the station.

Radius dimpling. A process of preparing a hole in sheet metal for flush riveting. A cone-shaped male die forces the edges of the rivet hole into the depression in a female die. Radius dimpling forms a round-edged depression into which the rivet head fits.

Range markings. Colored marks on an instrument dial that identify certain ranges of operation as specified in the aircraft maintenance or flight manual and listed in the appropriate aircraft Type Certificate Data Sheets or Aircraft Specifications. Color coding directs attention to approaching operating difficulties. Airspeed indicators and most pressure and temperature indicators are marked to show the various ranges of operation. These ranges and colors are the most generally used: Red radial line, do not exceed. Green arc, normal operating range. Yellow arc, caution range. Blue radial line, used on airspeed indicators to show best single-engine rate of climb speed. White arc, used on airspeed indicators to show flap operating range.

RDF. Radio direction finding.

Rebreather oxygen mask. A type of oxygen mask used with a continuous flow oxygen system. Oxygen continuously flows into the bottom of the loose-fitting rebreather bag on the mask. The wearer of the mask exhales into the top of the bag. The first air exhaled contains some oxygen, and this air goes into the bag first. The last air to leave the lungs contains little oxygen, and it is forced out of the bag as the bag is filled with fresh oxygen. Each time the wearer of the mask inhales, the air first exhaled, along with fresh oxygen, is taken into the lungs.

Receiver-dryer. The component in a vapor-cycle cooling system that serves as a reservoir for the liquid refrigerant. The receiver-dryer contains a desiccant that absorbs any moisture that may be in the system.

Rectangle. A plane surface with four sides whose opposite sides are parallel and whose angles are all right angles.

Rectification (arc welding condition). A condition in AC-electric arc welding in which oxides on the surface of the metal act as a rectifier and prevent electrons flowing from the metal to the electrode during the half cycle when the electrode is positive.

Reducing flame. See carburizing flame.

Reed valve. A thin, leaf-type valve mounted in the valve plate of an air conditioning compressor to control the flow of refrigerant gases into and out of the compressor cylinders.

Reinforcing tape. A narrow strip of woven fabric material placed over the fabric as it is being attached to the aircraft structure with rib lacing cord. This tape carries a large amount of the load and prevents the fabric tearing at the stitches.

Rejuvenator. A finishing material used to restore resilience to an old dope film. Rejuvenator contains strong solvents to open the dried-out film and plasticizers to restore resilience to the old dope.

Relative wind. The direction the wind strikes an airfoil.

Relay. An electrical component which uses a small amount of current flowing through a coil to produce a magnetic pull to close a set of contacts through which a large amount of current can flow. The core in a relay coil is fixed.

Relief hole. A hole drilled at the point at which two bend lines meet in a piece of sheet metal. This hole spreads the stresses caused by the bends and prevents the metal cracking.

Relief valve. A pressure-control valve that relieves any pressure over the amount for which it is set. They are damage-preventing units used in both hydraulic and pneumatic systems. In an aircraft hydraulic system, pressure relief valves prevent damaging high pressures that could be caused by a malfunctioning pressure regulator, or by thermal expansion of fluid trapped in portions of the system.

Repair. A maintenance procedure in which a damaged component is restored to its original condition, or at least to a condition that allows it to fulfill its design function.

Restrictor. A fluid power system component that controls the rate of actuator movement by restricting the flow of fluid into or out of the actuator.

Retard breaker points. A set of breaker points in certain aircraft magnetos that are used to provide a late (retarded) spark for starting the engine.

Retarder (finishing system component). Dope thinner that contains certain additives that slow its rate of evaporation enough to prevent dope blushing.

Retread. The replacement of the tread rubber on an aircraft tire.

Retreating blade. The blade on a helicopter rotor whose tip is moving in the direction opposite to that in which the helicopter is moving.

Retreating blade stall. The stall of a helicopter rotor disc that occurs near the tip of the retreating blade. A retreating blade stall occurs when the flight airspeed is high and the retreating blade airspeed is low. This results in a high angle of attack, causing the stall.

Return manifold. The portion of a fluid power system through which the fluid is returned to the reservoir.

Reverse polarity welding. DC-electric arc welding in which the electrode is positive with respect to the work.

Rib thread. A series of circumferential grooves cut into the tread of a tire. This tread pattern provides superior traction and directional stability on hard-surfaced runways.

Ribbon direction. The direction in a piece of honeycomb material that is parallel to the length of the strips of material that make up the core.

Rigid conduit. Aluminum alloy tubing used to house electrical wires in areas where they are subject to mechanical damage.

Rigidity in space. The characteristic of a gyroscope that prevents its axis of rotation tilting as the earth rotates. This characteristic is used for attitude gyro instruments.

Rime ice. A rough ice that forms on aircraft flying through visible moisture, such as a cloud, when the temperature is below freezing. Rime ice disturbs the smooth airflow as well as adding weight.

Rivet cutters. Special cutting pliers that resemble diagonal cutters except that the jaws are ground in such a way that they cut the rivet shank, or stem, off square.

Rivet set. A tool used to drive aircraft solid rivets. It is a piece of hardened steel with a recess the shape of the rivet head in one end. The other end fits into the rivet gun.

RMI. Radio magnetic indicator.

Rocking shaft. A shaft used in the mechanism of a pressure measuring instrument to change the direction of movement by 90° and to amplify the amount of movement.

Roll (aircraft maneuver). Rotation of an aircraft about its longitudinal axis.

Roots-type air compressor. A positive-displacement air pump that uses two intermeshing figure-8-shaped rotors to move the air.

Rosette weld. A method of securing one metal tube inside another by welding. Small holes are drilled in the outer tube and the inner tube is welded to it around the circumference of the holes.

Rotary actuator. A fluid power actuator whose output is rotational. A hydraulic motor is a rotary actuator.

Roving. A lightly twisted roll or strand of fibers.

RPM. Revolutions per minute.

Ruddervators. The two movable surfaces on a V-tail empennage. When these two surfaces are moved together with the in-and-out movement of the control yoke, they act as elevators, and when they are moved differentially with the rudder pedals, they act as the rudder.

Saddle gusset. A piece of plywood glued to an aircraft structural member. The saddle gusset has a cutout to hold a backing block or strip tightly against the skin to allow a nailing strip to be used to apply pressure to a glued joint in the skin.

Sailplane. A high-performance glider.

Sandwich material. A type of composite structural material in which a core material is bonded between face sheets of metal or resin-impregnated fabric.

Satin-weave fabric. Fabric in which the warp threads pass under one fill thread and over several others. Satin-weave fabrics are used when the lay-up must be made over complex shapes.

Scarf joint. A joint in a wood structure in which the ends to be joined are cut in a long taper, normally about 12:1, and fastened together by gluing. A glued scarf joint makes a strong splice because the joint is made along the side of the wood fibers rather than along their ends.

Schematic diagram. A diagram of an electrical system in which the system components are represented by symbols rather than drawings or pictures of the actual devices.

Schrader valve. A type of service valve used in an air conditioning system. This is a spring-loaded valve much like the valve used to put air into a tire.

Scissors. A name commonly used for torque links. See torque links.

Scupper. A recess around the filler neck of an aircraft fuel tank. Any fuel spilled when the tank is being serviced collects in the scupper and drains to the ground through a drain line rather than flowing into the aircraft structure.

Sea level engine. A reciprocating engine whose rated takeoff power can be produced only at sea level.

Sector gear. A part of a gear wheel containing the hub and a portion of the rim with teeth.

Series circuit. A method of connecting electrical components in such a way that all the current flows through each of the components. There is only one path for current to flow.

Series-parallel circuit. An electrical circuit in which some of the components are connected in parallel and others are connected in series.

Selcal system. Selective calling system. Each aircraft operated by an airline is assigned a particular four-tone audio combination for identification purposes. A ground station keys the signal whenever contact with that particular aircraft is desired. The signal is decoded by the airborne selcal decoder and the crew alerted by the selcal warning system.

Selsyn system. A DC synchro system used in remote indicating instruments. The rotor in the indicator is a permanent magnet and the stator is a tapped toroidal coil. The transmitter is a circular potentiometer with DC power fed into its wiper which is moved by the object being monitored. The transmitter is connected to the indicator in such a way that rotation of the transmitter shaft varies the current in the sections of the indicator toroidal coil. The magnet in the indicator on which the pointer is mounted locks with the magnetic field produced by the coils and follows the rotation of the transmitter shaft.

Segmented-rotor brake. A heavy-duty, multiple-disk brake used on large, high-speed aircraft. Stators that are surfaced with a material that retains its friction characteristics at high temperatures are keyed to the axle. Rotors which are keyed into the wheels mesh with the stators. The rotors are made in segments to allow for cooling and for their large amounts of expansion.

Selector valve. A flow control valve used in hydraulic systems that directs pressurized fluid into one side of an actuator, and at the same time directs return fluid from the other side of the actuator back to the reservoir. There are two basic types of selector valves: open-center valves and closed-center valves. The four-port closed-center valve is the most frequently used type. See closed-center selector valve and open-center selector valve.

Selvage edge. The woven edge of fabric used to prevent the material unraveling during normal handling. The selvage edge, which runs the length of the fabric parallel to the warp threads, is usually removed from materials used in composite construction.

Semiconductor diode. A two-element electrical component that allows current to pass through it in one direction, but blocks its passage in the opposite direction. A diode acts in an electrical system in the same way a check valve acts in a hydraulic system.

Semimonocoque structure. A form of aircraft stressed skin structure. Most of the strength of a semimonocoque structure is in the skin, but the skin is supported on a substructure of formers and stringers that give the skin its shape and increase its rigidity.

Sensible heat. Heat that is added to a liquid causing a change in its temperature but not its physical state.

Sensitivity. A measure of the signal strength needed to produce a distortion-free output in a radio receiver.

Sequence valve. A valve in a hydraulic system that requires a certain action to be completed before another action can begin. Sequence valves are used to assure that the hydraulically actuated wheel-well doors are completely open before pressure is directed to the landing gear to lower it.

Servo. An electrical or hydraulic actuator connected into a flight control system. A small force on the flight deck control is amplified by the servo and provides a large force to move the control surface.

Servo amplifier. An electronic amplifier in an autopilot system that increases the signal from the autopilot enough that it can operate the servos that move the control surfaces.

Servo tab. A small movable tab built into the trailing edge of a primary control surface of an airplane. The flight deck controls move the tab in such a direction that it produces an aerodynamic force moving the surface on which it is mounted.

Setback. The distance the jaws of a brake must be set back from the mold line to form a bend. Setback for a 90° bend is equal to the inside radius of the bend plus the thickness of the metal being bent. For a bend other than 90°, a K-factor must be used. See also K-factor.

Shake (wood defect). Longitudinal cracks in a piece of wood, usually between two annual rings.

SHF. Super-high frequency.

Shear section. A necked-down section of the drive shaft of a constant-displacement engine-driven fluid pump. If the pump should seize, the shear section will break and prevent the pump from being destroyed or the engine from being damaged. Some pumps use a shear pin rather than a shear section.

Shear strength. The strength of a riveted joint in a sheet metal structure in which the rivets shear before the metal tears at the rivet holes.

Shelf life. The length of time a product is good when it remains in its original unopened container.

Shielded wire. Electrical wire enclosed in a braided metal jacket. Electromagnetic energy radiated from the wire is trapped by the braid and is carried to ground.

Shimmy. Abnormal, and often violent, vibration of the nose wheel of an airplane. Shimmying is usually caused by looseness of the nose wheel support mechanism or an unbalanced wheel.

Shimmy damper. A small hydraulic shock absorber installed between the nose wheel fork and the nose wheel cylinder attached to the aircraft structure.

Shock mounts. Resilient mounting pads used to protect electronic equipment by absorbing low-frequency, high amplitude vibrations.

Shock wave. A pressure wave formed in the air by a flight vehicle moving at a speed greater than the speed of sound. As the vehicle passes through the air, it produces sound waves that spread out in all directions. But since the vehicle is flying faster than these waves are moving, they build up and form a pressure wave at the front and rear of the vehicle. As the air passes through a shock wave it slows down, its static pressure increases, and its total energy decreases.

Shop head. The head of a rivet which is formed when the shank is upset.

Show-type finish. The type of finish put on fabric-covered aircraft intended for show. This finish is usually made up of many coats of dope, with much sanding and rubbing of the surface between coats.

Shunt winding. Field coils in an electric motor or generator that are connected in parallel with the armature.

Shuttle valve. An automatic selector valve mounted on critical components such as landing gear actuation cylinders and brake cylinders. For normal operation, system fluid flows into the actuator through the shuttle valve, but if normal system pressure is lost, emergency system pressure forces the shuttle over and emergency fluid flows into the actuator.

Sidestick controller. A flight deck flight control used on some of the fly-by-wire equipped airplanes. The stick is mounted rigidly on the side console of the flight deck, and pressures exerted on the stick by the pilot produce electrical signals that are sent to the computer that flies the airplane.

Sight glass (air conditioning system component). A small window in the high side of a vapor-cycle cooling system. Liquid refrigerant flows past the sight glass, and if the charge of refrigerant is low, bubbles will be seen. A fully charged system has no bubbles in the refrigerant.

Sight line. A line drawn on a sheet metal layout that is one bend radius from the bend-tangent line. The sight line is lined up directly below the nose of the radius bar in a cornice brake. When the metal is clamped in this position, the bend tangent line is in the correct position for the start of the bend.

Silicon controlled rectifier (SCR). A semiconductor electron control device. An SCR blocks current flow in both directions until a pulse of positive voltage is applied to its gate. It then conducts in its forward direction, while continuing to block current in its reverse direction.

Silicone rubber. An elastomeric material made from silicone elastomers. Silicone rubber is compatible with fluids that attack other natural or synthetic rubbers.

Single-acting actuator. A linear hydraulic or pneumatic actuator that uses fluid power for movement in one direction and a spring force for its return.

Single-action hand pump. A hand-operated fluid pump that moves fluid only during one stroke of the pump handle. One stroke pulls the fluid into the pump and the other forces the fluid out.

Single-disk brakes. Aircraft brakes in which a single steel disk rotates with the wheel between two brake-lining blocks. When the brake is applied, the disk is clamped tightly between the lining blocks, and the friction slows the aircraft.

Single-servo brakes. Brakes that uses the momentum of the aircraft rolling forward to help apply the brakes by wedging the brake shoe against the brake drum.

Sintered metal. A porous material made by fusing powdered metal under heat and pressure.

Skydrol hydraulic fluid. The registered trade name for a synthetic, nonflammable, phosphate ester-base hydraulic fluid used in modern high-temperature hydraulic systems.

Slat. A secondary control on an aircraft that allows it to fly at a high angle of attack without stalling. A slat is a section of leading edge of wing mounted on curved tracks that move into and out of the wing on rollers.

Slip roll former. A shop tool used to form large radius curves on sheet metal.

Slippage mark. A paint mark extending across the edge of an aircraft wheel onto a tube-type tire. When this mark is broken, it indicates the tire has slipped on the wheel, and there is a good reason to believe the tube has been damaged.

Slipstream area. For the purpose of rib stitch spacing, the slipstream area is considered to be the diameter of the propeller plus one wing rib on each side.

Slot (aerodynamic device). A fixed, nozzle-like opening near the leading edge of an airplane wing ahead of the aileron. A slot acts as a duct to force high-energy air down on the upper surface of the wing when the airplane is flying at a high angle of attack. The slot, which is located ahead of the aileron, causes the inboard portion of the wing to stall first, allowing the aileron to remain effective throughout the stall.

Slow-blow fuse. An electrical fuse that allows a large amount of current to flow for a short length of time but melts to open the circuit if more than its rated current flows for a longer period.

Smoke detector. A device that warns the flight crew of the presence of smoke in cargo and/or baggage compartments. Some smoke detectors are of the visual type, others are photoelectric or ionization devices.

Snubber. A device in a hydraulic or pneumatic component that absorbs shock and/or vibration. A snubber is installed in the line to a hydraulic pressure gauge to prevent the pointer fluctuating.

Softwood. Wood from a tree that bears cones and has needles rather than leaves.

Soldering. A method of thermally joining metal parts with a molten nonferrous alloy that melts at a temperature below 800 °F. The molten alloy is pulled up between close-fitting parts by capillary action. When the alloy cools and hardens, it forms a strong, leak-proof connection.

Solenoid. An electrical component using a small amount of current flowing through a coil to produce a magnetic force that pulls an iron core into the center of the coil. The core may be attached to a set of heavy-duty electrical contacts, or it may be used to move a valve or other mechanical device.

Solidity (helicopter rotor characteristic). The solidity of a helicopter rotor system is the ratio of the total blade area to the disc area.

Solution heat treatment. A type of heat treatment in which the metal is heated in a furnace until it has a uniform temperature throughout. It is then removed and quenched in cold water. When the metal is hot, the alloying elements enter into a solid solution with the base metal to become part of its basic structure. When the metal is quenched, these elements are locked into place.

Sonic venture. A venture in a line between a turbine engine or turbocharger and a pressurization system. When the air flowing through the venture reaches the speed of sound, a shock wave forms across the throat of the venture and limits the flow. A sonic venture is also called a flow limiter.

Specific heat. The number of BTUs of heat energy needed to change the temperature of one pound of a substance 1 °F.

Speed brakes. A secondary control of an airplane that produces drag without causing a change in the pitch attitude of the airplane. Speed brakes allow an airplane to make a steep descent without building up excessive forward airspeed.

Spike knot. A knot that runs through the depth of a beam perpendicular to the annual rings. Spike knots appear most frequently in quartersawed wood.

Spin. A flight maneuver in which an airplane descends in a corkscrew fashion. One wing is stalled and the other is producing lift.

Spirit level. A curved glass tube partially filled with a liquid, but with a bubble in it. When the device in which the tube is mounted is level, the bubble will be in the center of the tube.

Splayed patch (wood structure repair). A type of patch made in an aircraft plywood structure in which the edges of the patch are tapered for approximately five times the thickness of the plywood. A splayed patch is not recommended for use on plywood less than $1/10$ inch thick.

Split bus. A type of electrical bus that allows all of the voltage-sensitive avionic equipment to be isolated from the rest of the aircraft electrical system when the engine is being started or when the ground-power unit is connected.

Split-rocker switch. An electrical switch whose operating rocker is split so one half of the switch can be opened without affecting the other half. Split-rocker switches are used as aircraft master switches. The battery can be turned on without turning on the alternator, but the alternator cannot be turned on without also turning on the battery. The alternator can be turned off without turning off the battery, but the battery cannot be turned off without also turning off the alternator.

Split (wood defect). A longitudinal crack in a piece of wood caused by externally induced stress.

Spoilers. Flight controls that are raised up from the upper surface of a wing to destroy, or spoil, lift. Flight spoilers are used in conjunction with the ailerons to decrease lift and increase drag on the descending wing. Ground spoilers are used to produce a great amount of drag to slow the airplane on its landing roll.

Spongy brakes. Hydraulic brakes whose pedal has a spongy feel because of air trapped in the fluid.

Spontaneous combustion. Self-ignition of a material caused by heat produced in the material as it combines with oxygen from the air.

Springwood. The portion of an annual ring in a piece of wood formed principally during the first part of the growing season, the spring of the year. Springwood is softer, more porous, and lighter than the summerwood.

Square. A four-sided plane figure whose sides are all the same length, whose opposite sides are parallel, and whose angles are all right angles.

Squat switch. An electrical switch actuated by the landing gear scissors on the oleo strut. When no weight is on the landing gear, the oleo piston is extended and the switch is in one position, but when weight is on the gear, the oleo strut compresses and the switch changes its position. Squat switches are used in antiskid brake systems, landing gear safety circuits, and cabin pressurization systems.

Squib. An explosive device in the discharge valve of a high-rate-discharge container of fire-extinguishing agent. The squib drives a cutter into the seal in the container to discharge the agent.

SRM. Structural Repair Manual.

Stabilator. A flight control on the empennage of an airplane that acts as both a stabilizer and an elevator. The entire horizontal tail surface pivots and is moved as a unit.

Stability. The characteristic of an aircraft that causes it to return to its original flight condition after it has been disturbed.

Stabilons. Small wing-like horizontal surfaces mounted on the aft fuselage to improve longitudinal stability of airplanes that have an exceptionally wide center of gravity range.

Stagnation point. The point on the leading edge of a wing at which the airflow separates, with some flowing over the top of the wing and the rest below the wing.

Stall. A flight condition in which an angle of attack is reached at which the air ceases to flow smoothly over the upper surface of an airfoil. The air becomes turbulent and lift is lost.

Stall strip. A small triangular metal strip installed along the leading edge of an airplane wing near the wing root. Stall strips cause the root section of the wing to stall before the portion of the wing ahead of the ailerons.

Standpipe. A pipe sticking up in a tank or reservoir that allows part of the tank to be used as a reserve, or standby, source of fluid.

Starter-generator. A single component starter and generator used on many of the smaller gas-turbine engines. It is used as a starter, and when the engine is running, its circuitry is shifted so that it acts as a generator.

Static. Still, not moving.

Static air pressure. Pressure of the ambient air surrounding the aircraft. Static pressure does not take into consideration any air movement.

Static dischargers. Devices connected to the trailing edges of control surfaces to discharge static electricity harmlessly into the air. They discharge the static charges before they can build up high enough to cause radio receiver interference.

Static stability. The characteristic of an aircraft that causes it to return to straight and level flight after it has been disturbed from that condition.

Stoddard solvent. A petroleum product, similar to naphtha, used as a solvent and a cleaning fluid.

STOL. Short takeoff and landing.

Stop drilling. A method of stopping the growth of a crack in a piece of metal or transparent plastic by drilling a small hole at the end of the crack. The stresses are spread out all around the circumference of the hole rather than concentrated at the end of the crack.

Straight polarity welding. DC-electric arc welding in which the electrode is negative with respect to the work.

Strain. A deformation or physical change in a material caused by a stress.

Stress. A force set up within an object that tries to prevent an outside force from changing its shape.

Stressed skin structure. A type of aircraft structure in which all or most of the stresses are carried in the outside skin. A stressed skin structure has a minimum of internal structure.

Stress riser. A location where the cross-sectional area of the part changes abruptly. Stresses concentrate at such a location and failure is likely. A scratch, gouge, or tool mark in the surface of a highly stressed part can change the area enough to concentrate the stresses and become a stress riser.

Stringer. A part of an aircraft structure used to give the fuselage its shape and, in some types of structure, to provide a small part of fuselage strength. Formers give the fuselage its cross-sectional shape and stringers fill in the shape between the formers.

Stroboscopic tachometer. A tachometer used to measure the speed of any rotating device without physical contact. A highly accurate variable-frequency oscillator triggers a high-intensity strobe light.

Sublimation. A process in which a solid material changes directly into a vapor without passing through the liquid stage.

Subsonic flight. Flight at an airspeed in which all air flowing over the aircraft is moving at a speed below the speed of sound.

Summerwood. The less porous, usually harder portion of an annual ring that forms in the latter part of the growing season, the summer of the year.

Sump. A low point in an aircraft fuel tank in which water and other contaminants can collect and be held until they can be drained out.

Supercooled water. Water in its liquid form at a temperature well below its natural freezing temperature. When supercooled water is disturbed, it immediately freezes.

Superheat. Heat energy that is added to a refrigerant after it changes from a liquid to a vapor.

Super heterodyne circuit. A sensitive radio receiver circuit in which a local oscillator produces a frequency that is a specific difference from the received signal frequency. The desired signal and the output from the oscillator are mixed, and they produce a single, constant intermediate frequency. This IF is amplified, demodulated, and detected to produce the audio frequency that is used to drive the speaker.

Supersonic flight. Flight at an airspeed in which all air flowing over the aircraft is moving at a speed greater than the speed of sound.

Supplemental Type Certificate (STC). An approval issued by the FAA for a modification to a type certificated airframe, engine, or component. More than one STC can be issued for the same basic alteration, but each holder must prove to the FAA that the alteration meets all the requirements of the original type certificate.

Surface tape. Strips of aircraft fabric that are doped over all seams and places where the fabric is stitched to the aircraft structure. Surface tape is also doped over the wing leading edges where abrasive wear occurs. The edges of surface tape are pink, or notched, to keep them from raveling before the dope is applied.

Surfactant. A surface active agent, or partially soluble contaminant, which is a by-product of fuel processing or of fuel additives. Surfactants adhere to other contaminants and cause them to drop out of the fuel and settle to the bottom of the fuel tank as sludge.

Surveyor's transit. An instrument consisting of a telescope mounted on a flat, graduated, circular plate on a tripod. The plate can be adjusted so it is level, and its graduations oriented to magnetic north. When an object is viewed through the telescope, its azimuth and elevation may be determined.

Swashplate. The component in a helicopter control system that consists basically of two bearing races with ball bearings between them. The lower, or nonrotating, race is tilted by the cyclic control, and the upper, or rotating, race has arms which connect to the control horns on the rotor blades. Movement of the cyclic pitch control is transmitted to the rotor blades through the swashplate. Movement of the collective pitch control raises or lowers the entire swashplate assembly to change the pitch of all the blades at the same time.

Synchro system. A remote instrument indicating system. A synchro transmitter is actuated by the device whose movement is to be measured, and it is connected electrically with wires to a synchro indicator whose pointer follows the movement of the shaft of the transmitter.

Symmetrical airfoil. An airfoil that has the same shape on both sides of its chord line, or center line.

Symmetry check. A check of an airframe to determine that the wings and tail are symmetrical about the longitudinal axis.

System-pressure regulator (hydraulic system component). A type of hydraulic system-pressure control valve. When the system pressure is low, as it is when some unit is actuated, the output of the constant-delivery pump is directed into the system. When the actuation is completed and the pressure builds up to a specified kick-out pressure, the pressure regulator shifts. A check valve seals the system off and the pressure is maintained by the accumulator. The pump is unloaded and its output is directed back into the reservoir with very little opposition. The pump output pressure drops, but the volume of flow remains the same. When the system pressure drops to the specified kick-in pressure, the regulator again shifts and directs fluid into the system. Spool-type and balanced-pressure-type system pressure regulators are completely automatic in their operation and require no attention on the part of the flight crew.

TACAN (Tactical Air Navigation). A radio navigation facility used by military aircraft for both direction and distance information. Civilian aircraft receive distance information from a TACAN on their DME.

Tack coat. A coat of finishing material sprayed on the surface and allowed to dry until the solvents evaporate. As soon as the solvents evaporate, a wet full-bodied coat of material is sprayed over it.

Tack rag. A clean, lintless rag, slightly damp with thinner. A tack rag is used to wipe a surface to prepare it to receive a coat of finishing material.

Tack weld. A method of holding parts together before they are permanently welded. The parts are assembled, and small spots of weld are placed at strategic locations to hold them in position.

Tacky. Slightly sticky to the touch.

Tailets. Small vertical surfaces mounted underside of the horizontal stabilizer of some airplanes to increase the directional stability.

Takeoff warning system. An aural warning system that provides audio warning signals when the thrust levers are advanced for takeoff if the stabilizer, flaps, or speed brakes are in an unsafe condition for takeoff.

Tang. A tapered shank sticking out from the blade of a knife or a file. The handle of a knife or file is mounted on the tang.

TCAS. Traffic Alert Collision Avoidance System.

Teflon. The registered trade name for a fluorocarbon resin used to make hydraulic and pneumatic seals, hoses, and backup rings.

Tempered glass. Glass that has been heat-treated to increase its strength. Tempered glass is used in bird-proof, heated windshields for high-speed aircraft.

Terminal strips. A group of threaded studs mounted in a strip of insulating plastic. Electrical wires with crimped-on terminals are placed over the studs and secured with nuts.

Terminal VOR. A low-powered VOR that is normally located on an airport.

Tetraethyl lead (TEL). A heavy, oily, poisonous liquid, $Pb(C_2H_5)^4$, that is mixed into aviation gasoline to increase its critical pressure and temperature.

Therapeutic mask adapter. A calibrated orifice in the mask adapter for a continuous-flow oxygen system that increases the flow of oxygen to a mask being used by a passenger who is known to have a heart or respiratory problem.

Thermal dimpling. See hot dimpling.

Thermal relief valve. A relief valve in a hydraulic system that relieves pressure that builds up in an isolated part of the system because of heat. Thermal relief valves are set at a higher pressure than the system pressure relief valve.

Thermistor. A special form of electrical resistor whose resistance varies with its temperature.

Thermistor material. A material with a negative temperature coefficient that causes its resistance to decrease as its temperature increases.

Thermocouple. A loop consisting of two kinds of wire, joined at the hot, or measuring, junction and at the cold junction in the instrument. The voltage difference between the two junctions is proportional to the temperature difference between the junctions. In order for the current to be meaningful, the resistance of the thermocouple is critical, and the leads are designed for a specific installation. Their length should not be altered. Thermocouples used to measure cylinder head temperature are usually made of iron and constantan, and thermocouples that measure exhaust gas temperature for turbine engines are made of chromel and alumel.

Thermocouple fire-detection system. A fire-detection system that works on the principle of the rate-of-temperature rise. Thermocouples are installed around the area to be protected, and one thermocouple is surrounded by thermal insulation that prevents its temperature changing rapidly. In the event of a fire, the temperature of all the thermocouples except the protected one will rise immediately and a fire warning will be initiated. In the case of a general overheat condition, the temperature of all the thermocouples will rise uniformly and there will be no fire warning.

Thermoplastic resin. A type of plastic material that becomes soft when heated and hardens when cooled.

Thermosetting resin. A type of plastic material that, when once hardened by heat, cannot be softened by being heated again.

Thermostatic expansion valve (TEV). The component in a vapor-cycle cooling system that meters the refrigerant into the evaporator. The amount of refrigerant metered by the TEV is determined by the temperature and pressure of the refrigerant as it leaves the evaporator coils. The TEV changes the refrigerant from a high-pressure liquid into a low-pressure liquid.

Thixotropic agents. Materials, such as microballoons, added to a resin to give it body and increase its workability.

TIG welding. Tungsten inert welding is a form of electric arc welding in which the electrode is a nonconsumable tungsten wire. TIG welding is now called GTA (gas tungsten arc) welding.

Toe-in. A condition of landing gear alignment in which the front of the tires are closer together than the rear. When the aircraft rolls forward, the wheels try to move closer together.

Toe-out. A condition of landing gear alignment in which the front of the tires are further apart than the rear. When the aircraft rolls forward, the wheels try to move farther apart.

Torque. A force that produces or tries to produce rotation.

Torque links. The hinged link between the piston and cylinder of an oleo-type landing gear shock absorber. The torque links allow the piston to move freely in and out of the landing gear cylinder, but prevent it rotating. The torque links can be adjusted to achieve and maintain the correct wheel alignment. Torque links are also called scissors and nutcrackers.

Torque tube. A tube in an aircraft control system that transmits a torsional force from the operating control to the control surface.

Torsion rod. A device in a spring tab to which the control horn is attached. For normal operation, the torsion rod acts as a fixed attachment point, but when the control surface loads are high, the torsion rod twists and allows the control horn to deflect the spring tab.

Total air pressure. The pressure a column of moving air will have if it is stopped.

TMC. Thrust management computer.

Toroidal coil. An electrical coil wound around a ring-shaped core of highly permeable material.

Total air temperature. The temperature a column of moving air will have if it is stopped.

TR unit. A transformer-rectifier unit. A TR unit reduces the voltage of AC and changes it into DC.

Tractor powerplant. An airplane powerplant in which the propeller is mounted in the front, and its thrust pulls the airplane rather than pushes it.

Trammel (verb). To square up the Pratt truss used in an airplane wing. Trammel points are set on the trammel bar so they measure the distance between the center of the front spar, at the inboard compression strut, and at the center of the rear spar at the next compression strut outboard. The drag and antidrag wires are adjusted until the distance between the center of the rear spar at the inboard compression strut and the center of the front spar at the next outboard compression strut is exactly the same as that between the first points measured.

Trammel bar. A wood or metal bar on which trammel points are mounted to compare distances.

Trammel points. A set of sharp-pointed pins that protrude from the sides of a trammel bar.

Transducer. A device that changes energy from one form to another. Commonly used transducers change mechanical movement or pressures into electrical signals.

Transformer rectifier. A component in a large aircraft electrical system used to reduce the AC voltage and change it into DC for charging the battery and for operating DC equipment in the aircraft.

Translational lift. The additional lift produced by a helicopter rotor as the helicopter changes from hovering to forward flight.

Transonic flight. Flight at an airspeed in which some air flowing over the aircraft is moving at a speed below the speed of sound, and other air is moving at a speed greater than the speed of sound.

Transverse pitch. See gauge.

Triangle. A three-sided, closed plane figure. The sum of the three angles in a triangle is always equal to 180°.

Tricresyl phosphate (TCP). A chemical compound, $(CH_3C_6H_4O)_3PO$, used in aviation gasoline to assist in scavenging the lead deposits left from the tetraethyl lead.

Trim tab. A small control tab mounted on the trailing edge of a movable control surface. The tab may be adjusted to provide an aerodynamic force to hold the surface on which it is mounted deflected in order to trim the airplane for hands-off flight at a specified airspeed.

Trimmed flight. A flight condition in which the aerodynamic forces acting on the control surfaces are balanced and the aircraft is able to fly straight and level with no control input.

Trip-free circuit breaker. A circuit breaker that opens a circuit any time an excessive amount of current flows, regardless of the position of the circuit breaker's operating handle.

Troubleshooting. A procedure used in aircraft maintenance in which the operation of a malfunctioning system is analyzed to find the reason for the malfunction and to find a method for returning the system to its condition of normal operation.

True airspeed (TAS). Airspeed shown on the airspeed indicator (indicated airspeed) corrected for position error and nonstandard air temperature and pressure.

Trunnion. Projections from the cylinder of a retractable landing gear strut about which the strut pivots retract.

Truss-type structure. A type of structure made up of longitudinal beams and cross braces. Compression loads between the main beams are carried by rigid cross braces. Tension loads are carried by stays, or wires, that go from one main beam to the other and cross between the cross braces.

Turbine. A rotary device actuated by impulse or reaction of a fluid flowing through vanes or blades that are arranges around a central shaft.

Turn and slip indicator. A rate gyroscopic flight instrument that gives the pilot an indication of the rate of rotation of the aircraft about its vertical axis. A ball in a curved glass tube shows the pilot the relationship between the centrifugal force and the force of gravity. This indicates whether or not the angle of bank is proper for the rate of turn. The turn and slip indicator shows the trim condition of the aircraft and serves as an emergency source of bank information in case the attitude gyro fails. Turn and slip indicators were formerly called needle and ball and turn and bank indicators.

Turnbuckle. A component in an aircraft control system used to adjust cable tension. A turnbuckle consists of a brass tubular barrel with right-hand threads in one end and left-hand in the other end. Control cable terminals screw into the two ends of the barrel, and turning the barrel pulls the terminals together, shortening the cable.

Twist drill. A metal cutting tool turned in a drill press or handheld drill motor. A twist drill has a straight shank and spiraled flutes. The cutting edge is ground on the end of the spiraled flutes.

Twist rope. A stripe of paint on flexible hose that runs the length of the hose. If this stripe spirals around the hose after it is installed, it indicates the hose was twisted when it was installed. Twist stripes are also called lay lines.

Two-terminal spot-type fire detection system. A fire detection system that uses individual thermoswitches installed around the inside of the area to be protected. These thermoswitches are wired in parallel between two separate circuits. A short or an open circuit can exist in either circuit without causing a fire warning.

Type Certificate Data Sheets (TCDS). The official specifications of an aircraft, engine, or propeller issued by the Federal Aviation Administration. The TCDS lists pertinent specifications for the device, and it is the responsibility of the mechanic and/or inspector to ensure, on each inspection, that the device meets these specifications.

UHF. Ultrahigh frequency.

Ultimate tensile strength. The tensile strength required to cause a material to break or to continue to deform under a decreasing load.

Ultraviolet-blocking dope. Dope that contains aluminum powder or some other pigment that blocks the passage of ultraviolet rays of the sun. The coat of dope protects the organic fabrics and clear dope from deterioration by these rays.

Undamped oscillation. Oscillation that continues with an unchanging amplitude once it has started.

Underslung rotor. A helicopter rotor whose center of gravity is below the point at which it is attached to the mast.

Unidirectional fabric. Fabric in which all the threads run in the same direction. These threads are often bound with a few fibers run at right angles, just enough to hold the yarns together and prevent their bunching.

Unloading valve. This is another name for system pressure regulator. See system pressure regulator.

Utility finish. The finish of an aircraft that gives the necessary tautness and fill to the fabric and the necessary protection to the metal, but does not have the glossy appearance of a show-type finish.

Vapor lock. A condition in which vapors form in the fuel lines and block the flow of fuel to the carburetor.

Vapor pressure. The pressure of the vapor above a liquid needed to prevent the liquid evaporating. Vapor pressure is always specified at a specific temperature.

Variable displacement pump. A fluid pump whose output is controlled by the demands of the system. These pumps normally have a built-in system pressure regulator. When the demands of the system are low, the pump moves very little fluid, but when the demands are high, the pump moves a lot of fluid. Most variable displacement pumps used in aircraft hydraulic systems are piston-type pumps.

Varnish (aircraft finishing material). A material used to produce an attractive and protective coating on wood or metal. Varnish is made of a resin dissolved in a solvent and thinned until it has the proper viscosity to spray or brush. The varnish is spread evenly over the surface to be coated, and when the solvents evaporate, a tough film is left.

Varsol. A petroleum product similar to naphtha used as a solvent and cleaning fluid.

Veneer. Thin sheets of wood "peeled" from a log. A wide-blade knife held against the surface of the log peels away the veneer as the log is rotated in the cutter. Veneer is used for making plywood. Several sheets of veneer are glued together, with the grain of each sheet placed at 45° or 90° to the grain of the sheets next to it.

Vertical axis. An imaginary line, passing vertically through the center of gravity of an airplane.

Vertical fin. The fixed vertical surface in the empennage of an airplane. The vertical fin acts as a weathervane to give the airplane directional stability.

VFR. Visual flight rules.

VHF. Very high frequency.

Vibrator-type voltage regulator. A type of voltage regulator used with a generator or alternator that intermittently places a resistance in the field circuit to control the voltage. A set of vibrating contacts puts the resistor in the circuit and takes it out several times a second.

Viscosity. The resistance of a fluid to flow. Viscosity refers to the "stiffness" of the fluid, or its internal friction.

Viscosity cup. A specially shaped cup with an accurately sized hole in its bottom. The cup is submerged in the liquid to completely fill it. It is then lifted from the liquid and the time in seconds is measured from the beginning of the flow through the hole until the first break in this flow. The viscosity of the liquid relates to this time.

Vixen file. A metal-cutting hand file that has curved teeth across its faces. Vixen files are used to remove large amounts of soft metal.

V_{NE}. Never-exceed speed. The maximum speed the aircraft is allowed to attain in any conditions of flight.

Volatile liquid. A liquid that easily changes into a vapor.

Voltmeter multiplier. A precision resistor in series with a voltmeter mechanism used to extend the range of the basic meter or to allow a single meter to measure several ranges of voltage.

VOR. Very high frequency Omni Range navigation.

VORTAC. An electronic navigation system that contains both a VOR and a TACAN facility.

Vortex (plural vortices). A whirling motion in a fluid.

Vortex generator. Small, low-aspect-ratio airfoils installed in pairs on the upper surface of a wing, on both sides of the vertical fin just ahead of the rudder, and on the underside of the vertical stabilizers of some airplanes. Their function is to pull high-energy air down to the surface to energize the boundary layer and prevent airflow separation until the surface reaches a higher angle of attack.

Warp clock. An alignment indicator included in a structural repair manual to show the orientation of the piles of a composite material. The ply direction is shown in relation to a reference direction.

Warp threads. Threads that run the length of the roll of fabric, parallel to the selvage edge. Warp threads are often stronger than fill threads.

Warp tracers. Threads of a different color from the warp threads that are woven into a material to identify the direction of the warp threads.

Wash in. A twist in an airplane wing that increases its angle of incidence near the tip.

Wash out. A twist in an airplane wing that decreases its angle of incidence near the tip.

Watt. The basic unit of electrical power. One watt is equal to $1/746$ horsepower.

Way point. A phantom location created in certain electronic navigation systems by measuring direction and distance from a VORTAC station or by latitude and longitude coordinates from Loran or GPS.

Web of a spar. The part of a spar between the caps.

Weft threads. See fill threads.

Wet-type vacuum pump. An engine-driven air pump that uses steel vanes. These pumps are lubricated by engine oil drawn in through holes in the pump base. The oil passes through the pump and is exhausted with the air. Wet-type pumps must have oil separators in their discharge line to trap the oil and return it to the engine crankcase.

Wing fences. Vertical vanes that extend chordwise across the upper surface of an airplane wing to prevent spanwise airflow.

Wing heavy. An out-of-trim flight condition in which an airplane flies hands off, with one wing low.

Wire bundle. A compact group of electrical wires held together with special wrapping devices or with waxed string. These bundles are secured to the aircraft structure with special clamps.

Woof threads. See fill threads.

Work. The product of force times distance.

Yaw. Rotation of an aircraft about its vertical axis.

Yaw damper. An automatic flight control system that counteracts the rolling and yawing produced by Dutch roll. See Dutch roll. A yaw damper senses yaw with a rate gyro and moves the rudder an amount proportional to the rate of yaw, but in the opposite direction.

Yield strength. The amount of stress needed to permanently deform a material.

Zener diode. A special type of solid-state diode designed to have a specific breakdown voltage and to operate with current flowing through it in its reverse direction.

Zeppelin. The name of large, rigid, lighter-than-air ships built by the Zeppelin Company in Germany prior to and during World War I.

Zero-center ammeter. An ammeter in a light aircraft electrical system located between the battery and the main bus. This ammeter shows the current flowing into or out of the battery.

Index

A

Accelerometers 10-32
Accumulators 12-30
   Cylindrical 12-31
   Maintenance of accumulators 12-32
   Operation 12-31
   Spherical 12-30
Actuators 12-32
   Hydraulic motor 12-34
   Linear actuators 12-32
   Rotary actuators 12-33
Air conditioning systems 16-34
Aircraft brakes 13-42
Aircraft fuel systems 14-13
Aircraft heaters 16-58
Aircraft oxygen systems 16-3
Aircraft pneumatic systems 12-47
Aircraft pressurization systems 16-21
Aircraft tires and tubes 13-75
Aircraft tubes 13-89
   Tire inspection 13-89
   Tube construction and selection 13-89
   Tube storage and inspection 13-89
Aircraft wheels 13-34
Air cycle air conditioning 16-35
   Cabin temperature control system 16-41
      Typical system operation 16-41
   Component operation 16-36
      Bleed air bypass 16-36
      Pack valve 16-36
      Primary heat exchanger 16-38
      Refrigeration bypass valve 16-40
      Refrigeration turbine unit or air cycle
      Machine and secondary heat exchanger 16-38
      Water separator 16-39
   Pneumatic system supply 16-36
   System operation 16-36
Air in the brake system 13-68
Amplifiers 11-21
   Common-collector amplifier 11-22
   Common-emitter amplifier 11-21
   Common-base amplifier 11-23
Antennas 11-38
   Length 11-38
   Transmission lines 11-41
   Types 11-40
      Loop antenna 11-41
      Marconi antenna 11-40
Anti-skid 13-60
   Control valves 13-63
   System maintenance 13-67
      Control unit 13-67
      Control valve 13-67
      Wheel speed sensor 13-67
   Anti-skid system tests 13-65
      Ground test 13-66
      In-flight test 13-67
   Auto brakes 13-65
   Control units 13-62
   System operation 13-60
   Touchdown and lock wheel protection 13-65
   Wheel speed sensors 13-61
Approval of new avionics equipment
Installations 11-72
Aromatic fuels 14-8
Automatic Flight Control System (AFCS) 10-65
Autopilot components 10-61
   Autopilot functions 10-64
   Command elements 10-63
   Computer and amplifier 10-61
   Feedback or followup element 10-63
   Output elements 10-61
   Sensing elements 10-61
   Yaw dampening 10-65
Autopilot systems 10-60
Aviation fuel 14-7
Avionics in aviation maintenance 11-2
   History of avionics 11-2

B

Basic analog circuits 11-19
Basic fuel system requirements 14-1

Basic hydraulic systems 12-6
    Closed-center hydraulic systems 12-6
    Open center hydraulic systems 12-6
Basis for autopilot operation 10-60
Bladder fuel tanks 14-25
Bleed air systems 16-58
Bleeding master cylinder brake systems 13-68
Bleeding power brake systems 13-70
    Fluid quantity and type 13-70
    Inspection for leaks 13-70
    Proper bolt torque 13-71
Bleeding shock struts 13-13
Boeing 737 next generation hydraulic system 12-38
    Filter units 12-40
    Indications 12-42
    Landing gear transfer unit 12-41
    Power Transfer Unit (PTU) 12-40
    Pumps 12-38
    Reservoirs 12-38
    Standby hydraulic system 12-42
Boeing 777 hydraulic system 12-42
    Center hydraulic system 12-45
        Center Hydraulic Isolation System (CHIS) 12-46
        Central hydraulic system reset 12-47
        Filter 12-45
        Nose gear isolation valve 12-46
        Reservoir 12-45
    Left and right system description 12-43
        Filter module 12-45
        Indication 12-45
        Pumps 12-45
        Reservoir 12-45
Bonding 11-74
Brake actuating systems 13-52
    Boosted brakes 13-54
    Independent master cylinders 13-52
    Power brakes 13-55
        Brake control valve/brake metering valve 13-56
Brake inspection and service 13-67
Brake malfunctions and damage 13-74
    Chattering or squealing 13-74
    Dragging 13-74
    Overheating 13-74

C

Carbon brakes 13-50
Carbon monoxide detectors 17-9
Carburetor icing 14-7
Cargo and baggage compartment fire detection
And extinguisher system 17-15
    Cargo compartment extinguishing system 17-16

Smoke detector system 17-16
Cargo compartment classification 17-15
Cargo fire detection 17-14
Checking for fuel system contaminants 14-54
    Detection of contaminants 14-56
    Foreign fuel contamination 14-56
    Fuel contamination control 14-58
    Microorganisms 14-55
    Solid particle contaminants 14-55
    Surfactants 14-55
    Water 14-54
Chemical anti-icing 15-10
Chemical or solid oxygen 16-5
Chemical oxygen systems 16-16
Chemical rain repellant 15-27
    Windshield surface seal coating 15-28
Chemical stability 12-2
Classes of fires 17-2
Clocks 10-76
Cockpit and cabin interiors 17-11
    Extinguisher types 17-11
Combustion heaters 16-58
    Combustion air system 16-59
    Controls 16-61
    Fuel system 16-60
    Ignition system 16-60
    Maintenance and inspection 16-61
    Safety features 16-61
    Ventilating air system 16-60
Composition of the atmosphere 16-1
Considerations 11-72
Construction and installation of deice boots 15-19
Continuous-loop systems 17-4
Control of cabin pressure 16-27
    Air distribution 16-34
    Cabin air pressure regulator and outflow
    Valve 16-30
    Cabin air pressure safety valve operation 16-31
    Cabin pressure controller 16-28
    Cabin pressurization troubleshooting 16-34
    Pressurization gauges 16-32
    Pressurization modes 16-27
Cooling and moisture 11-73

D

Defueling 14-61
Deice boot maintenance 15-21
Deice system for turboprop aircraft 15-14
Deicing and anti-icing of transport type aircraft 15-25
    Critical surfaces 15-25
    Deicing fluid 15-25

Holdover Time (HOT)..15-25
Deicing system components 15-14
    Control valve 15-17
    Deflate valve...15-18
    Distributor valve...15-18
    Dry-type engine-driven air pump.........................15-16
    Inlet filter 15-19
    Manifold assembly 15-19
    Oil separator 15-17
    Regulators and relief valves 15-18
    Timer/control unit...15-18
    Wet-type engine-driven air pump.........................15-14
Detonation..14-8
Digital aircraft systems 11-29
Digital building blocks..11-26
    AND gate..11-27
    Buffer gate 11-27
    EXCLUSIVE OR gate..11-28
    NAND gate...11-28
    Negative logic gates 11-28
    NOR gate..11-28
    NOT gate..11-26
    OR gate...11-27
Digital data displays..11-29
Digital electronics 11-26
Digital tuners and audio panels...............................11-30
Diodes 11-4
Direction indicating instruments.............................10-43
Dry powders...17-10
Dual-disc brakes...13-46

E

Electrically driven gyroscopic instrument
Systems 10-52
Electrical temperature measuring indication 10-36
    Electrical resistance thermometer 10-36
    Ratiometer electrical resistance thermometers.......10-38
Electric deice boots...15-22
Electric heating systems..16-58
Electron control valves 11-4
Electronic flight information systems 10-68
    Electronic Centralized Aircraft Monitor
    (ECAM)...10-71
    Electronic Flight Instrument System (EFIS) 10-70
    Engine Indicating and Crew Alerting System
    (EICAS)...10-72
Electronic instruments 10-67
    Electronic Attitude Director Indicator (EADI) 10-67
    Electronic Horizontal Situation Indicators
    (EHSI) 10-68
Electronic oscillation 11-25

Emergency backup systems 12-51
    Dump valve 12-51
    Emergency extension sequence............................12-52
    Gear emergency extension cable and handle 12-51
    Nitrogen bottles 12-51
Emergency brake systems 13-58
    Brake deboosters...13-60
    Parking brake...13-60
Emergency extension systems 13-22
Engine instruments..10-3
Evolution of hydraulic systems...............................12-7
Exhaust shroud heaters 16-58
Expander tube brakes..13-51
Extinguishing agents and portable fire
Extinguishers 17-10

F

Fenwal system..17-4
Field Effect Transistors (FET)................................11-16
Filling LOX systems...16-19
Filters 12-13
    Filter bypass valve..12-14
    Filter differential pressure indicators 12-14
    Maintenance of filters...12-14
    Micron-type filters..12-14
Fire detection/overheat systems..............................17-2
Fire detection system maintenance 17-18
Fire detection system troubleshooting 17-19
Fire extinguisher system maintenance 17-20
    Agent containers...17-20
    Container pressure check.....................................17-20
    Discharge cartridges 17-20
Fire hazards when fueling or defueling 14-61
Fire point...12-3
Fire prevention...17-21
Fire zones 17-8
Fixed and retractable landing gear 13-5
Flame detectors..17-9
Flash point...12-3
Flight director systems 10-65
Flight instruments 10-3
Flight Management System (FMS)..........................10-72
Flow between interconnected tanks 14-3
Frost removal...15-25
Fuel filters 14-36
Fuel flow...14-3
Fuel heaters and ice prevention...............................14-39
Fuel identification 14-10
Fueling 14-59
Fueling and defueling procedures 14-59
Fuel jettisoning system 14-6

Fuel lines and fittings 14-26
Fuel pumps... 14-5, 14-31
    Centrifugal boost pumps 14-32
    Ejector pumps..14-32
    Hand-operated fuel pumps 14-31
    Pulsating electric pumps...14-34
    Vane-type fuel pumps 14-35
Fuel strainer or filter..14-6
Fuel system components 14-5, 14-22
Fuel system drains...14-6
Fuel system hot weather operation 14-3
Fuel system independence 14-2
Fuel system indicators..14-40
    Fuel flowmeters 14-44
    Fuel pressure gauges 14-47
    Fuel quantity indicating systems 14-40
    Fuel temperature gauges..14-46
    Pressure warning signal..14-48
    Valve-in-transit indicator lights..............................14-48
Fuel system lightning protection 14-2
Fuel system lines and fittings..14-5
Fuel system repair 14-49
Fuel system servicing...14-54
Fuel tank expansion space 14-4
Fuel tank filler connection 14-4
Fuel tank installation 14-4
Fuel tank outlet 14-5
Fuel tank repair 14-50
    Bladder tanks 14-51
    Fire safety 14-52
    Integral tanks 14-52
    Riveted tanks 14-51
    Soldered tanks 14-51
    Welded tanks 14-50
Fuel tanks 14-3,14-22
Fuel tank sump...14-4
Fuel tank tests 14-3
Fuel tank vents and carburetor vapor vents 14-4
Fuel valves 14-26
    Cone valves 14-28
    Hand-operated valves 14-28
    Manually-operated gate valves...............................14-29
    Motor-operated valves..14-30
    Poppet valves..14-29
    Solenoid-operated valves 14-31
Fuel valves and controls 14-5
Fundamentals of electronics 11-3
    Analog electronics..11-4
    Analog versus digital electronics 11-3

G

Gaseous oxygen 16-4
Gaseous oxygen systems...16-6
    Continuous-flow systems 16-7
    Demand-flow systems 16-10
    Flow indicators 16-11
    Oxygen plumbing and valves 16-14
    Oxygen storage cylinders 16-6
    Oxygen systems and regulators...............................16-7
Ground deicing of aircraft..15-23
Gyroscopic instruments 10-52
    Electric attitude indicators......................................10-57
    Gyroscopic Direction Indicator or Directional
    Gyro (DG) 10-58
    Mechanical gyros 10-52
    Solid state gyros and related systems 10-54
        Microelectromechanical based attitude and
        directional systems..10-55
        Other attitude and directional systems...............10-55
        Ring Laser Gyros (RLG) 10-54
    Turn-and-slip indicator..10-58
    Turn coordinators 10-58
    Vacuum-driven attitude gyros 10-56

H

Halogenated hydrocarbons...17-10
Heat exchangers 12-32
Helicopter fuel systems...14-22
High-pressure systems 12-48
Human respiration and circulation..............................16-2
    Carbon monoxide poisoning 16-3
    Hyperventilation...16-3
    Oxygen and hypoxia..16-2
Hydraulic fluids...12-2
    Compatibility with aircraft materials 12-3
    Health and handling...12-5
    Hydraulic fluid contamination..................................12-4
        Contamination check 12-4
            Hydraulic sampling schedule 12-4
            Sampling procedure...12-4
        Contamination control 12-5
    Hydraulic system flushing 12-5
    Intermixing of fluids 12-3
    Mineral-based fluids..12-3
    Phosphate ester-based fluid (Skydrol®)...................12-3
    Polyalphaolefin-based fluids 12-3
Hydraulic Motor-Driven Generator (HMDG) 12-35
Hydraulic power pack system 12-7
Hydraulic power systems...12-7
Hydraulic system components 12-8
    Reservoirs...12-8

    Air-pressurized reservoirs 12-10
    Fluid-pressurized reservoirs 12-11
    Nonpressurized reservoirs 12-9
    Pressurized reservoirs 12-10
    Reservoir servicing 12-12

I

Ice and snow removal 15-27
Ice control systems 15-1
Ice detector system 15-3
Ice prevention 15-3
Icing effects 15-2
Inert cold gases 17-10
Inertial Navigation System (INS)/Inertial Reference
System (IRS) 11-71
Inspection of masks and hoses 16-19
Installation of aircraft antenna systems 11-75
Installation of communication and navigation
Equipment 11-72
Installed fire extinguishing systems 17-11
    CO_2 fire extinguishing systems 17-11
    Containers 17-12
    Discharge indicators 17-13
        Thermal discharge indicator (red disk) 17-13
        Yellow disk discharge indicator 17-14
    Discharge valves 17-13
    Fire switch 17-14
    Halogenated hydrocarbons fire extinguishing
    Systems 17-11
    Pressure indication 17-13
    Two-way check valve 17-13
Instrument housings and handling 10-77
Instrument installations and markings 10-77
    Instrument mounting 10-80
    Instrument panels 10-77
    Instrument power requirements 10-80
    Instrument range markings 10-81
Integral fuel tanks 14-25

J

Jet transport aircraft fuel systems 14-17

K

Kidde system 17-4
    Automatic self-interrogation 17-6
    Combination fire and overheat warning 17-5
    Dual-loop systems 17-6
    Fault indication 17-6
    Fire detection control unit (fire detection
    card) 17-6
    Sensing element 17-4

    Support tube mounted sensing elements 17-6
    System test 17-5
    Temperature trend indication 17-5

L

Landing gear alignment, support, and retraction 13-14
Landing gear arrangement 13-2
    Tail wheel-type landing gear 13-2
    Tandem landing gear 13-2
    Tricycle-type landing gear 13-3
Landing gear rigging and adjustment 13-26
    Adjusting landing gear latches 13-26
    Drag and side brace adjustment 13-28
    Gear door clearances 13-27
    Landing gear retraction test 13-29
Landing gear safety devices 13-22
    Ground locks 13-23
    Landing gear position indicators 13-23
    Nose wheel centering 13-24
    Safety switch 13-22
Landing gear system maintenance 13-24
Landing gear types 13-1
Large aircraft hydraulic systems 12-38
Large aircraft retraction systems 13-18
Large reciprocating-engine aircraft fuel systems 14-16
Lavatory fire extinguisher system 17-18
Lavatory smoke detectors 17-17
Lavatory smoke detector system 17-17
Leading edge slat anti-ice system 15-6
    WAI control system 15-6
    WAI ducts 15-6
    WAI indication system 15-9
    WAI pressure sensor 15-6
    WAI valve 15-6
Light emitting diodes 11-18
Lining wear 13-67
Liquid oxygen 16-4
Loading information onto a radio wave 11-32
    Amplitude Modulation (AM) 11-34
    Frequency Modulation (FM) 11-35
    Single Side Band (SSB) 11-36
Low-pressure systems 12-52
LOX systems 16-16

M

Magnetic compass 10-43
Maintenance of instruments and instrument
Systems 10-81
    Altimeter tests 10-82
    Autopilot system maintenance 10-85

Lcd display screens 10-86
Magnetic compass maintenance and
Compensation 10-84
Pitot-static system maintenance and tests 10-82
Tachometer maintenance......................................10-83
Vacuum system maintenance 10-85
Maintenance procedure 11-77
Mechanical movement indicators 10-29
Medium-pressure systems..12-52
Metal Oxide Semiconductor Field Effect Transistors
(MOSFETs) and Complementary Metal Oxide
Semiconductor (CMOS) 11-17
Multiple-disc brakes...13-46

N

Navigation instruments 10-4
Noise 11-4
Non-electric temperature indicators.............................10-36
Nose wheel steering systems 13-30
Large aircraft 13-30
Small aircraft 13-30

O

Octane and performance number rating........................14-9
Off aircraft brake servicing and maintenance 13-71
Automatic adjuster pins..13-71
Bolt and threaded connections 13-71
Brake housing and piston condition 13-72
Discs 13-71
Seal condition 13-72
Torque tube...13-72
On aircraft servicing 13-67
Onboard Oxygen Generating Systems (OBOGS).........16-5
Operation and handling tips...13-93
Braking and pivoting..13-93
Hydroplaning..13-94
Landing field and hangar floor condition 13-93
Takeoffs and landings 13-94
Taxiing 13-93
Oscillator circuits 11-24
Oxygen system inspection and maintenance 16-20
Oxygen systems and components 16-6
Oxygen system servicing 16-16

P

Pentodes 11-6
Photodiodes and phototransistors 11-18
Physiology of flight...16-1
Pitot-static pressure-sensing flight instruments 10-16
Airspeed indicators...10-24

Altimeters and altitude 10-16
Vertical speed indicator..10-22
Pitot-static systems..10-12
Air Data Computers (ADC) and Digital Air
Data Computers (DADC)................................10-14
Pitot tubes and static vents 10-12
Pneumatic continuous-loop systems 17-6
Averaging function 17-7
Discrete function 17-7
Pneumatic deice boot system for GA aircraft 15-12
GA system operation 15-13
Pneumatic power system maintenance 12-52
Pneumatic rain removal systems.................................15-28
Pneumatic system components 12-48
Air compressors...12-49
Check valves..12-49
Chemical drier 12-50
Control valves 12-49
Desiccant/moisture separator 12-50
Filters 12-50
Relief valves 12-49
Restrictors..12-50
Variable restrictor..12-50
Portable water tank ice prevention..............................15-32
Power Transfer Unit (PTU) 12-35
Pressure 10-7
Pressure-driven gyroscopic instrument systems 10-51
Pressure fueling systems 14-5
Pressure instruments 10-8
Engine oil pressure 10-8
Engine pressure ratio (EPR) 10-9
Fuel pressure..10-10
Hydraulic pressure...10-10
Manifold pressure..10-9
Pressure switches...10-11
Vacuum pressure 10-11
Pressure measuring instruments....................................10-5
Pressure of the atmosphere 16-21
Pressure type sensor responder systems 17-6
Pressurization issues 16-23
Pressurization terms 16-23
Prevention of oxygen fires or explosions...................16-20
Propeller deice system 15-23
Chemical propeller deice.....................................15-23
Electrothermal propeller device system 15-23
Pumps..12-15
Hand pumps...12-15
Power-driven pumps..12-16
Classification of pumps................................12-16
Constant-displacement pumps 12-17
Gear-type power pump 12-17

I-6

Gerotor pump 12-17
Piston pump 12-18
Bent axis piston pump 12-18
Inline piston pump 12-19
Vane pump 12-19
Variable-displacement pump 12-20
Basic pumping operation 12-20
Depressurized mode 12-22
Normal pumping mode 12-21
Purity 14-10

R

Radio communication 11-31
Radio navigation 11-41
Area Navigation (RNAV) 11-53
Automatic Direction Finder (ADF) 11-46
Collision avoidance systems 11-58
ADS-B 11-60
Traffic Collision Avoidance Systems (TCAS) ... 11-58
Distance Measuring Equipment (DME) 11-52
Emergency Locator Transmitter (ELT) 11-66
Global Positioning System (GPS) 11-69
Instrument Landing Systems (ILS) 11-49
Compass locators 11-52
Glideslope 11-49
Localizer 11-49
Long Range Aid to Navigation System
(LORAN) 11-68
Radar beacon transponder 11-54
Altitude encoders 11-58
Transponder tests and inspections 11-57
Radio altimeter 11-62
Radio Magnetic Indicator (RMI) 11-48
VOR navigation system 11-42
Weather radar 11-62
Radio transmitters and receivers 11-37
Receivers 11-37
Transceivers 11-38
Transmitters 11-37
Radio waves 11-31
Rain control systems 15-27
Ram Air Turbine (RAT) 12-35
Reciprocating engine fuel—AVGAS 14-7
Rectifiers 11-19
Reducing radio interference 11-74
Remote indicating compass 10-45
Remote indicating slaved gyro compass (flux
Gate compass) 10-45
Remote sensing and indication 10-26
Replacement of brake linings 13-72
Cleveland brakes 13-72

Goodyear brakes 13-72
Replacing tubing, valves, and fittings 16-20
Requirements for overheat and fire protection
Systems 17-2
Rigid removable fuel tanks 14-23
Rubber deicer boot systems 15-19
Adjustments 15-21
Inspection 15-21
Operational checks 15-19
Troubleshooting 15-21

S

Seals 12-35
Backup rings 12-37
Gaskets 12-37
O-Rings 12-35
O-Ring color coding 12-36
O-Ring installation 12-38
Seal materials 12-37
U-Ring 12-35
V-Ring packings 12-35
Wipers 12-38
Segmented rotor-disc brakes 13-46
Semiconductor diodes 11-9
Semiconductors 11-7
Servicing gaseous oxygen 16-16
Draining an oxygen system 16-17
Filling an oxygen system 16-17
Leak testing gaseous oxygen systems 16-16
Purging an oxygen system 16-19
Servicing shock struts 13-12
Shielding 11-74
Shimmy dampers 13-32
Non-hydraulic shimmy damper 13-33
Piston-type 13-33
Steering damper 13-32
Vane-type 13-33
Shock absorbing and non-shock absorbing
Landing gear 13-6
Bungee cord 13-7
Leaf-type spring gear 13-6
Rigid 13-7
Shock struts 13-8
Shock strut operation 13-11
Silicon controlled rectifiers 11-13
Single disc brakes 13-43
Fixed-disc brakes 13-44
Floating disc brakes 13-43
Small aircraft retraction systems 13-16
Pump feed systems 14-14

I-7

Small multiengine (reciprocating) aircraft fuel
Systems 14-15
   High-wing twin 14-16
   Low-wing twin 14-15
Small single-engine aircraft fuel systems 14-13
   Gravity feed systems 14-13
   High-wing aircraft with fuel injection system........ 14-14
Smoke detectors 17-8
   Ionization type 17-8
   Light refraction type 17-8
Smoke, flame, and carbon monoxide detection
Systems 17-8
Solid state magnetometers 10-46
Sources of operating air 15-12
   Turbine engine bleed air................................... 15-12
Sources of power for gyroscopic instruments........... 10-46
Sources of pressurized air 16-24
   Reciprocating engine aircraft 16-25
   Turbine engine aircraft 16-26
Stall warning and angle of attack (AOA)
indicators 10-34
Static discharge wicks.. 11-74
Surface ignition and preignition............................... 14-9
Synchroscope 10-32
Synchro-type remote-indicating instruments............ 10-26
   AC synchro systems 10-28
   DC selsyn systems.. 10-26
System servicing 16-55
   Charging the system 16-57
   Checking compressor oil 16-56
   Evacuating the system 16-57
   Feel test 16-56
   Leak test 16-56
   Performance test 16-56
   Purging the system 16-56
   Visual inspection 16-55

T

Tachometers... 10-29
   Electric tachometers 10-30
   Mechanical tachometers 10-29
Technician certification... 16-58
Temperature and altitude 16-22
Temperature measuring instruments....................... 10-35
Tetrodes... 11-6
Theory of refrigeration.. 16-41
   Basic vapor cycle.. 16-44
Thermal electric anti-icing....................................... 15-10
Thermal pneumatic anti-icing.................................. 15-4
Thermal switch system 17-2
Thermocouple system 17-3

Thermocouple temperature indicators 10-38
   Turbine gas temperature indicating systems 10-39
Tire balancing 13-92
Tire classification 13-75
   Bias ply or radial 13-76
   Ply rating 13-76
   Tube-type or tubeless 13-76
   Types 13-75
Tire construction 13-77
   Bead.. 13-78
   Carcass plies 13-78
   Sidewall 13-79
      Chine 13-79
   Tread 13-78
Tire inspection off of the aircraft.............................. 13-86
Tire inspection on the aircraft 13-79
   Inflation 13-79
   Tread condition... 13-80
      Tread damage... 13-82
      Tread depth and wear pattern 13-80
Tire mounting... 13-89
   Tubeless tires... 13-90
   Tube-type tires... 13-91
Tire removal 13-84
Tire repair and retreading....................................... 13-88
Tire storage 13-88
Total air temperature measurement 10-42
Transistors... 11-11
Transmission lines 11-76
Triacs... 11-14
Triodes 11-5
Troubleshooting the fuel system 14-49
   Fuel leak classification 14-50
   Location of leaks and defects 14-49
   Replacement of gaskets, seals, and packings 14-50
Turbine engine fuels 14-11
   Turbine engine fuel issues................................ 14-13
   Turbine engine fuel types 14-13
   Turbine fuel volatility.. 14-12

U

Unijunction Transistors (UJT) 11-15
Unusable fuel supply.. 14-3

V

Vacuum systems 10-48
   Engine-driven vacuum pump 10-48
   Twin-engine aircraft vacuum system operation 10-51
   Typical pump-driven system 10-49
   Venturi tube systems 10-48
Vacuum tubes.. 11-4

Valves 12-23
    Flow control valves 12-23
        Check valve 12-25
        Hydraulic fuses 12-27
        Mechanically operated sequence valve 12-26
        Orifice-type check valve 12-25
        Pressure-controlled sequence valve 12-26
        Priority valves 12-26
        Selector valves 12-23
        Sequence valves 12-25
    Pressure control valves 12-27
        Pressure reducers 12-28
        Pressure regulators 12-28
        Relief valves 12-27
    Shuttle valves 12-29
        Shutoff valves 12-30
Vapor cycle air conditioning 16-41
Vapor cycle air conditioning servicing
Equipment 16-51
    Full service refrigerant recovery, recycling, evacuation,
    and recharging units 16-52
    Leak detectors 16-54
    Manifold set, gauges, hoses, and fittings 16-51
    Refrigerant source 16-53
    Vacuum pumps 16-53
Vapor cycle air conditioning system
Components 16-45
    Compressor 16-48
    Condenser 16-49
    Evaporator 16-47
    Expansion valve 16-46
    Receiver dryer 16-46
    Refrigerant 16-45
    Service valves 16-50
Vapor lock 14-7
Vertical magnetic compass 10-45
Vibration isolation 11-73
Viscosity 12-2
Volatility 14-7

W

Warnings and cautions 10-74
    Annunciator systems 10-74
    Aural warning systems 10-75
Water 17-11
Wheel construction 13-34
    Inboard wheel half 13-35
    Outboard wheel half 13-36
Wheel inspection 13-36
    Off aircraft wheel inspection 13-37
        Balance weights 13-42

Bearing handling and lubrication 13-40
Cleaning the wheel assembly 13-38
Cleaning the wheel bearings 13-38
Disassembly of the wheel 13-38
Fusible plug inspection 13-42
Inspection of the wheel halves 13-41
Key and key screw inspection 13-42
Loosening the tire from the wheel rim 13-37
Wheel bearing inspection 13-38
    Brinelling 13-39
    Bruising 13-40
    Flase brinelling 13-39
    Galling 13-38
    Overheating 13-39
    Staining and surface marks 13-40
Wheel tie bolt inspection 13-41
On aircraft inspection 13-37
Proper installation 13-37
    Axle nut torque 13-37
Wide Area Augmentation System (WAAS) 11-70
Windshield frost, fog, and ice control systems 15-28
    Chemical 15-31
    Electric 15-28
    Pneumatic 15-30
Windshield wiper systems 15-27
Wing and horizontal and vertical stabilizer
anti-icing systems 15-4
Wing and stabilizer deicing systems 15-12
Wing Anti-ice (WAI) System 15-4

Z

Zener diodes 11-11

www.ingramcontent.com/pod-product-compliance
Lightning Source LLC
Chambersburg PA
CBHW082018300426
44117CB00015B/2270